Microsoft

Microsoft® Visual Basic® 2010 Developer's Handbook

D1203907

Klaus Löffelmann
Sarika Calla Purohit

Published with the authorization of Microsoft Corporation by:
O'Reilly Media, Inc.
1005 Gravenstein Highway North
Sebastopol, California 95472

ISBN: 978-0-7356-2705-5

1 2 3 4 5 6 7 8 9 TG 6 5 4 3 2 1

Printed and bound in Canada.

Microsoft Press books are available through booksellers and distributors worldwide. If you need support related to this book, email Microsoft Press Book Support at mspinput@microsoft.com. Please tell us what you think of this book at http://www.microsoft.com/learning/booksurvey.

Microsoft and the trademarks listed at http://www.microsoft.com/about/legal/en/us/IntellectualProperty/Trademarks/EN-US.aspx are trademarks of the Microsoft group of companies. All other marks are property of their respective owners.

The example companies, organizations, products, domain names, email addresses, logos, people, places, and events depicted herein are fictitious. No association with any real company, organization, product, domain name, email address, logo, person, place, or event is intended or should be inferred.

Acquisitions and Developmental Editor: Russell Jones
Production Editor: Kristen Borg
Production Services: Octal Publishing Services.
Technical Reviewer: Evangelos Petroutsos
Copyeditor: Bob Russell
Indexer: Lucie Haskins
Cover Design: Twist Creative • Seattle
Cover Composition: Karen Montgomery

To Adriana, in love. Thanks for always letting me be myself, and taking me the way I am.

— Klaus

Contents at a Glance

Table of Contents

What do you think of this book? We want to hear from you!

Microsoft is interested in hearing your feedback so we can continually improve our
books and learning resources for you. To participate in a brief online survey, please visit:

microsoft.com/learning/booksurvey

Part II **Object-Oriented Programming**

Part III Programming with .NET Framework Data Structures

Foreword

Visual Studio 2010 is an exciting version for the Visual Basic language, which reaches a double digit version in Visual Basic 10. This is a phenomenal achievement for a programming language, and it demonstrates the enormous utility that the language continues to provide, year after year. Visual Basic has always been a premier tool for making Microsoft platforms accessible and easy to use. And even though the specific technologies and devices have changed over time, the core mission of Visual Basic has remained the same. Starting in 1991 with Visual Basic 1 and continuing through to Visual Basic 3, Visual Basic revolutionized Windows application development by making it accessible in a way that simply wasn't possible before its arrival. Moving forward to Visual Basic 4 through Visual Basic 6, the language greatly simplified component programming with the Component Object Model (COM), Object Linking and Embedding (OLE) automation, and ActiveX controls. Finally, with Visual Basic 7 and beyond, the language has enabled developers to take advantage of the Common Language Runtime (CLR) and many .NET Framework technologies. This book covers examples of this, using Visual Basic to access .NET Framework data types, Language Integrated Query (LINQ), Windows Presentation Foundation (WPF), and the Task Parallel Library. LINQ in particular has had a significant impact on the language, providing a unified way to access data from objects, XML, or relational data sources. One of the most revolutionary features introduced as part of LINQ is XML literals, which makes Visual Basic the most productive language for programming with XML.

Looking ahead, there are three major development trends that we see influencing the Visual Basic language, now and in the future: declarative, dynamic, and concurrent programming.

Declarative programming lets developers state what the program should do, rather than requiring them to specify in great detail how the compiler should do it. This has always been a design principle for Visual Basic, in which we strive to increase the expressiveness of the language so that you can "say more with less code." Some recent examples of this in Visual Basic 9 are LINQ and type inference. Visual Basic 10 introduces similar efficiencies with multi-line lambdas, array literals, collection initializers, autoimplemented properties, and implicit line continuation—all of which are covered in this book.

Dynamic programming is another style that has influenced the design of Visual Basic. Late binding is an important feature that has made Visual Basic a great language for Microsoft Office development and COM programming. In Visual Basic 10, we extended Visual Basic's late-binding support to work with other dynamic type environments, such as JavaScript and IronPython. This was made possible by the Dynamic Language Runtime (DLR), which was introduced in .NET Framework 4.

Finally, concurrency is an undeniable trend that we see influencing many forms of development. Whether your application is running on a multicore machine, a clustered environment on premises, via distributed computing in the Cloud, or even on a single-core computer performing IO-bound operations, concurrency can help speed up its execution. .NET Framework 4 provides some great tools for concurrent programming, such as the Task Parallel Library and Parallel LINQ. Part VI of this book shows how to use these technologies in Visual Basic.

Visual Basic is a vibrant environment, and we invite you to dive into it in Visual Studio 2010. Whether you've used previous versions of Visual Basic or other object-oriented programming (OOP) languages, or you are new to OOP altogether, this book has the information you need to quickly become productive. It explains programming concepts, Visual Basic, Visual Studio, and the .NET Framework from the bottom up, and it establishes a strong foundation. For the more experienced reader, this book also goes deeply into these topics and includes dedicated sections on what's new in the 2010 release of Visual Studio. The book covers a variety of topics; some of them are technology-specific (such as WPF), while others are application agnostic (such as garbage collection and serialization). This book establishes a solid foundation that you can leverage when developing applications for any platform that Visual Studio 2010 targets, including Microsoft SharePoint, the Web, and the Cloud.

As Visual Studio Community Program Manager, I always enjoy meeting members of the Visual Studio community. One of the first times Klaus wrote to me, he quoted a motto he had learned from his grandmother: "the worst attempt is the one that you'll never make." I knew at that point that he was an ambitious person! Klaus has been writing computer books for more than 20 years. The subjects of those books include, Commodore 16, Commodore 64, Commodore 128, Atari ST, Amiga, Visual Basic 1, Visual Basic 3, Visual Basic 4, Visual Basic 5, Visual Basic 6, Visual Studio 2003, Visual Studio 2005, Visual Studio 2008, and now Visual Studio 2010. I've met with Klaus in various cities around the world: Antwerp, Berlin, and Seattle. His first trip to Seattle was for the Microsoft Most Valuable Professional (MVP) Summit. The MVP program honors Microsoft technology experts for their impact in the community, and Klaus was recognized as a Visual Basic MVP for the great support he's provided through writing books, delivering webcasts, and reviewing German content on MSDN. Klaus made his second trip to Seattle while writing this book. He found great inspiration in being at the place where "the magic happens." I took Klaus on a tour through the Microsoft offices, where he was able to connect with other members of the Visual Basic product team. It was a really exciting visit and I could see how passionate Klaus is about Visual Basic.

I was happy to connect Klaus with Sarika, who has been a great partner in writing this book. As a Test Lead on the Microsoft Visual Studio Professional team, Sarika has extensive expertise in Visual Studio. She joined the team in 2002, and has worked on the releases for Visual Studio 2003, Visual Studio 2005, Visual Studio 2008, and Visual Studio 2010. During this time, she's been deeply involved in the evolution of the Visual Basic language and Integrated Development Environment (IDE). As Test Lead, Sarika spends a lot of time thinking about how Visual Basic developers use Visual Studio and the .NET Framework to create client, web, and other types of applications. She also interacts with the Visual Basic community at various phases of the product cycle to gather feedback, review bugs, and present to customers.

Sarika's and Klaus's backgrounds were key assets in writing this well-thought-out book. Sarika has spent nearly a decade working on the Visual Studio IDE, which was a significant area of investment in this release. The Visual Studio 2010 user interface was rewritten in Windows Presentation Foundation, which enabled richer user experiences in Visual Studio itself as well as greater extensibility capabilities for third-party add-ins. Sarika shares her insight on this topic in the "sightseeing tour" of the Visual Studio 2010 IDE in Chapter 4. Klaus's experience draws from many years of work as a consultant on Visual Basic .NET and Visual Basic 6 migrations. He's worked with many development teams on a variety of projects, and he knows which concepts can be the most challenging for developers to pick up. He has a true passion for compiling the most useful information for his readers and presenting it in a way that's easy to understand. While writing a book can be an arduous task, Klaus tackles it with enthusiasm. He has a great sense of humor that shines through in the playful writing style and makes it fun to follow along.

So as Klaus's grandma would advise, give this book a try! I'm sure you will find that the 10th version of Visual Basic helps you to tackle your software development projects with greater ease and productivity than ever before.

Lisa Feigenbaum
Community Program Manager
Microsoft Visual Studio

August, 2010

Introduction

When someone asks me what I do for a living, I don't really know what to say. That might be because some 25 years ago I wrote my first book, *Programming Graphics for the Commodore 128*, (in German, and out of print) at age 16, when it was uncool, freaky, geeky, and nerdy to even work with computers at all, much less to write about programming them. Perhaps that feeling is etched on my memory and helps explain why the answer still causes me some embarrassment. "I write technical books about software development," also sounds a bit out-of-touch with the real world, doesn't it?

It isn't quite that bad nowadays, because the truth is, it's not just about writing anymore. The small company I own (ActiveDevelop—there are ten of us working there now, located in the only high-rise office building in Lippstadt, Germany) doesn't just write about *developing* software, it also actually *develops* software. We also help other companies with their software development efforts, bringing their teams up to speed on the latest technologies localizing software from English to German and vice versa, and helping them to migrate from Microsoft Visual Basic 6.0 to Microsoft Visual Basic .NET (or reluctantly, and often unnecessarily, to C#). One of us has even been the recipient of a Microsoft MVP award three times—and, er, that would be me. And to capitalize on this promotional opportunity, if you live in a German or English-speaking country, and need competent support for .NET, training, and project coaching in Visual Basic or C#, localization expertise, and a motivated team with good connections (hey, my co-author even works on the Visual Studio team), you now know where to find us: just send an email to info@activedevelop.de. Oh, and you can always follow me on Twitter @loeffelmann.

Because writing about software development has always been my passion, every once in a while I write a new book. Usually, this happens when Microsoft releases new products or new versions. That's the only way to explain why the book you are holding right now is the thirtieth book I have either written or co-authored. While I still find it exciting (just as it was back in the time of the Commodore 64) to learn new technologies and to receive beta versions of the latest Microsoft software, writing books has become more of a routine. In any case, that was true until my last book, *The Visual Basic 2008 Developer Handbook*, came out in Germany.

When writing this book, however, I experienced a second spring because it fulfilled a long-held wish. Remember? I live in a comparatively small town in the northwestern part of Germany. And I *always* wanted to write a programming book in the Microsoft metropolis, Seattle. And so I did. In June 2010 I flew about 6000 miles from Frankfurt to Seattle, where I spent almost four weeks writing a large part of this book at the "origin location." I wrote most of this material in an apartment in Bellevue, in the Japanese restaurant Blue Fin, at the Northgate Mall (I can recommend the large sushi selection); on the Boeing air field (OK, not really *on* the air field); in the hundreds of Starbucks in and around Seattle; at the pier overlooking Puget Sound; at Pike Place Market; in pubs overlooking Lake Washington; in the cafeteria between building 41 and 42 on the Microsoft campus; and on the lawn in front of Microsoft's Building 41 (home of the compiler teams and of my co-author, Sarika Calla). I wrote everywhere. One time I even travelled to Whidbey Island, from which Visual Studio 2005 got its code name. I wrote there, too. It was a lot of fun getting to know all the talented and competent people at Microsoft. They answered my questions even when they were really busy. I'm still impressed when I remember back to that time.

Getting the assistance of Sarika Calla was the icing on the cake; not even in my wildest dreams did I imagine I might work with someone from the Visual Studio team. Among other things, Sarika took care of the completely new Visual Studio user interface—and not only in this book! I can't think of anyone who could have done better: Sarika was the test lead for the new WPF-supported user interface of Visual Studio 2010. And finally, at this very moment, I'm reviewing the English translation of this book, which I originally wrote in German. All this is so exciting that I wanted to tell you about it at the beginning of this book. And in case we ever meet in person: since you already know what I do for a living—don't bother to ask... I still don't really know what to say.

Who Should Read This Book

Visual Basic has always had a special target audience. Typically, a Visual Basic programmer expects his favorite programming language to allow him to focus primarily on domain-specific knowledge and achieve a great solution in an exceptionally short time. That's the reason Visual Basic 6 became so popular to begin with, and why so many great business solutions are still programmed in older Visual Basic versions. Now, Visual Basic has grown up: what was missing from Visual Basic 6 is here now, and is often better and easier to use than in any other .NET language. Yet the typical Visual Basic developer can still expect Visual Basic to help him provide an architecture for his domain-specific application in a comparatively short time. Version 2010 is—in terms of OOP and being team enabled—as powerful as C#. BASICally, it provides developers the best of both worlds.

This book is for those developers who want to reach the high bar Visual Basic sets. The book doesn't start at square one, but it doesn't require a lot of previous knowledge, either. It leads you and teaches you the things you need to know to become as skilled in modern software development methodologies and object-oriented programming as you already are in your domain-specific area. You'll get results that are as fast as is possible with Visual Basic 6, but at the same time you'll develop quality applications that don't need to hide behind the C# or C++ competitors.

Assumptions

This book expects that you have at least a minimal understanding of procedural programming concepts. If you have not yet picked up the basic principles of Visual Basic programming, you might consider reading Michael Halvorson's *Microsoft Visual Basic 2010 Step by Step* (Microsoft Press, 2010).

Other than that, you're good to go!

Who Should Not Read This Book

Not every book is aimed at every possible audience. If you don't want to become an expert in Visual Basic and have fun learning at the same time, this book is not for you! Just kidding. But honestly, if you (as already stated in the previous section) don't have a basic knowledge about what programming is, or maybe have only had some basic (or, even better—BASIC) classes in high school or college, you should consider starting with a book that teaches the BASIC language from scratch. This book focuses on the Visual Basic language itself; it only scratches the surface of topics like Windows Forms programming or Windows Presentation Foundation. While this book provides sufficient information for you to build your first applications based on those technologies, it doesn't focus on them; there are whole books written about those topics alone, so don't expect this book to cover those subjects in depth.

Organization of This Book

This book is divided into six sections.

- Part I, Beginning with Language and Tools, provides an introduction to the Visual Basic language and the Visual Studio Integrating Development Environment. It also shows you how to develop applications based on Windows Forms or Windows Presentation Foundation (WPF) in practical step-by-step lessons.

- Part II, Object-Oriented Programming, lets you become an expert software developer and provides you with all the tools and techniques for building professional and robust .NET business applications that can compete with industrial standards.

- Part III, Programming with .NET Framework Data Structures, shows the important details that you need to hone your Visual Basic skills to perfection. It covers topics like programming with generic data types, Nullables, Tuples, Events, Delegates, and Lambdas. Most of all, this part provides you with the in-depth knowledge of arrays and collections that you need.

- Part IV, Development Simplification in Visual Basic 2010, shows you how to use features which are unique to Visual Basic, and provides shortcuts for many of the tasks you need to solve in your daily programming routine.

- Part V, Language-Integrated Query—LINQ, is all about querying data stored in various data source types. It demonstrates how to construct queries that filter, order, and group information from internal lists and object collections, as well as from data that comes from external data sources like SQL Server or XML documents.

- Part VI, Parallelizing Applications, is another important part of this book. Have you noticed that the clock speeds of modern processors haven't increased much over the last years? Well, the processor core counts certainly have. So, to really get all the performance you need (even from smaller computers like tablet PCs or netbooks), you need to parallelize your applications. This final section shows you how to do that—and what pitfalls might result.

Conventions and Features in This Book

This book presents information by using conventions designed to make the information readable and easy to follow.

- Boxed elements with labels such as "Note" provide additional information or alternative methods for completing a step successfully.

- Text that you type (apart from code blocks) appears in bold.

- A plus sign (+) between two key names means that you must press those keys at the same time. For example, "Press Alt+Tab" means that you hold down the Alt key while you press the Tab key.

- When the constraints of the printed page require code lines to break where they normally wouldn't, an arrow icon (➥) appears at the beginning of the new line.

- A vertical bar between two or more menu items (such as File | Close), means that you should select the first menu or menu item, then the next, and so on.

System Requirements

You will need the following software to complete the practice exercises in this book:

- One of Windows XP with Service Pack 3, Windows Vista with Service Pack 2 (except Starter Edition), Windows 7, Windows Server 2003 with Service Pack 2, Windows Server 2003 R2, Windows Server 2008 with Service Pack 2, or Windows Server 2008 R2.

- Visual Studio 2010, any edition (multiple downloads may be required if using Express Edition products)

- Computer that has a 1.6GHz or faster processor (2GHz recommended)

- 1 GB (32 Bit) or 2 GB (64 Bit) RAM (Add 512 MB if running in a virtual machine or SQL Server Express Editions, more for advanced SQL Server editions)

- 3.5GB of available hard disk space

- 5400 RPM hard disk drive

- DirectX 9 capable video card running at 1024 x 768 or higher-resolution display

- DVD-ROM drive (if installing Visual Studio from DVD)

- Internet connection to download software or chapter examples

Depending on your Windows configuration, you might require local administrator rights to install or configure Visual Studio 2010 and SQL Server 2008 products.

Code Samples

Most of the chapters in this book include exercises that let you interactively try out new material learned in the main text. All sample projects are available for download here:

http://go.microsoft.com/FWLink/?Linkid=223982

Follow the instructions to download the VbDevBook2010Samples.zip file.

Alternatively, you can download the files from the author's company website:

http://www.activedevelop.de/download/VbDevBook2010Samples.zip

 Note In addition to the code samples, your system should have Visual Studio 2010 and SQL Server 2008 installed. The instructions below use SQL Server Management Studio 2008 to set up the sample database used with the practice examples. If available, install the latest service packs for each product.

Installing the Code Samples

Follow these steps to install the code samples on your computer so that you can use them with the exercises in this book.

1. Unzip the VbDevBook2010Samples.zip file that you downloaded from the book's website.

2. If prompted, review the displayed license agreement. If you accept the terms, select the accept option, and then click Next.

Using the Code Samples

The folder created by the Setup.exe program is structured by chapters. In the chapters of this book when the text refers to a certain sample, it shows the relevant part of the folder where you unzipped the samples to. In every sample folder you'll find a Visual Basic solution file with the file extension .sln. Open this solution from within Visual Studio and run the sample according to what is stated in the text.

Acknowledgments

From Klaus Löffelmann:

First I would like to thank Lisa Feigenbaum. She put a lot of effort into the concept of this book and not only helped me to work out the relevant topics but also to perfect the English version. As community manager, Lisa is the primary contact for MVPs, and provides us with first-hand information. I'm sure I can speak for all MVPs: we are lucky to work with Lisa. Lisa, you rock!

Next I want to thank Sarika Calla, who not only agreed to reveal many aspects of the new Visual Studio user interface but who also was always at hand with help and advice while I was writing this book. It is great to be able to ask the real experts—those who developed Visual Basic and Visual Studio—while researching new topics for a book this size. Thank you for co-authoring this book!

I would also like to thank Ramona Leenings, our IT specialist trainee. Ramona not only created more than 90 percent of the screen shots of the original book (even though she hated it; it's not really a great job) but also edited and converted many examples, and wrote the practical WPF examples in Chapter 5. At age 20, Ramona is already a first-class developer, and has a knack for aesthetics and design. She is ambitious and linguistically able. I expect the Visual Basic and .NET communities to encounter her name more often in the upcoming years. Ramona, I'm your fan!

I want to thank the ActiveDevelop lead developer Andreas Belke (our database expert), who helped me with the LINQ part. It is always a lot of fun to work with Andreas. We are united by the fact that—like me—Andreas is a big fan of the Pacific Standard time zone.

Thomas Irlbeck, as the technical German editor,had the thankless task of checking the book to ensure the content was both correct and plausible. He attacked this task bravely, and his efforts ensured the quality of this book. His eye for detail is incredible, and he catches discrepancies that the authors overlook even after reading the text ten times.

Also, thanks to the folks at Octal Publishing, Inc., who handled the production of this book. I appreciate their commitment to get the first page proofs of this book to the printing press on time, and I enjoyed working with you, and I really had fun playing a Word-comment match while reviewing this book!

A big thank you also goes to Russell Jones from O'Reilly whose task was to convert my more-German-than-English-speech into a readable form. And thanks to this book's production editor, Kristen Borg, for giving me five more days for the review—I really needed the sleep! ;-)

And of course I want to thank my parents. First, I literally couldn't be here without you, and for that alone, I have to thank you! You had to put up with me while I was writing. I won't say anything too personal here. Instead I'll give you each a big kiss on the cheek.

And finally, there is my girlfriend: Adriana, I know I can be difficult, especially when I'm swamped with writing and contemplating chapters, screenshots, and debugging samples, and therefore, often trapped in a parallel universe. But your patience with me seems endless, and I so appreciate the extraordinary care you give to me. Thanks for always letting me be myself and for taking me the way I am—I love you so much! Please know, this book is dedicated to you.

From Sarika Calla:

In co-authoring this book, I have been helped by many people. I would like to thank Manish Jayaswal, Microsoft, and my father-in-law, Mr. R.K. Purohit for the care with which they reviewed my original manuscript. I am deeply indebted to Klaus Löffelmann, co-author of this book, and to Lisa Feigenbaum, who provided invaluable advice from inception to conclusion of this project. Last, but not least, I owe a great debt of gratitude to my husband Bhanu, my children, Shubham and Soham, my parents (Dr. S.K. Calla and Dr. Sudha Calla), my mother-in-law (Mrs. Sharda Purohit), and other family members (Surabhi, Nitesh, Dr. Veena, Dr. Rajesh, Yogi) and friends for their tremendous support and encouragement.

Thanks,
Sarika

Errata and Book Support

We've made every effort to ensure the accuracy of this book and its companion content. Any errors that have been reported since this book was published are listed on our Microsoft Press site at oreilly.com:

http://go.microsoft.com/FWLink/?Linkid=224787

If you find an error that is not already listed, you can report it to us through the same page.

If you need additional support, email Microsoft Press Book Support at mspinput@microsoft.com.

Please note that product support for Microsoft software is not offered through the addresses above.

We Want to Hear from You

At Microsoft Press, your satisfaction is our top priority, and your feedback our most valuable asset. Please tell us what you think of this book at:

http://www.microsoft.com/learning/booksurvey

The survey is short, and we read every one of your comments and ideas. Thanks in advance for your input!

Stay in Touch

Let's keep the conversation going! We're on Twitter: *http://twitter.com/MicrosoftPress*.

Part I
Beginning with Language and Tools

Chapter 1
Beginners All-Purpose Symbolic Instruction Code

Looking at the chapter title, you're probably thinking, "What a strange name for a chapter!" Why this name? Well, if you take the first letter of each word in the phrase *"Beginners All-purpose Symbolic Instruction Code"* they form the acronym, "BASIC." Developed in 1964 by John George Kemeny and Thomas Eugene Kurtz at Dartmouth College (they also came up with the name), BASIC, as it was originally conceived, had very little to do with the programming language we know today as Microsoft Visual Basic 2010. It was as far removed from the object-oriented programming we use today as Columbus was from India at the end of his famous voyage of discovery.

However, the modern version of the language contains fundamental linguistic elements, such as variable declarations and the use of structural commands, that are still very much "basic-esque," according to the original definition of BASIC. In this chapter, you will learn all that you need to know about these fundamental language elements.

Don't roll your eyes now, and say, "Oh, come on! I already know all that stuff!" It's possible that you really *do* already know everything contained in this chapter, in which case, by all means, you can pat yourself on the back and praise yourself, saying "Man—I'm good! I'm going to continue with object oriented-programming right away!" And then, highly motivated, you apply yourself to those much more challenging topics elsewhere in the book.

Or...you can read through the following sections and maybe catch yourself once in a while saying, "What? That works too?"

Either way, let me point out here that this chapter is not meant as a beginner's handbook, explaining the language at length, and it certainly doesn't start at square one. You should already be familiar with basic programming–preferably *in* BASIC; the following sections are meant to summarize Visual Basic for you, while showing you the differences between the BASIC dialects that you might have worked with so far—all in as concise a format as possible. It is not the purpose of this chapter to teach Visual Basic from scratch.

Starting Visual Studio for the First Time

These days, programming in Visual Basic means that you are very likely to spend 99.999 percent of your time in Microsoft Visual Studio. The rest of the time you probably spend searching for code files from other projects and binding them into your current project—or rebooting Visual Studio after it has crashed, which, thankfully, has become extremely rare after Service Pack 1 became available.

The integrated development environment (IDE) in Visual Studio 2010 provides tools in a user interface that help you to design your programs. Sorted according to importance these tools are:

- The Visual Basic 2010 Compiler, which becomes active when you use a command to start the compilation (in the *Create* menu or the corresponding Toolbar).

> **Note** The compiler translates programs that you write into Microsoft Intermediate Language (MSIL), which then is converted into processor code at runtime, taking the specific machine characteristics into account. You will learn more about this in Chapter 2, "Introduction to the .NET Framework." In the interest of being thorough, Visual Studio also provides other compilers for C++ or C#, but we're not worried about those in this context. Visual Basic Express provides a leaner version of Visual Studio, which only contains the Visual Basic Compiler. Of course, you have the option of adding Visual C# Express or C++ Express. You can find the link to Express downloads at *http://www.microsoft.com/Express/*.

- The Visual Studio Editor, which provides syntax highlighting support, IntelliSense, and other aids while you are editing the source code of your program.

- Various designers with corresponding tool dialogs, which support you as you create forms and other visual objects.

- The Solution Explorer, which manages and organizes the code files in your project.

However, starting Visual Studio 2010 for the first time doesn't take you directly to this IDE. Instead, the Choose Default Environment Settings dialog box appears, as presented in Figure 1-1.

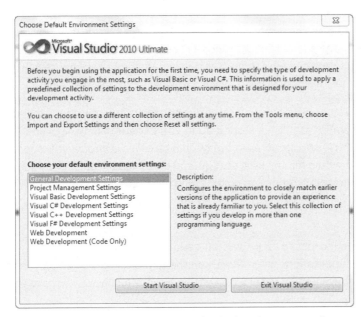

FIGURE 1-1 When starting the program for the first time, you need to customize the default settings for the development environment.

In this dialog, you decide which default settings to use to configure the development environment. Your best bet is to select General Development Settings.

Tip General Development Settings is the default for most Visual Studio 2005/2008 and 2010 installations. Visual Basic Development Settings include specific customizations, which provide the possibility to quickly adjust certain Visual Basic commands for dialog layout, command menus, and shortcuts. For example, the dialog for creating a new project is limited to Visual Basic projects only; some options, such as creating a solution directory along with a new project, are automatically hidden when you create a new project. You are able to create projects without naming them, and then later, at the end of your development session, you can choose whether to save them with a specific name. The same concepts apply to commands, which you can call by using drop-down menus: "Customized" means that many functions, which could also affect Visual Basic projects, are simply hidden.

Try different variations to see what works best for you. If, later on, you are no longer happy with the default settings you selected here, see Chapter 3, "Sightseeing," for help on how to reset your Visual Studio settings.

Console Applications

If you are developing for end users, you are probably creating programs that use the Windows graphic user interface. In Microsoft .NET jargon, such applications are called *Windows Forms applications*, or *WinForms applications* for short. For end users, this is currently the simplest and most familiar way to navigate a program; however, that project type is not necessarily appropriate when it comes to teaching developers, because the bells and whistles of the Windows UI, with all its graphic elements (such as buttons, dialog boxes, mouse control, and so on) can distract learners from focusing on each particular language element.

In .NET, you can use another project type, as well, which results in applications that older programmers will remember fondly (I'll leave it up to you to determine what "older" is) and server administrators will know about, even today. They're called *console applications*. These are programs that start with a minimalistic user interface. You launch such programs directly from the Windows command prompt and control them exclusively by using the keyboard. The only interface between the user and the program is a character-oriented monitor output and the keyboard.

The following sections concentrate exclusively on designing console applications. As mentioned before, console applications let you focus on the fundamentals. The following step-by-step instructions show you how to set up a console application, after you have started Visual Studio:

1. From the File menu, select the New command, and then click Project. Visual Studio will display the dialog box shown in Figure 1-2.

2. Under Installed Templates, open the branch Visual Basic, and then select Windows.

3. In the center pane, select Console Application, as shown in Figure 1-2.

4. Enter the name of your new project. If you would like to create an explicit solution directory, be sure to select the Create Solution Directory check box.

Note Visual Studio is designed to support anything from tiny sample programs to extremely complex and extensive projects. So extensive in fact, that on the one hand, a single project can lose clarity and transparency, but on the other hand, by dividing a project into parts, you can often make some of those parts available for use in other projects. This is why you would usually not simply create projects, but also a "project folder", called a solution (Visual Basic Express uses slightly different terminology, but in general it manages solutions, as well). In the simplest case a solution contains only one project—your Windows or console application. A solution directory makes sense, when you expect your solution to contain several projects. In addition to your main application these other projects might include, for example, additional class libraries or completely different project types, such as web services. In this case, the root directory contains only the solution file, which, by the way, has the extension *.sln*.

Tip Because there are quite a lot of templates for different purposes and different programming languages, you can always use the search box in the upper-right corner to find the template you're looking for in no time: simply type in keywords or keyword abbreviations like "visual basic" ("vb" works just as well) or "console" to narrow the list down to those templates that match the keyword.

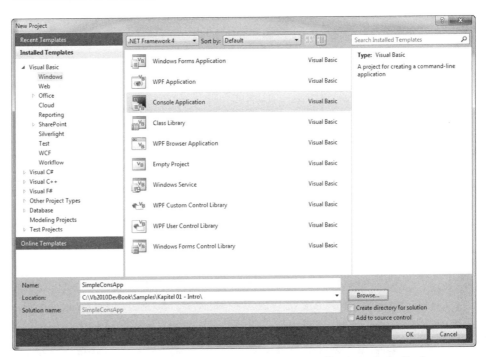

FIGURE 1-2 Use the New Project dialog box to create a new project for a console application.

5. Click the Browse button located in the lower-right portion of the window, specify the *path* to the location where you would like to save your project, and then click OK when you are done.

After you click OK, the Visual Basic Code Editor opens. Enter the following lines between the commands *Sub Main* and *End Sub*.

```
Sub Main()

    Dim dateOfBirth As Date
    Dim age As Integer

    Console.Write("Please enter your date of birth (mm/dd/yyyy): ")
    dateOfBirth = Date.Parse(Console.ReadLine())
    age = (Now.Subtract(dateOfBirth)).Days \ 365
    Console.Write("You are {0} years old", age)
    Console.ReadKey()
End Sub
```

Your results should look similar to Figure 1-3.

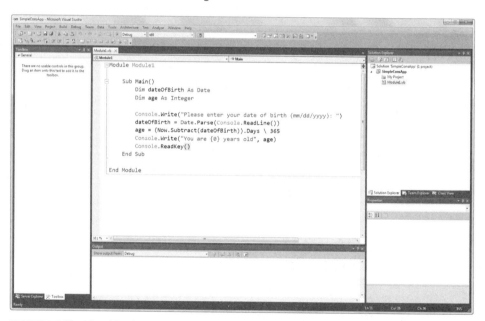

FIGURE 1-3 The Visual Studio 2010 IDE showing a new console application and a few lines of code.

Starting an Application

Start your new application by either pressing F5, clicking the start icon on the Toolbar, or clicking the Start Debugging command on the Debug menu. Upon startup, you are asked to enter your date of birth. You can see immediately how very different console applications are from the much more familiar Windows applications. You interact with the program solely by using the keyboard and the text-only display on your monitor. Figure 1-4 shows you how this first console application should look.

FIGURE 1-4 A typical console application. The user interacts with the application via the keyboard and the text-only output.

Important When you start an application following the steps just described, the speed at which it runs (regardless of whether it's a console application or a Windows Forms application) does not correspond at all to the speed at which it will run outside the Visual Studio user environment. The Visual Studio IDE can help you to check the application for errors and bugs by using the automatically attached debugger. For example, you can insert breakpoints at certain lines (by placing your cursor in a line and pressing F9 to automatically stop your program when it reaches a breakpoint). You can then examine the state of your program as it runs and even step through the program line by line (F11) or procedure by procedure (F10). This all takes time during program execution, whether you are actually using these features or not.

You can circumvent this overhead to see your application run at a more normal speed by instead pressing Ctrl+F5 to start it, or by selecting Start Without Debugging on the Debug menu. Of course, you won't be able to avail yourself of the Debugger functionality when you launch the application this way.

Tip You can also add a toolbar to make the entire debugging functionality more easily available by right-clicking an empty space within the Visual Studio IDE Toolbar to display the context menu and then selecting Debug, which displays the Toolbar, as shown in Figure 1-5.

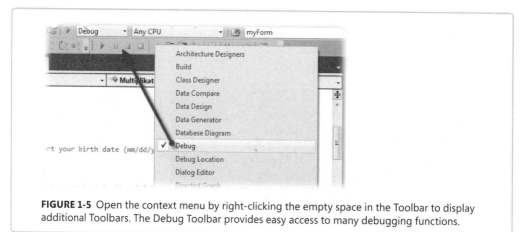

FIGURE 1-5 Open the context menu by right-clicking the empty space in the Toolbar to display additional Toolbars. The Debug Toolbar provides easy access to many debugging functions.

Anatomy of a (Visual Basic) Program

The initial methods to store computer data weren't magnetic; they didn't use diskettes or hard disks. Instead, early computers used punched tape, which was a paper tape with small holes stamped in it in specific patterns that represented the data. The punched tapes were fed through a special reader, and based on the configuration of these holes, the previously punched bits and bytes found their way into the computer. Interestingly, punched-tape devices were first used in the textile industry, not in the shape of an early computer, and not for storing sales volume or customer information; instead, they were used in looms. The information needed to control the loom was stored in the form of small wooden plates, arranged behind one another in a certain order.

This early scheme corresponds to how we define what a computer should do today, and thus to the anatomy of a program:

1. You need something that you process: namely data (or wool, in the textile industry).

2. You need instructions to control how something is processed: the program statements (or the knitting pattern).

Of course, this is an extreme simplification, and it doesn't even begin to suggest the incredible variety and number of the possibilities. This first application is but the tip of the iceberg. To demonstrate this, Figure 1-6 presents another, slightly more polished version of the first example. This version is intended to give you a better understanding of the different aspects of typical Visual Basic program anatomy (even though it's still only a console application).

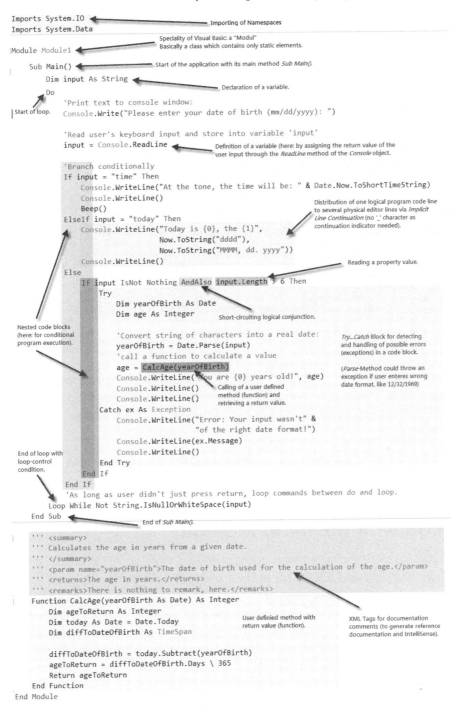

```vbnet
Imports System.IO          ◄──────────── Importing of Namespaces
Imports System.Data

                              Speciality of Visual Basic: a "Modul"
                              Basically a class which contains only static elements.
Module Module1     ◄────────

    Sub Main()     ◄──────────── Start of the application with its main method Sub Main().

        Dim input As String    ◄────────── Declaration of a variable.

        Do
                'Print text to console window:
Start of loop.  Console.Write("Please enter your date of birth (mm/dd/yyyy): ")

                'Read user's keyboard input and store into variable 'input'
                input = Console.ReadLine    ◄────── Definition of a variable (here: by assigning the return value of the
                                                    user input through the ReadLine method of the Console object.

            'Branch conditionally
            If input = "time" Then
                Console.WriteLine("At the tone, the time will be: " & Date.Now.ToShortTimeString)
                Console.WriteLine()
                                                        Distribution of one logical program code line
                Beep()                                  to several physical editor lines via Implicit
            ElseIf input = "today" Then                 Line Continuation (no '_' character as
                Console.WriteLine("Today is {0}, the {1}",  continuation indicator needed).
                            Now.ToString("dddd"),
                            Now.ToString("MMMM, dd. yyyy"))

                Console.WriteLine()                     ◄────── Reading a property value.
            Else
                If input IsNot Nothing AndAlso input.Length > 6 Then
                    Try
                        Dim yearOfBirth As Date
                        Dim age As Integer          Short-circuiting logical conjunction.

                        'Convert string of characters into a real date:    Try...Catch Block for detecting
                        yearOfBirth = Date.Parse(input)                    and handling of possible errors
                        'call a function to calculate a value              (exceptions) in a code block.
                        age = CalcAge(yearOfBirth)
                        Console.WriteLine("You are {0} years old!", age)   (Parse-Method could throw an
                        Console.WriteLine()          Calling of a user defined   exception if user enteres wrong
                        Console.WriteLine()          method (function) and       date format, like 12/32/1969)
                    Catch ex As Exception            retrieving a return value.
                        Console.WriteLine("Error: Your input wasn't" &
                                        "of the right date format!")
                        Console.WriteLine(ex.Message)
                        Console.WriteLine()
                    End Try
                End If
            End If
                'As long as user didn't just press return, loop commands between do and loop.
        Loop While Not String.IsNullOrWhiteSpace(input)
    End Sub     ◄────────── End of Sub Main().
```

Nested code blocks (here: for conditional program execution).

End of loop with loop-control condition.

```vbnet
    ''' <summary>
    ''' Calculates the age in years from a given date.
    ''' </summary>
    ''' <param name="yearOfBirth">The date of birth used for the calculation of the age.</param>
    ''' <returns>The age in years.</returns>
    ''' <remarks>There is nothing to remark, here.</remarks>
    Function CalcAge(yearOfBirth As Date) As Integer
        Dim ageToReturn As Integer
        Dim today As Date = Date.Today            User defined method with    XML Tags for documentation
        Dim diffToDateOfBirth As TimeSpan         return value (function).    comments (to generate reference
                                                                              documentation and IntelliSense).
        diffToDateOfBirth = today.Subtract(yearOfBirth)
        ageToReturn = diffToDateOfBirth.Days \ 365
        Return ageToReturn
    End Function
End Module
```

FIGURE 1-6 The anatomy of a small Visual Basic application.

Figure 1-6 also demonstrates that while an application consists of data and program state-ments, program statements can obviously have a variety of different structures. These struc-tures are easier to understand by looking at how the example program works again (see Figure 1-7), before focusing on its internal functions and the individual components of the BASIC language.

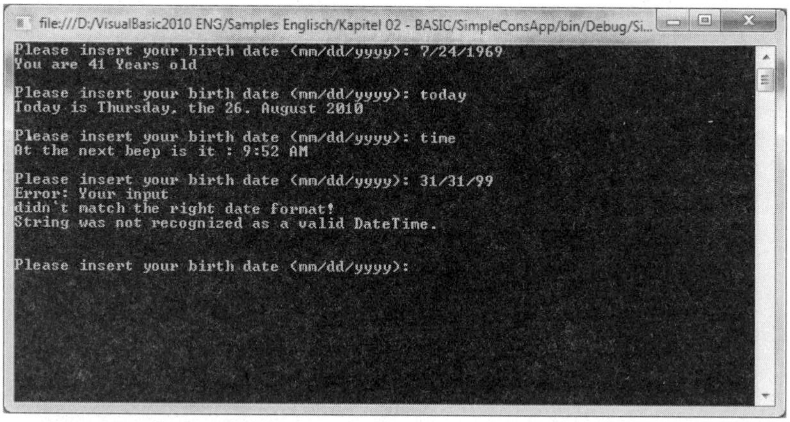

FIGURE 1-7 The Professional Edition of this example has a few more features up its sleeve than the first "lite" version.

To begin, after starting the application, you either enter a birth date or one of the commands **today** or **time**. The program responds as shown in Figure 1-7. If you enter a date using an invalid format, the program recognizes and catches the error and displays a corresponding message.

Internally, this application functions rather simply. The schematic provides an admittedly alternative glimpse into the elements used to build the application.

Starting Up with the *Main* Method

Each console application starts with a certain method, which in Visual Basic (and many other languages) always has the name *Main*, and contains statements that are encapsulated between *Sub* and *End Sub* commands (in Visual Basic only). A *Sub* in Visual Basic defines a method without return values. A console application needs at least this one *Main* method so that Windows knows where your program begins. In Visual Basic, you define methods that return values with the *Function* keyword and designate the return value with the *Return* key-word. The following section explains this in more detail.

The History of Important Programming Languages, and the History of *Sub Main*

In today's business world, when we talk about programming languages, we essentially only encounter two separate concepts: procedurally-structured and object-oriented programming. As the following section shows, procedural means that the code can be reused or used multiple times because it can be called from different points within the program and always returns to the same place from which it was called. By the way, another word for *method* is *procedure*, and this is where reusable code is placed, which is why this form of conceptional structuring is called procedural programming.

The term structured programming comes from certain structural constructs, such as *If ... Then ... Else* or *Switch* constructs. And object-oriented programming adds another abstraction level on top of that, but this is not of interest to us at the moment. What we are focusing on here is where it all started.

We need to go back to 1958; a time when developers still had to program their computers, on foot, so to speak, in direct machine code. A programmer at IBM named John Backus became so annoyed with this way of developing that he approached his supervisors with a request that he be allowed to develop a utility program to alleviate the problem.

At the time, Backus worked on an IBM System 704 mainframe computer. His utility was designed to help programmers by using commands that were a little closer to human language, and which also permitted the analysis and calculation of mathematical functions directly. The high-falutin' name of this project was *The IBM Mathematical Formula Translation System*. However, for Backus to pronounce this name each time he talked about the project would have probably delayed the completion of the project by another year, so he decided on a shorter nickname made up of a couple of first syllables. Thus, one of the first standard languages was born: ForTran (written here with a capital "T" to clarify the syllable origin).

At that time, all standard languages followed the so-called imperative concept, by which commands are handled one after the other. There were really no structures, not to mention procedures. The few deviations from the normal program execution took place when jump targets were reached (for example, a *GOTO* statement) or when one of the three passable jump targets could be reached with an *IF* statement (depending on whether the expression to be examined was less than, equal to, or greater than 0). With each subsequent development, the programming languages slowly evolved via various Fortran and Algol versions until eventually CPL (*Combined Program Language*) was created. This was a programming language that tried to unite the best aspects of Fortran and Algol (the languages for scientific applications) as well as Cobol (the language for finance-mathematical applications). Unfortunately the result was a monster, which, in spite of possessing the ideal requirements to serve as a platform for a language compiler, was much too large and sluggish.

Martin Richards of Cambridge University took CPL under his wing (some say the abbreviation stands for *Cambridge Program Language*, because it was developed in part at Cambridge[1]). He slimmed it down and thus created the language BCPL, which could only be used correctly on mainframe computers, but which was now suitable as a platform for further compiler development.

Just as an aside, BCPL was the first programming language that marked language structures{

```
    well, {
    let's say:
            { a basic approach }
        }
    }
```

for the first time with curly brackets.

Around 1969, Ken Thompson and Dennis Ritchie of the famous Bell Laboratories set for themselves the goal of getting BCPL to run on mini-computers. At the time, mini-computers were also minimalists with respect to hardware, so this was an ambitious goal. To complicate matters even further, there was only one way to do things: *every* element that wasn't absolutely vital for the language had to be removed. Thompson and Ritchie did exactly that and more; in their eagerness to save space, they didn't even spare the name. Therefore, BCPL became simply "B," which was—as you might begin to suspect—the daddy of C and the grand-daddy of C++ (and eventually C#). As a point of interest, the tutorial about B implementation by B.W. Kernighan and Murray Hill states right away on the first page, directly below Section 2, "General Program Layout":

```
main( ) {
            statements
        }
newfunc(arg1, arg2) {
            statements
        }

fun3(arg) {
              more statements
        }
```

---

[1] To be accurate, CPL was a common project between Cambridge University and the computer department of London University, which led to assertions that that was the reason to change the original name *Cambridge Programming Language* to *Combined Programming Language,* rather than being a combination of two computer language worlds.

And further:

> " All B programs consist of one or more "functions", which are similar to the
> functions and subroutines of a Fortran program, or the procedures of PL/I. main
> is such a function, and in fact all B programs must have a main. Execution of the
> program begins at the first statement of main, and usually ends at the last. Main
> will usually invoke other functions to perform its job, some coming from the same
> program, and others from libraries."[2]

So now you know a little more about the evolution of the important programming languages of today as well as the historical significance of the *Main* function, which existed more than 35 years ago in B, and whose name survived until today as a symbol identifier for the entry point to start a program.

Methods with and Without Return Values

The *Main* method enjoys a special status within an application because it needs at least one user-defined (custom) type, within which it can reside, and it defines the starting point of the application solely by its name. A custom type is essentially a class—Visual Basic also has a special kind of class called a *module*. A module is essentially just a class that has methods available to any caller who can access the module. These methods are also called *static* methods.

Methods are the units into which your program is arranged. Just as the operating system calls the *Main* method, you can call methods in your programs. These can be custom methods that you write or methods exposed by objects that the .NET Framework provides.

You can assign general requirements to methods for completing their tasks—but you don't have to. Such general requirements are called *parameters* or *arguments*. Whether a method can accept arguments is determined by its *signature*. The signature specifies which arguments and which types of arguments the method expects as well as the order or sequence in which it expects them.

Referring back to Figure 1-6, you can see several methods and how those methods are defined in the program. For example, *Console.WriteLine* calls a method of the class *Console*. The method displays whatever is passed as an argument in a certain format—also defined by an argument—in the console window.

---

[2] FTP://cm.bell-labs.com/cm/cs/who/dmr/scbref.pdf

Defining Methods Without Return Values by Using *Sub*

In Visual Basic, you define methods in two ways. One way is to use the keyword *Sub*. These are methods that can take arguments but will not return a result, as shown in the following:

```
Sub MethodName([Parameter1 As Typ1[, Parameter2 As Typ2]])
    [Statements]
    [Exit Sub|Return]
End Sub
```

To end method execution early, you can use either *Exit Sub* or *Return* statements—it doesn't matter which one you use. Exiting early makes sense only when you're checking for a certain condition or state, which you might do by using *If ... Then ... Else* constructs (you will learn more about them later in this chapter).

Defining Methods with Return Values by Using *Function*

Methods can also return a function result. In Visual Basic, you define such a method with the *Function* keyword, as follows:

```
Function MethodName([Parameter1 As Typ1[, Parameter2 As Typ2]]) as ReturnType
    [Statements]
    [Exit Sub]
    [Statements]
    Return FunctionResult
End Sub
```

The method *CalcAge* in Figure 1-6 is an example of this. This method receives a birth date as an argument and returns an integer to the calling instance. The return value type is specified with the words *As Integer* at the end of the method definition.

For methods that return values (*Functions* in Visual Basic), *Return* has a different meaning than for methods, which don't return values (*Sub* methods). *Return* not only ends execution as it does in a *Sub* method, but it also specifies *which* value to return. The value follows the *Return* keyword.

Declaring Variables

The application example *declares* a variable in the first line of its *Main* method. Variables are places in which a method or program can store data during its lifetime. Thus, the following line determines that the variable *input* can take content of the type *string*:

```
Dim input As String
```

The *String* type restricts the *input* variable to character strings: in other words, any kind of text. The *String* keyword, therefore, represents a type that contains text. If you were to specify *Integer* as the type, the variable *input* could save numbers between approximately −2 billion and +2 billion, but only integers, no fractions. If you were to specify *Double* as the type, the *input* variable could also hold fractions. However, their range of value becomes smaller as the fractions become more accurate. Fractions are also called *floating point numbers*, because the decimal point can be moved.

> **Important** In .NET (not just in Visual Basic), *type safety* is very important, because using the wrong types is a common source of errors. For example, if you write and sort a date in the Irish date format (dd.mm.yyyy) as a string, then 11.10.2002 is bigger than 10.11.2005, because 11 is greater than 10. But when you look at it as a date, the second date is of course later (greater) than the first, which is the earlier or smaller date value. One way to look at it is in the form of the number of elapsed time units. For dates further in the past, fewer seconds have passed than for later dates. Sorting dates as strings leads to a completely different result than sorting by date.

For a description of the different types you can use in .NET Framework, and therefore also in your Visual Basic programs, see Chapter 6, "The Essential .NET Data Types."

Visual Basic and the *Dim* Keyword: a Brief History

There are historical reasons why variables in Visual Basic are typecast by using the keyword *Dim*. This process is correctly called *Declaring of Variables*. In early versions of BASIC, it was possible to use a variable by simply providing a name, without defining anything about the type of that variable beforehand. The BASIC interpreter created and typed variables only at runtime, according to the context of their assignment. However, this was not the case for so-called arrays (groups of variables), which could be accessed by using one or more index values. For example, you can access individual array elements within loops by using counter variables. Of course, that is still possible, because arrays are still a central part of all .NET languages. The point is that even in early BASIC, you already had to define the dimensions and limits of an array (upper and lower bounds and number of dimensions). You did that by using the *DIM* statement.

Simply declaring a variable doesn't give it a value. However, when a variable type has some kind of basic state, it automatically receives an appropriate default value; for example, all numeric data types have the value 0, *False* is the default value for *Boolean* variables, and *Null (nothing)* for strings. Here, *Null* can actually be a value or state of a variable (and philosophically speaking, the computer therefore creates a contradiction in terms: "the state *is* nothing"), but just accept that for now. (You can find some good background information about *Null* on Wikipedia.)

The .NET Framework—or more precisely, the Common Type System (CTS), which regulates different data types throughout the .NET Framework—differentiates between two data types: value types and reference types. The essential and highly optimized value types, built directly into .NET Framework, are, for example, *Integer, Long, Single, Double, Decimal, Date,* and *String*. Because they are so deeply embedded into the .NET Framework and at the same time so highly optimized and not derived from some other type, they are also called *primitive data types*.

> **Note** Technically speaking, this last statement isn't entirely correct. For example, you might have heard someone say correctly that all data types are based on *Object*. Conceptually, however, this statement is inaccurate, because all primitive data types are handled specially by the Common Language Runtime (CLR), even if they are based on *ValueType* and therefore on *Object*.

Many different data types are required to save all the different kinds of data correctly—after all, you wouldn't necessarily put your coats in a drawer while hanging your socks in the closet; that might work, but it wouldn't be very practical. So the .NET Framework has a number of primitive data types that are designed for various tasks, as presented in the following list:

- *Byte, Short, Integer, Long, SByte, UShort, UInteger, ULong*   These data types save numerical values without decimal places. Using these types, you couldn't save the constant *Pi* with anything close to its actual value; it would end at 3 and drop the post-decimal fractional portion. These so-called integer data types differ only by value range and the memory space they require. For example, *Long* requires 8 bytes, but it covers a wide value range, from about −9 billion to +9 billion. The *Byte* type, on the other hand, needs only one byte, but only covers values between 0 and 255.

> **Note** This value of 255, which appears so arbitrary and uneven to mere mortals, in fact has historic underpinnings. The smallest unit of information a computer can handle is one *Bit*: A stream flows or it doesn't, which corresponds to *True* or *False* or *0* or *1*. However, just 0 and 1 aren't sufficient to represent the world around us.
>
> During the design phase of one of the first IBM mainframe computers, a design engineer named Werner Buchholz placed a few bits (initially 6) behind each other and thus turned them into a *Bite*. However, because the terms Bite and Bit were so often mixed up, *Bite* became *Byte*. But 6 Bits corresponds to a value range of 0–63 (2^6 = 64), which even back then often didn't cover a large enough value range. Thus, with the passing of time, 8 Bits became the basic size unit for a *Byte*.

All data storage in computing is based on the byte as a size unit: a *Short* requires 2 bytes, and therefore covers a value range from −32768 to +32767. The *UShort* type (the *U* before the data type name indicates that it is *unsigned*) does not have a sign (− or +). Therefore, the data range changes to 0 to 65,535—negative values are not allowed for integer data types that start with "U." The most commonly used integer data type is called *Integer*: it consists of 4 bytes, which corresponds to 32 bits, and 32 bits can naturally be handled most quickly by a 32-bit processor. Typically, using *Integer* data types is the fastest way to count within your programs.

- *Single* and *Double*   These data types require four and eight bytes, respectively, and can represent decimals. They are floating-point types, which means that the accuracy depends on the size of the value range. Rounding errors are very common with these data types. Therefore, you should not use them for financial or mathematical applications, but rather for calculating graphs and the like, where speed is more essential than accuracy.

- *Decimal*   This data type is more suitable for high accuracy. Rounding errors, such as when converting from a base-2 to a base-10 system, cannot happen with these because the values are saved differently internally than when using *Single* or *Double*. However, the processor cannot calculate the data type directly, so calculations using this type execute more slowly than those that use *Single* or *Double*. But *Decimal* is still fast enough for financial calculations.

- *Date*   This type stores date values (calendar data). Internally, a *Date* is an 8-byte floating-point number, where the pre-decimal places represent the actual date (day, month, and year) and the post-decimal places represent the time. You will find more details about this data type in Chapter 6.

- *Boolean*   This one is easy because it corresponds to one bit and saves only the numbers 0 and 1, which you can think of as *False* and *True*.

- *Char*   This data type saves a character. For modern programming purposes, characters require 2 bytes, because 256 different characters are no longer enough.

- *String*   This type saves character strings (text). Strictly speaking, strings are arrays of *Char* values.

In addition to these primitive value types, the .NET Framework has "normal" value types, which are composed of primitive data types. For example, the type *Size* is made up of two integer values; it provides methods and properties to define the size of objects or perform size calculations. Another example is the *Location* type, which saves coordinates.

You provide a variable with a value by using an assignment statement, which is explained in the next section.

Nullables

You can declare all value types as *nullables*. A nullable is unique because in addition to a value, it can also have *no* stored value, which is normally not possible for a value type.

As an example, if you declare the following *Integer* variable, you can use it directly— remember, that's part of the nature of value types. They don't need to have an initial value assigned to them in Visual Basic:

```
Dim count As Integer ' Count is 0
```

```
count = count + 1    ' Works, count is now 1
```

In the first line of the preceding code, the integer value type cannot support the idea that *count* has not been assigned a value. This is only possible when a variable has been defined as nullable for a specific type, which you do by appending a type literal (the question mark) to the end of the type name (*Integer*, in this example), as demonstrated in the following:

```
Dim nullableCount As Integer?         ' Count is now Nothing
nullablecount = 0                     ' Assign initial value
nullablecount = nullablecount + 1     ' Works, count is now 1
```

An interesting and useful characteristic of the nullable value type is that you can query it to determine if it has a value by using the *HasValue* property, as shown in the following example:

```
Dim nullableCount As Integer?
nullableCount = 0
nullableCount = nullableCount + 1

Dim anotherNullable As Integer?

Console.WriteLine("Does nullableCount have a value: " & nullableCount.HasValue.ToString)
Console.WriteLine("Does anotherNullable have a value: " & anotherNullable.HasValue.ToString)
```

The preceding sample code produces the following output in the console window:

```
Does nullableCount have a value: True
Does anotherNullable have a value: False
```

To delete the value of a nullable, assign *Nothing* to it:

```
    nullableCount = Nothing
```

Nullables *don't* cause an error when you try to access their value to perform calculations; the result stays "Nothing, unknown, I don't know what it contains"—in short, *Nothing*. The sample code could be explained as follows:

```
    Dim anotherNullable As Integer?         ' Doesn't have a value or value is unknown.
    anotherNullable = anotherNullable + 1   ' and that's how it stays.
    Console.WriteLine("anotherNullable is: " & anotherNullable.ToString)
```

When you run that code, the output is:

```
anotherNullable is:
```

There is literally no output. When trying to perform an addition, Visual Basic can determine that there is nothing in *anotherNullable*. It's not defined, and Visual Basic interprets this state with "I don't know what's in *anotherNullable*." The response is as follows: when Visual Basic doesn't know what a variable contains, and a value is supposed to be added to it, it also doesn't know what the result is. Therefore, the result is again *Nothing*.

Note Nullables are used mainly in database applications, wherein it's customary to define database tables in which the columns of some rows don't contain values. Therefore, there's a difference between a field in a table that contains the value 0 and one that contains no value. Nullables in .NET accommodate such situations. You'll find more detailed explanations about nullables in Chapter 18, "Advanced Types."

Expressions and Definitions of Variables

For numeric as well as date calculations or string operations, it is important to have an understanding of expressions. The following line (see Figure 1-6) is a *String* expression. The *ReadLine* method returns a string (in this case, whatever text the user has entered via the keyboard) and assigns the result to the variable *input*.

```
input = Console.ReadLine()
```

Another example of an expression in the code in Figure 1-6 is the static *Parse* method of the *Date* data type, as shown here:

```
birthyear = Date.Parse(input)
```

By assigning this expression in this manner, the string, which represents the date, is converted into a true date type. Remember, it's important to use the correct type in the correct place. A computer doesn't sort a string that happens to represent a date value as a true date (refer to the sidebar earlier in this chapter for more information). Therefore, you must instruct the *Date* type to parse the string (to go through it character by character and analyze it), to interpret the characters as a date and then convert them accordingly.

Defining and Declaring Variables at the Same Time

You can declare and assign of variables in one operation. So, instead of writing this

```
Dim christmas10 As Date
christmas10 = #12/24/2010#
```

you can condense it to the following:

```
Dim christmas10 As Date = #12/24/2010#
```

> **Note** Beginning with Visual Basic 2008, the *As <type>* portion of a variable declaration is no longer required within procedures (for example, within methods defined with *Sub* or *Function*) when the declaration and assignment happen at the same time. When the option *Local Type Inference* is set (more about this in the section, "Local Type Inference," later in this chapter), the Visual Basic compiler can recognize or *infer* the type for the declaration from the expression type during the expression assignment. Without Local Type Inference, you need to write an assignment and declare a *String* variable as follows:
>
> ```
> Dim almostGerman as String = "Bratwurst und Sauerkraut are yummy!"
> ```
>
> Using Local Type Inference, it's sufficient to write the statements as shown here:
>
> ```
> Dim almostGerman = "Bratwurst und Sauerkraut are yummy!"
> ```
>
> The compiler recognizes, that the constant expression "Bratwurst und Sauerkraut are yummy!" is a string, and infers the correct type when assigning a type. It doesn't recognize, though, that the expression is fundamentally false. Bratwurst only works with French fries—NEVER with Sauerkraut.

Complex Expressions

The result, or the return value, of a method can also serve as the operand of an operator, and you can therefore combine the return values of multiple methods into a complex expression. Just to make this a little more clear, first let's review the method from the initial example:

```
Function CalcAge(ByVal birthYear As Date) As Integer

    Dim retAge As Integer
    Dim today As Date = Date.Now
    Dim diffToBirthdate As TimeSpan

    diffForBirthdate = today.Subtract(bithyear)
    retAge = diffToBirthdate.Days \ 365
    Return retAge

End Function
```

This is constructed in such a way that the result is calculated in several intermediate steps. It's possible not only to calculate the value (which is stored in the next-to-last line in *retAge* and returned with *Return* in the last line), but also to return it at the same time. This is how the code would look rewritten as a complex expression:

```
Function CalcAge(ByVal birthyear As Date) As Integer

    Return Date.Now.Subtract(birthYear).Days \ 365

End Function
```

The preceding condensed code and the longer form shown in the prior example provide the exact same result.

It's not too hard to understand numeric expressions. Most of us were probably confronted with them for the first time in grade school. String expressions behave similarly. For example, the following declaration, expression calculation, and the subsequent definition for *dbl* is 55:

```
Dim dbl As Double
dbl = 5
dbl = dbl +5 * 10
```

> **Note** This calculation follows the rules of priority during the evaluation: "Power before parenthesis, before period, before prime."

Using this as a guide, you can see why "Adriana Ardelean" is stored in the *str* variable as the resulting value in the following:

```
Dim str As String
str = "-> Adriana Ardelean <-"
str = str.Substring(3, 16)
```

Therefore, you can also see why the following code always results in a date that represents two days in the future:

```
Dim dayaftertomorrow As Date
dayAfterTomorrow = Date.Now
dayAfterTomorrow = dayAfterTomorrow.AddDays(2)
```

Boolean Expressions

Numeric expressions, expressions that calculate date values, and string expressions are relatively easy to read and understand. They are similar to the typical curve sketching formulas we all learned in ninth or tenth grade.

How would you read the following expression?

```
Dim var = 5 = 5
```

Is this line valid? If yes, which type has *var* been assigned and what value does it carry?

To begin, yes, this line of code is valid. Second, it defines a variable of type *Boolean*. As mentioned earlier, variables of this type don't have a very large number range because they can only return one of two states, *True* or *False*.

Now let's look at the expression from a slightly more analytical standpoint: 5 = 5 is a true assertion. The result of the expression 5 = 5 is therefore *True*. In this case, the operator is the equal operator (not the assignment operator, which defines a variable; it's is the same operator character, but different context and different meaning), which always returns a *Boolean* result, the variable *var* will also be defined as *Boolean* by Local Type Inference. Try printing the result by using the statement following:

```
Console.WriteLine(var.ToString)
```

This statement prints the value, *True*.

Boolean variables and *Boolean* statements are important because they are used as arguments in statements for conditional program edits or for testing a loop exit criterion. For example, during an *If* query, the block of code between *If* and *End If* is run only when the result of the *Boolean* expression behind *If* is *True*. And if the construct contains an *Else* branch, that branch is run when the result is *False*. The section "*If ... Then ... Else ... ElseIf ... End If*," later in this chapter, provides more detail about how this works.

Comparing Objects and Data Types

In the real world, objects are things that you might or might not be able to touch, but you can at least describe them in some way. Take for example a bucket: you can clearly picture it in your mind, but you fail to imagine a repository *per se*, because it's not concrete enough a definition. The only way to think about it is to manifest it into something defined: If your repository becomes a drawer, a bowl, a can, or a bottle, you'd be able to picture it in your mind. But you can't think of just a repository. It's the same in programming, with some slight differences: objects are abstract entities. Apart from threads, which we'll discuss later in the book, they are pretty much the most abstract entities known in programming.

The best way to begin to explain what an object is would be to explain what it is not. For example, an *Integer* variable is not an object. Neither is a date variable nor a *Boolean* variable. A data type called *Point* (which determines a position for drawing) isn't an object, either.

However, the entity on which you draw things, the content of a window or a *PictureBox*, or a printer context are all objects. A brush that you use for drawing is an object. A button is an object. A *TextBox*, into which you can enter text in a Windows or web application, is also an object. A ToolTip is an object; a TCP/IP connection can also be an object (one that controls that connection). Strings are a little more tricky. Is a string an object? In principle, yes; by definition, no.

As you might have already noticed, objects and value data types have something in common. Both save data, and both regulate access to this data. But in general, objects are more complex; they need more memory and have more methods that let you do something with the object; for instance, setting focus to a *TextBox*, establishing a connection, bringing a button to the foreground. They also have more complex properties. Examples of these include specifying or determining the text inside a *TextBox*, setting or querying the buffer size of a TCP/IP connection, toggling a menu and thus setting or determining its "active" state, specifying or retrieving the background color of a button, and so on. And objects can trigger events (a button was *clicked*, the text in a *TextBox changed*, the data *received* in an open connection, and so forth).

Simple variable types, such as *Integer, Double, Date*, or *Boolean* can be used directly after declaration. Among other things, the .NET Framework infrastructure—the CLR to be exact— also ensures that the appropriate amount of memory is reserved on the processor stack for these value data types. A variable in your program is therefore connected to a memory address in the processor stack.

> **Note** The processor stack is a special memory range for caching temporary information, which the processor (or a running process with the help of the processor) can access extremely fast.

Essentially, there is no space for more complex objects. There might be room for one, but if you want to program a picture organizer, you will need to have more than one object in memory at the same time. And that's why space must be reserved in memory for these complex objects. The memory to be reserved is called the *Managed Heap* in .NET-speak. This is because you don't need to worry about other data structures infringing upon the memory space for your pictures; it's all managed for you. And you don't need to free up memory space manually when the object is no longer needed—that's managed for you, as well.

Thus, the difference between objects in programming and real life is that in the latter we don't distinguish between small objects which we can handle very, very fast and normal or large size objects. In programming, we do this when we talk about data stores for the different purposes:

The rule of thumb is a follows:

- **Value Types**   Can make due with very little memory space, but they are extremely fast
- **Reference Types**   Can use a lot of memory space, but they are slower (but still relatively fast)

Deriving from Objects and Abstract Objects

Objects in .NET have another interesting characteristic: they build upon each other. This is no different from objects in daily life. For example, as I mentioned before, a container is an abstract object, which we can classify in general but not in concrete terms. A milk carton is certainly a container, but a container is not necessarily a milk carton. A container could also be a bottle, or a bucket, or a barrel. The intersection of certain properties makes all these objects a container. Therefore, we can say that all objects that contain liquid, such as milk cartons, bottles, barrels, or buckets, are *derived* from container.

Programming works the same way. You can create a template (called a *class*) for an object but only use this template for creating further templates. The differences between these templates then flow into the derivations; by using additional properties and methods, the abstract class *Container* becomes the more specific class *Bottle*, or *MilkCarton*, or *Barrel*. And then you use this new template to bring into being (to *instantiate*) the actual barrel. You are instantiating an object from a class.

Here's another analogy: molds and sand. The mold is a class, the instantiation is the sand, which you take from a sand heap. You only have one mold—one class—but by filling it with sand, you can create countless objects. In .NET-speak: "You are reserving memory on the Managed Heap, so a class can be instantiated into an object."[3] For a more complete discussion of classes and objects, see Chapter 8, "Class Begins."

This is also the reason why objects for new creations (for instantiating) need the keyword *New*. So for example, to add a new button to a Windows Form, the following lines are required:

```
'Instantiate new button object
Dim t As New System.Windows.Forms.Button

'Set Text property
t.Text = "New button"

'Add to form
myForm.Controls.Add(t)

'Focus button
t.Focus()
```

Classes and objects are such an extensive topic that they have their own section in this book. With a basic idea of how this works, however, it will be easier for you to use classes and objects in the many examples that you'll see prior to reaching that part of the book. Most important, you need to be able to distinguish objects (reference types) from primitive data types (value types).

Properties

Objects and value types can have *properties*. Properties describe states that can be determined or changed. In contrast, methods typically perform a task. Even in everyday language, these things can't always be separated very easily. Properties are very similar to methods. Setting a property initially corresponds to calling a method that doesn't return a value, and reading a property corresponds to a function call to a method that returns a result.

---

[3] Translated into "sandbox speech" this means: "You take sand from the sand heap, so a mold can make a mud pie with it".

For example, the length of a string is a property. Let's start by declaring and defining a *String* variable, as follows:

```
Dim aName as String = "Adriana Ardelean"
```

You can then determine the string's length (the number of characters it contains) by using the appropriate property, as shown here:

```
Dim lengthOfName As Integer = aName.Length
```

Some properties, such as the current date (*Date.Now*) or the length of a string (*stringVar. Length*), can only be read, but not changed. Such properties are called, not surprisingly, *read-only* properties.

Other properties can be both read and written. For example, by using the *Enabled* property of a control, such as a button, you can determine whether a user is able to select it in a window:

```
aButton.Enabled = True      ' now it is usable
aButton.Enabled = False     ' now it isn't any longer.

'Query property and respond:
If aButton.Enabled Then
    ' The code here will be run only when the button is enabled.
End If
```

Type Literal for Determining Constant Types

Type literals force a constant to be a certain type. (Thus, in my opinion, I think they should be called "Type forcing literals for constants.") You have already learned about type literals in several examples. To assign a string to a variable, you define it as having the type *String*, and put whatever you would like to assign to it between quotes, as illustrated here:

```
Dim AText As String = "Put in quotes"
```

You don't do this for numeric variables, however:

```
Dim Pi as Double = 3.1415926
```

To force a numeric constant to be a string so that you can assign it to a *String* variable without having to convert it, you also place it in quotes. Quotes turn a number into a string:

```
Dim PiAsText As String="3.141592657"
```

Be aware that by using this technique, you can't calculate with *PiAsText*. The variable *PiAsText* is a string (like *AText* in the previous code line), which in this case happens to contain a string that we humans can interpret to be a number. From the computer's point of view, though, there is no difference between "3.1415926" and "Hello, nice weather today!".

In the .NET versions of Visual Basic (all versions since Visual Basic 2002), type literals aren't just limited to strings; they are also used with other data types. For example, to assign a date constant to a variable of the type *Date*, use the # (number) character, as follows:

```
Dim KlausBirthday As Date=#07/24/1969#
```

It is important to write the date using the United States format: month first, then day, then year, even if you're on a Spanish, Italian, French or German Windows system.

Apart from quotes for strings, this is the only other literal type character that you use to wrap a constant. Other type literals are simply placed behind the constant. In some cases, these can consist of two letters instead of just one.

Table 1-1 shows how to define constants with type literals. If a variable type character exists for a specific type, it is also presented.

TABLE 1-1 **Type Literal and Variable Type Characters of Primitive Data Types, as of Visual Basic 2005**

Type name	Type character	Type literal	Example
Byte	–	–	`Dim var As Byte = 128`
SByte	–	–	`Dim var As SByte = -5`
Short	–	S	`Dim var As Short = -32700S`
UShort	–	US	`Dim var As UShort = 65000US`
Integer	%	I	`Dim var% = -123I` or `Dim var As Integer = -123I`
UInteger	–	UI	`Dim var As UInteger = 123UI`
Long	&	L	`Dim var& = -123123L` or `Dim var As Long = -123123L`
ULong	–	UL	`Dim var As ULong = 123123UL`
Single	!	F	`Dim var! = 123.4F` or `Dim var As Single = 123.4F`
Double	#	R	`Dim var# = 123.456789R` or `Dim var As Double = 123.456789R`
Decimal	@	D	`Dim var@ = 123.456789123D` or `Dim var As Decimal = 123.456789123D`
Boolean	–	–	`Dim var As Boolean = True`
Char	–	C	`Dim var As Char = "A"C`
Date	–	#MM/dd/yyyy HH:mm:ss# or #MM/dd/yyyy hh:mm:ss am/pm#	`Dim var As Date = #12/24/2008 04:30:15 PM#`
Object	–	–	In a variable with the type *Object*, any type can be boxed or referenced
String	$	"String"	`Dim var$ = "String"` or `Dim var As String = "String"`

Type Safety

.NET languages follow the rule of type safety. Type safe means that you can't just mix different types randomly during assignments. For example, the following line will not compile and
causes the error message shown in Figure 1-8:

```
Dim aDifferentString As String
aDifferentString = 1.23
```

```
Module TypeSafety

    Sub TypeSafety()

        Dim aString As String

        aString = 3.14159
                  ⓘ ▾
        ┌──────────────────────────────────────────────┐
        │ Option Strict On disallows implicit conversions from │
        │ 'Double' to 'String'.                          │
        │ ⋀  │ Replace '3.14159' with 'CStr(3.14159)'.   │
        │    ┌────────────────────────────────────────┐ │
        │    │     Dim aString As String              │ │
        │    │                                        │ │
        │    │     aString = CStr(3.14159)3.14159     │ │
        │    │ End Sub                                │ │
        │    └────────────────────────────────────────┘ │
        │ ☑ Expand All Previews                          │
        └──────────────────────────────────────────────┘
    End Sub

End Module
```

FIGURE 1-8 Type safety in .NET enforces the rule that only equal or safe types can be
assigned implicitly to each other.

> **Note** By default, Visual Basic .NET simulates the non-existent type safety used by Visual Basic
> 6.0 and Visual Basic for Applications (for example, for macro programming in Microsoft Word or
> Microsoft Excel). You can (and should) change this default behavior for all new projects. To do
> that, from the Tools menu, select Options | Projects And Solutions, and then select all the check
> boxes under VB Defaults.
>
> That customizes the settings for all future projects. To customize the settings for the currently
> open project only, from the Project menu, select Properties, and then click the Compile tab. Set
> the drop-down lists for all compilation options to On.

To view what the problem is, click the red bar in the squiggly line (see Figure 1-8) to activate
autocorrect for intelligent compiling. The problem arises in this example because in .NET, you
can only assign the same types implicitly, or types that are different but for which an implicit
conversion is definitely safe. And what does "definitely safe" mean? It is definitely safe, for
example, to assign an *Integer* type to a *Long* type, as shown in the following:

```
Dim aLong As Long
Dim anInt As Integer = 10000
aLong = anInt
```

The computer would not complain about that assignment in any .NET language, because nothing can go wrong. *Integer* covers a much smaller number range than *Long*; therefore, an implicit conversion is *widening* the type, without possible risk.

Figure 1-9 demonstrates that it's a different story the other way around.

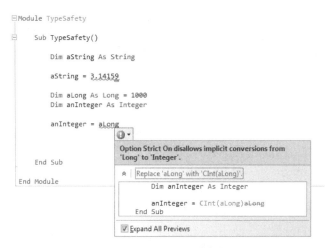

```
Module TypeSafety

    Sub TypeSafety()

        Dim aString As String

        aString = 3.14159

        Dim aLong As Long = 1000
        Dim anInteger As Integer

        anInteger = aLong
```

Option Strict On disallows implicit conversions from 'Long' to 'Integer'.

    Replace 'aLong' with 'CInt(aLong)'.

```
                Dim anInteger As Integer

                anInteger = CInt(aLong)aLong
            End Sub
```

☑ Expand All Previews

FIGURE 1-9 Whereas *smaller* types can safely be converted into *larger* ones, converting larger to smaller types is not type safe and, therefore, not permitted implicitly.

When converting from *Long* to *Integer*, information can become lost, so .NET doesn't classify these *narrowing* kinds of conversions as type safe. Of course, you *can* perform such a conversion—just not implicitly. You need to instruct .NET explicitly that you are aware of the risk and perform appropriate actions to be able to do the conversion. As you can see in Figure 1-9, autocorrect for intelligent compiling makes a direct suggestion: *"Replace 'aLong' with 'CInt(aLong)'"* The *CInt* (Convert to *Int*eger) command tells the compiler explicitly that you want to make the conversion from *Long* to *Integer*.

By now, you can probably guess the purpose of type literals in Visual Basic, which you saw in the previous section. Type safety also applies to constants. Therefore, there must be a way to force a constant to be a certain type. This is exactly what happens when you use type literals. Does the following work implicitly?

```
Dim aChar As Char
Dim aString As String = "Hello"
aChar = aString
```

No. Because *Char* can contain only one character, the *"ello"* portion of the "Hello" string would be lost during the conversion. A *Char* type can take only a single Unicode character, not an entire *String*. Even this code will not work properly:

```
Dim aChar As Char = "H"
```

String is *String*, and *Char* is *Char*. You define a *String* in quotes, no matter how many characters it has. And even if it could be converted (as in the preceding code line), type safety would be compromised. You need to turn "H" into a *Char* type, which you can do by placing the "c" (for character) type literal behind it, as shown in Figure 1-10.

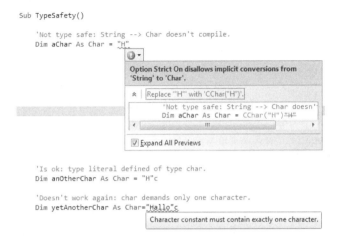

FIGURE 1-10 Use type literals to force constants to have a certain type.

The type safety rule doesn't apply only to *String* and *Char* types; it also applies to the various numeric data types. The following code section shows a few examples that demonstrate when it makes sense to employ type literals:

```
'Error: Implicit doesn't work from Double to Decimal.
Dim decimal1 As Decimal = 1.2312312312312
'Here it is a Decimal, because of the D at the end:
Dim decimal2 As Decimal = 1.2312312312312D

Dim decimal3 As Decimal = 9223372036854775807   ' OK.
' Overflow - without type literal it is implicitly a
' Long value, and in this case it is outside its value range:
Dim decimal4 As Decimal = 9223372036854775808
' With the type literal "D" Decimal is forced as a constant, and it's correct:
Dim decimal5 As Decimal = 9223372036854775808D  ' No overflow.

'Error: Without type literal it's again implicitly a Long,
'but outside of the Long value range:
Dim ushort1 As ULong = 9223372036854775808

' With the type literal Decimal is forced as a constant, and it's correct:
Dim ushort2 As Decimal = 9223372036854775808UL  ' No overflow.
```

Local Type Inference

Beginning with Visual Basic 2008, you can assign types to variables, based on their initial assignments. This becomes apparent in the following assignment:

```
Dim blnValue = True
```

When you assign the value *True* to a primitive variable and type safety is defined, then the variable must have the *Boolean* data type. The same logic applies to the following assignment:

```
Dim strText = "A string."
```

In this case, *strText must* be a string—the assignment defines it. It's different for numeric variables. It's important to know that by assigning an integer to a variable, which hasn't yet been assigned a type, the compiler assigns the type *Integer*, and by assigning a floating-point number, the compiler gives the variable the type *Double*. These standard types of constants already existed; in the end, it's the constants that determine, according to their type literals, which type they represent. Here are a few more examples:

```
Dim anInteger = 100 ' Integer, simple number without floating point defines integer constant
Dim aShort = 101S  ' Short, because the type literal S defines a Short constant
Dim aSingle = 101.5F  ' Single, because the type literal F defines a Single constant
```

> **Important** Local type inference works only at the procedure level, not at class level (which is why it's called *local* type inference).

You control whether local inference is in effect with the statement *Option Infer*, which takes either the parameter *Off* or *On*. By default, local type inference is enabled. To turn it off, use the following statement.

```
Option Infer Off
```

You would place the *Option Infer Off* (or *On*) statement directly at the beginning of the code file for the classes or modules of this code file, or globally for the entire project. To do this, in Solution Explorer, right-click the project (not the solution) to open the context menu, and then select Properties (see Figure 1-11).

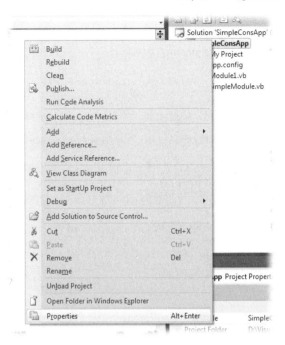

FIGURE 1-11 Opening the context menu of the project in Solution Explorer.

In the dialog box that appears, click the Compile tab, and then set the option for Option Infer, as desired (see Figure 1-12).

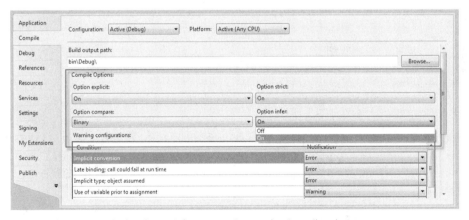

FIGURE 1-12 Setting the local type inference option on the Compile tab.

Arrays and Collections

This chapter has already presented two ways of storing data:

- Value types and primitive value types for saving fast, but small data structures, such as date values, integer values, floating-point values, True/False values, positions and sizes, and characters and strings.

- Reference types for saving larger amounts of data, such as controls and pictures.

You use both types within a program by employing variables. However, in some cases this can pose a problem: what do you do when you need to find another value in a table, based on the value of a variable?

Suppose that you have saved five names in variables. This, in and of itself, is not a problem:

```
Dim Name1 As String = "Lisa Feigenbaum"
Dim Name2 As String = "Sarika Calla"
Dim Name3 As String = "Ramona Leenings"
Dim Name4 As String = "Amanda Silver"
Dim Name5 As String = "Tanja Gelo"
```

Now you would like to access a name, and its number is saved in a variable, as shown in Figure 1-13.

```
Sub ArrayTest()
    Dim Name1 As String = "Lisa Feigenbaum"
    Dim Name2 As String = "Sarika Calla"
    Dim Name3 As String = "Ramona Leenings"
    Dim Name4 As String = "Beth Messi"
    Dim Name5 As String = "Tanja Gelo"

    Dim NameNo As Integer = 3
    Console.WriteLine(Name NameNo)
    |                   Comma, ')', or a valid expression continuation expected.
End Sub
```

FIGURE 1-13 To find a variable by using another variable, such as in a list, you won't get very far by using normal variable names.

The solution to this problem lies in a concept called *arrays*. An array can save as many values as you determine, under a specified name. Each name is associated with a unique index value. You can then use the index value to identify which value you want to access:

```
Dim Names(0 To 4) As String
Names(0) = "Adriana Ardelean"
Names(1) = "Sarika Calla"
Names(2) = "Ramona Leenings"
Names(3) = "Beth Messi"
Names(4) = "Lisa Feigenbaum"

Dim NameNo As Integer = 3
Console.WriteLine(Names(NameNo))
```

> **Important** In contrast to Visual Basic 6.0 or VBA, arrays in .NET are always 0-based. This means that the first element in an array has an index of 0. When dimensioning an array in Visual Basic, you always specify the upper limit, not the number of elements (as you would in C#, for example). While setting the dimensions, you can also use a short form. So, for example, the first line (highlighted in bold), in the previous code sample can also be written as follows:
>
> ```
> Dim Names(4) As String
> ```

> **Tip** You can also define arrays with array initializers. Using the following syntax, you specify the elements directly, which saves typing:
>
> ```
> Dim Names() As String = {"Adriana Ardelean",
>                          "Sarika Calla",
>                          "Ramona Leenings",
>                          "Beth Messi",
>                          "Lisa Feigenbaum"}
>
> Dim NameNo As Integer = 3
> Console.WriteLine(Names(NameNo))
> ```
>
> When you define an array this way, note that you don't specify the upper limit; the compiler derives the upper limit from the number of elements that lie between the curly braces.

If you don't know how many elements the array might have when you first create it, you should use a *List* type instead. With a *List*, you can easily add new elements by using the *Add* method, as shown in the following example:

```
Dim OtherNames As New List(Of String)
OtherNames.Add("Adriana Ardelean")
OtherNames.Add("Sarika Calla")
OtherNames.Add("Ramona Leenings")
OtherNames.Add("Beth Messi")
OtherNames.Add("Lisa Feigenbaum")

'You can also access a dynamic list,
'as in arrays, via the index:
Dim NameNo As Integer = 3
Console.WriteLine(OtherNames(NameNo))
```

For the moment, this is all the information we're going to cover about arrays and lists. You will learn more about them in Chapter 19, "Arrays and Collections," which is dedicated to these concepts, and you will encounter them again in the context of loops and in other places throughout the book.

Executing Program Code Conditionally

The *Boolean* data type is usually required when evaluating decisions, and used to control whether program code is executed or not, depending on its value. Such decision-making statements include *If*, *Case [Is]*, *While*, or *Until*.

The function *IIf* does not control the program execution but should be mentioned here because of its resemblance to the *If* statement. *IIf* returns a function result based on a passed-in *Boolean* value or expression. When the passed-in value or expression is *True*, *IIf* returns one result; if it is *False*, it returns the second.

If ... Then ... Else ... ElseIf ... End If

It is likely that you have employed the *If* statement many, many times, and you probably have its use down pat. But in the interest of being complete, let's examine it a little more closely.

In its simplest form, *If* causes code to run that's placed between *If* and *End If* when the *Boolean* expression behind *If* evaluates to *True*. The following construct demonstrates the concept of comparisons with *Boolean* expressions:

```
locBoolean = True
If locBoolean Then
    'Only runs when locBoolean is True.
End If
```

Some developers might unnecessarily use the following expression:

```
locBoolean = True
If locBoolean = True Then
    'Only runs, if locBoolean is True.
End If
```

In fact, in this identification, `locBoolean = True` is not a characteristic of the *If* statement, but basically just a normal variable assignment. When *locBoolean* has a value of *True*, the entire expression is *True*, as well. The only thing the statement *If* does is examine the *Boolean* value that follows it. It then runs the following statements only if the expression evaluates to *True*. That's why the value doesn't need to be additionally checked by the programmer—it's redundant. The equal sign here is the comparison operator. In other words, if you replace *locBoolean* with its current value, the preceding code looks as follows:

```
If True = True Then
```

You can quite confidently replace this by *If True Then* ... or *If locBoolean Then* ... (if it is true, then ...).

However, it's certainly confusing in BASIC (not only in Visual Basic), that assignment operators and comparison operators use the same character (the equal sign). For example, the following expression is a valid statement:

```
Dim locBoolean = "Klaus" = "Uwe"
```

The first equal sign functions as an assignment operator; the second is a *Boolean* comparison operator. The comparison operator has a higher priority than the assignment operator, so in this example *locBoolean* takes the value *False*, because the string "Klaus" does not equal "Uwe." Otherwise, this example would produce a type conversion error.

However, other languages aren't that much better. For example, C++ uses a single equal sign (=) for assignment, and a double equal sign (==) for comparison, which is not intuitive at all. As many as 5–8 percent of all errors in C++ programs can be traced back to this confusion, which is a much higher number than the errors caused by the incorrect use of the equals character in Visual Basic.

The *If* code block can be followed by an *Else* code block, which runs when the *Boolean* expression behind the *If* evaluates to *False*. In addition, you can use an *ElseIf* code block to insert further evaluations into the *If* construct. The code block behind the last *Else* code block, if present, runs only when none of the conditions of the individual *If* or *ElseIf* sections returned *True*, as shown in the example that follows:

```
locString1 = "Santa Claus, you think he's in town already?"
locString2 = "Santa Klaus*"
locBoolean = (locString1 Like locString2)    ' returns False; checks for similarity (see
➡below)

If locBoolean Then
    'Boxing is possible, too:
    If locString2 = "Santa Klaus" Then
        Console.WriteLine("Name found!")
    Else
        Console.WriteLine("No name found!")
    End If
ElseIf Now = #12:00:00 PM# Then
    Console.WriteLine("Noon!")
ElseIf Now = #12:00:00 AM# Then
    Console.WriteLine("Still up so late?")
Else
    Console.WriteLine("It is any other time or locString1 was not like locString1...")
End If
```

The Logical Operators *And*, *Or*, *Xor*, and *Not*

Visual Basic has a variety of logical operators, which can be applied to numerical as well as *Boolean* date types. The latter are mainly of interest because they can be used to formulate almost natural language conditions for program sequencing, for example in *If* constructs.

If you act on the assumption that the two numeric values 0 and 1, represented by the *Boolean* type, correspond to *True* and *False*, it's possible to formulate connections such as, "If statement1 *and* statement2 are true, then..."

The most important logical operators are:

- *And*   Executes a logical AND operation. Both statements must be true to make the expression true, as illustrated in the following table:

Statement 1	Statement 2	Result
False (0)	False (0)	False (0)
True (1)	False (0)	False (0)
False (0)	True (1)	False (0)
True (1)	True (1)	True (1)

- *Or*   Executes a logical Or operation. When at least one of the statements is true, the expression is true:

Statement 1	Statement 2	Result
False (0)	False (0)	False (0)
True (1)	False (0)	True (1)
False (0)	True (1)	True (1)
True (1)	True (1)	True (1)

- *Xor*   Executes a logical exclusive Or operation. Only when exactly *one* of the two statements is true is the statement true; otherwise, it's false:

Statement 1	Statement 2	Result
False (0)	False (0)	False (0)
True (1)	False (0)	True (1)
False (0)	True (1)	True (1)
True (1)	True (1)	False (0)

- *Not*   Negates the statement. If it is true, it becomes false, and if it is false, it becomes true:

Statement	Result
False (0)	True (1)
True (1)	False (1)

The following example illustrates how to use some of the logical operators. This code checks whether the character a user enters when selecting an option in a console application is within a certain range:

```
Sub ConditionCheck()

    'Output options and read characters from the keyboard.
    Console.Write("Which function would you like to execute (1-9, 0 or 'end' to
➥end): ")
    Dim input = Console.ReadLine

    'When entering "0" or "end",
    If input = "0" Or input.ToUpper = "END" Then
        'End method.
        Exit Sub
    End If

    'When the pressed character (string length=1) is greater than or equal to "1"
    'and lesser or equal to "9"...
    If input.Length = 1 And input >= "1" And input <= "9" Then
        '...then it was a valid selection, ...
        Console.WriteLine("This function is possible!")
        '...otherwise...
    Else
        '...not.
        Console.WriteLine("You have made the wrong choice.")
    End If
End Sub
```

Note   Logical operators can be applied to *Boolean* values and other numeric data types. By doing this, the bits that compose the values internally are linked. For example, the following code results in 5:

```
13 And 7
```

This is because the following operation is executed in binary:

```
    1101 (13)
And 0111 (07)
-------------
    0101 (05)
```

Each bit of the initial value is linked with each bit of the second value using *And*—and it then returns the result.

Comparison Operators That Return *Boolean* Results

Visual Basic understands the following comparison operators, which compare two expressions and return a *Boolean* result:

- *Expression1 = Expression2*   Checks for equality; returns *True* when both expressions are the same.

- *Expression1 > Expression2*   Returns *True* when *Expression1* is greater than *Expression2*.

- *Expression1 < Expression2*   Returns *True* when *Expression1* is less than *Expression2*.

- *Expression1 >= Expression2*   Returns *True* when *Expression1* is greater than or equal to *Expression2*.

- *Expression1 <= Expression2*   Returns *True* when *Expression1* is less than or equal to *Expression2*.

- *Expression1 <> Expression2*   Checks for inquality; returns *True* when *Expression1* is not the same as *Expression2*.

- *Expression1 Is [Expression2|Nothing]*   Checks for equality of an object reference (only applicable to reference types); returns *True* when *Expression1* points to the same data memory range as *Expression2*. When *Expression1* is not assigned to a range of memory (defined object variable, but not an instantiated object), the comparison with *Is* uses *Nothing* to return the *Boolean* value of *True*.

- *Expression1 IsNot [Expression2|Nothing]*   Check for the non-equality of an object reference (only applicable to reference types); returns *True* when *Expression1* points to a different data memory range than *Expression2*. When *Expression1* points to a valid memory range with instance data, the comparison with *IsNot* uses *Nothing* to return the *Boolean* value of *True*.

- *String1 Like String2*   Checks for similarity between two strings; a sample comparison can make the comparison more flexible. If both strings are equal, according to certain rules *True* is returned, otherwise *False*.

You can find more details in MSDN under the item, Like Operator.

The following lines of code demonstrate the use of comparison operators:

```
Dim locString1 As String = "Uwe"
Dim locString2 As String = "Klaus"

locBoolean = (locString1 = locString2)      ' Returns False.
locBoolean = (locString1 > locString2)      ' Returns True.
locBoolean = (locString1 < locString2)      ' Returns False.
locBoolean = (locString1 >= locString2)     ' Returns True.
locBoolean = (locString1 <= locString2)     ' Returns False.
locBoolean = (locString1 <> locString2)     ' Returns True.
locBoolean = (locString1 Is locString2)     ' Returns False.

locString2 = "Uwe"
String.Internal(locString2)                 ' Now returns True, because both
locBoolean = (locString1 Is locString2)     ' String objects point to a range. (see
➥chapter 7)

locString1 = "Santa Claus, you think he's in town already?"
locString2 = "Santa Klaus*"
locBoolean = (locString1 Like locString2)   ' Returns True.
```

Short Circuit Evaluations with *OrElse* and *AndAlso*

Take a look at the following code block:

```
'Short circuit evaluation speeds up the process.
If locChar < "0" OrElse locChar > "9" Then
    locIllegalChar = True
    Exit For
End If
```

Note the keyword *OrElse*. Another keyword that you can use that functions in a similar manner to *OrElse* is *AndAlso*. Both correspond to the commands *Or* and *And*, and they also serve to logically link and evaluate *Boolean* expressions—they just operate differently (and sometimes faster). Let's look at an example from our daily life to clarify the concept.

Suppose that you're wondering whether you should bring an umbrella along for your daily walk; it might rain, *or else* at least it looks pretty dark outside. But you would no longer need to consider how the sky looks if just before you leave, you discover that it actually *is* raining. If it's raining right now, there is no need for you to check the second criterion—the umbrella must come along; otherwise, you're going to get wet. That's exactly what *OrElse* does (or *AndAlso* respectively). This approach is called *Short Circuit Evaluation*.

Especially with objects or when calling methods, short circuit evaluation can help make your programs safer, as the following example shows:

```
Private Sub btnAndAlsoDemo_Click(ByVal sender As System.Object, ByVal e As System.
EventArgs) _
Handles btnAndAlsoDemo.Click
    Dim aString As String = "Klaus is the word that starts the sentence"
    If aString IsNot Nothing AndAlso aString.Substring(0, 5).ToUpper = "KLAUS" Then
        MessageBox.Show("The string begins with Klaus!")
    End If

    If aString IsNot Nothing And aString.Substring(0, 5).ToUpper = "KLAUS" Then
        MessageBox.Show("The string begins with Klaus!")
    End If
End Sub
```

As expected, this program code displays the message text twice, because *aString* has content in both cases, and in both cases, the string starts with "Klaus" (after all, it's the same string). Now replace the bold-highlighted line in preceding example with the line that follows:

```
    Dim aString As String = Nothing
```

Figure 1-14 shows the results when you run the program one more time.

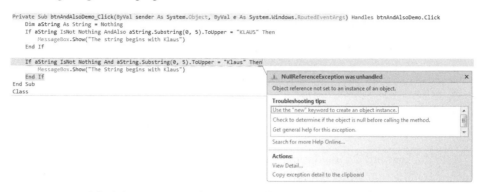

```
Private Sub btnAndAlsoDemo_Click(ByVal sender As System.Object, ByVal e As System.Windows.RoutedEventArgs) Handles btnAndAlsoDemo.Click
    Dim aString As String = Nothing
    If aString IsNot Nothing AndAlso aString.Substring(0, 5).ToUpper = "KLAUS" Then
        MessageBox.Show("The string begins with Klaus")
    End If

    If aString IsNot Nothing And aString.Substring(0, 5).ToUpper = "Klaus" Then
        MessageBox.Show("The String begins with Klaus")
    End If
End Sub
Class
```

FIGURE 1-14 *AndAlso* helps you with combined queries for *Nothing* and the use of instance methods.

Here, it becomes apparent how *AndAlso* works. The first query works because the second part, which is linked with *AndAlso,* doesn't even execute the code aString.Substring(0, 5).ToUpper = "KLAUS" any more. That's because the object *aString* was *Nothing*. When using *AndAlso,* if the first test evaluates to false, the rest of the checks are no longer of interest, and they are therefore ignored.

In the second version that uses *And,* the second part executes—even though it makes no sense to execute the code because the first expression is false. But because *aString* now has the value *Nothing,* you can't use its instance functions (*SubString, ToUpper*), so the program aborts with a *NullReferenceException.*

Select ... Case ... End Select

As shown in the previous section, you can use *ElseIf* for option analysis when you want to evaluate several *Boolean* expressions and you need to respond by running the corresponding program code. You can achieve the same result in a much more elegant fashion by using a *Select* construct. *Select* prepares an expression for comparison with a *Boolean* result; the actual comparison takes place by using one or several different *Case* statements, each of which must be followed by a corresponding comparison argument of the same type (or implicitly convertible). If none of the conditions following the *Case* statements apply, an optional *Case Else* at the end can execute statements that you want to run when none of the *Case* statements prove true. The *End Select* command completes the construct. When a *Case* expression evaluates to *True, Select* runs the code for that *Case,* but doesn't perform any further evaluations.

When evaluating conditions, *Case* by default checks only for equality; however, by adding the keyword *Is,* you can also use other comparison operators. The following example shows how to apply them:

```
Dim locString1 as String = "Miriam"

Select Case locString1
   Case "Miriam"
      Console.WriteLine("Hit!")
   Case Is > "N"
      Console.WriteLine("Name comes after 'M' in the alphabet")


   Case Is < "M"
      Console.WriteLine("Name comes before 'M' in the alphabet")

   Case Else
      Console.WriteLine("Name starts with 'M'")

   'Case Like "Miri"
      'This doesn't work!!!

End Select
```

However, comparison operations and conditional execution happen in one go here. This means that the following construct won't work:

```
'It doesn't work this way!!!
Select Case locBoolean

   Case
Console.WriteLine("Was true!")

End Select
```

The compiler has every right to complain.

The *If* Operator and *IIf* Function

If exists not only as a structure statement (*If … Then … Else*), but also as a function—and in two variations. The *IIf* function (mentioned briefly earlier, and yes, it's spelled with a double "I") takes three parameters, and returns either the first or the second expression as a result, depending on the result of the first *Boolean* expression:

```
Dim c As Integer
'Returns 10
c = CInt(IIf(True, 10, 20))
'Returns 20
c = CInt(IIf(False, 10, 20))
```

IIf has one big disadvantage: when using the *IIf* function, the result needs to be cast to the correct type, because the *IIf* function only returns a base *Object* type, as shown here:

```
Dim c As Integer
'Returns 10
c = CInt(IIf(True, 10, 20))
```

Beginning with Visual Basic 2008, this has become easier because the keyword *If* (with one "I") has been extended, so you can use it the same way as the *IIf* function:

```
Dim c As Integer
'Returns 20
c = If(False, 10, 20)
```

For even fewer keystrokes, combine the *If* operator with local type inference, as follows:

```
'Returns 20
Dim c = If(False, 10, 20)
```

However, be careful; mixing various return types can cause the compiler to stumble, as shown in Figure 1-15.

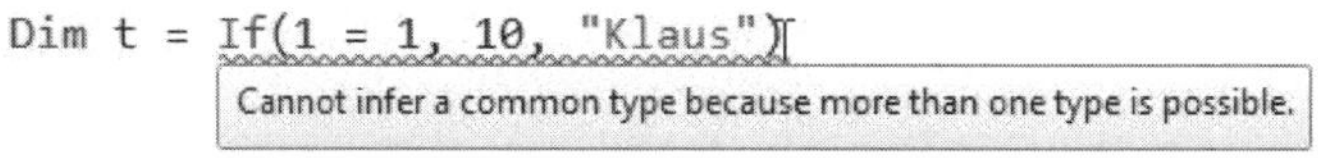

```
Dim t = If(1 = 1, 10, "Klaus")
```
Cannot infer a common type because more than one type is possible.

FIGURE 1-15 Using *If* instead of *IIf* only works if the compiler has the chance to clearly determine the corresponding types.

Loops

Loops let you to run the commands and the statements they contain over and over again, until a certain loop end state (called an *exit condition*) is achieved. Referring back to Figure 1-6, you can see an example of a loop in a *Do … Loop* construct, which allows users to repeatedly enter birth dates or commands until they type a whitespace (a space or a tab or a return) at the command prompt. When that happens, the variable *input* stays empty, and the loop reaches its exit condition, which was defined after the keyword *Loop*.

In addition to *Do … Loop*, Visual Basic recognizes *For … Next* loops, which repeat all internal statements until a counter variable has exceeded or dropped below a specified value. Also, in Visual Basic, you can use *For Each … Next* loops, which repeat their internal statements as often as there are elements in an object list, as well as *While … End While* loops, which repeat their internal statements as long as a certain exit condition is still valid (defined right after the *While* keyword). When there is no exit condition for a loop, it is called an *infinite loop*— and the content of the loop will run until you can no longer pay your electric bill (which, in a manner of speaking, constitutes an exit condition.)

For ... Next Loops

For ... Next loops let you repeat the statements within the code block for a predefined number of times. The syntax for such a construction is as follows (elements in square brackets are optional, which means that they don't *need* to appear in each *For ... Next* loop construct):

```
For counterVariable [As dataType] = Start To End [Step by step]
    [Statements]
    [Exit For]
    [Continue For]
Next [counterVariable]
```

The *counterVariable* of the *For* statement is a central part of the entire loop construct; it is therefore not optional—you must define it. *DataType* determines which numeric type *counterVariable* should be (for example, *Integer* or *Long*), but you can omit that when your project has the local type inference turned on, or if you already defined the variable beforehand. The latter is important when you want the variable to be valid after the loop exits and you want to use the value.

> **Important** Theoretically, you can also use floating point variable types, such as *Double* and *Single*, but you should try to avoid those. Because of rounding inaccuracies, which are normal during the conversion from the internal binary system to the decimal system, you can't specify the query for marginal values precisely. Therefore, a loop could potentially be repeated one too many or too few times, even though you don't expect it, or a targeted check for a certain value could fail because of rounding errors. For example, even though the value 63.0000001 is close to 63, it's still not 63. Checking the variable to see if it's equal to 63 by using the *If* command would fail.
>
> If you can't do without floating-point numbers in loops, consider using the more accurate but much slower *Decimal* type, or test for certain values in ranges rather than total equality, such as:
>
> ```
> If doubleVar >= 10.3 And doubleVar < 10.4 Then
>     [Statements]
> End If
> ```

The *Start* and *End* are required and define the initial value for *counterVariable*. In other words, they specify where the counting starts as well as the limiting value, which determines how many times the loop will execute. By default, the loop counter is incremented by using a step size of one for every loop iteration; however, by using the *StepSize* parameter you can define the increment.

Another way to exit a *For ... Next* loop is with the *Exit For* command. Using *Exit For* makes sense only if you place it inside an *If* query within a loop. *Exit For* exits the loop and continues running the program by running statements that follow the *Next* keyword, which marks the end of the loop. The keyword *Next* at the end of the loop is required; it delimits the bottom of the *For* loop.

Tip Use a *For … Next* loop construct when you already know how many loop iterations to expect. For example, a *For … Next* loop is perfectly suited for an array with a certain number of elements that to process:

```
Dim Names() As String = {"Lisa Feigenbaum",
                         "Sarika Calla",
                         "Ramona Leenings",
                         "Adriana Ardelean"}

'Run through For loop and return:
For index As Integer = 0 To Names.Length - 1
    Console.WriteLine(Names(index))
Next
```

For cases in which you don't know beforehand how many iterations will be necessary, it is better to use a *Do … Loop*, which is described in more detail later in this chapter.

The previous code example displays the following output:

```
Lisa Feigenbaum
Sarika Calla
Ramona Leenings
Adriana Ardelean
```

Note that the elements of an array or a list are always 0-based. That's why the value 1 is subtracted from the length of the array; that's the upper limit for running through the array (Length returns the number of array elements).

You can "nest" *For … Next* loops, placing an inner loop inside an outer loop; however, they can't overlap. You can also explicitly tie a *Next* statement to a particular *For* statement by adding the counter variable name after the *Next* statement. When a *Next* statement of an outer nesting level has been placed before the *Next* statement of an inner level loop, the compiler complains, and you will see a corresponding message in the error list. On the one hand, the compiler can recognize the overlap error only when you specify the corresponding counter variable in each *Next* statement; on the other hand, it assumes the correct counter variable, when you don't name one explicitly. Therefore, the latter (omitting the counter variable after the *Next* statement) is often the better solution.

Note The *stepSize* value can be positive or negative for integers. If the step size is negative, you need to adjust the loop's start and end values accordingly—in this case, the start value must then be greater than the end value so that several loop iterations can take place. If you don't specify a value for *stepSize*, the default is 1, as mentioned earlier. Also important: if *start* is greater than *end*, the step size is not automatically set to –1; unless you want 1 as the step size, you must explicitly specify the step size so that several loop iterations can take place.

> **Important** *start*, *end* and *stepSize* can be either constant values or calculated and complex expressions, as presented here:
>
> ```
> For dayCounter= 1 To (Now.Date - New Date(Now.Year, Now.Month, 1)).TotalDays
>     (Statements)
> Next
> ```
>
> This example states, as applicable to all expressions: they are evaluated only once, then the loop begins to run. It is important to be aware of that when considering performance issues (constructs, as in the example, don't slow the program down, because they are evaluated only once) and program flow. You cannot change the limit value that controls the end of the loop while the loop is running. Also important: you shouldn't manipulate the counter variable in code within the loop, because that can lead to unforeseen results or errors.

Nesting *For* Loops

For loops can be nested within each other, which means that within a *For* loop, you can place other *For* loops. Remember that the total number of iterations of the innermost loop will be the inner loop count multiplied by the outer loop count when all loops use constant values. For example:

```
For count1 As Integer = 1 To 10
    For count2 As Integer = 1 To 10
        For count3 As Integer = 1 To 10
            'The statements are run through a total of 10*10*10=1000 times.
        Next count3
    Next
Next count1
```

> **Tip** You don't need to specify the *counterVariable* after a *Next* statement. However, it sometimes makes your program easier to read, especially for deeply nested code.

For ... Each Loops

A *For ... Each* loop is similar to a *For ... Next* loop, but it repeats the inner statements for each element of a specified list or array. In general, you use *For ... Each* as follows:

```
For Each element [As DataType] In list
    [Statements]
    [Exit For]
    [Statements]
    [Continue For]
Next [element]
```

The variable *element* represents an item in the list. The *For ... Each* loop thus runs through the list elements—one list element is assigned to the *element* variable for each loop iteration. The inner statements in the loop are run repeatedly, once for each element contained in the list or array *list*.

Optionally, you can use *Exit ... For* to prematurely end the loop iterations. This is why it makes sense to put *Exit ... For* into its own *If* block.

The *Next* statement is required; it ends the definition of the *For* loop. However, you don't need to specify *element* after *Next*.

> **Note** Chapter 19 contains detailed information about lists as well as more in-depth coverage of the functionality of *For ... Each* loops.

The following example shows how to use a *For ... Each* loop to run through the *String* array created in the previous example. It displays the contents of all the array elements in the console window, as shown in the following:

```
Dim Names() As String = {" Adriana Ardelean",
                         "Sarika Calla",
                         "Ramona Leenings",
                         "Beth Messi",
                         " Lisa Feigenbaum "}

'Iteration using ForEach loop and return:
For Each name In Names
    Console.WriteLine(name)
Next
```

This code displays the following output in the console window:

```
Adriana Ardelean
Sarika Calla
Ramona Leenings
Beth Messi
Lisa Feigenbaum
```

> **Tip** Sometimes you need to know when the last element in a list has been reached. In such cases, don't use *For ... Each*; use *For ... Next* instead:
>
> ```
> 'Last element is treated differently:
> For index As Integer = 0 To Names.Length - 1
>     If index < Names.Length - 1 Then
>         Console.WriteLine(Names(index))
>     Else
>         Console.WriteLine("and last but not least: " & Names(index))
>     End If
> Next
> ```

Of course, it's possible to use an additional counter variable in the *For ... Each* loop, but that's pretty much redundant here, because you can just use *For ... Next*.

This code displays the following output in the console window:

```
Adriana Ardelean
Sarika Calla
Ramona Leenings
Beth Messi
and last but not least: Lisa Feigenbaum
```

Do ... Loop and *While ... End While* Loops

The *Do ... Loop* and *While ... End* loops repeat statements inside the program, either as long as a condition is *True*, or until the condition becomes *True*. Together with *Do*, the keyword *Until* indicates that a condition must become *True*. To run a loop as long as the condition is *True*, use *While*.

The *While* and *Until* keywords are placed either after the loop start (*Do*) or after the loop end (*Loop*).

Note that a *Do While ... Loop* provides the same result as a *While ... End While* loop. For historic reasons you can use a different syntax to get to the same result. You can create a loop construct with the appropriate exit conditions using the following code variations:

```
Do {While|Until} condition
    [statements]
    [Exit Do]
    [statements]
Loop
```

Or:

```
Do
    [statements]
    [Exit Do]
    [statements]
Loop {While|Until} condition
```

Or:

```
While condition
    [statements]
    [Exit While]
    [statements]
End While
```

When using a *While ... End While* or *Do ... Loop*, *Boolean* variables or expressions serve as exit conditions. The following lines of code show a few examples for using these loop types:

```
Dim Names() As String = {"Adriana Ardelean",
                         "Sarika Calla",
                         "Ramona Leenings",
                         "Beth Messi",
                         "Lisa Feigenbaum"}

'Return the names in ascending order ...
Dim index As Integer = 0
Do While index < Names.Length
    Console.WriteLine(Names(index))
    index += 1
Loop

Console.WriteLine("------------------------")
Console.WriteLine("      and backwards:")
Console.WriteLine("------------------------")

'... and in descending order.
index = Names.Length - 1
While index > -1
    Console.WriteLine(Names(index))
    index -= 1
End While
```

These lines of code display the following on the monitor:

```
Adriana Ardelean
Sarika Calla
Ramona Leenings
Beth Messi
Lisa Feigenbaum
------------------------
      and backwards:
----------------------
Lisa Feigenbaum
Beth Messi
Ramona Leenings
Sarika Calla
Adriana Ardelean
```

Exit—Leaving Loops Prematurely

The *Exit* statement causes a program to exit the loop and continue execution after the end of the loop. For a *For* loop, program execution continues after the *Next* statement; for a *Do* loop, it continues after the *Loop* command; and for a *While* loop, the program continues after *End While*. Sometimes, you want to end a loop early, such as when you discover a condition that makes continuation unnecessary, impossible, or undesirable; for instance, an inaccurate value, or a call for exiting. As an example, when you catch an exception in a *Try ... Catch ... Finally* statement (see the section "Error Handling in Code," later in this chapter), you can, for example, use *Exit For* at the end of the *Finally* block.

You can insert the desired number of *Exit* statements at any point within a loop. *Exit* is often used after the evaluation of a condition; for example, in an *If ... Then ... Else* structure.

Continue—Repeating Loops Prematurely

You can also run a loop early, which means that in *For ... Next* loops, you can, in certain cases, treat *Next* preferentially. You can do this by using *Continue*. Of course, you can use *Continue* in all other loop types, as well.

Simplified Access to Object Properties and Methods Using *With ... End With*

By using *With ... End With*, you can include a number of elements (properties, methods) of an object within a code block repeatedly without to the need to name the object name each time anew. When the fully-qualified name for the corresponding object variable is very long, *With ... End With* can be used not only to save keystrokes, but also to enhance performance. At the same time, you lower the risk of misspelling one of its elements.

For example, if you'd like to use several different properties of a single object, write the statements for property assignments into a *With ... End With* structure. When you do this, you no longer need to point to the object in each property assignment. A single reference to the object, by which you place a period just before the property name, is enough (see Figure 1-16).

FIGURE 1-16 In a *With ... End With* block, use the period to access the list of methods and properties of the object, which was specified behind *With*.

Note Remember that *With ... End With* builds a structure, as well. Variables that are defined between *With* and *End With* only exist in this scope. The following section addresses this topic further.

The Scope of Variables

Declaring variables at procedure level (for instance, within the *Sub* and *Function* methods, or *Property* procedures, which are covered in Chapter 9, "First Class Programming") has an effect on their scope. While in VBA and Visual Basic 6.0, for example, variables within procedures are still valid throughout that procedure from the moment they are declared, in .NET versions of Visual Basic, they are valid from the moment they are declared only within the code block in which they are defined. A "code block" in this context basically means a construct that encapsulates code in some way; for example, *If ... Then ... Else* blocks, *For ... Next* or *Do ... Loop* loops, or even *With* blocks, among others. The Visual Studio IDE makes it relatively easy to see where blocks apply: each structure statement that causes the editor to indent code placed between the start and end commands for the block automatically limits the scope of the variables defined in that block. Figure 1-17 shows an example of this.

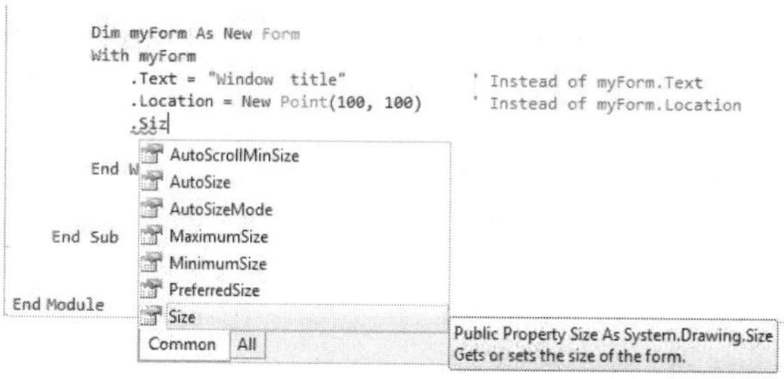

FIGURE 1-17 Variables are scoped to the structure block in which they are declared.

Figure 1-17 illustrates how the second time the program tries to access *fiveFound*, after completing the loop structure range (and thus also leaving the scope of the variable), an error occurs.

To make *fiveFound* accessible in both the *For ... Next* and the *If* structure block, you need to move the *fiveFound* definition to the procedure level, making the changes highlighted in the following code:

```
Sub Main()

    Dim fiveFound As Boolean

    For counter As Integer = 0 To 10
        'Dim fiveFound As Boolean
        If counter = 5 Then
            fiveFound = True
        End If
    Next
```

```
        If fiveFound Then
            Debug.Print("The number 5 was part of the list of numbers!")
        End If
    End Sub
```

This variable scoping rule means that you can declare variables with the same name multiple times, as long as they are in different structural code blocks, as the following example shows:

```
Sub Main()
    For counter As Integer = 0 To 10
        Dim fiveFound As Boolean
        If counter = 5 Then
            fiveFound = True
        End If
    Next
    For counter As Integer = 0 To 10
        Dim fiveFound As Boolean
        If counter = 5 Then
            fiveFound = True
        End If
    Next
End Sub
```

The preceding code declares the variable *fiveFound* twice within a single procedure, but no error occurs, because each declaration is placed in a different scope.

Note, however, that you can't declare variables with the same name in nested structures; that won't work because variables in a parent structure are always accessible from a child structure. Figure 1-18 shows how the corresponding error message would look.

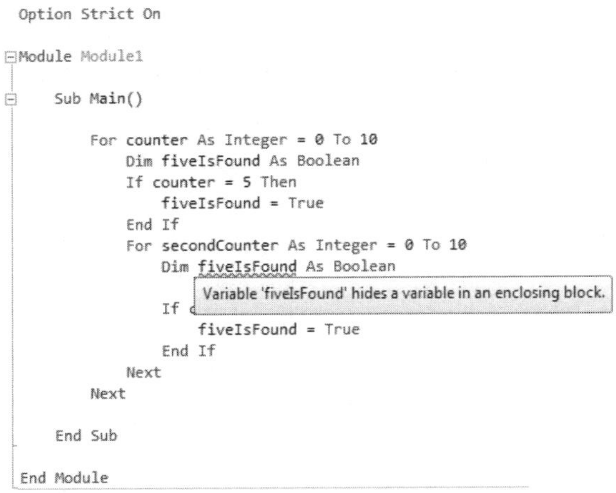

```
Option Strict On

Module Module1

    Sub Main()

        For counter As Integer = 0 To 10
            Dim fiveIsFound As Boolean
            If counter = 5 Then
                fiveIsFound = True
            End If
            For secondCounter As Integer = 0 To 10
                Dim fiveIsFound As Boolean
```
Variable 'fiveIsFound' hides a variable in an enclosing block.
```
                If c
                    fiveIsFound = True
                End If
            Next
        Next

    End Sub

End Module
```

FIGURE 1-18 Variables of a parent scope must not hide the variables in a child scope.

The += and –= Operators and Their Relatives

Visual Basic provides abbreviation operators for numeric calculations, such as the += and –= operators, which add or subtract and assign values in one operation, and for string concatenations, the &= operator, which appends and assigns a string to another string in one operation. The following example (from the next section) shows how you would use +=:

```
Do
    If (helpValue And 1) = 1 Then
        resultValue += value1
    End If
    value1 = value1 << 1
    helpValue = helpValue >> 1
Loop Until helpValue = 0
```

There are other abbreviation operators in Visual Basic that work in much the same way. Table 1-2 shows these operators, along with a brief description:

TABLE 1-2 Operator Abbreviations in Visual Basic

Operation	Abbreviation	Description
var = var + 1	*var += 1*	Increase the variable content by one
var = var—1	*var –= 1*	Decrease the variable content by one
*var = var * 2*	*var *= 2*	Multiply the variable content by two (double it)
var = var / 2	*var /= 2*	Divide the variable content by two (floating-point division)
var = var \ 2	*var \= 2*	Divide the variable content by two (integer division)
var = var ^ 3	*var ^= 3*	Raise the variable content to the power of three
varString = VarString & "Ramona"	*varString &= "Ramona"*	Add the string "Ramona" to the content of the string *varString*

Note Using abbreviations simply saves keystrokes, which means it's less work, but doesn't cause the code to run any faster.

It doesn't matter whether you write the following:

```
intvar = intvar + 1
```

Or, whether you use this, instead:

```
intvar += 1
```

The compiler generates the same code with either syntax.

The Bit Shift Operators << and >>

In addition to the previously mentioned operators, Visual Basic 2003 already introduced bit shift operators. These operators shift the individual bits of integer values to the left or to the right. This book doesn't discuss the functionality of the binary system in depth, but briefly, shifting the bits of an integer value to the left doubles the value; shifting it to the right divides it by two (without a remainder).

For example, a binary 101 (decimal 5) becomes binary 10 (decimal 2) when shifted one bit to the right. For right shifts, the rightmost value simply falls off. Similarly, binary 101 becomes binary 1010 (decimal 10) with a shift to the left; left shifts add zeroes at the right.

The code that follows demonstrates a multiplication algorithm at bit level. Older developers might remember their times with the Commodore 64. Back then, such algorithms were used in Assembler every day.

```
Private Sub MultiplicationWithBitShift
    Dim value1,value2, resultValue, helpValue As Integer
    value1 = 10
    value2 = 5
    resultValue = 0
    helpValue = value2

        'This algorithm works the same as multiplying
        'the old fashioned way in the decimal system:
        '
        '(10)   (5)
        '1010 * 101 =
        '------------
        '      1010 +
        '     0000  +
        '    1010
        '------------
        '    110010 = 50

    'The "5" is shifted to the right bitwise,
    'to test its outer right bit. If it is set,
    'the value 10 is first added, and then its
    'complete "bit content" is moved one place to the left;
    'when it is not set, nothing happens.
    'This process repeats until all
    'bits of "5" are used up, i.e. the variable helpValue,
    'which processes this value, has become 0.
    'For a multiplication, as many additions are necessary
    'as there are bits set in the second value.
```

```
    Do
        If (helpValue And 1) = 1 Then
            resultValue += wert1
        End If
        value1 = value1 << 1
        helpValue = helpValue >> 1
    Loop Until helpValue = 0
    Console.WriteLine("The result is:" & resultValue)
End Sub
```

Error Handling in Code

To be honest, error handling in the old Visual Basic versions, which still function in .NET today, has always been anathema to me. If an error occurred after a very long routine in the finished program, it was difficult and required a lot of effort to locate the exact position of the error. The system variable *Erl* made it possible to show the line in which the error occurred in the error handler, but to achieve this, you had to number the code lines manually—a procedure that seemed rather antediluvian, even back then.

Today, discovering the exact location of an error is much, much easier, even though Visual Basic still allows the original error-handling syntax. Here's a look at the before and after versions. The following example shows a small VBA routine, which reads a file into a *String* variable, or at least it tries to do that. Watch for comments in the list, which mark the program execution in case of an error with numbers.

 Note   The following example is Visual Basic 6.0/VBA Code.

```
Private Sub Command1_Click()

    Dim fileNotFoundFlag As Boolean
    On Local Error GoTo 1000

    Dim ff As Integer
    Dim myFileContent As String
    Dim lineMemory As String
    ff = FreeFile
    '1: The error occurs here
    Open "C:\ATextFile.TXT" For Input As #ff
    '3: then go here
    If fileNotFound Then
        '4: to show this message.
        MsgBox ("The file does not exist")
```

```
    Else
        'This block is only run,
        'when everything was ok.
        Do While Not EOF(ff)
            Line Input #ff, lineMemory
            myFileContent = myFileContent & lineMemory
        Loop
        Close ff
        Debug.Print myFileContent
    End If
    'And that's also important so that the
    'program doesn't run into the error routine.
    Exit Sub

    '2: Then the program jumps here
1000 If Err.Number = 53 Then
        fileNotFound = True
        Resume Next
    End If

End Sub
```

Amazing, isn't it? Just to catch a simple error, the program must jump back and forth like mad all over the code. And this example catches only one single error!

What's even more uncomfortable for me is that the *On Error GoTo* statement is still possible in all VB.NET derivations—even though it's now completely unnecessary—as you will see in a moment. Reading a text file functions a little differently here in the following example, because *Open* and *Close* don't exist in this Visual Basic 6.0 format any longer. But that's not what this section is about.

Important The only difference, at least concerning the error handling, is that the line numbers must have colons, like other jump labels. Translating the program above into VB.NET might yield the following possible result (unfortunately):

```
Private Sub btnFileReadDotNet_Click(ByVal sender As System.Object, _
    ByVal e As System.EventArgs) Handles btnFileReadDotNet.Click
    'IMPORTANT:
    'To access the IO objects, "Imports System.IO" must be
    'placed at the beginning of the code file!

    Dim FileNotFoundFlag As Boolean
    'Same rubbish here!
    On Error GoTo 1000
```

```
        Dim myFileContent As String
        '1: If an error occurs here
        Dim fileStreamReader As New StreamReader("C:\ATextFile.txt")
        '3: to land here again with Resume Next
        If FileNotFoundFlag Then
            '4: and to catch the error
            MessageBox.Show("File was not found!")
        Else
            'When no error occured, this block is run
            myFileContent = fileStreamReader.ReadToEnd()
            fileStreamReader.Close()
            'And the file content is displayed.
            Debug.Print(myFileContent)
        End If
        Exit Sub
        '2: program execution continues here
1000:   If Err.Number = 53 Then
            FileNotFoundFlag = True
            Resume Next
        End If
End Sub
```

Elegant Error Handling with *Try/Catch/Finally*

VB.NET offers a much more elegant way of implementing error handling. In contrast to *On Error GoTo*, with the *Try/Catch/Finally* structure you can handle errors at the spot where they actually occur. Take a look at the following example, which is an adaptation of the previous example, this time using *Try/Catch*:

```
Private Sub btnFileReadDotNet_Click(ByVal sender As System.Object, ByVal e As System.
➥EventArgs) _
Handles btnFileReadDotNet.Click
    'IMPORTANT:
    'To access the IO objects, "Imports System.IO"
    'must be placed at the beginning of the code file!

    Dim myFileContent As String
    Dim fileStreamReader As StreamReader

    Try
        'Try the following commands.
        fileStreamReader = New StreamReader("C:\myTextFile.txt")
        myFileContent = fileStreamReader.ReadToEnd()
        fileStreamReader.Close()
        Debug.Print(myFileContent)
```

```
        Catch ex As FileNotFoundException
            'Here only FileNotFoundExceptions are caught
            MessageBox.Show("File not found!" & vbNewLine & _
                vbNewLine & "The exception text was:" & vbNewLine & ex.Message, _
                "Exception", MessageBoxButtons.OK, MessageBoxIcon.Error)
        Catch ex As Exception
            'Here all other exceptions, which
            'have not been handled yet, are caught
                'Here all other exceptions, which
                'have not been handled yet, are caught
                MessageBox.Show("An exception occured while processing the file!" & _
                    vbNewLine & "The exception had the type:" & ex.GetType.ToString & _
                    vbNewLine & vbNewLine & "The exception text was:" & vbNewLine & _
                    ex.Message, "Exception", MessageBoxButtons.OK, MessageBoxIcon.Error)
        End Try
    End Sub
```

What happens here? All the statements placed between the *Try* statement and the first *Catch* statement occur in a kind of "trial mode." If an error occurs during execution of any of these wrapped statements, the program automatically jumps to the *Catch* block that most closely matches the error that occurred.

Catching Multiple Exception Types

If you enter the command *Try* in the Visual Studio Code Editor and then press Return, the Editor automatically inserts the following block:

```
Try

Catch ex As Exception

End Try
```

Exception is the name of the class that is highest in the Exception inheritance hierarchy, so it can catch all exceptions—without exception (sorry... I had to do it). In the preceding code, any exception that occurs is instantiated in the variable *ex*. But sometimes you want to handle different errors differently, so it makes sense (as seen in the sample code) to differentiate between the many different exception types. Perhaps your program needs to react differently to an exception triggered by a non-existent file than to one in which the file does exist, but is currently in use.

You can try this out by using the sample code. When you run it, you see an exception called *FileNotFoundException*. A *Catch* block using this class name for the exception type (*Catch ex As FileNotFoundException*) catches only exceptions of that particular type. In the preceding example, that exception produces the message box shown in Figure 1-19.

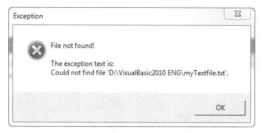

FIGURE 1-19 The sample code returns this message when the file didn't exist; in other words, when a *FileNotFoundException* occurred.

If you now create a text file on drive C under this name, and then open that file in Word, for example, the line again produces an exception, as illustrated here:

```
fileStreamReader = New StreamReader("C:\myTextFile.txt")
```

This time, however, it's not a *FileNotFoundException*, it's an *IOException*, which produces the error output shown in Figure 1-20.

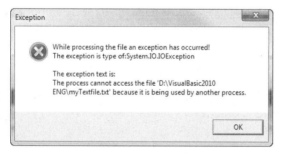

FIGURE 1-20 Now this file exists, but it's already open in Word.

This exception is caught with *Catch ex as Exception*, even though it has the type *IOException* because, *IOException* is derived from *Exception*. In object-oriented programming, you create extended classes by inheriting from existing classes, and from those classes you can derive others that are even further specialized, and so on. It's the same for exception classes. *Exception* is the base class. The exception class *SystemException* is derived from *Exception*, and *IOException* is derived from *SystemException*. Because the example doesn't explicitly handle *IOException* separately, the runtime chooses the *Catch* block that represents at least one of the base classes of the exception class that occurred. Using *Exception* is the catch-all method, because *all* other exception classes are based on it. The exception *FileNotFoundException* is handled separately, but for all other exceptions the *Catch ex as Exception* block executes.

Important You can implement as many *Catch* branches into a *Try-Catch* block as you like, and therefore, target and catch all conceivable exception types. However, be sure that you put the more specialized exception types at the top, and those they are based on further below. Otherwise, you'll get into trouble because the runtime executes the *Catch* block that first match-es a base exception class, which can occur before the *Catch* block with the specialized exception. Figure 1-21 illustrates the potential problem:

```
Try
    fileStreamReader = New StreamReader("D:\VisualBasic2010 ENG\myTextfile.txt")
    myFileContent = fileStreamReader.ReadToEnd()
    fileStreamReader.Close()
    Debug.Print(myFileContent)
    Console.Write(myFileContent)
Catch ex As Exception
    MessageBox.Show("While processing the file an exception has occurred!" & vbNewLine & _
                    "The exception is type of:" & ex.GetType.ToString & vbNewLine & _
                    vbNewLine & "The exception text is:" & vbNewLine & ex.Message, _
                    "Exception", MessageBoxButtons.OK, MessageBoxIcon.Error)
Catch ex As FileNotFoundException
    'Catch' block never reached, because 'System.IO.FileNotFoundException' inherits from 'System.Exception'.
                    "Exception", MessageBoxButtons.OK, MessageBoxIcon.Error)
End Try
```

FIGURE 1-21 Place *Catch* blocks with specialized exception classes before *Catch* blocks that handle base exception classes; otherwise, the computer complains.

Using the *Finally* Block

Program code placed in a *Finally* block *will always be executed*. Even when an error occurs and is caught with *Catch*, or even if that *Catch* block contains a *Return* statement, the *Finally* block will still execute.

Normally, *Return* is the last command in a procedure, no matter where *Return* was placed. In certain cases, however, it doesn't make much sense, especially when working with error han-dling, and therefore, *Finally* is the golden exception here.

Suppose that you are reading from a file, and to do so, you have opened the file. When opening the file, there was no error, but there was an error while reading it. Maybe you have read past the file end, and now lines which you are trying to process are empty (therefore, *Nothing*). You have handled this case (catching a *Null* reference) with the corresponding *Catch* block, and because there is nothing else to do, you want to leave your read routine directly from the *Catch* block, with *Return*, after an error message has been displayed. The problem is that the file is still open, and you should close it. With *Finally*, it is possible to implement such a process elegantly.

The following example simulates such a process. It reads the file c:\aTextFile.txt line by line, converting the individual lines into uppercase letters before combining them into a text block. However, because it tries to read too many lines, the *ToUpper* string method, which converts the line into uppercase letters, stops working at the point where the *ReadLine* func-tion finds no more content, and therefore, returns *Nothing*:

```vb
Private Sub btnTryCatchFinally_Click(ByVal sender As System.Object,
  ByVal e As System.EventArgs) Handles btnTryCatchFinally.Click
    'IMPORTANT:
    'To access the IO objects, "Imports System.IO"
    'must be placed at the beginning of the code file!

    Dim meinDateiInhalt As String
    Dim fileStreamReader As StreamReader
    Try
        'Try the following commands.
        fileStreamReader = New StreamReader("C:\aTextFile.txt")
        Dim locLine As String
        myFileContent = ""
        'Now we read line by line, but too many lines,
        'and therefore shoot past the end of the file:
        Try
            ' If your file "C:\aTextFile" doesn't contain
            ' exactly 1001 lines, it goes bust somewhere in here:
            For lineCounter As Integer = 0 To 1000
                locLine = fileStreamReader.ReadLine()
                'locLine is now Nothing, and the conversion into
                'capitals can no longer work.
                locLine = locLine.ToUpper
                myFileContent &= locLine
            Next
        Catch ex As NullReferenceException
            MessageBox.Show("The line could not be converted, " &
                "because it was empty!")
            ' Return? But the file is still open!!!
            Return
        Finally
            ' No matter! Even with Return in the Catch block
            ' Finally is still executed!
            fileStreamReader.Close()
        End Try
        'But this line runs only when the Try succeeds:
        Debug.Print(myFileContent)
    Catch ex As FileNotFoundException
        'Only FileNotFoundExceptions are caught here
        MessageBox.Show("File not found!" & vbNewLine &
            vbNewLine & "The exception text was:" & vbNewLine & ex.Message,
            "Exception", MessageBoxButtons.OK, MessageBoxIcon.Error)
    Catch ex As Exception
        'Here all other exceptions, which
        'have not been handled yet, are caught
        MessageBox.Show("An exception occured while processing the file!" &
            vbNewLine & "The exception had the type:" & ex.GetType.ToString &
            vbNewLine & vbNewLine & "The exception text was:" & vbNewLine &
            ex.Message, "Exception", MessageBoxButtons.OK, MessageBoxIcon.Error)
    End Try
End Sub
```

Tip You can retrace this process quite well by setting a breakpoint (press F9) in the line that contains the *Return*, statement, and then running the program. When you step through the program by pressing F11, you will notice that even after the *Return* statement, the code in the *Finally* block is still executed.

Chapter 2

Introduction to the .NET Framework

Microsoft .NET and the Microsoft .NET Framework are among the least understood terms in the IT industry. Microsoft isn't entirely innocent in this regard; the original marketing promotions didn't quite use the terms properly either and marketing campaigns ended up using them for pretty much any purpose anyone could think of as the first version of .NET Framework approached release.

So, the first version of Windows Server 2003 was still called .NET Server, but the only thing it contained that had anything to do with .NET was a pre-installed .NET Framework. The *user interface* (UI) of the operating system itself didn't rely on the .NET Framework for even a single line of code. Other than the .NET Framework being pre-installed in Version 1.1, only Internet Information Services, which supported ASP.NET (which *was* based on that .NET Framework version) website hosting, provided any connection to .NET.

If you asked people back then what .NET actually was, and which components it contained, you might have received all kinds of answers—and not necessarily any that came close to the truth.

OK—so let's start there: what on earth is .NET?

What Is .NET, and What Is It Composed Of?

.NET is a collection of various technologies that share a common infrastructure, and that offer software developers the opportunity to develop safe, stable, easily maintainable, multi-platform software—both web browser oriented and smart client applications.

A lot of terms connected to the .NET Framework are tossed around at software symposia and the like by programmers and others who don't always seem to be clear on what these terms actually mean. Even experienced developers don't always know the background of certain .NET terms right away. It's evident that many programmers know only the half of it at best, and they might supply you with either half-truths or even completely wrong information.

One feature that concerns application compilation that applies to the entire .NET Framework platform deserves a special mention: in contrast to some other popular programming languages, none of the .NET language compilers (not even the Microsoft Visual Basic compiler) produce machine commands that are directly executable on the processor. Instead, the .NET compiler produces intermediary code that isn't converted to native processor code until runtime. This makes your applications both much more platform independent, and also provides a runtime opportunity to perform optimizations on the target operating system and available processor or processors. These features would not be possible if the program were translated to machine language from the start.

The following sections introduce and briefly explain the most important .NET terms and technologies. But don't worry: even if the copious abbreviations and acronyms seem confusing at first, the underlying concept is sheer genius and basically quite easy to understand. At the very least, after you finish the following sections, you should recognize a recurrent theme that flows elegantly throughout the entire .NET concept.

What Is an Assembly?

In the simplest case, when you write a program in Windows, a compiler converts your source code into an executable file (.exe). For bigger projects that group functions used repeatedly by various parts of the program, the compiler produces Dynamic Link Libraries (DLLs), which can be called from the outside, thus avoiding redundancies and saving space. You can picture a DLL as a set of classes and methods that cannot run on their own, but that can make those classes and methods available to any number of .exe files.

Under .NET, all this works pretty much the same way, but there is one fundamental difference. In their compiled intermediary code state (more about that later in the section about Just-in-Time compilers), the .exe files or the DLLs are called *assemblies*.

An executable .NET .exe file is an assembly. A .NET DLL is also an assembly. Therefore, an assembly basically just represents a directly (.exe) or an indirectly (DLL) executable entity that contains program code. An assembly is the smallest deliverable entity of .NET programming.

Admittedly, there are more complicated concepts and many more possibilities associated with assemblies. But for the daily use of .NET technologies, this description is quite sufficient.

What Is a Namespace?

A namespace is a way of grouping and separating code. One purpose of namespaces is to group classes within assemblies. Another is to ensure that names are unique. Namespaces have no bearing on their containing assembly name, but they do have a direct bearing on the fully-qualified name of the class or structure *within* an assembly. Namespaces also don't have any bearing on file names (unlike assemblies); therefore, they are an abstract quantity.

The definition of namespaces primarily serves the same purpose as the division of a book into chapters. If the individual sections of a book were just arranged randomly, making sense of the content would be enormously difficult. It's the same issue for objects. For example, the object name *AddressDetails* only hints at the object's purpose. But when that object resides in the namespace *MyFibu.Suppliers*, that naming hierarchy suddenly provides more clarity and order. Namespaces make it easier to find the appropriate object and also eliminate the possibility that another object called *AddressDetails*, created in a different namespace, such as *MyFibu.Customers*, would have the same name as this *MyFibu.Suppliers.AddressDetails* class.

Namespaces can span several assemblies. It's conceivable that you might want to put two classes of the namespace *MyFibu.Suppliers* in one assembly and two other classes belonging to the same namespace in another assembly. In that respect, namespaces and assemblies are completely independent.

The Framework Class Library (FCL), which contains all the .NET Framework classes, uses namespaces extensively (more details more about that in just a bit). For example, classes that deal with Windows Forms belong to the namespace *System.Windows.Forms*. However, that namespace is defined not only in the *System.Windows.Forms* assembly, which contains the most important objects for form control; other objects that belong to the same namespace (*System.Windows.Forms*) reside in the *System.dll* assembly. It is only due to a decision by Microsoft programmers that the namespace and assembly have the same name. As mentioned earlier, that's not a requirement.

> **Note** Namespaces permit a "clean" definition of classes with the same name, but it's possible that an imported namespace might obscure a class or structure of the *System* namespace, and you are therefore no longer able to access it. The *Global* keyword provides a remedy.

Embedding of Namespaces and Assemblies in Code Files and Projects: a Practical Example

Now that you know theoretically what namespaces and assemblies are, let's look at how this works in real life by using the following scenario. You are creating a console application from which you want to call a *MessageBox*; for example, a typical Windows message dialog.

To follow along, go to File | New | Project. In the Installed Templates, click Visual Basic and Windows, and then select the Console Application template. Name the sample project something like **NamespaceDemo**.

When you try to enter the name of the *MessageBox* class, the compiler quits and displays an error message, as shown in Figure 2-1.

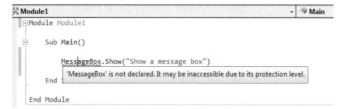

FIGURE 2-1 A method can only access objects that have their own defined assembly or reside in assemblies that it references.

The compiler doesn't recognize *MessageBox* because the *MessageBox* class is defined in an assembly that, by default, isn't embedded in the Console Application template. That makes sense, because a message box is a graphical window—and this is a console application. Nonetheless, you can still use the *MessageBox* class in your console application; but first you need to establish a reference to the assembly that contains it—in this case, the *System. Windows.Forms.dll* assembly. Here's how to do that:

1. In Solution Explorer, move the mouse pointer to the project name (*not* the solution name; when working with a solution that contains a single project, position the mouse pointer over the second entry from the top).

2. Right-click to open the context menu (see Figure 2-2), and then select Add Reference.

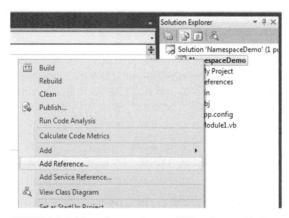

FIGURE 2-2 Add a reference to an additional assembly to your project by opening the context menu in Solution Explorer and then clicking Add Reference.

3. In the dialog box that opens, on the .NET tab, select the entry System.Windows.Forms, as shown in Figure 2-3.

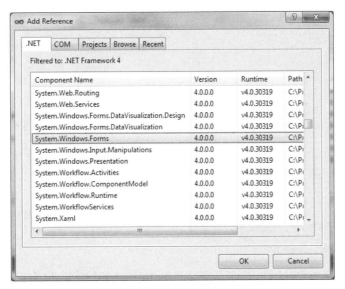

FIGURE 2-3 Use the Add Reference dialog box to select the assemblies that your project should reference.

4. Click OK to close the dialog.

Simply adding the reference doesn't eliminate the error (the error message hasn't gone away), but you can now access the *MessageBox* class. The namespace of many classes is the same as the assembly itself—at least that's true in this example. Therefore, if you replace the *MessageBox* class name with its fully-qualified name (the one that contains the namespace), the error message disappears, as shown in Figure 2-4.

```
Module Module1

    Sub Main()

        System.Windows.Forms.MessageBox.Show("Show a message box")

    End Sub

End Module
```

FIGURE 2-4 Using the fully-qualified name, you can *always* reach a class in a referenced assembly.

Of course, you would type your fingers raw if you always had to write out the fully-qualified name completely when using any method from a class in a referenced external assembly, because you normally use not only one but many classes of such assemblies. Fortunately, you can use the *Imports* statement to import a namespace for a code file globally. Figure 2-5 shows how this works.

```
Imports System.Windows.Forms
Module Module1

    Sub Main()

        MessageBox.Show("Show a message box")

    End Sub

End Module
```

FIGURE 2-5 With the Imports statement, you can embed a namespace globally for a code file.

Visual Basic also offers the ability to embed namespaces globally for a project. To embed global namespaces, follow these steps:

1. Open the project context menu again, as shown in Figure 2-2.

2. Select Properties.

3. In the Properties dialog box, click the References tab.

   On this tab, you'll find references to all the assemblies added to your project that contain classes that you can use as well as a list of existing and pre-imported namespaces that supply these assemblies. The selected (checked) assemblies (see Figure 2-6), have been pre-imported—you can access their classes without adding *Imports* statements in each file. Check any assemblies that you want to import on a project-wide basis, and then close the dialog.

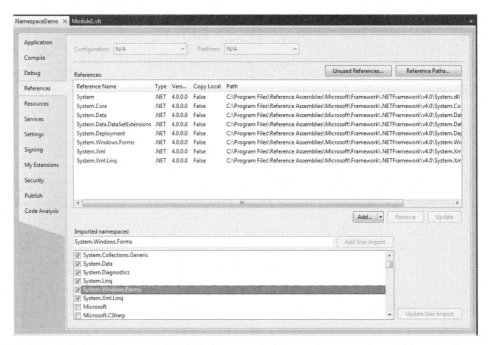

FIGURE 2-6 In the project properties, the References tab shows a reference to all assemblies as well as the namespaces. The selected namespaces are pre-imported automatically.

Common Language Runtime and Common Language Infrastructure

The *Common Language Runtime* (CLR) contains the base assembly of the .NET Framework (the assembly itself is called *mscorlib.dll*). It makes up the lowest layer—the foundation, so to speak—on which all other .NET Framework objects reside. This assembly is called *Base Class Library* (*BCL*; more on this in the following section). The BCL is only one part of the CLR, which contains equally important components. For example, the CLR provides the Just-in-Time compilation functionality (which you'll see later in this chapter), which compiles .NET assemblies from Microsoft Intermediate Language (MSIL) to native machine code just prior to execution.

> **Note** Some developers use the abbreviation *MSIL*, some *MIL*, and some just *IL*.

Another extremely important CLR role is its implementation of the .NET Framework-specific *Garbage Collector*. As opposed to C or C++, you don't need to worry about picking up your data garbage (objects you have used and no longer need after a certain point in time) when developing with the .NET Framework. The Garbage Collector tracks all .NET objects, removing objects that are no longer referenced, and thus no longer needed.

Finally, CLR uses its execution engine, which resides in the DLL mscoree.dll, to ensure that your .NET programs can be executed. The Execution Engine adjusts the comparatively new .NET technology to the start processes of a regular Windows program, by using JIT compilation.

The CLR itself is based on the Common Language Infrastructure (CLI), defined as "the specification of an international standard for the creation of development and program execution environments," a standard that defines how different programming languages (the code that they generate) and different libraries can work seamlessly together. This concept makes it possible to develop.NET projects that work with code written in multiple programming languages. For example, it is perfectly possible to formulate financial program libraries in Visual Basic, but to call them from a Windows application written in C#.

The Framework Class Library and the Base Class Library

These two terms form the base of a mountain of incorrect explanations. Even some experts will argue that the Framework Class Library (FCL) and the Base Class Library (BCL) are the same—but they aren't. Others differentiate the two by declaring the BCL the parent of the CLR—but it isn't.

The BCL is a *part* of the CLR and contains all the base objects you need during your everyday life as a developer. The BCL is always there, but developers hardly ever see it or are even are aware they're using it. It also defines all primitive data types and thus implements the

Common Type System (CTS; see the next section) in the form of usable objects and types, most of which are contained in the *System* namespace or in *mscorlib.dll* assembly. When developing under .NET, you will probably use mostly objects and methods from the BCL. No matter whether you are using a variable of a primitive data type, saving large amounts of data in arrays, handling character strings, or using regular expressions—all the necessary classes and methods are contained in the BCL.

The BCL is designed to the greatest extent possible to be platform independent. It is standardized because it is based on the CLI, which is certified by ECMA. ECMA itself is (by their own description) an *"industry association founded in 1961 and dedicated to the standardization of Information and Communication Technology (ICT) and Consumer Electronics (CE)."* The abbreviation originates from the name *European Computer Manufacturers Association*—a name that's no longer used. You can find more information about ECMA at *http://www.ecma-international.org*.

By the way, don't confuse ECMA with the *European Carton Makers Association*, which, if cartons happen to be a particular interest of yours, you can find at *www.ecma.org*.

This is the reason why its source code is currently freely available in version 1.0 as part of the free CLI implementation called *Rotor*. It's also relatively easy to port to other platforms. There are currently executable implementations of the CLI for Mac OS, FreeBDS, and—of course—Windows.[1] In plain English, this means:

- The BCL is the equivalent of the CLI under Windows, and is therefore part of the CLR.

- The FCL combines *all* .NET functional areas under one name.

The Common Type System

The Common Type System (CTS) establishes rules for data type implementations and data type concepts in the CLI. To use the acronyms you've seen: the BCL of the CLR converts the CTS according to the CLI. (Now there's a sentence to brag about! However, I strongly discourage you from using it for romantic self-promotional purposes.)

In plain language, this means that the CTS defines how the CLR declares, uses, and manages types, and it plays an important role in how the CLR integrates the different .NET languages. It does this by enforcing unconditional type safety (you can't just assign a character string to an integer variable) and guaranteeing high performance during code execution. It defines a fixed set of rules that .NET languages must follow, and thus ensures that objects developed in one .NET language can be used in another .NET language.

---

[1] The "Mono" project under Linux goes one step further and implements a complete FCL, which is even compatible to the Microsoft FCL in many areas.

This is a huge step forward compared to older Microsoft technologies for data exchange between different programs and programming environments (such as COM). Formerly, if you wanted to write a Visual Basic program to pass a *string* to a statement written in C/C++, for example, (which was the case as soon as you wanted to use Windows functions from Visual Basic), you needed to know a great deal about both environments—a string in C is different than a string in Visual Basic—otherwise, you'd get strange effects, and probably crash the application.

The conversion concept of these rules almost incidentally yields another significant advantage that you will learn about in the next section.

Microsoft Intermediate Language and the Just-In-Time Compiler

Due to the CTS concept and the rules it enforces, the compilers of the various .NET programming languages don't directly translate their source code into the machine language understood by the computer's processor. Rather, the programs are first converted into *Common Intermediate Language* or *CIL*. It's called an intermediate language because it is more abstract and a level higher than a processor machine language, but it's still closer to machine language than a full-fledged high-level language, such as Visual Basic or C#. Like the CLI, the CIL is also a technology carrier; the actual implementation Microsoft uses for Windows platforms is called *Microsoft Intermediate Language (MSIL)*. MSIL is a processor-independent language that can be easily translated into actual machine language for any processor.

An assembly, therefore, doesn't usually contain any commands a processor can understand directly; instead, it contains program code, from which the *Just-in-Time compiler* (JIT) creates the actual machine program at runtime. Initially, this sounds like a performance problem waiting to happen, but it's not. (OK, fine, let's say: In very few cases. OK, fine, let's say: not usually.) The JIT compiler is optimized so that it compiles only the methods of a class that a program requires immediately. Your programs will eventually recover some of the time lost to method compilation, because the JIT compiler typically creates much more efficient code than other compilers. That's because the JIT compiler understands the characteristics of the computer on which the code that needs to be compiled will run.

A conventional compiler wouldn't know the computer, because the computer on which an application is developed and compiled is usually completely different than the computer on which it will eventually run. The JIT compiler considers the processor characteristics. For example, if it recognizes that the computer running a .NET application has an Intel I7 processor, it can optimize the code for that processor. A conventional compiler, however, must always create machine code with average optimization, because it must guarantee that the code will work on all compatible processors (Intel Atom, I3, I5, I7, AMD Athlon II, Phenom, and so on). Thus, the JIT compiler has a large number of optimization possibilities available that typical compilers can't take advantage of—but we won't get into them in detail here.

> **Note** One exception is the FCL itself, which is pre-compiled so that it's not necessary to JIT-compile the entire .NET Framework (or the parts needed by the application) at each application start. This could lead to the impression that the FCL, in contrast to your own programs, might not be optimally adjusted for your system, because if it has been pre-compiled internally at Microsoft, it couldn't possibly be optimized to your own personal system. However, that's not the case, and here's why: while working in .NET you might have noticed that installing .NET Framework on a speedy machine goes quickly, but still takes noticeably longer than expected. That's because during installation the FCL does more than just *copy* the appropriate directories; it actually compiles the FCL into them. The FCL installation files in the .NET Framework setup exist in MSIL. During installation on a computer, they are translated into native machine code and then—optimized for that computer—are set up in the target directories.

This approach has one more advantage: programs developed under the .NET Framework can be processor-independent. An application created with the target type *Any* (meaning, *targets any .NET-supported architecture*) also runs independently of the processor. Therefore, if you develop a project with the target type *Any*, it would run, for example, not only on a 32-bit Windows XP system, but also on a 64-bit Windows Vista installation with full 64-bit support.

Chapter 3
Sightseeing

Introduction

The intent of this chapter is to provide an overview of the Microsoft Visual Studio 2010 integrated development environment (IDE). Although the breadth of the functionality in the IDE warrants its own book, by the end of this chapter, you should generally feel comfortable with the IDE, know the key functionality and strengths of Visual Studio 2010, and have developed the ability to explore further on your own.

Instead of describing all the user interface (UI) elements, the flow of this chapter follows the major tasks that developers need to perform. These include:

- Getting started by picking the right development settings.

- Creating new projects or upgrading existing projects.

- Increasing productivity with the power of the Windows Presentation Foundation-based Visual Studio UI.

- Browsing, understanding, and navigating code.

- Creating code by using Test-Driven Development.

- Extending Visual Studio with third-party extensions.

This chapter makes extensive reference to shortcut key combinations. The precise shortcut keys used in the chapter are based on the Microsoft Visual Basic Development Settings—the keystrokes can vary if you are using a different setting. When using the shortcut keys, treat the sequences of keys in the pattern "key+key" (for example Alt+>) as an instruction to press those keys simultaneously.

Note Shortcut key combinations are provided for the United States keyboard layout, and they are not necessarily localized to other cultures. So, for example, the shortcuts for switching the IntelliSense tabs from Common to All are Alt+< and Alt+>. The keys position in the layout of the keyboard will most likely stay the same, which means in this sample, the shortcuts for switching the IntelliSense tabs on a German keyboard will be Alt+Comma (,) and Alt+Period (.).

This chapter also uses illustrations lavishly to explain various UI elements.

Starting Visual Studio for the First Time: Selecting the Profile

When you start Visual Studio 2010 for the first time, a dialog box opens (see Figure 3-1) that provides an option to choose your development settings.

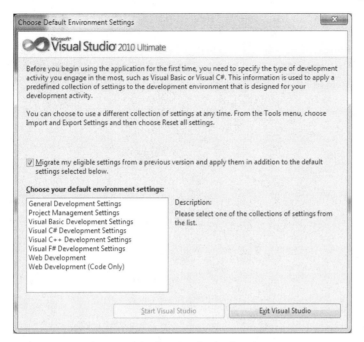

FIGURE 3-1 Starting Visual Studio 2010 for the first time.

To optimize the IDE experience for a specific development project, Visual Studio supports the concept of *settings*. Settings (also referred to as a *Profile*) determine various customizations made to the IDE to configure the window layout, show or hide specific tool windows and menu items, determine keyboard shortcut bindings, filtering and ordering of project templates, and so on. As a developer, you can choose settings that correspond to the type of development that you do most frequently, modifying the IDE to meet your needs. You can then save the new modified settings—or even share them, if you like. If you're unsure of which setting to choose; the General Development Settings choice is a good place to start. However, if you're starting software development with a specific language, such as Visual Basic, it's probably best to start with the Visual Basic Development Settings. With that pointed out, the Visual Basic Development Settings hide some UI elements and functionality that you might need later. So, for learning purposes, or as a hobby programmer, the Visual Basic Development Settings choice is recommended, but if you use Visual Basic for professional purposes, the General Development Settings option is likely more suitable.

If you upgrade to another edition of Visual Studio, you will have the option to apply the previous edition's settings by using the Migrate My Eligible Settings option.

To change the settings, from the Tools menu, select Import And Export Settings, as shown in Figure 3-2.

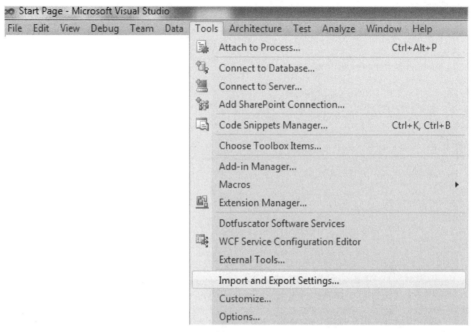

FIGURE 3-2 To reset the Visual Studio IDE settings, use the Import And Export Settings command.

The Import And Export Settings Wizard appears, in which you can perform operations such as importing user-defined settings, exporting your current environment settings, or resetting configurations to a default list. This is useful because developers often switch gears to a different programming language or move from a client development to a web development project.

> **Tip** When changing settings, the wizard provides an option to save your current settings—which can be useful when you get back to your current development project. Visual Studio persists settings in an XML-formatted file named currentsettings.vssettings in the folder \Documents\Visual Studio 2010\Settings. Visual Studio updates the currentsettings file automatically whenever you change any setting in the IDE, such as moving a tool window, changing the color mapping for text or comments, and so on.

Visual Studio applies settings as layers. A settings file can contain information on all the IDE settings or on only a subset of the available IDE settings. This means that you can import multiple .vssettings files. When you do that, the new file overlays the section of settings defined in the file. You can find a sample settings file in the downloadable code for the book.

The Start Page: Where Your Developing Endeavors Begin

Now that you have selected the Development Settings, the first document launched in Visual Studio IDE is the Start Page. The Start Page is a "welcome" page that provides one-stop access to common tasks, such as creating new projects, opening existing projects, and getting learning resource and news updates on Visual Studio itself. Figure 3-3 shows the various parts of the Start Page.

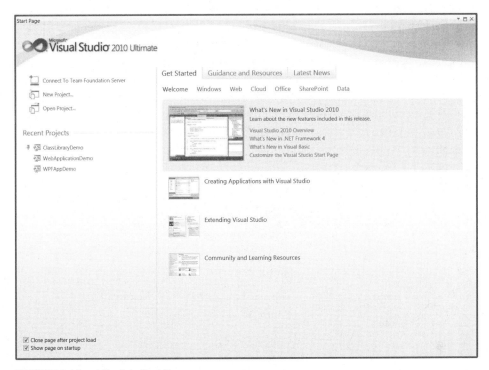

FIGURE 3-3 Visual Studio's Start Page.

The Start Page is divided into three main sections: a command section that displays the New Project and Open Project commands, a Recent Projects list (which will be empty when you first get started), and a tabbed content area that has a Get Started tab and an RSS Feed tab. The command section hosts the New Project and Open Project commands. The Recent Projects list displays links to recent projects. Clicking a link opens the corresponding project in Visual Studio. If you right-click a link, you can select one of the options presented in the following table.

Option	Description
Open Project	Loads the solution in the IDE.
Open Containing Folder	Launches Windows Explorer and opens the directory containing the solution file.
Remove From List	Removes the entry from the Recent Projects list. This action does not delete the project from disk.

Hovering over an item in the Recent Projects list highlights that item and exposes a "pushpin" icon. Clicking the pushpin icon "pins" the project to the list so that it remains in the list even after you open and close other projects. Clicking the pushpin on a pinned project unpins it from the list. In Figure 3-3, the ClassLibraryDemo project is pinned. You can also use the project's context menu (right-click the project to access the menu) to remove it from the list. You can choose the number of projects that display in the Recent Projects list (the list shows ten projects by default). To change the number of projects, click Tools | Options | Environment | General, and then enter the desired number (within a range of 1 to 24) in the Items Shown In Recently Used Lists text box, as demonstrated in Figure 3-4.

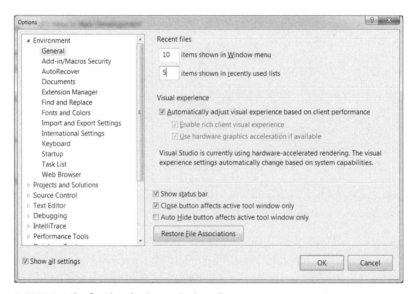

FIGURE 3-4 Configuring the Recent Projects list.

The content area hosts a Get Started tab, Guidance And Resources tab, and Latest News tab. The Get Started tab displays a list of Help topics, web sites, technical articles, and other resources that can help you increase your productivity and learn about features in the product. You can change the list by clicking one of the following categories from the category row, just below the tabs: Welcome, Windows, Web, Cloud, Office, SharePoint, and Data. Clicking an icon in the Get Started section displays a description of the resource, together with a list of links that pertain to that resource. The Guidance And Resources tab provides more general guidance on coding and development, and follows the same format as the Getting Started tab. It includes categories for Development Process, MSDN Resources, and Additional Tools. The Latest News tab lists featured articles from the selected news channel. You can switch to a different news channel by changing the address in the RSS feed box at the top of the article list.

The Visual Studio startup can be customized by clicking Tools | Options | Environment | Startup, as illustrated in Figure 3-5.

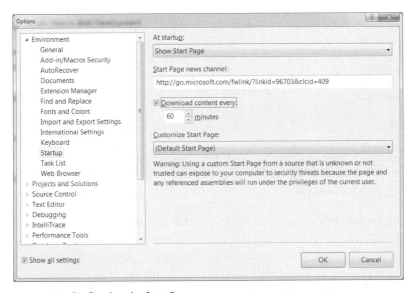

FIGURE 3-5 Configuring the Start Page.

Although the Start Page is useful, most often, once the project is opened, developers just close the Start Page. You can do this by selecting the Close Page After Project Load check box, which is located at the bottom of the Start Page. You can also determine if the Start Page is displayed when starting Visual Studio by selecting the Show Page On Startup check box.

Beginning Development Experience—Creating New Projects

When you are ready to create a new project, you need to open the New Project dialog box. You can do so either from the Start Page, or by clicking File | New menu, by using the icon , or by pressing Ctrl+N. Figure 3-6 shows the New Project dialog box.

FIGURE 3-6 The New Project dialog box.

The New Project dialog box categorizes the installed templates and enables the creation of new projects. Project templates are files that store information about the Visual Studio version, the target framework, the list of references, file imports, and so on that Visual Studio should add when you create a project. To create one, simply select a template from the list, provide a name for the project or solution, and then click OK.

The templates are filtered based on the .NET Framework version that you select in the drop-down list at the top-center of the dialog. The drop-down list is populated based on the framework versions you have installed on your machine. You'll see a discussion of the different .NET Framework versions in the section "The History of Multitargeting," later in this chapter.

Because there is large number of templates and the list is growing continuously, the search functionality of the New Project Dialog comes in handy. To search for templates, use the Search Installed Templates box on the upper-right corner of the New Project dialog. Similar to Windows Explorer and Internet Explorer, pressing Ctrl+E sets the focus to the search box on the dialog.

The search performs case-insensitive substring matches over the title and description of the templates in all categories. Search uses *AND* criteria to find matches when you pass in multiple words as search criteria. For example, if you search for "proj test VB," the search results will contain templates that have words (in the title or description) that contain all three substrings, in any order. You can also use the New Project dialog box to search for and install online templates or user-created templates. To search for online templates, click Online Templates to view the categorized list of online templates. Selecting a template from the list provides more information on the template, such as Type, Version, Downloads, Rating, and so on. Double-click the template to download it and add it to the solution.

You can expand projects by adding project items through the Add New Item dialog. The project item templates shown in the dialog are filtered based on the current project and the targeted version of the .NET Framework. Just like project templates, item templates store information about the files, references and imports to be added to the project when you add a project item to a project. The Add New Item dialog box shown in Figure 3-7 is very similar in functionality to that of New Project.

FIGURE 3-7 The Add New Item dialog box.

Managing Templates

This section applies to anyone who wants to create custom templates or organize the installed templates differently from their default categorization. If you're not interested in that, you can skip this section.

To appear in the New Project and Add New Item dialog boxes, template files must reside in a location that Visual Studio recognizes. You can create custom subcategories for templates so that those subcategories also appear in the user interface. By default, Visual Studio searches two locations for project and item templates. If a compressed file that includes a .vstemplate file exists in these locations, that template will appear in the New Project or Add New Item dialog boxes. The default templates installed with Visual Studio are located in the directories shown here (note that *Locale* is *1033* for English and *1031* for German):

\VisualStudioInstallationDirectory\Common7\IDE\ItemTemplates\Language\Locale\

\VisualStudioInstallationDirectory\Common7\IDE\ProjectTemplates\Language\Locale\

In contrast, custom Visual Basic project and item templates are located in these folders:

\My Documents\Visual Studio 2010\Templates\ProjectTemplates\Visual Basic\

\My Documents\Visual Studio 2010\Templates\ItemTemplates\Visual Basic\

You can change the location of custom templates by clicking Tools | Options | Projects And Solutions | General Categories in the New Project and Add New Item dialog boxes. The locations reflect the directory structure that exists in the installed and custom template locations, so you can modify these directory structures to organize your templates in some more desirable way. Note that you cannot create new categories at the programming language level, only at the individual language level.

Similarly, you can organize installed templates by creating subdirectories in the programming language folder. These subdirectories appear in the New Project and Add New Item dialog boxes as virtual folders within each language.

Changes to the organized templates are not reflected instantaneously. For the changes to be picked up, you must do the following:

1. Close all instances of Visual Studio.
2. Run the Visual Studio command prompt as administrator.
3. Type **devenv /setup**.
4. Open Visual Studio.

   The changes will be visible in the New Project and New Item dialogs.

Modifying Templates

To change the templates, simply extract the files for the specific .zip file corresponding to the template that you need to modify, make the desired changes, and then re-zip all the files.

Migrating from Previous Versions of Visual Studio to Visual Studio 2010

Now let's switch gears and discuss the process of taking projects and solutions created with previous versions of Visual Studio and upgrading them to Visual Studio 2010.

Upgrading Projects created with Visual Studio 2003 Through 2008

The process of migrating the projects created in earlier versions of Visual Studio to a newer version is referred to as *upgrading*. When you open projects created in Visual Studio 2003 through Visual Studio 2008 in Visual Studio 2010, Visual Studio detects the target framework version of the upgraded projects. To retain the continuity of the development process, Visual Studio 2010 keeps the target framework for upgraded projects. This behavior is, however, different from the Visual Studio Express SKU, which automatically upgrades older projects to target the 4.0 version of the .NET Framework. (Visual Studio can only maintain the earlier target framework if you have the targeted versions of the framework installed on your computer.) You need .NET 3.5 SP1 installed to be able to target Frameworks 2.0–3.5. Figure 3-8 shows that if the targeted framework version is not on your computer, the Upgrade Wizard provides options to:

- Change the target framework of the projects to 4.0.

- Download the needed framework version.

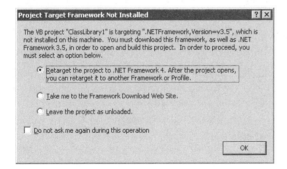

FIGURE 3-8 Upgrading a project when the target framework is not on the computer.

The upgrade process upgrades project and solution files to Visual Studio version 10.0 (2010). It also escapes identifiers in the code files that match any of the new keywords introduced since that project was created. As an example, when you upgrade a Visual Studio 2003 project to Visual Studio 2010, if there are any identifiers named *Global*, *Using*, *IsNot*, *Partial*, *Custom*, *UShort*, *Uinteger*, *ULong*, or *Of*, those identifiers are "escaped" by enclosing them in square brackets [ ]. When Visual Studio upgrades projects that use obsolete APIs or have code patterns for which warnings were added in newer versions of Visual Studio, it populates the upgraded project's error list with obsolete APIs and other warnings.

Note The following is a list of issues about which you should be aware when converting projects to Visual Studio 2010:

- After a solution or any of its projects has been converted, it might no longer be possible to edit, build, or run the upgraded project in previous versions.

- If the solution or project is under source control, it will be checked out automatically during conversion.

- Creating a backup (an option available from the conversion wizard) is always a safe option.

- For Office projects, the Upgrade Wizard will modify your project to target the version of Office you have installed. If you do not want to change the version of Office this project targets, cancel the wizard and clear the Always Upgrade To Installed Version Of Office option, which you can access by clicking Tools | Options | Office Tools.

- Upgrading of Smart Device projects is not currently supported in Visual Studio 2010.

- To automate the conversion of many solutions or projects, you can create a batch file that uses the command-line upgrade tools. The script that follows upgrades a solution file named MyProject.sln.

  ```
  devenv "MyProject.sln" /upgrade
  ```

  This automatically creates a backup copy in the current folder.

The conversion report contains useful information when a project or solution does not
upgrade smoothly. The following table presents a list of errors that can occur if conversion
fails.

Error	Description
Error creating backup file	A backup copy of the solution file cannot be created. Check whether there is already a file that has the same name.
Error creating backup of project file	A backup copy of the project file cannot be created. Check whether there is already a file that has the same name.
File is not writable	The file is read-only or is located on a read-only network share. Source-controlled files that are exclusively checked out by another user are read-only.
Internal Non Fatal Error	An error has occurred with Visual Studio. To try to repair Visual Studio. In the Add or Remove Programs dialog box, select the product you have installed, and then click Change/Remove.
Unable to open project file to per-form upgrade	The project file cannot be opened. Check whether the project file has been opened and locked by another application.
Unable to parse project file	The project file is corrupt or is a version that cannot be upgraded.
Unable to save upgraded project file	An internal error might have occurred.
Web project component not installed. Unable to upgrade project	The project is a web project. Visual Web Developer Express edition is the only Express edition that can be used to convert web projects.

Upgrading Visual Basic 6.0 Applications to Visual Studio 2010

Visual Studio 2010 does not directly support upgrading Visual Basic 6.0 applications. However, you can accomplish such an upgrade in two ways:

■ Download the free Visual Basic 2008 Express edition, upgrade the Visual Basic 6.0 projects to Visual Studio 2008 format, and then upgrade to Visual Studio 2010 by using the Upgrade Wizard as discussed earlier.

■ Use third-party tools. Both free and more advanced commercial versions are available. Which you are able to use depends on the individual needs of the project. ArtinSoft is one company that provides such upgrades.

Note   The second option is recommended—even by Microsoft.

Multitargeting of Visual Basic Applications by Using Visual Studio 2010

Often, software developers and large companies are restricted from adopting newer versions of Visual Studio until their customer base moves to the new framework. This becomes a bigger challenge when some companies or individuals develop applications catering to multiple target frameworks. In Visual Studio 2002–2005, the only option was to have side-by-side installation of multiple versions of Visual Studio and maintain multiple copies of the application. In Visual Studio 2010, however, the *multitargeting* feature allows developers to create applications that target Framework versions 2.0, 3.0, 3.5, and 4.0, as well as various profiles within those framework versions. The key benefit of multitargeting is that you can use Visual Studio 2010 to create and develop new projects that target earlier versions of the .NET Framework (such as 2.0, 3.0, and 3.5). Multitargeting in Visual Studio 2010 also lets you continue to develop projects that were created using earlier versions of Visual Studio, including Visual Studio 2005 and Visual Studio 2008, and reap the benefits of the latest and greatest tooling support in Visual Studio 2010.

The History of Multitargeting

Visual Studio took its first step toward multitargeting in Visual Studio 2008, but it was a baby step. Even though with Visual Studio 2008 you could target different versions of the .NET Framework 2.0, 3.0, and 3.5, the underlying Common Language Runtime (CLR) for all these frameworks remained the same: the .NET CLR version 2.0. Figure 3-9 illustrates how you can think of it as an "onion model," where CLR 2.0 is the core and the .NET Framework 2.0, .NET Framework 3.0, and .NET Framework 3.5 are layers built on top of one another.

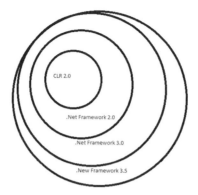

FIGURE 3-9 The "onion model" of multitargeting in Visual Studio 2008.

The multitargeting challenge grew with the release of the new .NET 4.0 Framework for Visual Studio 2010, which runs on top of the .NET CLR version 4.0. This version of the CLR does not overwrite previous versions; instead, it installs side-by-side with earlier versions of the .NET CLR.

Visual Studio took another step forward in Visual Studio 2010 by enabling targeting for .NET Framework versions that span multiple versions of the CLR (CLR 2.0 and CLR 4.0).

Also, the addition of Microsoft Silverlight project templates in Visual Studio 2010 meant that it should have maintained the ability to create projects targeting Silverlight 2.0 through Silverlight 4.0, as shown in Figure 3-10.

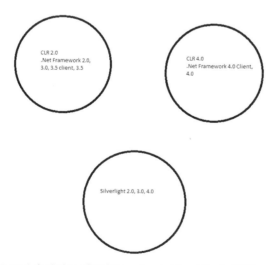

FIGURE 3-10 A depiction of multitargeting in Visual Studio 2010.

Multitargeting in Visual Studio 2010 is well supported in the IDE. Microsoft added several features that help when you work on a project that targets an earlier version of the .NET Framework. The following list presents some of the filters provided by Visual Studio to ensure that the applications targeting a specific framework will work well when deployed on a computer with only the target framework installed.

- Items in the New Project dialog box, Add New Item dialog box, Add New Reference dialog box, and Add Service Reference dialog box are filtered to omit choices that are unavailable in the target framework version.

- Custom controls in the Toolbox are filtered to remove those that are not available in the target version, and to show the latest version when multiple controls are available for the targeted version.

- IntelliSense filters out language features that are not available in the targeted version. Because this filtering is based on the referenced assemblies for the target framework, there are some exceptions.

- Properties in the Properties window are filtered to omit those that are not available in the target version.

- Menu options filter out options that are not available in the target version.

- It compiles and builds with the appropriate version of the compiler (or uses the 4.0 compiler with appropriate compiler switches).

Multitargeting for New Projects

Visual Studio 2010 lets you choose .NET 2.0, 3.0, 3.5 or 4.0 as the target framework when you create a new application. You can select the target framework by using the drop-down list in the the New Project dialog box. The drop-down list is populated based on the framework versions installed on your computer, as shown in Figure 3-11.

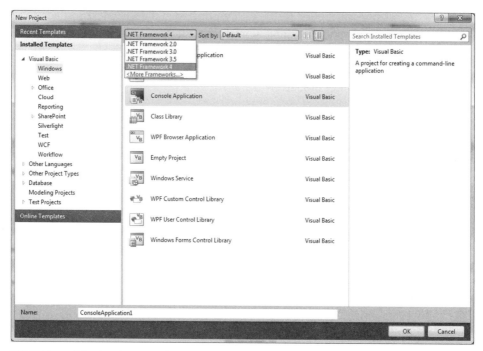

FIGURE 3-11 Selecting the target framework for a new project.

Note Multitargeting through the New Project dialog box is not available in Express editions of Visual Studio.

Changing the Target Framework for Applications

You can change the target .NET Framework version or profile for an existing project by modifying the project properties.

1. Open the Project Properties page by double-clicking the My Project node in Solution Explorer.

2. Navigate to the Compiler Tab.

3. Click the Advanced Compiler Options button.

4. On the Compile tab, select the target framework from the Target Framework (All Configurations) drop-down list (see Figure 3-12). Note that the drop-down shows only the frameworks installed on your computer, but it includes an option to install other frameworks from the Web. Clicking that option opens the .NET Framework Developer Center page in your browser.

When you change the target framework of a project, Visual Studio makes any required changes to references and configuration files.

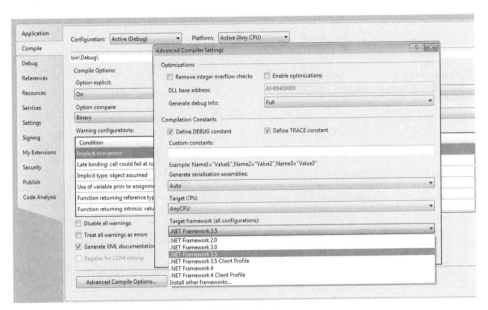

FIGURE 3-12 Changing the target framework of a project.

As an example, if you create a new WinForms application that targets the 3.5 version of the framework, all references use runtime version v2.0.50727, as shown in Figure 3-13.

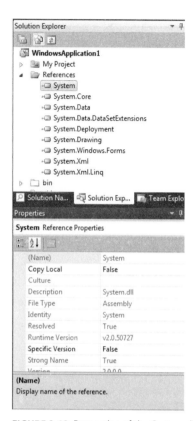

FIGURE 3-13 Properties of the System.dll for a project targeting .NET Framework 3.5.

Now upgrade the project to Visual Studio 2010. Notice that the reference version is modified to v4.0.30319, as illustrated in Figure 3-14.

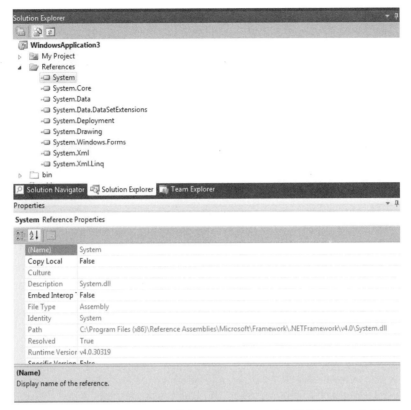

FIGURE 3-14 Properties of System.dll for a project targeting .NET Framework 4.0.

Understanding Profiles

When you expanded the drop-down list to select a target framework, you probably noticed entries such as.NET Framework 4 Client Profile and.NET Framework 3.5 Client Profile.

The .NET Framework profile is a subset of the .NET Framework that provides a limited set of libraries and features. The key benefit of profiles is that they reduce the size of the deployment package for applications by including only the relevant set of assemblies. This also helps because you do not need to worry about installing patches issued for assemblies that are not a part of the profile on your computer.

The .NET Framework 4 Client Profile contains the features needed to develop client applications, such as WinForms, Windows Presentation Foundation (WPF), and so on, and omits server-side features such as ASP.NET and the .NET Framework Data Provider for Oracle. An application that targets the .NET Framework 4 Client Profile has a smaller redistribution package that installs the minimum set of client assemblies on the user's computer, without requiring the full version of the .NET Framework 4.

For a complete list of reference assemblies included in the .NET Framework 4 Client Profile, see Assemblies in the .NET Framework Client Profile, which is available at http://msdn.microsoft.com/en-us/library/ff462634.aspx.

You might have also noticed in the drop-down list that the 3.5 Framework had a client profile, so you're probably wondering what the difference is between the 3.5 Client Profile and the 4.0 Client Profile. The .NET Framework Client Profile was introduced in .NET Framework 3.5 SP1 to improve deployment and installation of the .NET Framework. The following table lists the differences between the .NET Framework 3.5 SP1 Client Profile and the .NET Framework 4 Client Profile. Note that the 4.0 version is more versatile and better supported than the 3.5 version.

.NET Framework 3.5 SP1 Client Profile	.NET Framework 4 Client Profile
Web install only.	Local package and web install.
Only supports Microsoft Windows XP SP2 or SP3 and x86 architecture, where no previous version of the Microsoft .NET Framework is installed.	All platforms and CPU architectures supported by the .NET Framework 4, except IA64.
Single entry in Add or Remove Programs. When the full version of the .NET Framework is installed, it replaces the Client in Programs And Features and cannot be reverted.	Part of the .NET Framework. The .NET Framework is made up of the .NET Framework 4 Client Profile and .NET Framework 4 Extended components that exist separately in Programs And Features.
Windows Update will upgrade it to the full version of the .NET Framework.	Independent component. Can be serviced separately. Does not need the .NET Framework 4 Extended component of the .NET Framework.

Client Profile is Default for Client Projects

Upon creating a new 4.0 targeting client application (Winform, WPF, Office, Workflow, Console, and so forth), the Target Framework by default is set to the .NET Framework 4 Client Profile.

For non-client applications such as web, and deployment projects, the target is set to.NET Framework 4 Full Profile.

Because profiles are not shown in the New Project dialog box, you can change them only through the Project Properties page.

Interesting Read for Multitargeting

The other two questions that come up about multitargeting are:

1. How does Visual Studio ensure that the application is allowed to execute only against a specified SKU?

   The answer lies in the additional app.config file added to .exe project templates, which specifies the profile and CLR runtime version. Visual Studio adds enforcement to prevent apps specified as NETFX4 Full in app.config to run on NETFX4 Client. If the app.config file is missing, the application will run only on the Client Profile.

2. For down-targeted projects, what compiler does Visual Studio use to compile my project?

   For non-web applications, Visual Studio uses the 4.0 compiler to compile projects that target all the framework versions. The 4.0 compiler includes a language version switch that lets it generate IL compatible with different target frameworks. Using the 4.0 compiler allows developers to use newer language features for down-targeting than would otherwise be possible.

Limitations of Multitargeting

Multitargeting—for all its capabilities—does have a few gotchas, or perhaps stated more diplomatically, "room for improvement."

Lack of Round-Tripping Support

Round-tripping is the ability to use a current or previous version of Visual Studio to target a platform supported by both versions of Visual Studio. For example, with round-tripping, you can open projects from a previous version of Visual Studio in a newer IDE without performing a conversion; thus, you canwork side-by-side on older and upgraded projects. This means that companies with some developers using Visual Studio 2008 while others are using Visual Studio 2010 need to keep their solutions separate. The source files can be shared across solutions if they're not impacted by the design-time compatibility issue discussed in the following section.

Compromised Design Time Compatibility

When you use the 4.0 compiler in the IDE, you get the new tooling support for Visual Studio 2010 as well as the ability to use new language features that are supported in the Base Class Library (BCL) for the targeted framework. On the flip side, being able to use Visual Studio 2010 features for down-targets results in the potential problem of source files not being design-time compatible when used with earlier versions. That might be an issue for source code shared over projects that target different versions of the framework.

As an example, when you paste the following code in a class, it can be compiled by using Visual Studio 2010 for any version from 2.0 onward.

```
Property test As String
Sub DesignTimeCompatDemo()
        Dim query = Aggregate process In System.Diagnostics.Process.GetProcesses()
                    Into Average(process.Threads.Count) ' notice no explicit line -
                    ' continuation character
    End Sub
```

The preceding code uses both the implicit line continuation and autoimplemented property features introduced in the Visual Studio 2010 version. This means that the generated assembly is runtime compatible. However, if you try to compile this same source code by using either the 3.5 or 2.0 version of the compiler, you will generate errors, because the 3.5 compiler does not recognize these language features, so it treats this as invalid code. This limitation is referred to as the "lack of design-time compatibility in source files." To make this code design-time compatible, you would need to use only features that were available in the 3.5 compiler.

Non-Optimal Experience with Mixed Target Solutions

For most applications, the majority of developers would use a single target framework version for all projects in the solution. However, if your application requires you to use multiple target framework versions in your solution, you might need to compromise on the IDE experience. For Visual Basic projects, Project-to-Project References that target different framework silos are treated as File References. As an example, if you have a project that targets the 4.0 Framework and another project in the solution targets the 3.5 Framework version, Visual Studio will convert any project references between the two projects to file references. The limitation of a file reference is that it does not provide live IntelliSense and error/warning squiggles in the code, or support rename/find-all references across projects, or Go To Definition on symbols spanning both projects. This behavior is similar to having multilanguage projects in your solution (such as a Visual Basic and a C# project). When adding a reference across silos, you will see the message shown in Figure 3-15. The good news is that if you then change the target framework of projects so that they match, the file references are automatically converted back to project to project references.

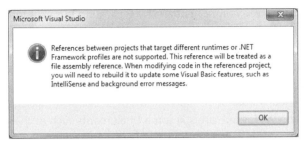

FIGURE 3-15 Crossing the silos with project references.

Framework Silos for Visual Basic projects are listed in the following:

- 4.0 Client Profile, 4.0 Full Profile
- 2.0, 3.0, 3.5 Client Profile, 3.5 Full Profile

Third-Party User Controls

The Add Reference dialog box disables system assemblies that do not pertain to your target .NET Framework version. (System assemblies are .dll files that are part of a .NET Framework version.) This helps you to avoid adding references to assemblies that are not in your target version. If you modify your project file to include references that belong to a .NET Framework version that is newer than the one currently targeted by your project, your reference will not resolve. Also, you cannot add or use controls that depend on this reference. This ability to limit user controls also blocks adding controls created by using the 4.0 Full target framework in projects that target the 4.0 Client Profile (which is the default for new Winforms and WPF applications).

You can resolve this problem by switching the .NET Framework target of your project to one that includes this reference, which you can do from the Project Property page as explained earlier. Another option is to create a custom template for client projects that targets the full framework. This book's code includes a modified WinForms template that targets the full profile. To change the target framework of a template, modify the corresponding .vbproj file in the template.

Zooming In the New and Improved WPF-Based IDE

If you have been following any of the marketing campaigns for Visual Studio 2010, you must have heard the phrase "New, Improved WPF IDE," and you might have wondered why. During development of Visual Studio 2010, Microsoft placed special emphasis on ensuring that that Visual Studio had the most modern look and feel. That includes some new and upcoming UI gestures and also includes extensibility features built into Visual Studio. Because of the mature code base of Visual Studio components, these goals could be accomplished only by upgrading the codebase, making it more componentized by separating business logic from the presentation layer. As a technology, WPF leads naturally to this "separated presentation" architecture, often called "Model, View, Controller" or "Model, View, Presenter." As a side effect with the adoption of WPF, Visual Studio now functions as a great example of how large and complex applications can be built successfully by using WPF. Although all the major UI components, including the Visual Studio Shell, Start Page, editor, window management system, and so on, are handled by WPF, there are still some UI elements such as the Object browser, classview, and so forth that are based on Windows Forms and are hosted within a WPF control. Altogether, Visual Studio 2010 is a very interesting mix of technologies. To see for yourself which pieces of the IDE are written in WPF, you can use the "Snoop" tool (*http:// snoopwpf.codeplex.com*), which is a WPF spy tool that inspects the WPF visual tree for Visual Studio, as shown in Figure 3-16.

FIGURE 3-16 The Snoop tool on Visual Studio 2010 IDE.

Managing Screen Real Estate

With the shift in coding and designing paradigms toward a more modular approach, the arrangement of various code files, designer files, and tool windows has become a personal preference. Visual Studio 2010 has taken a step forward in adding customizability, letting developers arrange IDE windows within one monitor or across multiple monitors.

Split Window

Suppose that you have a large Visual Basic code file, and you would like to be able to see two different parts of the same file at the same time. Visual Studio's split window support is the feature you need.

To use the feature, click and hold the splitter control located in the upper-right corner of the code window, and then drag the split window down to your desired location.

Alternatively, you can select Split from the Window menu, as illustrated in Figure 3-17.

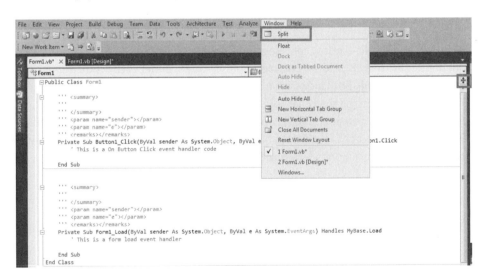

FIGURE 3-17 Options for managing document windows.

Figure 3-18 shows the file Form1.vb split into two views. One view shows the *Button1_Click* event; the other view shows the *Form1_Load* event.

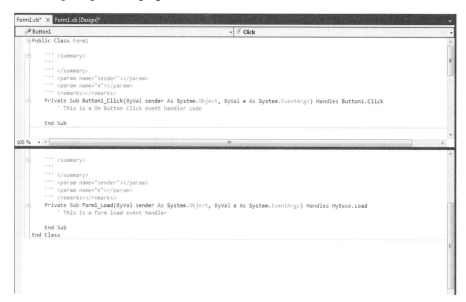

FIGURE 3-18 A file window split horizontally.

Each view in the split window can show a different part of the code and can scroll or zoom independently. To switch focus between split windows, either click inside the desired view or press F6 or Alt+F6. Both views have separate identities in the sense that editing code in one view does not scroll the other view. On the other hand, common elements such as dropdowns and invoking error correction via the error list are associated with the active view. Outlining (expanded/collapsed state of code blocks/regions) is same in all the views. If you expand a code block in one view, it will show as expanded in all views.

Figure 3-19 shows different highlight references invoked in the two views of the Form1.vb file.

FIGURE 3-19 Highlighted references in split windows.

Horizontal and Vertical Tab Group

Document windows can be stacked horizontally or vertically. Use the Windows menu to make the selection.

Figure 3-20 shows horizontally tabbed documents, and Figure 3-21 shows vertically tabbed documents.

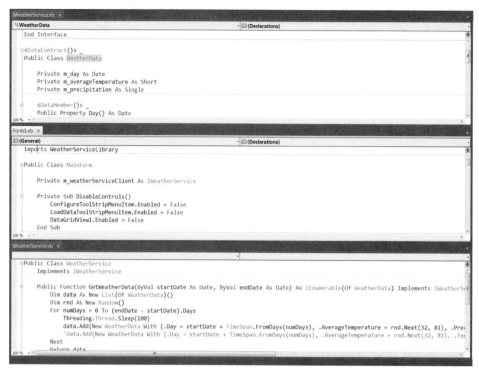

FIGURE 3-20 Horizontally tabbed document windows.

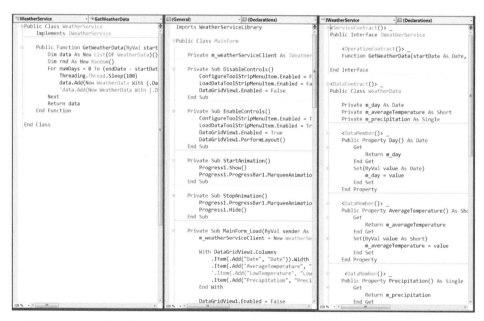

FIGURE 3-21 Vertically tabbed document windows.

Multimonitor Support or Tear-Away Windows

Monitors have become affordable and many developers today use two or more monitors for their daily work.

Visual Studio 2010 lets developers spread out their coding and design windows across multiple screens by enabling documents and tool windows to be dragged outside of the IDE. To drag the window outside the IDE, click the tab for that window, drag it outside the Visual Studio window and outside of the Visual Studio shell window. You can also accomplish this by floating the window and using the Window key + arrow keys to move it

To re-dock the window, click the title bar and drag it back inside the IDE space, aligning the title bar to the tabs of other windows. When re-docking, you'll see a visual clue (as shown in Figure 3-22) that indicates when the window is properly aligned. To re-dock, you can also press Ctrl, and then double click the window's title bar.

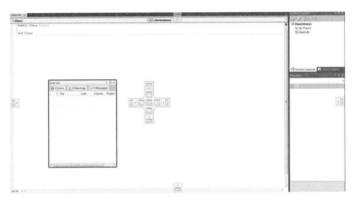

FIGURE 3-22 Visual clue on moving error list tool window.

Persistence of Window Layout

Document screen locations are stored in the per-user Visual Studio store on the local computer. This means that if you work on the same solution on different computers, you can maintain separate window locations on each one. It also means that each user can keep his window layout when working on projects between multiple people under source control. If a number of monitors attached to the computer are changed, Visual Studio detects whether you have a second monitor enabled or not. If not, it moves documents from your second screen to your primary screen. That way you won't "lose" any documents.

Common Use Scenarios

Although document layout is a personal choice, the following are a few case examples in which this feature will likely help increase productivity.

- View designer and code files simultaneously

- View application and test tool windows simultaneously

- View multiple code files simultaneously

Normal View

In the normal/default view, different document windows are tabbed, as shown in Figure 3-23.

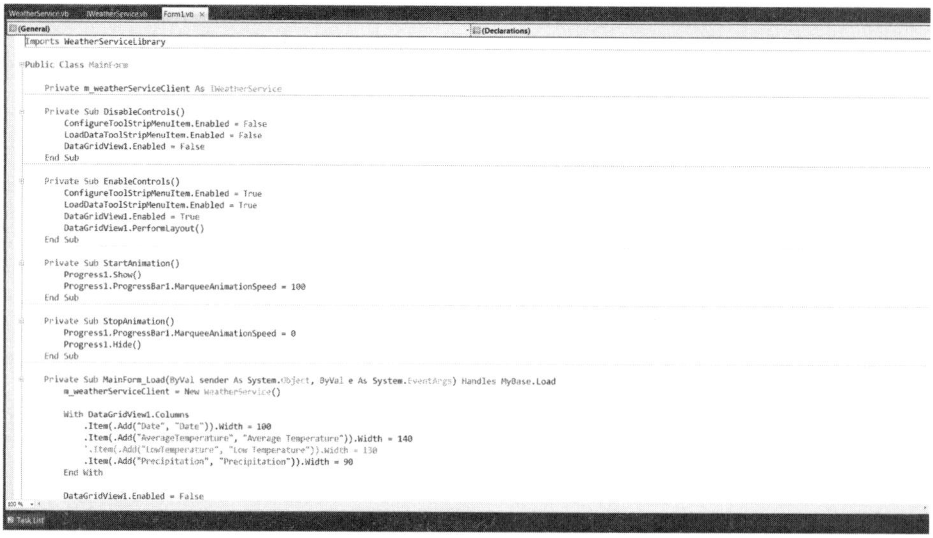

FIGURE 3-23 Docked view of document windows.

Windows In Float

Figure 3-24 demonstrates how you can arrange windows in a "float" style in Visual Studio 2010.

FIGURE 3-24 Windows can be arranged in a "floating" style.

Docking the Windows

You can also dock windows by clicking and holding the mouse on the title bar of the window. This displays the visual clue that shows the docking options for the window. Figure 3-25 shows the ability to dock the Weatherservice.vb file to either center, top, down, right, or left.

FIGURE 3-25 Docking clue for document window

Beyond docking inside the IDE, Visual Studio 2010 developers can also dock outside the IDE. Windows outside the IDE can be maximized to use the entire screen real estate, or they can be placed side by side in different configurations. As you've seen, the possible window layouts are vast, indeed, leaving it up to developers to maximize their own productivity.

Searching, Understanding, and Navigating Code

Rapid Application Development (RAD) is a necessity in the current software development environment. But RAD requires tools to easily search, browse, and understand the code base. This section discusses some features in Visual Studio 2010 with which developers can efficiently search and navigate code.

Navigate To

Navigate To lets you search and explore files and symbols in a solution and navigate to a specific location in the solution. You can access the Navigate To dialog box (see Figure 3-26) from the Edit menu or by using the new Ctrl+Comma keyboard shortcut. Navigate To provides fast and incremental search across Visual Basic, C#, and C++ projects in the solution. The "incremental" search feature begins to display results as soon as you start typing the search item. Results are filtered with each added keystroke character (they also change as you remove characters). To navigate to the location of a symbol, double-click the symbol (or press Enter with the item selected in the results view). If the file is not already open in the Editor, the file opens and highlights the symbol.

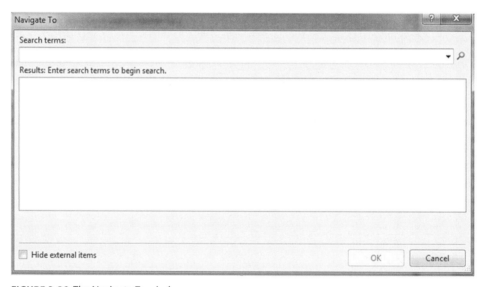

FIGURE 3-26 The Navigate To window.

Smart Searching Capabilities

The Navigate To feature supports some nice "fuzzy search" capabilities with which you can perform smart filters and searches without having to know the exact name of the item you are looking for. The search characteristics can be described as follows:

- **Substring matching**   The search executes a substring match, which means that search results will include items where the search string is at the beginning, end, or anywhere in the middle of the matching term. For example, the search string "class" will find *myclass*, *classname* and *myclassname* symbols.

- **Multiple substring searches**   To find items that contain two sequences of strings, type the two sequences, seperated by a space. Note that the order of these strings does not matter. For example, the search string "hi world" will find both *myhigher-world*, and *myworldishigh*. Instead of a space, you can also use the asterisk (*) wildcard character.

- **Pascal searching**   Types and members within the .NET Framework using a naming design-guideline pattern called "Pascal Casing," which means that the first letter of each word in a type or member name is capitalized. Navigate To supports the Pascal Casing convention to quickly filter types. Just type the uppercase first letter of names in a type/member and it will automatically filter for results that match the uppercase Pascal naming convention. For example, typing GWD finds items composed of words that start with G, then W, and then D , such as GetWeatherData

- **Case sensitivity**   If the search string contains uppercase characters, the search is case-sensitive; otherwise, it is case-insensitive.

The search results might include symbol definitions and file names in the solution, but the results do not include namespaces or local variables.

Navigating Between Code Blocks

To navigate between methods in a code file, from the Edit menu, select either the menu option Next Method or Previous Method, or use the shortcut keys Ctrl+Down Arrow or Ctrl+ Up Arrow (for the next and previous method, respectively).

Highlighting and Navigating Between Symbol References

Highlighting references is a simple and very easy concept that helps developers understand a scoped piece of code. You can think about this as a "Find All Referenced" feature within an open document. Suppose that you need to see where code in the file calls a specific method overload. By using the Highlight Reference feature, you can achieve that with a single click. Simply place your cursor on the specific method (declaration or call), and the declaration and all the call sites for that overload are highlighted. All you need to do is scroll up or down to see the complete view. You can navigate to the next reference or the previous reference by pressing Ctrl+Shift+Up Arrow or Ctrl+Shift+Down Arrow, respectively. Although this feature does not work in XML document sections or XAML, it is a useful feature to browse the structure of a code file. Figure 3-27 shows highlighted references to the method *ShowDialog*.

FIGURE 3-27 Using the Highlight References functionality to find overloads.

Another extension of this feature is to highlight the boundaries of the code flow; for example, module, class, loop constructs, try catch blocks, and so on. Figure 3-28 shows a *Try ... Catch* block highlighted.

FIGURE 3-28 Highlighting the code boundaries of a *Try ... Catch* block.

Note So it doesn't interfere with regular typing, the Highlight References feature is invoked 750 milliseconds after you place your cursor on a symbol.

The scope of the Highlight References feature is within a single file. However, there are some notable points.

When multiple files are open, each view can have its own highlighted reference set. Even if several instances of a file are open at the same time, each view can have its own set of references. All visible views show references as highlighted.

Split windows count as multiple views; therefore, you can have different highlights in each split window.

Changing the Highlight Color

The default highlight color is gray, but you can configure this to your preference by clicking Tools | Options | Fonts And Colors. In the Display Items list, click Highlighted Reference, and then change the Item Background to the color of your choice (see Figure 3-29). You can also change the border color of the rectangle by specifying a color in the Item Foreground.

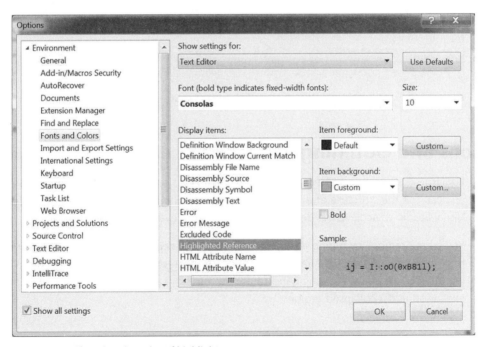

FIGURE 3-29 Changing the color of highlights.

Disabling Highlight References

If you don't like the Highlight References feature, you can simply turn it off. From the Tools Options menu, select Text Editor | Basic | VB Specific, and then clear the check box for Enable Highlighting Of References And Keywords (see Figure 3-30). The setting is persisted across all IDE sessions.

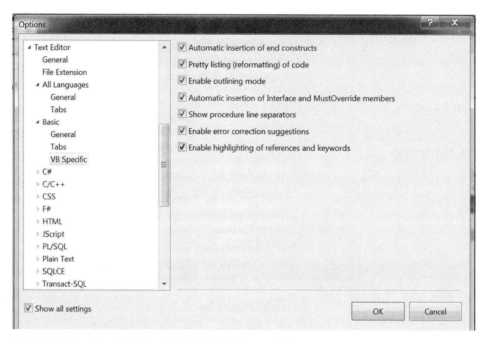

FIGURE 3-30 Enabling/Disabling the Highlight References feature.

Regions and Outlining

For large code files, it is often very useful to be able to collapse some code blocks so that you can see the structure of the file. You can use the Regions and Outlining menu options in Visual Studio to achieve the desired file compression level.

You create regions by typing **# Region** *"name of the region"* in the Code Editor. End a region by inserting an *#End Region* statement. You can expand and collapse regions by clicking the plus and minus outlining indicators on the left margin. Figure 3-31 shows both an expanded and a collapsed region.

```
Class test
private members
#Region "public members"
    Public Sub MyPublicMethod()

    End Sub
    Public Function MyFunction1() As Boolean
        Return False
    End Function
#End Region
End Class
```

FIGURE 3-31 Expanded and collapsed regions and outlining glyphs.

In addition to regions, you can invoke several other outlining options by right-clicking an item, such as a block of code, to display the Editor context menu. From the context menu, you can select the following:

- **Hide Selection**   Hides the currently selected text. Text must be selected to execute this command. Shortcut keys are Ctrl+M and then Ctrl+H. This can be used to mimic regions-like behavior inside a method body.

- **Toggle Outlining Expansion**   Reverses the current hidden or expanded state of the innermost outlining section in which the cursor is positioned when you are in a nested collapsed section. Shortcut keys are Ctrl+M and then Ctrl+M.

- **Toggle All Outlining**   Sets all procedures to the same hidden or expanded state. If some regions are expanded and some hidden, then the hidden regions are expanded. Shortcut keys are Ctrl+M and then Ctrl+L.

- **Stop Outlining**   Removes all outlining information for the entire document. All procedures are visible and the outlining symbols are removed, but the underlying code is undisturbed. Shortcut keys are Ctrl+M and then Ctrl+P.

- **Stop Hiding Current**   Removes the outlining information for the currently selected user-defined region. Shortcut keys are Ctrl+M and then Ctrl+U.

- **Collapse To Definitions**   Collapses the members of all types so that all members belonging to a type are clearly seen. This is identical to the Collapse Block command, except that the environment automatically runs through all of the code in the document, creates regions in each of your procedures, and then hides them. Shortcut keys are Ctrl+M and then Ctrl+O.

Architecture Explorer

In Visual Studio Ultimate, you can select vertical sections or "slices" of code that you want to visualize by using Architecture Explorer. You can use this feature to deepen your understanding of the code by drilling into the code structure. You can launch Architecture Explorer by clicking Architecture | Windows | Architecture Explorer or from the Sequence diagram. Figure 3-32 shows the *classview* domain being used to drill down to the calls within a specific method (*IncreaseBet* in this case).

FIGURE 3-32 The Architecture Explorer window.

Sequence Diagram

A picture is worth a thousand words. Visual Studio 2010 can generate a sequence diagram on the fly for any given method. You can invoke the generator by selecting Generate Sequence Diagram from the method declaration. Invoking the generator displays a dialog, with which you can customize the diagram generation by specifying what to visualize, and the call depth.

Figure 3-33 illustrates a sample sequence diagram showing the call hierarchy, looping, and exception handling in the constructor of the *BlackJackForm* class. You can edit or browse the generated sequence diagram by using several options provided in the context menu on the diagram.

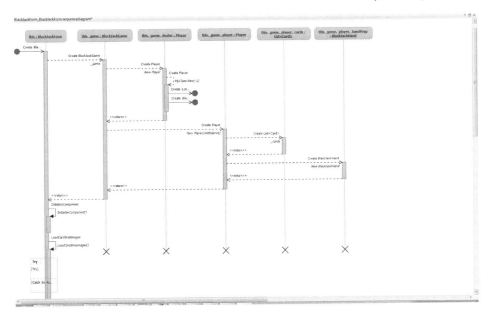

FIGURE 3-33 A sequence diagram.

Class Diagram

Using a class diagram, you can visually create, edit, and manage classes, structures, enums, methods, interfaces, delegates, and more. To open a class diagram, on the Solution Explorer Toolbar, click View Class Diagram. Figure 3-34 shows a snapshot of a class diagram. The View Class Diagram icon is highlighted in the figure.

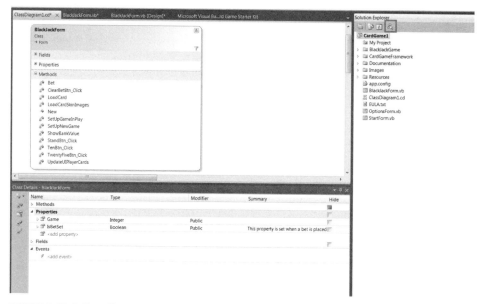

FIGURE 3-34 A Class diagram.

Coding Bottom Up

IntelliSense is one of the most-used features in the Visual Studio IDE, and it has been a primary influencer of the flow of writing code.

In previous versions of Visual Basic Editor, IntelliSense was based on the top-down paradigm of authoring code. But as the new programming paradigm of Test-Driven Development (TDD) gained popularity, Microsoft extended IntelliSense to support the bottom-up coding style. Because this had to work in addition to the existing IntelliSense functionality, IntelliSense in Visual Studio 2010 has dual modes: Declare First mode and Consume First mode. You can toggle which mode is in effect by pressing Ctrl+Alt+Space, or from the menu, select Edit | Intellisense | Toggle Completion Mode.

Declare First Mode

If you have used a previous version of IntelliSense, this mode works just as it did before. In this mode IntelliSense shows the elements declared in the code at the call site and constrains you to pick one of those declarations, as shown in Figure 3-35.

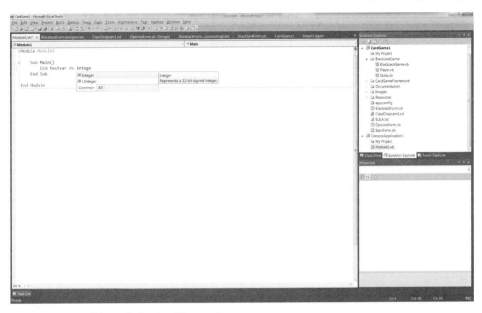

FIGURE 3-35 IntelliSense in Declare First mode.

Consume First Mode

In consume first mode, you have the flexibility of consuming or using the code elements before declaring them. In Figure 3-36, note that there is an extra item box that shows the user-typed element name.

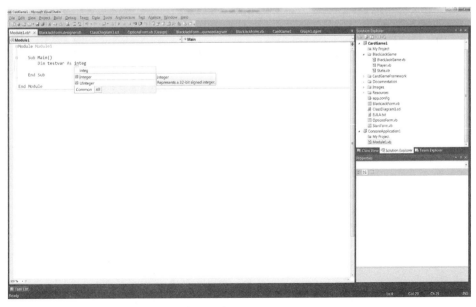

FIGURE 3-36 IntelliSense in Consume First mode.

In addition to enabling a different coding paradigm, Microsoft added several other incremental benefits to IntelliSense in Visual Studio 2010, some of which are listed below:

- **Substring filtering instead of prefix filtering.**   One great Visual Basic IntelliSense feature is that the list is filtered as you type. This helps to narrow down the item that you want to select and use in IntelliSense. However, the feature does not help when you're unsure of the starting characters of the name of the symbol that you're looking for. In the 2010 version, Intellisense is now filtered based on substrings. As an example, if you start typing "dir" in the method body, IntelliSense will show all directory-management methods, as shown in Figure 3-37.

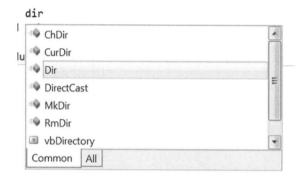

FIGURE 3-37 The IntelliSense filtering feature.

- **Pascal Filtering in IntelliSense.**   Pascal Search refers to the ability to search for multiple-word phrases by using a single abbreviation. The single word abbreviation must be strictly capitalized for IntelliSense to understand that it's a Pascal Case IntelliSense search.

  For example, when you type **Dim x as DC**, IntelliSense responds as shown in Figure 3-38, because *DataColum* and *DataColumnCollection* would follow the Pascal Case search, but **DataRowCollection** would not.

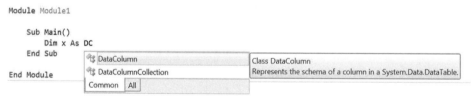

FIGURE 3-38 Pascal filtering in the IntelliSense window.

Note To switch between the Common and All tabs in the IntelliSense window, press Alt+< and Alt+>. Holding the Ctrl key down makes the IntelliSense list transparent, in case you need to see what's behind it.

Note If you have used previous versions of Visual Studio, you might notice a change in IntelliSense behavior with regard to the enum list. In previous versions, the enum IntelliSense list used to be a flat list that contained only enum members, but in Visual Studio 2010, it has two tabs. The Common tab contains the enum members and the All tab contains generic list members. This can disrupt the flow of typing in some cases. The Visual Basic team was aware of this issue, and it has been addressed in Service Pack 1 for Visual Studio 2010.

The Generate From Usage Feature

With the Generate From Usage feature, you can generate classes and members from the consumption site. You can generate a stub for any class, constructor, method, property, field, or enum that you want to use but have not yet defined, all without leaving your current code location. This feature minimizes interruption to your workflow. The feature was added as an extension to the error-correction functionality in Visual Basic. To invoke the feature, click the small red rectangle (called a glyph or smart tag) or double-click the corresponding item in the error list. Alternatively, you can use the shortcut key combinations Shift+Alt+F10 or Ctrl+Period.

For example, you can use the feature to create the code elements shown in the following list (depending on the context):

- Generate property stub
- Generate field stub
- Generate method stub
- Generate class
- Generate interface
- Generate new type (Class, Structure, Interface, Enum, Delegate, or Module)

Customizing Types by Using the Generate New Type Dialog

The Generate New Type option provides additional flexibility when you generate a class, structure, interface, enum, delegate or module. It provides options to place the class in an existing file, specify its access modifiers, or add the new file to another project in the solution. Figure 3-39 shows the Generate New Type dialog box.

FIGURE 3-39 The Generate New Type dialog box.

The following table presents the choices available in the Generate New Type dialog box.

Option	Choices
Access	Default, Friend, or Public
Kind	Class, Structure, Interface, Enum, Delegate, or Module
Project	Current project or another project in the solution
File name	Create new file with file name, or Add to existing file with file name

If you generate the type in a new file, that file will contain the default set of imports for a class generated by the Add New Item dialog box. If you generate the type in another project in the solution, Visual Studio adds project reference and imports statements to the project automatically.

Extending Visual Studio

IDE extensibility is one of the most powerful features introduced in Visual Studio 2010. The WPF architecture has led to easily extensible hooks in Visual Studio UI elements. As an example, the Start Page and the IntelliSense window can easily be customized to suit individual needs. New refactorings are easy to add to the Visual Basic Editor. In fact, there are numerous free extensions available online, including the Pro Power Pack Tools released by Microsoft. The Start Page includes several useful links in the section Extending Visual Studio. Because creating extensions is a community activity, you need to be aware that extensions can conflict with each other.

Managing Visual Studio Extensions

With a large number of extensions already available (640 as of June 2010) and growing rapidly, it has become a necessity to pick and choose (and discard) the extensions you
want installed locally on your development computer. Visual Studio 2010 includes a feature
named Extension Manager that lets you add, remove, enable, and disable Visual Studio
extensions. Click Tools | Extension Manager to open the Extension Manager, which is shown
in Figure 3-40.

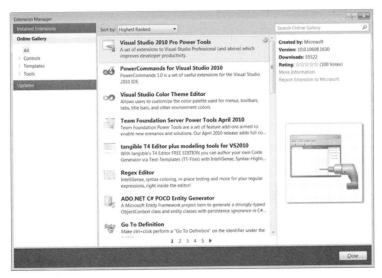

FIGURE 3-40 The Extension Manager window.

The Extension Manager window is divided into three panes. The left pane categorizes extensions by group: installed extensions, new extensions from the online gallery, or updates to
installed extensions. The middle pane displays extensions in the selected group. You can
apply various filters to sort the list. The right pane provides information on the selected
extension. If the extension is not yet installed, you can download it; if it is already installed,
you can disable or enable it, or uninstall it.

Extension Manager can install extensions from the Visual Studio Gallery on MSDN (*http://
go.microsoft.com/FWLink/?Linkid=178891*). These extensions can be packages, templates, or
other components that add functionality to Visual Studio.

Extension Types

Extension Manager supports extensions in the VSIX package format, which might include project templates, item templates, toolbox items, Managed Extension Framework (MEF) components, and VSPackages. Extension Manager can also load and install MSI-based extensions, but it cannot enable or disable them. The Visual Studio Gallery contains both VSIX and MSI extensions. Visual Studio continues to support deployment technologies such as the Visual Studio Content Installer (VSI) and the Microsoft Installer (MSI)—but not through Extension Manager. You can use the VSI format for macros, add-ins, code snippets, and certain other Visual Studio extension types. The MSI format, which is used extensively for applications, can also be used for extensions. Both .vsi files and .msi files comprise complete packages that you can distribute, and that users can install by double-clicking.

Note Chapter 4, "Introduction to Windows Forms—Designers and Code Editor by Example," and Chapter 5, "Introduction to Windows Presentation Foundation," explore many more features of the Visual Studio IDE, including the Windows Forms Designer, the Code Editor, the WPF Designer, and the XAML Editor in a learning-by-doing fashion.

Chapter 4

Introduction to Windows Forms— Designers and Code Editor by Example

Apart from what you need for debugging, the two basic tools for developing Windows Forms applications (also known as "Smart Clients") are the Forms Designer and the Code Editor.

There are two approaches when trying to explain the important tools of a development environment: a theoretical approach, and a practical one. The theoretical approach gives you a quick overview as to what possibilities each tool offers, but it doesn't teach you how to use the tools. The practical approach offers many more advantages. Keep in mind as you proceed that as a developer you might feel slightly under-challenged by this example, but you need to follow it from beginning to end to get the most out of this chapter and to learn the intricacies and the features of the tools. After completing the exercise, you will be better prepared to develop applications on your own.

You'll be using a concrete example to introduce the Forms Designer and the Code Editor. The example even overshoots the chapter's thematic limits a bit, and provides some information on completely different topics that I consider sensible in the context. Of course, you will cover most of the topics in more detail later in this book. Just remember that, first and foremost, we're trying to provide you with adequate knowledge in a short amount of time so that you can create some small projects right away—even though you haven't read the book in its entirety.

Case Example: the DVD Cover Generator

It's impressive how magazines, newspapers, gas stations, book clubs, and other institutions are courting the favor of their customers these days by using digital media. Thanks to their efforts, I have come to enjoy a sizable DVD collection for which I had to invest relatively little money. But what's often missing is a decent cover (and solid case) with which you can store your DVD on a shelf like a book and actually find it again, if necessary. This is even more important for movies that you recorded from pay-per-view channels or video that you shot yourself. Sure, there are lots of different cover designers on the market, most of which don't cost much. And everybody who has purchased a DVD burner along with a computer will most likely be the proud owner of such a program anyway. Most of these burn programs feature quite powerful designers (see Figure 4-1).

FIGURE 4-1 A basic DVD cover design with a beautiful theme: simply cut out the printed inlay along the marked lines and insert it into the plastic cover.

In my view, however, they offer a bit too much of a good thing. If I had time, I'm sure I could design a cover with them, which might even be as good as many an original. But I usually don't have time, and when I do, I don't want to spend it designing a complex cover. What I need—and maybe you do, too—is a program that allows me to enter the title, the actors, and a brief description, and maybe add a picture, and then the program magically cooks up a cover from these ingredients. This can be achieved quickly and easily, as you will see in the following sections.

Specifications for "Covers"

We'll call our application "Covers," and it should work as follows:

- The program should provide a simple but dynamically resizable window in which the basic data about the film can be entered into simple text fields: film title, actors, brief description, and a picture that will be printed on the cover's front page. Refer back to Figure 4-1 to see how the result might look for a typical German-styled vacation video; Figures 4-2 and 4-3 show how the program is used.

FIGURE 4-2 The *Covers* application captures information about a film and prints a cover—literally at the push of a button.

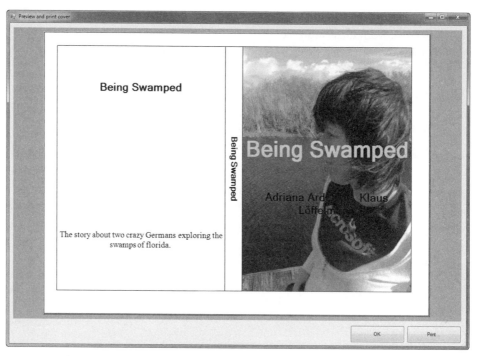

FIGURE 4-3 The print preview window sets up the author's girlfriend as a true cover girl!

- When you adjust the size of the *Covers* main window, all controls should automatically adjust to the size of the form. The controls will grow dynamically along with the form. When you enlarge the form to the right, the buttons on the right follow the right window margin. The data entry controls should take up all available space.

- Users should be able to load a picture onto the form; the application would then scale the image automatically to fit the exact dimensions of the cover's front page. Should the picture not fit into the form's picture element, the application will display scroll bars automatically, which you can use to preview the picture in its entirety.

- You can reset all entries by clicking the Delete Entry button. This button is particularly useful when you want to print several different covers in succession.

- The program must remember all entries between sessions. When you leave the program and restart it, all the entries should appear exactly as they were when you terminated the previous program session.

- After you have entered data into the form, you can use *Print Inlay* to bring up the print preview window, which shows you the inlay on the monitor as it will be printed later. The preview window must be dynamically resizable, as well.

- Before printing, you have the option to select and set up the printer that you want to use. No matter what the settings are, however, the printer must always print the inlay in landscape format.

The following several sections show you how to create the software from A to Z in Microsoft Visual Studio 2010 with Microsoft Visual Basic 2010, step by step. You will be surprised how little code you will need to write—most of the code you will write applies to the actual printing process.

> **Companion Content** The code files that accompany this book contain the complete project. However, I recommend that you avoid using them and instead type the code segments as they're presented here. This will help you to get a better feel for and understanding of the Code Editor and its rich feature set. Typing the relatively large print routine would be a too much of a good thing though, and therefore, you'll find the code for that as a text file in \VB 2010 Developer Handbook\Chapter 04\Covers\Print Routine for Covers.txt.

Creating a New Project

To begin, create a new project. If you haven't launched Visual Studio yet, do so now.

> **Note** To specify the location where the project should be saved as you design it, click Tools | Options to open the Option dialog box, and then verify that the Save New Projects When Created check box in the section Projects And Solutions/General is selected.

To create a new project, click the upper-left area of the Visual Studio Start Page on the New Project link. Figure 4-4 provides some orientation.

FIGURE 4-4 To set up a new project, click the New Project link directly from the start page.

In the New Project dialog box, select Installed Templates in the tree structure, and then click Visual Basic/Windows. In the large list field, select Windows Forms Application. Under Name, enter the name of your new project; for this example, type **Covers**. In the Location box, specify the directory in which you want to save all the project files. The Browse button opens a dialog that can help you specify the directory by browsing for it in your file system. Ensure that the check box adjacent to Create Directory For Solution is selected. Figure 4-5 shows you how the window should look now. Click OK when you are done.

> **Tip** To combine several projects into one solution—for example, to divide an application into several layers (data layer, business logic, user interface, controls, and so on), and put these layers into different class libraries—you can integrate your Windows Forms application project into a solution at this point. The solution gets its own directory. Each Windows Forms project contained within the solution is located in its own subdirectory, below the parent solution directory. In this case, you need to select the Create Directory For Solution check box and enter the name of the solution into the Solution Name text field.

FIGURE 4-5 Use the New Project dialog to set up a new Windows Forms application.

Designing Forms with the Windows Forms Designer

The first step in building the sample application is to design a form. Because you'll be using the Toolbox frequently, it makes sense to always keep it in the foreground. On the left side of your Visual Studio integrated development environment (IDE), there is a collapsed tab group that contains the Server Explorer and the Toolbox.

Move the mouse pointer over the Toolbox icon to expand it. Click the pin icon in the window title, located in the upper-right corner of the Toolbox (see Figure 4-6). When you pin it, the Toolbox stays where it is and doesn't automatically collapse when you move the mouse pointer away from it.

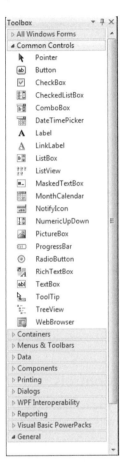

FIGURE 4-6 The Visual Studio Toolbox.

To give yourself as much room as possible for experimenting, resize the form to fill most of your workspace.

Positioning Controls

Referring back to Figure 4-2, you can see that the form has three buttons that each trigger different actions. You will position these buttons on the form first.

1. In the Toolbox, click the Button icon. Move the mouse pointer into the form and draw a button of approximately the same size as those in Figure 4-2.

2. Draw another button somewhere in the form (it doesn't matter where). The size and position of the buttons are not important at this point; you will learn shortly how to adjust the position and size of the various controls on the form.

> **Tip** You can select a control in the Toolbox (such as the button) and then click the desired position in the form surface to insert the control on the form at a default size.

3. Drag the button labeled Button1 into the upper-right corner of the form. Once there, you will notice that the button snaps to the corner. You will see two guidelines that keep the button at specific distances from the form's edges, as demonstrated in Figure 4-7.

FIGURE 4-7 Guidelines help you to position the controls along the form's border or below each other.

Guidelines and the Margin/Padding Properties of Controls

Each control you place on your form is based on a base control type named *Control*. This control not only provides the foundation upon which other controls can build (for example, the mechanism for displaying their actual contents—a button must represent totally different contents than a *CheckBox* control) but it also provides a designer functionality. For more information about this topic, see the sidebar "Who's the 'Owner' of the Forms Designer Anyway?," on the next page).

This is why any control you position in the form automatically has a *Margin* property that determines the distance between the controls. This is also the distance at which the guidelines appear and the control snaps into position.

When controls act as "containers" for other controls (such a control is called a *ContainerControl*), another property comes into play: the *Padding* property. This property determines how much distance should be maintained to the outer border when you position a control within a container control.

Note The forms themselves make an exception here: when positioning controls at the border of a form, a few additional pixels of distance are maintained when the designer displays the guidelines, possibly to conform with the Microsoft Style Guide for designing forms.

Tip Snapping to a position doesn't only happen in areas that work with the distances set by the *Margin* or *Padding* properties. Visual Studio also supplies this functionality to align controls exactly along their base lines when they are positioned next to each other. This is often the case when you are using a *Label* control to label a *TextBox* control in the form, as shown in Figure 4-8.

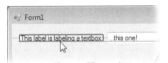

FIGURE 4-8 When labeling *TextBox* controls with the *Label* control, the guideline assists you by snapping the controls to the text box base lines.

Tip Developers who prefer working with the grid functionality that they were used to in Visual Studio 2003 or Visual Basic 6.0 don't need to do without in Visual Studio 2010. In the Visual Studio Options dialog (Tools | Options) you can change the *LayoutMode* property from *SnapLines* to *SnapToGrid* in the Windows Forms Designer tab. If you prefer to work in the layout mode of Visual Studio 2010, but you don't need the snap functionality, you can set the *SnapToGrid* property in this dialog to *False*.

Who's the "Owner" of the Forms Designer Anyway?

From a strictly legal point of view, *you* are the owner, of course. After all, you have purchased Visual Studio, and therefore also the Forms Designer. But that's not what I'm referring to. The actual question is: in which program part of the entire Visual Studio/.NET Framework complex does the designer functionality reside? The answer might surprise you, because it's not, as one would probably assume, that Visual Studio is responsible for the editing of controls in the Designer completely by itself. Visual Studio basically just works as an event-passing mechanism to the affected component. That's because a control basically consists of two parts: the control that provides the actual functionality required at runtime, and a second component, the designer. That's right. Each component has its own designer. Of course, there weren't hundreds of developers who programmed hundreds of different designers. Just like *Control* provides all the base functionality for a new actual control that just builds upon them, there is another component called *ControlDesigner* that contains all the base design functionalities. Visual Studio only plays the role of generous host here, providing the environment for designing forms. The technical term is *Designer Host*. It doesn't matter

> if a new control is created and doesn't have its own designer (whether totally new or based on *ControlDesigner*), because Visual Studio uses the *ControlDesigner* itself for this control—and its base functions at least permit moving, copying, snapping, and other functions you need when building a form. For those of you who are pretty well versed in .NET assemblies and are interested, the designers of all the controls of .NET are located in the assembly System.Design.Dll.

Adjusting the Size and Position of Controls

At this point, all three buttons are placed randomly on the form (see Figure 4-9). The goal now is to align them vertically, one below the other, and make them all the same size. You can make these changes manually by resizing and moving the buttons around with the mouse, until they are in the right place and at the right size. Thanks to the guideline functionality, that's no big deal, but it's still a bit of a hassle.

There's an easier way. You can select several controls (in this exercise, your buttons) and then perform size and position operations on them all at once. By doing this, all controls orient themselves using the first-selected control as a reference point. When you have selected the controls (remember: the first one marked is always the reference control), Visual Studio offers several options, which are described in the section, "Functions for Control Layout in the Designer," later in this chapter.

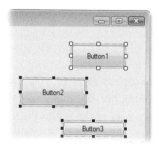

FIGURE 4-9 The button controls randomly placed in the form (with the exception of the Button1, which is already in its final position and size).

Selecting Multiple Controls and Specifying the Reference Control

To select several controls on the form simultaneously, click the first control normally, and then consecutively click all the other controls while simultaneously pressing the Ctrl key. You can also use the mouse to draw a frame around the controls you want to select. The reference control for the functions described in Table 4-4 is whichever control you select first when selecting the controls with the Ctrl key pressed. To change the reference control after selecting a set of controls, just click the control you want to use as the reference (*without* pressing the Ctrl key). Unlike many other selection procedures in Windows, doing this doesn't cancel the selection, and the newly clicked element isn't selected; instead, you are actually just changing the reference control. To cancel the entire selection, click any open area within the form or on a previously unselected control.

> **Tip** You can identify the reference control by its white sizing handles; all other selected controls have black sizing handles.

1. Select all the controls on the form by using the Ctrl key method.

   It's important that you use the button in the upper-left corner as the reference control, which means that you need to click that button first.

> **Note** For the following step you might need to activate the Layout toolbar. To do this, right-click an empty space next to a displayed toolbar, and then select Layout from the context menu. The same commands are also available through the Format menu.

2. In the Layout Toolbar, select the Make Same Size function (the table in the section "Functions for Control Layout in the Designer," later in this chapter, can help you find the correct icon).

3. Click the Align Left icon to align the buttons along their left edges.

   The buttons are now aligned along their left edges, but their vertical positions are still unchanged.

4. You can adjust the distances between the buttons by dragging them with the mouse with the support of the guidelines, or you can use the Make Vertical Spacing Equal function, and then use the Increase Vertical Spacing or Decrease Vertical Spacing functions, until you are happy with the result. Figure 4-10 shows the results of the positioning.

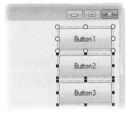

FIGURE 4-10 Use the functions Make Same Size, Align Left, Make Vertical Spacing Equal, and Increase/Decrease Vertical Spacing to size and position the button controls.

Ideally, you don't need to handle the buttons individually after drawing them on the form. The options in the Layout Toolbar help you to adjust them to achieve a clean layout on the form within seconds.

Performing Common Tasks on Controls by Using Smart Tags

There are complex controls, such as the *TableLayoutPanel* (which you will use in the next step in this example), that provide "Smart Tags" with which you can easily specify common behaviors (see Figure 4-11). Smart Tags contain a list of context-sensitive tasks associated with the control that provide you with a shortcut to the control properties. At the same time, they provide you with the means to specify them more comfortably.

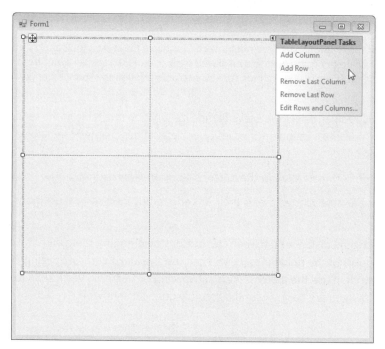

FIGURE 4-11 One click on the Smart Tag of a control opens the task window, which provides functions for performing the most common tasks.

1. Select the *TableLayoutPanel* by clicking it in the Toolbox, and then draw the control on the form at approximately the same proportional size as the control shown in Figure 4-11.

2. The list of context tasks behind the Smart Tag opens. You can open and close the context task list any time by clicking on the Smart Tag.

> **Note** Not every control has a Smart Tag with a list of context tasks behind it, but if a control does a have a Smart Tag, this list is always available.

Dynamically Arranging Controls at Runtime

Implementing a user interface such as Windows Explorer in Visual Basic 6.0 used to take a considerable effort. It took many hours to develop the code to dynamically rearrange the controls if the user adjusted the window size at runtime.

With the release of the .NET versions of Visual Basic, this has become demonstrably easier. If you do it right, you don't need to write a single line of code to reposition and re-align controls to adjust for changes in form size. And beginning with Visual Basic 2008, this task became disproportionately simpler, because Visual Basic 2008 provided new container controls that exclusively serve this purpose. The following features are available in Visual Basic 2010. With them, you can get a handle on the resize issue—without programming:

- **Anchor**   Use this property to anchor each side of the control to the form. If you change the form size, the sides of the control maintain their distance to the sides of the form to which they are anchored.

- **Dock**   With this property, you can dock a control to a form border or to a previously docked control. This ensures that the docked sides of the control always reach the form border—or to the first previously docked control.

- **SplitContainer**   This control provides a double container for further controls. It lets you increase the size of one container part at the expense of the other container part. As an example, think of Windows Explorer: you can grab the dividing vertical bar in the middle with the mouse and move it left or right—the left *TreeView* control containing the directories and other main elements (such as the control panel, mobile devices, and so on) becomes wider or narrower accordingly, while the *ListView* control in the right container part becomes narrower or wider respectively.

- **TableLayoutPanel**   This control provides a container for further elements. It arranges multiple contained controls in a table, whose columns and lines increase in adjustable relationships when the *TableLayoutPanel* control itself increases or decreases in size. This makes it possible not only for certain controls to become larger when the form size increases, but also causes controls to increase or shrink in size proportionately to form size changes.

- **FlowLayoutPanel**   This control is easiest to explain by using the example of a text editor with word wrap activated. When a word no longer fits at the end of a line, it is automatically moved to the next line. *FlowLayoutPanel* works the same way—not with words, but with controls. Controls aren't arranged at fixed positions, but are below or next to each other. When the form's size increases, *FlowLayoutPanel* fits as many controls as possible on a line. If some of the controls no longer fit on that line because there isn't enough space on the form, they automatically jump to the next line, just like word wrap in a text editor.

The following sections demonstrate the most important features with the example.

Anchoring Controls with the Anchor Property

The *Anchor* property solves the most important and most frequent problem quickly and elegantly. It lets you anchor the sides of controls to the sides of a form or to the container control in which they reside. Each anchored side of a control maintains a fixed distance from the matching side of its container's border, even when the container's size changes. This means that a control anchored at two opposite sides of a container that's being enlarged or reduced becomes larger or smaller as the size of its container changes, or when it is anchored only on the right side of the container, its position will change.

In this next example, you'll anchor the three controls to follow the right window border so that they'll move when the user increases or decreases the form's width. The *TableLayoutPanel* (which will later contain the input fields, the labels, and the picture), will be anchored at all four sides, allowing it to grow dynamically with the form. This way, you ensure that all the controls contained in the *TableLayoutPanel* will adjust themselves proportionately, as well.

1. Select all three buttons.

2. In the Properties window, select *Anchor*, open the list field, and then click one of the four long rectangles (which form a cross) to specify the anchor positions.

    Active anchors are displayed in gray (see Figure 4-12). Clicking a gray area turns off the anchoring.

> **Tip** You don't need to set the properties of the different controls to which you want to assign the same values one after another. Instead, select the controls that you want to have the same property value, and then use the Properties window to assign that property to all the selected controls at once. Visual Studio finds the largest common denominator concerning existing properties when multiple controls are selected, which means it displays only those properties in the Properties window that apply to all the selected controls.

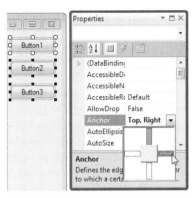

FIGURE 4-12 Changing the *Anchor* property from the initial *Top, Left* setting to *Top, Right* causes the controls to always maintain the same distance, relative to the top and right form border, and to follow the border when enlarging the form to the right.

3. Increase the size of the *TableLayoutPanel* so that the three sides in question are as close to the form borders as possible.

4. Set the *Anchor* property of the *TableLayoutPanel* so that all four sides are anchored, as shown in Figure 4-13.

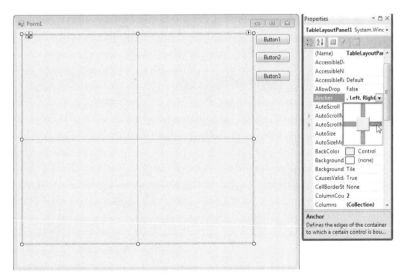

FIGURE 4-13 When you set the *Anchor* property of a control to all four sides, the control increases and decreases in size in all directions, relative to the form.

After defining these settings, you can view the new Anchor properties in action by increasing or decreasing the size of the form in Design mode. Notice how the controls automatically adjust to the changing form dimensions.

Adjusting Controls Proportionately to Form Size Changes with *TableLayoutPanel*

When you look at the *TableLayoutPanel* in Figure 4-13, you can see that it is made up of four cells. Like a *Panel* control, each cell serves as a container for another control. As the size of the *TableLayoutPanel* changes, the controls in the cells also change size proportionately. So by arranging the controls in these cells, you essentially pass any parent size change on to these child controls. Your controls will grow dynamically as the form expands, creating more space on the screen and using the extra space efficiently.

Creating Columns and Rows for the *TableLayoutPanel*

By default, when you draw a *TableLayoutPanel* in the form for the first time, it contains four cells: two columns and two rows. To increase the number of columns or rows, you can either use the Properties window (as with all controls), or you can access the context task list via the control's Smart Tag.

1. Click the Smart Tag of the *TableLayoutPanel* already in the form, and then click Edit Rows And Columns, as shown in Figure 4-14.

2. Open the Show drop-down list, and then select Rows.

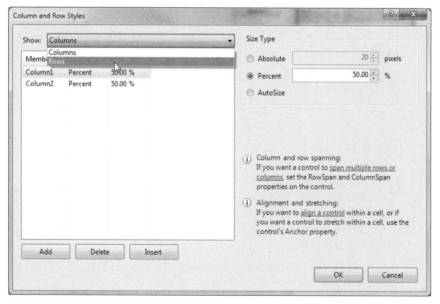

FIGURE 4-14 To specify the number of the rows on the control, click the Smart Tag, select the element Edit Rows And Columns in the context task list of the *TableLayoutPanel*, and then select Rows from the Show drop-down list.

3. Click Add twice to add two rows to the *TableLayoutPanel*.

4. Click the first row to select it, and then set the Size Type to *Absolute*.

5. Enter **25** pixels as the height of the first row.

Your screen should look like that shown in Figure 4-15. By setting the row height, you're specifying that the row's height should remain fixed at 25 pixels. Because this row will later contain the input field for the film title, which should be entered in a single row, the input field does not need to resize vertically no matter how large the form becomes. In fact, it makes sense to keep the height of this field constant, so that other rows containing controls can have more space available for their contents.

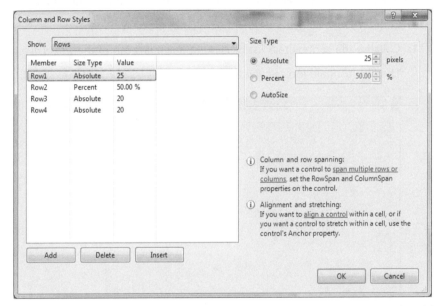

FIGURE 4-15 Use the Column And Row Styles dialog dialog box to configure the heights of the individual rows.

Tip After performing value changes to the *TableLayoutPanel*, do *not* press Enter if you want to make further changes to size types or values; simply click the next row in the list. Pressing Enter triggers an OK button click, which closes the dialog entirely, so you would have to open it again.

Note When using a combination of Absolute and Percent size types, the absolute number of pixels you specify is subtracted from the amount of available space (for both height and width settings). The remaining space is divided among the other lines proportionally, according to their value settings.

6. For Row2, keep the Size Type setting at Percent, but enter the value **25**.

7. For Row3 and Row4, change the Size Type setting to Percent, and then enter the values **25** and **50**, respectively.

8. From the Show drop-down list, select Columns. Click the line Column1, set the Size Type to Absolute, and then enter **120** as the fixed pixel width.

9. Change Column2 by setting its percent value to **100**.

    With these settings, the left column, which will always have the same labels, will always maintain a width of 120 pixels, while the right column will resize dynamically.

10. Confirm your changes and close the dialog by pressing Enter.

11. Collapse the context task list by clicking the Smart Tag of the *TableLayoutPanel*.

    The result should look similar to Figure 4-16.

FIGURE 4-16 This is how your form should look after specifying the example row and column parameters.

Arranging Controls in the Cells of the *TableLayoutPanel*

Looking at the form again in Figure 4-2, you can see that the next thing you need to tackle is arranging the *TextBox* and *Label* controls. To position the controls, drag them from the Toolbox into the cells of the *TableLayoutPanel*. Figure 4-17 illustrates you how this works.

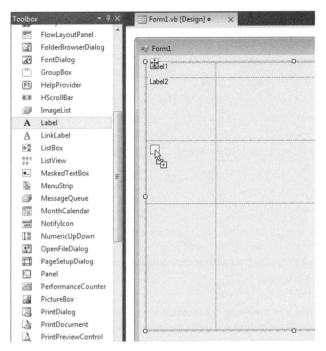

FIGURE 4-17 To place the controls, just drag them from the Toolbox into the respective cells of the *TableLayoutPanel*.

1. Drag three *Label* elements into the three upper-left cells.

2. Drag three *TextBox* elements into the three upper-right cells.

3. Insert a *Panel* control into the lower-left cell.

   This will later serve as a container for the ellipsis button (...) that users can click to select a graphic file. It will also contain another *Panel* and a nested *PictureBox* control.

4. The result should look similar to Figure 4-18.

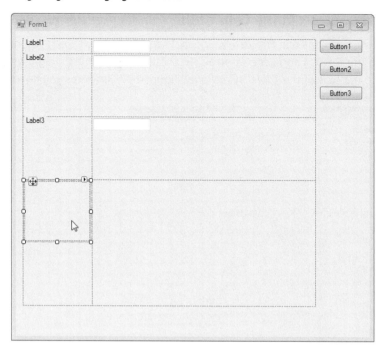

FIGURE 4-18 After you place all the controls, your form should look like this.

> **Note** What is the purpose of the *Panel* in the lower-left corner (after all, you want a picture there, as well as an ellipsis button for selecting the picture)? The answer is, each cell of the *TableLayoutPanel* can contain only one control. That doesn't mean, however, that a *TableLayoutPanel* can't function as a container for other controls. That opens the door for complex constructions, but the more complex and nested they are, the more they can pose a disadvantage. Arranging such constructions from scratch at runtime takes time— especially if you have a slow graphics card—because the contents of all the controls need to be updated after each resize operation. You should try to make do with just one container per cell and limit the number of controls in each container as much as possible. Only in special cases (the following section shows you just such a case) should you consider a deeper nesting level.

Anchoring Controls in the *TableLayoutPanel*

As Figure 4-18 shows, the arrangement isn't very elegant yet. The labels are "hanging" in the upper-left corner, and the *TextBox* elements don't extend over the entire width of the form. To take care of this, you can turn again to the *Anchor* property of the individual controls, as follows:

1. Set the *Anchor* property of the upper *Label* control to *Left, Right*.

2. Set the *Anchor* property of the remaining *Label* control to *Top, Left, Right*.

3. To make the *Label* elements look better, select them all, and then set all their *BorderStyle* properties to *Fixed3D*.

4. Set the *TextAlign* property of all *Label* controls to *MiddleRight*.

5. Set the *Anchor* of the upper *TextBox* control to *Left, Right*.

6. Before you can change the *Anchor* property of the two lower *TextBox* controls, you need to set them to accept multiline input.

    This must be done in order for a *TextBox* to use the entire available area of a cell, and be anchored at all four sides of the cell that contains it.

    a. Select both lower *TextBox* controls, and set their *Multiline* property to *True*.

    b. For these text boxes to automatically receive a visible scroll bar (in case a user enters more lines of text than fit in the control), set the *Scrollbars* property to *Vertical*.

7. Select the *Panel* by holding down the Ctrl key while clicking the control.

8. Set the *Anchor* property for all the selected controls to *Top, Bottom, Left, Right*.

    The form should now look similar to Figure 4-19.

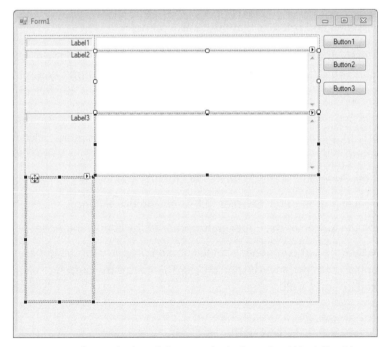

FIGURE 4-19 After anchoring all the controls, the form should look like this.

Spanning Rows or Columns of the *TableLayoutPanel*

In addition to the properties discussed thus far, the *TableLayoutPanel* also functions as a *Property Extender.*

> ### What Is a Property Extender?
>
> A control or component that functions as a Property Extender provides other controls located in the same container with additional properties.
>
> Such a component discovers the controls within its reach for which it makes sense to provide extended properties in the current context, and then extends them with those new properties. These properties, however, exist only for these reachable controls, because these new properties refer to an interaction with the property extender control.
>
> Controls located outside the property extender's reach or controls in other forms are not affected.

This is why all controls located in a *TableLayoutPanel* cell have four additional properties: *Column*, *ColumnSpan*, *Row*, and *RowSpan*. *Column* and *Row* specify the row and column where the control is located. *ColumnSpan* and *RowSpan* are more interesting; they determine the number of rows and columns that the control spans.

If you look closely, the *Panel* that will later contain the *PictureBox* and the ellipsis button spans the entire table width (see Figure 4-2) because its *ColumnSpan* property is set to *2* (the number of columns in the *TableLayoutPanel*). To set this value, perform the following:

1. Deselect any selected controls so that you don't accidentally also set the *ColumnSpan* property of the most recently selected controls. To do so, simply click an empty space in the form.

2. Select the *Panel* and set its *ColumnSpan* property to **2**.

3. Add a small button to the *Panel* as well as an additional *Panel*.

4. Position the button at the upper-right corner of the containing *Panel*.

   Ensure that the *Left* component of the *Location* property for the upper-left corner of the control is not negative. It should be 0. This causes the button to align at the top, as depicted in Figure 4-20.

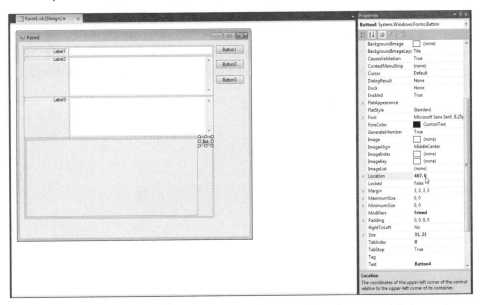

FIGURE 4-20 The bottom row of the *TableLayoutPanel* now contains only one panel that spans two columns. It contains a second panel as well as a button for selecting a picture.

5. Increase the size of the second *Panel* that you just inserted, until it's as close to the outer borders of the containing *Panel* as possible. Use the *Location* and *Size* properties to fine-tune its position.

6. Set the *Anchor* property of the button to *Top, Right*.

7. Set the *Anchor* property of the second *Panel* to *Top, Bottom, Left, Right*.

Your form should now look like the one presented in Figure 4-20.

Automatic Scrolling of Controls in Containers

If you're curious as to why you placed another *Panel* next to the button rather than inserting a *PictureBox* control directly, the answer reveals itself if you take another look at Figure 4-2. The area for the cover picture needs to be scrollable because the picture might not fit in it. But unfortunately, the *PictureBox* control doesn't provide scrollbars.

Fortunately, the container controls offer the functionality you need. By setting the *AutoScroll* property of a container control to *True*, the controls it contains (which might not be visible because of the size of the viewing area) can be scrolled into view by using the scroll bars automatically generated by the container. Figure 4-21 demonstrates this behavior.

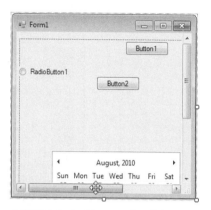

FIGURE 4-21 In this example, all the controls are located in one panel, which functions as a container. Not all controls fit into the viewing window, but by setting the *AutoScroll* property of the *Panel*, users can view the entire area with the help of the automatically generated scroll bars, both at design time and at runtime.

You can take advantage of this behavior: the *PictureBox* supports a setting that resizes the *PictureBox* control to the size of the picture it contains. This property is called *SizeMode*, and for this exercise, you set it to *AutoSize*. If the *PictureBox* is located in a *Panel* whose *AutoSize* property is set, and you load a picture that forces the *PictureBox* to increase in size until it no longer fits into the *Panel*, the *Panel* automatically displays the scroll bars. If only the *Panel* has a frame and the *PictureBox* has no other visible borders, to users, it looks as if they're scrolling the picture in the *PictureBox*. In reality, though, the *Panel* scrolls the entire *PictureBox*. From a development point of view, you have not only just saved several days' worth of development work (no joke: developing a control with scrollable content is no piece of cake), but you did it without even having to write a single line of code. Figure 4-22 shows the results of this scripting *legerdemain*.

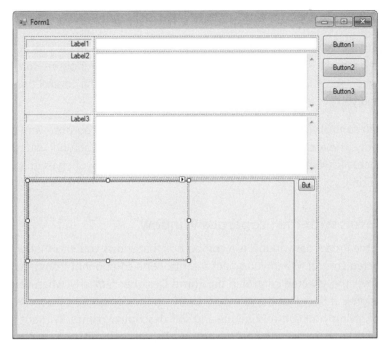

FIGURE 4-22 The nested combination of a *Panel*, another *Panel*, and a *PictureBox* will display the scroll bars if a picture is too large.

1. Select the *Panel* next to the ellipsis button, if it isn't already selected.

2. Set the *BorderStyle* property to *FixedSingle*.

3. Set the *AutoScroll* property to *True*.

4. Drop a *PictureBox* in the *Panel*.

5. Instead of positioning the *PictureBox* control with the mouse, set its *Location* property by typing **0,0**.

> **Note** Remember that the coordinates of a control are always relative to its current container.

6. Set the *SizeMode* property of the *PictureBox* to *AutoSize*.

Your form should look similar to Figure 4-22.

Selecting Controls That Users Can't Reach with the Mouse

When working with containers and nested controls like those you saw in the preceding section, it sometimes becomes difficult to select certain controls with the mouse—sometimes you simply miss when you're intending to click inside the borders of the control that you are trying to reach, and you accidentally select a different one.

To experiment with control selection, select some random control on purpose, and then press Tab repeatedly. The focus switches controls. Continue pressing Tab until you reach the control that you actually want to select. And when even *that* doesn't work (yes, this happens), read the next section.

Selecting Controls with the Properties Window

The upper line of the Properties window is a combo box that shows you information about the currently selected control. When you select a control or a component from the drop-down list, it becomes the selected control in the Forms Designer. Similarly, when you select a control in the Designer, it becomes the selected control in the combo box. Figure 4-23 shows the importance of giving your controls unique and self-descriptive names. Without functional names, you'll need quite some luck to find the desired *TextBox* in the list among controls with the default names, such as *TextBox1*, *TextBox2,* and so forth.

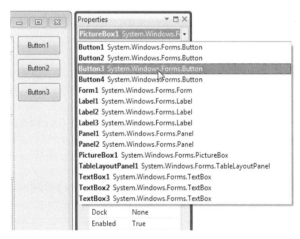

FIGURE 4-23 Using the Properties window, you can select any control in the Designer.

Determining the Tab Order of Controls

The *tab order* determines the sequence in which controls will become active when users press the Tab key to move between screen elements. Figure 4-24 shows the tab order for the elements in the *Cover* application.

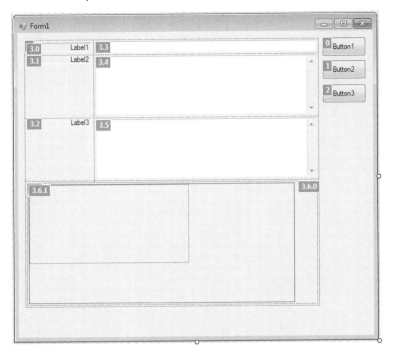

FIGURE 4-24 By choosing View | Tab Order, you can determine the sequence in which controls acquire focus at runtime when the user presses the Tab key. To do this, you must first select the form.

Setting the tab order In Visual Studio 2010 is fast and easy:

1. Select the form itself. Click on the title of the form to select it.

2. From the View menu, select the Tab Order item.

    The form display changes, adding numbers to each control, as shown in Figure 4-24.

3. Click the controls one after another in the sequence in which you want them to activate with Tab at runtime. Include the containers, as well. The process becomes a little tricky when specifying the first control—the *TableLayoutPanel*—whose tab order number ends up shifted to the background (it sits slightly behind the label *3.0* in Figure 4-24). Try clicking the outermost border of the upper-left corner to grab it. After clicking all the controls, the numbering sequence should look similar to that in Figure 4-25.

> **Tip** When you are in tab order mode and you move the mouse pointer over a control, its border changes into a thicker frame. This is to help you see where you are. In Figure 4-25 you can see this effect on *Panel1* (the only control with a solid border).

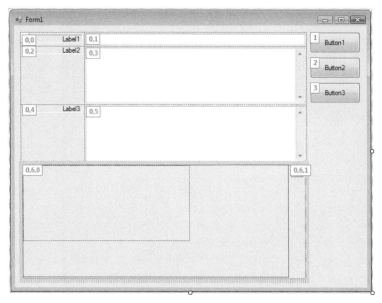

FIGURE 4-25 The tab order numbers for the controls you have already specified are displayed with a white background. Press Esc when you've completed the tab order assignment operation.

4. After you have clicked the last button, press Esc to leave Tab Order mode.

> **Tip** The tab order is set by the *TabIndex* property of a control, which means that you can also change the tab order by manually changing the *TabIndex* properties of the controls. However, because they are re-numbered automatically, If you insert a new control between the controls with the *TabIndex* 3 and the one with the *TabIndex* 4, you will need to increase all tab index entries after *TabIndex* 4 by 1. Hopefully your form doesn't have 36 controls.

At this point, you've completed the actual setup of the form, including all the control resizing and tab order. To sum up: what you have achieved in the past hour or so would have taken hours of design and possibly some non-trivial code in Visual Basic 6.0—maybe even several days' worth, when you take into account a *PictureBox* control with scrolling functionality for its contents.

Using the *Name*, *Text*, and *Caption* Properties

On the design side, this example is still missing the labels for its controls as well as the names of the controls. You will use these names later to access the controls from within your application's code. They are specified by using the *Name* property (the name of a control, which you use to address the control) and the *Text* property (for labels, buttons, and most other controls).

> **Note** All controls have a *Text* property. This is because this property is implemented in *Control*, which each subsequent control builds upon. There are controls that don't display their *Text* property in the properties window, but they still have the *Text* property.

> **Important** The *Caption* property, as you know it from Visual Basic 6.0 for specifying the label of buttons and *Label* controls, no longer exists in .NET. It has been replaced by the *Text* property.

> **Tip** When assigning *Text* and *Name* properties, you should do so one after another, not by switching between them. First, specify all *Name* properties, and then all *Text* properties. Here's why: when you have clicked the first control and specified, for example, the *Text* property in the Properties window, then you just need to click the next control and start typing. Visual Studio remembers that you had last set the *Text* property in the Property window, so as soon as you start typing in the next selected control, it automatically directs the keyboard entry to the latest property in the Property window.

Specifying Accelerator Keys

For many controls, the *Text* property has another function. When you place an "&" (ampersand) character in front of another character, that marks it as an *accelerator key*. You can recognize the accelerator key of a control, because it is underlined. At runtime, users can access a control or activate a button, for example, by pressing the accelerator key together with the Alt key. For example, if you want to users to be able to jump to a *TextBox* by using an accelerator key, you can put a *Label* control in the tab order *before* the *TextBox* and specify the label's accelerator key with the "&" character. Because labels do not receive focus, Windows sets the focus to the next control in the tab order—the *TextBox* in this case. The following example shows how this works.

Figure 4-26 and Table 4-1 demonstrate how you specify the *Text* property for all *Label* and *Button* controls.

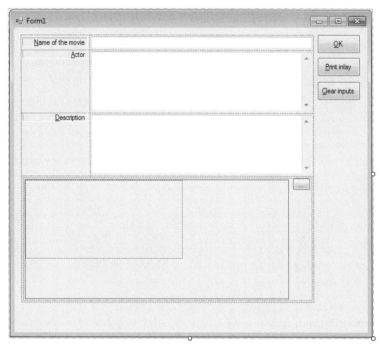

FIGURE 4-26 This graphic shows all the controls. You can use it to help you to assign labels and accelerator keys to the controls as shown in Table 4-1.

TABLE 4-1 The *Name* and *Text* properties for the Controls in the Covers Application

Control	Name (Name property)	Label (Text property)
Label (Left, Top)	*lblNameofFilm*	"&Name of Film"
Label (Left, Center)	*lblActors*	"&Actors"
Label (Left, Bottom)	*lblBriefDescription*	"&Brief Description"
Button (Right, Top)	*btnOK*	"&OK"
Button (Right, Center)	*btnPrintInlay*	"&Print Inla"
Button (Right, Bottom)	*btnDeleteEntries*	"&Delete Entries"
TextBox (Center, Top)	*txtNameofFilm*	"" (empty string—delete the entry)
TextBox (Center, Center)	*txtActors*	""
TextBox (Center, Bottom)	*txtBriefDescription*	""
Button (next to the PictureBox)	*btnSelectCoverPicture*	"..."
PictureBox	*picCoverPicture*	(not applicable)

Notice the specific convention when naming the controls; the three letter prefix specifies the type of control. You can choose your own naming convention for control names, of course. Many developers do that, some don't—Microsoft advises that you *not* do that. The section "Naming Conventions for Controls," later in this chapter, contains a table that lists the conventions for the most important controls.

> **Note** The form itself also has a *Text* property, but the form's *Text* property specifies the text that should appear in the title bar of the form.

1. Select the form.

2. In the Property window, specify an appropriate value for the *Text* property, such as **VB Developer Handbook Cover Inlay Generator**, or something to that effect.

Setting up Accept and Cancel Buttons for a Form

You have already learned how to set up accelerator keys in the previous section. There are two keys for each form that provide a specific functionality: the Enter key, which activates the OK button (and applies the data entered on the form), and the Esc key, which activates the Cancel button (and closes the form without applying the data).

Visual Basic 6.0 developers will search the button properties in vain for these settings—they were moved to forms in .NET. In the end, this makes more sense; after all, only one button at a time can be used for cancelling and another for applying changes in a dialog.

You specify the OK and Cancel buttons on a form through the *AcceptButton* and *CancelButton* properties. To set these properties, open a combo box that contains all of the form's buttons and select the appropriate one.

This example deviates a little from the standard method. Here, the Cancel functionality is assigned to the OK button and the Apply functionality to the Print Inlay button. It makes more sense for users this way, because they leave the dialog with OK; therefore, accidentally pressing the Enter key doesn't cancel the dialog (and thus quit the program).

1. Select the form in the Designer.

2. Set the *AcceptButton* property to the button *btnPrintInlay*.

3. Set the *CancelButton* property to the button *btnOK*.

Adding Multiple Forms to a Project

Smart Client applications seldom consist of just one form. You need a second form that will later contain the print preview, and that you can use to trigger the printing process. Later, during runtime, this form receives the printable data. It must then take over the printing process and display a preview on its own.

> **Note** If you haven't done so yet, try to separate yourself from the procedural way of thinking when designing the forms of your application. It's generally bad programming style to access the elements of a form from another form, module, or class, for example. It's better to provide very few public methods in the form, and their only purpose should be to accept parameters. Leave the evaluation of these parameters to the form itself. And in continuing your preparation for object-oriented programming, you should view each form as a small enclosed application that can only receive data, interact with the user, and then return results.

> **Important** The functionality of forms (setting or querying of input fields, evaluating user actions) should be handled by the form class itself. Avoid manipulating the contents of user controls directly from other modules, classes, or forms.

Follow these steps to add a second form to the project:

1. In the Project Explorer, right-click the name of the project (not the solution) to display the context menu.

   If you don't see a solution for your project, go to Tools |Options | Projects And Solutions | General, and then select the option Always Show Solution.

2. From the context menu, select Add, and then Windows Form, as shown in Figure 4-27.

3. In the New Form dialog that appears, leave the default name as **Form2.vb**.

4. Click Add to add the new form to the project and close the dialog.

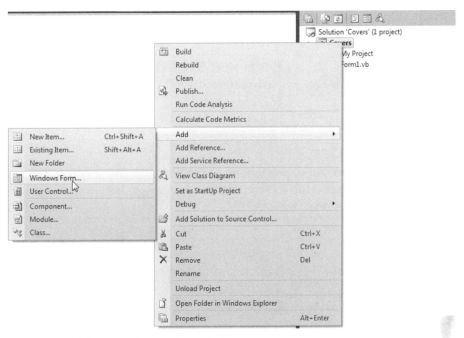

FIGURE 4-27 Adding a new form to the project.

5. Using Figure 4-28 as a guide, increase the size of the new form (which displays immediately) so that you'll have enough space for the required controls.

6. In the Print section of the Toolbox, look for the *PrintPreviewControl*. (You might need to open it.)

Draw the control large enough on the form, and then adjust each side of the control with the help of the guidelines so that they have the same distance from the upper-left and upper-right form border.

7. Set the Anchor property of the control to *Top Bottom*, *Left*, *Right*.

8. Insert two buttons into the form next to each other. Set the Anchor properties of these buttons to *Bottom*, *Right*.

9. Assign *Name* and *Text* properties of the controls according to the values shown in Table 4-2.

TABLE 4-2 The *Name* and *Text* Properties Settings for the Controls in the Second Form (Print Form)

Control	Name (Name property)	Label (Text property)
PrintPreviewControl	(keep the default name)	–
Left Button	btnOK	&OK
Right Button	btnPrint	&Print
Form	(keep the default name)	Show cover preview and print the cover

Save the entire project by either going to the File menu and selecting Save All, or using the corresponding icon in the Toolbar, as shown in Figure 4-28.

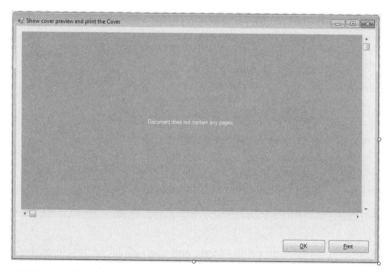

FIGURE 4-28 Here's how the print form should look in the Designer.

What's Next?

The design part of this software project is finished. You now need to supply the appropriate programming logic. The following two sections are meant as look-up references. Take a quick peek, and when you are ready to start programming and finish the software, continue with the section, "The Code Editor," later in this chapter.

Naming Conventions for Controls in this Book

Microsoft states explicitly that the naming of object variables should not include any hints as to what type they are. Various tools for checking style and security for source code (for example, FxCop, which is implemented in the project properties in some SKUs of Visual Studio) even send you a reminder during source code analysis.

You can use IntelliSense to determine the type of an object variable explicitly. All you need to do is position the mouse pointer over the object variable to display the type of variable as a ToolTip.

Nevertheless, for the examples in this book I have decided to forego Microsoft's suggestion, at least when it comes to naming object variables that reference controls. I believe that doing so simplifies reading lists on paper, and that it contributes to a better understanding of code. Besides, IntelliSense is only available in the Visual Studio Code Editor. With that in mind, Table 4-3 offers some naming suggestions.

TABLE 4-3 Suggestions Naming Conventions for Naming Controls

Component	Prefix/Name Combination
Label	lblName
Button	btnName or cmdName[1]
TextBox	txtName
CheckBox	chkName
RadioButton	optName[2] or rbtName
GroupBox	grpName
PictureBox	picName
Panel	pnlName
ListBox	lstName
ComboBox	cmbName
ListView	lvwName
TreeView	tvwName

[1] From *CommandButton*—this was the official name of the button in Visual Basic 6.0/VBA. In .NET, this is no longer common; it appears only once in a while with Visual Basic 6.0/VBA porting.

[2] From *OptionButton*, the name of the option button in Visual Basic 6.0/VBA.

Functions for Control Layout in the Designer

Figure 4-29 shows the original position of the three controls in the form. Table 4-4 juxtaposes the functions that hide behind the icons in the Layout Toolbar. In the table's right column, you can see the result of the arrangement after you have clicked the corresponding icon.

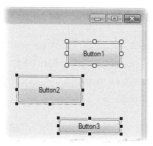

FIGURE 4-29 This is the initial arrangement of the buttons in Table 4-4. Ensure that certain functions orient themselves at the upper-right button.

TABLE 4-4 The Icons to Control Extended Functionalities of the Output Window

Icon	Function	Effect on the *Cover* application controls
🔲	*Align Lefts*	Button1, Button2, Button3
🔲	*Align Centers*	Button1, Button2, Button3
🔲	*Align Rights*	Button1, Button2, Button3
🔲	*Align Tops*	Button2, Button3, Button1

Icon	Function	Effect on the *Cover* application controls
	Align Middles	
	Align Bottoms	
	Make Same Width	
	Make Same Height	
	Make Same Size	
	Make Horizontal Spacing Equal	
	Increase Horizontal Spacing	n/a

Icon	Function	Effect on the *Cover* application controls
	Decrease Horizontal Spacing	n/a
	Remove Horizontal Spacing	n/a
	Make Vertical Spacing Equal	
	Increase Vertical Spacing	n/a
	Decrease Vertical Spacing	n/a
	Remove Vertical Spacing	n/a
	Center Horizontally	n/a
	Center Vertically	n/a
	Bring to Front	n/a
	Send to Back	n/a

Keyboard Shortcuts for Positioning Controls

Although dragging controls with the mouse is an excellent technique for placing them into their approximate positions, you'll find that for precise sizing and positioning, using the keyboard is far more accurate. Table 4-5 lists the important keyboard shortcuts for positioning controls.

TABLE 4-5 Keyboard Shortcuts for Positioning Controls

Key	Task
Arrow keys	Moves the selected control in the corresponding direction.
Ctrl+arrow keys	Moves the selected control in the corresponding direction. The control stops automatically at each guideline that comes next.
Shift+arrow keys	Changes the selected control's size by pixel.
Ctrl+Shift+arrow keys	Changes the control's size so that the respective side touches the next guideline.
Alt	Turns off the guideline function as long as the key remains pressed while moving controls with the mouse.

The Code Editor

The Code Editor is definitely the Visual Studio element in which you will spend most of your time. Over the years it has become a truly ingenious tool that can relieve you of a lot of work, and it has been improved enormously over the years.

But that's only the case if you get know it and really master all its subtleties—and its occasional quirks.

Setting the Editor Display to the Correct Size

In Visual Studio 2010, you can increase or decrease the size of the contents of documents to whatever is comfortable for your viewing (see Figure 4-30).

The easiest way to work in the editor is with the mouse. To increase or decrease the font size, press the Ctrl key and move the mouse wheel.

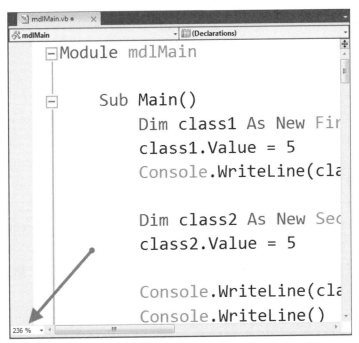

FIGURE 4-30 In Visual Studio 2010 (and in most other document windows), you can zoom in or out on the text in the editor as desired.

Alternatively, you can directly enter a value into the text field at the lower-left corner of the window (see Figure 4-30), or you can open the combo box and select the zoom factor.

It's pretty comfortable to work in the default editor font in Visual Studio 2010 (it is for me, anyhow). If you would like to change to a different font for editing, go to Tools | Options | Fonts And Colors, and then set the default font and colors as you prefer.

> **Note** Custom view sizes for the Editor window are not persisted (the custom size is maintained only as long as the Editor window is open). When you close and open the Editor window again, the view returns to the default font size.

Many Roads Lead to the Code Editor

There are many different ways to call the Code Editor. The simplest method to edit modules or pure class files is via Solution Explorer. Double-click a class or module file to open the file directly in the Editor. To view the class code of a form, you need to select the form in Solution Explorer, and then click the Display Code icon in the top line of Solution Explorer (the ToolTip helps you find the correct icon). You have several different options for calling the Code Editor:

- Double-click a pure class or module file in Solution Explorer.
- With a form class selected, click the View Code icon in Solution Explorer.
- At compiler error: double-click the corresponding error message in the output window.
- At compiler error: double-click the corresponding error message in the error list.
- With comments in the task list: double-click the corresponding comment.
- Double-click an element in a designer. Double-clicking a button in a form, for example, takes you to the existing event handler for that button or opens the Form Editor window and inserts the code body for the event handling routine.
- The editor appears after an error occurs while executing an application in debug mode.

IntelliSense—The Strongest Workhorse in the Coding Stable

IntelliSense is the feature that saves you the most work during development, because it provides you with all conceivable information about the objects and language elements you're currently editing.

To demonstrate the flexibility of IntelliSense, you'll implement the first few lines of code in the example.

1. Open *Form1* in the Designer by double-clicking the form file in Solution Explorer.
2. Double-click the OK button.

Visual Studio takes you to the Code Editor for the class code of *Form1* and automatically provides the outline of the subroutine that will handle the click event of the OK button. This is the method that is called and executed when the user clicks the OK button at runtime.

3. Enter **me.** (including the period) into the line between *Private Sub...* and *End Sub*.

   As soon as you type the period, a list of all the members applicable to the object appears. (In this case, *me* is the form itself, because you are in the class file *Form1;* you will learn the exact meaning in the class chapters—this section concentrates on the editor capabilities.) The list is called the "completion list."

4. To close the form with a single click of the OK button, you can use the *Close* method of the form. If you type in the first letters of the method's name, *Close*, the selection eventually jumps to the method you're trying to specify (see Figure 4-31).

> **Note** You will notice that IntelliSense not only provides you with a complete element list for the object, but also a brief description of the respectively selected elements as a ToolTip—as seen in Figure 4-31.

5. You don't need to enter any more letters in the method name. As soon as the correct method name is selected, just press Enter; the Code Editor will insert the remaining letters of the method name automatically and then move the cursor to the next line.

By doing this, you have already implemented some of the application's functionality. Run the application by pressing F5 and verify that the OK button works and closes the form.

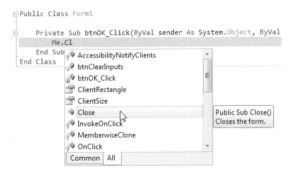

FIGURE 4-31 Typing the period after the object name opens the completion list (thanks to IntelliSense), which displays elements that can be used for the object.

Filtering Elements in the Completion List

In Figure 4-32, notice the two tabs at the bottom of the IntelliSense list. You can use these tabs to filter the elements by importance. Microsoft has predetermined which elements are "common" (but they don't tell us how they arrive at this selection).

The Online Help states, "The Common tab, which is selected by default, displays items that are most often used to complete the statement that you are writing. The All tab displays all items that are available for automatic completion, including those that are also on the Common tab."

Displaying Element Parameter Information

To demonstrate another feature of IntelliSense, we will implement the function "Delete Entries."

1. Navigate back to the Design view of the form *Form1*.

2. Double-click the Delete Entries button.

   This inserts the function body for the button's event handling routine and displays the Code Editor.

3. Start entering the following code:

   ```
   Dim locDr As DialogResult
   ```

   Notice that IntelliSense offers you the completion list after you have typed the keyword *As*. Enter as much of the word *DialogResult* as it takes to reach and highlight that item in the list, and then press Enter.

4. In the next line, type the following:

   ```
   locDr=
   ```

   IntelliSense becomes active here, too. This time it shows you all the possible members of the *DialogResult* enumeration, because it assumes that you want to assign one of those members to the variable *locDr*. Just ignore the list in this case, and continue typing (you don't need to completely type *Show* either, thanks to the completion function).

   ```
   locDr = MessageBox.Show(
   ```

   As soon as you type the opening parenthesis, IntelliSense shows you complete parameter information for the *MessageBox.Show* method (see Figure 4-32), which displays a message box on the screen.

   ```
   Private Sub btnClearInputs_Click(ByVal sender As System.Object, ByVal e As System.Eve
       Dim locDr As DialogResult
       locDr = MessageBox.Show(
   End Sub
   Class        ▲ 2 of 21 ⬆ Show(text As String, caption As String) As System.Windows.Forms.DialogResult
                             Displays a message box with specified text and caption.
                             text: The text to display in the message box.
   ```

FIGURE 4-32 For methods that contain parameters, IntelliSense shows all the parameters, including explanations. The current parameter, whose value you're entering, is marked in bold.

Multiple Command Lines, Implicit Line Continuation, and Parameter Information

Many of you already know from using Visual Basic 6.0 or VBScript that you can distribute a logical line of code in Visual Basic over several physical lines in the editor by using the "_" (underscore) character, which makes the code much easier to read. At the end of the (physical) line, you type a space followed by an "_" (underscore) character. Then you continue writing the actual (logical) line as if you had inserted a word wrap.

Beginning with Visual Basic 2010, this is no longer required. As Figure 4-33 illustrates, in most cases, you just wrap to the next line and continue typing there. This works after a comma, a bracket, a period—but not always.

```
Dim locDr As DialogResult
locDr = MessageBox.Show("Are you sure?", "Delete entry",
                        MessageBoxButtons.YesNo,
                        MessageBoxIcon.Question,
                        MessageBoxDefaultButton.Button2)
```

FIGURE 4-33 With Visual Basic 2010, in most cases, you no longer need to employ the word wrap character.

For example, you still need to use the underscore to wrap the line preceding a *Handles* keyword. When you're unsure, you're always free to use the underscore line-continuation character, which is why this book shows line breaks with the underscore, as well—it always works. In many cases, you can leave it off when using Visual Basic 2010 or later. Feel free to experiment to find out which method works best for you!

Now, let's continue with the example. Add the following to the line (because it hasn't been completely typed in):

```
"Are you sure?", "Delete entries?", _
```

Press Enter. After the line break, the parameter information is gone. To show the parameter information for the new line, as well, press Ctrl+Space. Now enter the rest of the logical command line:

```
MessageBoxButtons.YesNo, _
MessageBoxIcon.Question, MessageBoxDefaultButton.Button2)
```

Automatic Completion of Structure Keywords and Code Indentation

To complete the method for deleting the input fields, enter the following line:

```
If locDr = Windows.Forms.DialogResult.Yes Then
```

As soon as you press Enter at the end of the current line, the Editor automatically inserts an *End If* statement two lines below and then places the cursor between the two lines.

Now enter the remaining lines:

```
txtBriefDescripton.Text = ""
txtNameOfFilm.Text = ""
txtActors.Text = ""
picCoverPicture.Image = Nothing
myPictureFileName = ""
```

As you do that, you will notice that no matter which column you begin to type in, the lines always adjust to the structure specified by *If ... End If*, and are indented accordingly.

> **Note**   This also works for nested structures. This automatic indentation helps you to keep track of which nesting level of the structure you are currently working in.

Error Detection in the Code Editor

Visual Basic has a *background compiler* feature. The background compiler does a lot of preparation work for the actual compiler, which becomes active only when you execute an application. One advantage of the background compiler's work is that applications you develop in Visual Basic have a much shorter turnaround time—the amount of time it takes from compiler start via project compilation to the actual application start—than applications developed in other .NET languages. The background compiler also saves you considerable time during development because unlike other languages, such as C++ or C# (or Visual Basic 6.0/VBA), it detects syntax errors as soon as you enter each complete code line.

> **Note**   C++, C#, and Visual Basic 6.0/VBA also feature background compilers, but those are no-where near as consistent as in Visual Basic 2010. In these other languages, it often happens that the compiler only finds syntax errors or undeclared variables during project creation. In Visual Basic 2010, this almost never happens.

Simple Error Detection in the Editor

If you constructed the example code exactly as shown, you will have noticed an error in the last line you entered. This error wasn't difficult to notice, because the Code Editor marks the line, as shown in Figure 4-34.

```
If locDr = Windows.Forms.DialogResult
    txtDescription.Text = ""
    txtNameOfTheMovie.Text = ""
    txtActor.Text = ""
    picCoverPic.Image = Nothing
    myImagename = ""
```
'myImagename' is not declared. It may be inaccessible due to its protection level.

FIGURE 4-34 Errors detected by the background compiler are marked directly in the Editor while creating the project, before the actual compilation.

The variable in question, which you will need later in the form to save the file name, is not yet declared; you'll do that next.

Editor Support for Runtime Errors

Directly below the class definition, enter the following bold line:

```
Public Class Form1

    Private myPictureFileName As Integer
```

> **Note** Before I'm deluged with emails, let me point out that the error in the preceding code example was indeed intentional.

After you do that, you'll see that the error is no longer marked with a squiggly underline.

Now, test the application in its current state.

1. Start the program by pressing F5

2. Enter a few lines into the input fields

3. Click Delete Entries

4. Confirm the message field by clicking Yes

Instead of deleting the entries, the program quits with an error message (see Figure 4-35).

FIGURE 4-35 If an error (also called an *exception*) occurs during program execution in Debug mode, Visual Studio displays the Editor, highlights the affected area with a yellow background, and shows the corresponding message.

Errors that occur in a .NET application during runtime that cause the program to terminate execution are called *exceptions*. In this case, there's a mistake in the declaration of the *myPictureFileName* variable (OK, OK... I made the mistake, not you.) that led to this exception, the details of which you can view in the Exception Snapshot window (see Figure 4-36). At runtime, .NET tried to assign an empty space to the variable, which, unfortunately, was declared as an *Integer* variable. This led to an *InvalidCastException* (an exception due to invalid type conversion).

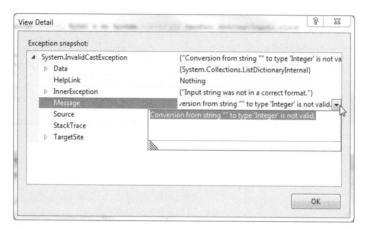

FIGURE 4-36 You can use the Exception Snapshot window to learn more about what circumstances caused the exception.

If you need further information about the exception, click View Details, located under Actions, in the lower part of the dialog box. The Editor will display another dialog box (Figure 4-36) through which you can get extended information.

Let's continue with the example:

1. Click the OK button on the dialog.

2. Close the dialog underneath by clicking the Close button in the upper-right corner.

3. End debugging by selecting Debug | Stop Debugging, or by clicking in the Toolbar on the square icon.

Forcing Type Safety: Error Correction Options for Type Conflicts

None of this would have happened if we had forced Visual Studio to enforce type safety from the get-go. The Code Editor would have detected the error before you even had a chance to run the application.

Since version 2002, Visual Basic has supported a setting statement, *Option Strict [On|Off]*. If you enable *Option Strict*, the background compiler ensures that you can only assign compatible types; this means either the same type, or that a clean type conversion is available (for example from *Integer* to *String*).

Try entering the following code:

```
Option Strict On
```

As soon as you insert the statement at the very top of the code (even before the class definition statement *Class Form1*) and then scroll back to the line in question, you will notice that a long rectangle with a red border and yellow fill has been added at the end of the squiggly line. This marks the code that probably led to the exception.

Smart Tags in the Visual Basic

You can recognize a Smart Tag by the small, long rectangle (it could be confused with an underline) in a code line. A Smart Tag is displayed in the Code Editor when Visual Basic thinks that something should be changed or remarked.

If you move the mouse pointer onto this Smart Tag (the thin rectangle), it changes into a small symbol in the form of an exclamation mark, signifying that it offers different kinds of support, depending on the case at hand, not just help with type conflicts, as in this example.

Smart Compile Auto-Correction

In many cases a dialog behind the Smart Tag provides a correction suggestion for a recognized error. Such help dialogs are called "Smart Compile Auto-Correction." If the auto-correction is indeed correct, and the probable error is an actual error, all you need to do is click the blue correction suggestion, and the Editor performs the correction in the program code.

Important Unfortunately, in this example, Smart Compile Auto-Correction doesn't work for the error, because it's an inherited error. But you can see that you would have at least saved a complete test run if *Option Strict* had been enabled from the beginning. For this reason, you should turn on *Option Strict* across all your projects, to save yourself the work of writing individual *Option Strict On* statements in each code file. You also should set your Visual Studio options so that *Option Strict* is always turned on by default when you create a new project. The sidebar that follows shortly explains how to do this.

To fix the error, just change the line

```
Private myPictureFileName As Integer
```

to:

```
Private myPictureFileName As String
```

Setting up Forced Type Safety (Option Strict) Across the Project

You can make sure that type safety is always in effect in a project—without having to write *Option Strict On* at the top of each code file. To do that, open the project's context menu (not the solution) in Solution Explorer, and then select Properties. The project properties now open as a document window in the document tab group, and you can globally turn on *Option Strict* from the Compile tab.

Forced Type Safety for all Subsequent New Projects

To force the setting to be in effect whenever you create a new project, use the Visual Studio Options dialog. Bring that up by selecting Tools | Options, and then click the area Projects and Solutions. On the VB Defaults tab, specify your preferred setting for Option Strict.

XML Documentation Comments for IntelliSense for Customized Objects and Classes

You have already learned how IntelliSense can help you find the correct classes, objects, methods, and other elements when developing applications. But it can do a lot more for you.

To show more IntelliSense capabilities, you need to do a bit of prep work. First, you'll implement a method that loads a picture from a file into an *Image* object. The actual functionality isn't of primary interest here, since you're still concentrating on how to use the Code Editor features.

1. Insert the following lines into the class code of *Form1*:

```
Function CoverPictureFromFileName(ByVal CoverPictureFromFileName As String) As Image
    Dim locImage As Image
    If CoverPictureFromFileName IsNot Nothing AndAlso CoverPictureFromFileName <> ""
Then
        locImage = Image.FromFile(CoverPictureFromFileName)
        Return locImage
    End If
    Return Nothing
End Function
```

2. Go to Design mode (the designer window) by pressing F7. (By the way, F7 toggles between Design view and Code view of a form.)

3. Double-click the ellipsis button next to the *PictureBox* to open the Code Editor and edit the event handling routine for this button.

4. Enter the following lines into the stub (meaning into the function body (between *Private Sub btnSelectCoverPicture ...* and *End Sub*):

```
Dim locOfd As New OpenFileDialog

With locOfd
    locOfd.CheckFileExists = True
    locOfd.DefaultExt = "*.bmp"
    locOfd.Filter = "Jpeg pictures (*.jpg)|*.jpg|Windows bitmap (*.bmp)|*.bmp|" & _
        "All files (*.*)|*.*"
    Dim locDr As DialogResult = locOfd.ShowDialog()
    If locDr = Windows.Forms.DialogResult.Cancel Then
        Return
    End If

    myPictureFileName = locOfd.FileName
End With
```

5. Between the last two lines, add an additional, incomplete statement:

```
picCoverPicture.Image = CoverPictureFromFileName(
```

As soon as you type the opening parenthesis, you will see that IntelliSense includes your custom methods (and other elements you create, such as properties and so on). Take a look at Figure 4-37. Do you notice anything?

FIGURE 4-37 IntelliSense works for your custom methods, as well. Of course, initially there are no explanations.

Just as for built-in methods, IntelliSense does get activated, but the helpful explanations are missing. Where do those come from, anyhow? Up to Visual Basic 2003 that was the end of IntelliSense for custom methods, unless you used third-party tools. But it's different in Visual Basic 2010, as you will soon see:

1. Before you complete the line, position the cursor over the following line:

```
Function CoverPictureFromFileName(ByVal CoverPictureFromFileName As String) As Image
```

2. Type three apostrophes (''').

3. As soon as you have typed the third apostrophe, the Code Editor inserts a set of comment lines for documenting the method, as shown in Figure 4-38.

```
''' <summary>
'''
''' </summary>
''' <param name="CoverpicFileName"></param>
''' <returns></returns>
''' <remarks></remarks>
Function CoverFromImage(ByVal CoverpicFileName As String) As Image
    Dim locImage As Image
    If CoverpicFileName IsNot Nothing AndAlso CoverpicFileName <> "" Then
        locImage = Image.FromFile(CoverpicFileName)
        Return locImage
    End If
    Return Nothing
End Function
```

FIGURE 4-38 The Editor inserts an XML skeleton above the method, where your documentation goes.

4. For the following steps, use Figure 4-39 as a guide. Enter a function explanation between *<summary>* and *</summary>*.

```
''' <summary>
''' Loads an Image(if avaiable) out of a file and returns the picture as Image(or Nothing)
''' </summary>
''' <param name="CoverpicFileName">Name of the image file</param>
''' <returns>Image from the Imagefile with the given name as image-object.</returns>
''' <remarks>Created by Klaus Löffelmann at 10/26/2005</remarks>
Function CoverFromImage(ByVal CoverpicFileName As String) As Image
    Dim locImage As Image
    If CoverpicFileName IsNot Nothing AndAlso CoverpicFileName <> "" Then
        locImage = Image.FromFile(CoverpicFileName)
        Return locImage
    End If
    Return Nothing
End Function
```

FIGURE 4-39 Complete the XML tags according to this template.

5. Enter the description of the parameter *CoverPictureFileName* between *<param name= "CoverPictureFileName">* and *</param>*.

> **Note** Should you later need to work with methods or properties that accept multiple parameters, you can add more *param* tags and insert the parameter descriptions between them.

6. Type the description of the return value between *<returns>* and *</returns>*.

7. Optionally, you can enter a note between *<remarks>* and *</remarks>*.

> **Note** There are more commenting tags than those discussed here. See the topic "Recommended XML Tags for Documentation Comments," in the documentation.

8. After completing your entries, return to the incomplete line.

```
picCoverPicture.Image = CoverPictureFromFileName(
```

Delete characters from the end of the line until only *"Cov"* of *"CoverPictureFromFileName"* is left, and then press Ctrl+Space. You will now see not only the function name in the completion list (as before), but also the description you specified in the XML documentation (see Figure 4-40).

FIGURE 4-40 After you have documented your methods and property procedures with the appropriate XML tags, IntelliSense shows a function description.

9. Press Space to complete the function name.

10. When you type the opening parenthesis, IntelliSense becomes active again, as illustrated in Figure 4-41. You can see that IntelliSense now shows the parameter name and the parameter type as well as the parameter documentation.

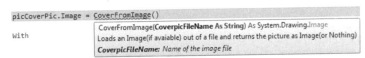

FIGURE 4-41 IntelliSense also shows the corresponding parameter description.

11. Complete the line so it looks as follows:

```
picCoverPicture.Image = CoverPictureFromFileName(myPictureFileName)
```

Note Along the way, you now have implemented the complete picture display in the form with just a few lines of code. And thanks to the settings you specified earlier in the Designer, the picture selection already works with a scroll bar. You can see this for yourself: start the program by pressing F5, click the ellipsis button, and then select a picture file in the dialog. The picture displays on the form.

> **Tip** On top of what you just learned, you can make real HTML-Reference help files out of the documentation tags, which is very helpful if you create class and function libraries in a team. Take a look at Eric Woodruff's wonderful Sandcastle Helpfile Builder, which you can find at CodePlex (*http://shfb.codeplex.com/*).

Adding New Code Files to the Project

You need a data structure to pass user entries in the main form to the print form. In the example, the program uses this data structure to first cache the individual data fields in the data structure—let's call them *CoverData*—and then pass it all at once to the print form.

Using this structure, the data collection task and the print task are cleanly separated from each other. The main form takes care of the data collection, and an auxiliary form handles printing the data. The main form doesn't need to access the print and preview form directly or manipulate its controls or variables; instead, it instructs the print form how to display the cover in the preview pane or output it on a printer by calling a single public function and passing the appropriate data through an instance of a custom class.

To do this elegantly, you should put the data structure in its own code file. This should be a class file that has the same name as the data structure (the class): *CoverData*.

> **Note** Visual Basic 6.0/VBA programmers know data structures in their simplest form, as custom types. Without jumping ahead to the class section of the book, the simplest class corresponds more or less to the definition of a new type with *Type*.

You add a class file to a project in a similar manner as adding a new form (which adds a new form class file).

1. Open the context menu of the *Covers* project (not the solution) in Solution Explorer.
2. Select Add, and then from the drop-down menu that appears, select Class, as demonstrated in Figure 4-42.

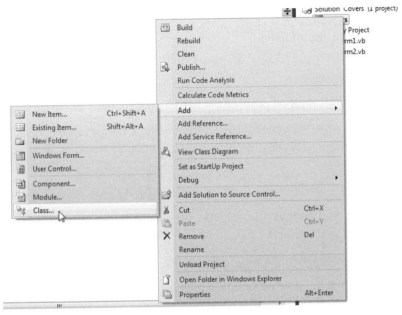

FIGURE 4-42 Adding a new class file to the project.

3. In the dialog box that opens, enter the name of the class file (without the file exten-sion); in this example, type **CoverData**.

4. Click Add or press Enter.

    The Code Editor opens, and the class definitions are already specified. Now, enter the following lines between *Public Class CoverData* and *End Class*:

    ```
    Public Property FilmTitle As String
    Public Property Actors As String
    Public Property Description As String
    Public Property CoverPicture As Image
    ```

Using this new class, you can read data from the main form and pass it to the print form. And that's exactly what you'll implement next.

> **Companion Content** To avoid typing too much for this section, you can take the easy route and copy the printing code into the form. You can find the code at \VB 2010 Developer Handbook\Chapter 04\Covers\Print Routine for Covers.txt.

1. Open the text file Print Routine for Covers.txt in Notepad.

2. Press Ctrl+A to select all the text in the file, and then press Ctrl+ C to copy it to the clipboard.

3. Close Notepad.

4. Go back to Visual Studio.

5. In Solution Explorer, click Form2.vb, and then in the Toolbar of Solution Explorer, click the Show Code icon.

6. Press Ctrl+A, and then press Ctrl+V to paste the contents of the clipboard.

This completes the code for the print form. Right now, you don't need to worry about the specific functionality; explaining that thoroughly would entail jumping ahead too many topics.

7. Save all your changes and close the document Form2.vb.

To implement the code that creates a new instance of the *CoverData* class, feeds it data from the input fields, and passes the class to the print form for processing, do the following:

1. Press F7 to switch to the Design mode of Form1.vb.

2. Double-click the Print Inlay button to insert the stub for the *btnPrintInlay_Click()* event handler into the code.

3. Type in the following code (the comments just briefly explain the code, and of course you don't need to add them):

```
'Instantiate CoverContent class in an object
Dim locCoverData As New CoverData

'Assign data to CoverData object
locCoverData.FilmTitle = txtNameOfFilm.Text
locCoverData.Actors = txtActors.Text
locCoverData.Description = txtBriefDescription.Text
locCoverData.CoverPicture = picCoverPicture.Image

'Call print preview and pass CoverContent object
'with data.
Dim locCoverPrintForm As New Form2
locCoverPrintForm.DialogActors(locCoverData)
```

Refactoring Code

Basic refactoring functionalities were introduced in Visual Studio 2008. Unfortunately, Visual C# 2008 received many more refactoring tools than Visual Basic 2008. Visual Basic 2008 had only a single function for automatic code refactoring: renaming methods, properties, objects, and events. With the release of Visual Basic 2010, Microsoft added the "Consume First" functionality, which you learned about in Chapter 3, "Sightseeing."

Note You can download a free version of the Add-Ins Refactor tool from *http://tinyurl.com/66u4la*.

What exactly does refactoring mean?

Suppose that you are developing a relatively complex function, and after a while you notice that your function already has 1,000 lines of code. At that point, it becomes clear that you should have broken your function up into several smaller functions. But it's not too late for that; you can generate a new function that performs a basic task from the larger function. You are now performing active refactoring.

The biggest problem occurs when the names you have given to methods are wrong, or are not sufficiently unique or self-explanatory. You might already have encountered this problem once or twice, especially when working as a team. And everyone who ever had to rename a function knows that this can be a lot of work, because functions are always referenced much more often than you would expect.

You can't always simply use a find-and-replace routine for this purpose either. Consider the following scenario: you want to rename a property called *bindControl* to *BoundControl*. But there is also a method called *UnbindControl*, which you have completely forgotten about, and which (using search and replace) you are now accidentally and unwittingly renaming, as well—to *UnboundControl*.

This problem becomes even more serious when renaming variables that are used multiple times in several scopes. For example, if you have implemented a method in two classes, you might want to change only the name of the method in one class and everywhere you have used it. To do this by using find-and-replace without any mistakes is virtually impossible.

Visual Basic 2010 includes a new refactoring tool called the renaming tool to handle just such tasks. Renaming by using refactoring always refers only to the element that you are renaming, and not to other elements by the same name in other parts of the code. Moreover, refactoring renames all references to the new element name. Try it out by doing the following:

1. In the code for *Form1.vb*, search for the function *CoverPictureFromFileName*.

2. Right-click the function name to open the context menu.

3. Select Rename from the context menu.

4. In the dialog, enter the new name for the function—for example, type **GetCoverImage**, as shown in Figure 4-43.

FIGURE 4-43 You can use the Rename dialog box to rename a method (of a function) as well as all its references.

5. Click OK.

6. Move the cursor to the function *btnSelectCoverPicture_Click*.

You can see here that not only is the name of the function changed, but also the reference to the function has changed changed, as seen in bold in the following function list:

```
    Private Sub btnSelectCoverPicture_Click(ByVal sender As System.Object, ByVal e As
System.EventArgs) _
Handles btnSelectCoverPicture.Click
        Dim locOfd As New OpenFileDialog

    With locOfd
        locOfd.CheckFileExists = True
        locOfd.DefaultExt = "*.bmp"
        locOfd.Filter = "Jpeg pictures (*.jpg)|*.jpg|" & _
            "Windows Bitmap (*.bmp)|*.bmp|All files (*.*)|*.*"

        Dim locDr As DialogResult = locOfd.ShowDialog()
        If locDr = Windows.Forms.DialogResult.Cancel Then
            Return
        End If

        myPictureFileName = locOfd.FileName
        picCoverPicture.Image = GetCoverImage(myPictureFileName)
    End With
    End Sub
```

Refactoring Code (Adjusting Class Names) by Renaming Project Files or Object Properties

As long as you name your class files or form files exactly the same as the classes or form classes that define them, renaming works in the same manner, with the difference being that you also rename the physical file that contains the actual class code.

Give it a try:

1. Open the context menu of *Form2.vb* in Solution Explorer.

2. Select Rename.

3. Enter a new name for the form file; for example, type **frmPrintCover.vb**.

> **Note** You are renaming a physical file; therefore, ensure that you add the file extension.

4. Press Enter. If a security question pops up, answer it accordingly.

5. Move the cursor to the function *btnPrintInlay_Click* in the code of *Form1*.

   The last few lines of the function now look as follows:

   ```
   'Call print preview and pass the CoverContent object
   'with the data.
   Dim locPrintCoverForm As New frmPrintCover
   locPrintCoverForm.DisplayDialog(locCoverContent)
   ```

   You can see why this is the case when you open the code of the former *Form2.vb* (now *frmPrintCover.vb*). When you renamed the file, the class name was changed to *frmPrintCover*, and the reference to it in the *btnPrintInlay_Click* was changed accordingly.

> **Note** For large projects with many form files or class files, refactoring classes and form classes by renaming code files can become bothersome. You can turn off Enable Refactoring On Rename in the Options dialog of Visual Studio. To do this, select Tools | Options, and then click the Windows Forms Designer tab, as shown in Figure 4-44. Set the EnableRefactoringOnRename property to *False*.

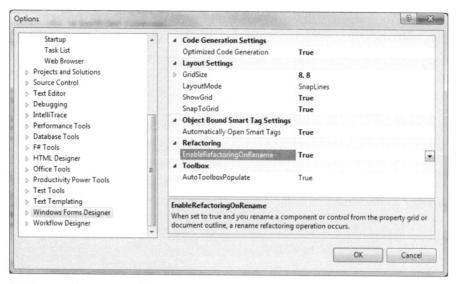

FIGURE 4-44 You can turn off the refactoring by renaming code files.

Note The refactoring tools in Visual Studio 2010 are based on the tools of a company called Developer Express. If you would like to use the complete refactoring tool, you can get it as a test version or buy the complete version by going to *http://tinyurl.com/5z32yt*.

Code Snippets Library

The sample program already looks pretty good, but it doesn't run without errors yet, and it's not protected against unintentional misuse. What does that mean? Some user might try, for example, to load a text file as the cover image instead of a picture file. If a user supplies the wrong file type (or if they choose a file with a .jpg extension that's not really an image), the program quits abruptly with an exception (a runtime error message, as shown in Figure 4-45) that the code currently doesn't handle.

FIGURE 4-45 Loading a small text file leads to an "OutOfMemoryException" error.

There is room for speculation, but the error might be caused by the internal graphic filters, which erroneously interpret text bytes as size specifications for a graphic that is about to be loaded. The error occurs when reserving space for the graphic rather than later when reading the "incorrect" byte sequence.

Of course, a professional application shouldn't crash with a runtime exception—especially if the exception displays such a misleading message to the user (see Figure 4-45).

It would be nice if errors didn't cause the application to come to a screeching halt, but instead, were handled gracefully by the application as well as being reported to an adminis-trator (by email, for example).

I'd love to explain to you how that works, but you know what? I can't. I would need to do hours of research, and even then, it would still be questionable whether I'd find information for programming such a feature.

But, thankfully, I don't need to do that, because Visual Basic 2010 has a code snippet library that provides something to match many common needs. For example, there's a snippet to handle errors that might occur in a code segment. Here's how it works:

1. Close the exception dialog.

2. Stop the program by clicking the Stop Debugging icon (use the ToolTip to help you find the correct icon).

3. Move the cursor to the *GetCoverImage* method so that it's exactly at the beginning of the line:

   ```
   locImage = Image.FromFile(CoverPictureFileName)
   ```

4. Right-click to display the context menu, and then select Insert Snippet.

   You'll see a folder list that contains all the various code snippet categories. Double-click Code Patterns - If, For Each, Try Catch, Property, Etc.

5. Double-click the item Error Handling (Exceptions).

6. In the list that opens, double-click the statement Try...Catch...End Try Statement (Figure 4-46).

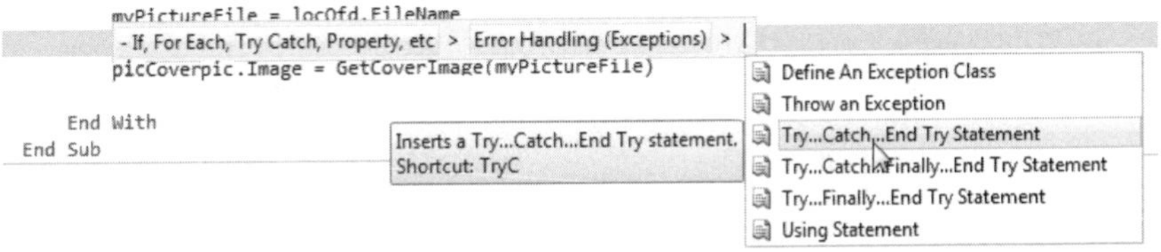

FIGURE 4-46 When inserting a code snippet, you can see the various categories hierarchically next to each other. A ToolTip provides you with further information about the selected snippet. Also pay attention to the displayed shortcut string for "next time."

Note You should try to remember the shortcut the ToolTip shows if you need a code snippet repeatedly. That way you can insert the code snippet later by typing the shortcut, with less hassle.

The Editor inserts the necessary error handling code, which you just need to rearrange a little bit, as follows:

```
If CoverPictureFileName IsNot Nothing AndAlso CoverPictureFileName <> "" Then
    Try
        'Try to load the image and...
        locImage = Image.FromFile(CoverPictureFileName)
        '...when no error occurs, return the following result:
        Return locImage
    Catch ex As Exception
        'If an error occurs you end up here.

    End Try
End If
```

Note Remember to convert *ApplicationException* to *Exception* so that your code catches not only *ApplicationException* exceptions, but also all other conceivable exceptions, as explained in Chapter 1, "Beginners All-Purpose Symbolic Instruction Code."

With this code change, the application can now catch the error. Now you need to react to the error properly in the *Catch* block; for example, you need to send an email to the administrator or the software manufacturer.

Inserting Code Snippets with the Help of Connections

Code snippets help here as well. In the snippet category Other—Connectivity, Security, Workflow, in the subcategory Connectivity And Networking, you'll find an entry called Create An Email Message, which also has the shortcut *conEmail*. If you know the shortcut, you only need to insert it into the location where the entire snippet should appear in the code, and then press Tab twice (Tab, Tab), as shown in the following example:

```
Function GetCoverImage(ByVal CoverPictureFileName As String) As Image
    Dim locImage As Image
    If CoverPictureFileName IsNot Nothing AndAlso CoverPictureFileName <> "" Then
        Try
            'Try to do this without error, and...
            locImage = Image.FromFile(CoverPictureFileName)
            '...when no error occurs, return the following result:
            Return locImage
```

```
        Catch ex As Exception
            'If an error occurs you end up here.
                conEmail
        End Try
    End If
    Return Nothing
End Function
```

The function is changed when you press Tab Tab after *conEmail*, as shown in Figure 4-47.

```
If CoverPicFileName IsNot Nothing AndAlso CoverPicFileName <> "" Then
    Try
        'Try this without errors and ...
        locImage = Image.FromFile(CoverPicFileName)
        '... once there is no error, this solution will me send:
        Return locImage
    Catch ex As Exception
        'When there is an error, you will be send here
        Return Nothing

        Dim message As New MailMessage("sender@address", "from@adress", "Subject", "Message Text")
        Dim emailClient As New SmtpClient("Email Server Name")
        emailClient.Send(message)

    End Try
```

FIGURE 4-47 The inserted code snippet. By pressing Tab, you can easily jump from parameter to parameter and change them in one go.

Just press Tab to jump from parameter to parameter, and then enter the appropriate values, until the *Catch* block shows the following code:

```
        .
        .
        .
        Catch ex As Exception
            'If an error occurs you end up here.

            Dim message As New MailMessage("covers@loeffelmann.de", _
                        "klaus@loeffelmann.de", _
                        "Error during program execution", ex.Message)
            Dim emailClient As New SmtpClient("192.168.0.1")
            emailClient.Send(message)
        End Try
        .
        .
        .
```

Note For this example to run on your system, you need to have an appropriately configured SMTP (mail) server in your network. Enter your own data to replace the email data in the list and then replace the TCP/IP number (192.168.0.1) with your own TCP/IP number or the host name of your SMTP server. Should you need to access SMTP servers that don't support an open relay function,[3] add the bold line shown in the following code to pass the logon information.

---

[3] Relaying to and from any email address without login shouldn't be possible with most SMTP servers (hopefully!), unless they permit relaying due to the integrated security in Active Directory networks. In such cases the network logon when starting Windows also takes care of the implicit logon to the SMTP server, if necessary.

```
      .
      .
      .

          Catch ex As Exception
              'If an error occurs you end up here.

          Dim message As New MailMessage("covers@loeffelmann.de", _
                      "klaus@loeffelmann.de", _
                      "Error during program execution", ex.Message)
          Dim emailClient As New SmtpClient("192.168.0.1")
          emailClient.Credentials = New Net.NetworkCredential("Username", "Password")
          emailClient.Send(message)
      End Try

      .
      .
      .
```

Saving Application Settings with the Settings Designer

Many applications need to save settings when the application is terminated. This used to be a relatively labor-intensive issue because applications had to handle serializing their settings themselves.

> **Note** Serialization is the process where an object that saves data in the main storage within an application puts that data via a data stream into a target storage, either for the purpose of making this data available for re-utilization by an object of the same "structure," or to save it permanently on a data carrier. In the reverse process, a data stream becomes the original instance of the object again, so the process actually corresponds to the loading of data into the main storage. You'll read more about serialization in Chapter 20, "Serialization."

Custom methods within the application had to make sure that important data was prepared so it could be saved in the correct format. The conversion into the correct format (for example, numeric values into strings when serializing, or strings into numeric values when deserializing) represented the biggest amount of work, because incorrect type conversions (a date exists as a string, but the program attempts to convert the string into a numeric variable) had to be caught and excluded, which consumed a comparatively large amount of time and effort.

In .NET 4.0 and Visual Studio 2010, this is much easier. You can interactively specify setting variables by using a special designer, which you can then access from your application and use to save application settings. And the best part is that Visual Basic applications automatically ensure that the contents of these variables are saved when the program is ended, and will be automatically restored at the next program launch.

Setting Up Settings Variables

You'll find the designer for defining settings variables in the project properties.

1. in Solution Explorer, right-click the project (not the solution) to open the context menu, and then select Properties.

2. Go to the Settings tab.

   For this sample program, you want the entries the user has input into the text fields at runtime to be saved to the program code at program end, and to be loaded and written into the input fields at the next program start.

3. Call the first settings variable *LastFilmName* and assign it as type *String* (it saves character strings).

4. Click the first name cell of the settings table (see Figure 4-48) and enter **LastFilmName** as the variable name, and then press Tab.

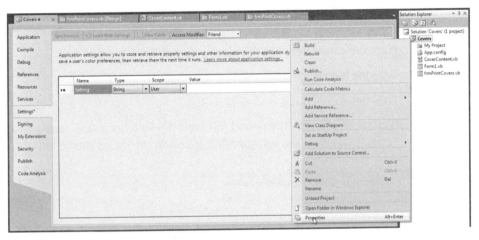

FIGURE 4-48 The Settings Designer window.

5. In the next column, you would normally select the desired variable type in the combo box; however, you don't need to do that here because *String* is already correct for text entries, so simply press Tab.

6. Under Scope, select whether the Settings variable should be read-only or editable in the program.

   Select *User* if you want the variable content to change at runtime and save the new content when the program ends. Select *Application* when the value is a constant that can be set only at design time and never changes at runtime. For this example, leave the setting set to *User*.

7. Leave the Value field empty.

You could enter a default value that the *Settings* variable would have at the first application start from any user account, but you don't need a default value here.

8. Press Tab to go to the next line, which the Settings Designer creates automatically.

9. Set up further variables (all the ones with the *String* type and *User* scope) in this manner, and call them **LastActor**, **LastDescription**, and **LastCoverPictureFileName**.

10. Click the Save Selected Elements icon to apply the changes.

Using Settings Variables in Code

If you have created the setting variables as described in the previous section, it's a piece of cake to actually use them from your code—you can access all of them via the *My* keyword, as the following procedure shows:

1. Switch to the Design mode of Form1.vb by pressing Ctrl+Tab.

2. Double-click somewhere on the form—the best place is below the three buttons, so you don't accidentally hit one of the other controls.

3. Place the cursor between *Private Sub Form1_Load* and *End Sub*.

4. Type the following line:

```
txtBriefDescription.Text = My.Settings.
```

5. As soon as you type the period following *My.Settings*, IntelliSense activates and all the Settings variables you just specified appear in the list, as shown in Figure 4-49.

FIGURE 4-49 You can access the Settings variables via *My.Settings*; IntelliSense will help you find the appropriate Settings variable.

6. Select LastDescription from the completion list.

7. Repeating your settings selection in this manner, add the following lines to the code so that the code block looks like this:

```
Private Sub Form1_Load(ByVal sender As System.Object, ByVal e As System.EventArgs)

    Handles MyBase.Load
    txtBriefDescription.Text = My.Settings.LastDescription
    txtNameOfFilm.Text = My.Settings.LastFilmName
    txtActors.Text = My.Settings.LastActors
```

```
    Dim locImage As Image = GetCoverImage(My.Settings.LastCoverPictureFileName)
    picCoverPicture.Image = locImage
End Sub
```

> **Note** IntelliSense initially marks the element in the completion list that you have used most frequently, as long as you haven't yet entered any letters to identify another word for completion. For example, if you enter **My.** for the third time, *Settings* is automatically selected.

What exactly does *Form1_Load* do? Adding the code *Handles Mybase.Load* determines that *Form1_Load* is called automatically when the .NET Framework displays the form, which is the case at program start. *Form1_Load* then transfers the program settings already located in the Settings variables to the text fields. Because you can't save pictures directly in Settings variables, here's a trick: you save the last known file name, and then try to load the most recent picture at startup from the same source. Because the cover picture loading function can catch errors, you can afford the risk that the picture no longer resides at its original location.

To complete this example, you still need to add the reverse operation. When a user closes the form, you need to save the strings in the text fields as well as any current picture file name in the Settings variables so that the application can display the field contents the next time a user loads the form.

The best time to take care of this is when the form is just about to close. At that point, the contents of the controls still exist; therefore, the most appropriate place to handle such tasks is when the *FormClosing* event occurs. You'll implement a corresponding event handling routine next:

1. Select Form1.vb in Design mode by pressing Ctrl+Tab.

2. Click the title bar of the form to select it.

3. In the Properties window, click the *Events* icon (the lightning bolt icon) to display the names of the events.

4. Under the Behavior category, double-click the *FormClosing* event.

   The *FormClosing* event should be immediately visible, unless you have chosen to display the members names sorted alphabetically.

5. The Editor inserts stub code for the *FormClosing* event; all you need to do is complete it by adding the following lines of code:

```
Private Sub Form1_FormClosing(ByVal sender As System.Object, _
ByVal e As System.Windows.Forms.FormClosingEventArgs) Handles MyBase.FormClosing
    My.Settings.LastDescription = txtBriefDescription.Text
    My.Settings.LastFilmName = txtNameOfFilm.Text
    My.Settings.LastActor = txtActors.Text
    My.Settings.LastCoverPictureFileName = myPictureFileName
End Sub
```

Binding of Settings Values with Form and Control Properties

You can also use Settings values to save properties of forms and controls. The appropriate property values are bound directly to the Settings values. Here's how you can benefit from this capability.

Suppose that when a user opens a form at runtime, the form should automatically display at whatever position it was in the last time the user displayed it. In this case, you could use Settings values to save the *Location* property which specifies the position of the form. You would have to read the corresponding property values from the settings within the form's *Load* event handler, and then when closing the form in *FormClosing*, apply them to the settings again.

However, you can also automate this process by binding the property to a Settings value, using following these steps:

1. Open *Form1* by double-clicking the corresponding class file in Solution Explorer.

2. Click the title bar of the form to select the form itself.

3. In the Properties window (ensure that you switch back to the properties list), open the entry (ApplicationSettings) by clicking the adjacent triangle icon.

4. Click Location, and then open the combo box, as shown in Figure 4-50.

FIGURE 4-50 Binding a form property to Settings value.

5. In the list that opens, click New.

   Visual Studio opens an additional dialog, from which you can directly set up a new Settings value with the correct property type, without the need to go to the application settings table.

6. Enter a default position for the form under DefaultValue (remember to separate the two numbers with a semicolon, not a comma), and then specify the name for the Settings value; for example, **MainFormPosition**, as demonstrated in Figure 4-51.

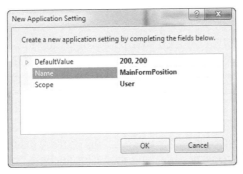

FIGURE 5-51 Specifying a name for a new Settings value in the New Application Setting dialog box.

7. Click *OK* to finish.

Now, when you start the program, the main form opens at position 200; 200. If you then move the form and close it, the next time you start it, it will automatically display at the position it had when you last closed the program.

> **Note** Unfortunately you can't bind the *size* of the form to the Settings values in this manner, because the *Size* property isn't bindable to application properties, due to reasons related to .NET Framework. It is possible to bind the form size indirectly to a Settings value by using the *ClientSize* property, but if you do that, the *Anchor* settings of the other controls are not correctly accounted for when the size is recreated. The workaround is to assign properties manually in the event handling routines *FormLoad* and *FormClosing* by using the *Size* property for the form size.

Where Are Settings Stored?

Visual Studio stores settings values in the user's personal application data directory under *Local Settings* on the Windows installation drive, and in further subfolders. The naming of those subfolders follows a specific pattern. The folder path is a combination of the user's name, the company's name (defined in the containing .NET assembly), and the application's name, followed by and a mysterious letter-combination that is probably a secret message from extraterrestrials (they forced me!) and the version number of the application.

To make it easier to understand (or, to make it understandable all together), here's the path on my machine:

C:\Documents and Settings\loeffel.ACTIVEDEVELOP\Local Settings\Application Data\
OtherCompany\Covers.vshost.exe_Url_ohvclojvckpztoiykwlhs3ba2acq2v4i\1.0.0.0

To break this long path down a bit:

My logon name in our Active Directory network is *loeffel-* (which, by the way, means "spoon" in English and is derived from my last name Löffelmann, thus Spoonman). Our domain is *ActiveDevelop* (my birth date is *07/24/1969*, but even with this knowledge you wouldn't be able log on to our domain server).

For the company name, I specified *Other Company* in the Assembly Information dialog. You can open this dialog by selecting Properties in the project context menu in Solution Explorer. Open the Applications tab (default property page), and then click the Assembly Information button. The last-but-two directory in the path is created from the name you specified under Company.

The next directory comes from the program name. It is created from the runtime program name, which can vary. When you start the program in debug mode, the .NET Framework doesn't start the program itself; instead, it launches a host process, which makes sure that you can edit the program code during debugging,[4] and that the debug speed is tolerable. The application name of this host process is a combination of the actual application name (*Covers*) and *.vshost.exe*. The string *Url_* and other identifying information is appended, but I haven't been able to determine the exact meaning at the time of this writing.

This is followed by the version number of the program in yet another subfolder, where the file user.config is located. user.config is an XML file that saves the actual settings, as shown in the following example:

```xml
<?xml version="1.0" encoding="utf-8"?>
<configuration>
    <userSettings>
        <Covers.My.MySettings>
            <setting name="LastFilmName" serializeAs="String">
                <value>Terminator III-Rise of the Machines</value>
            </setting>
            <setting name="LastActor" serializeAs="String">
                <value>Arnold Schwarzenegger, Kristanna Loken, Nick Stahl,
                Claire Danes</value>
            </setting>
            <setting name="LastDescription" serializeAs="String">
                <value>Kristanna tries to park the crane, but doesn't succedd.
                    Arnie
                        helps, but turns it upside down.</value>
            </setting>
            <setting name="LastCoverPictureFileName" serializeAs="String">
                <value>C:\Documents and Settings\All Users\Documents\
                        Personal Pictures\Sample Pictures\Arnie.jpg</value>
            </setting>
```

---

[4] This debugging mode is the much-discussed "Edit & Continue" feature, which didn't exist in Visual Basic 2002, but was introduced in Visual Basic 2008.

```
        <setting name="PrintFormPosition" serializeAs="String">
            <value>303, 123</value>
        </setting>
    </Covers.My.MySettings>
  </userSettings>
</configuration>
```

Note User and application settings are not saved in the same configuration file. If you selected *Application* scope in the Settings Designer, and thus have specified a read-only property that applies to all users, you'll find those settings in the file *appname*.exe.config—where *appname* is your project's application name. This file is located in the *bin* subfolder of the directory and has the name configured for the project. By default, you'll find *Debug* and *Release* configuration settings—which may initially have the same parameters—with the exception that the compilation is saved in different subfolders because of the different configuration names.

For example, if you created your project in the main directory of the "D" drive under the name *Covers*, the executable files (and also appname.exe.config) will be located in *D:\covers*. The sidebar that follows provides you with more information about these configuration settings.

About the Configuration Settings "Debug" and "Release" and Code Execution Speed

Many developers, especially developers who are taking their first baby-steps within the Visual Studio IDE, tend to initially misunderstand the configuration management of project compiler settings. They often discover that the code execution speed in *Debug* configuration setting doesn't represent the actual program speed, and are disappointed when switching to *Release* doesn't break any speed records either.

But it just can't do that. The difference in speed is because the Visual Studio Debugger is appended to the process at application start, which makes it noticeably slower. The default configuration settings *Debug* and *Release*, on the other hand, control the degree of optimization of the finished compilation. In release mode, the compiler does not generate debug symbols, which is a requirement for optimizing the speed of the executable code. However, in both versions you can append the Debugger, which always slows down execution speed to the point that you will no longer notice any optimizations.

If you want to find out how fast your program will eventually be for the user, launch it by going to the Debug menu and selecting the command Start Without Debugging, or by pressing Ctrl+F5.

With the configuration settings, you can determine, for example, which platforms the compilation should target ("x86", —"Any", and so on), which project within a solution you want to compile, and similar options. You can also specify the project subfolders where the compiler should generate executable files.

Important If you start a program in debug mode (such as with F5), it always runs more slowly than if you start it without debugging (Ctrl+F5).

Congratulations!

You have just finished your first functional (and quite useful) Windows .NET Framework 4.0 application. Have fun working with the *Covers* application. Test it! Use it to create covers for your vacation videos. Print things until the printer smokes!

Chapter 5

Introduction to Windows Presentation Foundation

"You must please the eye, too!"

That's what my Mom used to say when she had me set the table when I was a little boy. I certainly tried to comply with her aesthetic needs, but my own principle of "form follows function" contradicted hers, and I admit that that's probably the reason why, ever since Microsoft Visual Basic 4.0, I've focused more on Windows Forms applications than on web applications. (And it's also why I never tried to become an interior designer.) Many web applications can be created in a very pleasing manner from a graphical and design point of view, often much more pleasing than Windows Forms applications. Unfortunately, that's true only when the right people create the web application—and I have to admit that I'm not one of them.

What Is the Windows Presentation Foundation?

Such was life for those born without the gift of design creativity. And then Microsoft released the graphics-based framework called *Windows Presentation Foundation* (WPF) together with Microsoft .NET Framework 3.0. As the name indicates, the goal was to create a technique for presenting information in a graphically oriented form. But it went beyond that: WPF also had to make sure these graphic functions can be used to implement any user interface; in other words, it must support all the events and features that allow users to interact with it, including mouse, pen, and touch input from notebook, tablets, notepads, or special table displays.

 More Information Would you like a demonstration? YouTube can help, and *http://tinyurl.com/6gaoln* shows you where.

For Windows Forms programmers that means only one thing: rethink, and rethink hard, because these days *function is design*, and form follows function.

During the past two years, WPF has undergone a near constant evolutionary process spurred on by nobody and by everybody all at once. Even though originally Microsoft did not design WPF to be the successor to Windows Forms, it looks more and more as if that's exactly what's happening. Many of the large existing Visual Basic 6.0 and C++ COM applications had to be migrated (and are still supposed to!) to a new platform, because they cause serious problems in Vista, Windows 7, and Windows Server 2008, and often it happens that they don't work at all in 64-bit versions of Windows, which are becoming increasingly common. The only solution is to migrate these older applications to .NET Visual Basic 6.0; VBA should preferably be migrated to .NET versions of Visual Basic. And during this migration process, while the decisions about the best way to transition thousands of different developer teams out there is being put into place, the same question always arises: how should we design new front-ends and user interfaces? During this process, many teams have come to the conclusion that WPF makes a good substitute for the aging user interface (UI) in Windows Forms. The long-term benefits seem to outweigh the disadvantages and the enormous additional work that still needs to be done when replacing Windows Forms with WPF. This additional work consists mainly of the following:

- It's not easy to adapt to WPF functionality. This is especially true for teams coming from Visual Basic 6.0, who still need to get used to the concept of object-oriented programming. And I'm talking about object-*oriented* here—many developers who have squeezed the last drop out of Visual Basic 6.0 and know all its peculiarities and pitfalls inside and out are familiar only with object-based programming, due to the way Visual Basic 6.0 worked. There is a big difference, especially when it comes to the best possible application construction. In the .NET versions of Visual Basic, which are object-oriented, this can lead to a completely different approach, during which everything is rearranged until it's nothing like the original application.

- The construction of forms, or at least their WPF counterparts, follows an entirely different concept than in Windows Forms. In WPF, you use an XML-based language called XAML (similar to HTML) for describing web pages. There is a huge learning curve, especially if you are not familiar with the concept of markup languages, such as HTML, that describe page construction and layout.

- Windows Forms uses a time-tested designer. As of this writing, even the .NET Designer for Windows Forms applications is already five years old, and the earliest .NET designer was conceptually based on what already existed in Visual Basic 6.0. The WPF Designer has quite a bit of potential for improvement (to put it nicely), even in .NET 4.0; therefore, you should be prepared to type a lot of code directly into XAML for things that you would do interactively in the Windows Forms designer. Even though your initial exposure to the WPF designer in Visual Studio might amaze you, don't be surprised if you later find yourself uttering the occasional curse.

Note If you are planning to develop professional WPF applications, you won't be able to avoid a designer specifically intended for WPF called Microsoft Expression Blend, which is already in version 4.

Incomprehensibly, Expression Blend is not part of Visual Studio 2010—you have to purchase it separately. That increases the attractiveness of getting an MSDN subscription: the MSDN Professional Edition of this subscription includes Microsoft Visual Studio 2010 Professional as well as Expression Blend 4. Of course, you will also get access to all the operating systems, servers, and the most common development applications from Microsoft with that subscription. You can find out more about MSDN at *http://tinyurl.com/3a9dkm7*.

What's So New About WPF?

My good friend and colleague, Marcus, once told me that what he hates most about computer books is that they don't just get to the point and describe issues or problems in a step-by-step manner, using simple examples. (He was also referring directly to the rough draft of the text you are reading right now.) As he pointed out at that time, he was two pages into the chapter, and he still didn't have a clue how to draw a simple line on the screen with WPF; how hard could that be? Maybe he's right, but at the same time he obviously hasn't understood the very basics of WPF, because his question by itself already shows that he assumes that the WPF rendering engine works similarly to what he knows; for example, a line can become a rectangle, and a rectangle a button.

More Information To learn more about the concept of rendering, go to *http://tinyurl.com/34omj3v*.

Unfortunately, WPF is quite different. To understand how WPF works, you should know something about its development history. Why? I'll use a metaphor for simplicity; otherwise, you'd be the fellow with the washboard who sees a washing machine for the first time and asks why anyone would build something so totally un-ergonomic, where the washboard is on the inside of the drum and the user has to crawl inside to scrub the laundry.

My friend will get his simple example, but not without a little side excursion into the *History of Windows* and how its graphic elements have found their way onto the screen.

25 Years of Windows, 25 Years of Drawn Buttons

Windows applications have been around for more than 25 years. And let's be honest: Even though Windows 1.0 and 2.0 already existed, it wasn't until Windows 2.11, which was shipped bundled with Adobe Pagemaker, that Windows became widely known. Even then, its mainstream breakthrough didn't come until Windows 3.0, thanks to that version's new look and feel when using applications (see Figure 5-1). Since then the basic concept hasn't really changed fundamentally. That holds true for Windows 95, Windows NT, and even for Windows 2000, and Windows XP.

More Information For more detailed look at the early years of Windows, go to *http://www.winhistory.de/more/win1.htm*.

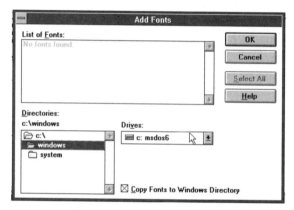

FIGURE 5-1 The dialog box for adding fonts in Windows 3.0.

One thing is certain: Windows has become a lot more stable over time, especially when it reached the Windows NT-based versions. Windows 95 and Windows NT 4.0 brought many new graphical elements that became even more colorful and modern with the advent of Windows XP, which was crowned with even more color gradients. But one thing hasn't changed since the first version of Windows: the manner in which the graphic finds its way onto the screen.

For 99 percent of all programs, this happens with the help of the Windows *Graphics Device Interface* (GDI). This *Application Programming Interface* (API) contains functions for two-dimensional drawing (drawing lines, rectangles, and circles, as well as various brush sizes, forms and patterns) that are supported by graphic cards. *Graphic Card Support* means that graphic card drivers don't need to convert certain commands (for example for drawing a line) themselves, which entails a costly use of algorithms and processor time; instead, these commands are passed directly to the graphic card processor so that the graphic card draws the line by itself—and of course much, much faster than the processor in your computer could ever do it. The example that follows serves as a reminder of how this used to look in practice.

> **Companion Content** Open the solution SimpleSampleGDIPlus.sln, which you can find in the \VB 2008 Developer Handbook\Chapter 05\SimpleSampleGDIPlus folder.

Figure 5-2 is only of marginal interest right now. But it's worth exploring *how* such lines end up on the screen, and how Windows ensures that they stay there as long as they're needed.

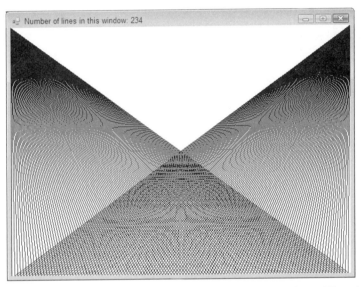

FIGURE 5-2 The result after double-clicking in a window—the fanned lines show the much dreaded Moiré[1] effect.

---

[1] You can find more about the Moiré effect at *http://tinyurl.com/bt6zjf.*

Here's a small code sample that draws these lines in the window upon a mouse double-click:

```
Public Class Form1

    Private myDoubleClicked As Boolean

    'Overwrite OnLoad - handle Load load result with it, ...
    Protected Overrides Sub OnLoad(ByVal e As System.EventArgs)
        MyBase.OnLoad(e)
        '...and insert window text.
        Me.Text = "Double-click in the window to show the graphic."
    End Sub

    'We could have also handled the Load result...
    Private Sub Form1_Load(ByVal sender As Object, ByVal e As System.EventArgs) _
            Handles Me.Load
        'but why handle an instance result in the instance,
        'which triggers the result? Better to interfere at the position,
        'which triggers the result, and that is OnLoad.
    End Sub
    'Graphic is drawn into the window as soon as the user double-clicks.
    Protected Overrides Sub OnDoubleClick(ByVal e As System.EventArgs)
        MyBase.OnDoubleClick(e)
        Dim g As Graphics = Graphics.FromHwnd(Me.Handle)
        DrawDemo(g)
        myDoubleClicked = True
    End Sub

    'And draw here.
    Public Sub DrawDemo(ByVal g As Graphics)

        'First delete the window content.
        g.Clear(Color.White)

        'Determine and remember actual width of client scope
        Dim actualWidthRemembered = Me.ClientSize.Width
        Dim lineCounter = 0

        'Take every 5th pixel into account
        For x = 0 To actualWidthRemembered Step 5

            'First draw the line from top left to bottom right.
            g.DrawLine(Pens.Black, 0, 0, x, Me.ClientSize.Height)

            'Then another one from top right to bottom left.
            g.DrawLine(Pens.Black, actualWidthRemembered, _
                        0, actualWidthRemembered - x, _
                        Me.ClientSize.Height)
```

```
            'Update line counter
            lineCounter += 2
        Next

        'Display number of drawn lines in window title.
        Me.Text = "Number of lines in the window: " & lineCounter
    End Sub
End Class
```

When drawing objects in GDI and GDI+ (more about GDI+ later), you should keep in mind that they are highly volatile. If you don't ensure that the window content is restored after it has been destroyed (because something else has been moved over the window, or because someone has resized the window) the content disappears, as shown in Figure 5-3. To create that figure, the window size was first increased by a few pixels horizontally and vertically, and then the Windows Calculator was moved over the window.

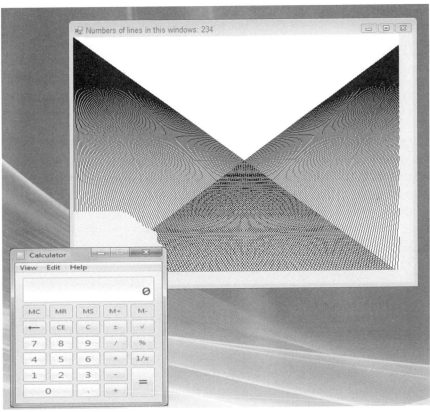

FIGURE 5-3 To avoid the effects shown here in GDI and GDI+, the developer must take care to restore the window content when it is enlarged or covered.

> **Note** Beginning with Windows Vista, you need to turn off the Aero display to reproduce the original behavior of the GDI. In Windows Vista and Windows 7, every application is assigned a dedicated video storage space so that application windows do not overlap in video storage, so you no longer see the behavior demonstrated in Figure 5-3. That's also why Vista seems to react more slowly than Windows 7. Simply put, access to GDI functions in Windows 7 is better optimized and the various windows can't influence each other much. In addition, Vista GDI operations are not hardware-supported, but as of Windows 7, they are supported again. In Windows Vista, applications can hinder each other when accessing the GDI, and therefore, the interface doesn't seem as fluent as in Windows 7. Pure application performance, however, is often faster in Windows Vista than in Windows 7; conversely, the screen display of GDI operations is faster in Windows 7, because those operations are supported by the hardware.

To ensure that issues such as that illustrated in Figure 5-3 don't happen, developers must take charge manually: the *Paint* event, triggered when something is moved in front of the window—thus requiring that area of the window to be redrawn when the window comes back into view—is used to let the application know that the window content needs to be updated. Thus, adding the following lines fixes the artifacts in the first example:

```
'Is triggered when the window content is destroyed
'and needs to be redrawn
Protected Overrides Sub OnPaint(ByVal e As System.Windows.Forms.PaintEventArgs)
    MyBase.OnPaint(e)

    'Only after double-clicking.
    If myDoubleClicked Then
        '
        DrawDemo(e.Graphics)
    End If
End Sub
```

In some cases, you also need to handle the *Resize* event, which fires when the window's size changes.

This basic principle for displaying document content in Windows Forms has been in place since the first version of Windows. That's true not only for graphics, but for everything. And at the same time, it in fact is true only for graphics, which are displayed in windows, because many people don't know why Windows is called Windows. Why? Because not only document contents of any kind are displayed in windows, which are recognized as such, but almost every element in Windows, with few exceptions, is a window. A button is a window. A list box is a window. An open combo box is made up of two windows. A text box is a window, and the text it contains is a window. Strictly speaking, even a ToolTip or the speech bubble from the notification area is a window—and all the classes that represent those windows must ensure that they redraw their content as soon as it has been destroyed by any overlapping window. As far as the hardware is concerned, the graphic card helps only in the following ways:

- It copies picture blocks at extremely high speed.

- It draws baseline figures, such as lines, rectangles, and ovals, and fills them with content. Unfortunately, it does this only when the native character commands of the operating system (GDI commands) are used. The .NET graphic commands are converted by a more modern graphic library, GDI+. Unfortunately, that library doesn't provide corresponding hardware support on many graphic cards. So even though it offers much more convenient graphic operations, they are *considerably* slower than their GDI equivalents.

> **Note** There are two exceptions when rendering text in .NET: the *TextRenderer* which is actually the only direct graphic object that uses GDI, and the *ControlPaint* class in the *System.Windows. Forms* namespace for drawing certain UI elements. Some of the static methods use GDI (for example, *DrawReversibleFrame* for inverse drawing of a frame or *DrawReversibleLine* for inverse drawing of a line).

Games and Protagonists

For many years, graphic cards have been able to do a lot more than just boring old rendering. The DirectX library has been around since Windows 95, and I'm sure the older developers among us can remember the original first-person-shooter game *Wolfenstein 3D* (from id Software), which had a highly controversial subject, but nevertheless demonstrated the capabilities of an office computer of the early 1990s when it came to games, and therefore when it came to graphics and sound. Back then, the fundamental problem was that such an extremely high performance required the application to run completely alone, without troublesome "competition" from other applications. And that was possible only in MS-DOS, even though Windows 3.11 already existed as a quasi-multitasking operating system. DirectX eventually fulfilled the requirements (Windows 95 had been launched in the meantime) that made a multitasking operating system possible. Again it was the company id Software that ushered in a DirectX revolution by porting the computer game *Doom* to Windows 95 with DirectX version 3.0. Enough game developers regarded that version of DirectX as a true multimedia alternative to the standalone concept of MS-DOS for it to become widely accepted.

Gamers in particular witnessed the evolution of breathtaking user interfaces for their beloved games during that time, which were surpassed only by three-dimensional virtual reality AI systems in science fiction movies. Let's be honest: which Windows user back then didn't consider the movie *Disclosure* with Michael Douglas and Demi Moore a special UI treat—albeit with the bitter aftertaste of knowing that 45 minutes later you had to be back in the real world at your many-years-old and therefore rather boring Windows NT 4.0 SP4a user interface.

For Windows users, the situation remained mostly static for approximately the next 10 years. During that time, many users (I'm sure not just developers) began to crave at least a small move in the direction of game UIs. But through Windows 2000 and its numerous Service Packs; through Windows XP and its unfortunately not-so-numerous Service Packs, Windows continued to disappoint us in that regard. But then Windows Vista and the .NET Framework 3.0 arrived.

With Windows Vista, a new graphic system was finally introduced, which permitted display-ing certain items with the help of a function library based on DirectX—and that was WPF. WPF-based applications run most smoothly and with the most hardware-support since Windows Vista. With a special version of Windows XP, users get to enjoy WPF-based applica-tions as well, but not in the same display perfection as in Windows Vista.

At the time of this writing, the multimedia developer community has arrived at version 11 of DirectX, which contains the newest and most elaborate multimedia function libraries yet. And if you've been watching the development of Windows Vista, you know that DirectX is exclu-sively reserved for Vista and Windows 7 users and developers as of Version 10, and you're probably also aware of how hard it was to create stable NVIDIA and ATI graphic card drivers for complete DirectX 10 support.

Theoretically, as developers we were able to create demanding applications with WPF (which, by the way, originated based on DirectX 9) since .NET Framework 3.0 or Windows Vista, as the case may be. The emphasis here is on *theoretically*, because there was one small problem: at that time no truly functional tool was available to make such programming possible in the real world. Sure, a quickly assembled addition to Visual Studio 2005 was available for learning and baby steps, but nothing at all for real-world WPF application development.

Narrating all these events from recent WPF history has laid a foundation so that you can really get going with WPF in Windows Vista SP1 and Visual Studio 2008 SP1 or .NET Framework 3.5 SP1.

Well, maybe not quite yet.

Keeping in mind that the concept of how graphics find their way onto the screen with GDI or GDI+ and what developers need to do to ensure graphics stay persistent (or at least seem that way), we now have the background to provide the ever-patient Marcus with a demon-stration that will show on one hand how WPF draws lines, and why, on the other hand, draw-ing lines with WPF—as we know it from GDI—must not be what this is about.

Companion Content Open the solution SimpleSampleWPF solution.sln, which you can find in the \VB 2010 Developer Handbook\Chapter 05\SimpleSampleWPF folder.

At first glance, drawing the lines in WPF doesn't look very different from the GDI+ version you saw earlier, as is demonstrated in Figure 5-4. However, the lines are cleaner, and unlike GDI+, drawing in Vista is more orderly with less flicker, so subjectively, it seems a little faster.

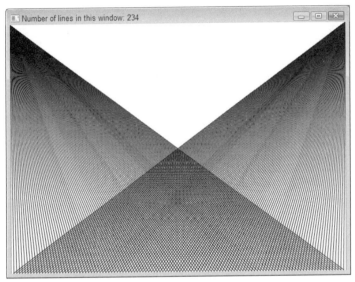

FIGURE 5-4 The WPF version of the line magic initially looks very similar to the GDI version.

You can already discover the first basic differences when you drag another window on top of this one, as discussed in connection with Figure 5-3. Nothing becomes lost anymore when you overlap it with another window, even though in the WPF example, the actual drawing process takes place in the window's *SizeChanged* event. Therefore, the redrawing of the content during resize is already taken care for us, as shown in the following code example:

```
Imports System.Windows.Media.Animation

Class Window1

    Private Sub Window1_SizeChanged(ByVal sender As Object, ByVal e As
    System.Windows.SizeChangedEventArgs) Handles Me.SizeChanged
        'myCanvas comes from the XAML definition
        'where we have removed the default grid
        'and replaced it with the canvas.
]
        myCanvas.Children.Clear()

        'Determine and remember actual canvas width
        Dim actualCanvasWidthRemembered = myCanvas.ActualWidth
        Dim lineCounter = 0

        'Take each 5th pixel into account
        For x = 0 To actualCanvasWidthRemembered Step 5
```

```
                        'Create new line object and set parameters
                        Dim aLine As New Line()
                        'Set parameter accordingly
                        aLine.Stroke = Brushes.Black
                        aLine.X1 = 0
                        aLine.Y1 = 0
                        aLine.X2 = x
                        aLine.Y2 = myCanvas.ActualHeight
                        aLine.HorizontalAlignment = HorizontalAlignment.Left
                        aLine.VerticalAlignment = VerticalAlignment.Center
                        aLine.StrokeThickness = 1
                        'Add to canvas
                        myCanvas.Children.Add(aLine)

                        'Define the other line
                        aLine = New Line()
                        'Set parameter accordingly again
                        aLine.Stroke = Brushes.Black
                        aLine.X1 = actualWidthRemembered
                        aLine.Y1 = 0
                        aLine.X2 = actualWidthRemembered - x
                        aLine.Y2 = myCanvas.ActualHeight
                        aLine.HorizontalAlignment = HorizontalAlignment.Left
                        aLine.VerticalAlignment = VerticalAlignment.Center
                        aLine.StrokeThickness = 1
                        'Add to canvas
                        myCanvas.Children.Add(eineLinie)

                        'Update line counter
                        lineCounter += 2
                Next

                Me.Title = "Number of lines in the window: " & lineCounter
            End Sub
            .
            .
            .
End Class
```

The fact is that unlike in GDI or GDI+, what you draw in a WPF window is persistent. This becomes clear when you double-click the graphic again. Notice that each individual line becomes animated and thus generates a very nice effect, as illustrated in Figure 5-5.

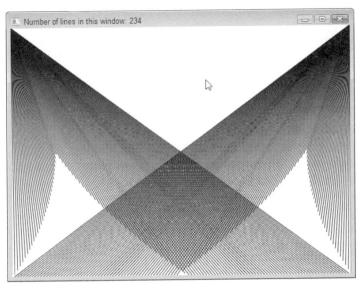

FIGURE 5-5 When you double-click the screen again, it looks very different, because it starts a simple animation process which affects each of the 234 lines in the window.

Maybe you can guess how much work it would take for GDI+ or GDI to make this animation as flicker-free as in our example. You would need to double-buffer and cache the display image, and you would have to cache the current lengths of the individual lines and control them yourself. Not so in WPF:

```
Private Sub Window1_MouseDoubleClick(ByVal sender As Object, _
     ByVal e As System.Windows.Input.MouseButtonEventArgs) Handles Me.MouseDoubleClick
        Dim count = 0

        'Of course it only works, because there
        'are lines on the canvas object.
        For Each lineItem As Line In myCanvas.Children
            'Y2 property is animated, thus the name.
            'The class DoubleAnimation animates properties
            'of the type Double.

            'Animate from the current line height
            'to half the line hight.
            Dim Y2Animation As New DoubleAnimation(lineItem.ActualHeight, _
                        lineItem.ActualHeight / 2, TimeSpan.FromSeconds(3))

            'Specifies that the animation becomes automatic,
            'after it has been run through completely once.
            Y2Animation.RepeatBehavior = RepeatBehavior.Forever

            'Specifies that DoubleAnimation counts up initially and
            'when AutoReverse=True it counts backwards.
            Y2Animation.AutoReverse = True
```

```
                'The animation for each following line begins delayed by
                '500 milliseconds after the previous one
                Y2Animation.BeginTime = New TimeSpan(500000 * count)

                'Start animation...
                lineItem.BeginAnimation(Line.HeightProperty, Y2Animation)
                count += 1
        Next
    End Sub
```

In WPF, each individual line isn't just a simple method that causes changes to occur in graphic memory; instead, its representation gives the impression of a drawn line. A line, as used in WPF, is an object derived from a class that already brings a huge amount of infrastructure with it. Not only does it make sure that an instance of that class renders and updates itself as needed, but it also inserts itself into an animation infrastructure, and therefore behaves like most of the other objects that WPF recognizes as a *visible entity*, (a so-called *visual*) and can control.

But you've really seen only the tip of the iceberg. A demonstration by David Teitlebaum shows what WPF is capable of since Service Pack 1 of .NET 3.5. You can watch it at *http://tinyurl.com/5kmpz7* (very impressive on Channel 9 [*http://channel9.msdn.com/*]), the number one developer's resource for what's going on in product and technology development at Microsoft. The site includes numerous screencasts, video interviews, blogs, forum discussions, and much, much more). You can also find the demonstration files on David Teitlebaum's blog; however, they are only available in C#.

How WPF Brings Designers and Developers Together

When designing and programming a user interface, design and logic were often mixed together. In a Windows Forms application, the look of a window is specified by using Visual Basic code in the method *InitializeComponent* in a class, which is derived from *System.Windows.Forms.Form*. A graphic designer usually isn't interested in program code. She uses certain tools to create beautiful and colorful graphics, but rarely writes code to change the look of a window or a control. On the other hand, despite efforts to create a purely visual programming environment, it's restrictive to implement the logical part of the application, for example, data access or number calculations, by using a visual tool.

Unfortunately, there are very few programmers who are also great designers. But you can also look at it the other way around: there are very few top designers who are also expert programmers.

At the application interface level, the two worlds collide, so it's important to build a bridge that's acceptable to both sides. On one side is the graphic designer with his tools who delivers something that a software developer on the other side combines with the application logic. At the same time the graphic designer shouldn't have to deal with much programming;

similarly, the developer should be able to get by without much knowledge of the tools used by designers. The goal is to enable top designers and top software developers to combine their expertise and create high-quality applications.

Here's a brief exercise that can help clarify this discussion. Let's start the old-fashioned way and write a WPF application with only Visual Basic code. Initially, we won't separate design and code. Of course, we'll be using yet another version of the well-known *Hello World!* program. So here we go:

1. Start Visual Studio 2010, and then select File | New |Project.

2. In the New Project dialog box, select Visual Basic as the programming language. In the large combo box, click Empty Project.

3. Use references to the following libraries: *System, WindowBase, PresentationFramework, System.Xaml*, and *PresentationCore*.

   To do this, in Solution Explorer, right-click the command Add Reference. Select the specified references on the context menu that appears, and then click OK to add them to the project.

4. In Solution Explorer, add a new Visual Basic class code file and name it **Hello.vb** (select Add | New Item from the menu).

5. Type in the following code segment:

```vb
Imports System
Imports System.Windows

Namespace Hello

    Public Class Hello
        Inherits System.Windows.Window

        <STAThread()> _
        Shared Sub main()
            Dim w As New Window With {.Title = "Hello World!", .Width = "200",
➥.Height = "200"}
            w.Show()

            Dim app As New Application
            app.Run()
        End Sub

    End Class
End Namespace
```

6. On the Application tab, in the project properties, set Windows Forms Application as the Application Type.

7. Run the program by clicking the command Start Without Debugging from the Debug menu.

When you run the program, you'll see a rather boring window with the words "Hello World!" in the title bar, as shown in Figure 5-6.

FIGURE 5-6 Your first WPF window.

Let's take a closer look at the code of this example. After inserting the required namespaces from the references, the code defines a namespace called *Hello*, which contains the class *Hello*. In WPF, the attribute *<STAThread()>* must be used before the static method to set the threading model for the application to "single-threaded apartment." This is a relic from the old *Component Object Model* (COM) days, but it takes care of compatibility with the COM world, if necessary.

The *Main* method first creates a *Window* object, which contains the text for the title line via the *Title* property. The *Show* method from the *Window* class handles the appearance of the window on the screen. If you omit the last two code lines in the *Main* method and run the program, the window is displayed only for a very brief moment, because the application shuts down immediately. This is where those last two lines come into play. The *Run* method on the newly created *Application* object creates a message loop for this main window. Now the little program can receive messages. The window stays visible until the message loop ends, such as when a user clicks the Close button in the upper-right corner of the window's title bar.

However, now we've put the designer out of work, because as software developers, we have implemented the design in the Visual Basic code. Actually, the design of this application consists of only one line:

```
Dim w As New Window With {.Title = "Hello World!", .Width = "200", .Height = "200"}
```

In this simple example, I'm calling everything else application logic. Because a designer doesn't want to work with Visual Basic code or other programming languages, we need to employ another "language" so that designers can "declare" user interfaces and graphics.

For that, WPF uses the Extensible Application Markup Language.

Extensible Application Markup Language

The Extensible Application Markup Language (XAML) is, like XML, a hierarchically oriented description language. With it, you can declare both user interface elements and graphics. Let's go back to our first example (Figure 5-6). This time we'll declare the designer part by using XAML. A note in advance: a designer wouldn't type in the XAML code manually, of course, as we'll be doing it in the example. Instead, he uses tools such as Expression Blend that turn their designs into XAML code. The following code sample shows the required XAML code for our first program:

```
<Window x:Class="Hello2.Window1"
    xmlns="http://schemas.microsoft.com/winfx/2006/xaml/presentation"
    xmlns:x="http://schemas.microsoft.com/winfx/2006/xaml"
    Title="Hello World!"
    Height="250"
    Width="250"
       >
  </Window>
```

The code here is clearly not overwhelming. These few lines of XAML code basically just declare a *Window* object, set the window's title to "Hello World!," and define the window size as 250 × 250 pixels. In essence, the code sets the properties *Title*, *Width*, and *Height* of the *Window* object to the desired values.

XAML is basically XML, so all properties in XAML take text values. Therefore, the values must be embedded in double quotes. To use the XAML code, you must declare two namespaces:

```
xmlns="http://schemas.microsoft.com/winfx/2006/xaml/presentation"
xmlns:x="http://schemas.microsoft.com/winfx/2006/xaml"
```

Visual Studio 2010 automatically inserts these namespaces into XAML files in your .NET Framework 4.0 projects.

This project was created with Visual Studio, which takes over the rest of the work. In the background, it creates another file that contains Visual Basic code and (among other things), creates an *Application* object and calls its associated *Run* method. The Visual Studio-generated code isn't important here. When you start the application, you see the same window as in the first example.

For the second example, the procedure with Visual Studio 2010 is as follows:

1. Start Visual Studio 2010, and then select File | New | Project.

2. In the New Project dialog box, select Visual Basic as the programming language.

3. In the large combo box, select WPF Application.

4. In Solution Explorer, open the XAML file named MainWindow.xaml.

5. Type in the same code as the last example, just change the Visual Studio-created code accordingly.

6. Run the program by clicking the command Start Without Debugging from the Debug menu.

Now, you have supplied the interface declaration with XAML. Let's return to the application logic. In the next example, you'll implement some minimal logic. For the user interface, you'll use XAML again, and for the logic you'll use Visual Basic.

The example shows how the user interface and application logic work together in a WPF application. To illustrate, you'll declare a button of a certain size in the middle of the window (see the following code). Assume that this is your user interface, created by a designer.

```
<Window x:Class="Hello3.Window1"
    xmlns="http://schemas.microsoft.com/winfx/2006/xaml/presentation"
    xmlns:x="http://schemas.microsoft.com/winfx/2006/xaml"
    Title="Hello 3" Height="200" Width="200">
    <Grid>
        <Button Click="OnClick" Width="120" Height="40" Margin="28,58,21,64"
                >Please click!</Button>
    </Grid>
</Window>
```

Within the declaration of the main window the code defines another WPF element: the button. In XAML, this element is called *Button*. Of course, the button has properties that you can set, such as the *Width* (here set to 120 units) and its *Height* (set to 40 units). "Please click!" is used for the button's text.

When a user clicks the button, the application should display some text. Can you guess which text? Of course, "Hello World!" This is the application logic that the software developer creates (see the next code sample). The connection between the *Button* element and the Visual Basic code is created with the help of an event. In XAML, the *Button* element exposes the *Click* event (see the previous code sample), which points to the event handler *OnClick*. This method now is implemented in Visual Basic.

This project was also created with Visual Studio 2010. At first, only the *System* and *System.Windows* namespaces are required. Visual Studio generates almost all the code shown in the following example. All you need to do is enter the *OnClick* method (highlighted in bold):

```
            Private Sub OnClick(ByVal sender As System.Object, _
                           ByVal e As System.Windows.RoutedEventArgs)
            MessageBox.Show("Hello World!")

                ' After the Messagebox: change button
                With btn
                    .Content = "Good morning!"
                    .FontSize = 20
                    .Foreground = Brushes.Red
                End With


            End Sub
        End Class
    End Namespace
```

Figure 5-8 shows the window after the *OnClick* event method has executed. The button property has been changed after the OK button was clicked in the *MessageBox* element.

FIGURE 5-8 The window display after calling *MessageBox.Show*.

Now we can use XAML and code "in both directions." We use events to call the application logic from XAML. A large number of events are fired by the various WPF elements. We then implement event handler methods that contain the application logic. Alternatively, to work the other way around, changing the WPF elements that were declared in XAML at runtime, we use the common object model of these elements to call the properties and methods from the program code. Each object can be identified by its name. The property values declared in XAML are therefore the *initial* settings for displaying the WPF elements.

As mentioned previously, the XAML declaration of the user interface represents the initial state of the application. However, if necessary, you can change the start values even before the application becomes visible from within our code by implementing a method to handle the *Loaded* event, as shown in the two code samples that follow.

For the main window with the class name *Window1*, the *Loaded* event is bound to the method *OnLoaded*. The code implemented in the corresponding Visual Basic method is executed directly after the constructor call for *Window1*. Now, when the window is displayed on the screen, it already contains the enlarged button because the properties *Width* and *Height* in the *OnLoaded* method have been changed appropriately. If a user clicks the button, the application still calls the *OnClick* event handler and executes the code in it (see Figure 5-9). First, the XAML code:

```
<Window x:Class="Hello5.Window1"
    xmlns="http://schemas.microsoft.com/winfx/2006/xaml/presentation"
    xmlns:x="http://schemas.microsoft.com/winfx/2006/xaml"
    Title="Hello 5" Height="300" Width="300"
    Loaded="OnLoaded">
        <Button Name="btn" Click="OnClick" Width="120" Height="40"
                Margin="34,61,24,61">Please click!</Button>
</Window>
```

And the Visual Basic code:

```
Imports System
Imports System.Windows

Namespace Hello5
    Partial Public Class Window1
        Inherits System.Windows.Window

        Public Sub New()
            InitializeComponent()
        End Sub

        Private Sub OnClick(ByVal sender As System.Object, _
                        ByVal e As System.Windows.RoutedEventArgs)
            MessageBox.Show("Hallo Welt!")

            ' After the Messagebox: change button
            With btn
                .Content = "Good morning!"
                .FontSize = 20
                .Foreground = Brushes.Red
            End With
        End Sub

        Private Sub OnLoaded(ByVal sender As System.Object, _
                        ByVal e As System.Windows.RoutedEventArgs)
            btn.Height = 80
            btn.Width = 150
        End Sub
    End Class
End Namespace
```

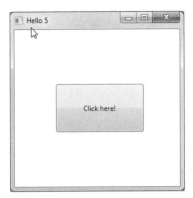

FIGURE 5-9 The window looks like this following execution of the *OnLoaded* method.

> **Important** Everything that can be specified and declared in XAML can also be created in Visual Basic via program code. However, that statement doesn't work in reverse. In other words, not everything that you can do in program code can be specified and declared in XAML.

We can now change the design of the last sample application without modifying the application code. So let's get a little crazy and display the button in a skewed form (let's try it with angled sides). To do that, you need a *transformation*. For now, just use the XAML code to perform the transformation, as shown in the following code sample:

```
<Window x:Class="Hello5a.Window1"
    xmlns="http://schemas.microsoft.com/winfx/2006/xaml/presentation"
    xmlns:x="http://schemas.microsoft.com/winfx/2006/xaml"
    Title="Hello 5a" Height="300" Width="300"
    Loaded="OnLoaded">
        <Button Name="btn" Click="OnClick" Width="120" Height="40" Margin="34,61,24,61">
            Please click!
            <Button.RenderTransform>
                <SkewTransform AngleX="10" />
            </Button.RenderTransform>
        </Button>
</Window>
```

The logic implemented in Visual Basic (the event methods *OnLoaded* and *OnClick*) remains unchanged for this example. The code of the last example is still used to react to the *Click* event. When this program starts, you see a skewed button (see Figure 5-10, left), but the functionality behind the button has not changed. Clicking it triggers the method *MessageBox. Show*, and later the properties of the now-skewed button are changed as before (Figure 5-10, right).

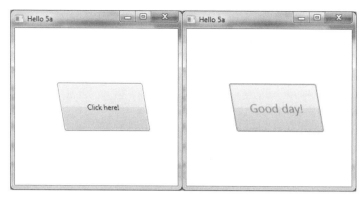

FIGURE 5-10 The application with a modified button design.

What is evident here is that this application has clearly achieved a clean separation between design and logic. The software developer can change the application logic without accidentally modifying the design. Conversely, the designer can change the appearance of the application without having to deal with program code.

Note Today's WPF and Microsoft Silverlight applications often take the degree of separation between design and coding even further: when using the fundamental knowledge of object-oriented programming for developing of large business applications, you would probably use a technique called *MVVM* (Model View ViewModel). This book focuses on how to learn everything you need to learn and use MVVM—but it does not cover MVVM itself—that topic is out of scope for this book; however, a good starting point for more information is *http://en.wikipedia.org/wiki/MVVM*). For an additional learning resource, you can read *Building Enterprise Applications with Windows® Presentation Foundation and the Model View ViewModel Pattern* (2011, Microsoft Press; ISBN: 978-0-735-65092-3) by Raffaele Garofalo.

Event Handling in WPF and Visual Basic

I'd like to elaborate a bit more on the binding of event handling in WPF applications. When developing Windows Forms applications in Visual Studio, Visual Basic developers are used to binding event procedures by double-clicking the appropriate control—Chapter 4, "Introduction to Windows Forms—Designers and Code Editor by Example," shows how this works. In principle, this is possible in WPF applications with the designer, as well. In both cases, Visual Basic inserts the event routine body with an appropriate name, which automatically contains the correct signature for handling the event. The keyword *Handles* instructs the Visual Basic compiler that it must create the infrastructure for adding the event delegate to the *Form* class (or *Window* class in WPF).

WPF applications offer an additional possibility that you should always prefer during development: specifying which event procedure should be called for a specific event within the XAML code itself. Doing that works just as simply as double-clicking a control (see Figure 5-11).

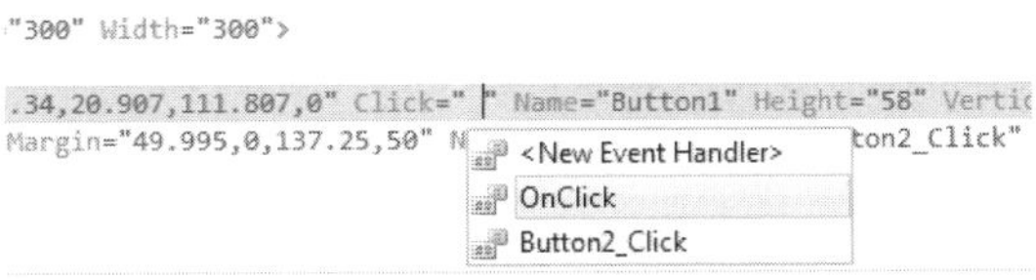

FIGURE 5-11 In WPF, you can wire up event procedures in Visual Basic programs via XAML code, which is a little different than you are used to with Windows Forms applications.

You can write the event name directly into the XAML element definition; IntelliSense then helps you to either link the result with an existing method (which of course must have the appropriate event signature) or to insert the body of a new event handling routine. To do the latter, you would simply select the first entry, <New Event Handler>, in the IntelliSense object list.

XAML Syntax Overview

This section contains a brief overview of XAML syntax. The XAML code will also be compared to regular Visual Basic code. Many of you probably have prior experience with XML; nevertheless, for those who don't, we'll explain the XAML syntax with the help of a few examples.

An XAML hierarchy always starts with the root element, a *Window* or *Page* element. The required XML namespaces are defined there.

Next, it declares the user interface hierarchy. All elements that can be used in XAML exist as normal classes in the .NET Framework 4.0. As a programmer, you know that a class can contain properties, methods, and events, among other elements. Let's see how this works in XAML:

```
<Button Name="btnClear" Width="80" Height="25" Click="OnClear">Delete</Button>
```

The preceding XAML line declares an element of the type *Button* with the name *btnClear*. At runtime the .NET Framework generates an object of type *Button*. The properties *Width* and *Height* are specified, and the *Click* event is bound to the event handler *OnClear*. The text on the button is set by using the default property for the *Button* element. You could achieve the same result with the following Visual Basic code:

```
Dim btnClear As New Button
btnClear.Width = 80
btnClear.Height = 25
btnClear.Content = "Delete"
AddHandler btnClear.Click, AddressOf OnClear
Me.Content = btnClear
```

Due to the WPF content model, you need the last Visual Basic line to add the button as content into the parent element (*Me* being the Window element, in this case). In XAML, that's taken care of by the declaration hierarchy:

```
<Window ...
  Width="300" Height="300">
  <!-The following button is the window content -->
  <Button Click="OnClear">Test</Button>
</Window>
```

The *OnClear* event method is implemented in Visual Basic code, and it normally has the following signature:

```
        Public Sub OnClear(ByVal sender As System.Object, _
                       ByVal e As System.Windows.RoutedEventArgs)
```

When you need to access the properties of the parent element, you use a concept called *attached properties*, as illustrated below:

```
<Grid>
...
  <Button Grid.Row="0" Grid.Column="0">Button 1</Button>
  <Button Grid.Row="1" Grid.Column="0">Button 2</Button>
</Grid>
```

In the preceding code, the properties *Row* and *Column* of the outer *Grid* element are accessible as attached properties in the *Button* declaration (you'll see more about *Grids*, later).

You will often declare elements in XAML without using their location property. In this case, you can use an abbreviated form. So, instead of using

```
<TextBox Name="text" Width="100"></TextBox>
```

you can write:

```
<TextBox Name="text" Width="100" />
```

Frequently, you need to assign not just a number or text, but a complex element (which itself has one or more properties) to a property. As an example, we will assign an element of the type *RotateTransform* to the property *RenderTransform* of a *Button*. For this element the properties *Angle*, *CenterX*, and *CenterY* must be set:

```
<Button Name="btnClear" Width="80" Height="25" Click="OnClear">
  Delete
  <Button.RenderTransform>
    <RotateTransform Angle="25" CenterX="40" CenterY="12.5" />
  </Button.RenderTransform>
</Button>
```

First, several properties (*Name*, *Width*, and so on) are set "directly" for the button itself. The *Button* class provides the property *RenderTransform*, to which the *RotateTransform* object is assigned. Therefore, the *RotateTransform* element is declared within the hierarchy, and the properties *Angle*, *CenterX*, and *CenterY* are specified. The corresponding Visual Basic code appears as follows:

```
' Generate Button element
Dim btnClear As New Button
btnClear.Width = 80
btnClear.Height = 25
btnClear.Content = "Delete"
AddHandler btnClear.Click, AddressOf OnClear

' Generate rotation
Dim rot As New RotateTransform
rot.Angle = 25
rot.CenterX = 40
rot.CenterY = 12.5

' Assign rotation to button
btnClear.RenderTransform = rot
Me.Content = btnClear
```

These hierarchies can be nested as deeply as desired. As the previous example shows, the definition of hierarchies in XAML is usually much easier and more transparent than in regular programming languages.

WPF objects often have properties that can be assigned several elements of a type. For example, you can insert several *ListBoxItem* elements into a *ListBox*:

```
<ListBox>
  <ListBox.Items>
    <ListBoxItem>Test1</ListBoxItem>
    <ListBoxItem>Test2</ListBoxItem>
    <ListBoxItem>Test3</ListBoxItem>
  </ListBox.Items>
</ListBox>
```

The three *ListBoxItem* elements are placed into a *Collection* object and assigned to the *ListBox* property *Items*. There is an easier way to write this, as shown here:

```
<ListBox>
  <ListBoxItem>Test1</ListBoxItem>
  <ListBoxItem>Test2</ListBoxItem>
  <ListBoxItem>Test3</ListBoxItem>
</ListBox>
```

For comparison, look at the following corresponding Visual Basic code for generating the *ListBox*:

```
Dim lb As New ListBox
Dim item As New ListBoxItem
item.Content = "Test1"
lb.Items.Add(item)
```

```
item = New ListBoxItem
item.Content = "Test2"
lb.Items.Add(item)
item = New ListBoxItem
item.Content = "Test3"
lb.Items.Add(item)
Me.Content = lb
```

With XAML, you can declare and assign entire object lists very easily. The following example initializes a *MeshGeometry3D* element with data:

```
<MeshGeometry3D Positions="0,0,0 5,0,0 0,0,5"
                TriangleIndices="0 2 1"
                Normals="0,1,0 0,1,0 0,1,0" />
```

In the example, the property *Positions* is initialized with three elements of type *Point3D*. Each *Point3D* element is itself initialized with three comma-separated *Double* numbers. The property *Normals* is specified similarly. There are only three numbers for the property *TriangleIndices*, which are simply added. The corresponding Visual Basic code looks like this:

```
Dim mesh As New MeshGeometry3D
mesh.Positions.Add(New Point3D(0.0, 0.0, 0.0))
mesh.Positions.Add(New Point3D(5.0, 0.0, 0.0))
mesh.Positions.Add(New Point3D(0.0, 0.0, 5.0))
mesh.TriangleIndices.Add(0)
mesh.TriangleIndices.Add(2)
 mesh.TriangleIndices.Add(1)
 mesh.Normals.Add(New Vector3D(0.0, 1.0, 0.0))
 mesh.Normals.Add(New Vector3D(0.0, 1.0, 0.0))
 mesh.Normals.Add(New Vector3D(0.0, 1.0, 0.0))
```

In the preceding example, for the properties *Positions*, *TriangleIndices*, and *Normals* of the *MeshGeometry3D* class, there is always one *Add* method, which handles the data from the XAML entries correctly and adds them.

With these few examples, you have learned the rudiments of the most important syntax elements of XAML, and these limited examples should be sufficient for you to read and understand the XAML hierarchies in this book. With a bit of practice you'll soon be able to create your own code using XAML.

> **Note** Remember that in the future, you won't enter these XAML hierarchies manually; they'll be generated by visual tools (not necessarily by the built-in WPF Designer—but Microsoft does provide additional tools, which you can find out about at *http://www.microsoft.com/expression/*).

ImageResizer—a Practical WPF Example

As in Chapter 4, we'll stick to our motto here, as well: the best way to learn about new thematic blocks and features of Visual Studio is to implement a non-trivial sample application. To demonstrate the basics of WPF and the corresponding tools, we came up with something really cool—well, at least we think so—which not only represents a typical example, but also gives you something that you can use later on a daily basis (some of you anyway).

It all starts with curiosity—one of the strongest human motivators, which, since the appearance of social networks, has sparked a lot of excitement. If I want to show my vacation pictures to my envious colleagues at home on the same day that I take them, doing so no longer presents a technical problem. There are countless possibilities for distributing the pictures via the Internet, but they are all hiding one problem: thanks to the resolution of millions of modern camera pixels, pictures are extremely sharp, but that sharpness is reflected in the size of the files. And that file size problem is the basis for the project idea in this chapter.

This chapter provides you with a quick, effortless, and above all practical introduction to WPF application development. If you have been programming with Windows Forms and similar technologies, this chapter will help you apply your knowledge to a new style of application development and open the door to a completely new world view.

You will find out how to save time by avoiding the work of reducing picture sizes manually, and still make your colleagues envious (which is ultimately the goal, right?). The result, the *ImageResizer* (see Figure 5-12), is a WPF-based project that lets you adjust the format and size of pictures by using your computer's resources effectively and with minimal user effort.

FIGURE 5-12 The user interface of the *ImageResizer* program.

1. Start Visual Studio (if you haven't done so already).

2. On the Start Page, click the New Project link, and then select the type WPF Application.

3. Give the project the name **ImageResizer**, as shown in Figure 5-13, and then confirm by clicking OK.

FIGURE 5-13 Setting up a new project on the Start page.

By default, Visual Studio adds two new files to a new WPF project: *MainWindow* and *Application*. *MainWindow* represents a class file that contains the code for the default window of the WPF application. Here's where most of your program logic will take place. You can, of course, add more project files of this type to your project. This data type may contain XAML code as well as program code (in a code-behind file).

The *Application* file contains global project settings, including such things as the appearance of a button, but also methods that, among other things, handle the starting and ending of the application—basically anything that affects the entire application. This project type can also contain XAML code as well as a code-behind file.

Visual Studio initially opens the window *MainWindow* in Design view so you can edit the application's user interface. Design view shows both the designer and the code, just like when you're designing a website in most HTML applications. Figure 5-14 illustrates how the bottom pane contains the HTML code and the top pane contains the design, which shows the page as it would be rendered by the browser. The language for WPF is XAML, so the Visual Studio designer shows XAML in the bottom pane and shows how the window looks at runtime in the designer. How the window looks is determined by tags, their nesting, and order.

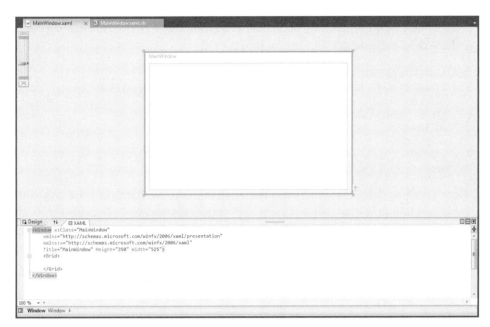

FIGURE 5-14 The WPF window in Design mode.

The code in Figure 5-14 can be translated as follows, starting with the *Window* tag:

```
<Window x:Class="MainWindow">...</Window>
```

The tags *<Window>...</Window>* define a WPF window with the name *MainWindow*. Everything that's defined between these tags belongs to the window, as shown here:

```
<Window x:Class="MainWindow"
        Title="MainWindow" Height="350" Width="525">

</Window>
```

In the preceding example, three properties are set: the window *Title* (which is initially *MainWindow*), the *Height* (350 pixels) and the *Width* (525 pixels).

The following two lines of code represent the schema for the XAML that determines the appearance of the window. The lines register two namespaces that define all WPF objects. Remember this principle, because you can use it later to access your own controls in XAML code.

```
xmlns="http://schemas.microsoft.com/winfx/2006/xaml/presentation"
xmlns:x="http://schemas.microsoft.com/winfx/2006/xaml"
```

Register the assembly in which your program runs, and give it a prefix under which it can be reached, for example:

```
xmlns:loc="clr-namespace:ImageResizer"
```

Now all assembly elements are accessible in the window with *<loc:NameDesElements>* *</loc:NameDesElements>* and can be thus bound.

```
<Window x:Class="MainWindow"
    xmlns="http://schemas.microsoft.com/winfx/2006/xaml/presentation"
    xmlns:x="http://schemas.microsoft.com/winfx/2006/xaml"
    Title="MainWindow" Height="350" Width="525">
    <Grid>

    </Grid>
</Window>
```

Notice that, by default, a WPF *Grid* is nested in the window. The *Grid* is the only content of a top-level window. This is one of the major differences between Windows Forms and WPF: in Windows Forms you can put as many controls as you like directly on a form (which is the equivalent of a window in WPF), but that doesn't work in WPF with a window. Each window can contain only *one* control, and, ninety percent of the time, the window content in WPF is a *Grid*. The WPF *Grid* is essentially the equivalent of an HTML table (*<table></table>*); it divides a space into rows and columns, and it can, unlike the window, hold multiple child elements.

> **Note** Basically, there are only two kinds of controls in WPF: those that can contain content (for instance, another control), which have a *Content* property, and those that are *containers*, which nest other controls and arrange them in a certain way. Containers themselves do not have a visual representation. There is no such separation in Windows Forms, where each control may also function as a container (just like the form itself). This takes some getting used to when developing in WPF.
>
> You can see this yourself. Delete the *Grid* in the window and drag a button from the Toolbox into the window. Run the program. That works. But if you add another button and try again, the process fails—the designer refuses to let you arrange the second button. After all, the window is a *Content* control, which means it can contain only one control. If you want the window to contain multiple controls, then the window's single control *must* be a container control, and by default, a *Grid* control is a container control. It has the most flexible layout options.

What you've learned so far about WPF provides a solid theoretical base. But before you put any of it into practice, try to figure out how you'd like your interface to look. Don't underestimate this step. It will save you a lot of work later when designing the interface in WPF.

You should consider questions such as:

- What information does the program need, and which controls should be used to display that information?
  - ○ Picture/folder paths must be entered into the program:

    TextBox, Button
  - ○ The output folder must be entered into the program:

    TextBox, Button
  - ○ Entering a postfix:

    TextBox
  - ○ Users must select a file type:

    ComboBox
  - ○ A graphic resolution must be entered into the program:

    TextBox
  - ○ Start the process:

    Button
- What controls do I need to display information to users?
  - ○ Labels for each *TextBox*:

    Label
  - ○ List of all selected pictures

    ListBox
- What additional controls, such as titles, progress bars, and so on, do I need?
  - ○ Title of the window

    TextBlock
  - ○ Progress bar for the status and display of the current picture

    StatusBar, ProgressBar, TextBlock
- How should the controls behave when a user enlarges the window?
  - ○ The title and the *StatusBar* stay static. The size of input fields should not increase, but the file name list should increase proportionally. The *ListBox* should expand dynamically.
- How do I arrange controls sensibly so that they won't be misunderstood?

For this last step you should picture what your ideas should look like in practice. It's best to do this with pen and paper. Draw your window as you think it should look when it's finished, and then think about how to achieve that design with WPF; for example, you might consider a *Grid*, which permits you to define rows and columns.

Figure 5-15 shows a design suggestion for dividing the *ImageResizer* interface that you should try to follow.

FIGURE 5-15 A proposed user interface design for the *ImageResizer* application.

Figure 5-16 shows a possible interface divided into 6 rows and 5 columns.

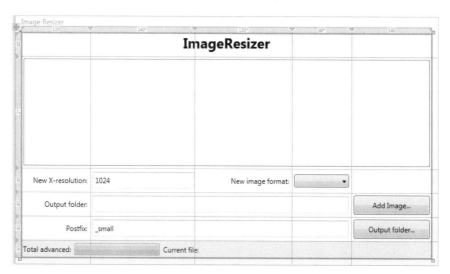

FIGURE 5-16 Dividing the interface into rows and columns.

There are generally two possibilities for implementing an interface in WPF: either with the Designer or through code. In my view, the best option is to define as much as possible in code, because that way, you can ensure that the code is clean, maintainable, and understandable, and thus can be debugged easily later on. In the beginning, this can take a bit of effort, but in the end, it might save you time. Creating a complicated nested interface in the Designer can lead to unwanted results at runtime and leave you searching the Designer-generated code for its cause. A Designer is universal and can implement your ideas to a certain extent, but not necessarily in the most convenient way. Nevertheless, a Designer can take care of tedious typing, for example, when defining the rows and columns of the *Grid*.

Defining Grid Columns and Rows for Arranging Controls

The following procedure describes how to set up your grid columns and rows and prepare them to contain the controls in your design.

1. In the Design view of the Visual Studio *MainWindow*, click the window and enlarge it to your preferred size by using the small blue rectangle in the lower-right corner, as shown in Figure 5-17.

FIGURE 5-17 Enlarge the Design window to your desired size.

2. Click the grid inside the window and move the mouse pointer along its blue frame.

   A line is displayed for defining a row (along the left border) or column (along the top border). As depicted in Figure 5-18, move the pointer to the desired spot to determine the correct dimensions of a row or column, and then click at that point to create that row or column.

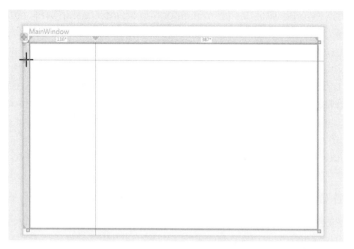

FIGURE 5-18 Dividing the grid in the Designer into rows and columns.

3. Continue this procedure until your window is divided similar to that shown in Figure 5-19.

FIGURE 5-19 The grid after division into rows and columns.

A quick look tells you that the first column is too big and the last one a little too small. You can now fine tune the division easily and quickly in the XAML code. The WPF Designer has already produced some XAML code, as shown in the following:

```
<Grid>
        <Grid.RowDefinitions>
            <RowDefinition Height="45*" />
            <RowDefinition Height="163*" />
            <RowDefinition Height="54*" />
            <RowDefinition Height="57*" />
            <RowDefinition Height="55*" />
            <RowDefinition Height="41*" />
        </Grid.RowDefinitions>
        <Grid.ColumnDefinitions>
            <ColumnDefinition Width="164*" />
            <ColumnDefinition Width="156*" />
            <ColumnDefinition Width="157*" />
            <ColumnDefinition Width="90*" />
            <ColumnDefinition Width="142*" />
        </Grid.ColumnDefinitions>
    </Grid>
```

The * (asterisk) character next to the values for row height and column width indicates "partial or proportional." Thus, the first row contains "45 parts" of the total, while the second row uses "163 parts" of the total. The WPF Designer always attaches the * specification when you create rows and columns. If you want fixed pixel widths, just delete the asterisk from the XAML code.

Note In principle, this also works with the Designer (see Figure 5-20), but it takes a lot longer, so we won't concern ourselves with it in this example.

FIGURE 5-20 Fixed column and row dimensions can also be set with the Designer, but it's a lot more cumbersome and time consuming.

In this design, the title will be located in the first row of the grid, and the status bar in the last, so those two rows should have a fixed height.

4. Go to the source code and change the height of the first row to *40* and the last row to *30*.

5. The input fields are located in rows 3, 4, and 5. Specify the height for these rows as *40*.

6. Only the row with the *ListBox* remains, which should be resized dynamically. Change the height to "*".

Now everything else maintains its fixed size, and only the *ListBox* with the file names can be resized dynamically, according to the window's dimensions, as illustrated here:

```
<Grid.RowDefinitions>
    <RowDefinition Height="40" />
    <RowDefinition Height="*" />
    <RowDefinition Height="40" />
    <RowDefinition Height="40" />
    <RowDefinition Height="40" />
    <RowDefinition Height="30" />
</Grid.RowDefinitions>
```

7. Repeat the same procedure with the columns. Try to determine which columns should have a fixed width and which should resize dynamically. The first column contains the text blocks for labeling the input fields, and the last column contains the buttons for using the program. These two columns should not change size, because buttons and text blocks don't look very good when they become larger, and there is no good reason for allowing them to enlarge. The remaining columns should grow dynamically with the window. Change the values for the width of the first and last columns to *120* and *140* respectively, and adjust the values of the dynamic columns as shown in the following:

```
<Grid.ColumnDefinitions>
    <ColumnDefinition Width="120" />
    <ColumnDefinition Width="140*" />
    <ColumnDefinition Width="130*" />
    <ColumnDefinition Width="80*" />
    <ColumnDefinition Width="140" />
</Grid.ColumnDefinitions>
```

At this point, you have laid the foundation for your user interface and, you are now ready to arrange the controls inside the cells of the grid.

> **Important** The first row of a *Grid* is always 0 (then 1, 2, and so on). Remember to start counting at zero, when assigning a *Grid* row to a control. The same logic applies to the columns in the *Grid*.

"Begin at the beginning," the King said very gravely," and go on till you come to the end: then stop!" —Lewis Carroll, *Alice in Wonderland*.

We will follow the spirit of the King's advice and start at the top of our interface, with the title.

8. Move the mouse pointer to the left border of the Visual Studio IDE, and then click the Toolbox icon to display it.

9. Drag a *TextBlock* from the Toolbox (see Figure 5-21) to the second cell of the top row of the grid.

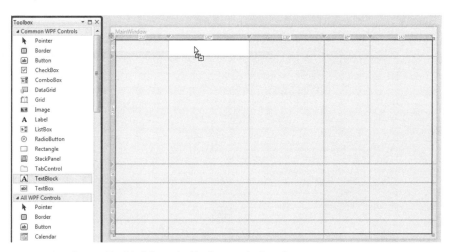

FIGURE 5-21 Drag a *TextBlock* from the Toolbox to the interface.

10. Position the *TextBlock* approximately as shown in Figure 5-22. Right-click the *TextBlock* and select *Reset Layout/All*.

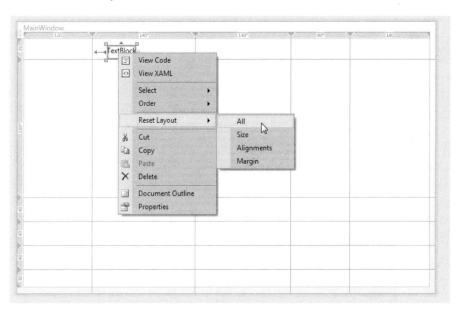

FIGURE 5-22 Position the *TextBlock* and adjust the layouts.

The result is a *TextBlock* that completely fills the cell.

11. In the Properties window on the right side of Visual Studio, change the value of the Text property from *TextBlock* to *ImageResizer* (see Figure 5-23). You can also reach the Properties window by right-clicking the control and selecting Properties on the context menu.

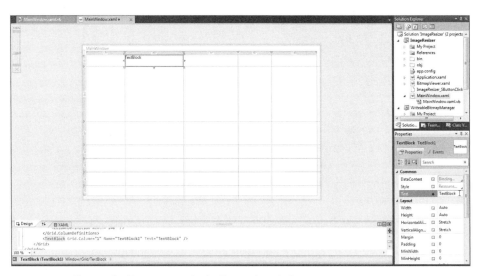

FIGURE 5-23 Change the Text property in the Properties window.

12. Change the properties in the Text category until they look like those shown in Figure 5-24.

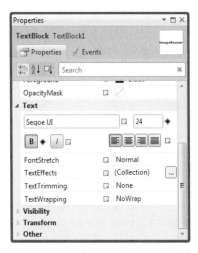

FIGURE 5-24 Adjust the properties of the Text category in the Properties window.

This sets the text size appropriately for a title, but the title should be located in the middle of the top line and span all five columns.

13. Change the following properties in the *Layout* category (see Figure 5-25):

- *HorizontalAlignment*: **Center**
- *Grid.ColumnSpan*: **5**
- *Grid.Column*: **0**

FIGURE 5-25 Adjust the properties in the Layout category to match those shown here.

The *TextBlock* is located in column 0, spans five columns, and is centered horizontally in that space. All these properties are also written into the XAML code. The WPF Designer has generated XAML code that represents our changes:

```
<TextBlock Grid.Column="0" Name="TextBlock1" Text="ImageResizer" FontSize="24"
FontWeight="Bold" HorizontalAlignment="Center" Grid.ColumnSpan="5" />
```

Next, you add a *ListBox* for presenting the file names to the user. This time, you won't work in the WPF Designer; instead, you'll use the XAML Editor for training purposes, to show how quickly and simply you can do that.

14. Position the cursor in the XAML code, one line below the *TextBox* that you just inserted, and then type **<Listb**. You will notice that IntelliSense is active in the XAML Editor too, and gives you suggestions (Figure 5-26).

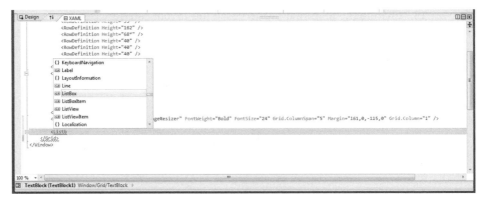

FIGURE 5-26 IntelliSense also supports you in the XAML Editor.

15. Select *ListBox* from the list and type **>**.

   Visual Studio completes your entry with the corresponding end tag.

16. Complete the line as follows:

```
<ListBox Name="FilenamesListBox" Grid.ColumnSpan="5"></ListBox>
```

   The *ListBox* can now be called in the code-behind file by using the name
   FilenamesListBox—in other words, you've done the same thing that you already know
   from Windows Forms (give names to elements to call them from the Visual Basic code)
   directly in XAML. You'll see how to insert code into the code-behind file a little later.

   The *Grid.ColumnSpan* property in the XAML code also directly specifies that the *ListBox*
   should span all five columns of the *Grid*. But there is one problem: The *ListBox* is still in
   the same row as the *TextBlock*, because the default setting for the row is 0. If there is no
   explicit row setting in the code, the control is placed in the top row of the *Grid* (in row
   0). This is also the case for columns. It would also be nice if the *ListBox* weren't glued to
   the edge, but would maintain a certain distance from the top. Fortunately the *Margin*
   property can take care of that.

17. Complete the line of code with the following:

```
<ListBox Name="FilenamesListBox" Grid.ColumnSpan="5" Grid.Row="1"
Margin="4,4,4,4"></ListBox>
```

> **Tip** Instead of entering all four distances for the *Margin* property individually, you can
> also use this shorter version when all the values are the same:
>
> ```
> <ListBox Name="FilenamesListBox" Grid.ColumnSpan="5" Grid.Row="1"
> Margin="4"></ListBox>
> ```
>
> This saves time and space, and adds clarity.

The result should look similar to Figure 5-27.

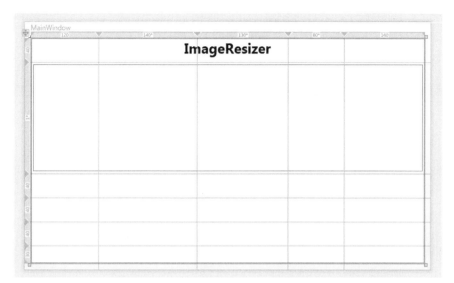

FIGURE 5-27 The user interface after inserting the *TextBlock* and the *ListBox* controls.

You now possess enough knowledge to arrange your interface further. You can add more controls with the designer or manually in the XAML pane. How you want to proceed from here is up to you.

Next, you should add the buttons to the user interface. Each *Button* has a *Content* property that specifies the button's caption.

18. Insert three controls of the type *Button* (see Figure 5-28) with the following properties:

Name	Row	Column	Content	Margin
			Button Property	
AddImagesButton	2	4	Add Pictures...	4
ChooseOutputFolderButton	3	4	Output folder...	4
StartButton	4	4	Start!	4

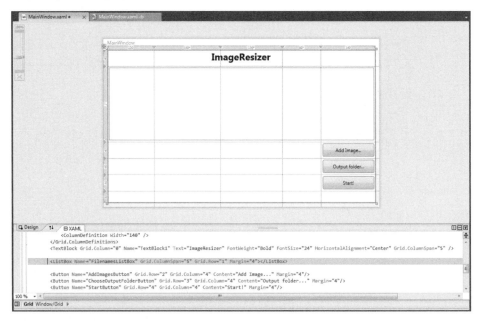

FIGURE 5-28 Add three buttons to the interface.

Next, you'll add the labels. To do that, position four *Label* controls in the *Grid* and specify each label's text with the *Content* property (see Figure 5-29). You can use the four labels from the table below or derive your own from the design. You don't need to set the *Name* property for the labels, because their purpose is merely decorative, and you don't need to access them later via code. Nevertheless, the designer always gives them a name by default.

Note If you enter the code for the labels manually, remember that the default value for rows and columns is 0. Therefore, you don't need to set the column value for the first three labels.

The properties *HorizontalContentAlignment* and *VerticalContentAlignment* determine the alignment of the content *within* the control (left, center, right, top, bottom).

Content	Row	Column	HorizontalContentAlignment	VerticalContentAlignment
New x resolution:	2	0	Right	Center
Output folder:	3	0	Right	Center
Postfix:	4	0	Right	Center
New picture format:	2	2	Right	Center

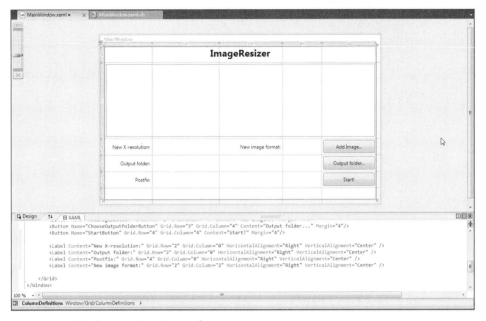

FIGURE 5-29 Add four labels to the interface.

To gather user input at runtime, you still need input fields (see Figure 5-30). We'll take care of those next.

19. Add three controls of the type *TextBox* with the following properties to the window:

Name	Row	Column	Grid. ColumnSpan	Text	Margin	VerticalContent Alignment
X_ResTextBox	2	1	(no properties)	1024	4,6,0,6	Center
OutputFolderTextBox	3	1	3	(empty)	4,6	Center
PostfixTextBox	4	1	3	_small	4,6	Center

The values for *Margin* are shown differently here than you've seen previously. When only a single decimal number is specified, the value applies to all four margins—you learned about this input help earlier; when *two* values are specified, the left/right values and top/bottom values are combined; the first number represents the left and right margin, and the second number is the margin to the top and bottom. When all four values are specified, they should be read as follows: left, top, right, bottom—(in a clockwise fashion, starting with the left side).

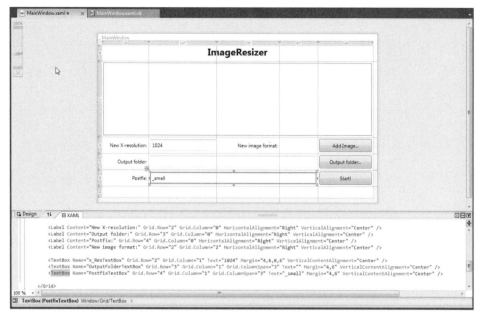

FIGURE 5-30 Almost finished: only two elements are missing on the interface.

Now we'll add a control to enable users to specify the picture type.

20. Add the following code in the XAML Editor:

```
<ComboBox Grid.Column="3" Grid.Row="2" Name="FormatComboBox" Margin="4"
          VerticalContentAlignment="Center">
    <ComboBoxItem>.jpg</ComboBoxItem>
    <ComboBoxItem>.bmp</ComboBoxItem>
    <ComboBoxItem>.png</ComboBoxItem>
    <ComboBoxItem>.tif</ComboBoxItem>
</ComboBox>
```

What does this code do? It inserts a *ComboBox* into the cell in row 3 and column 4, names it *FormatComboBox*, sets its margin to 4, and centers it vertically. It also adds four *ComboBox* elements to the control that will be available in the drop-down list so that users can select a value at runtime. (This procedure corresponds to adding elements to the *Items* list code of the *ComboBox* with the Add method.)

To complete the interface, you still need to add the *StatusBar* in the last row.

21. Add the status bar with the following XAML segment:

```
<StatusBar Grid.ColumnSpan="5" Grid.Row="5" Name="StatusBar1">
    <StatusBarItem>
        <TextBlock Text="Total progress:"/>
    </StatusBarItem>
    <StatusBarItem>
        <ProgressBar Height="20" Width="150" Name="TotalProgressBar" />
    </StatusBarItem>
```

```
<StatusBarItem>
    <TextBlock Text="Current file:" Name="CurrentFileTextBlock" />
</StatusBarItem>
</StatusBar>
```

The *StatusBar* nests three child elements: two *TextBlock* controls, and one *ProgressBar* control. The *ProgressBar*, called *TotalProgressBar*, shows the progress of the picture conversion at runtime, and the text block *CurrentFileTextBlock* informs the user which file is being processed.

The interface is complete and contains 18 controls altogether, as depicted in Figure 5-31. If you didn't know XAML before, you've probably learned a lot about it now by designing a user interface.

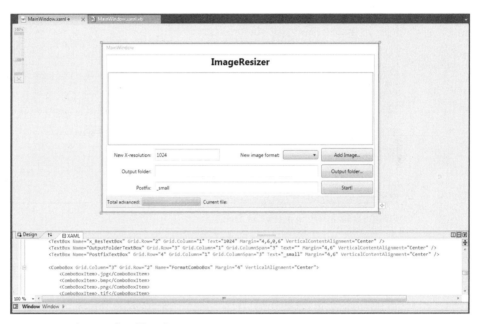

FIGURE 5-31 The completed interface.

Inserting a New Row Retroactively

Maybe by now the process of creation has stimulated your imagination and creativity to the point that suddenly you have this really cool idea for your interface. How about a menu for the *ImageResizer*, with entries that let you end the program, reset entries, or change certain settings? Unfortunately there is no room left in this carefully designed window. All the rows are occupied and you'd need to move all the controls down by one position to make room for a new row; and that's quite a bit of work. But every problem has a solution: in this situation, the Designer is faster than the XAML Code Editor (one of the very few cases where it is faster). Here is a little trick that you can use:

1. In the Designer, click the grid, and place the mouse pointer on the blue frame so that the line divides the first row in half, as seen in Figure 5-32.

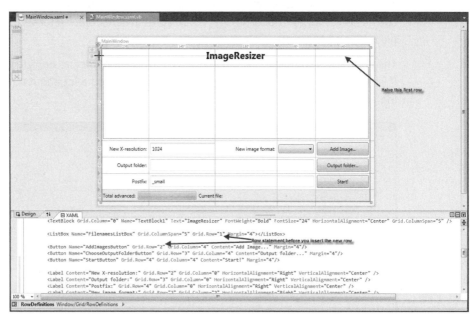

FIGURE 5-32 Inserting a new line: Step 1.

2. Click to define a new line.

   You will notice that the WPF Designer has adjusted the row definition. The first row, which previously had the height of 40 has now been divided into two rows, as shown in the following highlighted code (you might have hit the middle better than I did, and you now see two lines with a height of 20):

```
<Grid.RowDefinitions>
        <RowDefinition Height="17" />
        <RowDefinition Height="23" />
        <RowDefinition Height="*" />
        <RowDefinition Height="40" />
        <RowDefinition Height="40" />
        <RowDefinition Height="40" />
        <RowDefinition Height="30" />
    </Grid.RowDefinitions>
```

The WPF Designer has also automatically adjusted the row settings of all the controls, as illustrated in Figure 5-33.

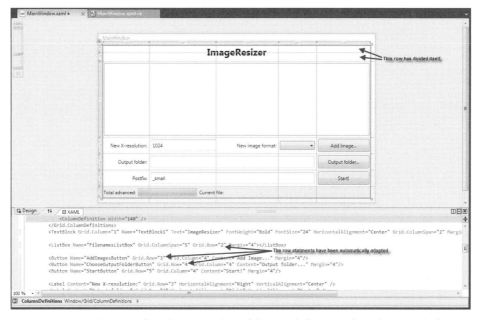

FIGURE 5-33 Inserting a new line: the row settings of the rows below are adjusted automatically.

That was pretty fast, wasn't it? As you have probably surmised, the same principle applies to columns, as well. Adjust the new row heights so that the top row has the value *35* and the next row has the value *40*. The Designer has changed the position settings for the *TextBlock* so that its previous position in the *Grid* does not change:

```
<TextBlock Grid.Column="1" Name="TextBlock1" Text="ImageResizer" FontSize="24"
FontWeight="Bold" HorizontalAlignment="Center" Grid.ColumnSpan="2" Margin="159,0,37,0"
Grid.RowSpan="2" />
```

The *RowSpan* property now has the value *2*, which means that the *TextBlock* spans both rows. At the same time, the Designer noticed that the *TextBlock* is too tall for one row and requires a span of two rows. Furthermore, the *TextBlock* now has a left and right margin for which the Designer has added the *Margin* property. This truly is a textbook example for Designer code. The Designer has moved the *TextBlock* into the second column (*Column="1"*, due to the zero-based counting), assigned it two columns' worth of space, and given it a margin—which puts it exactly where it was before the row division. The *TextBlock* is located at the correct position, but still this way of positioning seems a bit confusing because the *TextBlock* should actually be only in the first row and be positioned in the center of *all* five columns. To make this happen, change the code as follows:

- Delete the settings for *Margin*.
- Delete the settings for *RowSpan*.
- Change the setting for *ColumnSpan* to *5*.

- Change the setting for *Column* to *0*.

- Set the value for *Row* to *1*.

The result then looks as follows:

```
<TextBlock Grid.Column="0" Grid.Row="1" Grid.ColumnSpan="5"
HorizontalAlignment="Center"
                   Name="TextBlock1" Text="ImageResizer" FontSize="24"
FontWeight="Bold" />
```

You could argue that this is nitpicking. But keep in mind that if you are ever forced to manually change the code of a complex user interface created with the Designer, you need to understand how the Designer "thinks" and how it structures code to fully comprehend the code and all the possible consequences of your changes.

The Main Menu

To implement the menu, perform the following procedure:

1. Insert the following code above the *TextBlock* with the title:

```
<Menu Grid.ColumnSpan="5" Margin="5"></Menu>
```

If you are a fan of menus from Windows Forms and their menu designer, you will most likely be disappointed by the WPF Designer, even in Visual Studio 2010. You can create a menu only manually in the XAML Editor; there is no Designer support. But this also has an advantage: creating a menu manually by entering the code is both fast and exceptionally flexible because you can build any structure you like. For example, the menu can have menu items, which themselves can contain menu items—or any other control. So, theoretically, you can create a menu item that contains a *ComboBox* that shows videos upon opening—the concept of the *Context* property makes this possible. Menu items have a property called *Header*, whose value normally defines the text of the menu item, but which can also contain pictures, videos, or any other control.

A classic simple menu structure in which a user clicks the *File* menu to get to the *Exit* command looks as follows, with Figure 5-34 displaying the results:

```
<Menu Grid.ColumnSpan="5" Margin="5">
    <MenuItem Header="File">
        <MenuItem Header="Exit"></MenuItem>
    </MenuItem>
</Menu>
```

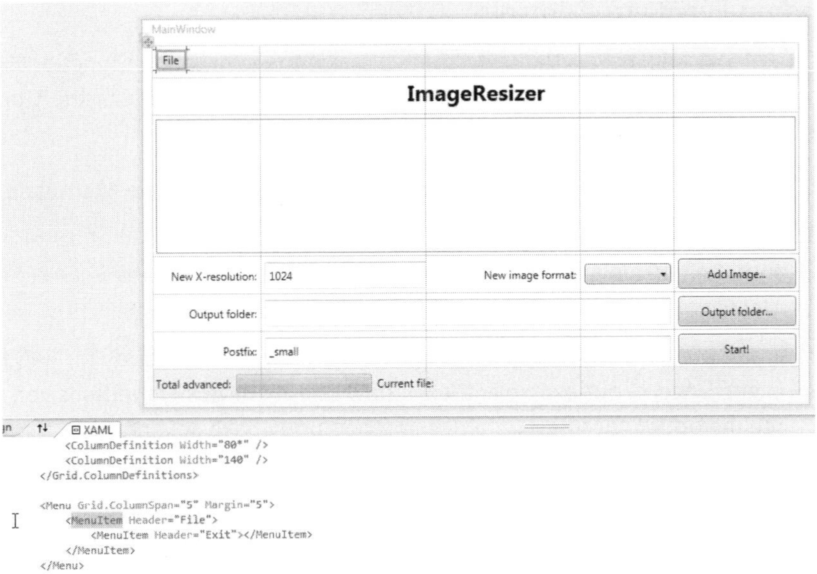

```
        <ColumnDefinition Width="80*" />
        <ColumnDefinition Width="140" />
    </Grid.ColumnDefinitions>

    <Menu Grid.ColumnSpan="5" Margin="5">
        <MenuItem Header="File">
            <MenuItem Header="Exit"></MenuItem>
        </MenuItem>
    </Menu>
```

FIGURE 5-34 The added File menu: Code and Designer view.

The menu item with the label *Exit* is actually a child element of the element with the label File and will be seen as a subitem at runtime (see Figure 5-35).

2. Complete the code according to the preceding example and start the program by pressing F5 or going to the Debug menu and clicking the command Start Debugging.

FIGURE 5-35 The menu at runtime.

Binding Events to Controls

Because looks aren't everything, it's time to tackle the application's functionality. First, discontinue debugging by clicking the Close button (X) in the window or the Stop Debugging button in Visual Studio.

1. Place your cursor on the menu item *Exit* and give it the name **MenuItemExit**.

2. Type **Click=**. IntelliSense will show you all available methods that are already in the code-behind file and which correspond to the signature of the *Click* event of the *MenuItem*.

   It also provides you with the option to add a new method body for handling the *Click* event. Since, in our example, the window doesn't have any methods yet, you will only see the option for inserting a new method body. Take advantage of this opportunity and double-click *<New event handler>*, as shown in Figure 5-36.

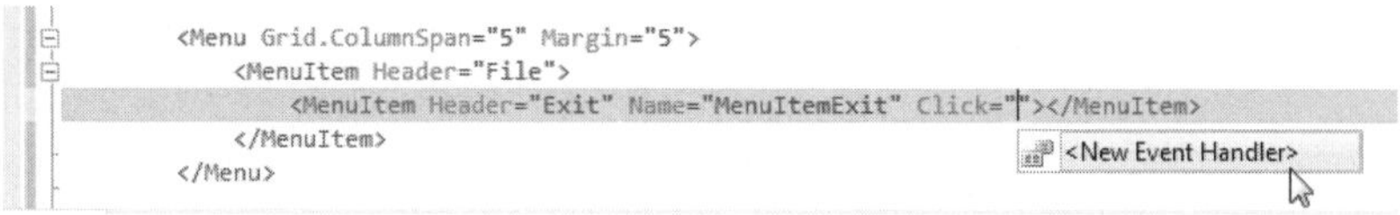

   ```
   <Menu Grid.ColumnSpan="5" Margin="5">
       <MenuItem Header="File">
           <MenuItem Header="Exit" Name="MenuItemExit" Click=""></MenuItem>
       </MenuItem>
                                          <New Event Handler>
   </Menu>
   ```

   FIGURE 5-36 Binding the menu item's *Click* event to a method.

3. Press F7 to get to the code-behind file, or double-click the file MainWindow.xaml.vb in Solution Explorer to open it. You will notice that Visual Studio inserts the method body for the event handler.

4. Verify that the name in the *Click* attribute and the name of your event handler procedure match.

5. Complete the method body as follows, and then start debugging:

   ```
   Private Sub MenuItemExit_Click(ByVal sender As System.Object,
       ByVal e As System.Windows.RoutedEventArgs)
           Me.Close()
       End Sub
   ```

   Now, when you click the menu item Exit at runtime, the window (and thus the program) closes.

Loading the Default Settings

The folder where the logged-on user's edited picture will most likely end up is the default Window directory *My Pictures* or *Pictures* (or possibly a custom subfolder of that folder). So you want that to be the default path when the window loads. Furthermore, you want the picture format .jpg to be selected automatically by default.

You can also wire methods directly to the event by using code. Type in the method body of the event routine and bind it via the keyword *Handles* to the desired event:

```
Private Sub MainWindow_Loaded(ByVal sender As Object,
                              ByVal e As System.Windows.RoutedEventArgs) Handles
➥Me.Loaded

    End Sub
```

This routine is bound to the window's *Loaded* event, which means that any code you add to it will execute as soon as the window loads—the ideal time to set default values.

> **Note** The object-oriented programming experts among you will search in vain for an overridable *OnLoaded* method in the *Windows* class. Why some event-triggering methods of the *Windows* class (and its base classes—*Windows* is derived from *FrameworkElement*) are overridable while others aren't, I can't tell you. The fact is that the *Loaded* event can be reached only by binding the actual event. This is important to remember if you are accustomed (from Windows Forms) to relying on the IntelliSense list of overridable methods when looking for events, which you receive when you type **overrides** followed by a space within a Windows class in the Editor.

Write the preceding code, if you haven't done so yet, and complete it as follows:

```
Class MainWindow

    Private Sub MainWindow_Loaded(ByVal sender As Object,
                                  ByVal e As System.Windows.RoutedEventArgs)
                                  Handles Me.Loaded

        'Preselect JPeg
        FormatComboBox.SelectedIndex = 0

        'Set My Pictures + ImageConverter + date as default directory
        Dim myOutputFolder As String
        myOutputFolder = Environment.GetFolderPath(Environment.SpecialFolder.MyPictures)
        myOutputFolder &= "\ImageConverter\" & Now.ToString("yyyy-MM-dd")
        OutputFolderTextBox.Text = myOutputFolder
    End Sub

    Private Sub MenuItemExit_Click(ByVal sender As System.Object,
        ByVal e As System.Windows.RoutedEventArgs)
        Me.Close()
    End Sub

End Class
```

Start the program by pressing F5. You see the path to your picture folder displayed in the appropriate *TextBox* control (Figure 5-37).

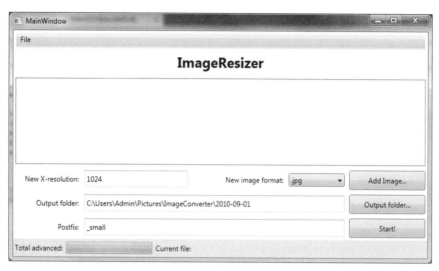

FIGURE 5-37 When loading the window, the picture format is preselected, and the output folder is set to the user's picture folder by default.

Organization Is Everything: Making the Output Path Freely Definable

If the default output location needs to be changed, you need an appropriate user-friendly dialog. Fortunately, .NET Framework provides this dialog, so the effort involved consists of specifying only a few settings.

1. Bind the *Click* event to the *ChooseOutputFolderButton* button's *Click* event with a routine. How you do this—in code via a *Handles* keyword or by defining the *Click* event handler in XAML code—is up to you. In XAML code, it would look as follows:

```
<Button Name="ChooseOutputFolderButton" …
    Click="ChooseOutputFolderButton_Click"></Button>
```

The class that provides this dialog is the *FolderBrowserDialog*. A bit of prep-work is required to be able to instantiate and use it, because the dialog isn't (yet) available in the WPF function library. However, it does exist in Windows Forms, and it's possible to "borrow" its functionality from Windows Forms for our WPF user interface. This is how you do that:

2. Right-click the project *ImageResizer* (not the solution), and then select Add Reference as illustrated in Figure 5-38.

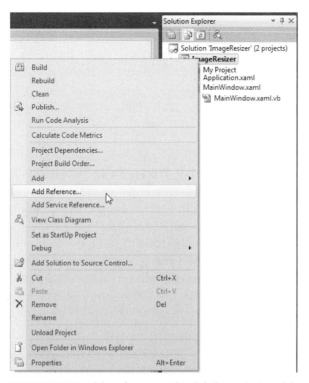

FIGURE 5-38 To add a reference, right-click the project, and then select the appropriate menu item.

3. In the dialog box that opens, look for the assembly *System.Windows.Forms* on the *.NET* tab (Figure 5-39). Select it and confirm the dialog by clicking OK.

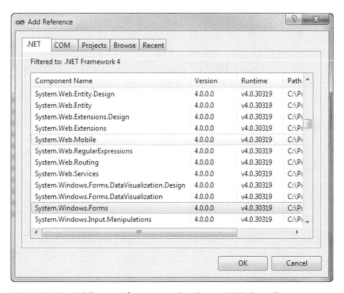

FIGURE 5-39 Adding a reference to the *System.Windows.Forms* namespace to the project.

Now you can use classes from the assembly that you just referenced in your *MainWindow* code. To do this, type in the code that follows. Be sure to add this above the class definition (add only the line in bold text—the other lines are there only to show positioning).

```
Imports System.Windows.Forms

Class MainWindow
    ...
End Class
```

Because you can now access the class that displays the folder selection dialog on the screen, you can instantiate it with typical code and then use it. Setting the value of the *ShowNewFolderButton* property to *True* allows users to create new folders by using the dialog. The *Description* property gives the dialog the title *Select Target Folder*. The dialog is called with the *ShowDialog* method and the program waits until the dialog closes before executing the following statement. At that point, the dialog was either canceled or confirmed. If the dialog was confirmed (the user clicked OK), then she has selected a folder, so you can display that path in the corresponding input field. The code should look as follows:

```
Private Sub ChooseOutputFolderButton_Click(ByVal sender As System.Object,
                                           ByVal e As System.Windows.
                                           RoutedEventArgs)

    Dim folderBrowser = New FolderBrowserDialog
    folderBrowser.ShowNewFolderButton = True
    folderBrowser.Description = "Select target folder"
    Dim dr = folderBrowser.ShowDialog
    If dr = Forms.DialogResult.OK Then
        OutputFolderTextBox.Text = folderBrowser.SelectedPath
    End If
End Sub
```

Press F5 to start a test run. Click the Output Folder button, and then select a new path to confirm that changing the path in the dialog sets a new output path.

Making Final Preparations: Adding Pictures

The stage is set, but the actors are missing: you still need the pictures that you want to edit. When a user clicks the Add Pictures button, you want to display a dialog that allows them to select the pictures to be added. First, wire the *Click* event of the button *AddImagesButton* to a method that calls the file selection dialog. Two versions of this dialog are available in different libraries, one in Win32 and in one in Windows Forms, so you must fully reference the dialog to avoid mix-ups:

```
Private Sub AddImagesButton_Click(ByVal sender As System.Object, _
                                  ByVal e As System.Windows.RoutedEventArgs) _
Handles AddImagesButton.Click

        'We are using OpenFileDialog from Win32, because it's "made" for WPF -
        'but we need to fully qualify it, because it exists in .Forms and .Win32.
        Dim fod = New Microsoft.Win32.OpenFileDialog
    End Sub
```

There are several properties that you must set before calling this dialog. For the program to run smoothly, file paths and files must exist, and file names must be valid and accepted by the operating system. The following code prepares the dialog:

```
        'Only existing files and paths can be selected.
        fod.CheckPathExists = True
        fod.CheckFileExists = True

        'Only valid Win32 file names are accepted.
        fod.ValidateNames = True
```

To make the interface friendlier for users, you can let them select multiple pictures simultaneously:

```
        'Several files can be selected.
        fod.Multiselect = True
```

The dialog filters out all files but well-known image file extensions, and by default, the file type .jpg should be preselected:

```
        'The filter should filter for picture files
        fod.Filter = "Jpeg Files (*.jpg; *.jpeg)|*.jpg; *.jpeg" &
                "|Bitmap Files (*.bmp)|*.bmp" &
                "|TIFF Files (*.tif;*.tiff)|*.tif;*.tiff" &
                "|PNG Files (*.png)|*.png" &
                "|All Files (*.*)|*.*"

        'By default the filter is set to "*.jpg"
        fod.DefaultExt = "*.jpg"
```

Now that the dialog has been confirmed, the names of the selected files need to appear as elements in the *ListBox*. The following code shows you a new feature of Visual Basic 2010: multi-line statement lambdas. (You will learn more about these useful helpers in Chapter 17, "Developing with Generics.") For each element in the list of selected file names, a small routine is executed to add the element list in the *ListBox*:

```
        'Save the DialogResult
        Dim dr = fod.ShowDialog
        'and check for success
        If dr = True Then
            Array.ForEach(fod.FileNames, Sub(filename)
                                FilenamesListbox.Items.Add(filename)
                         End Sub)
        End If
```

On to the Finish Line: Reducing Picture Size

Now all the information necessary for execution is available, and the actual editing of the pictures can begin. The program will go through the following steps:

1. Reading the information from the user interface

2. Editing the pictures

3. Saving each edited picture

4. Displaying the progress to the user

But there's a catch: unlike Windows Forms, the WPF libraries don't provide a picture class for manipulating images. With this book you have also acquired a functional workaround that permits you to save pictures in WPF, as well. You can find the library written by the author (along with some extra tools) in the subfolder WriteableBitmapManager, in the solution of this example (*ImageResizer*). Of course, you can also use this component in your other projects.

By executing the following steps, you will also learn how to add program libraries to a solution and how to add the appropriate references, so you can use them for your own projects, later on.

Adding a Project to an Existing Solution and Setting References

1. Copy the project *WriteableBitmapManager* into a folder of your choice; for example, the project folder of the *ImageResizer* which, by default, is located in the Windows documents folder under Visual Studio 2010\Projects.

2. Go to Visual Studio and right-click the solution ImageResizer in Solution Explorer.

3. Click Add/Existing Project, as illustrated in Figure 5-40.

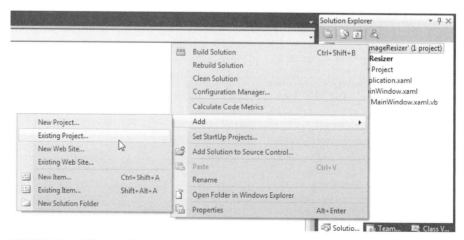

FIGURE 5-40 Adding an existing project to the solution.

4. Navigate to the correct folder, select the project file of the project WriteableBitmapManager, and then click Open, as depicted in Figure 5-41.

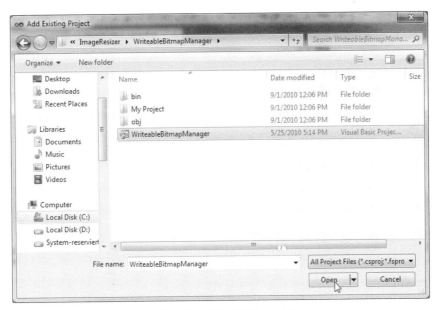

FIGURE 5-41 Select the project file of the WriteableBitmapManager.

The project will now be located in the solution.

5. Proceed as described earlier to add a reference to the project *WriteableBitmapManager* to your *ImageResizer* project (see Figure 5-42). To do this, click the Projects tab, and then click WriteableBitmapManager. Click OK to close the dialog box and add the selected reference to the current project.

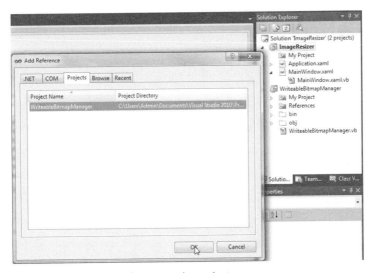

FIGURE 5-42 Adding a reference to the project.

6. Complete the code in the *MainWindow* with the following line (highlighted in bold):

```
Imports System.Windows.Forms
Imports ActiveDevelop.Wpf.Imaging
Class MainWindow
…
End Class
```

The Heart of the Program: Image Resizing

The process of resizing an image is triggered by the *StartButton* button. Wire the *Click* event of that button to a method that will reduce image size based on the following information:

- The size of the picture
- The type of picture it should act upon
- The list of pictures to be resized

The method pulls the required information from data entered by the user on the interface. Enter the following code into the method's body:

```
Dim myReduceToX = Integer.Parse(X_ResTextBox.Text)
Dim newExtension = DirectCast(FormatComboBox.SelectedItem, ComboBoxItem).Content.ToString
```

Initialize the *ProgressBar* by determining the maximum value and creating a counter to monitor the progress:

```
Me.TotalProgressBar.Maximum = FilenamesListbox.Items.Count
Dim progressCount = 0
```

Perform the following steps for each picture:

1. Display the name of the picture currently being edited on the interface.

2. Save the file name of the picture in a new instance of the *FileInfo* class (you'll use it later to retrieve information about the image).

3. Instantiate the class *WriteableBitmapManager*, and then request a copy of the picture.

4. Calculate the factor by which the picture should be resized.

5. Resize the picture copy by the calculated factor and find out the time it took for the conversion.

6. Rename the picture according to the selected file type.

7. Save the picture with the help of the *WriteableBitmapManager* instance in the specified folder with the specified postfix.

8. Increase the progress counter by one, and then display the progress in the *ProgressBar*.

To use the *FileInfo* class, import the following namespace:

```
Imports System.IO
```

Add yet another reference to the *ImageResizer* project by right-clicking the project in Solution Explorer. In the context menu that appears, select *Add Reference*, and then select the library *System.Drawing* on the tab .NET. In code, the procedure looks as follows:

> **Note** The following code, which is located in the *StartButton_Click* method might a bit much to type in. If you have been following along by typing the code, you can save yourself some time by opening the text file ImageResizer_SButtonClick.txt in the example directory of this chapter, which contains the entire code, and copy it from there into the event handler.

```vbnet
Private Sub StartButton_Click(ByVal sender As System.Object, ByVal e As System.Windows.
RoutedEventArgs)

        'Read new width:
        Dim myReduceToX = Integer.Parse(X_ResTextBox.Text)
        'Read file type
        Dim newExtension = DirectCast(FormatComboBox.SelectedItem, _
                                    ComboBoxItem).Content.ToString

        'Determine number of iterations and assign to progress bar
        Me.TotalProgressBar.Maximum = FilenamesListBox.Items.Count
        'Counter for thus far completed calculations = progress
        Dim progressCount = 0

        'For each picture ...
        For Each filenameItem As String In FilenamesListBox.Items
            'display file name
            CurrentFileTextBlock.Text = filenameItem
            'and save
            Dim fileInfo As New FileInfo(filenameItem)

            'Instantiate manager and make a copy of the picture
            Dim currentPicture As New WriteableBitmapManager(filenameItem)
            Dim mySmallWbm = currentPicture.CreateCompatible(myReduceToX)
            'Calculate resize factor
            Dim pixelFakt As Double = currentPicture.WriteableBitmap.PixelWidth / _
                myReduceToX

            'Measure time
            Dim sw = Stopwatch.StartNew
            'Reduce picture size
            For y = 0 To mySmallWbm.WriteableBitmap.PixelHeight - 1
                For x = 0 To myReduceToX - 1
                    mySmallWbm.SetPixel(x, y, _
                        currentPicture.GetPixel(CInt(Math.Truncate(pixelFakt * x)), _
                                            CInt(Math.Truncate(pixelFakt * y))))
                Next
            Next
```

```
            'and update
            mySmallWbm.UpdateBitmap()
            'Stop clock
            sw.Stop()

            'Adjust file type
            Dim newFilename = fileInfo.Name.Replace(fileInfo.Extension, "")
            'Combine path and new extension
              newFilename = OutputFolderTextBox.Text &
                        "\" & newFilename & PostfixTextBox.Text & newExtension

            'Save
            mySmallWbm.SaveBitmap(newFilename)

            'and display progress
            progressCount += 1
            TotalProgressBar.Value = progressCount


        Next
    End Sub
```

Press F5 to start a test run of your program.

From Coach to Business Class

Without being clairvoyant, I can say without much doubt that you have browsed to the output folder and have taken a look at the smaller pictures.

To polish our program a bit and give it a certain amount of user comfort, wouldn't it be nice to see the small pictures immediately in a preview? No problem. Right-click the *ImageResizer* project, select Add from the context menu, and then click New Item (Figure 5-43).

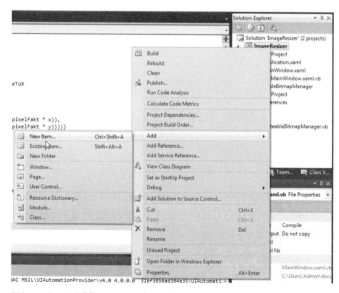

FIGURE 5-43 Adding a new element.

In the displayed dialog, select Window (WPF), and name it **BitmapViewer.xaml** (Figure 5-44). Confirm the dialog by clicking Add.

FIGURE 5-44 Adding a new window.

The new window doesn't need much of an interface. Insert a *ScrollViewer* control into the *Grid* and place an *Image* into it. Set the *Stretch* property of the *Image* to *None* so that the picture displays at its original size, and name it **PreviewImage**.

Enlarge the window by dragging until it is big enough to hold the image, and set the start position to the center of the screen by using the *WindowStartupLocation* property and the *CenterScreen* value:

```
<Window x:Class="BitmapViewer"
    xmlns="http://schemas.microsoft.com/winfx/2006/xaml/presentation"
    xmlns:x="http://schemas.microsoft.com/winfx/2006/xaml"
    Title="BitmapViewer" Height="448" Width="656" WindowStartupLocation="CenterScreen">
    <Grid>
        <ScrollViewer Name="ScrollViewer1" HorizontalScrollBarVisibility="Visible">
            <Image Name="PreviewImage" Stretch="None" />
        </ScrollViewer>
    </Grid>
</Window>
```

Now, navigate to the code-behind file and insert a subroutine called *ShowPicture*, which accepts a variable of type *WriteableBitmapManager* and a variable of type *String* as parameters. Add the following code to complete the preview window:

```
Public Sub ShowPicture(ByVal wbm As WriteableBitmapManager, ByVal statusText As String)
     PreviewImage.Width = wbm.WriteableBitmap.Width
     PreviewImage.Height = wbm.WriteableBitmap.Height
     PreviewImage.Source = wbm.WriteableBitmap
     Me.Title = statusText
 End Sub
```

This window is also still missing the namespace for the *WriteableBitmapManager* class, as illustrated in Figure 5-45.

Tip To import missing namespaces, you can take advantage of Visual Studio's error correction capabilities, as shown in Figure 5-45. Letting Visual Studio insert the missing namespace saves you not only from having to scroll to the beginning of the code file, but also eliminates having to search for the namespace that you want to import.

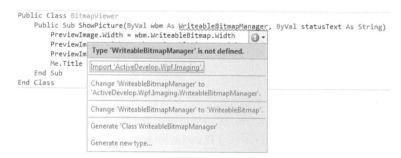

FIGURE 5-45 Visual Studio suggests corrections for errors, such as missing references.

Insert the lines of code highlighted in bold in the following listing into your image resizing routine to call the window, display the individual pictures, and then close the window:

```
Private Sub StartButton_Click(ByVal sender As System.Object, ByVal e As _
System.Windows.RoutedEventArgs)

    'Instantiate and display the preview window
    Dim picViewer As New BitmapViewer
    picViewer.Show()

    'Read new width:
    Dim myReduceToX = Integer.Parse(X_ResTextBox.Text)
    'Read file type
        ...
```

```
'For each picture ...
For Each filenameItem As String In FilenamesListBox.Items
    'display the file name
    CurrentFileTextBlock.Text = filenameItem

    ...
    'and update
    mySmallWbm.UpdateBitmap()
    'Stop clock
    sw.Stop()

    'Display reduced picture
    picViewer.ShowPicture(mySmallWbm, "Duration of conversion in ms: " &
              sw.ElapsedMilliseconds.ToString("#,##0.00"))


    ...
Next

picViewer.Close()

End Sub
```

If you start the program now, the preview window displays only one picture—the last one that was converted. Why?

Because the program runs on a single thread, it is so busy during the calculations that it neglects the interface, and doesn't get a chance to update it. However, if you move the calculation to a different thread, then the main program will have the time to update its interface. Unfortunately, this topic is fairly advanced, but you'll see an in-depth discussion of threading in Chapter 28, "Programming with the Task Parallel Library (TPL)."

For now, let's solve the problem by triggering the Windows message loop. By doing this, you are giving the program the opportunity to process accrued messages very quickly, even though you would normally be blocking the calculation performance of the UI thread. Make the following change:

```
    ...
    picViewer.ShowPicture(mySmallWbm, "Duration of conversion in ms: " &
              sw.ElapsedMilliseconds.ToString("#,##0.00"))

    'Evil workaround—more about this in the chapter about threading:
    System.Windows.Forms.Application.DoEvents()
    ...
Next

picViewer.Close()

End Sub
```

Chapter 6
The Essential .NET Data Types

In Chapter 1, "Beginners All-Purpose Symbolic Instruction Code," you learned about variables, including what the different types of variables are, and you saw a few examples of declaring and using variables of various data types. However, there's still a lot to learn about the base data types, which are part of the Microsoft .NET Framework. These are the data types that you'll be using over and over as a developer.

The base data types are mainly *primitive* data types, such as *Integer, Double, Date, String*, and so on, with which you're already familiar. They are an integral part of the C# and Microsoft Visual Basic.NET languages; you can recognize them easily because the Microsoft Visual Studio code editor colors them blue as soon as you declare them.

Base data types include all the types that are part of any .NET programming language, and they expose the following characteristics:

- **They can be used as variable values.** You can set the value of each base data type directly. For example, specifying a value of *123.324D* identifies a variable of type *Decimal* with a specific magnitude.

- **They can be used as constant values.** It is possible to declare a base data type as a constant. When a certain expression is exclusively defined as a constant (such as the expression *123.32D*2+100.23D*), it can be evaluated during compilation.

- **They are recognized by the processor.** Many operations and functions of certain base data types can be delegated by the .NET Framework directly to the processor for execution. This means that no program logic is necessary to calculate an arithmetic expression (for example, a floating-point division). The processor can do this by itself, so such operations are therefore very fast. Most of the operations of the data types *Byte, Short, Integer, Long, Single, Double*, and *Boolean* fall into this category.

Numeric Data Types

For processing numbers, Visual Basic provides the data types *Byte, Short, Integer, Long, Single, Double,* and *Decimal.* The data types *SByte, UShort, Uinteger,* and *ULong* were introduced with Visual Basic 2005. They differ in the range, the precision, or *scale,* of the values that they can represent (for instance, the number of decimal points), and their memory requirements.

> **Note** The nullable data types have been around since Visual Basic 2005, and we discussed them briefly in the introduction to Chapter 1. Nullable data types behave similarly to their regular data type counterparts, but they can also reflect a non-defined state, namely *null*[1] (or *Nothing* in Visual Basic). With the release of Visual Basic 2008, these data types are also part of the Visual Basic language syntax, and they are defined by the question mark symbol as type literal. Here's how you declare an *Integer* data type as nullable:
>
> ```
> Dim t As Integer?
> ```
>
> You'll see more about nullable data types in Chapter 18, "Advanced Types."

Defining and Declaring Numeric Data Types

All numeric data types (as with all value types) are declared *without* the keyword *New.* Constant values can be directly assigned to numeric types in the program's code. There are certain keywords that define the type of a constant value. A variable of the type *Double* can, for example, be declared with the following statement:

```
Dim aDouble As Double
```

You can then use *aDouble* immediately in the code. Numeric variables can be assigned values, which are strings made up of digits followed (if necessary) by a type literal. In the following example, the type literal is the *D* following the actual value:

```
aDouble = 123.3D
```

Just as with other base data types, declaration and assignment can take place in a single statement. Therefore, you can replace the two preceding statements with the following single statement:

```
Dim aDouble As Double = 123.3D
```

If you use local type inference (refer to Chapter 1 for more information), you don't even need to specify the type or procedure level (for example, in a *Sub,* a *Function* or a *Property,* but not for module or class variables); you can let the compiler infer the correct type from the type of the expression or the constant from which the variable is assigned:

---

[1] Not to be confused with the value *0!* Null denotes the absence of a value.

```
Dim aDouble = 123.3D
```

> **Note** Local type inference must be switched on through the property settings of your project. Alternatively, you can place *Option Infer On* at the top of the code file in which you want to use local type inference.

The example applies to all other numeric data types equally—the type literal can of course differ from type to type.

TABLE 6-1 **Type Literals and Variable Type Declaration Characters of the Base Data Types in Visual Basic 2010**

Type name	Type declaration character	Type literal	Example
Byte	–	–	`Dim var As Byte = 128`
SByte	–	–	`Dim var As SByte = -5`
Short	–	S	`Dim var As Short = -32700S`
UShort	–	US	`Dim var As UShort = 65000US`
Integer	%	I	`Dim var% = -123I` or `Dim var As Integer = -123I`
UInteger	–	UI	`Dim var As UInteger = 123UI`
Long	&	L	`Dim var& = -123123L` or `Dim var As Long = -123123L`
ULong	–	UL	`Dim var As ULong = 123123UL`
Single	!	F	`Dim var! = 123.4F` or `Dim var As Single = 123.4F`
Double	#	R	`Dim var# = 123.456789R` or `Dim var As Double = 123.456789R`
Decimal	@	D	`Dim var@ = 123.456789123D` or `Dim var As Decimal = 123.456789123D`
Boolean	–	–	`Dim var As Boolean = True`
Char	–	C	`Dim var As Char = "A"c`
Date	–	#MM/dd/yyyy HH:mm:ss# or #MM/dd/yyyy hh:mm:ss am/pm#	`Dim var As Date = #12/24/2008 04:30:15 PM#`
Object	–	–	In a variable of the type *Object*, any type can be boxed or referenced by it
String	$	"String"	`Dim var$ = "String"` or `Dim var As String = "String"`

Delegating Numeric Calculations to the Processor

The example that follows shows how to leave some mathematical operations to the processor. To do this, you need to know that, due to its computational accuracy, the *Decimal* type is calculated not by the floating-point unit of the processor, but by the corresponding program code of the Base Class Library (unlike *Double* or *Single*).

Note This example goes a little deeper into the system. You will learn how to view the Assembler and machine language representation—the concrete compilation of your program, the way the processor sees it. Although this is not a requirement for developing applications by any means, it's definitely an interesting experiment, and it will help you understand how the processor processes data.

Companion Content Open the solution Primitives01.sln, which you can find in the \VB 2010 Developer Handbook\Chapter 06\Primitives01 folder.

Before you run the following sample code, press F9 to set a breakpoint in the highlighted line.

```vb
Public Class Primitives
    Public Shared Sub main()
        Dim locDouble1, locDouble2 As Double
        Dim locDec1, locDec2 As Decimal

        locDouble1 = 123.434D
        locDouble2 = 321.121D
        locDouble2 += 1
        locDouble1 += locDouble2
        Console.WriteLine("Result of the Double calculation: {0}", locDouble1)

        locDec1 = 123.434D
        locDec2 = 321.121D
        locDec2 += 1
        locDec1 += locDec2
        Console.WriteLine("Result of the Decimal calculation: {0}", locDec1)

    End Sub
End Class
```

When you start the program, it will stop at the line with the breakpoint. On the Debug/Window menu, select Disassembly. This window will display what the Just-in-Time (JIT) compiler has done with the program, which is first compiled in the IML, as shown in the code that follows.

Note The Disassembly window can display only assembly code, which is not very well optimized. No setting can change that—you will always see the debug code, not the optimized code. Later, in the optimized code, the processor registers are used as carriers for local variables, whenever possible, which drastically increases the execution speed of your applications.

```
        Dim locDouble1, locDouble2 As Double
        Dim locDec1, locDec2 As Decimal

           locDouble1 = 123.434D
00000055  movsd      xmm0,mmword ptr [000002E8h]
0000005d  movsd      mmword ptr [rsp+50h],xmm0
           locDouble2 = 321.121D
00000063  movsd      xmm0,mmword ptr [000002F0h]
0000006b  movsd      mmword ptr [rsp+58h],xmm0
           locDouble2 += 1
00000071  movsd      xmm0,mmword ptr [000002F8h]
00000079  addsd      xmm0,mmword ptr [rsp+58h]
0000007f  movsd      mmword ptr [rsp+58h],xmm0
```

The numbered lines correspond to assembly language statements and show the operations required by the processor to execute the preceding Visual Basic statement. These are the statements that the processor understands, and no matter what language you're using to write your applications, at the end of the day, your code must be translated into a series of assembly statements. That's what compilers do for you. The listings in this section demonstrate (if nothing else) what a "high-level" language is all about.

Unlike what you might have expected, no special methods of the *Double* structure were called. Instead, the addition happens via the floating-point functionality of the processor itself (*addsd*,[2] marked in bold). It's quite different further down in the disassembly, where the same operations are carried out by using the *Decimal* data type:

```
locDec2 += 1
0000017e  mov       rcx,129F1180h
00000188  mov       rcx,qword ptr [rcx]
0000018b  add       rcx,8
0000018f  mov       rax,qword ptr [rcx]
00000192  mov       qword ptr [rsp+000000A8h],rax
0000019a  mov       rax,qword ptr [rcx+8]
0000019e  mov       qword ptr [rsp+000000B0h],rax
000001a6  lea       rcx,[rsp+000000A8h]
000001ae  mov       rax,qword ptr [rcx]
000001b1  mov       qword ptr [rsp+000000E0h],rax
000001b9  mov       rax,qword ptr [rcx+8]
000001bd  mov       qword ptr [rsp+000000E8h],rax
000001c5  lea       rcx,[rsp+40h]
000001ca  mov       rax,qword ptr [rcx]
000001cd  mov       qword ptr [rsp+000000D0h],rax
```

---

[2] Scalar Double-Precision Floating-Point Add

```
000001d5  mov        rax,qword ptr [rcx+8]
000001d9  mov        qword ptr [rsp+000000D8h],rax
000001e1  lea        r8,[rsp+000000E0h]
000001e9  lea        rdx,[rsp+000000D0h]
000001f1  lea        rcx,[rsp+000000B8h]
000001f9  call       FFFFFFFFEF381460
// Here the addition routine of …
000001fe  mov        qword ptr [rsp+00000128h],rax
00000206  lea        rcx,[rsp+000000B8h]
0000020e  mov        rax,qword ptr [rcx]
00000211  mov        qword ptr [rsp+40h],rax
00000216  mov        rax,qword ptr [rcx+8]
0000021a  mov        qword ptr [rsp+48h],rax
          locDec1 += locDec2
0000021f  lea        rcx,[rsp+40h]
00000224  mov        rax,qword ptr [rcx]
00000227  mov        qword ptr [rsp+00000110h],rax
0000022f  mov        rax,qword ptr [rcx+8]
00000233  mov        qword ptr [rsp+00000118h],rax
0000023b  lea        rcx,[rsp+30h]
00000240  mov        rax,qword ptr [rcx]
00000243  mov        qword ptr [rsp+00000100h],rax
0000024b  mov        rax,qword ptr [rcx+8]
0000024f  mov        qword ptr [rsp+00000108h],rax
00000257  lea        r8,[rsp+00000110h]
0000025f  lea        rdx,[rsp+00000100h]
00000267  lea        rcx,[rsp+000000F0h]
0000026f  call       FFFFFFFFEF381460
// … Decimal is called. Here also.
                .
                .
                .
```

The preceding code demonstrates that the addition requires many more preparations. This is because the values to be added must first be copied to the stack. The actual addition isn't performed by the processor itself, but by the corresponding routines of the Base Class Library (BCL), which is called by using the *Call* statement, shown in the disassembly (highlighted in bold).

Tip This example illustrates why the performance of the *Decimal* data type is only about one tenth of the performance of the *Double* data type. Therefore, you should use *Decimal* only when you need to perform exact financial calculations and can't tolerate any rounding errors. (For more information, read the section, "Numeric Data Types at a Glance," later in this chapter.)

A Note About Common Language Specification Compliance

Some of the data types introduced in Visual Basic 2005 don't conform to the Common Language Specification (CLS), or they simply aren't CLS-compliant. Some generic data types and some primitive data types that save integer values without prefixes (as well as the base data type *SByte*) belong to this group. Methods that accept types that are not CLS-compliant as arguments (or return values) should not be provided in components intended for use by other .NET programming languages. You must not assume that these types are "accessible" in all .NET languages. Visual Basic does not automatically check for CLS compliance. If you have components checked for compliance by the Visual Basic compiler, you can use the *CLSCompliant* attribute at class level, as follows:

```
<CLSCompliant(True)> _
    Public Class AClass

    Private myMember As UShort

    Public Property NotCLSCompliant() As UShort
        Get
            Return myMember
        End Get
        Set(ByVal value As UShort)
            myMember = value
        End Set
    End Property
End Class
```

Checking a single method for CLS compliance works the same way:

```
<CLSCompliant(True)> _
Public Shared Function ANonCLSComplianceMethod() As UShort
    Dim locTest As ClassLibrary1.AClass
    locTest = New ClassLibrary1.AClass
End Function
```

Note Contrary to common belief, it's not true that a method, an assembly, or even your entire application is non–CLS-compliant if you are using just a single non-compliant type. Your assembly becomes non–CLS-compliant only when you expose variables of non–CLS-compliant types by making them *Public*.

Numeric Data Types at a Glance

The following short sections describe the use of numeric data types and the range of values that you can represent with each numeric type.

Byte

.NET data type: *System.Byte*

Represents: Integer values (numbers without decimal points) in the specified range

Range: 0 to 255

Type literal: Not available

Memory requirements: 1 byte

Declaration and example assignment:

```
Dim aByte As Byte
aByte = 123
```

Description: This data type stores only unsigned positive numbers in the specified numeric range.

CLS-compliant: Yes

Conversion of other numeric types: *CByte(objVar)* or *Convert.ToByte(objVar)*

```
aByte = CByte(123.45D)
aByte = Convert.ToByte(123.45D)
```

SByte

.NET data type: *System.SByte*

Represents: Integer values (numbers without decimal points) in the specified range

Range: –128 to 127

Type literal: Not available

Memory requirements: 1 byte

Declaration and example assignment:

```
Dim aByte As SByte
aByte = 123
```

Description: This data type saves negative and positive numbers in the specified numeric range.

CLS-compliant: No

Conversion of other numeric types: *CSByte(objVar)* or *Convert.ToSByte(objVar)*

```
aByte = CSByte(123.45D)
aByte = Convert.ToSByte(123.45D)
```

Short

.NET data type: *System.Int16*

Represents: Integer values (numbers without decimal points) in the specified range

Range: –32,768 to 32,767

Type literal: S

Memory requirements: 2 bytes

Declaration and example assignment:

```
Dim aShort As Short
aShort = 123S
```

Description: This data type stores signed numbers (both negative and positive) in the specified range. Conversion to the *Byte* data type can cause an *OutOfRangeException*, due to the larger scope of *Short*.

CLS-compliant: Yes

Conversion of other numeric types: *CShort(objVar)* or *Convert.ToInt16(objVar)*

```
'Decimal points are truncated
aShort = CShort(123.45D)
aShort = Convert.ToInt16(123.45D)
```

UShort

.NET data type: *System.UInt16*

Represents: Positive integer values (numbers without decimal points) in the specified range

Range: 0 to 65,535

Type literal: US

Memory requirements: 2 bytes

Declaration and example assignment:

```
Dim aUShort As UShort
aUShort = 123US
```

Description: This data type stores unsigned numbers (positive only) in the specified numeric range. Conversion to the *Byte* or *Short* data types can cause an *OutOfRangeException*, due to the (partially) larger scope of *Byte* or *Short*.

CLS-compliant: No

Conversion of other numeric types: *CUShort(objVar)* or *Convert.ToUInt16(objVar)*

```
'Decimal points are truncated
aUShort = CUShort(123.45D)
aUShort = Convert.ToUInt16(123.45D)
```

Integer

.NET data type: *System.Int32*

Represents: Integer values (numbers without decimal points) in the specified range

Range: –2,147,483,648 to 2,147,483,647

Type literal: I

Memory requirements: 4 bytes

Declaration and example assignment:

```
Dim anInteger As Integer
Dim anDifferentInteger%      ' also declared a integer
anInteger = 123I
```

Description: This data type stores signed numbers (both negative and positive) in the specified range. Conversion to the *Byte*, *Short*, and *UShort* data types can cause an *OutOfRangeException*, due to the larger scope of *Integer*. By appending the "%" (percent) character to a variable, the *Integer* type for the variable can be forced. However, in the interest of better programming style, you should avoid this technique.

CLS-compliant: Yes

Conversion of other numeric types: *CInt(objVar)* or *Convert.ToInt32(objVar)*

```
anInteger = CInt(123.45D)
anInteger = Convert.ToInt32(123.45D)
```

UInteger

.NET data type: System.UInt32

Represents: Positive integer values (numbers without decimal points) in the specified range

Range: 0 to 4,294,967,295

Type literal: UI

Memory requirements: 4 bytes

Declaration and example assignment:

```
Dim aUInteger As UInteger
aUInteger = 123UI
```

Description: This data type stores unsigned numbers (positive only) in the specified range. Conversion to the data types *Byte*, *Short*, *Ushort*, and *Integer* can cause an *OutOfRangeException*, due to the (partially) larger scope of *UInteger*.

CLS-compliant: No

Conversion of other numeric types: *CUInt(objVar)* or *Convert.ToUInt32(objVar)*

```
aUInteger = CUInt(123.45D)
aUInteger = Convert.ToUInt32(123.45D)
```

Long

.NET data type: *System.Int64*

Represents: Integer values (numbers without decimal points) in the specified range.

Range: −9,223,372,036,854,775,808 to 9,223,372,036,854,775,807

Type literal: L

Memory requirements: 8 bytes

Declaration and example assignment:

```
Dim aLong As Long
Dim aDifferentLong& ' also defined as long
aLong = 123L
```

Description: This data type stores signed numbers (both negative and positive) in the specified range. Conversion to all other integer data types can cause an *OutOfRangeException*, due to the larger scope of *Long*. You can force a variable to a *Long* by appending the "&" (ampersand) character to a variable. However, in the interest of better programming style, you should avoid this technique.

CLS-compliant: Yes

Conversion of other numeric types: *CLng(objVar)* or *Convert.ToInt64(objVar)*

```
aLong = CLng(123.45D)
aLong = Convert.ToInt64(123.45D)
```

ULong

.NET data type: *System.UInt64*

Represents: Positive integer values (numbers without decimal points) in the specified range

Range: 0 to 18.446.744.073.709.551.615

Type literal: UL

Memory requirements: 8 bytes

Declaration and example assignment:

```
Dim aULong As ULong
aULong = 123L
```

Description: This data type stores unsigned numbers (positive only) in the specified numeric range. Conversion to all other integer data types can cause an *OutOfRangeException*, due to the larger scope of *ULong*.

CLS-compliant: No

Conversion of other numeric types: *CULng(objVar)* or *Convert.ToUInt64(objVar)*

```
aULong = CULng(123.45D)
aULong = Convert.ToUInt64(123.45D)
```

Single

.NET data type: *System.Single*

Represents: Floating-point values (numbers with decimal points whose scale becomes smaller with the increasing value) in the specified range

> **Note** Scale in this context refers to the number of decimal points of a floating-point number.

Range: $-3.4028235 * 10^{38}$ to $-1.401298 * 10^{-45}$ for negative values; $1.401298 * 10^{-45}$ to $3.4028235 * 10^{38}$ for positive values

Type literal: F

Memory requirements: 4 bytes

Declaration and example assignment:

```
Dim aSingle As Single
Dim aDifferentSingle! ' also defined as Single
aSingle = 123.0F
```

Description: This data type stores signed numbers (both negative and positive) in the specified range. By appending the "!" (exclamation) character to a variable, you can foce the variable to the *Single* type. However, in the interest of better programming style, you should avoid this technique.

CLS-compliant: Yes

Conversion of other numeric types: *CSng(objVar)* or *Convert.ToSingle(objVar)*

```
aSingle = CSng(123.45D)
aSingle = Convert.ToSingle(123.45D)
```

Double

.NET data type: *System.Double*

Represents: Floating-point values (numbers with decimal points whose scale becomes smaller with the increasing value) in the specified range

Range: −1.79769313486231570*10308 to −4.94065645841246544*10−324 for negative values; 4.94065645841246544*10−324 to 1.79769313486231570308 for positive values

Type literal: R

Memory requirements: 8 bytes

Declaration and example assignment:

```
Dim aDouble As Double
Dim aDifferentDouble# ' also defined as Double
aDouble = 123.0R
```

Description: This data type stores numbers (both negative and positive) in the specified range. By appending the "#" (hash) character to a variable, you can force it to the *Double* type. However, in the interest of better programming style, you should avoid this technique.

CLS-compliant: Yes

Conversion of other numeric types: *CDbl(objVar)* or *Convert.ToDouble(objVar)*

```
aDouble = CDbl(123.45D)
aDouble = Convert.ToDouble(123.45D)
```

Decimal

.NET data type: *System.Decimal*

Represents: Floating-point values (numbers with decimal points whose scale becomes smaller with the increasing value) in the specified range

Range: Depends on the number of used decimal places. If no decimal places are used (called a scale of 0) the max/min values are between ±79,228,162,514,264,337,593,543,950,335. When using a maximal scale (28 places behind the period; only values between –1 and 1 can be stored at this scale) the max/min values are between ±0.9999999999999999999999999999.

Type literal: D

Memory requirements: 16 bytes

Declaration and example assignment:

```
Dim aDecimal As Decimal
Dim aDifferentDouble@ ' also defined as Decimal
aDecimal = 123.23D
```

Description: This data type stores signed numbers (both negative and positive) in the specified range. By appending the "@" (ampersand) character to a variable you can force the *Decimal* type. However, in the interest of better programming style, you should avoid this technique.

Important For very high values, you must attach the type literal to a literal constant to avoid an *Overflow* error message.

Note No arithmetic functions are delegated to the processor for the data type *Decimal*. Therefore, this data type is processed much more slowly than the floating-point data types *Single* and *Double*. At the same time, however, there will be no rounding errors due to the internal display of values in the binary system. You will learn more about this in the following section.

CLS-compliant: Yes

Conversion of other numeric types: *CDec(objVar)* or *Convert.ToDecimal(objVar)*

```
aDecimal = CDec(123.45F)
aDecimal = Convert.ToDecimal(123.45F)
```

The Numeric Data Types at a Glance

Table 6-2 presents a list of the numeric data types, along with a brief description.

TABLE 6-2 The Numeric Base Data Types in .NET 2.0/3.5/4.0 and Visual Basic 2010

Type name	.NET type name	Task	Scope
Byte	*System.Byte*	Stores unsigned integer values with a width of 8 bits (1 byte)	−0 to 255
SByte	*System.SByte*	Stores signed integer values with a width of 8 bits (1 byte)	−127 to 128
Short	*System.Int16*	Stores signed integer values with a width of 16 bits (2 bytes)	−32,768 to 32,767
UShort	*System.UInt16*	Stores unsigned integer values with a width of 16 bits (2 bytes)	0 to 65,535
Integer	*System.Int32*	Stores signed integer values with a width of 32 bits (4 bytes) **Note:** On 32-bit systems, this integer data type is processed most quickly	−2,147,483,648 to 2,147,483,647
UInteger	*System.UInt32*	Stores unsigned integer values with a width of 32 bit (4 bytes)	0 to 4,294,967,295
Long	*System.Int64*	Stores signed integer values with a width of 64 bits (8 bytes)	−9,223,372,036,854,775,808 to 9,223,372,036,854,775,807
ULong	*System.UInt64*	Stores unsigned integer values with a width of 64 bits (8 bytes)	0 to 18,446,744,073,709,551,615
Single	*System.Single*	Stores floating-point numbers with single precision; requires 4 bytes for display	−3.4028235E+38 to −1.401298E-45 for negative values; 1.401298E-45 to 3.4028235E+38 for positive values
Double	*System.Double*	Stores floating-point numbers with double precision; requires 8 bytes for display. **Note:** This is the fastest data type for floating-point number calculations because it is delegated directly to the math unit of the processor for calculation.	1.79769313486231570E+308 to -4.94065645841246544E-324 for negative values; 4.94065645841246544E-324 to 1.79769313486231570E+308 for positive values
Decimal	*System.Decimal*	Stores floating-point numbers in binary-coded decimal format. **Note:** This is the lowest data type for floating-point number calculations, but its special form of representing values excludes typical computer rounding errors.	0 to ±79,228,162,514.264,337.593,543,950,335 (±7.9...E+28) without decimal character; 0 to ±7.9228162514264337593543950335 with 28 places to the right of the decimal character; smallest number not equal 0 (zero) is ±0.0000000000000000000000000001 (±1E-28)

Avoiding Single and Double Rounding Errors

It's not unusual that some numeric systems are unable to display exact values for fractions. However, programmers repeatedly believe that they have found an error in a programming language or claim that the computer can't calculate correctly. You have already experienced rounding and conversion errors from one numeric system into another in your daily life with the base-10 system. For example, dividing the number 1 by 3 results in a number with infinite decimal points (0.333333333333...). Representing the fraction one-third using a base-3 system requires considerably fewer numbers; it's simply 0.1.

It doesn't really matter how many numbers you use to display a fraction, but as long as you use a finite number of digits in numeric systems to display a fraction, there will be situations in which rounding errors are unavoidable.

For example, 3*1/3 in a base-3 system leads to the following calculation:

```
 0.1
+0.1
+0.1
=============================================
+1.0
```

In the decimal system, this also corresponds to 1.0. But performing this same addition in the decimal system is imprecise, because even if you use 60 decimal places to represent the number, you never reach the value 1 in the addition, as shown here:

```
 0,333333333333333333333333333333333333333333333333333333333333
+0.333333333333333333333333333333333333333333333333333333333333
+0.333333333333333333333333333333333333333333333333333333333333
==============================================================
 0.999999999999999999999999999999999999999999999999999999999999
```

The total value in the preceding calculation is very close to 1—but it's not quite 1. If you have multiple intermediate results during the course of a calculation, such representation errors can quickly lead to bigger mistakes that will become relevant at some point.

The computer has the same problem with certain numbers when it calculates in the binary system. Even though it can display the number 69.82 in the decimal system correctly, it runs into problems with the binary system. Converting 69 works without issues, but it becomes difficult with 0.82.

Once you know that decimal places are represented by negative powers of the base number, you can try to approximate the fractional part (0.82) by using the following calculations:

```
0.5         1*2^-1  intermediate result: 0.5
0.25        1*2^-2  intermediate result: 0.75
0.125       1*2^-3  intermediate result: 0.8125
0.0625      0*2^-4  intermediate result: 0.8125
0.03125     0*2^-5  intermediate result: 0.8125
```

```
0.015625         0*2^-6  intermediate result: 0.8125
0.0078125        0*2^-7  intermediate result: 0.8125
0.00390625       1*2^-8  intermediate result: 0.81640625
0.001953125      1*2^-9  intermediate result: 0.818359375
0.0009765625     1*2^-10 intermediate result: 0.8193359375
0.00048828125    1*2^-11 intermediate result: 0.81982421875
```

At this point, the computer has generated the binary digits 0.11100001111, but we have not reached the desired goal. The truth is that you can play this game for all eternity, but you will never be able to represent the number 0.82 in the decimal system with a finite number of digits in the binary system.

> **Companion Content** What's the impact to programming in Visual Basic? Take a look at the sample program in the \VB 2010 Developer Handbook\Chapter 06\Primitives02 folder.

```vb
Public Class Primitives

    Public Shared Sub main()

        Dim locDouble1, locDouble2 As Double
        Dim locDec1, locDec2 As Decimal

        locDouble1 = 69.82
        locDouble2 = 69.2
        locDouble2 += 0.62

        Console.WriteLine("The statement locDouble1=locDouble2 is {0}",
            locDouble1 = locDouble2)
        Console.WriteLine("but locDouble1 is {0} and locDouble2 is {1}", _
                        locDouble1, locDouble2)


        locDec1 = 69.82D
        locDec2 = 69.2D
        locDec2 += 0.62D
        Console.WriteLine("The statement locDec1=locDec2 is {0}", locDec1 = locDec2)

        Console.WriteLine()
        Console.WriteLine("Press key to exit!")
        Console.ReadKey()

        ...

    End Sub

End Class
```

At first glance, you'd think that both *WriteLine* methods return the same text. You don't need to use a calculator to see that the value (and thus the first variable) within the program represents the addition of the second and third value; therefore, both variable values should

be the same. Unfortunately that's not the case. Although the second part of the program achieves the correct result using the *Decimal* data type, the *Double* type fails in the first part of the program.

The second *WriteLine* method is even more confusing, because both variables appear to contain the same value to the last decimal place. Here's the output from the preceding code:

```
The statement locDouble1=locDouble2 is False
but locDouble1 is 69.82 and locDouble2 is 69.82
The statement locDec1=locDec2 is True

Press key to exit!
```

So what happened here? During the conversion from the internal binary number system to the decimal number system, a rounding error takes place that conceals the true result. Based on this experiment, the following remarks can be made. If at all possible, try to avoid using fractioned *Double* or *Single* values as counters or conditions within a loop; otherwise, you run the risk that your program becomes bogged down in endless loops as a result of the inaccuracies just mentioned. Therefore, follow these rules:

- Use *Single* and *Double* data types only where the umpteenth number behind the comma is not important. For example, when calculating graphics, where rounding errors are irrelevant due to a smaller screen resolution, you should always choose the faster processor-calculated data types, *Single* and *Double*, over the manually calculated Decimal data type.

- When working with finance applications you should *always* use the *Decimal* data type. It's the only data type that ensures that numeric calculations that cannot be represented exactly will not result in major errors.

- If possible, never use the *Decimal* data type in loops, and do not use it as a counter variable. The type is not directly supported by the processor, so it degrades your program's performance. Try to get by with one of the many integer variable types.

- When you need to compare *Double* and *Single* variables to one another, you should query their deltas rather than comparing the values directly, as in the following code:

```
If Math.Abs(locDouble1 - locDouble2) < 0.0001 then
    'Values are nearly the same, i.e. the same.
End If
```

Methods Common to all Numeric Types

All numeric data types have methods that are used the same way for all types. They convert a string into the corresponding numeric value or a numeric value into a string. Other methods serve to determine the largest or smallest value a data type can represent.

Converting Strings into Values and Avoiding Culture-Dependant Errors

The static functions *Parse* and *TryParse* are available to all numeric data types to convert a string into a value. For example, to convert the numeric string "123" into the integer value 123, you can write:

```
Dim locInteger As Integer
locInteger = Integer.Parse("123")
```

> **Important** Beginning with Visual Basic 2005, you can no longer write the following:
>
> ```
> locInteger = locInteger.Parse("123")    'Should not be done like this any longer!
> ```
>
> Because *Parse* is a static function, you should no longer call it via an object variable—use only the corresponding class name. A program that addresses the static function via an object variable can still be compiled, but the Code Editor will display a warning.

You can also try to convert the string into a numeric value, as shown here:

```
Dim locInteger As Integer
If Integer.TryParse("123", locInteger) Then
    'Conversion successful
Else
    'Conversion not successful
End If
```

If the conversion is successful, the converted number is displayed in the output variable—*locInteger* in this example. The .NET Framework equivalent of *Integer* also permits conversions via this code:

```
locInteger = System.Int32.Parse("123") 'This would work, too.
```

And of course, it's also possible to make the conversion via the *Convert* class in .NET Framework style by using the following:

```
locInteger = Convert.ToInt32("123")      'And this would work.
```

Finally, there's an old-fashioned way in Visual Basic:

```
locInteger = CInt("123")                 'Last option.
```

But watch out: you might find differences when running programs on a non–English-language system because of the default cultural setting. For example, if you run the following program on a German system, it will not act the way you might expect:

```
Dim locString As String = "123.23"
Dim locdouble As Double = Double.Parse(locString)
Console.WriteLine(locdouble.ToString)
```

You might expect the string to be converted correctly into the value 123.23. Instead the program returns the following:

```
12323
```

This is definitely not the expected result. However, if you run the program on an English system, the result will be correct, as expected:

```
123.23
```

Well, maybe not quite. Germans are used to separating the decimal places from integer places by a comma. English speaking countries use a period, and the preceding output uses the correct English formatting. What's the impact of this behavior on your programs? To begin, you should avoid saving numeric constants as text in the program code itself if you want to convert them to a numeric type later on (as shown in the example). When you define numeric data types within your programs, make those definitions directly in code. Do not use strings (text in quotes) and the corresponding conversion functions. You have probably already noticed that numeric strings placed in code (without quotes) for assigning a value must always adhere to the English formatting.

> **Note** To be accurate, the behavior that was just described isn't caused by an English-language system; it is because that operating system has default cultural settings. Of course, a German or other non–English-language system can also be configured to yield the same result.

As long as you don't need to exchange files with information saved as text across cultural borders for which your program has to generate values, you have nothing to worry about: if your application is run on an English-language system, your numbers are written into the file with a period as separator; in the German-speaking areas, a comma is used. Because cultural settings are taken into account when reading a file, your application should be able to generate the correct values back from the text file.

It becomes a bit more problematic when the files containing the text are exchanged across cultural borders. This can happen pretty easily; for example, you might access a database server in a company with a .NET Windows Forms application from a German Windows 7 system, because many IT departments exclusively run English-language versions on their servers for a variety of reasons. Therefore, a platform in the United States would export the file with a period separator, and in Germany, the *Parse* function would recognize the period as a thousands-separator, and thus erroneously treat the fractional digits as significant integer digits. In this case, you need to ensure that any export of a text file is culturally neutral, which you can achieve as follows:

You can use the *Parse* function and the *ToString* function of all numeric types to control the conversion by a *format provider*. For numeric types, .NET offers many different format providers: some help you control the format depending on the application type (financial, scientific, and so on), others control it depending on the culture, namely the classes *NumberFormatInfo* and *CultureInfo*. You can pass either to the *ToString* or the *Parse* function (assuming they have been properly initialized).

Important You should always use the following procedure for applications that will be used internationally to avoid type conversion errors from the start:

```
Dim locString As String = "123.23"
Dim locdouble As Double

locdouble = Double.Parse(locString, CultureInfo.InvariantCulture)
Console.WriteLine(locdouble.ToString(CultureInfo.InvariantCulture))
Console.ReadLine()
```

Note To be able to access classes and functions that control globalization, you must bind the namespace *System.Globalization* with the *Imports* statement at the beginning of the program, as follows:

```
Imports System.Globalization
```

The static property *InvariantCulture* returns an instance of a *CultureInfo* class that represents the current system locale.

Note Should the conversion fail simply because the string doesn't contain a convertible format, and thus can't be converted into a value, .NET Framework generates an exception (see Figure 6-1). The exception can either be caught with *Try … Catch*, or alternatively, you can use the static method *TryParse*, which never causes an exception during conversion attempts.

```
locDec1 = 69.82D
locDec1 = Decimal.Parse("123.123.123") '69.2D
locDec2 = 69.2D
locDec2 += 0.62D
Console.WriteLine("The statement locDec
Console.WriteLine()
Console.WriteLine("Press a key to exit!
Console.ReadKey()
'End
```

FIGURE 6-1 If a string that represents a numeric value cannot be converted due to its format, the .NET Framework generates an exception.

Performance and Rounding Issues

If you are using type-safe programming in Visual Basic .NET (which you should always do by using *Option Strict On* in the project properties), it is customary to convert a floating-point number into a value of the type *Integer* by using the conversion operator *CInt*. But a lot of programmers don't know that the Visual Basic compiler behaves completely differently than the casting operator in C#. *CInt* in Visual Basic uses commercial rounding, so the compiler turns

```
Dim anInt = CInt(123.54R)
```

into:

```
Dim anInt = CInt(Math.Round(123.54R))
```

It is *not possible* to implement a simple *CInt* (as used by the Visual Basic compiler itself, and as is the default in C#) in Visual Basic itself. When converting a floating-point in C#, the decimal places after the integer are simply truncated—they are not rounded. To simulate this, you need to use the following construct:

```
Dim anInt = CInt(Math.Truncate(123.54R))
```

The problem is that the compiler generates the following completely redundant code from it:

```
Dim anInt = CInt(Math.Round(Math.Truncate(123.54R)))
```

When it comes to processing graphics, for example, this means a huge performance compromise, of course, because two functions are called from the Math Library. C# is noticeably faster because it provides a *CInt* directly.

> **Tip** If you do run into performance problems due to this behavior, create a C# assembly that provides a function for converting *Double*, *Single*, or *Decimal* directly to *Integer* values. It's quite probable that this function will be inlined (the JIT compiler transfers the code of the C# function to the assembly without generating a function call jump), and therefore, you can achieve almost the same performance as in C#.

Determining the Minimum and Maximum Values of a Numeric Type

The numeric data types recognize two specific static properties that you can use to determine the largest and smallest representable value. These properties are called *MinValue* and *MaxValue*—and just like any static function, you can call them through the type name as shown in the following example:

```
Dim locDecimal As System.Decimal

Console.WriteLine(Integer.MaxValue)
Console.WriteLine(Double.MinValue)
Console.WriteLine(locDecimal.MaxValue) ' Compiler gives a warning - use type name instead.
```

Special Functions for all Floating-Point Types

Floating-point types have certain special properties that simplify processing of abnormal results during calculations (such as the *Infinity* and the *NaN* properties). To check for non-numeric results in your calculations, use the following members of the floating-point data types.

Infinity

When a floating-point value type is divided by 0, the .NET Framework does not generate an exception; instead, the result is *infinity*. Both *Single* and *Double* can represent this result, as shown in the following example:

```
Dim locdouble As Double
locdouble = 20
locdouble /= 0
Console.WriteLine(locdouble)
Console.WriteLine("The statement locDouble is +infinite is {0}.",
    locdouble = Double.PositiveInfinity)
' I suggest using the IsPositiveInfinity method and replacing the last statement
' with an If statement:
If locdouble.IsPositiveInfinity Then
...
Else
...
End If
```

When you run this example, no exception occurs, but the program displays the following on the screen:

```
+infinite
The statement locDouble is +infinite is True.
```

Instead of performing the comparison to infinity by using the comparison operator, you can also use the static function *IsInfinity*, as follows:

```
Console.WriteLine("The statemdnt locDouble is +infinity is {0}.", locdouble.
IsInfinity(locdouble))
```

You can also use the *IsPositiveInfinity* and *IsNegativeInfinity* methods to determine whether a value is infinitely large or infinitely small (a very large negative value).

To assign the value *infinite* to a variable, use the static functions *PositiveInfinity* and *NegativeInfinity*, which return appropriate constants.

Not a Number: *NaN*

The base floating-point types cover another special case: the division of 0 by 0, which is not mathematically defined and *does not return a valid number*:

```
'Special case: 0/0 is not mathematically defined and returns "Not a Number"
aDouble = 0
aDouble = aDouble / 0
If Double.IsNaN(aDouble) Then
    Debug.Print("aDouble is not a number!")
End If
```

If you run this code, the output window will display the result of the *If* query.

Important You can test these special cases only via properties that static functions directly "append" to the type. With the floating-point type constant *NaN*, you can assign the value "not a valid number" to a variable, but you can't use the constant to test for the not-a-number state, as shown in the example that follows.

```
Dim aDouble As Double

'Special case: 0/0 is not mathematically defined and returns "Not a Number"
aDouble = 0
aDouble = aDouble / 0

'The text should be returned as expected,
'but isn't!
If aDouble = Double.NaN Then
    Debug.Print("Test 1:aDouble is not a number!")
End If

'Now the test can be performed!
If Double.IsNaN(aDouble) Then
    Debug.Print("Test 2:aDouble is not a number!")
End If
```

The preceding example displays only the second message in the output window.

Note Both features, *NaN* and *Infinity*, let your programs behave totally differently in contrast to Visual Basic for Applications (or the old Visual Basic 6.0 for that matter). So be careful if you migrate applications, or even only methods, from Visual Basic 6.0 to VB.NET: some algorithms in VBA/Visual Basic 6.0 *expect* errors at certain points to occur, but since a division by zero doesn't necessarily lead to an error in VB.NET (this happens only with integer data types), those algorithms might return incorrect results in certain cases.

Converting with *TryParse*

All numeric data types expose the static method *TryParse*, which attempts to convert a string into a value. Unlike *Parse*, the *TryParse* method doesn't generate an exception when the conversion fails. Instead, you pass a variable name as a reference argument to the method, and the method returns a result, indicating whether the conversion was successful (*True*) or not (*False*), as shown here:

```
Dim locdouble As Double
Dim locString As String = "Onehundredandtwentythree"

'locdouble = Double.Parse(locString) ' Exception
'Not working, either, but at least no exception:
Console.WriteLine("Conversion successful? {0}", _
        Double.TryParse(locString, NumberStyles.Any, New CultureInfo("en-En"), locdouble))
```

Special Functions for the *Decimal* Type

The value type *Decimal* also has special methods, many of which aren't of any use in Visual Basic (you can use them, but it doesn't make much sense—they were added for other languages that don't support operator overloading). Take, for example, the static *Add* function, which adds two numbers of type *Decimal* and returns a *Decimal*. You can use the + operator of Visual Basic instead, which can also add two numbers of the type *Decimal*—and does so in much more easily readable code. Therefore, it makes sense to use the functions presented in Table 6-3.

TABLE 6-3 The Most Important Functions of the *Decimal* Type

Function name	Task
Remainder(Dec1, Dec2)	Determines the remainder of the division of both decimal *Decimal* values.
Round(Dec, Integer)	Rounds a *Decimal* value to the specified number of decimal places.
Truncate(Dec)	Returns the integer part of the specified *Decimal* value.
Floor(Dec)	Rounds the *Decimal* value to the next smaller number.
Negate(Decimal)	Multiplies the *Decimal* value by –1.

The *Char* Data Type

The *Char* data type stores a character in Unicode format (more about this topic later in the chapter) using 16 bits, or 2 bytes. Unlike the *String* type, the *Char* data type is a value type. The following brief overview gives you more details:

.NET data type: *System.Char*

Represents: A single character

Range: 0–65.535, so that Unicode characters can be displayed

Type literal: c

Memory requirements: 2 bytes

Delegation to the processor: Yes

CLS-compliant: Yes

Description: *Char* values are often used in arrays, because in many cases it's more practical to process individual characters than it is to process strings. Like any other data type, you can define *Char* arrays with constants (you'll see an example shortly). The following section on strings contains examples on how to use *Char* arrays instead of *strings* for character-by-character processing.

Even if *Char* is saved internally as an unsigned 16-bit value, and is therefore like a *Short*, you cannot implicitly convert a *Char* into a numeric type. In addition to the possibility described in the Online Help, however, you can use not only the functions *AscW* and *ChrW* to convert a *Char* to a numeric data type, and vice versa, but also the *Convert* class, for example:

```
'Normal declaration and definition
Dim locChar As Char
locChar = "1"c
Dim locInteger As Integer = Convert.ToInt32(locChar)
Console.WriteLine("The value of '{0}' is {1}", locChar, locInteger)
```

When you run this example, it displays the following output:

```
The value of '1' is 49
```

You can also use the functions *Chr* and *Asc*, but they work only for non-Unicode characters (ASCII 0–255). Due to various internal scope checks, they also have an enormous overhead; therefore, they are nowhere near as fast as *AscW, ChrW* (which are the fastest, because a direct and internal type conversion of *Char* into *Integer*, and vice versa, takes place) or the *Convert* class (which has the advantage of being easily understood by non-Visual Basic developers as well).

Declaration and Sample Assignment (also as Array):

```
'Normal declaration and definition
Dim locChar As Char
locChar = "K"c

'Define and declare a Char array with constants.
Dim locCharArray() As Char = {"A"c, "B"c, "C"c}

'Convert a Char array into string.
Dim locStringFromCharArray As String = New String(locCharArray)
```

```
'Convert a string into a Char array.
'Of course that's also possible with a string variable.
locCharArray = "This is a string".ToCharArray
```

The *String* Data Type

Strings are used to store text. Unlike in Visual Basic for Applications (or Visual Basic 6.0), the modern versions of Visual Basic offer an object-oriented programming (OOP) approach for working with strings, which makes string processing much easier. Your programs will be easier to read if you follow the OOP concepts.

You have already encountered strings several times in the previous chapters. Nevertheless, it's worth taking another look behind the scenes. In conjunction with the Regular Expression (*Regex*) class, the .NET Framework offers the best possible string support.

In contrast to other base types, strings are reference types. However, you don't have to define a new *String* instance with the keyword *New*. The compiler intervenes here because it has to generate special code anyhow.

> **Note** Similar to nullables (see Chapter 18) when boxing, CLR interrupts the default behavior for reference types and changes it. Strictly speaking, since strings are reference types, they need to be instantiated with *New*. The equal operator would also need to assign just one reference. For strings, however, when assigning an instance to an object variable, the content is cloned, which also deviates from the default. You can read more about reference types in Chapter 12, "Typecasting and Boxing Value Types."

The following sections provide an overview of the special characteristic of strings in the BCL. At the end of this section, you'll find an example application that illustrates the most important string manipulation functions.

Strings—Yesterday and Today

Beginning with Visual Studio 2002 and .NET Framework 1.0, Microsoft introduced a completely new way to approach string programming in Visual Basic. This was the result of the new implementation of the data type *String*, which is created by instantiating a class, like other objects.

Almost all commands and functions that were "standalone" in Visual Basic 6.0 and VBA still exist in the .NET Framework versions of Visual Basic. But they are not only superfluous—you can reach the same goal much more elegantly with the existing methods and properties of the *String* object—but they also slow down programs unnecessarily, because internally they call the *String* object functions anyhow.

For (almost) all the old string functions, there is a corresponding class function that you should use as a substitute. The following sections demonstrate the handling of strings with the help of a few short examples.

Declaring and Defining Strings

As with all other base data types, you can declare strings without using the *New* keyword; you can perform assignments directly in the program. For example, you can declare a string with the statement:

```
Dim aString As String
```

You can then immediately use the new string variable. The instance of the *String* object is created at IML level. Strings are defined as a list of characters between quotes, as shown in the following example:

```
aString = "Susan Kallenbach"
```

Just as with other base data types, declaration and assignment can both take place in an assignment. Therefore, you can combine the two single statements shown in the preceding statements into the following shorter, single statement:

```
Dim aString As String = "Susan Kallenbach"
```

Handling Empty and Blank Strings

For decades, Visual Basic developers have become accustomed to using the code pattern shown in the following to check whether a string variable is not defined (*Nothing*) or points to an empty string:

```
Dim myString As String
myString = WinFormsTextBox.Text

If myString Is Nothing Or myString = "" Then
    MessageBox.Show("myString is empty.")
End If
```

Initially, the data type *String* acts like a regular reference type. As soon as it is declared, it becomes *Nothing*, because its content points to *nothing*. But it also has a second state that corresponds to the value "empty," which occurs when it points to a memory area reserved for saving characters, but that doesn't contain any characters. In this case, the *String* variable saves an empty string. Yet a third possibility occurs when the string *does* contain data (at least from the computer's standpoint), but that data does not represent visible content, because it's not printable (or more precisely, it's not visible on the screen or when printed). Such characters are called whitespace characters, which include space characters, tabs, and other control characters.

All these states are checked by a static method of the *String* type, and it simplifies testing for such states:

```
If String.IsNullOrWhiteSpace(myString) Then
    MessageBox.Show("my string is empty.")
End If
```

When you run this code, you always receive the message "my string is empty" when the *myString* variable is empty (points to an empty string), is *Nothing*, or contains only one or more whitespaces.

The method *IsNullOrWhiteSpace* has been available since .NET Framework 4.0. If you need to maintain backward compatibility with earlier versions of the .NET Framework, or if you want to allow whitespaces as valid entries, it is better to use the *IsNullOrEmpty* method, which returns *True* for *Nothing* and empty strings, as illustrated in the following:

```
If String.IsNullOrEmpty(myString) Then
    MessageBox.Show("myString is empty.")
End If
```

Automatic String Construction

Normally, a class constructor creates an instance and a structure to pre-assign certain values to parameters—you'll find a lot more on constructors in this book's OOP section.

Even though you create strings in the same manner as all other base data types, you still have the option of calling a constructor method. However, you don't employ the constructor exclusively for re-instantiating an empty *String* object (the parameterless constructor is not permitted), but you actually emulate, among others, the old *String$* function from Visual Basic 6.0 or VBA.

With their help it was possible to generate a string programmatically and save it in a *String* variable.

 Note While many of the old Visual Basic 6.0/VBA commands are still available all of the .NET Framework versions up to 4.0, the *String* function itself no longer exists in the .NET versions of Visual Basic—possibly due to the type identifier of the same name.

To use the *String* constructor as a *String$* function substitute, do the following:

```
Dim locString As String = New String("A"c, 40)
```

The type literal "c" indicates that you need to pass a value of the type *Char* in the constructor. Unfortunately this limits the repetition function to one character, which wasn't the case with *String$*. Fortunately, it's no problem to implement a *Repeat* function, which resolves this issue:

```
Public Function Repeat(ByVal s As String, ByVal repetitions As Integer) As String
    Dim sBuilder As New StringBuilder

    For count As Integer = 1 To repetitions
        sBuilder.Append(s)
    Next

    Return sBuilder.ToString
End Function
```

> **Note** This construct mainly serves as an example, and you should only construct strings in this manner if there are very few characters. You should use the larger text segments of the *StringBuilder* class for performance reasons. The *StringBuilder* class is described in the section, "*StringBuilder* vs. *String*: When Performance Matters," later in this chapter. Why this is the case is explained in the section, "No Strings Attached, or Are There? Strings are Immutable!"

Apart from using a constructor to generate strings by repeating the same character, you can also use one to create a string from a *Char* array or a portion of a *Char* array, as shown in the following example:

```
Dim locCharArray() As Char = {"K"c, "."c, " "c, "L"c, "ö"c, "f"c, "f"c, "e"c, "l"c, "m"c,
➥"a"c, "n"c, "n"c}
Dim locString As String = New String(locCharArray)
Console.WriteLine(locString)
locString = New String(locCharArray, 3, 6)
Console.WriteLine(locString)
```

When you run this program, the console window displays the following output:

```
K. Löffelmann
Löffel
```

Assigning Special Characters to a String

To include quotes in the string itself, use repeated double quotes. For example, to define the string "Adriana said, "it's only 1pm, I'm going to sleep in a little longer!" in a program, you would write the assignment as follows:

```
locString = "Adriana said, ""it's only 1pm, I'm going to sleep in a little longer!""."
```

To include other special characters, use the existing constants in the Visual Basic vocabulary. For example, to build a paragraph into a string, you need to insert the ASCII codes for *line-feed* and *carriage return* into the string. You achieve this by using the constants shown in the following example:

```
locOtherString = "Adriana said ""I'm going to sleep in a little longer!"""" & vbCr & vbLf & _
                 "She fell asleep again immediately."
```

You could use *vbNewLine* or the shorthand *vbCrLf* character constants instead. For example, you can save keystrokes with the following version, which delivers the same result:

```
locOtherString = "Adriana said ""I'm going to sleep in a little longer!"""" & vbNewLine & _
                 "She fell asleep again immediately."
```

Table 6-4 presents the special character constants that Visual Basic offers.

TABLE 6-4 The Constants That Correspond to the Most Common Special Characters

Constant	ASCII	Description
vbCrLf or vbNewLine	13; 10	Carriage return/line feed character
vbCr	13	Carriage return character
vbLf	10	Line feed character
vbNullChar	0	Character with a value of 0
vbNullString		String with a value of 0. Doesn't corresponds to a string with a length of 0 (""); this constant is meant for calling external procedures (COM Interop).
vbTab	9	Tab character
vbBack	8	Backspace character
vbFormFeed	12	Not used in Microsoft Windows
vbVerticalTab	11	Control characters for the vertical tab which isn't used in Microsoft Windows

Memory Requirements for Strings

Each character in a string requires two bytes of memory. Even though strings are returned as letters, each character is represented in memory by a numeric value. The values from 1 to 255 correspond to the *American Standard Code for Information Interchange*—ASCII for short—which standardizes only values up to 127 for each character set. Special characters are defined in the 128–255 range, and those characters depend on the specific character set used. Generally the codes for the special characters of the European countries, such as "öäüÖÄÜâéè", have the same code for each font (the exception proves the rule, as usual). Values above 255 represent special characters that are used, for example, for the Cyrillic, Arabic, or Asian characters. This coding convention, called Unicode, permits a considerably larger total number of characters. The .NET Framework generally saves strings in *Unicode* format.

No Strings Attached, or Are There? Strings are Immutable!

Generally, strings are reference types, but they are strictly static in memory and are therefore immutable. In practice, that means that there is no restriction as to how you handle strings: even though you might think you have changed a string, you have actually created a new one that contains the changes. You need to know that when it comes to applications that perform many string operations, you should use the *StringBuilder* class instead, which is noticeably more powerful, even though it doesn't offer the flexibility of the string manipulation methods or the advantages of the base data types. (The section, "When Speed Matters," discusses this topic in more detail.)

You can read more about reference and value types in Chapter 8, "Class Begins."

Much more important is the impact of the immutability of strings in your programs: even though strings are considered reference types, they behave like value types, because they cannot be changed. When two string variables point to the same memory area and you change the content of a string, it appears as though you are changing the value of the original variable, but in reality, such operations create a completely new *String* object in memory and change the existing variable to point to it. This way, you never end up in the situation you know from reference types, in which changing the object content via the object variable never causes another string variable, which points to the same memory area, to return the edited string. This explains why strings are reference types, but at the same time, they "look and feel" like value types.

You will see more about this in the following section along with some practical examples.

Memory Optimization for Strings

For saving strings the .NET Framework uses an *internal pool* that to avoids redundancies in string storage. If you define two strings within your program using the same constant, the Visual Basic compiler recognizes that they're the same and places only one copy of the string in memory. At the same time, it allows both object variables to point to the same memory area, as the following example proves:

```
Dim locString As String
Dim locOtherString As String

locString = "Adriana" & " Ardelean"
locOtherString = "Adriana Ardelean"
Console.WriteLine(locString Is locOtherString)
```

When you start this program, it returns *True*—meaning that both strings point to the same memory area. This condition exists only as long as the compiler can recognize the equality of the strings, and to do this, their values must be specified in a single statement. For example, in the following code, the compiler can no longer recognize the equality of the strings, so the result would be *False*:

```
Dim locString As String
Dim locOtherString As String

locString = "Adriana"
locString &= " Ardelean"
locOtherString = "Adriana Ardelean"
Console.WriteLine(locString Is locOtherString)
```

It's obvious that a behavior to avoid redundancies at runtime would take too much time and can't be used in a sensible way. If there are a lot of strings, the BCL would waste too much time searching for strings that already existing. However, you do have the option to specifically add a string created at runtime to a pool. If you add several identical strings to the internal pool, they are not assigned redundantly—several identical strings then share the same memory. Of course, this only makes sense when you can predict that there will be many conformant strings within a program. The example that follows shows how you explicitly add a string with the static function *Intern* to the internal pool:

```
Dim locString As String
Dim locOtherString As String

locString = "Adriana"
locString &= " Ardelean"
locString = String.Intern(locString)
locOtherString = String.Intern("Adriana Ardelean")
Console.WriteLine(locString Is locOtherString)
```

When you start this program, the output is again *True*.

Determining String Length

VBA/Visual Basic 6.0 compatible command: Len

.NET versions of Visual Basic: *strVar.Length*

Description: With this command you determine the length of a string in characters, and not in bytes.

Example: The following example accepts a string from a user and returns the string's characters in inverse order:

```
Dim locString As String
Console.Write("Enter a text: ")
locString = Console.ReadLine()
For count As Integer = locString.Length - 1 To 0 Step -1
   Console.Write(locString.Substring(count, 1))
Next
```

You can find the same example with Visual Basic 6.0 compatibility commands in the next section.

Retrieving Parts of a String

VBA/Visual Basic 6.0 compatible command(s): *Left, Right, Mid*

.NET versions of Visual Basic: *strVar.SubString*

Description: Use this command to retrieve a certain part of a string as another string.

> **Note** Why the good-old *Left* and *Right* methods of the class *String* were omitted is a question only the programmer can answer. Maybe they were simply forgotten, or the programmer knew only C and couldn't imagine a world as simple as BASIC.

Example: The following example reads a string from the keyboard and then returns its characters in inverse order. You can find the same example in the previous section with the functions of the *String* object.

```
Dim locString As String
Console.Write("Enter a text: ")
locString = Console.ReadLine()
For count As Integer = Len(locString) To 1 Step -1
    Console.Write(Mid(locString, count, 1))
Next
```

Padding Strings

VBA/Visual Basic 6.0 compatible command(s): *RSet, LSet*

.NET versions of Visual Basic: *strVar.PadLeft; strVar.PadRight*

Description: With these commands, you can increase the length of a string to a certain number of characters; the string is padded with blank characters at the beginning or the end.

Example: The following example demonstrates the use of the *PadLeft* and the *PadRight* method:

```
Dim locString As String = "This string is so long"
Dim locString2 As String = "Not this one"
Dim locString3 As String = "This"
Len(locString)
locString2 = locString2.PadLeft(locString.Length)
locString3 = locString3.PadRight(locString.Length)

Console.WriteLine(locString + ":")
Console.WriteLine(locString2 + ":")
Console.WriteLine(locString3 + ":")
```

When you run this program the following output is generated:

```
This string is so long:
          Not this one:
This               :
```

> **Note** The strings are so perfectly aligned only because the Console window uses a monospaced font by default. You can't align strings in a typical window that uses a proportional font with the *PadLeft* and *PadRight* methods.

Find and Replace Operations

VBA/Visual Basic 6.0 compatible command(s): *InStr, InStrRev, Replace*

.NET versions of Visual Basic: *strVar.IndexOf; strVar.IndexOfAny; strVar.Replace; strVar. Remove*

Description: With the Visual Basic 6.0 compatible command *InStr*, you can search for the occurrence of a character or a string within a string. *InStrRev* does the same, but it starts the search from the end of the string. *Replace* lets you to replace a substring within a string with another string.

Using the *IndexOf* method of the *String* class, you can search for the occurrence of a character or a string within the current string. Furthermore, the *IndexOfAny* method lets you find the occurrences of a group of characters passed as a *Char* array within the string. The *Replace* method replaces individual characters or strings with others in the current string, and the *Remove* method removes a specific substring from the string.

Example: The following examples demonstrate how to use the *Find* and *Replace* methods of the *String* class:

> **Companion Content** Open the corresponding solution (.sln) for this example, which you can find in the \VB 2010 Developer Handbook\Chapter 06\Strings – Find and Replace folder.

```
Imports System.Globalization

Module Strings
    Sub Main()
        Dim locString As String = _
            "Common wisdoms:" + vbNewLine + _
            "* If you would shout for 8 years, 7 months, and 6 days," + vbNewLine + _
            " you would have produced enough energy to heat a cup of coffee." + _
 ➥vbNewLine + _
            "* If you hit your head against the wall, you use up 150 calories." +
```

```
➥vbNewLine + _
            "* Elephants are the only animals who can't jump." + vbNewLine + _
            "* A cockroach can live for 9 days without a head before it dies of
➥hunger." + vbNewLine + _
            "* Gold and other metals originate solely from" + vbNewLine + _
            "  supernovae." + vbNewLine + _
            "* The Moon consists of debris from a collision of a" + vbNewLine + _
            "  planet the size of Mars with the Earth." + vbNewLine + _
            "* New York is called the ""Big Pineapple"", because ""Big Pineapple"" in
➥the language of" + vbNewLine + _
            "  Jazz musicians meant ""hitting the jackpot"". To have a career in New
➥York" + vbNewLine + _
            "  meant their jackpot." + vbNewLine + _
            "* The expression ""08/15"" for something unoriginal was originally " +
➥vbNewLine + _
            "  the label of the machine gun LMG 08/15;" + vbNewLine + _
            "  It become the metaphor for unimaginative, military drills." +
➥vbNewLine + _
            "* 311 New Yorkers are being bit by rats per year in average." +
➥vbNewLine + _
            "  But 1511 New Yorkers have been bit by other New Yorkers at the same
➥time."
        'Replace number combination with letters
        locString = locString.Replace("08/15", "Zero-eight-fifteen")

        'Count punctuation
        Dim locPosition, locCount As Integer

        Do
            locPosition = locString.IndexOfAny(New Char() {"."c, ","c, ":"c, "?"c},
➥locPosition)
            If locPosition = -1 Then
                Exit Do
            Else
                locCount += 1
            End If
            locPosition += 1
        Loop

        Console.WriteLine("The following text...")
        Console.WriteLine(New String("="c, 79))
        Console.WriteLine(locString)
        Console.WriteLine(New String("="c, 79))
        Console.WriteLine("...has {0} punctuation.", locCount)
        Console.WriteLine()
        Console.WriteLine("And after replacing 'Big Pineapple' with 'Big Apple' it
➥looks as follows:")
        Console.WriteLine(New String("="c, 79))
```

```
            'Another substitution
            locString = locString.Replace("Big Pineapple", "Big Apple")
            Console.WriteLine(locString)
            Console.ReadLine()

    End Sub

End Module
```

The example displays the following output on the screen:

```
The following text...
=================================================================================
Common wisdoms:
* If you would shout for 8 years, 7 months, and 6 days,
  you would have produced enough energy to heat a cup of coffee.
* If you hit your head against the wall, you use up 150 calories.
* Elephants are the only animals who can't jump.
* A cockroach can live for 9 days without a head before it dies of hunger.
* Gold and other metals originate solely from
  Supernovae.
* The Moon consists of debris from a collision of a
  planet the size of Mars with the Earth.
* New York is called the "Big Pineapple", because "Big Pineapple" in the language of
  Jazz musicians meant "hitting the jackpot". To have a carreer in New York
  meant their jackpot.
* The expression "08/15" for something unoriginal was originally
  the label of the machine gun LMG 08/15;
  It become the metaphor for unimaginative, military drills.
* 311 New Yorkers are being bit by rats per year in average.
  But 1511 New Yorkers have been bit by other New Yorkers at the same time.
=================================================================================
...has 23 punctuation marks.

And if you replace 'Big Pineapple' with 'Big Apple' it looks as follows:
=================================================================================
Common wisdoms:
* If you would shout for 8 years, 7 months, and 6 days,
  you would have produced enough energy to heat a cup of coffee.
* If you hit your head against the wall, you use up 150 calories.
* Elephants are the only animals who can't jump.
* A cockroach can live for 9 days without a head before it dies of hunger.
* Gold and other metals originate solely from
  Supernovae..
* The Moon consists of debris from a collision of a
  planet the size of Mars with the Earth.
* New York is called the "Big Apple", because "Big Apple" in the language of
  Jazz musicians meant "hitting the jackpot". To have a carreer in New York
  meant their jackpot.
```

```
* The expression "08/15" for something unoriginal was originally
  the label of the machine gun LMG 08/15;
  It become the metaphor for unimaginative, military drills.
* 311 New Yorkers are being bit by rats per year in average.
  But 1511 New Yorkers have been bit by other New Yorkers at the same time.
```

> **Tip** The example presented in the section "Splitting Strings," contains a custom function called *ReplaceEx*, which you can use to search for several characters, replacing found occurrences with a specified character.

Trimming Strings

VBA/Visual Basic 6.0 compatible command(s): *Trim, RTrim, LTrim*

.NET versions of Visual Basic: *strVar.Trim, strVar.TrimEnd, strVar.TrimStart*

Description: These methods remove characters from both the beginning and the end of a string (*Trim*) or at either end of a string (*TrimStart* and *TrimEnd*). For these methods, the object methods of the strings are preferable to the compatibility functions, because for the former you can also specify which characters should be trimmed, as the following example demonstrates. In contrast, the Visual Basic 6.0 compatibility functions only allow space characters to be trimmed.

Example: The following example generates a *String* array whose individual elements have unwanted characters at the beginning and the end (not just space characters), which are removed by using the *Trim* function.

> **Note** This example also shows that strings act differently than common objects, even though they are considered reference types, because they are immutable. If you assign two object variables to an object and change the content of a variable, the object variable will also represent the changed object content. Even if a string seems to be changed, in fact, it's not. Rather, another completely new instance is created, which reflects the changes. The original string is discarded (you can read more about this topic in the section, "No Strings Attached, or Are There? Strings are Immutable!," earlier in this chapter).

```
Dim locStringArray() As String = { _
    "  - Here the actual text starts!", _
    "This text ends with strange characters! .-    ", _
    "  - Here both sides are problematic -  "}
```

```
For Each locString As String In locStringArray
    locString = locString.Trim(New Char() {" "c, "."c, "-"c})
    Console.WriteLine("Clean and neat: " + locString)
Next

'Important: String is a reference type, but nothing has changed for the array.
'That's because strings aren't changed directly, but are always created anew and thus
changed.
For Each locString As String In locStringArray
    Console.WriteLine("Still messy: " + locString)
Next
```

If you run this program, the following output is generated:

```
Clean and neat: Here the actual text starts!
Clean and neat: This text ends with strange characters!
Clean and neat: Here both sides are problematic
Still messy:    - Here the actual text starts!
Still messy: This text ends in strange characters! .-
Still messy:    - Here both sides are problematic -
```

Splitting Strings

VBA/Visual Basic 6.0 compatible command(s): *Split*

.NET versions of Visual Basic: *strVar.Split*

Description: The .NET *Split* method of the *String* class is superior to the compatibility function in that it permits you to specify several separator characters in a *Char* array. This makes
your programs more flexible when it comes to analyzing and rebuilding text.

Example: The following example separates the individual terms or sections of a string into
partial strings separated by different separator characters. These separated strings are later
presented as elements of a *String* array and are further prepared with additional functions.

> **Companion Content** Open the corresponding solution (.sln) for this example, which you can
> find in the \VB 2010 Developer Handbook\Chapter 06\String – Split folder.

```
Module Strings
    Sub Main()
        Dim locString As String = _
            "Individual, elements; separated by, different - characters."
        Console.WriteLine("From the line:")
        Console.WriteLine(locString)
        Console.WriteLine()
        Console.WriteLine("Becomes a string array with the following elements:")
        Dim locStringArray As String()
        locStringArray = locString.Split(New Char() {","c, ";"c, "-"c, "."c})
```

```
        For Each locStr As String In locStringArray
            Console.WriteLine(ReplaceEx(locStr, New Char() {","c, ";"c, "-"c, "."c}, _
                Convert.ToChar(vbNullChar)).Trim)
        Next
        Console.ReadLine()
    End Sub

    Public Function ReplaceEx(ByVal str As String, ByVal SearchChars As Char(), _
                    ByVal ReplaceChar As Char) As String
        Dim locPos As Integer
        Do
            locPos = str.IndexOfAny(SearchChars)
            If locPos = -1 Then Exit Do
            If AscW(ReplaceChar) = 0 Then
                str = str.Remove(locPos, 1)
            Else
                str = str.Remove(locPos, 1).Insert(locPos, ReplaceChar.ToString)
            End If
        Loop
        Return str
    End Function
End Module
```

When you run this program, it generates the following output:

```
The line:
Individual, elements; separated, by, different- characters.

Becomes a string array with the following elements:
Individual
elements
separated
by
different
characters
```

Iterating through Strings

The following code segment uses a further variation for iterating through the individual characters in a string. The *Chars* property of a *String* object is an array of *Char* values, which represent the individual characters in the string. Because the *String* object also offers the function *GetEnumerator*, you have the following option for iterating via a string:

```
For Each locChar As Char In "This is a string"
    'Do something.
Next
```

Thanks to the power of the *String* class, the functions *Find* and *Replace* are surprisingly easy to implement. In the following code, assume that the *fneFiles* collection contains a list of file names:

```
Private Sub btnCheckFound_Click(ByVal sender As System.Object, ByVal e As System.
➥EventArgs) _
              Handles btnCheckFound.Click
    For Each locFEI As FilenameEnumeratorItem In fneFiles.Items
        Dim locFilename As String = locFEI.Filename.Name
        If locFilename.IndexOf(txtSearch.Text) > -1 Then
            locFEI.Checked = True
        Else
            locFEI.Checked = False
        End If
    Next
End Sub

Private Sub btnReplaceChecked_Click(ByVal sender As System.Object,ByVal e As System.
➥EventArgs) _
    Handles btnReplaceChecked.Click
    For Each locFEI As FilenameEnumeratorItem In fneFiles.Items
        Dim locFilename As String = locFEI.SubItems(1).Text
        If locFEI.Checked Then
            If locFilename.IndexOf(txtSearch.Text) > -1 Then
                locFilename = locFilename.Replace(txtSearch.Text, txtReplace.Text)
                locFEI.SubItems(1).Text = locFilename
            End If
        End If
    Next
End Sub
```

StringBuilder vs. *String*: When Performance Matters

As you saw earlier in this chapter, .NET provides you with extremely powerful tools for processing strings. If you read the section on memory management, you probably noticed that string processing speed in certain scenarios leaves much to be desired. The reason is simple: strings are immutable. If you are working with algorithms that build strings character-by-character, then for every character you add to the string, a completely new string must be created—and that takes time.

The *StringBuilder* class represents an alternative for such operations. In no way does it provide the functionality of the *String* class in terms of methods, but it does offer an essential advantage: it is managed dynamically, and therefore, it is disproportionately faster. When it comes to building strings (by appending, inserting, or deleting characters), you should use a *StringBuilder* instance—especially when you're dealing with large amounts of data.

Using the *StringBuilder* class is quite simple. First, you need to declare the *System.Text* namespace, which you can bind into your class or module file with an *Imports* statement, as follows:

```
Imports System.Text
```

Next, you simply declare a variable with the type *StringBuilder*, and then initialize it with one of the following constructor calls:

```
'Declaration without parameters:
Dim locSB As New StringBuilder
'Declaration with capacity reservation
locSB = New StringBuilder(1000)
'Declaration from an existing string
locSB = New StringBuilder("Created from a new string")
'Declaration from string with the specification of a capacity to be reserved
locSB = New StringBuilder("Created from string with capacity for more", 1000)
```

Note that you can specify an initial capacity when defining a *StringBuilder* object. This way, the space that your *StringBuilder* object will eventually require is reserved immediately—no additional memory needs to be requested at runtime, which improves performance.

To add characters to the string, use the *Append* method. Using *Insert*, you can place characters anywhere into the string stored in the *StringBuilder* object. *Replace* lets you replace one string with another, whereas *Remove* deletes a specified number of characters from a specific character position onward. Here's an example:

```
locSB.Append(" - and this gets appended to the string")
locSB.Insert(20, ">>this ends up somewhere in the middle<<")
locSB.Replace("String", "StringBuilder")
locSB.Remove(0, 4)
```

When you have finished building the string, you can convert it into a "real" string by using the *ToString* function:

```
'StringBuilder has finished building the string
'Convert to string
Dim locString As String = locSB.ToString
Console.WriteLine(locString)
```

When you execute the preceding statements, the console window displays the following text:

```
StringBuilder Create>>this ends up somewhere in the middle<<d from string with capacity for
more - and that is added to the StringBuilder
```

Performance Comparison: *String* vs. *StringBuilder*

Companion Content   Open the solution (.sln) for this example, which you can find in the \VB 2010 Developer Handbook\Chapter 06\StringVsStringBuilder folder.

This section's project demonstrates the efficiency of the *StringBuilder* class. The program creates a number of *String* elements, each consisting of a fixed number of random characters. When you start the program, enter the values of the following parameters as prompted:

```
Enter the string length of an element: 100
Enter a number of elements to be generated: 100000

Generating 100000 string elements with the String class...
Duration: 2294 milliseconds

Generating 100000 string elements with the StringBuilder class...
Duration: 1111 milliseconds
```

The preceding code demonstrated that using the *StringBuilder* class with an element length of *100* characters already doubles the speed. Restart the program. To see a really impressive increase in speed, enter an element length of *1000* and specify the value of *10000* for the number of elements to be generated, as shown in the following example:

```
Enter the string length of an element: 1000
Enter a number of elements to be generated: 10000

Generating 10000 string elements with the String class...
Duration: 6983 milliseconds

Generating 10000 string elements with the StringBuilder class...
Duration: 1091 milliseconds
```

With these parameters, the *StringBuilder* is approximately six times faster than the *String* class. The lengthier the generated strings, the more sense it makes to use a *StringBuilder* object.

The program relies on the *StopWatch* class for timing the operations. With this class, you can measure time durations with extreme precision—and it's simple to use. The following code sample, which reuses some code from earlier in the chapter, shows its use:

```vb
Imports System.Text

Module StringsVsStringBuilder

    Sub Main()
        Dim locAmountElements As Integer
        Dim locAmountCharsPerElement As Integer
        Dim locVBStringElements As VBStringElements
        Dim locVBStringBuilderElements As VBStringBuilderElements

        'StringBuilderExamples()
        'Return

        Console.Write("Enter the string length of an element: ")
        locAmountCharsPerElement = Integer.Parse(Console.ReadLine)
        Console.Write("Enter a number of elements to be generated: ")
```

```
                locAmountElements = Integer.Parse(Console.ReadLine)
                Console.WriteLine()
                Console.WriteLine("Generating " & locAmountElements &
                          " string elements with the String class...")
                Dim locTimeGauge = Stopwatch.StartNew
                locVBStringElements = New VBStringElements(locAmountElements,
        ➥locAmountCharsPerElement)
                locTimeGauge.Stop()
                Console.WriteLine("Duration: " & locTimeGauge.ElapsedMilliseconds.ToString())
                locTimeGauge.Reset()
                Console.WriteLine("Generating " & locAmountElements &
                          " string elements with the StringBuilder class...")
                locTimeGauge.Start()
                locVBStringBuilderElements =
                          New VBStringBuilderElements(locAmountElements,
        ➥locAmountCharsPerElement)
                locTimeGauge.Stop()
                Console.WriteLine("Duration: " & locTimeGauge.ElapsedMilliseconds.ToString())
                locTimeGauge.Reset()
                Console.WriteLine()
                Console.ReadLine()
            End Sub


        Sub StringBuilderExamples()


            'Declaration without parameters:
            Dim locSB As New StringBuilder
            'Declaration with capacity reservation
            locSB = New StringBuilder(1000)
            'Declaration from an existing string
            locSB = New StringBuilder("Created from a new string")
            'Declaration from string with the specification of a capacity to be reserved
            locSB = New StringBuilder("Created from string with capacity for more", 1000)

            locSB.Append(" - and this gets appended to the string")
            locSB.Insert(20, ">>this ends up somewhere in the middle<<")
            locSB.Replace("String", "StringBuilder")
            locSB.Remove(0, 4)

            'StringBuilder has finished building the string
            'Convert to string umwandeln
            Dim locString As String = locSB.ToString
            Console.WriteLine(locString)
            Console.ReadLine()
        End Sub

    End Module

    Public Class VBStringElements

        Private myStrElements() As String
```

```vb
    Sub New(ByVal AmountOfElements As Integer, ByVal AmountChars As Integer)

        ReDim myStrElements(AmountOfElements - 1)
        Dim locRandom As New Random(DateTime.Now.Millisecond)
        Dim locString As String

        For locOutCount As Integer = 0 To AmountOfElements - 1
            locString = ""
            For locInCount As Integer = 0 To AmountChars - 1
                Dim locIntTemp As Integer = Convert.ToInt32(locRandom.NextDouble * 52)
                If locIntTemp > 26 Then
                    locIntTemp += 97 - 26
                Else
                    locIntTemp += 65
                End If
                locString += Convert.ToChar(locIntTemp).ToString
            Next
            myStrElements(locOutCount) = locString
        Next
    End Sub

End Class

Public Class VBStringBuilderElements

    Private myStrElements() As String

    Sub New(ByVal AmountOfElements As Integer, ByVal AmountChars As Integer)

        ReDim myStrElements(AmountOfElements - 1)
        Dim locRandom As New Random(DateTime.Now.Millisecond)
        Dim locStringBuilder As StringBuilder

        For locOutCount As Integer = 0 To AmountOfElements - 1
            locStringBuilder = New StringBuilder(AmountChars)
            For locInCount As Integer = 0 To AmountChars - 1
                Dim locIntTemp As Integer = Convert.ToInt32(locRandom.NextDouble * 52)
                If locIntTemp > 26 Then
                    locIntTemp += 97 - 26
                Else
                    locIntTemp += 65
                End If
                locStringBuilder.Append(Convert.ToChar(locIntTemp))
            Next
            myStrElements(locOutCount) = locStringBuilder.ToString
        Next
    End Sub

End Class
```

The *Boolean* Data Type

The data type *Boolean* saves binary states, which means it doesn't save much. Its value can be *False* or *True*—it can't save anything else. This data type is most frequently used when running conditional program code (you saw the basics of conditional code in Chapter 1).

.NET data type: *System.Boolean*

Represents: One of two states: *True* or *False*.

Type literal: Not available

Memory requirements: 2 bytes

Note: To define a *Boolean* variable, use the keywords *True* and *False* directly and without quotes in the program text, such as in the following example:

```
Dim locBoolean As Boolean
locBoolean = True 'Expression is true.
locBoolean = False 'Expression is false.
```

Converting to and from Numeric Data Types

You can convert a *Boolean* type to a numeric data type.

Important   Visual Basic deviates from the .NET Framework in its internal representation of the primitive *Boolean* data type. For example, when you convert a *Boolean* data type into an *Integer* data type using Visual Basic commands, the value *True* is converted to –1. But when using .NET Framework conversions, such as the *Convert* class, *True* is converted to +1.

The following example shows how this works:

```
Dim locInt As Integer = CInt(locBoolean)      ' locInt is -1
locInt = Convert.ToInt32(locBoolean)          ' locInt is now +1!!!
Dim locLong As Long = CLng(locBoolean)        ' locLong is -1
locLong = Convert.ToInt64(locBoolean)         ' locLong is +1
```

When converting it back, the behavior of the *Convert* class of .NET Framework and the conversion statements of Visual Basic are identical. Only the numeric value 0 returns the *Boolean* result of *False*, all other values result in *True*, as the following example shows.

Companion Content   Open the corresponding solution (.sln) for this example, which you can find in the \VB 2010 Developer Handbook\Chapter 06\Primitives03 folder.

```
locBoolean = CBool(-1)                   ' locBoolean is True.
locBoolean = CBool(0)                    ' locBoolean is False.
locBoolean = CBool(1)                    ' locBoolean is True.
locBoolean = Convert.ToBoolean(-1)       ' locBoolean is True.
locBoolean = Convert.ToBoolean(+1)       ' locBoolean is True.
locBoolean = CBool(100)                  ' locBoolean is True.
locBoolean = Convert.ToBoolean(100)      ' locBoolean is True.
```

Converting to and from Strings

When you convert a *Boolean* data type into a string—for example, to save its status in a file—the respective value is converted to one of two strings represented by the static read-only properties *TrueString* and *FalseString* of the *Boolean* structure. In the current version of .NET Framework (4.0, as of this writing), they result in "True" and "False," regardless of the computer's cultural settings. So, no matter if your programs run on a United States platform or, for example, on a German platform, it always becomes either "True" or "False", never "Wahr" or "Falsch". When converting a *String* into *Boolean*, these strings return the values *True* and *False*, respectively.

The *Date* Data Type

The *Date* data type stores and manipulates date values. It helps you to calculate time differences, parse date values from strings, and convert date values into formatted strings.

.NET data type: *System.DateTime*

Represents: Dates and time from 1.1.0001 (0 hours) to 31.12.9999 (23:59:59 hours) with a resolution of 100 nanoseconds (this unit is called a *tick*)

Type literal: Enclosed in pound-signs, *always* United States culture format (#MM/dd/yyyy HH:mm:ss#)

Memory requirements: 8 bytes

> **Note** *Date* also is a base data type, for which you can define a date variable directly by using literals in the program code. The same rules apply for numeric values: The United States date/time format is important. If you are not familiar with this format, here's a brief explanation.

For the United States, you write date values in the format month/day/year, separated by a slash. This syntax can easily cause confusion if you are not familiar with it. For example, the date 12/17/2011 is clearly a United States date, because there is no month 17. However, the date 12/06/2011 could be interpreted as either June 12th or December 6th. There is a similar

issue with the time of day. In the United States, you might find a 24-hour display for a bus schedule or in the military, but otherwise, the postfixes "AM" (for "ante meridian"—before noon) and "PM" (for "post meridian"—after noon) defines which 3 o'clock is intended. The formatting scheme becomes even more problematic with 12:00 (there is no 0:00!). Maybe you've had your own experience when trying to program a video recorder that recorded not your desired TV program, but another that was broadcast 12 hours later (or earlier). 12:00 AM corresponds to midnight or the 0:00 hour on the 24-hour clock; 12:00 PM corresponds to noon.

Value assignments to a *Date* data type in program code occur by surrounding the date/time string characters with "#" (hash) characters. The following example shows how this works:

```
Dim Midnight As Date = #12:00:00 AM#
Dim Noon As Date = #12:00:00 PM#
Dim NewYearsEve As System.DateTime = #12/31/2010#
Dim TimeForChampagne As System.DateTime = #12/31/2010 11:58:00 PM#
Dim TimeForAspirin As System.DateTime = #1/1/2011 11:58:00 AM#
```

The editor helps you to find the correct format by translating the 24-Hour format into the 12-hour format, automatically. For example, it converts the expression *#0:00#* to *#12:00:00 AM#* automatically.

It also adds missing entries for minutes and seconds if you inadvertently enter a value that contains only the hours portion. You can enter times in the 24-hour format; the editor will automatically convert them to the 12-hour format.

TimeSpan: Manipulating Time and Date Differences

What's unique about the *Date* data type is that it supports calculations to determine time differences, representing a length of time with *TimeSpan* objects. These objects represent time intervals, not time values. Unlike the *Date* type, *TimeSpan* is not a .NET base data type.

The *TimeSpan* data type is quite easy to use. You can subtract one data value from another to determine the time span between the two dates, or add a time span to a date, or subtract it from a date (see the following example) to calculate the date after so many months, days or hours.

> **Companion Content** Open the corresponding solution (.sln) for this example, which you can find in the \VB 2010 Developer Handbook\Chapter 06\DateTime folder.

```
Dim locDate1 As Date = #3:15:00 PM#
Dim locDate2 As Date = #4:23:32 PM#
Dim locTimeSpan As TimeSpan = locDate2.Subtract(locDate1)
Console.WriteLine("The time span between {0} and {1} is", _
                locDate1.ToString("HH:mm:ss"), _
                locDate2.ToString("HH:mm:ss"))
```

```
Console.WriteLine("{0} second(n) or", locTimeSpan.TotalSeconds)
Console.WriteLine("{0} minute(n) and {1} second(n) or", _
                  Math.Floor(locTimeSpan.TotalMinutes), _
                  locTimeSpan.Seconds)
Console.WriteLine("{0} hour(s), {1} minute(s) and {2} second(s) or", _
                  Math.Floor(locTimeSpan.TotalHours), _
                  locTimeSpan.Minutes, locTimeSpan.Seconds)
Console.WriteLine("{0} Ticks", _
                  locTimeSpan.Ticks)
```

A Library with Useful Functions for Date Manipulation

In the same example, you will find a class file called *DateCalcHelper.vb* that contains a static class of the same name. This class provides some useful functions that simplify the calculation of certain relative points in time, and shows how to perform calculations with date values.

Thanks to the XML comments in the example, the class is self-explanatory. When you develop you own programs that make intensive use of relative point-in-time calculations, just add this code file to your project (or the assembly of your project).

The following code shows the function names along with their explanations (in bold):

```
Public NotInheritable Class DateCalcHelper

    ''' <summary>
    ''' Calculates the date which corresponds to the 1st of the month,
    ''' which results from the specified date.
    ''' </summary>
    ''' <param name="CurrentDate">Date, whose month the calculation is based on.
➥</param>
    ''' <returns></returns>
    ''' <remarks></remarks>
    Public Shared Function FirstDayOfMonth(ByVal CurrentDate As Date) As Date
        Return New Date(CurrentDate.Year, CurrentDate.Month, 1)
    End Function

    ''' <summary>
    ''' Calculates the date which corresponds to the last day of the month,
    ''' which results from the specified date.
    ''' </summary>
    ''' <param name="CurrentDate">Date, whose month the calculation is based on.
➥</param>
    ''' <returns></returns>
    ''' <remarks></remarks>
    Public Shared Function LastDayOfMonth(ByVal CurrentDate As Date) As Date
        Return New Date(CurrentDate.Year, CurrentDate.Month, 1).AddMonths(1).
➥AddDays(-1)
    End Function
```

```
''' <summary>
''' Calculates the date which corresponds to the first of the year,
''' which results from the specified date.
''' </summary>
''' <param name="CurrentDate">Date, whose year the calculation is based on.
''' </param>
''' <returns></returns>
''' <remarks></remarks>
Public Shared Function FirstOfYear(ByVal CurrentDate As Date) As Date
    Return New Date(CurrentDate.Year, 1, 1)
End Function


''' <summary>
''' Calculates the date which corresponds to the first Monday of the first week of
''' the month, which results from the specified date.
''' </summary>
''' <param name="CurrentDate">Date, whose week the calculation is based on.
''' </param>
''' <returns></returns>
''' <remarks></remarks>
Public Shared Function MondayOfFirstWeekOfMonth(ByVal CurrentDate As Date) As Date
    Dim locDate As Date = FirstDayOfMonth(CurrentDate)
    If Weekday(locDate) = DayOfWeek.Monday Then
        Return locDate
    End If
    Return locDate.AddDays(6 - Weekday(CurrentDate))
End Function


''' <summary>
''' Calculates the date which corresponds to the Monday of the week,
''' which results from the specified date.
''' </summary>
''' <param name="CurrentDate">Date, whose week the calculation is based on.
''' </param>
''' <returns></returns>
''' <remarks></remarks>
Public Shared Function MondayOfWeek(ByVal CurrentDate As Date) As Date
    If Weekday(CurrentDate) = DayOfWeek.Monday Then
        Return CurrentDate
    Else
        Return CurrentDate.AddDays(-Weekday(CurrentDate) + 1)
    End If
End Function


''' <summary>
''' Calculates the date which corresponds to the first Monday
''' of the second week of the month,
''' which results from the specified date.
''' </summary>
''' <param name="CurrentDate">Date, whose week the calculation is based on.
''' </param>
```

```vb
''' <returns></returns>
''' <remarks></remarks>
Public Shared Function MondayOfSecondWeekOfMonth(ByVal currentDate As Date) As
➥Date
    Return MondayOfFirstWeekOfMonth(currentDate).AddDays(7)
End Function


''' <summary>
''' Calculates the date which corresponds to Monday of the last week of the month,
''' which results from the specified date.
''' </summary>
''' <param name="CurrentDate">Date, whose week the calculation is based on.
''' </param>
''' <returns></returns>
''' <remarks></remarks>
Public Shared Function MondayOfLastWeekOfMonth(ByVal CurrentDate As Date) As Date
    Dim locDate As Date = FirstDayOfMonth(CurrentDate).AddDays(-1)
    If Weekday(locDate) = DayOfWeek.Monday Then
        Return locDate
    End If
    Return locDate.AddDays(-Weekday(CurrentDate) + 1)
End Function


''' <summary>
''' Results in the date of the next work day.
''' </summary>
''' <param name="CurrentDate">Date the calculation is based on</param>
''' <param name="WorkOnSaturdays">True, if Saturday is a work day.</param>
''' <param name="WorkOnSundays">True, if Sunday is a work day.</param>
''' <returns></returns>
''' <remarks></remarks>
Public Shared Function NextWorkday(ByVal CurrentDate As Date,
        ByVal WorkOnSaturdays As Boolean, _
        ByVal WorkOnSundays As Boolean) As Date
    CurrentDate = CurrentDate.AddDays(1)
    If Weekday(CurrentDate) = DayOfWeek.Saturday And Not WorkOnSaturdays Then
        CurrentDate = CurrentDate.AddDays(1)
    End If
    If Weekday(CurrentDate) = DayOfWeek.Sunday And Not WorkOnSundays Then
        CurrentDate = CurrentDate.AddDays(1)
    End If
    Return CurrentDate
End Function


''' <summary>
''' Results in the date of the previous work day.
''' </summary>
''' <param name="CurrentDate">Date the calculation is based on</param>
''' <param name="WorkOnSaturdays">True, if Saturday is a work day.</param>
''' <param name="WorkOnSundays">True, if Sunday is a work day.</param>
''' <returns></returns>
''' <remarks></remarks>
```

```
        Public Shared Function PreviousWorkday(ByVal CurrentDate As Date,
            ByVal WorkOnSaturdays As Boolean, _
            ByVal WorkOnSundays As Boolean) As Date
        CurrentDate = CurrentDate.AddDays(-1)
        If Weekday(CurrentDate) = DayOfWeek.Sunday And Not WorkOnSundays Then
            CurrentDate = CurrentDate.AddDays(-1)
        End If
        If Weekday(CurrentDate) = DayOfWeek.Saturday And Not WorkOnSaturdays Then
            CurrentDate = CurrentDate.AddDays(-1)
        End If
        Return CurrentDate
    End Function
End Class
```

Converting Strings to Date Values

Just like the base numeric data types, you can also convert strings that represent date values into a *Date* data type. The *Date* data type provides two functions, *Parse* and *ParseExact*, that analyze a string and build the actual date value from it.

Conversions with *Parse*

When using *Parse*, the parser uses every trick in the book to convert a date, a time, or a combination of both into a time value, as shown in the following example:

```
Dim locToParse As Date
locToParse = Date.Parse("13.12.10") ' OK, basic European setting is processed.
locToParse = Date.Parse("6/7/10")   ' OK, but European date is used in spite of "/".
locToParse = Date.Parse("13/12/10") ' OK, as above.
locToParse = Date.Parse("06.07")    ' OK, is extended by the year.
locToParse = Date.Parse("06,07,10") ' OK, comma is acceptable.
locToParse = Date.Parse("06,07")    ' OK, comma is acceptable; year is added.
'locToParse = Date.Parse("06072010") ' --> Exception: was not recognized as a valid date!
'locToParse = Date.Parse("060705")   ' --> Exception: was not recognized as a valid date!
locToParse = Date.Parse("6,7,4")    ' OK, comma is acceptable; leading zeros are added.

locToParse = Date.Parse("14:00")    ' OK, 24-hour display is acceptable.
locToParse = Date.Parse("PM 11:00") ' OK, PM may be in front of...
locToParse = Date.Parse("11:00 PM") ' ...and behind the time specification.
'locToParse = Date.Parse("12,00 PM") ' --> Exception: was not recognized as a valid date!

'Both date/time combinations work:
locToParse = Date.Parse("6.7.10 13:12")
locToParse = Date.Parse("6,7,10 11:13 PM")
```

As you can see here, a format entry that is very common in European locales is not recognized: when the individual value groups of the date are written sequentially but without a separating character. However, there is a solution to this problem as well.

> **Note** The date 6/7/10 represents a July date, for example, in the Irish locale, and a June date in the United States locale.

Conversion with *ParseExact*

If, in spite of all its flexibility, *Parse* fails to recognize a valid date/time format, you can still set a recognition pattern for the entry by using the method *ParseExact* for string conversions.

> **Note** You should also use *ParseExact* if you don't want to allow as much flexibility as *Parse* permits.

This is especially true when you need to differentiate between time and date values. For a field in which the users of your program must enter a time, your program knows, for example, that the value 23:12 refers to the time 23:12:00, and not to the date 23.12.2000. *Parse* wouldn't work here, because it can't recognize the context.

Apart from the string to be analyzed, *ParseExact* requires at least two additional parameters: a string that contains the specific recognition pattern, and a *format provider* that provides further formatting requirements. There are several different format providers that you can use—but you can access them only after inserting the following line, which imports the required namespace at the beginning of your module or class file:

```
Imports System.Globalization
```

The simplest version that will recognize a time entry as the time of day, if it has been entered in the above format, it would look like this:

```
locToParse = Date.ParseExact("12,00", "HH,mm", CultureInfo.CurrentCulture)
```

The string "HH" specifies that hours are expressed in the 24-hour format. If you use the lower-case pattern "hh" instead, the parser will recognize only the 12-hour format. Next, the input contains a comma, which becomes the separator character, and finally the format specifies that minutes come last, using the string "mm."

In practice, it's rare that users follow specific requirements; therefore, your program should ideally recognize several different versions of time entries. With the *ParseExact* function, you can specify a range of possible formats for the parser to perform the conversion. All you need to do is define a *String* array containing the permitted formats, and then pass it to the *ParseExact* method along with the string to be parsed. If you decide to use this method, however, you also need to specify a parameter that regulates the parsing flexibility (for example, if the input strings that will be analyzed are allowed to contain whitespace, which then will be ignored). The entry is regulated by a parameter of the type *DateTimeStyles* which allows the settings listed in Table 6-5.

TABLE 6-5 The Extended Settings That Can Be Used with *Parse*

Member name	Description	Value
AdjustToUniversal	Date and time must be converted to Universal Time or Greenwich Mean Time (GMT)	16
AllowInnerWhite	Additional whitespaces within the string are ignored during parsing, unless the *DateTimeFormatInfo* format patterns contain spaces	4
AllowLeadingWhite	Leading whitespaces are ignored during parsing, unless the *DateTimeFormatInfo* format patterns contain spaces	1
AllowTrailingWhite	Trailing whitespaces are ignored during parsing, unless the *DateTimeFormatInfo* format patterns contain spaces	2
AllowWhiteSpaces	Additional whitespaces, which are located at any position within the string, are ignored during parsing, unless the *DateTimeFormatInfo* format patterns contain spaces. This value is equivalent to the combination of *AllowLeadingWhite*, *AllowTrailingWhite*, and *AllowInnerWhite*	7
NoCurrentDateDefault	Date and time are inseparately combined in the *Date* data type. Even if only a time is assigned, the *Date* value will always show a valid date. This setting specifies that the *DateTime.Parse* method and the *DateTime.ParseExact* method use a date according to the Gregorian calendar with year = 1, month = 1, and day = 1, when the string only contains the time, but not the date. If this value isn't specified, the current date is used.	8
None	Specifies that the default formatting options must be used; for instance, the default format for *DateTime.Parse*, and *DateTime. ParseExact*.	0

The following lines of code show how to use *ParseExact* to convert strings into date values with specific requirements for date formats:

```
Imports System.Globalization

Module Module1

    Sub Main()

        Dim locToParseExact As Date
        Dim locTimePattern As String() = {"H,m", "H.m", "ddMMyy", "MM\/dd\/yy"}

        'Works: it's in the time pattern.
        locToParseExact = Date.ParseExact("12,00", _
                        locTimePattern, _
                        CultureInfo.CurrentCulture, _
                        DateTimeStyles.AllowWhiteSpaces)
```

```
'Works: it's in the time pattern, and whitespaces are permitted.
locToParseExact = Date.ParseExact(" 12 , 00 ", _
                    locTimePattern, _
                    CultureInfo.CurrentCulture, _
                    DateTimeStyles.AllowWhiteSpaces)

'Doesn't work: it's in the time pattern, but whitespaces are not permitted.
'locToParseExact = Date.ParseExact(" 12 , 00 ", _
'                    locTimePattern, _
'                    CultureInfo.CurrentCulture, _
'                    DateTimeStyles.None)

'Works: it's in the time pattern.
locToParseExact = Date.ParseExact("1,2", _
                    locTimePattern, _
                    CultureInfo.CurrentCulture, _
                    DateTimeStyles.None)
'Works: it's in the time pattern.
'But the date corresponds to 1.1.0001 and is therefore
'not displayed as a Tooltip, contrary to all the other
'examples shown here.
locToParseExact = Date.ParseExact("12.2", _
                    locTimePattern, _
                    CultureInfo.CurrentCulture, _
                    DateTimeStyles.NoCurrentDateDefault)

'Works: it's not in the time pattern, because seconds are used
'locToParseExact = Date.ParseExact("12,2,00", _
'                    locTimePattern, _
'                    CultureInfo.CurrentCulture, _
'                    DateTimeStyles.NoCurrentDateDefault)

'Doesn't work: the colon is not in the time pattern.
'locToParseExact = Date.ParseExact("1:20", _
'                    locTimePattern, _
'                    CultureInfo.CurrentCulture, _
'                    DateTimeStyles.None)

'Now it works, because it's used as date in the time pattern.
'(third element in the string array)
locToParseExact = Date.ParseExact("241205", _
                    locTimePattern, _
                    CultureInfo.CurrentCulture, _
                    DateTimeStyles.AllowWhiteSpaces)

'Works: US format is used,
'as defined by the slashes and the group order.
'(fourth element in the string array).
locToParseExact = Date.ParseExact("12/24/05", _
                    locTimePattern, _
                    CultureInfo.CurrentCulture, _
                    DateTimeStyles.AllowWhiteSpaces)
  End Sub

End Module
```

When you define slashes as group separators, remember to always put a backslash in front so the separators aren't processed as control characters.

.NET Equivalents of Base Data Types

There is a .NET equivalent for each base data type in Visual Basic, as shown in Table 6-6.

TABLE 6-6 The Base Visual Basic Data Types and Their .NET Equivalents

Base data type in Visual Basic	.NET data type equivalent
Byte	System.Byte
SByte	System.SByte
Short	System.Int16
UShort	System.UInt16
Integer	System.Int32
UInteger	System.UInt32
Long	System.Int64
ULong	System.UInt64
Single	System.Single
Double	System.Double
Decimal	System.Decimal
Boolean	System.Boolean
Date	System.DateTime
Char	System.Char
String	System.String

Table 6-6 illustrates that it doesn't matter at all whether you declare a 32-bit integer with

```
Dim loc32BitInteger as Integer
```

or with

```
Dim loc32BitInteger as System.Int32
```

The object variable *loc32BitInteger* ends up with the exact same type in both cases. Take a look at the IML-generated code that follows:

```
Public Shared Sub main()

    Dim locDate As Date = #12/14/2003#
    Dim locDate2 As DateTime = #12/14/2003 12:13:22 PM#
    If locDate > locDate2 Then
        Console.WriteLine("locDate is larger than locDate2")
```

```
    Else
        Console.WriteLine("locDate2 is larger than locDate")
    End If
```

The generated lines of code verify that this is true:

```
.method public static void  main() cil managed
{
  // Code size       75 (0x4b)
  .maxstack  2
  .locals init ([0] valuetype [mscorlib]System.DateTime locDate,
           [1] valuetype [mscorlib]System.DateTime locDate2,
           [2] bool VB$CG$t_bool$S0)
  IL_0000:  nop
  IL_0001:  ldc.i8      0x8c58fec59f98000
  IL_000a:  newobj      instance void [mscorlib]System.DateTime::.ctor(int64)
  IL_000f:  nop
  IL_0010:  stloc.0
  IL_0011:  ldc.i8      0x8c59052cd35dd00
  IL_001a:  newobj      instance void [mscorlib]System.DateTime::.ctor(int64)
  IL_001f:  nop
  IL_0020:  stloc.1
  IL_0021:  ldloc.0
  IL_0022:  ldloc.1
  .
  .
  .
```

As the code highlighted in bold shows, both local variables have been declared as *System.DateTime* type. Notice also that *Date* variables are represented internally as *Long* values).

The GUID Data Type

GUID is the abbreviation for *Globally Unique Identifier*. The term "Global" refers to the fact that even though two GUID generators aren't aware of each other's existence and are spatially separated from each other, they are highly unlikely to produce two identical identifiers.

GUIDs are 16-byte (128-bit) values, usually represented in the format {XXXXXXXX-XXXX-XXXX-XXXX-XXXXXXXXXXXX}, where each "X"represents a hexadecimal number between 0 and F.

In .NET, the name of the data type (GUID) corresponds to its abbreviation.

> **Note** Don't use the GUID constructor to create a new GUID. Because a GUID is a value type, do-ing so wouldn't make any sense anyway. If you use the default constructor (the constructor with no parameters) with a value type, the value type is created on the Managed Heap but is then immediately discarded. Instead, use the static function *NewGuid* to create a new GUID, as shown in the following example:
>
> ```
> Dim t As Guid
> t = Guid.NewGuid
> ```

GUIDs are generally used as primary keys in databases, because it is extremely improbable that two computer systems generate identical GUIDs. Database tables with foreign key iden-tifiers based on GUIDs are particularly useful for synchronizing databases that cannot be constantly connected for technical reasons.

The *Guid* data type has a constructor with parameters that let you recreate an existing GUID via a string. Using it this way makes sense, for example, when a component (class, structure) that you have developed must always return the same unique identifier.

The following automatically implemented property of a class could therefore implement a *UniqueID* property:

```
Public Class AClass

    'The property always returns the same GUID:
    Property UniqueID As Guid = New Guid("{46826D55-6FDD-44FA-BADE-515E04770816}")
End Class
```

You can read more about classes and properties in Part II, "Object-Oriented Programming."

> **Tip** When you want only a new GUID string, you don't need to write an application that uses *NewGuid* to create one. Instead, you can use a feature already in Visual Studio. On the Tools menu, click Create GUID. The Create GUID dialog box appears. In the dialog box, select Registry Format, and then click Copy (see Figure 6-2). Go back to the Code Editor and paste the clipboard content as a parameter for the *Guid* constructor, as shown in the preceding example.

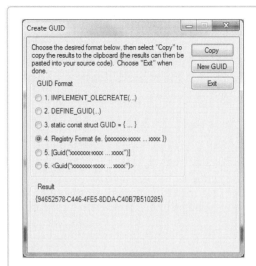

FIGURE 6-2 Using the Create GUID dialog box in the Visual Studio IDE, you can easily create a GUID constant.

Constants and Read-Only Fields (Read-Only Members)

Apart from the variable types discussed in this chapter, there are two *value storage types* in Visual Basic, which at first glance seem rather similar, *constants* and *read-only* fields. These two value storage types are defined only once during your program's lifetime, but they behave very differently under certain circumstances—and their contents are saved in completely different manners.

Before discussing the differences, let's examine what they have in common. Read-only fields and constants are used in similar contexts: namely, when a value must be used at different places within a program. For example, you would probably use a constant to return the name of your program or the expiration date of a demo version. When queried at different places within your program the constant must always have the same value. To avoid having to change the value in the source code in many different places (should you need to make any changes later on) you define this value as a constant or read-only field centrally, and then substitute the field or constant name for the value where you would use the value in the code.

Of course, you need to ensure that this value cannot be overwritten. Therefore, neither constants nor read-only fields can be changed.

Constants

You define constants with the *Const* keyword at the module level. Module level means that you can define a constant in a class, in a module, or in a structure. The syntax for defining a constant is just like a variable, but you need to add the keyword *Const*, as shown in the following example:

```
Public Const APPLICATIONNAME As String = "Type demo"
```

Or:

```
Private Const EXPIRATIONDATE as Date=#12/31/2010#
```

You can also define other constants this way—you just need to specify the appropriate type with the *As* clause and a value.

But watch out!

You can only define actual constants as constants. Even if, for example, the return value of a method, such as *Date.MaxValue* actually has the *characteristics* of a constant, you can't assign it to a constant. For example, the following statement will cause an error:

```
Private Const EXPIRATIONDATE as Date=Date.MaxValue
```

In this case, you should use a read-only field, as explained in the following section.

There's another important issue—the use of public constants across several assemblies.

Important You might think that a constant could therefore be "misused" as a field variable, which is read-only. However, that can backfire, when public constants are accessed in other assemblies.

When you give a constant a value, a concrete value is *never* created and saved at runtime. Therefore, constants don't need any memory space at runtime—neither on the Managed Heap, nor on the stack, nor within any processor registers. Instead, the actual value is hidden in the metafiles of the assembly in which the constant is defined. Unfortunately, that can lead to problems if different versions are used.

Because they are saved only in the metadata of the assembly, constants can be evaluated only at compilation time, not at design time. Therefore, for example, if you define a public constant in assembly A and access it from assembly B, you basically only need assembly A during the *creation* of assembly B. To put it simply, this is because the compiler only looks in assembly A, *while* it is creating assembly B, and transfers the values of the constants to assembly B where necessary. If assembly A is exclusively used to call constants, you could dispose of it afterward. And that's the problem. Because assembly A isn't actually accessed at runtime but only at compilation time, it's not enough to exchange assembly A, if the value of the constant defined there changes. Since assembly B accessed assembly A only at compilation time, it is not affected by the change.

For this reason you need to be careful with public constants and *always recreate an application with all connected assemblies when a scenario such as the one described above takes place*. To avoid this kind of behavior from the start, an alternative is to use read-only properties. The topic of properties is discussed in detail in Chapter 9, "First Class Programming."

Read-Only Fields

Read-only fields can also define constant values. These are also defined exclusively at module level (class, structure, module), and differ from a typical variable declaration by the keyword *ReadOnly*:

```
Private ReadOnly THEDATE As Date=#07/24/1969#
Friend ReadOnly MAXDATE As Date=Date.MaxValue
```

Or:

```
Public ReadOnly PERMITTED_CITIES As New List(Of String) From {"Lippstadt", "Las Vegas",
                                                "Kempen", "Los Angeles"}
```

These examples show that unlike regular constants, read-only fields are executable statements.

> **Important** An assignment to a read-only field might occur only in the constructor of the class, the structure, or the module, as you can see in the following code segment.

Therefore, the following construction is permitted:

```
Public Class Test
    Friend ReadOnly MAXDATE As Date
    Public ReadOnly PERMITTED_CITIES As List(Of String)

    Sub New()
        'Permitted only once!
        MAXDATE = Date.MaxValue
        PERMITTED_CITIES = New List(Of String) From {"Lippstadt", "Las Vegas",
➥"Kempen", "Los Angeles"}
    End Sub
    .
    .
    .
```

If you attempt to assign or re-assign a value to a read-only field from within a method, as in the following code segment, Visual Basic generates a design-time warning. The following code will cause the error *"A read-only variable cannot be the target of an assignment."*

```
Sub NewMethod()
    MAXDATE = Date.MaxValue
    PERMITTED_CITIES = New List(Of String) From {"Munich", "Paris", "London", "Seattle"}
```

Important With objects that can be defined as read-only fields, as we have seen in the code sample, the definition as *ReadOnly* only prohibits a completely new assignment. However, since in this case the variable is a pointer to an object, nothing stands in the way of manipulating the object content. Therefore, the following code is valid—although whether it's practical is a different question:

```
'But this works:
PERMITTED_CITIES.Clear()
PERMITTED_CITIES.AddRange(New List(Of String) From {"Munich", "Paris",
    "London", "Seattle"})
End Sub

End Class
```

Part II
Object-Oriented Programming

Chapter 7

A Brief Introduction to Object-Oriented Programming

Everything in Microsoft .NET works on the basis of classes and objects. This applies to Microsoft Visual Basic as well as the other .NET programming languages. Even in the era of Visual Basic 6.0, the notion that Visual Basic wasn't an Object-Oriented Programming (OOP) language was only partly true. Although no regular inheritance existed and polymorphism was available only through emulated late binding, Visual Basic 6.0 already used interfaces for Component Object Model (COM) development, extensively.

The most important OOP aspects are:

- **It saves development costs.** With OOP development, you can create useful reusable components. Software development departments or Independent Software Vendors (ISV) invest in the future with OOP. OOP components are the real capital because every successful project creates components that reduce the cost of the next project.

- **OOP regulates the cooperation of development teams.** It does this not in a patronizing or dictating way but in a supportive manner. Using object models, teams can design and prepare the code in such a way that other teams can seamlessly merge the code from team A with the code from team B without the need for constant collaboration between both teams during the development phase. Teams can even develop classes to process code that isn't written yet and guarantee that, even years later, this code will work flawlessly.

- **OOP ensures robust code.** OOP in .NET ensures that your application is reliable, protected against crashes, and robust as long as you adhere to some rules: late binding (enabling compilation of properties or methods for object variables that contain descendants of their class types) in Visual Basic should be allowed only in exceptional cases. In this way, for example, the .NET type system ensures that an attempt to use the variable type "JPEG image" as a string at runtime doesn't fail (as is possible in C++) causing an application to become unstable, or allowing it to be misused to run malicious code because of buffer overflows.

- **OOP provides the basis for functional language elements and LINQ.** Classes and collections let you use schema-bound data structures that can be treated as a single entity. In contrast, loose array elements are not connected, For example, using

Therefore, we want to put the cart before the horse and use an example to show how a program saves and organizes data without classes and the types of traps a developer can fall into by using that classless organization.

Mini Address Book—the Procedural Version

First, you'll see the old-style procedural version—which we have pompously named *Mini Address Book*.

Note In the following sections, the example programs are not Windows applications but console applications that can be executed in a Windows command prompt window. If you need a quick refresher on console applications, read Chapter 1, "Beginners All-Purpose Symbolic Instruction Code."

Companion Content Open the solution (.sln) for this example, which you can find in the \VB 2010 Handbook\Chapter07\MiniAddressBook folder.

When you start the program, you see a console window with a program output similar to that shown in Figure 7-1.

Tip If you use a 22-inch or 24-inch monitor with a comparable high resolution, you should set the font of the console window to the largest font (10×18). On the system menu, click either Default Values or Properties. Default Values applies to all future instances, and Properties applies only to the current instance of the console window.

```
file:///D:/VisualBasic2010 ENG/Samples Deutsch/Kapitel 09 - Klassentreffen/MiniAdressoClass/bin/...

003: Vüllers, Christian, 27548, München
004: Weichel, Thomas, 30758, Dortmund
005: Weichelt, Anne, 88462, Lippetal
006: Albrecht, Alfred, 31905, Hildesheim
007: Weichel, Katrin, 58575, Braunschweig
008: Sonntag, Franz, 81878, München
009: Neumann, Axel, 02869, Berlin
010: Braun, Katrin, 47669, Rheda

Addresses going to be sorted ... finished!

000: Ademmer, Daja, 28933, Wiesbaden
001: Ademmer, Hans, 88661, Bad Waldliesborn
002: Ademmer, Melanie, 60601, Hildesheim
003: Ademmer, Uwe, 99599, Bad Waldliesborn
004: Albrecht, Guido, 55501, Bielefeld
005: Albrecht, Alfred, 31905, Hildesheim
006: Braun, Michaela, 18984, Straubing
007: Braun, Katrin, 47669, Rheda
008: Braun, Uta, 12626, Wuppertal
009: Braun, Gabriele, 12368, Braunschweig
010: Englisch, Hans, 51025, Bielefeld

Press a key to exit...
```

FIGURE 7-1 The first version of the program seems to run as expected, but the procedural concept introduced a critical error that is not immediately obvious.

The following is the first version of this simple example program. It displays a few contact addresses, stores the data in arrays, sorts the contacts by last name, and then outputs the addresses. Here's an explanation of how the program generally handles data:

```
Module Main Module

    Dim LastName(0 To 100) As String
    Dim FirstName(0 To 100) As String
    Dim ZIP(0 To 100) As String
    Dim Location(0 To 100) As String

    Sub Main()
```

For each contact address, the program requires four single elements that are saved in a total of four arrays. This makes it difficult for the developer to keep the data for a single contact address together. Without a *connected* entity to bind the contact data programmatically based on their input, errors are bound to occur. Just such an error crept into this version of the program. (By "crept," of course, I mean that I entered this bug on purpose, but this example of procedural programming is typical for internal data management, as are the errors that can occur.)

```
Sub SortAdresses()

    'Example of a local type inference
    Dim numberElements = 101
    Dim delta = 1

    Dim externalCounter As Integer
    Dim internalCounter As Integer
```

You might have noticed something special about the sorting routine. This is known as *local type inference*, and it was introduced in Visual Basic 2008. This sets variable types automatically by analyzing the constant assignments. Chapter 1 explains how the local type inference works.

But let's get back to the original problem: in this example, the culprit is the program's sorting routine. With careful programming this routine is supposed to ensure that data integrity is not violated by logically sorting the address records. Here's the sorting routine:

```
Dim tempFirstName, tempLastName, tempZIP, temLocation As String

'Determine the highest value of the distance sequence
Do
    delta = 3 * delta + 1
```

```
        Loop Until delta > numberElements
        '
    Do
        'Future exit criteria - gets correcpondingly lower
        delta \= 3

        'Shellsort's Core Algorithm
        For externalCounter = delta To numberElements - 1
            tempFirstName = FirstName(externalCounter)
            tempLastName = LastName(externalCounter)
            tempZIP = ZIP(externalCounter)
            tempLocation = Location(externalCounter)

            internalCounter = externalCounter
            Do
                If tempLastName >= LastName(internalCounter - delta) Then Exit Do
                FirstName(internalCounter) = FirstName(internalCounter - delta)
                LastName(internalCounter) = LastName(internalCounter - delta)
                ZIP(internalCounter) = ZIP(internalCounter - delta)

                internalCounter = internalCounter - delta
                If (internalCounter <= delta) Then Exit Do
            Loop
            FirstName(internalCounter) = tempFirstName
            LastName(internalCounter) = tempLastName
            Location(internalCounter) = tempLocation
        Next
    Loop Until delta = 0
End Sub
```

On closer inspection, you'll see an error in the algorithm that impacts the data integrity. The triangle exchange of a contact element doesn't actually exchange all the array elements. In the first exchange, the location item falls by the wayside, and the return exchange omits the postal code. For a commercial program, this would be a catastrophe, especially because even with a list that contains only 100 contact addresses, this error doesn't immediately catch the eye.

Such errors are typical in older procedural programming for which developers didn't have object-oriented techniques that could simplify the task of keeping the data together. You'll see how to improve such operations and avoid errors by organizing the data and program code into classes in the next chapters.

Chapter 8
Class Begins

What Is a Class?

Think back to your childhood and picture yourself sitting in a sandbox, playing with molds and wet sand, and making all kinds of shapes. If sandboxes and wet sand didn't appeal to you, perhaps you used molds and clay. You might find this hard to believe, but back then you actually used the concept of classes for the first time. Basically a class is just a mold. The mold determines what the objects that it creates will look like, but the mold itself is not one of the objects; it's just a template—a class. When you want to create an object, you use the mold to instantiate an object of that class. To follow the analogy further, Figure 8-1 shows how you instantiate a "monkey" shape by putting clay into the mold. You squeeze the mold together, pull off the mold, and then reveal your masterpiece.

FIGURE 8-1 Even a child plays in an object-oriented way when she puts clay into a mold to make a shape.

Classes in programming are similar; they too serve as a kind of template for the actual objects in your application that store the actual application data. When you use the class, you need a specific portion of memory (called the *Managed Heap* in the .NET framework) with which to fill the class—just like you would put clay into the mold (see Figure 8-2). By calling a special *constructor* method, you squeeze that memory into place, and you can create many instances of your monkeys...er...classes (see Figure 8-3). The difference is that classes are of course not clay figures, but a memory address that contains information about a customer, a product, an image, or a TCP/IP connection—whatever the classes represent!

Of course, classes in the .NET Framework are a bit more abstract, and you don't get your hands dirty while building objects. Classes contain a number of *field variables*—also called *fields* or *member variables*—and a class body definition that includes these variables and gives the class a name.

This is the simplest version of a class that logically encapsulates its data (as you will soon see). Let's get it straight right off the bat by creating a simple class. In the example that follows, you'll build a class called *Contact* that contains four fields that make up a single address. You no longer need four unrelated arrays, but only one array consisting of elements that will each store a complete address.

For more information on arrays and lists, see Chapter 19, "Arrays and Collections."

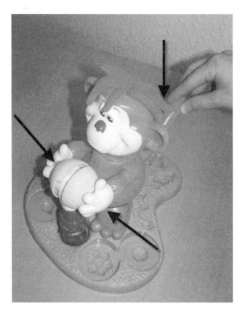

FIGURE 8-2 Using the method *"SqueezeTogether."*

For this purpose, let's take another look at the sample from Chapter 7, "A Brief Introduction to Object-Oriented Programming." Next, add a class file called *Contact.vb* to the existing program, and then add the following lines into this new class' code file:

```
Public Class Contact
    Public LastName As String
    Public FirstName As String
    Public Zip As String
    Public City As String
End Class
```

The *Contact* class is a simple class that contains only four publicly accessible fields, but it serves to combine those four fields logically into an entity that represents a person and an address.

FIGURE 8-3 Finally, making lots of clay monkeys—or in programmer-speak: from the class *Monkey* you can create many instances that can all have different properties. In this example, the instances can be differentiated by their *color property*, even though they all come from the same class (the mold).

Instantiating Classes with *New*

To create an object that is an instance of a class, you use the keyword *New*. Internally, the .NET Framework automatically appropriates sufficient memory for storing the field values[1]. An object variable declared with the same type as the class is used to access elements of the class instance. So for example, you create an object of the *Contact* class by using the following statements:

```
Dim adr As Contact
adr = New Contact
```

---

[1] To be accurate, this is a certain part of the memory that is "managed" (constantly cleaned up) by the .NET Framework called *Managed Heap*.

The first line of code creates an object variable of type *Contact*, and the second assigns a new instance. You can also combine both lines into one, as demonstrated in the following:

```
Dim adr As New Contact
```

Then you can use the class instance with the help of the defined object variables to access the individual fields, as follows:

```
adr.LastName = "Doe"
adr.FirstName = "Doe"
adr.Zip = "93111"
adr.City = "Los Angeles"
```

To get back to our clay mold analogy, the object instance represents the clay shape, which was created by the mold. The class is the mold. The object variable names the clay shape, which came out of the mold, and of course you can create any number of clay shapes from the mold.

Any number? Well, not quite: you can only create as many as the "managed clay heap" yields, from which you create the individual shapes. The clay in our analogy corresponds to the Managed Heap from which you get the memory space for your object instances.

In the beginning, many developers mistakenly try to use the class directly without instantiating it: of course, however, it doesn't work this way.

```
Contact.LastName = "Doe"
Contact.FirstName = "Joe"
Contact.ZIP = "93111"
Contact.City = "Los Angeles"
```

Why?

Think about it for a moment. Consider a base data type, such as an integer variable, declared and initialized with the following statements:

```
Dim i as Integer
i = 5
```

Would you ever write a statement like the following?

```
Integer = 5
```

You can't use the data type keyword as the variable name and expect to create a new variable. Needless to say, that won't work. Later on, you will see that there are actually properties and methods that you can call directly via the type name, such as with *if File.Exists("C:\windows\ calc.exe") then*—but those are called *static methods*, which act as an exception to the rule. You'll read more about static methods later.

Initializing Public Fields During Instantiation

Visual Basic 2008 and later versions permit a shorter way of initializing fields or properties with values: you can define public fields or properties directly during instantiation by using the keyword *With*, as shown in the following example:

```
Dim adr As New Contact With {.LastName = "Doe",
    .FirstName = "Joe", .ZIP = "93111", .City = "Los Angeles"}
```

New or Not New: About Objects and Reference Types

To make all of the later chapters easier to comprehend, it makes sense to talk a bit about saving objects; in other words, instances of classes. Object variables and objects aren't really as connected as you might think. In fact, it's just the opposite.

In reality, this is how it works: an object variable basically only saves a *memory address pointer* (typically just called a *pointer*) to the actual data in a specially monitored part of the main memory—the Managed Heap. Figures 8-4 and 8-5 demonstrate that the data of the objects you are instantiating from classes by using the *New* keyword are placed in this Managed Heap.

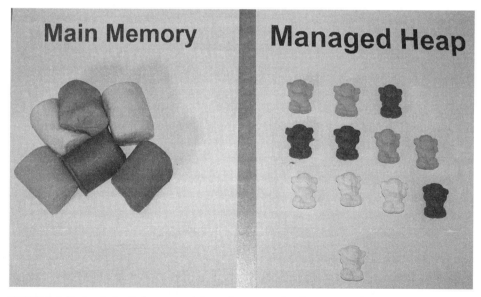

FIGURE 8-4 During instantiation, part of the main memory is taken away and made available to the new objects which are then on the monitored Managed Heap.

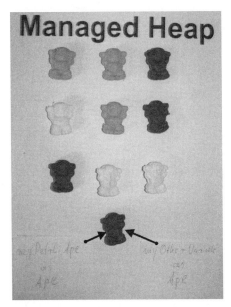

FIGURE 8-5 Object variables are simply sticky notes that identify an object (an object instance). Of course, you can place two sticky notes on a monkey, or in programmer-speech: several object variables can point to the same instance.

You might recall from the early days of the Commodore 64, Atari ST, Amiga, and machine language that a computer's memory is divided into memory areas, which all have individual memory addresses.

When you create an object based on a class—for example by instantiating a *Contact* data type with *New* into the object variable *objVarContact*—the .NET Framework places the data for this object instance, for example, at the memory location 460.386 on the Managed Heap, and the object variable internally becomes an *Integer* variable (or on a 64-bit system, a *Long* variable) with this address. Figure 8-6 shows this as a diagram.

Note For sake of clarity, in this explanation we used the data type name *Contact* instead of *Address*, so there won't be any confusion with the term memory *address*.

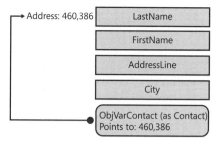

Instance of Class Contact

FIGURE 8-6 Object variables only save the memory addresses for the actual data that .NET Framework places on the Managed Heap

However, this fact has important consequences, as the following example demonstrates.

> **Companion Content** Open the corresponding solution (.sln), which you can find in the \VB 2010 Developer Handbook\Chapter 08\ClassObjectsMemory folder.

```
Module Module1

    Sub Main()

        'Instantiating with New and thus
        'creating memory for the Contact
        'object on the Managed Heap.
        'Simultaneously initialize the instance with data.
        Dim objVarContact As New Contact With {.LastName = "Doe", _
               .FirstName = "Joe", .ZIP = "93111", .City = "Los Angeles"}

        'Only create object variable,
        'but don't reserve memory space!
        Dim objVarContact2 As Contact

        'objVarContact2 now points to the
        'same instance as objVarContact
        objVarContact2 = objVarContact

        'It can be proven:
        'Changing of the instance happens...
        objVarContact2.LastName = "Smith"

        'via both object variables which
        'of course reflect the same.
        Console.WriteLine(objVarContact.LastName)
```

```
        Console.WriteLine()
        Console.WriteLine("Press button to exit")
        Console.ReadKey()
    End Sub

End Module

Public Class Contact
    Public FirstName As String
    Public LastName As String
    Public ZIP As String
    Public City As String
End Class
```

When you run this example, the following output is displayed:

```
Smith
```

```
Press button to exit
```

Note that this example contains a single data instance of the *Contact* class, but the same instance is referred to by two object variables, and the instance is therefore pointed to by two variables. During instantiation, the address of the memory where the instance data is placed is saved in the object variable *objVarContact*. The address is copied to the variable *objVarContact2*, but—and this is important—no copy is made of the instance in the Managed Heap, as shown in Figure 8-7.

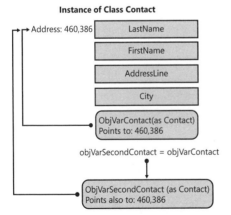

FIGURE 8-7 Copying an object variable into another object variable only copies the pointer to the instance, which then can be edited and called by both variables.

An object variable points to the data it represents. In other programming languages, such as C++, there are specific variables, called *memory address pointers*, as mentioned earlier. In Visual Basic, an object variable that manages the instance of a class automatically becomes such a pointer.

You should master the relationship between an object variable and the actual object (instance) it points to, because it is often the source of hard-to-find errors—after all, it's possible for an object variable to accidentally change the instance of an object that is also referred to by another variable. It can also come in handy when you don't want to copy objects, only the pointers to them. A sorting routine, for example, will be much faster if it doesn't have to copy the actual data when sorting the list, but only pointers to the data.

Nothing

You'd think writing about "nothing" wouldn't take very long, because there's nothing to write. But writing about nothing in Visual Basic or .NET is more than nothing—a lot more!

Nothing as a Null Reference Pointer

Using the knowledge you gained in Chapter 7, you can figure out for yourself why an object variable can have the value *Nothing* (*null* in C#—just for the sake of thoroughness). When you create an instance of a class by using *New*, you need to assign this instance (or more specifically, the address of this instance) to the object variable. Only then can you access the public fields, properties, and methods of the class instance (of the object) via the object variable, as illustrated in Figure 8-8.

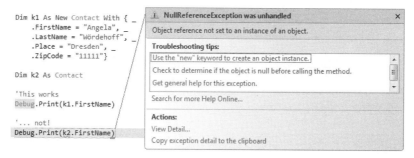

FIGURE 8-8 When you access class elements (fields, properties, methods) with an object variable that doesn't have a class instance assigned to it, a *NullReferenceException* is triggered.

Of course, you can also define an object variable without initializing it. But Figure 8-8 shows that if you then try to access the fields of an uninitialized object variable, you'll get a corresponding exception at runtime. The Visual Basic background compiler will detect this condition and display the appropriate warning as you write your code; your object variable doesn't point to an actual object—it points to *Nothing*.

To check whether a variable refers to a valid object or to *Nothing*, you need to use a special comparison operator in Visual Basic, the *Is Nothing* operator (you don't need a special operator in C#). The syntax of this operator is:

```
If objVariableName Is Nothing Then…
```

Note that the equals operator won't work in the case of object variables; for example, you cannot use the following statement:

```
If objVariableName = Nothing Then…
```

> **Important** *Nothing* works with *Is*, but not with the equals operator (=) because the equals operator in Visual Basic performs *value comparisons*, whereas *Is* performs *reference comparisons* (it is a pointer). The equals sign makes sure that the class calls a certain method, which compares the content to the memory content of another variable rather than the memory address.
>
> If you try it anyway (with *Option Strict* on) the compiler generates the following error: "*Option Strict On* does not permit operands of the type *Object* for the = operator. Use the *Is* operator, if you want to test object identity."

Of course, you can also assign *Nothing* to reference variables. You should always set an object variable to *Nothing* when you no longer need it in your code and want to free up the instance for disposal by the garbage collector, as shown in the following:

```
k2 = Nothing
```

After running the preceding line of code, if *k2* had been a pointer to a valid instance of a contact, it would no longer point to anything—it points to *Nothing*, and therefore, the garbage collector will dispose of it. Assigning *Nothing* to a variable can also make sense in other situations, as the following section describes.

Nothing and Default Values

In Visual Basic the keyword *Nothing* also has another meaning when used in connection with value types, such as the primitive data types *Integer*, *Double*, *Date*, or *Decimal*. In this case assigning *Nothing* actually assigns these data types their *default* value. The following lines will clarify this:

```
Dim intValue = 5
Debug.Print(intValue.ToString)

intValue = Nothing
Debug.Print(intValue.ToString)
```

```
Dim dateValue = #7/24/1969#
Debug.Print(dateValue.ToString)

dateValue = Nothing
Debug.Print(dateValue.ToString)
```

The above code generated the following output in the debug window:

```
5
0
24.07.1969 00:00:00
01.01.0001 00:00:00
```

> **Note** To be accurate, *Nothing* is only the supplier of default values of the corresponding data type, and the default value of reference values is a null-pointer. In this respect, *Nothing* is a misnomer, because it should be called *Default*.

Using Classes

Even though classes are custom data types, you can handle them just as you do all the other data types in the .NET Framework. This means that you can store multiple instances of the same class in an array or any other collection. As an example, in the next exercise, you will revise the address application by using classes to represent each address.

With all the information from the previous sections, you can now rewrite your original sample program so that it uses a single array, which contains elements from the newly created type, *Contact*. The conversion doesn't even require many changes.

> **Companion Content** Open the corresponding solution (.sln), which you can find in the \VB 2010 Developer Handbook\Chapter 08\MiniAddressoClass folder.

First, you must set up a data structure to store the contacts at the beginning of the program, as shown here:

```
Module MainModule

    Dim Contacts(0 To 100) As Contact
```

Unlike in the first version, you can now get away with a single array, which contains elements that encapsulate the fields of a complete contact. The sorting algorithm also looks a lot cleaner, as is demonstrated in the highlighted code that follows:

```
    Sub SortAddresses()

        Dim numberElements As Integer = 101
```

```
    Dim outerCounter As Integer
    Dim innerCounter As Integer
    Dim delta As Integer

    Dim tempContact As Contact

    delta = 1

    'Determine highest value of distance
    Do
        delta = 3 * delta + 1
    Loop Until delta > numberElements

    Do
        'Later exit criterion—let it get smaller again
        delta = delta \ 3

        'Shellsort's core algorithm
        For outerCounter = delta To numberElements - 1
            tempContact = Contacts(outerCounter)

            innerCounter = outerCounter
            Do
                If tempContact.LastName >= Contacts(innerCounter - delta).LastName Then
                    Exit Do
                End If
                Contacts(innerCounter) = Contacts(innerCounter - delta)

                innerCounter = innerCounter - delta
                If (innerCounter <= delta) Then Exit Do
            Loop
            Contacts(innerCounter) = tempContact
        Next
    Loop Until delta = 0
End Sub
```

Because the new data type *Contact* encapsulates the data of a complete contact address, the error that occurred in the previous version of the program is no longer possible. The three-way exchange now inevitably takes place for a complete contact. There is no longer any risk that individual fields can become lost. The bold code in the preceding example shows the clean-up.

Note There are more elegant built-in methods to sort an array, which you can find by exploring the *Array* class.

Value Types

Unlike reference types, which are created from classes, there is a further basic element for saving data in .NET Framework, namely the value type. Value types are the variables that store the humble base data types, such as integers, strings, and dates. But why not implement all data types as objects? There's a simple reason: it's a lot of work. Consider that even for the smallest integer variable, you need to reserve memory space, write the value that will be represented by the integer variable into this memory space, place the reference to this memory space into an object variable, and then retrieve this variable from the memory whenever you want to access it.. A purely object-oriented language would treat all variables as reference types, but the .NET Framework treats the most common variables in a different way for performance reasons.

And that's why value types have their place in the .NET Framework. They don't end up on the Managed Heap (the object memory heap), but instead they go on to something called the *processor stack*, which is a memory area that the processor can access most quickly. For some primitive data types, the CIL Compiler creates code that is so optimized, that it can use a processor register directly to save the value, for example, of an integer variable. This is particularly efficient because saving a value in a processor register eliminates the need to look up the value in a memory address variable. Primitive values can be placed *directly* on the stack or stored in a processor register. Thus the term *value type*.

> **Companion Content** Open the corresponding solution (.sln), which you can find in the \VB 2010 Developer Handbook\Chapter 08\ReferenceVsValueTypes folder.

This also impacts how value types are handled, because if the memory for a value type is assigned implicitly, it doesn't need to be explicitly requested with *New*. And this is exactly why the construct illustrated in Figure 8-9 makes no sense at all.

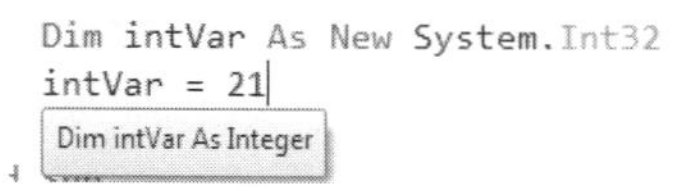

```
Dim intVar As New System.Int32
intVar = 21|
  Dim intVar As Integer
```

FIGURE 8-9 You can declare every primitive type via its .NET Framework equivalent—but there's no difference in the result.

The ToolTip shown in Figure 8-9 demonstrates how the construction doesn't differentiate when defining the variable type. Even though you have specified *System.Int32* (which is the .NET Framework integer type), the ToolTip says that the *intVar* variable is an *Integer* type.

> **Note** For those of you who are interested in the details of the previous example, here's what happens: you declare a variable of a value type as an object—because you have specified the keyword *New* without parameters. Then nothing at all happens with the instance of the *Int32* object. It is created on the Managed Heap and expires. The Garbage Collector disposes of this instance at the next opportunity. The Garbage Collector is described in more detail in Chapter 13, "Dispose, Finalize, and the Garbage Collector."

This actually happens when the optimized code is executed. The value is stored in a register of the processor because *System.Int32* is a value type and is used as such, as the ToolTip correctly states. The first statement simply declares the variable of the type *Int32*, which the compiler overrides with the keyword *Integer*.

> **Note** The construct *New Integer()* could have been rejected by the compiler directly with an error because it "knows" that the construct would only create *an instance* of *Int32* as an *object*, which can't be referenced; the *intVar* variable maintains its connection to the memory space for one integer value on the stack.

Remember the most important point: *Value types don't need to be instantiated. They can be used directly.* The Common Language Runtime (CLR) makes sure that value types are saved differently than reference types, to optimize performance.

This behavior makes sense not only for primitive data types, such as *Integer*, *Date*, or *Decimal*, but also for data types that you create yourself and which, first and foremost, should be handled extremely fast. You can create a custom value type as a *structure*, which is similar to a class, as you will learn in the following section.

Creating a Value Type with a Structure

In principle, value types are created the same way as reference types, but while reference types are created from classes, custom value types are created with structures (Visual Basic's precursor to classes). So, to create the sample class *Contact* as a value type, which we'll call *ContactStructure*, use the keyword *Structure* in the code. The class definition will be replaced by the following statements:

```
Public Structure ContactStructure
    Public FirstName As String
    Public LastName As String
    Public ZIP As String
    Public City As String
End Structure
```

The same rules that apply to base type variables also apply to this structure. You no longer need to instantiate it with *New*. The following code works:

```
'A contact is defined as a structure and can be
'used immediately, without the New keyword–the memory
'is allocated on the stack automatically.
Dim einContact As ContactStructure
aContact.FirstName = "Angela"
aContact.LastName = "Merkel"
aContact.ZIP = "09999"
aContact.City = "Berlin"
```

Assigning a Value Type to a Variable

There is another behavior that should be mentioned—and should be expected—because we are dealing with base data types: when you assign a value type variable to another one of the same type, the actual contents of the variable are copied. This behavior is called *cloning*. Take a look at the following code:

```
'The following statements demonstrate
'the cloning of value type variables:
'When assigning from value type to value type no references
'are copied, but the contents are.
Dim aDifferentContact As ContactStructure
aDifferentContact = aContact

'Changing the one "instance" has therfore
'no impact on changing the second instance.
aDifferentContact.LastName = "Schmidt"
Console.WriteLine(aContact.LastName & ", " &
                     aContact.FirstName)
Console.ReadLine()
```

This code produces the following output:

```
Schmidt, Angela
```

In contrast to reference types, the second variable, *aDifferentContact*, doesn't point to the first instance of *Contact*, because there is no actual "instance" in the object sense. Instead, the relevant data is sitting on the stack, and when your transfer the data to another value variable by assignment, the data is duplicated. Multiple value type variables can contain identical data, but never *one and the same* data.

> **Note** This description of the difference between value and reference types should suffice for most programming purposes. However, there's quite a bit to learn about copying values versus copying references, especially when saving data in collections and arrays. You'll find more information on this topic in Chapter 11, "Developing Value Types," and Chapter 12, "Typecasting and Boxing Value Types."

Chapter 9
First Class Programming

Here's another look at the earlier definition of a class:

"A class creates the structures for saving data and contains program code that regulates this data."

So far you've learned about one component of a class, its fields or variables, with which you can save certain things in a class instance. But you're still missing another important part—the part that regulates access to the data. The class concept supports data-regulating code to be present in a class in the form of two procedure types: in methods (*Sub*, *Function*) and in property procedures (*Property*).

In addition, it's possible (using a special routine called *constructor*) to specify what should happen when a class is instantiated. This means that in addition to the underlying procedures that the Common Language Runtime (CLR) performs anyway, such as reserving memory space for the actual data in your class instance, you can perform additional actions at instantiation time.

The sample class that you saw in Chapter 8, "Class Begins," consisted of just four field variables. You could access the four fields in each instance because they were defined with the keyword *public*, which makes them publicly accessible. Of course, that sample class had very little to do with the concept of data encapsulation; instead, it served only to combine different data values into a logical data unit. That isn't true data encapsulation, because data encapsulation uses some kind of class barrier to regulate the movement of data in and out of the class. Where external code can assign public field variables to any valid value, *properties* let you to execute custom code to enforce rules, ensuring that assigned values meet those rules.

Using Properties

Suppose that you want to abbreviate city names in the *Contacts* class sample (presented in the previous chapters) if those names exceed 30 characters in length. To confirm that the names were truncated, you want to add an ellipsis "..." to the city names.

In the procedural world you would create a function that checks whether a character chain has more than 30 characters, and if so, you would remove all characters after the 27th character and add three dots (...). That ensures that your city names would never exceed the maximum allowed 30 characters.

To enforce this data access rule, you must not allow direct access to the field variable that holds the city name. Instead, as in the following example, incorporate each access to the field *City* into a function call.

First, you must implement an *EllipsisString* routine to truncate names that are too long and add the ellipsis, as shown in the following code:

```
Function EllipsisString(ByVal text As String, ByVal MaxLength As Integer)
    As String
    Dim tmpText As String

    If text.Length > MaxLength Then
        tmpText = text.Substring(0, MaxLength - 3) + "..."
    Else
        tmpText = text
    End If
    Return tmpText
End Function
```

Then, you can call this routine every time you access the field variable *City* of an instance of the class *Contact*:

```
Sub HandleClass()
    .
    .
    .

    Dim tmpContact As New Contact
    .
    .
    .

    tmpContact.City = EllipsisString(Console.ReadLine, 30)
End Sub
```

However, there is a much more elegant—and equally important, a *safe* way—of ensuring that the *City* field variable of the *Contact* class never has a character string assigned to it that is too long: using a *property procedure*.

If you've been programming in Microsoft Visual Basic for a while (regardless of whether you've been working with a Microsoft .NET version or the pre-.NET Visual Basic 6.0) you've probably become familiar with properties a long time ago. With the help of properties, you can usually call *and* edit specific object states. From outside the class, it seems as if you are directly calling or manipulating a public field. For example, if you need to know whether a button on a form is enabled or not, use the property in the query form, as shown here:

```
If Button.Enabled Then DoSomething
```

If you want to ensure that the button is not enabled, you set a property by using the assignment form, as in the following line:

```
Button.Enabled = False     ' Disabled, the button cannot be pressed at the time
```

You know from experience that when setting a button property, you not only change the state of a variable of the *Button* class, but that setting this property will also cause something else: the button becomes disabled on the form and grayed-out. You can re-enable the button by setting its *Enabled* property to *True*. The code that makes all this work must reside somewhere within the class, so here's the question: how do you add properties to a custom class?

For this purpose Visual Basic provides a special type of procedure, called *property procedures*. You define a property in Visual Basic within a class in a property procedure, which has two distinct sections: one that's activated when the property is read, and another that's activated when the property is set, as shown here:

```
Property AProperty() As DataType

    Get
        Return DataTypeObjectVariable
    End Get

    Set(ByVal Value As DataType)
        DataTypeObjectVariable = Value
    End Set

End Property
```

After defining the property, you can access it on any instance of the class—just like a field variable, as you will see in the next section.

Note Editor support has changed slightly for property procedures with the introduction of *autoimplemented properties*. Until Visual Basic 2008, pressing Enter after writing the property body inserted the *Get* and *Set* parts of the property procedure automatically in Visual Basic. Now that the property is implemented automatically, it requires a bit more effort, as demonstrated in the following:

```
' A property that can be changed
Property SomeValue() As Integer
```

Simply write the keyword *Get* into the next line, and then press Enter:

```
' A property that can be changed
Property SomeValue() As Integer
Get
```

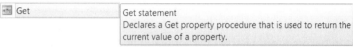

The editor now adds the outline of the *Set* and *Get* procedures for you, as follows:

```
' A property that can be changed
Property SomeValue() As Integer
    Get

    End Get
    Set(value As Integer)

    End Set
End Property
```

Assigning Values to Properties

The following statement assigns a value to the property *AProperty* of some object.

```
Object.AProperty = Something
```

In the *Set* accessor *Set(ByVal value as DataType)* of the property procedure, use the variable *value* to access the value in *Something*. When making an assignment, only the *Set* portion of the property procedure execute.

The statement can be used the other way around to retrieve a value from a property.

```
Something = Object.AProperty
```

In this case, only the *Get* accessor of the property procedure is executed. That accessor returns the result with *Return*, and in this case, assigns it to the object variable *Something* which, of course, needs to be of the same type as the property.

Using this knowledge, you can now rewrite the class as follows:

Companion Content Open the corresponding solution (.sln), which you can find in the \VB 2010 Developer Handbook\Chapter 09\MiniAddressoClass V2 folder.

```vb
Public Class Contact
    Private myFirstName As String
    Private myLastName As String
    Private myZip As String
    Private myCity As String

    Public Property FirstName() As String
        Get
            Return myFirstName
        End Get
        Set(ByVal value As String)
            myFirstName = value
        End Set
    End Property

    Public Property LastName() As String
        Get
            Return myLastName
        End Get
        Set(ByVal value As String)
            myLastName = value
        End Set
    End Property

    Public Property Zip() As String
        Get
            Return myZip
        End Get
        Set(ByVal value As String)
            myZip = value
        End Set
    End Property
```

```
    Public Property City() As String
        Get
            Return myCity
        End Get
        Set(ByVal value As String)
            myCity = EllipsisString(value, 30)¹
        End Set
    End Property

    Private Function EllipsisString(ByVal text As String, ByVal MaxLength
        As Integer) As String

        Dim tmpText As String

        If text.Length > MaxLength Then
            tmpText = text.Substring(0, MaxLength - 3) + "..."
        Else
            tmpText = text
        End If
        Return tmpText
    End Function

End Class
```

This simple example shows how property procedures protect the actual data structures. The data, which is saved in a class instance, has private access modifiers (for more information about access modifiers, see the section "Specifying Variable Scope with Access Modifiers," later in this chapter). Access modifiers prevent the data from being modified directly from the outside; only the class code itself has direct access to the field variable. Field variables are named differently, too. In this example, the field variables have the prefix *my* (because they are "my" variables from the class view or class instance view). This is a common convention, but it's not required. You can name your field variables as you please—but you should make sure that you name the field variables differently than the corresponding (and accessible from the outside) properties. Otherwise, a compile error occurs.

The property procedures in this example have the same name as the original public field variables. From a developer's point of view, nothing has changed as far as handling is concerned. However, the result did change because now, by using the property routines, access to the field variables is controlled exclusively by the class. The example shows that the *City* variable will never contain more than 30 characters as a result of this procedure. Whenever someone tries to assign a city name longer than 30 characters, the property *Set* accessor adjusts the string (adding the ellipsis) because it calls the *EllipseString* method. The actual data memory of the city—the field variable *myCity*—can no longer be accessed from the outside because its access is protected with the access modifier *private (*for this and all other

---

[1] A footnote in a code listing? Why not. The technical editor for this book rightly suggests an alternative at this point: instead of messing up *myCity*, it is possible to save the original assignment in its full length and call the method *EllipsisString* when *retrieving* the property. This way the original property definition can still be accessed, if necessary.

field variables). And this is exactly what a class does: *it encapsulates data and controls their access with code.*

The *autoimplemented properties* was introduced in Visual Basic 2010. In many cases, you will need properties for binding data for example in Windows Presentation Foundation (WPF) applications, but the code only sets the appropriate field variables of your class, as the following example shows:

```
Public Property LastName() As String
    Get
        Return _LastName
    End Get
    Set(ByVal value As String)
        _LastName= value
    End Set
End Property
```

Here, the field variable upon which the property is based only distinguishes itself from the property name by an underscore (_). Such properties, which don't really need any additional code, take a lot of time to write, and that's exactly what is no longer necessary with Visual Basic 2010. You can achieve exactly the same result by using the following line:

```
Public Property LastName() As String
```

The compiler ensures that the corresponding *Get* and *Set* procedures are created, and even creates an appropriate field variable.

Note As previously mentioned, Visual Basic creates a field variable "under the hood." But this field variable doesn't really lie that deep under the hood; you still access it directly from its class, even though it's not very obvious where it can be found. IntelliSense doesn't mention it, but that doesn't mean it doesn't exist.

As shown in the previous example, the Visual Basic compiler gives the field variable associated with the property the same name as the property itself, prefixed with an underscore character. Thus, if your property is called *LastName*, the corresponding field variable is called *_LastName*.

In this case, the field variable is also called a *Backing Field* (for instance, a help field). By the way, this backing field is always *Private*, no matter what access modifier you give the property itself. If you define the property statically (see the section, "Static Properties," later in this chapter), the backing field is also defined statically—exactly the same as when implementing a property with an explicitly defined field variable.

In the section "Public Variables or Properties—a Question of Faith?," later in this chapter, you can see clues as to why you should prioritize properties or autoimplemented properties over public fields.

Note To refresh your memory, IntelliSense is the name of the Code Editor's input assistance, which completes element names for you, shows all the elements of an object, and makes function overloads visible as you are writing code (you'll see more on overloading in the section "Overloading Methods, Constructors, and Properties," later in this chapter).

Pre-Allocating Default Property Values for Autoimplemented Properties

It is very common to pre-allocate default values to properties, usually in a class constructor. Pre-allocating default values is also possible with autoimplemented properties. And you can do it without bending yourself out of shape and having to write additional code in the constructor. It works exactly the same as when initializing variables. The following are a few examples, beginning with the following line, which defines a property of the type *String* and pre-allocates the string "Ramona Leenings".

```
Public Property LastName() As String = "Ramona Leenings"
```

This statement defines a property of the type *Integer Array* and pre-allocates three elements:

```
Property ConvertibleTemperatures As Integer() = New Integer() {23, 25, 31}
```

This statement defines a property of the generic type *List(Of String)* and uses a collection initializer to pre-allocate three strings for the generic list.

```
Public Property LastNames As New List(Of String) From {"Leenings", "Feigenbaum", "Löffelmann"}
```

Passing Arguments to Properties

In Visual Basic, properties can take any parameter, just like functions. The parameters are embedded in the property procedure (like functions) and can be accessed within the property's code. For example, assume a property is defined as follows:

```
Property PropertyWithParameters(ByVal Par1 As Integer, ByVal Par2 As String) As Integer

    Get
        If Par1 = 0 Then
            Return 10
        Else
            Return 20
        End If
    End Get

    Set(ByVal Value As Integer)
        If Par2 = "Klaus" Then
            'DoSomething
        ElseIf Par1 = 20 Then
            'DoSomethingElse
        End If
    End Set

End Property
```

You can then use statements to assign or query, such as the following:

```
'Set property with parameters.
locObjectInstance.PropertyWithParameters(10, "Klaus") = 5

'Query property with parameters.
If locObjectInstance.PropertyWithParameters(20, "Test") = 20 Then
    'Do something
End If
```

Note If you are adjusting very old code, or you are still working in Component Object Model (COM) (possibly written in Visual Basic 6.0) due to downward compatibility issues, you must remember that in contrast to Visual Basic 6.0, value type parameters are passed as a value, not as a reference. If you change a value within a property procedure in Visual Basic 6.0, the value of the variable in the calling code has also changed (unless it is explicitly protected by putting it between brackets before overwriting it, or you have passed it explicitly with *ByVal,* as happens automatically in .NET versions of Visual Basic). In .NET versions of Visual Basic, the *value* is passed by value to a property; therefore, you are always working with a *copy* of the passed variable.

The differentiation between *Set* and *Let* that existed in Visual Basic 6.0, no longer exists in .NET versions of Visual Basic. Because everything is derived from *Object*, and therefore, basically only objects are manipulated, the *Let* has also become redundant, so everything would need to be manipulated with *Set*—and then of course, you can just leave *Set* out.

Important Properties with parameters should be used only as an exception, because they are a special characteristic of Visual Basic. Unlike Visual Basic, C# also supports properties, but it can only access properties without parameters or default properties (more about this in the following section). Therefore, if you are developing classes as a team or for a broader public and expect your assemblies to be used by developers who are working in a .NET language other than Visual Basic, you should avoid parameterized properties.

Default Properties

In VBA and Visual Basic up to version 6.0 you can use a default property to determine which property is executed when the calling code did not specify a property. In Visual Basic 6.0/ VBA, default properties serve to simplify work for developers who might tend to be lazy writers. The type system in .NET does not allow type ambiguities. For example, in the following code, it is not clear whether you want to assign the *Textbox* itself to *anObject* or the result of the default property of the *Textbox*:

```
Dim ATextBox as TextBox
Dim anObject as Object
.
.
.
anObject = ATextBox
```

Exceptions here are parameterized properties, because the property signature shows that it's not the object itself but the result of a parameterized property that will be returned.[2] It makes sense in this case, and here's why.

Suppose that you are developing a *NumericList* class that saves and manages various numeric values as a list and provides access to the list elements via an index. If there were no properties with parameters, you would need to do the following to query a list element:

```
'Set index.
numList.Index = 5
'Query element.
DoSomethingWith = numList.Item
```

Of course, this would be rather laborious. It becomes easier if you specify the index and the query in one line (the way it actually works). In Visual Basic, this is no problem when you use a property with a parameter as follows:

```
DoSomethingWith = numList.Item(5)
```

It becomes even easier when the property *Item* in this example is declared the default property.[3] Then you don't even need to specify the property name; the following line would suffice:

```
DoSomethingWith = numList(5)
```

The appropriate definition for the *Item* property would look like this:

```
Default Public Property Item(ByVal Index As Integer) As Integer

    Get
        Return myInternalList(Index)
    End Get

    Set(ByVal Value As Integer)
        myInternalList(Index) = Value
    End Set

End Property
```

> **Important** In contrast to VBA and Visual Basic 6.0, the .NET versions of Visual Basic have no default properties without parameters. It's also important to know that you can't declare default properties as Static. However, that doesn't prevent you from implementing a property that behaves statically.

---

[2] This is similar to overloads, where you also only differentiate through signatures, which of the several available functions is the correct one.

[3] As mentioned before: in C#, default properties are the only way to pass a parameter to a property procedure.

Avoid the Ultimate Property-No-Go

Recently, when working on a project that involved migrating a complex project from English to German and simultaneously from Visual Basic 6.0 to VB.NET (and also migrating the team from Visual Basic 6.0 to object-oriented approaches), we stumbled across some performance issues that took some time to solve.

A few components seemed to slow down for no obvious reason. After a few tests, we finally discovered the reason for that: classes with property definitions like this were bound to *DataGridViews*, which, in turn, were then used in user or pop-up controls that users could resize at runtime:

```
Public ReadOnly Property AcountDescription As String
    Get
        Dim datalayer = AppConfig.GetDatalayer(Of AllEntities)()
        Dim uniCap = (From u In datalayer.UniCapAccountCap
            Where u.AccountCapID = TextNr1 And u.Company =
            CShort(datalayer.CompanySettings.UniCapCompany)).FirstOrDefault
            Return If(uniCap Is Nothing, "", uniCap.AccountCaption)
    End Get
End Property
```

 Warning The preceding code is just for demonstration purposes; don't do this at home!

What's happening here is that the property getter is executing time intensive code. Each time the property is accessed, the data is slooooowly pulled from the SQL-Database—in this case via *LINQ to Entities*, which you will learn about in Chapter 27, "LINQ to Entities: Programming with Entity Framework." Developers call this type of code "expensive." In this case, the class that contained this code was bound to a *DataGridView*, so every time the user made the *DataGridView* update itself, it had to retrieve the data from the database for the corresponding column. Now imagine this code running on a terminal server with "only" 20 users working on it concurrently.

 Note There is another technique called *lazy loading*, in which code retrieves property data only at the time when it is first used. Don't confuse lazy loading, which is perfectly OK in the appropriate scenarios, with what you saw here. With lazy loading, the expensive operation happens in the property getter all right, but only once! It's then buffered, and reused from that buffer for each subsequent call. In contrast, what you saw here has nothing to do with lazy loading—you might call it crazy loading at best.

Public Variables or Properties—a Question of Faith?

Now that you have learned so much about properties, you might ask why you should use them instead of simple public field variables.

As long as you only need the properties in a class to save some values, but you don't need to do anything in particular when querying or setting these values, public variables are actually sufficient. For example, the class illustrated here contains one public field variable:

```
Class WithAProperty
    Public TheProperty As Integer
End Class
```

It fulfills exactly the same purpose as the following class (which, beginning with Visual Basic 2010, doesn't even require more keystrokes):

```
Class AlsoWithAProperty

    'Self-implementing property
    Public Property TheProperty() As Integer

End Class
```

Generally, you should prefer the second version to the first for the following reasons, some of which you already know:

- **Data Encapsulation**   Properties encapsulate and regulate the access to data, as you have already seen in the previous example. Even if you pass a property value completely to a field variable (for possible expansions), you are at least prepared in case of regulation algorithms.

- **Data Binding**   Fields cannot be used for data binding. Many times you'll want to use not only data sources such as databases for binding, but also objects, such as collections. Public fields (public field variables) cannot be used as a data source.

 Note Data binding is a procedure that binds properties of one object to the properties of another. This way, you can synchronize data between objects. Often binding procedures are used in conjunction with controls to display the content of a data class so that the display automatically changes if the data class content changes.

- **Polymorphism**   Another important argument is the replacement of properties by so-called Polymorphism when inheriting from classes, which is addressed in Chapter 10, "Class Inheritance and Polymorphism." This much should be remembered for now: a variable, once declared as public, will always remain public. Inherited classes cannot take additional control to regulate its access. However, if you expose your data to the outside world by using only property procedures, you can later add additional rules (scope queries, error catching) or modify existing behavior. To achieve this, you don't need to change the original class at all.

Thus, properties are always preferable to public fields. If you cannot fall back on auto-implemented properties, the Visual Basic code snippet library (see the following sidebar) provides input assistance.

Save Time When Creating Property Procedures with Code Snippets

The sample class in the previous section demonstrates convincingly that it makes a lot of sense to manage, regulate, and protect the field variables of a class by using appropriate property procedures—even though that sometimes requires more typing, especially when you need to create access control code and can't fall back on auto-implemented properties. However, code snippets can simplify the process.

Code snippets can save you a lot of time when working with properties. To add a new property to your class based on a field variable, type the string **Pro** at the position where you want to create the new property. A dialog box opens, as shown in Figure 9-1.

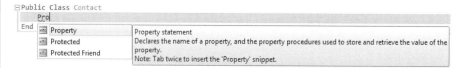

FIGURE 9-1 To add a property procedure by using code snippets, type the string **Pro,** and then Press Tab twice (as seen in the Note for the IntelliSense list) to insert the property code snippet.

Press the Tab key twice to insert the *Property* code snippet. The code should appear similar to Figure 9-2.

```
Public Class Contact

    Private newPropertyValue As String
    Public Property NewProperty() As String
        Get
            Return newPropertyValue
        End Get
        Set(ByVal value As String)
            newPropertyValue = value
        End Set
    End Property

End Class
```

FIGURE 9-2 Edit the selected field variable, and add the appropriate data type by pressing Tab.

Now change the field variable (which has been inserted with the default name *new-PropertyValue)* to a name that you prefer.

As soon as you press Tab, all the field variables references in the code block switch to the new name. At the same time, the next editable field of the code snippet is highlighted and ready to be modified. In this example, that would be the type definition of the property's backing field, as shown in Figure 9-3.

```
Public Class Contact

    Private myFirstName As String
    Public Property NewProperty() As String
        Get
            Return myFirstName
        End Get
        Set(ByVal value As String)
            myFirstName = value
        End Set
    End Property

End Class
```

FIGURE 9-3 You can change the default inserted property name and type.

Change the type, and then press Tab again. This changes all the types for the property procedure. Finally change the name of the property to complete the property procedure.

The result shows all properties and their corresponding field variables as pairs. Many developers don't like this format, preferring instead to define field variables at the beginning of the class code file. Of course, you can arrange the field variable definitions as you wish. Moving them around does not affect the class functionality.

Class Constructors: Defining What Happens in *New*

When instantiating a class into an object, the .NET Framework first creates the appropriate amount of memory space for the field variables on the Managed Heap (it's actually the Common Language Runtime [CLR] that controls this process). There are a few other things

happening internally, which are responsible for managing the object on the Managed Heap, but that's it for now.

In many cases, however, a certain amount of housekeeping work is necessary to prepare the class to function correctly. For example, think of what happens when you instantiate a new button for your Windows Forms application: the infrastructure creates enough space on the Managed Heap for the data (which holds the control information for the button), and then calls the *CreateWindow* function of the Windows operating system file Win32.Dll to create—in layman's terms—the button from the operating system's perspective.

Here's a simpler example. How would you implement into your previously used sample class a feature that automatically determines the class creation date as soon as an instance of the *Contact* class has been created? There are two possibilities:

- **You implement another property**   Create a property called *CreationDate that* determines the current date/time combination—whenever you create an instance of the *Contact* class you set the property to *Date.Now*. There is one danger: you might forget this step. And that's exactly opposite of the idea of good object-oriented programming: you should create objects that are so highly self-managing, that you simply *cannot* forget such things or do them the wrong way. This is similar to using property procedures to regulate the access to class members in such a way that you can't accidentally compromise them.

- **Here's a better alternative**   Implement a property that gives you read-access to the *CreationDate* property. You will see exactly how this works in the section, "Different Access Modifiers for Property Accessors," later in this chapter. But that part is less important. What's important here is that you can implement a special method that automatically supplies the creation date for the field variable on which the property is based, as soon as an object of the class is created. This ensures that the creation date will be set for every new instance of the class.

To put that last bullet point into practice, you'll implement a constructor for the sample class. The constructor code is executed immediately after the CLR has finished creating the default infrastructure for the new object. In Visual Basic, you create a constructor by inserting a subroutine called *Sub New:*

> **Companion Content**   Open the corresponding solution (.sln), which you can find in the \VB 2010 Developer Handbook\Chapter 09\MiniAddressoClass V3 folder

```
Public Class Contact

    Private myFirstName As String
    Private myLastName As String
    Private myZip As String
    Private myCity As String
    Private myCreationDate As Date

    Sub New()
        myCreationDate = Date.Now
    End Sub

    Public ReadOnly Property CreationDate() As Date
        Get
            Return myCreationDate
        End Get
    End Property
    .
    .
    .
End Class
```

The relevant changes in the list are formatted in bold. As soon as some code creates a new instance of the class, the CLR first creates the object structures internally, and then immediately calls the class constructor. In this case, the constructor—defined by the name *Sub New*—sets the field variable *myCreationDate* to the current date/time. Now, to discover when any instance of this class was created, simply access its creation date with the corresponding read-only property (*CreationDate*). This procedure fulfills all three requirements in our specifications:

- The class cannot be instantiated without the creation date being set; the constructor takes care of that with *Sub New*.
- The creation date can be retrieved with the property procedure.
- The creation date *can only be retrieved*, not changed, because it's a read-only property—there's no *Get* accessor. Therefore, it cannot be changed retroactively.

At this point, the function block is foolproof.

Parameterized Constructors

You probably noticed that the class of the first example was a little unwieldy. First, you had to instantiate it (which can never be avoided) but then we used properties to assign the appropriate contents from the derived object. However, you probably know of classes (that you might have already used in the .NET Framework) that instantiate new objects and set one or more parameter values at the same time. The sample class used so far is kind of pathetic in that respect, but that will change now.

As you've seen, to create a class constructor (which is where you'd likely want to initialize field variables), you implement a *Sub New*. A constructor differs from normal methods because the procedure name is a keyword (*New*). The Visual Studio editor and compiler recognize this as a keyword and mark it in blue.

> **Note** Constructors can only be *Sub* methods, not *Function* methods. The latter wouldn't make any sense anyway, because instantiating a class with *New* already returns the instantiated object as the "function result" of *New*. From a purely technical standpoint this explanation is wrong, of course. It is only meant as a mnemonic.

> **Companion Content** Open the corresponding solution (.sln), which you can find in the \VB 2010 Developer Handbook\Chapter 09\MiniAddressoClass V4 folder.

Let's go back to the sample program. To declare the class instance *and* assign initial values to it, the original sample application needs to be modified slightly. The required changes are marked in bold in the following listing:

```
Public Class Contact

    Private myFirstName As String
    Private myLastName As String
    Private myZip As String
    Private myCity As String
    Private myCreationDate As Date

    'Constructor without parameters
    Sub New()
        myCreationDate = Date.Now
    End Sub

    'Constructor takes initialization parameters
    Sub New(ByVal FirstName As String, ByVal LastName As String, _
            ByVal Zip As String, ByVal City As String)

        'And calls the constructor without parameters.
        'This can ONLY happen first or not at all.
        Me.New()

        'Initialize field variables with the parameters.
        myFirstName = FirstName
        myLastName = LastName
        myZip = Zip
        myCity = City
    End Sub
```

```
Public ReadOnly Property CreationDate() As Date
    Get
        Return myCreationDate
    End Get
End Property
    .
    .
    .
End Class
```

Using this updated version of the class, you can now instantiate a contact as follows, directly assigning default parameters at the same time:

```
Module MainModule

    Sub Main()

        'Use different colors than in the console window
        Console.BackgroundColor = ConsoleColor.White
        Console.ForegroundColor = ConsoleColor.Black
        Console.Clear()

        'Specify an address with a parameterized contructor:
        Dim AngiesContact As New Contact("Angela", "Wördehoff", _
                                "99999", "Bahamas")

        'Of course, it also works like this as of 2008, but it doesn't *replace*
        'the parameterized contructor. And it requires more writing.
        Dim LöffelsContact As New Contact With {.FirstName = "Klaus", _
                                .LastName = "Löffelmann", _




                                .Zip = "59555", _
                                .City = "Lippstadt"}
    End Sub
End Module
```

 Note You could argue that parameterized constructors have become a bit obsolete as of Visual Basic 2008, because Visual Basic now has property initializers for the constructor that you can write by using the *With* keyword, as shown in the second example. However, that argument is correct only to a certain extent. On the one hand, you can only control the property assignments with the property procedures themselves—a parameterized constructor might try to perform further value checks. On the other hand, passing default values for certain members with a parameterized constructor still requires fewer keystrokes, and maybe you want to pass parameters to the class constructor, which might not be covered or exposed by any property. It would be conceivable, for example, to pass a *Contact* instance to a constructor to clone an existing contact.

Furthermore, some other .NET languages don't support property initializers; they are converted exclusively by the compiler, which generates the appropriate code. If you are developing assemblies that other .NET languages will also access, creating parameterized constructors makes it easier for downstream developers using your classes.

Just like methods, constructors can be overloaded, but there are certain issues that you must keep in mind while performing recursive calls. The section "Overloading Methods, Constructors, and Properties" in this chapter provides more details.

Oh yes! The version of the sample program from the very beginning of this chapter has neither properties nor a default constructor in the source code, but in such cases the Common Type System (CTS) requires that the compiler take the appropriate actions to ensure that such a condition cannot happen.

> **More Information** In Chapter 2, "Introduction to the .NET Framework," you can see how the CTS requires strict type binding and code consistency, which thus forces code robustness in the CLR.

As an example, let's go back to the previous version of the sample program, in which there was only one constructor (version 3 of the example *Contact* class). Now, suppose that you were to comment out this constructor and pre-initialize one of the field variables with a default value, as shown below:

```
Public Class Contact

    'Sub New()
    '     myCreationDate = Date.Now
    'End Sub

    Private myFirstName As String
    Private myLastName As String
    Private myZip As String
    Private myCity As String


    Private myCreationDate As Date = Date.Now

    Public ReadOnly Property CreationDate() As Date
        Get
            Return myCreationDate
        End Get
    End Property
End Class
```

To summarize: in this version, the default constructor was eliminated (by commenting it out); at the same time, the current time/date combination is assigned to the corresponding field variable *myCreationDate* (which is obviously allowed, because the compiler doesn't complain). In this case, the question is, "when does the date initialization take place, and what makes it happen"?

As was briefly discussed in Chapter 3, the compiler doesn't translate your program directly into machine code, but into an *Intermediate Language* (IL). Your program's frame data, such as constants, defined attributes, as well as version information, is put into a special data scope in the same file. In .NET, this data is called *metadata*. When you first start a program,

at that point there isn't anything the processor can run because it understands only Pentium or x86 code, as far as Intel platforms are concerned. So, there must be some mechanism that translates your program into machine code at some point between program start and program execution. There is. This tool is part of the CLR and is called the Just-in-Time (JIT) compiler. You can view the "temporary" IL code with a specific tool from the .NET tool box— it displays the whole truth, even the parts that the compiler adds without your involvement.

Armed with this knowledge, you can view any compiled Visual Basic program in its "IL state" and find out what the Visual Basic compiler has turned it into. The individual commands are not so important here, what matters is the metadata that provides information about the components, types, signatures, and so on that your program is composed of.

Additional Tools for .NET

There are several additional useful tools for Microsoft Visual Studio 2010. After several attempts, Microsoft finally managed to put them in a place where you might expect them to be—in the Start menu of the Visual Studio program group under Microsoft Windows SDK Tools.

SDK stands for Software Development Kit. The SDK contains all the tools you need to compile and test programs as well as adjust resources and much more, even without Visual Studio (although you cannot edit programs or manage project files with these tools). Contrary to earlier versions, a complete version of the SDK seems to install with Visual Studio 2010.

In the following section you'll take a closer look at one of the SDK tools: the IL Disassembler. You can use this tool to view the CIL or MSIL code, as the case may be, as well as the metadata that comprises your assembly before the JIT compiler turns it into executable code.

With that brief digression out of the way, you can return to the task at hand:

1. Select Build Solution from the Build menu. The Visual Basic compiler recreates the IL code within the .exe file (in the output assembly).

2. In the Microsoft Windows SDK Tools program group, start the IL Disassembler (see the sidebar "Additional Tools for .NET").

3. Select Open from the File menu, and then Open in the dialog that opens the .exe file of the sample program. You will find the program file MiniAddressoClass.exe in the project directory, in the folder \bin\Debug\.

Note You will find two .exe files in the Debug directory—one ends with *vshost.exe*. Do *not* use that one; it's a small tool required by the Visual Studio IDE to speed up the creation time of your projects and to enable the much-desired *Edit and Continue* feature, which permits you to perform changes to your program *while* debugging it. Edit and Continue is still not available in Visual Studio on a 64-bit Windows operating system, and your project is also compiled against 64 bits (or if on a 64-bit operating system, the default setting "Any" has been selected). You can force x86 code by forcing the corresponding target platform with the configuration manager. Then Edit and Continue will be available to you.

4. In the window that appears, open the branch *MiniAddressoClass* and also the subbranch *MiniAddressoClass.Contact*, which contains all the elements of our *Contact* class.

5. In the View menu, select Show Source Lines.

When viewing the CIL code, the appropriate line of Visual Basic source code will be shown, as illustrated in Figure 9-4.

FIGURE 9-4 The meta data of the .exe file permits viewing the program structure in the IL Disassembler.

Figure 9-5 demonstrates the structure of the program. You'll see elements that you specified, such as function names, but you will also discover a method that you didn't author directly, the *.ctor* method (short for "constructor").

```
MiniAdressoClass.contact:.ctor : void()
Find  Find Next
.method public specialname rtspecialname
        instance void  .ctor() cil managed
{
    .custom instance void [mscorlib]System.Diagnostics.DebuggerNonUserCodeAttri
    // Code size        9 (0x9)
    .maxstack  8
    IL_0000:  ldarg.0
    IL_0001:  call        instance void [mscorlib]System.Object::.ctor()
    IL_0006:  nop
    IL_0007:  nop
    IL_0008:  ret
} // end of method contact::.ctor
```

FIGURE 9-5 The disassembled IML code of the default constructor.

The *.ctor* method in not a method in the conventional sense; it's a constructor, which is the part of the class that is created when you implement a *Sub New* in Visual Basic. But this is what you commented out in the source code before building the application and starting the IL Disassembler.

What has happened here is that the compiler has independently made sure that the class contains a constructor, which is exactly what the CTS requires; each class that can be instantiated must have a constructor. Whether that constructor can be called is a different question. For example, you can give the class constructor a *Private* access modifier so that the class can be instantiated only by itself; the private constructor is no longer callable from outside the class.

> **Note** At first glance, this makes no sense, correct? On the contrary! There is a *design pattern* called *Singleton* that defines a certain way to design a class. The design pattern has just one private constructor—but it also has a public static method that you can call to request an instance. This method can regulate, how instances are returned, and how many—for *Singleton* classes there can be only one instance of that class at a time. You'll see a full example of a *Singleton* class at the end of Chapter 10, "Class Inheritance and Polymorphism".

Even without knowing exactly which IL statement is responsible for which task, one thing is immediately clear: the first part of the method calls another constructor, and that's correct. Each new class that you create is derived implicitly from base types, or the *Object* type. If you don't specify otherwise, the constructor of this base class is called.

To learn more about what deriving from classes means and why the base class constructor is called at this point, see Chapter 10.

By displaying the source code, you can be sure that the variable declaration of the member *myCreationDate* (which was originally only located under the class body) has found its way into the constructor. There, it will be assigned the current time/date.

This example, therefore, shows that the Visual Basic compiler has saved you a lot of work. It made sure of the following:

- That a default constructor with the method *.ctor* exists, even though you didn't explicitly implement it with *Sub New()*.

- Within the default constructor, the default base class *Object* constructor (`call instance void [mscorlib]System.Object::.ctor()`) is called.

- All field variables, if required, are defined within this default constructor; that is, they are "filled" with values, as long as you have specified the variable below the class body during declaration.

> **Important** This demonstrates why you should always define the class field variables, which need to be pre-initialized, where they are declared. If you have defined several overloaded constructors in a class (see the following section), you run the risk of forgetting this pre-initialization of the variable in all constructors, because the Visual Basic compiler takes care of it. The following example shows what this means. The compiler adds the commented out lines to the code by itself, by defining the declared field variables with default values on the module level:

```
Public Class AClass

    'Class field initialization should happen here,
    'so the appropriate initialization code automatically moves into all constructors!
    Private myFieldVariable As Date = Date.Now
    Private myOtherFieldVariable As Integer = 5
    Private myName As String

    'Sub New()
    '    myFieldVariable = Date.Now
    '    myOtherFieldVariable = 5
    'End Sub

    Sub New(ByVal name As String)
        'myFieldVariable = Date.Now
        'myOtherFieldVariable  = 5
        myName = name
    End Sub
End Class
```

Class Methods with *Sub* and *Function*

Class code isn't executed only in property procedures. Methods defined in Visual Basic by *Sub* or *Function* are also a part of the class. Non-static methods (those not defined via the class instance. see the section "Static Method," later in this chapter) are methods that should act upon the field variables of a class.

As an example, consider that a function, such as *ContactText,* could take care of returning the text representative of the class field values; the corresponding routines would look as follows:

```
Public Function ContactText() As String

    Return LastName & ", " & FirstName & ", " & _
        Zip & ", " & City

End Function
```

This member method of the class uses the instance variable directly and returns all its fields concatenated in a continuous string. This means that the respective changes can also be performed at the output routine in the module, which uses the following individual instances:

```
Sub AddressOutput(ByVal from As Integer, ByVal to As Integer)

    For c As Integer = from To to
        Console.WriteLine(c.ToString("000") & ": " & Contacts(c).ContactText())
    Next

End Sub
```

The *ContactText* method is called here for each *Contact* instance, and, of course, it returns a different result for each instance. The preceding example shows very clearly that it's a member method.

Companion Content Open the corresponding solution (.SLN file), which you can find in the \VB 2010 Developer Handbook\Chapter 09\MiniAddressoClass V5 folder.

 Note An application always starts with a *Sub Main*. This is also true for Windows applications that you create as Windows Forms projects under Visual Basic. For more information, read Chapter 2, "introduction to the .NET Framework."

Overloading Methods, Constructors, and Properties

If you're a seasoned Visual Basic 6.0 developer, you probably know the advantage of having your language support optional parameters. At first glance, overloading functions in .NET seems similar, but it's actually a completely different concept. What both concepts have in common is that they permit a liberal passing of parameters to functions. But that's where the commonalities end.

By overloading functions you can give your classes an enormous amount of flexibility and adaptability. Overloading functions means that you create different functions with the same name, but which differ only by the type, the order, or the number of parameters that are passed to it. Take a look at the following code example:

```
Sub AProcedure()
    'Do something.
End Sub

Sub AProcedure(ByVal a_parameter As Integer)
    'Do something else.
End Sub

Sub AProcedure(ByVal a_different_parameter As String)
    'Do something else.
End Sub

Sub AProcedure(ByVal a_parameter As Integer, ByVal a_different_parameter As String)
    'Do something else.
End Sub

Sub AProcedure(ByVal a_completely_different_parameter As Integer)
    'Error: an integer as parameter already existed.
    'The method 'AProcedure' has been defined multiple times with identical signatures.
End Sub
```

In the preceding example, it seems as if the signature (which represents the combination of parameter types and parameter order when calling a function) becomes part of the name, and shows which of the existing versions of *AProcedure* should be called. The parameter names are immaterial—only the parameter *type* is critical for signature identification.

This is why the last *Sub* of the example creates problems. Just like the first one, it takes a parameter of type *Integer*. The variable name is different, but that's not what matters; the names are just hollow words.

The benefit of overloading methods is that using the classes becomes disproportionately simpler. Even with the companion example, you at least get to enjoy the comfort of over-loaded methods (or constructors) when you use the *Contact* class. You don't need to know which method is responsible for which partial task. You can just use a function (IntelliSense even suggests all available overloaded forms of the method as you write code). When you put the line that instantiates the class into an object in your program, IntelliSense shows you the individual constructor signatures after you have typed the open bracket following *New Contact*, as shown in Figure 9-6.

```
'Indicates an adress with parameterized constructor:
Dim AngisKontakt As New Contact(|
```

    ▲ 2 of 2 ▼   New(**FirstName As String**, LastName As String, ZipCode As String, Town As String)

```
'This works since 2008, too - this does not replace
'the parameterized constructor. Also this is more typing.
Dim LöffelsKontakt As New Contact With {.FirstName = "Klaus", _
                                        .Lastname = "Löffelmann", _
                                        .ZipCode = "59555", _
                                        .Town = "Lippstadt"}
```

FIGURE 9-6 IntelliSense helps you to select the correct signature for overloaded methods, such as constructors.

Unlike with optional parameters, overloading lets you implement methods or constructors, which depending on the versions, do completely different things. Of course, both constructor versions in this chapter's example are thematically linked (as they should be; otherwise, they should have completely different names). What's important is that the two overloaded procedures can—in contrast to *one* procedure with optional parameters—be implemented completely differently (the first initializes the class with an integer, the other by specifying a Roman numeral). Both methods are also clearly separated visually.

Note The principle of function overload works for *Sub* methods in the same way as for *Function* methods; however, when using functions, you need to know that the return type cannot be used as a signature differentiation criteria. This means:

```
Function AFunction() As Integer
    'Do something.
End Function

Function AFunction(ByVal DifferentSignature As Integer) As Integer
    'This works.
End Function

Function AFunction() As String
    '"Function AFunction() As Integer" and "Function AFunction() As String"
    ' can't overload each other, because they only differ by return type.
End Function
```

The first two functions are OK because the signatures differ. However, the last function differs from the first only by its return type. This is why the Visual Basic compiler raises an error at design time.

Tip You can use the keyword *Overloads* to show a method overload and make it easier to read, as follows:

```
Overloads Function AFunction() As Integer
    'If using overloads,...
End Function

Overloads Function AFunction(ByVal DifferentSignature As Integer) As Integer
    '...then with functions
End Function
```

If you decide to use the *Overloads* keyword, you need to use it for *all* method overloads.

As an alternative to overloading methods, Visual Basic provides optional parameters. Optional parameters have advantages and disadvantages when you compare them to overloaded methods:

- Optional parameters are possibly not supported by other .NET programming languages. This is the case for C# up to version 2008 or .NET Framework up to 3.5. Later versions of C# are able to handle optional parameters. If you use optional parameters in your classes, you need to keep in mind that other .NET languages might not support optional parameters, especially if you aren't developing against the newest version of the .NET Framework.

- Using optional parameters necessarily makes the code that handles the optional parameters within a method harder to read and less easy to reuse. When you use optional parameters, you need to perform case differentiation by querying default values, which are defined only from constants, to find out which parameters have been passed by the caller and which haven't; your code must react differently in each possible combination. A method that does two totally different things based solely on its parameter pretty much functions as squeezed "double code" in a function body. However, with overloaded functions, you can separate two problem solutions in a visually clean fashion.

- If you are working without strict type binding (*Option Strict Off*) while using overloaded functions and optional parameters for the same methods, performance is compromised immensely, because the runtime library of Visual Basic might first need to discover which routine best matches the specified parameter. When using very flexible parameter transfers you might create errors, which I, for one, honestly wouldn't want to debug.

- But developing Office applications with VSTO is definitely more comfortable in Visual Basic (or with C# as of version 2010), specifically *because* the Office libraries use optional parameters so intensively, which are then applicable in Visual Basic. When calling Office methods in earlier versions of C#, you must pass the keyword *System. Reflection.Missing.Value* for each optional parameter that you don't specify.

 Note Until .NET Framework 4.0, the .NET Framework itself had no methods that used optional parameters.

Using Optional Parameters

Defining optional parameters for a method is relatively simple—and using them to call the method is quite transparent. On one hand, the following example demonstrates how to

define optional parameters for a method, and on the other, how to call such a method, in different versions:

Companion Content   Open the corresponding solution (.sln), which you can find in the \VB 2010 Developer Handbook\Chapter 09\OptionalParametersDemo folder.

```vb
Module OptionalParametersDemo

    Private Const MAXDATEVALUE As Date = #12/31/9999 11:59:59 PM#
    Private Const DEFAULTDATEFORMAT = "dd.MM.yyyy"

    Sub Main()

        'Call with yesterday:
        PrintTimeDeltaOpt(Date.Now.AddDays(-1))

        'Call with day before yesterday, different than output format:
        PrintTimeDeltaOpt(Date.Now.AddDays(-2), DateFormatString:=
            "dddd, dd. MMMM yyyy")

        'It would have also worked this way:
        PrintTimeDeltaOpt(Date.Now.AddDays(-2), , , "dddd, dd. MMMM yyyy")

        'All of it self-selected:
        PrintTimeDeltaOpt(Date.Now.AddDays(-2), Date.Now, "TimeSpan: ", _
                        "dddd, dd. MMMM yyyy", "Start time: ", "End time: ", True)

        Console.WriteLine("Press key to end:")
        Console.ReadKey()

    End Sub

    Public Sub PrintTimeDeltaOpt(ByVal Starttime As Date, _
        Optional ByVal Endtime As Date = MAXDATEVALUE, _
        Optional ByVal TimeSpanCaption As String = "TimeDifference: ", _
        Optional ByVal DateFormatString As String = DEFAULTDATEFORMAT, _
        Optional ByVal StartTimeCaption As String = "StartTime: ", _
        Optional ByVal EndTimeCaption As String = "EndTime: ", _
        Optional ByVal PrintDelimitter As Boolean = True)

        'Typical for optional parameters:
        'Here we need to "discover" whether an optional parameter
        'was specified, and if not, replace it with the value
        'we actually "mean".
        If Endtime = MAXDATEVALUE Then
            Endtime = DateTime.Now
        End If
```

```
        Dim timeDifference = Endtime - StartTime

        Console.WriteLine(StartTimeCaption & "{0:" & DateFormatString & "}" & _
            vbNewLine & EndTimeCaption & "{1:" & DateFormatString & "}" & _
            vbNewLine & TimeSpanCaption & "{2:dd\.hh\:mm}", StartTime, EndTime, _
            timeDifference)

        If PrintDelimitter Then
            Console.WriteLine(New String("-"c, 75))
            Console.WriteLine()
        End If
    End Sub

End Module
```

There are three points worth mentioning in this demonstration:

First, in the first bold line you can see how to use *named parameters*. Named parameters let you specify parameters without the need to arrange them in any particular sequence in the parameter list (in other words, unlike normal calls, the parameter sequence does not need to match the sequence in which the parameters appear in the method signature.

This way of specifying parameters is another advantage of using optional parameters rather than method overloads, where named parameters aren't possible. As an added benefit, IntelliSense also supports named parameters, as shown in Figures 9-7 and 9-8.

FIGURE 9-7 IntelliSense also provides support for named parameters, which you can recognize by the string ":=".

```
Sub Main()

    PrintTimeDeltaOpt(|
    ┌─────────────────────────────────────────────────────────┐
    │ PrintTimeDeltaOpt(Starttime As Date,                      │
    │        [Endtime As Date = #12/31/9999 11:59:59 PM#],      │
    │        [TimeSpanCaption As String = "Zeitdifferenz: "],   │
    │        [DateFormatString As String = "dd.MM.yyyy"],       │
    │        [StartTimeCaption As String = "Startzeit: "],      │
    │        [EndTimeCaption As String = "Endzeit: "],          │
    │        [PrintDelimitter As Boolean = True])               │
    └─────────────────────────────────────────────────────────┘
End Sub

Public Sub PrintTimeDeltaOpt(ByVal Starttime As Date, _
                    Optional ByVal Endtime As Date = MAXDATEVALUE, _
                    Optional ByVal TimeSpanCaption As String = "Zeitdifferenz: ", _
                    Optional ByVal DateFormatString As String = DEFAULTDATEFORMAT, _
                    Optional ByVal StartTimeCaption As String = "Startzeit: ", _
                    Optional ByVal EndTimeCaption As String = "Endzeit: ", _
                    Optional ByVal PrintDelimitter As Boolean = True)
```

FIGURE 9-8 For signatures, IntelliSense not only shows you the variable names, but also the default values used to initialize the parameters when you omit them.

Second, the preceding example also shows how you can leave out specific parameters by using a comma sequence.

Finally, the example also demonstrates the negative aspects of optional parameters. Specifically, it shows a targeted replacement of values when a default value, which can only have a constant value (for example, *DateTime.Now* would not be possible as a default value because it's not a constant), needs to be replaced by a dynamic value. The example replaces the max date, which is the assumed default value when the parameter *Endtime* is omitted, with the current time (or the current date), which makes a lot more sense in this situation.

Mutual Calling of Overloaded Methods

You will run into overloaded methods in every corner of .NET Framework. Normally, the function overload feature of the .NET Framework simply facilitates handling for developers. Signatures for certain functions are offered with only a few parameters for safe and simple programming, whereas other versions of the same function have more parameters, ensuring the utmost flexibility.

The *WriteLine* method, which you have had the chance to admire several times already, serves as a very clear example of this; it has no less that 18 overloads. Enter the statement **Console.WriteLine** in the Visual Basic code editor, and then type the open bracket. IntelliSense shows you the signatures of all 18 different overloads, one at a time, as illustrated in Figure 9-9.

```
Console.WriteLine(
```

> ▲ 4 of 18 ▼ WriteLine(**buffer**() As Char)
>
> Writes the specified array of Unicode characters, followed by the current line terminator, to the standard output stream.
>
> **buffer:** A Unicode character array.

```
End
```

FIGURE 9-9 The *WriteLine* method has no fewer than 18 overloads.

Of course, overloading methods wouldn't be a true alleviation of labor if developers had to implement each one of them separately. Therefore, overloaded methods can—apart from the special case of *Sub New*—call each other without any restrictions.

The standard way to provide the user of your classes (and you're one of them) with the most flexibility is to develop a universal method that can do anything, and then "trim it down" by using overloads afterward.

Suppose, for example, that you have developed a class that provides a method to draw circles on the monitor. You call this method *Circle*. This method accepts, in its universal version, the following parameters:

```
Public Sub Circle(ByVal Xpos As Integer, ByVal YPos As Integer, ByVal XRadius As Integer, _
            ByVal YRadius As Integer, ByVal StartAngle As Integer, _
            ByVal EndAngle As Integer)
      'Here is the code for circle.
End Sub
```

Only rarely do you need this full form of the method, however. Typically, you don't need to specify the x *and* y radius of the ellipsis every time, and even more rarely do you need to specify the start and end angle of the circle. Calling the following simplified version is much more practical, which is why such methods are called *convenience methods*. A trimmed down version might look like this:

```
Public Sub Circle(ByVal Xpos As Integer, ByVal YPos As Integer, ByVal Radius As Integer)
    Circle(Xpos, YPos, Radius, Radius, 0, 359)
End Sub
```

At first glance it looks as if the function would call itself. But it doesn't, because the signature of the internally called *Circle* method in the second line doesn't correspond to its own signature. Therefore, the Visual Basic compiler checks which *Circle* method it should call; in this example, it calls the first universal form of the method.

Mutual Calling of Overloaded Constructors

It becomes a bit more problematic when overloaded constructors are supposed to call each other—there are operational limits. Armed with the knowledge from the previous section, you might want to follow your gut feeling and try to redesign the constructors of this example as shown in Figure 9-10.

FIGURE 9-10 If you try to call a different constructor method not at the first position within the constructor, Visual Basic will abort this with an error.

Visual Basic aborts this call with a basic syntax error and simply doesn't allow the call.

> **Note** A little nostalgia for you: the error message shown in Figure 9-10 existed for the Commodore 64, which also had a form of Microsoft-Basic. Amazingly, it has managed to stick around until today!

By the way, at this point, it's important to know and specify which *New* you are calling. Basically, each class has two versions of *New*, which were not created by an overload: the *New*, (the constructor of your class), and the *New* of the class from which you have derived your class. Because this example hasn't explicitly specified a class from which to derive, it automatically inherits from *Object*. Of course, *Object* has a constructor, as well. You can call base class methods as well as methods of your class. When you specify *Me*, you specify your class; to specify the base class—in this case the *Object* class—use the *MyBase* keyword. You will learn more about inheritance and calling functions of the base classes in Chapter 10.

Overloading Property Procedures with Parameters

Properties that accept parameters can be overloaded, just like functions. This principle comes into play almost exclusively with default properties (see the section "Default Properties," earlier in this chapter). As with "normal" functions, you can only differentiate by using the property signature (the order, the types, and the count of parameters), not by using the return type. Therefore, overloading properties is possible only if at least one property variation accepts parameters. Here's an example of overloading properties:

```
Property Overload() As Integer
    Get
        'Here the code for determining the property.
    End Get
    Set(ByVal Value As Integer)
        'Here the code for the assignment.
    End Set
End Property

Property Overload(ByVal Par1 As Integer) As Integer
    Get
        'Here the code for determining the property.
    End Get
    Set(ByVal Value As Integer)
        'Here the code for the assignment.
    End Set
End Property

Property Overload() As String
    Get
        'Doesn't work, because this property...
    End Get
    Set(ByVal Value As String)
        'only differs from the first by the return type.
    End Set
End Property
```

Note To overload properties, you need at least one property procedure that accepts parameters. But when using it, consider what you have already learned in this chapter: this is a Visual Basic-specific procedure (apart from default properties), and by using it, you might prevent other languages, such as C#, from using properties that accept parameters. For example, C# can't handle property procedures that accept parameters, except when using default properties.

Specifying Variable Scope with Access Modifiers

Access modifiers are keywords in Visual Basic that specify the *scope* of a variable. This means the segment of the application that can access the variable. You've already learned about the access modifiers *Private* and *Public*, which specify whether an element can be accessed only from within a specific scope (*Private*) or from anywhere (*Public*). The tables in the following sections present additional access modifiers that are available for objects, classes, and functions/properties.

> **Note** These tables are meant to show you the available access modifiers in a compact and clearly arranged form. You need the CTS label for the access modifiers when looking at the IML code of a class to determine, for example, the access mode of a property.

Access Modifiers and Classes

Table 9-1 explains the various Visual Basic access modifiers and their CTS equivalents for classes. The latter, by the way, are sometimes important to know, when you either use them in other languages than Visual Basic, or if you're looking for certain access-modifier-related *Enum* constants to use them in reflection, a technique that is discussed in detail in Chapter 21, "Attributes and Reflection."

> **Note** If you do not specify a scope, classes are declared as *Friend* by default.

TABLE 9-1 Possible Access Modifiers for Classes in Visual Basic

Access modifier	CTS label	Description
Private	*Private*	Classes are always *Public* or *Friend*, unless they're nested within another class, in which case they can be either *Public*, Friend or *Private*. For example:
		Public Class A
		Private Class B
		End Class
		End Class
		Public Class C
		'Acces denied, Class B is private!
		Dim b as A.B
		End Class
		Note: It's also possible (and common) to have nested public classes.

Access modifier	CTS label	Description
Public	*Public*	You have access to this class from the outside as well as from other assemblies.
Friend	*Assembly*	You can access this class from within the assembly but not from another assembly. If you omit the access modifier keyword, this is the default setting.
Protected	*Family*	Same as *Private*. In addition, classes derived from the class can access the marked and nested "inner" classes with *Protected*.
Protected Friend	*FamilyOrAssembly*	Access to the nested class is possible from derived classes and classes of the same assembly.

Access Modifiers and Procedures (Subs, Functions, Properties)

Table 9-2 explains the Visual Basic modifiers for methods (Subs and Functions).

> **Note** If you don't specify otherwise, *Subs*, *Functions*, and *Properties* are declared as *Public* by default. For these elements, you should always use an access modifier so that the element's scope is immediately evident when navigating through the source code.

TABLE 9-2 Possible Access Modifiers for Procedures in Visual Basic

Access modifier	CTS label	Description
Private	*Private*	The procedure can only be accessed from within the class that contains it.
Public	*Public*	The procedure can be accessed from any other class and from different assemblies. This is the default setting for methods and properties.
Friend	*Assembly*	The procedure can be accessed from within the assembly, but not from different assemblies.
Protected	*Family*	The procedure can only be accessed from within the class or a derived class.
Protected Friend	*FamilyOrAssembly*	The procedure can only be accessed from within the class, a derived class, or from within the assembly.

Access Modifiers and Variables

Variables declared at class level with *Dim* only are considered *Private*; they are accessible only from within the class. Variables declared within a code block or at procedure level apply only to that code block. Within a code block, you can use the *Dim* statement, but no other access modifier. At procedure level a variable can additionally be declared as *Static*. You'll see more about *Static* access modifiers in the section "Static Elements," later in the chapter. Table 9-3 sums up the access modifiers for variables.

TABLE 9-3 Possible Access Modifiers for Variables in Visual Basic

Access modifier	CTS label	Description
Private	*Private*	The variable can only be accessed from within the class that contains it. Variables within procedures or smaller scopes cannot be defined explicitly as *Private*, but are so by default.
Public	*Public*	The class variable can be accessed from outside the class. However, you should declare variables at most as *Protected* and only use properties to make them public. You can read more about this in section "Public Variables or Properties—a Question of Faith?," earlier in this chapter.
Friend	*Assembly*	The class variable can be accessed from within the assembly, but not from another assembly. (Same as for *Public*.)
Protected	*Family*	The variable can only be accessed from within the same or a derived class. In classes which might later get inherited several times, variables should be defined as *Protected*, so derived classes will be able to access them also.
Protected Friend	*FamilyOrAssembly*	The class variable can only be accessed from within the class, a derived class, or from within the assembly. You should avoid this combination.
Static	—	A special case in Visual Basic. For more information, read the section "Static Elements," later in this chapter.

Different Access Modifiers for Property Accessors

Beginning with Visual Studio 2005, the *Get* and *Set* accessors can have different access modifiers. For example, you can specify that a certain property can be read from anywhere (*Public*), but that properties can be written only from within the same class (*Private*). In code, such a property would look like this:

```
Module Module1

    Sub Main()
        Dim locPropertyTest As New PropertyTest("Text for property")

        'Reading from a property is possible without problems
        Console.WriteLine("Property contains: " & locPropertyTest.AProperty)

        'ERROR: The Set access modifier prohibits writing,
        'because it is 'private'.
        locPropertyTest.Aproperty = "Newer Text"
    End Sub

End Module

Public Class PropertyTest

    Private myAProperty As String

    Sub New(ByVal textForProperty As String)
        'It's allowed-the class may set
        'the property!
        AProperty = textForProperty
    End Sub

    Public Property AProperty() As String
        Get
            Return myAProperty
        End Get
        Private Set(ByVal value As String)
            myAProperty = value
        End Set
    End Property

End Class
```

This example consists of two units: a module and a class. The *PropertyTest* class has a param-eterized constructor as well as a property with accessors that have different access modifiers.

Within the constructor (*Sub New*), read access to the property is possible without a problem, because within the class itself, you can access elements whose access has been restricted with *Private*. Within the module, however, write access no longer works, because at the time of access, the program is outside the class, and because of the *Private* modifier, the code can't access the *Set* accessor of the property.

But why do you need properties that use different access modifiers for their *Set* and *Get* accessors? Consider, for example, a situation in which you'd like to make assemblies (class libraries) available to other developers. You want to be able to manipulate certain class prop-erties from any assembly position, but you want to prevent the developer who is using your assembly from doing the same. In this case, you define the *Get* accessor as *Public*—because

reading the property poses no risk, after all, so you can any code read the value, but you define the *Set* accessor as *Friend*. This way, you can update the class property from any code in your class library, but developers who embed the assembly (access it from outside your assembly), can no longer change the property value directly.

Such properties are particularly important when they are supposed to be quasi-constants. Your assembly defines the property whenever and however it wants, based on certain conditions. The assemblies you reference must live with this setting, however. For example, classes that reflect Windows registry settings can make use of this. It's also conceivable to expose a connection string to a SQL Server this way. By doing that, you'd be able to manipulate the connection string from your assembly, but an outside assembly could only read the connection string, getting the property value you set within your assembly.

Static Elements

So far you have learned about class members such as properties, methods, and fields that exclusively apply to class instances, because those elements rely on the ability to access the instance fields of a class to operate correctly. If you were to try to access these instance fields without first creating an instance of the class, the .NET Framework would have thrown the infamous *NullReferenceException*.

However, you also have the option to create components that don't access class members. This means that they can therefore be called without instantiation. The following sections show how this works.

> ## Don't Let the Keywords *Static* and *Shared* in Visual Basic Confuse You
>
> *Static* (contrary to *shared*) ensures that a variable used only within a procedure (*Sub* or *Function*) doesn't lose its content after leaving the subroutine. But you can access this variable only within the subroutine in which it is defined. In principle, a variable that has been defined with *Static* is a variable that has been defined as a *Shared* member for the class, and has received an internal attribute that regulates the access of the variable in the scope in which it was declared.
>
> By the way, *Static* variables exist only for compatibility with the old Visual Basic 6.0 (and earlier versions). And just to confuse you a bit more, in C#, *static* is what *Shared* is in .NET versions of Visual Basic—all clear?

Static Methods

Static methods are methods (*Sub*, *Function*) marked with the keyword *Shared* (not *Static*, as pointed out in the preceding sidebar) and which are therefore defined directly through the class, not through the class instance. This means that unlike instance methods, you can call a static method directly with the class name; you don't need an instance to access the method.

A good example of a static method is the *Parse* method of all the numeric data types. To convert a string into an *Integer* value, you use the following function:

```
Dim intVar as Integer = Integer.Parse("1234")
```

As you can see here, you don't use an instance method for the function call, because no field variables of the instance are required for the conversion. It's different the other way around: to convert an *Integer* value into a string, you use the *ToString* instance method, which, of course, uses the internal field variable of the *Integer* data type, as shown here:

```
Dim intVar as Integer = 5
Debug.Print(intVar.ToString())
```

> **Note** Basically, the *EllipseString* method of the class example should be defined as static and therefore, *Shared*, because it also encapsulates an algorithm that doesn't directly access a field variable of the class. Consequently, this method should then be defined as public, making the correct signature look as follows:

```
Public Shared Function EllipsisString(ByVal text As String,
   ByVal MaxLength As Integer) As String
.
.
.
End Function
```

The revised method would be called as shown below:

```
Dim s as String = Contact.EllipsisString("This is the truncated string", 20)
```

If you have an object variable for an instantiated *Contact* instance, you could theoretically use that object variable to access the static method. You shouldn't do that, however, because it causes confusion. Using object variables always implies that something is supposed to happen with the class instance (for instance, the data content of the class). But nothing happens in this case, because, as mentioned before, static methods don't (and can't) use field variables. The Visual Basic background compiler agrees, because when you attempt to call a static method with an object variable, you get the warning shown in Figure 9-11.

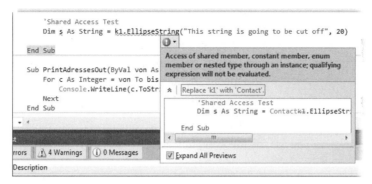

FIGURE 9-11 The background compiler of Visual Basic quits with a warning when you attempt to call a static method with an object variable. The error correction options help you to fix the problem.

Figure 9-11 also shows how Smart Tags appear in the Visual Studio editor after an object or object name has been edited—you might be familiar with Smart Tags from Microsoft Word. If you have read Chapter 4, "Introduction to Windows Forms—Designers and Code Editor by Example," you already know about them. The following sidebar provides a brief summary of the use of Smart Tags.

Smart Tags in the Visual Basic Editor

You can recognize a Smart Tag by a light-colored thin underline in a statement in the Visual Basic editor. It tells you that something needs to be improved or noted.

When you move the mouse pointer over the underline it changes into a small symbol in the form of an exclamation mark, which offers you several options (which ones depends on the context). In many cases, the Smart Tag brings up a dialog box that suggests a correction for the recognized *"mistake"*. Figure 9-12 shows it in context.

Using Smarttags

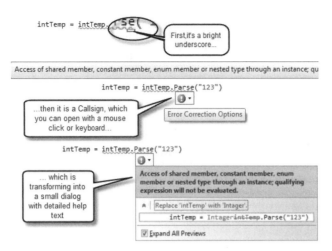

FIGURE 9-12 This is how you use the Smart Tags in the Visual Basic 2010 Code Editor.

Static Properties

Visual Basic also supports static properties. Just like static functions, you call static properties directly through the class, not through a class instance. This means that properties you mark as static should provide features that apply to all the instances of this class, not to a specific instance.

The best example of a static property is the *DateTime.Now* property, which returns the current time and, of course, is completely independent of the properties of individual *DateTime* instances. You declare static properties with the *Shared* keyword, just as with static functions.

Note As with regular properties, you can create autoimplemented static properties. In this case, the appropriate *Backing Fields* (the field variables) are also created statically. They have the same name as the property, prefixed by an underscore character. IntelliSense does not list these variables, but that doesn't mean you can't use them.

Distributing Class Code over Multiple Code Files by Using *Partial*

To distribute the definition of a class or structure over several files, you can use the *Partial* keyword. This means that you can put any number of partial definitions into as many different source files as you like; however, all definitions must be located in the same assembly and in the same namespace.

> **Note** Visual Basic uses partial class definitions to separate autogenerated code in its own source files from code files you create. For example, the Windows Form Designer defines classes for controls, such as *Form. You should not change the code in these generated code files.*

Normally, you don't distribute the code for a single class or structure over two or more code files, so you don't typically need the *Partial* keyword. However, it makes sense to use *Partial* when the code for a class grows so much that transparency would suffer. A good approach is to create an additional directory within the solution for the class files separated with *Partial*, and to place all the partial code files for the class there.

When creating a partial class or structure, all the same rules for creating classes and structures apply, such as those for the use of access modifiers and inheritance. By the way, only the additional code files require the keyword *Partial* to extend the class code—you *can* include that keyword with the initial class code, but that's not necessary.

Partial Class Code for Methods and Properties

What applies to the class itself also applies to method and property definitions, only in a slightly modified way. In particular, partial class code serves to maintain automatically generated code in connection with code that modifies it.

For example, suppose that you have generated code from an entity model of the Entity Framework for access to a database via an object model. For some reason you need to expand it. If you had to change the entity model code directly, and subsequently Visual Studio were to regenerate the code, your changes would be lost.

```
'Excerpt from a file generated by the code generator for an object model of an entity data
model:

    '''<summary>
    '''Initializes a new AWEntities object.
    '''</summary>
    Public Sub New(ByVal connection As Global.System.Data.EntityClient.EntityConnection)
        MyBase.New(connection, "AWEntities")
```

```
      'Here a method of the generated class is called ...
      Me.OnContextCreated
End Sub

    '...which only defines your method body with Partial here.
    'The actual code can be located in a separate code file,
    'and cannot be overwritten any longer when the code is recreated.
    Partial Private Sub OnContextCreated()
    End Sub
```

This is why you can define "empty" method bodies with *Partial* at the method level. The autogenerated code can create the method definitions, but your actual custom code that implements these methods resides in a different code file. The result: you can now recreate the generated code over and over again, without overwriting your manually edited code, which remains in a separate code file.

Chapter 10
Class Inheritance and Polymorphism

Reusing Classes Through Inheritance

Inheritance and reuse by extending classes is a central programming technique, one that the Microsoft .NET Framework itself uses frequently. You could go so far as to say that .NET wouldn't make sense without class inheritance.

To be competitive as a developer and to be able to create applications that are reliable, maintainable, and have a long lifespan, it is necessary to truly understand class inheritance and be able to build your own object models.

Grasping the concept of class inheritance is often difficult, especially if you're a beginner. You literally wait for the moment when the light bulb goes on in your head, and when that happens, suddenly new doors open. Any object-oriented programming (OOP) developer who has truly mastered these techniques will remember the moment when he suddenly "got it"—all the while grinning like the Cheshire cat.

But we actually already know the concept of object inheritance from our daily lives. When you see a dog, you recognize that creature as a dog, even though you might have never seen this particular dog, or the specific breed. Instead, you have an idea of a "base dog" in your head, and you can recognize its derivatives (such as Australian shepherds; Irish wolfhounds [unfortunately the favorite of the Author's girlfriend]; dachshunds [the typical retired German's favorite], golden retrievers [the Author's favorite]; and so on), because you can compare them to that base dog concept. All sorts of things work like this in real life. For example, think of

a container. You can certainly imagine what a container looks like. But what you are imagining is *derivative* (therefore an inheritance) of a *certain* container *type*; for example, a bucket or a bottle. But it's just not possible to imagine a container *per se*. Obviously, a bottle is a container, but a bucket and a bathtub are containers, too. Yet it's clear that a bottle is not a bathtub. All of these objects simply have a number of common properties that make them containers.

As human beings, we function in an object-oriented manner, so why not use inheritance in our programs? If objects have similar behaviors, but can be traced back to an original scheme—like a container—then why should you bother to reinvent the wheel over and over again in code? Suppose you were able to program a bottle (whatever that might look like), and then later needed to program a *beverage can*. I'd bet that you would use the same code to define the property *ContainerVolume* for both objects, because that would make sense. It would be easier though, if you could first program a completely abstract (non-imaginable and thus non-applicable) class called *Container* and then give this *Container* class all the basic properties; for example, the property *Volume*. Then you let *Bottle* and *beverage can* inherit from the *Container* class, so that both would also inherit the *Volume* property.

 Note Your mind is able to categorize objects such as buckets, barrels, beverage cans, bottles, cups, bathtubs, tanks, and all other manner of containers. This is something that Immanuel Kant described in the context of *transcendental schemata*.

For now, that will suffice for an introduction to the principles of inheritance. It would actually be nice to say that Microsoft Visual Basic can look back to a long history of inheritance—after all, classes have been available in Visual Basic since version 4.0. But even in version 6.0 or in the still in use Visual Basic for Applications (VBA), true inheritance was or is pretty much non-existent. Visual Basic's command of polymorphism—the possibility of addressing different classes via the same method names—was also insufficient at best. Until Visual Basic 6.0/VBA), classes could pass on inheritance only by using a technique called *delegation*, in which one class is included in another as a field variable, and its properties exposed to the outside through new functions and property procedures. In Visual Basic 6.0, true polymorphism was restricted to interfaces (you'll see more about this topic in the section titled "Interfaces," later in this chapter).

Before using inheritance in an example, let's take a moment to explain the syntax with a few simple code samples. Right now we don't want to use the time-honored example, because it can't take advantage of inheritance without some substantial changes, which might be a bit confusing in the beginning and might make it harder to understand the concept.

Companion Content Open the corresponding solution (.sln), which you can find in the \VB 2010 Developer Handbook\Chapter 10\Heredity01 folder.

> **Note** I would recommend that you follow this exercise step by step to build this project on your own and thus gain a better understanding of the process and concepts that it involves.

1. Create a new project. On the File menu, click New | Project.

2. Click Visual Basic Projects in the Project Types list, select Console Application below Templates, and then enter **Inheritance** for the project name.

3. Specify a directory of your choice in the appropriate field.

4. Click OK to create the new project.

5. Double-click Module1.vb in Solution Explorer to display the code for the project.

   Don't let the keyword *Module* confuse you. You will learn more about modules (which play a special role in Visual Basic from a .NET Framework point of view) later in this chapter.

6. Click the Rename command in the context menu and change the name from Module1.vb to **mdlMain.vb**. Remember to specify the file name extension as **.vb**.

7. In Project Explorer, double-click mdlMain.vb to open its code window.

Now enter the following line in the Code Editor underneath the module definition (behind *End Module*), and then press Enter:

```
Class FirstClass
```

Visual Basic automatically inserts the following line to complete the class code block.

```
End Class
```

This first class should contain a property and a method definition with which you can set and query the contents of the class. This sample class doesn't do anything special. It just saves an *Integer* value in its property. Enter the following code into your class:

```
Class FirstClass

    Private myAValue As Integer

    'Property for changing the value.
    Property AValue() As Integer

        Get
            Return myAValue
        End Get

        Set(ByVal Value As Integer)
            myAValue = Value
        End Set

    End Property
```

```
        'Function for returning the content as a string.
        Function AsString() As String

            Return CStr(myAValue)

        End Function

End Class
```

> **Note** You already covered the concept of autoimplemented properties in Chapter 9, "First Class Programming." Theoretically, the following examples could use autoimplemented properties without showing other definitions. Nevertheless, in the following chapters, you'll see code that does without autoimplemented properties every once in a while. The purpose of omitting them is to help you get a feel for what's actually happening. We won't let the compiler write the additional lines of code for *Get/Set* and perform the management of the field variables, but to recap, if you did use autoimplemented properties, the example would work like this: the property variable would be called *_AValue*, it would be defined by the compiler, and the example would be a few lines shorter, as shown in the following:
>
> ```
> Class FirstClass
>
>     'Property for changing the value.
>     Property AValue() As Integer
>
>     'Function for returning the content as a string.
>     Function AsString() As String
>
>         Return CStr(_AValue)
>
>     End Function
>
> End Class
> ```

You now create a small framework program in the module *mdlMain,* which uses the following code:

```
Module mdlMain

    Sub Main()
        Dim class1 As New FirstClass
        class1.AValue = 5
        Console.WriteLine(class1.AsString())

        Console.WriteLine()
        Console.WriteLine("Press key to exit")
        Console.ReadKey()
    End Sub

End Module
```

You can now start the program; the result will probably be exactly what you expected. For the next steps, just imagine that the source code for the *FirstClass* class is not available to you. So, create a new class called **SecondClass**, and underneath its class definition, insert the code *Inherits FirstClass*, as follows:

```
Class SecondClass
    Inherits FirstClass

End Class
```

You have now created a new class called *SecondClass*. This class doesn't appear to have any properties or methods—but it has them anyway. Place the cursor in the first procedure of the code file, after the following line:

```
Console.WriteLine(class1.AsString())
```

Insert the following statement:

```
Dim class2 As New SecondClass
```

Now, to see how IntelliSense displays the members of the new class (see Figure 10-1), insert the *class2* instance name, followed by a period.

```
Module mdlMain

    Sub Main()

        Dim class1 As New FirstClass
        class1.aValue = 5
        Console.WriteLine(class1.AsString())

        Dim class2 As New SecondClass
        class2.
                 AsString     Public Overridable Function AsString() As String
                 aValue
        Console  Common   All   ()
        Console.WriteLine("Press any key to exit!")
        Console.ReadKey()
    End Sub
```

FIGURE 10-1 Even though so far there is no definition for any member in the class *SecondClass*, IntelliSense still shows you a property and a method.

What happened? By adding the statement,

```
Inherit FirstClass
```

you specified that *SecondClass* inherits all members of *FirstClass*. Anything *FirstClass* can do, *SecondClass* can also do.

> **Important** Reusability is what OOP is all about; with inheritance you are writing code that is reusable. If you want to change an existing class to adjust it for a specific application or requirement, you need not touch the original class (you might not even have access to its code). You just create a new class that inherits from the original class, and then you change the inherited class, customizing and extending it according to your requirements.
>
> Here's one of the advantages of this methodology: if you discover that all classes that are based on some base class contain the same error, then removing the error in the base class also removes the error from all the derived classes. In contrast, in copy/paste inheritance, often used in Visual Basic 6.0 and VBA, the code is repeated ("when we need code at a different location in our code, we just copy it"). With that methodology, you need to know exactly how often you have reused the code and find all the places where that same error is located. Therefore, applications that are procedurally constructed are often faulty and are sometimes extremely difficult to maintain.

Suppose that for a specific problem, you need a class that can do exactly what *FirstClass* can do, only you now require an additional property that determines the current instance value increased by 10. In this case, *SecondClass* inherits from the class *FirstClass*, as you already saw in the example, so you can just add the new property procedure to *SecondClass* as follows:

```
Class SecondClass
    Inherits FirstClass

    ReadOnly Property IncreasedBy10 as Integer

        Get
            Return AValue + 10
        End Get
    End Property
End Class
```

And that's it. The functionality of *FirstClass* is now also in *SecondClass*, which even has one additional property. As a test, insert the code **Console.WriteLine(class2.** beneath the following line:

```
Dim class2 As New SecondClass
```

As soon as you type the last period, IntelliSense again displays the members of the class, and guess what: you now see all the old members as well as the new property in the list, as displayed in Figure 10-2.

```
Module mdlMain

    Sub Main()

        Dim class1 As New FirstClass
        class1.aValue = 5
        Console.WriteLine(class1.AsString())

        Dim class2 As New SecondClass
        class2.
                 ⊛ AsString
                 ≡ AValue      Public Property AValue As Integer
                 ≡ IncreasedBy10
        Console  Common  All
        Console                ress any key to exit!")
        Console.ReadKey()
    End Sub
```

FIGURE 10-2 The new property can now be found in *SecondClass* together with the old members.

Complete the line:

```
Console.WriteLine(class2.IncreasedBy10)
```

Launch the program, and notice what happens:

```
5
10

Press key to exit
```

Did you expect 15 to be returned as the second result? Of course not, because the instance *class1* created from *FirstClass* is completely independent of the instance *class2*, which was based on the class *SecondClass*. You have only borrowed the code as a template from *FirstClass*. The object instances you create from either class store their own—and thus different—data.

> **Note** It's very important to understand how classes are managed internally. The code for a class exists only once—even if you create many instances of a class. Therefore, it's absurd to believe that a class that has 10 times as much program code as class "X" would require 10 times as much memory space as class X if both classes were instantiated 10 times. The program code for a class always uses the same amount of memory, no matter how many instances you create from it. Of course, the program code isn't loaded in memory multiple times either when you derive one class from another. Only the additional program code for adding new members or overriding existing members uses up additional memory. The point to remember is that the memory requirements for a class instance are determined by the class's field variables.

To arrive at the expected result, you need to change the program as follows:

```
Module mdlMain

    Sub Main()
        Dim class1 As New FirstClass
        class1.AValue = 5
        Console.WriteLine(class1.AsString())

        Dim class2 As New SecondClass
        class2.AValue = 5
        Console.WriteLine(class2.IncreasedBy10)
        Console.WriteLine()
        Console.WriteLine("Press key to exit")
        Console.ReadKey()
    End Sub
End Module
```

Now you can take a look at the class by using the IL Disassembler and see whether the Visual Basic compiler has taken care of some of the work.

1. Start the IL Disassembler from the Windows Start menu (in the program group Microsoft Visual Studio 2010/Microsoft Windows SDK Tools) and open the file Inheritance.exe, which is located in the \bin\Debug\ directory of the folder where you created the *Inheritance* project.

2. Click the plus sign to open the branch *Inheritance*, and then the sub-branches *Inheritance.FirstClass* and *Inheritance.SecondClass*.

   You should then see a window resembling Figure 10-3.

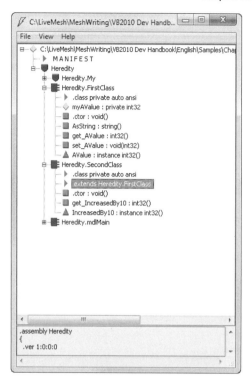

FIGURE 10-3 Both test classes in the IL Disassembler.

As in the earlier examples, Visual Basic has done the work for you and inserted the corresponding constructor procedures (*.ctor*) into the base class *FirstClass* as well as the derived class *SecondClass*.

Note   Figure 10-3 demonstrates that internally, properties are converted into functions or methods. The Visual Basic Compiler turns the *AValue* property of the base class, which has both *Get* and *Set* accessors, into the functions *get_AValue* and *set_AValue* respectively. The property itself is defined below and its IML code just specifies which of the functions in the class resolve the property. (Double-clicking the property name displays the code.)

```
.property instance int32 AValue()
{
  .set instance void Inheritance.FirstClass::set_AValue(int32)
  .get instance int32 Inheritance.FirstClass::get_AValue()
} // end of property FirstClass::AValue
```

As you might have guessed, *SecondClass* contains only the code for the additional members. Figure 10-3 illustrates how *extends Heredity.FirstClass* specifies that the class inherits from the base class, and can therefore use its members. Because the single property has only one *Get* accessor, there is only one property function in the form of *get_IncreasedBy10.*

> **Tip** Field variables you want to manipulate later directly in inherited classes should be declared as *Protected*, and only in exceptional situations. For base classes, you should follow the principle of encapsulating and protecting as much as possible. Field variables should be defined as *private*, if possible, but NEVER as *public*.

Now that you know that derived classes automatically call the default base class constructor, what happens if the base class doesn't have a default constructor? You already encountered such a case in the *Contact* example, in Chapter 8, "Class Begins." If a class has a constructor with parameters, the compiler will not generate any other default constructor.

So what happens when you add a constructor to the class *FirstClass* that receives a parameter (such as the initialization value for *myAValue*)? Try it out by adding the following line to the code of the *FirstClass* class:

```
Sub New(ByVal InitialValue As Integer)
```

As soon as you insert the new line, various error markings appear in the source code, and their descriptions appear in the error list, as shown in Figure 10-4.

	Description	File	Line	Column	Project
⊗ 1	Argument not specified for parameter 'InitialValue' of 'Public Sub New (InitialValue As Integer)'.	mdlMain.vb	5	13	Heredity03
⊗ 2	Class 'heredity.SecondClass' must declare a 'Sub New' because its base class 'heredity.FirstClass' does not have an accessible 'Sub New' that can be called with no arguments.	mdlMain.vb	45	7	Heredity03

FIGURE 10-4 After inserting a parameterized constructor, you immediately see two errors in the error list.

The reason the errors occur is that *class1* can no longer be instantiated in the module within *Sub Main*, because the code doesn't pass a parameter to the constructor:

```
Dim class1 As New FirstClass
```

Because the class's only constructor is now the parameterized constructor we inserted into the class definition, no default constructor exists. As soon as you add a constructor to a class yourself (whether it's parameterized or not), Visual Basic no longer generates a default constructor for you for that class.

To recap, if you don't implement a constructor (*Sub New...*) explicitly, the compiler inserts one for you automatically. However, as soon as you create any explicit constructor, you'll need to implement all constructors explicitly (even the default constructor—the one without parameters).

So now there's only one constructor, and it accepts a parameter. You can eliminate the first error by specifying the initialization value for the class during the *New FirstClass* method call, as follows:

```
Dim class1 As New FirstClass(5)
Console.WriteLine(class1.AsString())
      .
      .
      .
```

Not having a default constructor also means that the derived class doesn't know how to instantiate the base class (a necessary action). In this case, you need to ensure that the base class is called by calling its constructor with *MyBase.New*.

The following code shows the correct version (changes are highlighted in bold, and some sections are abbreviated with an ellipsis):

```
Module mdlMain

    Sub Main()
        Dim class1 As New FirstClass(5)
        Console.WriteLine(class1.AsString())

        Dim class2 As New SecondClass(5)
        Console.WriteLine(class2.IncreasedBy10)

        Console.WriteLine()
        Console.WriteLine("Press key to exit")
        Console.ReadLine()
    End Sub

End Module

Class FirstClass

    Protected myAValue As Integer
```

```
      Sub New(ByVal NewValue As Integer)
          myAValue = NewValue
      End Sub

      'Property for changing the value.
      Property AValue() As Integer
      ...
      End Property
      'Function for returning the content as a string.
    Function AsString() As String

          Return CStr(myAValue)

      End Function
End Class

Class SecondClass
    Inherits FirstClass

      Sub New(ByVal NewValue As Integer)
          MyBase.New(NewValue)
      End Sub

      ReadOnly Property IncreasedBy10 As Integer
      ...
      End Property

End Class
```

Initializing Field Variables for Classes Without Default Constructors

Let's take a look at what happens when you initialize field variables during object instantiation, as shown in the following example:

```
Class FirstClass

    Private myAValue As Integer = 9

    Sub New()
        'The following code line makes no sense but to fill the constructor with something.
        Console.WriteLine("WriteLine Test: Default Constructor")

    End Sub

    Sub New(somethingToWrite As String)
        'The following code line makes no sense but to fill the constructor with something.
        Console.WriteLine("WriteLine Test:" & somethingToWrite)

    End Sub.
    .
    .
```

The example has a default constructor and one constructor with parameters. As no code can be run "outside" a class, where does the assignment of `Private myAValue As Integer = 9` take place? To find the answer, you must go back to the IML code of the class again. The compiler does most of the work because it must build the code to initialize the field variables into each constructor (see Figure 10-5). That's the only way to ensure that all required variable initializations are performed.

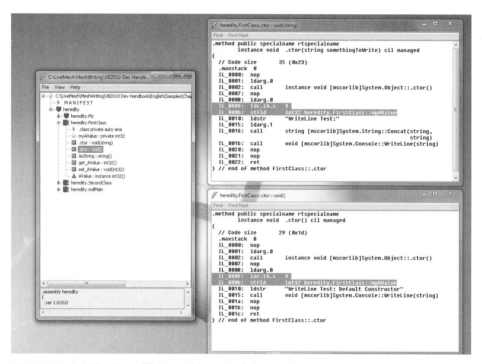

FIGURE 10-5 Initializations of field variables are built into each constructor procedure, if required.

 Tip This is the correct procedure or place for initializing field variables of a class with default values: you'll never forget the definitions in existing constructors because the compiler makes sure that the assignments of the default values to the field variables take place in *each* existing constructor.

Overriding Methods and Properties

By now, you probably agree that overriding classes is quite a brilliant concept. It helps you to structure your programs better, makes them easier to read, and helps you to build bigger and more complex projects, cleanly. But classes wouldn't be so evolutionary if it weren't for the ability to access certain functions of a base class from within the code of the derived class. Classes that bind to others can become extremely flexible.

Replacing methods or properties with others in a derived base class requires the base class to allow certain members to be overridden; these functions, methods, or properties must be explicitly marked so that they can be overridden later. In Visual Basic, the keyword *Overridable* is used to mark a base class procedure as enabled for possible override. All functions and properties, which are marked at least as *Protected* in the base class can also have the *Overridable* modifier. Similarly, the members of the derived class that override those in the base class must be marked with the keyword *Overrides*.

> **Note** It's important that you don't lump overriding and overloading together randomly. Visual Basic permits a derived class to overload a procedure of a base class. When you overload a procedure, you don't replace the base function, you just add another overload. But that means the only way to truly override (that is to say, replace) procedures in a base class is to create a procedure in the derived class that *has the same signature* as the overridden procedure in the base class.

> **Important** When overloading functions within a new class that you are implementing, you can get away without using the *Overloads* keyword and just use duplicate method names (with different signatures!). However, when you're overloading methods of a base class in a derived class, you absolutely *must* use *Overloads*.

Here's a little example of overriding methods. Assume that you don't like the way the string in the derived class *SecondClass* returns the variable value as a string (by using the function *AsString*). You want the *AsString* function to return the value in a different format: "The value is: xxx". Change the classes as follows:

> **Companion Content** Open the corresponding solution (.sln), which you can find in the \VB 2010 Developer Handbook\Chapter 10\Heredity02 folder.

```
Module mdlMain

    Sub Main()
        Dim class1 As New FirstClass(5)
        Console.WriteLine("Class1 result with AsString: " & class1.AsString())

        Dim klasse2 As New SecondClass(5)
        Console.WriteLine("Class2 result with AsString: " & Class2.AsString())

        Console.WriteLine()
        Console.WriteLine("Press Return to exit")
        Console.ReadLine()
    End Sub

End Module
```

```
Class FirstClass

    Private myAValue As Integer

    Sub New(ByVal NewValue As Integer)
        myAValue = NewValue
    End Sub
    'Property for changing the value.
    Property AValue() As Integer
       .
       .
       .
    End Property

    'Function for returning the content as a string.
    Public Overridable Function AsString() As String

        Return CStr(myAValue)

    End Function

End Class

Class SecondClass
    Inherits FirstClass

    Sub New(ByVal NewValueAs Integer)
        MyBase.New(NewValue)
    End Sub

    ReadOnly Property IncreasedBy10() As Integer
       .
       .
       .
    End Property

    Public Overrides Function AsString() As String
        Return "The value is: " & MyBase.AsString()
    End Function

End Class
```

When you run this version of the program, you see the following output:

```
Class1 result with AsString: 5
Class2 result with AsString: The value is: 5

Press key to exit
```

Overriding Existing Methods and Properties of .NET Framework Classes

The function name in the example doesn't actually sound too nice—*AsString* seems to be a bit of a fragment, somehow stilted, is grammatically arguable, and I think it should really be renamed to *ToString* to maintain consistency with the .NET Framework, don't you think?

However, if you change the existing function *AsString* in the first class to *ToString*, something unexpected happens, as illustrated in Figure 10-6).

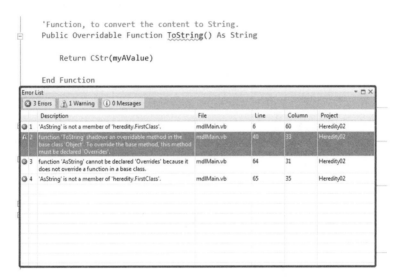

FIGURE 10-6 When you try to implement *ToString*, this error message appears.

Which method is it referring to? IntelliSense lists the existing methods of an object, as shown in Figure 10-2, but the object doesn't provide any method called *ToString*. That's because the IntelliSense settings you've used so far haven't displayed all the members. By default, IntelliSense doesn't display lesser important methods in the list. Only when you set the list to *All* are all the members shown, including *ToString*, as you can see in Figure 10-7.

> **Note** You can switch between IntelliSense tabs by using the keyboard shortcuts Alt+< and Alt+>.

```
Module mdlMain

    Sub Main()

        Dim class1 As New FirstClass(5)
        Console.WriteLine("Class1 returns by AsString: " & class1.ToString())
        class1.
                 AValue
                 Equals
                 GetHashCode        ass
        Dim cla  GetType            ss(5)
        class2   ReferenceEquals
                 ToString       Public Overrides Function ToString() As String
        Console Common  All     ss2 returns by AsString: " & class2.AsString())
```

FIGURE 10-7 Now you see all members of the instance *FirstClass*.

IntelliSense is very helpful here because you can immediately see the modifiers of the *ToString* function in the ToolTip description. They tell you that the function was declared with *Overridable*—so it's possible to override the *ToString* method in a derived class yourself, by using *Overrides* in *FirstClass*.

> **Companion Content** The modified version of the example with the overridden *ToString* function is located in the \VB 2010 Developer Handbook\Chapter 10\Heredity03 folder.

Polymorphism

You've now learned a lot about inheritance and overriding of class members. So, how can you put those techniques to use? For inheritance and function overriding to make complete sense, you use a technique called *polymorphism*.[1] If you asked me to describe polymorphism in one sentence, I would ask you to wait, and then give you the following answer: "Polymorphism in OOP describes a possibility for exchanging methods or properties in the classes of a class inheritance hierarchy, and to be able to reach a method that has the same name, but different functionality, of the modified classes in the inheritance hierarchy via the same object variable of the type base class dependent on the actual instantiated derived class."

Phew!

I realize that's terribly abstract—but that's exactly what polymorphism is.

---

[1] Something like "varied in shape and form."

It took me some time to come up with a relatively plausible example of polymorphism in daily life, just to make the abstract concept a little simpler to absorb. I have to admit that after hours of pondering, I became annoyed and gave up. But then something happened to a friend and former colleague of mine that I had never experienced myself.

Jürgen was standing at the cash register of a local supermarket, paying for his purchases, when his cell phone rang. It was his girlfriend. The cashier hadn't noticed the ringing, and couldn't see the phone because Jürgen was holding it between his shoulder and his ear. Jürgen tried to keep it short so that he wouldn't slow the line down. Then, as luck would have it, his quick answers happened to fit exactly into the conversation the cashier was having with him. So he was having two conversations at the same time (one voluntarily with his girlfriend, the other involuntarily with the cashier). This exchange continued until the cashier became aware of the misunderstanding, because Jürgen answered the cashier's statement, "That comes to 21.45 Euro," with "I love you, too!"

Jürgen had two completely independent conversations with totally different content, but he used the exact same method to "take care of business." His method—his choice of words—was polymorphous, even though his words were the same in both conversations.

So let's get back to programming. What do you think will happen in our *Heredity03* example, if you changed the line of the module *mdlMain* from,

```
Dim class2 As New SecondClass(5)
```

into:

```
Dim class2 As FirstClass
class2 = New SecondClass(5)
```

Do you think Visual Basic will trigger an error because you have declared *class2* as *FirstClass*, but then assigned an instance of the second class to the object variable? Not at all! Not only is this procedure correct, but you have just encountered the most powerful tool of object-oriented programming.

Inheritance and Polymorphism—We Know How It Works, but Why Use It?

In the last sections, you've already learned a lot about inheritance techniques and poly-morphism, such as how you can get a class to behave in a polymorphic manner. It's not very hard to illustrate this technique with examples, or to understand how it works. However, what good are examples—even if you understand them and are able to reproduce them yourself in your own code—if you don't really know how to recognize

problems that require you to create your own class models. So the challenge is to get you to understand why class inheritance and polymorphism make so much sense in certain situations. These techniques have the potential to make your programs more robust and let you structure them much more easily.

Basically developers can come much closer to real life when describing objects by using OOP than procedural programmers ever could. Unfortunately, long-time Visual Basic programmers tend to think along the lines of procedural programming. For programmers with an extensive Visual Basic 6.0 or Visual Basic for Applications background, it takes longer for the light to go on—even longer than for developers who started directly with a .NET version of Visual Basic.

When programming in OOP style, you need to understand object relationships to make them "work together."

For example, take a set of graphics applications such as Microsoft Publisher, Adobe Illustrator, or CorelDraw. All of these programs work with similar objects, which differ only in the way that they are formed. Even different objects, such as a line, a circle, a rectangle, an oval, a pentagon, or a complete picture can have elements in common; for example:

- They must be placed at a certain position on the paper or in a document window, and therefore, they have dimensions that are defined by coordinates pairs (x1, y1, x2, y2).

- They must render themselves; that is, they must be able to draw themselves in a specified graphic context (such as on a printer, a screen, a plotter, and so on).

- They must have properties that describe in detail how they should draw themselves; for example, their line width and color.

The idea of creating such an application in an object-oriented manner comes naturally. You implement a base class that provides all these basic functions, and you call it *GraphicsObject*, for example. Of course, you can't implement all the methods, such as the drawing itself, in this base class—because *GraphicsObject* itself is only the largest common denominator; concrete object drawing operations do not belong there.

Even though the *GraphicsObject* can't draw anything when it is defined, it can expose common properties, such as color or dimensions, because those are properties that all graphic objects must have. Later, you can derive the more specific objects from the *GraphicsObject* class.

Only when implementing the actual objects do you worry about the rendering itself (this takes place in the derived classes). The *Circle* derived class draws a circle, the *Line* derived class draws a line, and the *Rectangle* derived class draws a rectangle.

This object-oriented approach to a coding problem is also team-friendly. Different teams can solve different problems at the same time, without them being time-dependent. After the base class implementation of *GraphicsObject* has been completed, Team A can start implementing object management. Team A doesn't care what an object variable of the type *GraphicsObject* actually draws. Team A only manages a list of this type and ensures that the objects are drawn at the positions defined by *GraphicsObject* as well as in the correct color and line weight. For testing, Team A just needs a single implemented object. Similarly, what Team A draws when going through the list is not important to Team B. Even though Team A calls the *Render* method when drawing the object of *GraphicsObject*, the list of *GraphicsObject* doesn't actually contain real *GraphicsObject* objects; it contains other derived classes, which Team B implements in a concrete fashion—one after the other. Only one object variable of the base class type is used to draw the object, which is located behind the base class object variable in the list. So when Team A calls the *Render* method, the code that actually is executed is the concrete implementation in the derived classes. At this point, polymorphism pays off. Team A makes a call to *Render* and something happens. In this example, a shape is drawn, depending on which actual object type is in the list. Therefore, Team A programs with the help of the developed object model a functionality whose real result Team A doesn't know and—and here's the bottom line—doesn't *need* to know.

Compared to procedural programming, there is another advantage that I mentioned earlier, but that I would like to dig into a little further in this context: during procedural programming, "objects" used to be "passed on" in the form of code copy/paste. When the routine for drawing of a circle with all its attributes was done, then (unfortunately) the code was usually copied, and then the procedure for drawing lines was created from it. If an error was discovered in the first *Circle* routine, this error also had to be fixed in all the "derived" (the manually copied) lines of code. Of course, this led to a lot of errors which would find their way into the final version of the application. If the team had to "fix" 20 or 30 procedures, you can imagine how easy it would be to overlook the occasional error.

This can't happen with object-oriented procedures. An error in the base class *GraphicsObject* is corrected there, but the faulty code has been implemented only once. Therefore, all the derived classes not only inherit the basic functionality of the base class, but also all of its code fixes. It's clear to see that object-oriented development can guarantee more stable programs than procedural development.

It can get dangerous, however, when developers who have been used to procedural programming for many years try OOP for the first time while creating object models. These developers often become so fascinated by the new possibilities of inheritance and polymorphism, that they start creating unbelievably complex object models. Along

the way, they lose focus on what's really essential. Essentially, they build the foundation for a 100-story skyscraper even though they're building only a single-family home on top of it. It's therefore extremely important to install some kind of supervisory body, perhaps a project manager, who can ensure that an object model doesn't become so "full of itself" that it loses its OOP features.

A Simple Example of Polymorphism

This first simple example of polymorphism takes us to Windows Forms development for a moment—to a brief application that uses a *ListBox*.

Companion Content The basic structure for the following experiments is located in the \VB 2010 Developer Handbook\Chapter 10\ToStringDemo folder. Once there, open the corresponding solution (.sln file).

This project consists of two "elements," the form with a single button control, and a class that saves contact data as last and first name.

```
'The form code
Public Class frmMain

    Private Sub btnAddContact_Click(ByVal sender As System.Object, ByVal e As System.
➥EventArgs) _
             Handles btnAddContact.Click

        'Instantiate new contact object and
        'fill it with Textbox content
        Dim locContact As New Contact(txtFirstName.Text, txtLastName.Text)

        'Add to Listbox
        lstContacts.Items.Add(locContact)
    End Sub
End Class


'The Contact class
Public Class Contact

    Private myFirstName As String
    Private myLastName As String

    Sub New(ByVal FirstName As String, ByVal LastName As String)
        myFirstName = FirstName
        myLastName = LastName
    End Sub
```

```
     Public Property FirstName() As String
         Get
             Return myFirstName
         End Get
         Set(ByVal value As String)
             myFirstName = value
         End Set
     End Property

     Public Property LastName() As String
         Get
             Return myLastName
         End Get
         Set(ByVal value As String)
             myLastName = value
         End Set
     End Property
End Class
```

First, look at the code line highlighted in bold. As soon as the user enters the first and last names into the *TextBox* controls and clicks the button, the program creates a new instance of the *Contact* class and, with the help of the *Add* method of the *Items* collection, adds this contact to the *ListBox* control. This approach is possible because, unlike Visual Basic 6.0 or VBA, the *Add* method of the *ListBox* doesn't accept just *String* values as items; it accepts objects of any type and displays the string returned by their *ToString* method.

The problem: when the *ListBox* can receive objects of the type *Object* in its *Items* collection, you can pass all types to it (even our *Contact* object). As you already know, this is possible because an object variable can point to its "own type" as well as to each derived type (see the section "Polymorphism" and the sections that follow it, later in this chapter). And because all classes are implicitly derived from *Object*, each custom class you create is also based on *Object*. So far, so good.

But who or what makes sure that the text that is displayed in the *ListBox* makes sense? The current implementation of the program doesn't display the desired results in the *ListBox* yet, as you can discover when you run the program, which looks like Figure 10-8.

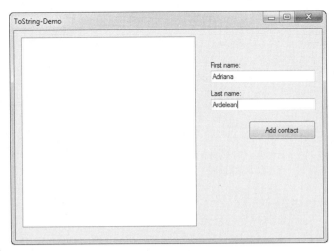

FIGURE 10-8 Adding an object to the *ListBox* initially leads only to the display of the fully-qualified object name.

The result is probably not quite what you expected, but it really can't be anything else. You will see why this is the case once you learn how the *ListBox* determines the text of an object.

You might have already guessed that when the *ListBox* fills its display area with text, it calls the *ToString* function of each item[2] added to its *Items* collection. It can do this without having to worry that an object it contains might not have a *ToString* method, because *ToString* is a part of *Object*. And *Object* itself is the base class for all base classes, so every derived object has a *ToString* method. The default implementation of the *ToString* method in *Object* only renders the type name of the object. That *Object.ToString* method looks like this:

```
Public Overridable Function ToString() As String
      Return Me.GetType.ToString
End Function
```

GetType returns an object type that is then translated by *ToString* into a readable string. This way *ToString* displays the type name for each object—thanks to polymorphism.

For example, for the *ToString* method of the example class to display a sensible text in a *ListBox*, you must implement the *ToString* function in the corresponding class with an override. You can extend the *Contact* class with the following code:

```
    Public Overrides Function ToString() As String
        Return LastName & ", " & FirstName
    End Function
```

---

2 To be exact, it calls *GetItemText* of its base class *ListControl* and *that's* what determines the text with *ToString*, in case the object isn't a control that can be bound to a different property. In this case *GetItemText* would determine the object text via *ToString*, which is bound to the control (or returns an empty string if there's no binding). Therefore, if you pass the instance of some control (such as a button or the form itself) to the *Items* collection, you will see an empty string in the list.

Now the program displays proper names on the list, as shown in Figure 10-9.

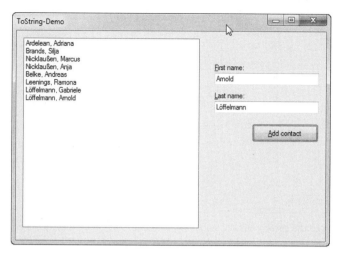

FIGURE 10-9 By overriding *ToString()* in a class whose object instance is added to the list, you can control the displayed text.

Using Polymorphism in Real World Applications

To create a new CorelDraw application as a prime example for polymorphism would probably be a bit too ambitious, but I'll use a typical real-world example to demonstrate polymorphism. Suppose that you are working in the IT department of a large mail-order company. It's your job to create software that processes product lists, formats them, and calculates a total. The products to be processed with your application can be data types with completely different properties: a movie Video and DVD product data type that stores the film's duration information and the leading actors' names along with the title; a Book data type that stores the author and title, and so on. All data types should also store price and state tax information.

Even though it would be quite possible to create this application without polymorphism, polymorphism enables us to write much more elegant and maintainable code. Without polymorphism you'd have to create a kind of "superset" that knows all the desired properties and then program each special case—which is simply asking for spaghetti code.

In this example, assume that the lists are text files and that they follow a specific format. Your application saves the data internally using that same format. The product list with the data to be processed should have a format like that presented in the following code example. Note that prices have been multiplied by 100 to make them integer values:

```
;Inventory list to be evaluated by the program Inventory
;Format:
;Type (1=book, 2=CD or video), order number, title, addition, pre-tax in Cent, addition2
1;0001;Night Watch;Terry Pratchett;1990;
```

```
1;0002;The Blessing Stone;Barbara Wood;2490;
1;0003;Dude, Where's My Country;Michael Moore;1290;
1;0004;The Guardian;Nicholas Sparks;1900;
2;0005;X-Men 2 - Special Edition;128;2299;Patrick Stewart
2;0006;Sex and the City: Season 5;220;2999;Sarah Jessica Parker
2;0007;Indiana Jones (Box Set 4 DVDs);359;4499;Harrison Ford
2;0008;The Pelican Brief;135;1499;Julia Roberts
```

The list contains different types of products that you need to consider. Your program must process the individual products in the list, and it should then return a list in the following format (the price line shows the gross price, tax, and the net price):

```
Choose (1) for brief or (2) for detailed display.
10001   Night Watch
18.60 $ 1.30 $  19.90 $

0002    The Blessing Stone
23.27 $ 1.63 $  24.90 $

0003    Dude, Where's My Country
12.06 $ 0.84 $  12.90 $

0004    The Guardian
17.76 $ 1.24 $  19.00 $

0005    X-Men 2 - Special Edition
19.32 $ 3.67 $  22.99 $

0006    Sex and the City: Season 5
25.20 $ 4.79 $  29.99 $

0007    Indiana Jones (Box Set 4 DVDs)
37.81 $ 7.18 $  44.99 $

0008    The Pelican Brief
12.60 $ 2.39 $  14.99 $


----------------------------
Gross amount: 189.66 $
----------------------------
----------------------------
```

Press Enter to finish. The product types differ in two ways: books have authors along with title and price information, but for films you need to add the duration, as well. The program must also offer the ability to create both short and detailed lists. The detailed list must show the additional properties of the respective product type, and must look like this:

```
Choose (1) for brief or (2) for detailed display.
10001   Night Watch
18.60 $ 1.30 $  19.90 $

0002    The Blessing Stone
23.27 $ 1.63 $  24.90 $
```

```
0003    Dude, Where's My Country
12.06 $ 0.84 $  12.90 $

0004    The Guardian
17.76 $ 1.24 $  19.00 $

0005    X-Men 2 - Special Edition
19.32 $ 3.67 $  22.99 $

0006    Sex and the City: Season 5
25.20 $ 4.79 $  29.99 $

0007    Indiana Jones (Box Set 4 DVDs)
37.81 $ 7.18 $  44.99 $

0008    The Pelican Brief
12.60 $ 2.39 $  14.99 $


------------------------------
Gross amount: 189.66 $
------------------------------
------------------------------
```

Press Enter to finish. When planning the program, because you don't know how many products the file will contain at design time, you must design the product storage dynamically. You have two possibilities:

- Prior to processing any products, you read the entire file and find out how many products you need to process. Then you dimension an array according to the number of products and you read the products into the array.

- Alternatively, you could create a class to store the products that resizes itself dynamically. The class itself could pre-define an array with an initial size of, for example, four elements. When those initial four elements are insufficient, the class creates a new temporary array with eight elements, copies the existing four elements of the "old" arrays into the new one, and then exchanges the two arrays, so that the old member array of the class now has space for eight elements. Copying the array elements from one to another only seems time-intensive at first glance, but actually, this process only copies the pointer to the product files (as you learned earlier), and modern 32-bit and 64-bit processors perform such operations at nearly the speed of light.

  If you chose the first option, you must process the imported file twice, which is very time-intensive, especially with larger files.

The products themselves are also saved in classes. Because both types of products have a lot in common and differ only marginally, it make sense to create a base class that covers the similarities, and implement the special cases for each product type in two derived classes.

> **Important** To ensure type safety, the "List class" that stores the individual products should accept only product classes and classes derived from it.

Polymorphism is invaluable in this application. You can control the product classes derived from the product base class via an object variable of the product base class. This means that you can manage an array that accepts only the type "product base class," even though different class instances (well, maybe not totally different, but extended) can be saved within. And this is the show-stopper: you specify, for example, a method of the product base class in the code for executing a certain function, but then that same method is exposed by all derived classes, so you can call it as if the base class method were overridden in the derived classes.

> **Companion Content** This might sound a little confusing at first. To clear things up, open the file Inventory01.sln, which you can find in the \VB 2010 Developer Handbook\Chapter 10\ Inventory01 folder.

Before getting into the polymorphism aspect of this example, it's worth exploring the techniques used to establish the preconditions for saving the data. First, take a look at the class *DynamicList,* which we'll use to store the products:

```
Class DynamicList

    private myStep As Integer = 4          ' Step size by which the array is increased.
    private myCurrentArraySize As Integer  ' Actual array size.
    private myCurrentCounter As Integer    ' Pointer to the current item.
    private myArray() As ShopItem          ' Array with the items.

    Sub New()
        myCurrentArraySize = myStep
        ReDim myArray(myCurrentArraySize - 1)
    End Sub

    Sub Add(ByVal Item As ShopItem)

        ' Store item in array.
        myArray(myCurrentCounter) = Item

        'Increase pointer to the next element
        myCurrentCounter += 1

        'Check if the current array limit has been reached
        If myCurrentCounter = myCurrentArraySize - 1 Then
            'Create new array with storage
            'and copy elements over. To do this:
```

```
                        'New array becomes larger:
                        myCurrentArraySize += myStep

                        'Create temporary array
                        Dim locTempArray(myCurrentArraySize - 1) As ShopItem


                        'Copy every element. With this method,
                        'this performs extremely fast, because firstly,
                        'only the pointers to the actual elements are being copied.
                        'And secondly, it is highly optimized native code.
                        Array.Copy(myArray, locTempArray, myArray.Length)

                        'Temp array becomes main array, and we're done!
                        'The previous list of pointers in myArray which is now orphaned
                        'gets disposed by the Garbage Collector.
                        myArray = locTempArray
                End If
        End Sub

        'Returns the number of the existing elements
        Public Overridable ReadOnly Property Count() As Integer
                Get
                        Return myCurrentCounter
                End Get
        End Property

        'Allows re-assignment of an item's value.
        Default Public Overridable Property Item(ByVal Index As Integer) As ShopItem
                Get
                        Return myArray(Index)
                End Get

                Set(ByVal Value As ShopItem)
                        myArray(Index) = Value
                End Set
        End Property
End Class
```

The *Add* method in this class is critical. It checks whether the array is large enough to accommodate a new item. If not, it performs the exchange described earlier. Now, *myArray* points to the new array elements—the pointers to the old array elements were literally "forgotten." By the way, .NET Framework recovers the memory from the previous array by using the *Garbage Collector*. To put it simply, the Garbage Collector ("GC" for short) checks whether objects that are using memory space still have some kind of connection to the object variables being used. If not, it discards them and reclaims the memory they were using. In this example, the pointers to the original elements that were saved in the member array *myArray*

have no connection to any object after the copying process. The object name is redirected to the new elements with the following line:

```
'assign temporary array to member array
myArray = locTempArray
```

The original elements are now sitting in the memory without any connection, so the GC disposes of them during its next run.

> **Important** Keep in mind that the data of the actual object instances during this process is not touched at all. And that's also the reason why copying an array with *Array.Copy* happens so unbelievably quickly (which is also the case if you do this yourself, and run the whole array in a *For* loop and assign the individual elements to the new array).

The *Add* method accepts objects of a specific type only. In this example, this type is called *ShopItem*. This class is the basis for the product storage and looks as follows:

```
Class ShopItem

    private myTitle As String                  ' Title
    private myNetPrice As Double               ' Net price
    private myOrderNumber As String            ' Order number
    private myPrintTypeSetting As PrintType    ' Output format

    Public Sub New()
        myPrintTypeSetting = PrintType.Detailed
    End Sub

    Public Sub New(ByVal StringArray() As String)
        Title = StringArray(FieldOrder.Titel)
        'FieldOrder is an Enum and is defined further below:
        GrossPrice = Double.Parse(StringArray(FieldOrder.GrossPrice)) / 100
        OrderNumber = StringArray(FieldOrder.OrderNumber)
        PrintTypeSetting = PrintType.Detailed
    End Sub

    Public Property Title() As String
        Get
            Return myTitle
        End Get
        Set(ByVal Value As String)
            myTitle = Value
        End Set
    End Property
```

```vb
    Public Property OrderNumber() As String
        Get
            Return myOrderNumber
        End Get
        Set(ByVal Value As String)
            myOrderNumber = Value
        End Set
    End Property


    Public Property NetPrice() As Double
        Get
            Return myNetPrice
        End Get

        Set(ByVal Value As Double)
            myNetPrice = Value
        End Set

    End Property

    Public ReadOnly Property NetPriceFormatted() As String
        Get
            Return NetPrice.ToString("#,##0.00") + " $"
        End Get
    End Property

    Public Overridable Property GrossPrice() As Double
        Get
            Return myNetPrice * 1.19
        End Get

        Set(ByVal Value As Double)
            myNetPrice = Value / 1.19
        End Set
    End Property

    Public ReadOnly Property GrossPriceFormatted() As String
        Get
            Return GrossPrice.ToString("#,##0.00") + " $"
        End Get
    End Property

    Public ReadOnly Property VATAmountFormatted() As String
        Get
            Return (GrossPrice - myNetPrice).ToString("#,##0.00") + " $"
        End Get
    End Property

    Public Overridable ReadOnly Property Description() As String
        Get
            Return OrderNumber & vbTab & Title
        End Get
    End Property
```

```
Public Property PrintTypeSetting() As PrintType
    Get
        Return myPrintTypeSetting
    End Get

    Set(ByVal Value As PrintType)
        myPrintTypeSetting = Value
    End Set
End Property

Public Overrides Function ToString() As String

    If PrintTypeSetting = PrintType.Brief Then
        'Shortform: The Description property of the object is used
        'according to the original implementation in the base class
        Return MyClass.Description & vbCr & vbLf & _
            Me.NetPriceFormatted & vbTab & Me.VATAmountFormatted & vbTab & _
            Me.GrossPriceFormatted & vbCr & vbLf
    Else
        'Longform: The overridden and extended Description property
        'of the object itself are used
        Return Me.Description & vbCr & vbLf & _
            Me.NetPriceFormatted & vbTab & Me.VATAmountFormatted & vbTab & _
            Me.GrossPriceFormatted & vbCr & vbLf
    End If

End Function

End Class
```

It's not difficult to understand this class, because it performs two simple tasks: saving data, which is made accessible by properties, and formatting the output. Some of the properties are also defined as *ReadOnly*, because it makes no sense to allow write-access to them.

Converting Numbers to Strings and Formatting Them

One of the characteristics of the *ToString* function of primitive data types (*Integer*, *Double*, and so on) is the formatted output of numbers. In this case, you use an overload of *ToString* which accepts a string as parameter. In this example, the string "#,##0.00" creates a decimal with exactly two places, independent of the actual value, and the integer portion to be formatted with thousand separators.

Now let's take a look at the classes derived from the base class:

```
Class BookItem
    Inherits ShopItem

    private myAuthor As String

    Public Sub New(ByVal StringArray() As String)
        MyBase.New(StringArray)
        Author = StringArray(FieldOrder.AdditionalRemarks1)
    End Sub

    Public Overridable Property Author() As String
        Get
            Return myAuthor
        End Get
        Set(ByVal Value As String)
            myAuthor = Value
        End Set
    End Property

    ' we're assuming that the state tax/sales tax/VAT is 7%
    Public Overrides Property GrossPrice() As Double
        Get
            Return NetPrice * 1.07
        End Get

        Set(ByVal Value As Double)
            NetPrice = Value / 1.07
        End Set
    End Property

    Public Overrides ReadOnly Property Description() As String
        Get
            Return OrderNumber & vbTab & Title & vbCr & vbLf & "Author: " & Author
        End Get
    End Property

End Class
```

With the *Inherits* keyword that follows the *Class* keyword, you specify that the new class that stores book information is derived from the base class *ShopItem*. This allows object variables defined as *ShopItem* to also reference instances of *BookItem*, because each derived class can be "addressed" by an object variable of the base class. For example, if you have declared an object variable called *AProduct* as follows:

```
Dim AProduct as ShopItem
```

and define it with:

```
AProduct=New ShopItem()
```

you can later return its content with the statement:

```
Console.WriteLine(AProduct.GrossPriceFormatted)
```

In this case, the *GrossPriceFormatted* method of the base class *ShopItem* is used, as expected. Interestingly, however, when you address an instance of a derived class using the same object variable *AProduct,* as shown here:

```
AProduct=New BookItem(…)
```

and later call that same member:

```
Console.WriteLine(AProduct.GrossPriceFormatted)
```

this time the call uses the *GrossPriceFormatted* member of the derived class *BookItem* instead of the *GrossPriceFormatted* function of the base class.

That's the unbeatable advantage of polymorphism: you have a control program that seems to be calling a member of a base class object variable, but it actually calls an overridden version in a derived class.

The base class for this example provides a parameterized constructor that accepts a *String* array. The data for the content of a class instance is taken from this *String* array, as shown in the following:

```
Public Sub New(ByVal StringArray() As String)
    Title = StringArray(FieldOrder.Titel)
    GrossPrice = Double.Parse(StringArray(FieldOrder.GrossPrice)) / 100
    OrderNumber = StringArray(FieldOrder.OrderNumber)
    PrintTypeSetting = PrintType.Detailed
End Sub
```

The passed-in array always contains the individual data values in elements with the same index. For easier source code comprehension, these are stored in an *Enum* collection (more about *Enums* in Chapter 16, "Enumerations") as demonstrated here:

```
Enum FieldOrder 'Takes care of the field order
    Type
    OrderNumber
    Title
    AdditionalRemarks1
    GrossPrice
    AdditionalRemarks2
End Enum
```

The derived class *BookItem* can now define an instance effortlessly. It just calls the constructor of the base class and completes its own constructor by assigning a specific array element of the parameter it received:

```
Public Sub New(ByVal StringArray() As String)
    MyBase.New(StringArray)
    Author = StringArray(FieldOrder.AdditionalRemarks1)
End Sub
```

Suppose that books have a different sales tax or VAT (*Value Added Tax*) than other products (as they do in most of the countries in Europe). In those countries, this is done to reduce the consumer tax burden for groceries or books as opposed to a new flat screen television or the latest Mercedes S Class, and thus be more fair to various income levels. To reflect different percentages of tax for different products, you need to override the function that calculates the gross price, as follows:

```
Public Overrides Property GrossPrice() As Double
    Get
        Return NetPrice * 1.07
    End Get

    Set(ByVal Value As Double)
        NetPrice = Value / 1.07
    End Set
End Property
```

Here again, you can see polymorphism in action: the derived class doesn't need to override the method that returns the formatted gross price as a *String*. Take a look at the base class function in the following code:

```
Public ReadOnly Property GrossPriceFormatted() As String
    Get
        Return GrossPrice.ToString("#,##0.00") + " $"
    End Get
End Property
```

Note that this function doesn't use a field variable directly, but instead uses a property that has been implemented in the class. From the viewpoint of the derived class *BookItem,* it's not the *GrossPrice* of the base class that is called, but that of the (overridden) derived class. Therefore, the formatted gross price of a book is taken into consideration. *GrossPriceFormatted* calls the overridden property procedure of the derived class, even though *GrossPriceFormatted* itself is found exclusively in the base class.

The functions *Description* and *VATAmountFormatted* work similarly.

The second class for saving Video and DVD products, called *DVDItem*, also takes advantage of polymorphism:

```
Class DVDItem
    Inherits ShopItem

    Protected myRunningTime As Integer
    Protected myActor As String

    Public Sub New(ByVal StringArray() As String)
        MyBase.New(StringArray)
        RunningTime = Integer.Parse(StringArray(FieldOrder.AdditionalRemarks1))
        Actor = StringArray(FieldOrder.AdditionalRemarks2)
    End Sub

    Public Overridable Property RunningTime() As Integer
        Get
            Return myRunningTime
        End Get
        Set(ByVal Value As Integer)
            myRunningTime = Value
        End Set
    End Property

    Public Overridable Property Actor() As String
        Get
            Return myActor
        End Get
        Set(ByVal Value As String)
            myActor = Value
        End Set
    End Property

    Public Overrides ReadOnly Property Description() As String
        Get
            Return OrderNumber & vbTab & Title & vbCr & vbLf & "Duration: " &
                myRunningTime & " Min." & vbCr & vbLf & "Leading actor: " & Actor
        End Get
    End Property

End Class
```

This example illustrates how well polymorphism supports code reuse, and how it saves you a huge amount of repetitive typing. If the base class works, the derived classes will work just as smoothly, except for the additional features they implemented themselves. Therefore, you don't need to spend so much time searching for errors.

At this point, you're done creating the classes for the example. All that's left to do is implement the main program, which reads the original text file, creates the elements from each line of text, adds them to the list, and finally, returns the results:

```
Module mdlMain

    'The inventory file must be located in the same folder as the executable.
    Private Filename As String = My.Application.Info.DirectoryPath & "\Inventory.txt"

    Sub Main()

        'StreamReader for reading text files
        Dim locSr As StreamReader
        Dim locList As New DynamicList   ' Dynamic list
        Dim locElements() As String      ' Individual ShopItem elements
        Dim locShopItem As ShopItem      ' One single ShopItem element
        Dim locDisplayMode As PrintType ' Display mode

        'Find out if the text file exists:
        'For simplicity's sake catch possible errors here …)
        Try
            locSr = New StreamReader(Filename, System.Text.Encoding.Default)
        Catch ex As Exception
            Console.WriteLine("Error while reading inventory file!" & _
                              vbNewLine & ex.Message)
            Console.WriteLine()
            Console.WriteLine("Press key to exit")
            Console.ReadKey()
            Exit Sub
        End Try

        Console.WriteLine("Select (1) for brief and (2) for detailed display")
        Dim locKey As Char = Console.ReadKey.KeyChar
        If locKey = "1"c Then
            locDisplayMode = PrintType.Brief
        Else
            locDisplayMode = PrintType.Detailed
        End If

        Do
            Try
                'Read line
                Dim locLine As String = locSr.ReadLine()

                'Nothing entered, so that's it!
                If String.IsNullOrEmpty(locLine) Then
                    locSr.Close()
                    Exit Do
                End If
```

```
                    'Overlook semi-colon
                    If Not locLine.StartsWith(";") Then
                        'You don't need to declare an explicit Char array
                        'to split the line into the comma-separated elements
                        locElements = locLine.Split(New Char() {";"c})

                        If locElements(FieldOrder.Type) = "1" Then
                            locShopItem = New BookItem(locElements)
                        Else
                            locShopItem = New DVDItem(locElements)
                        End If
                        locList.Add(locShopItem)
                    End If

                Catch ex As Exception
                    Console.WriteLine("Error while evaluating the inventory file!" & _
                                      vbNewLine & ex.Message)
                    Console.WriteLine()
                    Console.WriteLine("Press key to exit")
                    Console.ReadKey()
                    locSr.Close()
                    Exit Sub
                End Try

            Loop

            Dim locGrossAmount As Double = 0

            'Return all elements
            For count As Integer = 0 To locList.Count - 1
                locList(count).PrintTypeSetting = locDisplayMode
                Console.WriteLine(locList(count).ToString())
                locGrossAmount += locList(count).GrossPrice
            Next

            Console.WriteLine()
            Console.WriteLine("----------------------------")
            Console.WriteLine("Total: " & locGrossAmount.ToString("#,##0.00") & " $")
            Console.WriteLine("----------------------------")
            Console.WriteLine("----------------------------")
            Console.WriteLine()
            Console.WriteLine("Press Return to exit")
            Console.ReadLine()

        End Sub

    End Module
```

Notice that the *WriteLine* statements, which take care of the outputs and show the products on the screen, take up most of the listing. Because the product classes manage most of the required operations, the main program's task is to open the file, read an element from the list, and then save it.

The main program also uses polymorphism, specifically when it returns the list on the screen:

```
'Return all elements
For count As Integer = 0 To locList.Count - 1
    locList(count).PrintTypeSetting = locDisplayMode
    Console.WriteLine(locList(count).ToString())
    locGrossAmount += locList(count).GrossPrice
Next
```

It iterates through the elements of the list with a counter loop. Because the *Item* property of the *DynamicList* class is the default property, you don't need to specify the property name *Item* here; it's sufficient to index the desired element within parentheses.

The *ToString* method of the indexed object then shows the output on the screen. Which *ToString* method is executed depends on the specific class whose instance is saved in the array element. For example, if it is a *BookItem* object, the program calls *BookItem.ToString*; for a *DVDItem* object it calls the *DVDItem.ToString* function. The same applies later for calculating the state tax and the property *GrossPrice*.

Polymorphism and the Use of *Me*, *MyClass*, and *MyBase*

The option to provide the user either with a detailed list or a very brief list is a requirement of the program. Theoretically, there are two approaches to this problem: the main program could perform all the printing, in which case it would need to differentiate between the various special cases. Basically, you'd have to write two separate print routines responsible for printing the detailed and the brief version, respectively. The other approach is to embed the string processing into the appropriate classes.

It so happens that there's a property called *Description* in the base class that returns a compact descriptive text for the content of an object instance. You can override this property in the derived classes, extending the property to include the additional information in the output.

It would be much easier if the program could use (depending on the user input) either the property of the base class *or* of the respective derived class for the screen output. For this purpose, the base class would need to supply a property that would control whether to issue the brief or the detailed version for the product description output.

Therefore, you can add the property *PrintType* to the base class. This property can have only two states, defined in an *Enum*:

```
Enum PrintType  ' Print format
    Brief       ' Brief
    Detailed    ' Detailed
End Enum
```

Before the actual content of a product object can be displayed on the screen, the program controlling the output must ensure that the *PrintType* property is set to the appropriate value, as selected by the user at program start. After *PrintType* has been set, the product object can determine whether it should return the brief base class description or its own longer description. Because this "decision algorithm" is the same in the base class as in all derived classes, you can implement it exclusively in the base class. Thanks to polymorphism, it is then possible to query the "correct" *Description* property of the respective class and build the return string from it.

The last problem is implementing the compact form of the product printout. The *ToString* function must be able to cancel polymorphism and specifically call the *Description* property of the base class—whether the current object is derived or original. The keyword *MyClass* helps you achieve this; it lets you access a specific member of the class in which the keyword *MyClass* appears. By using it, you cancel the method override for the duration of the call and use the original version in the class containing the *MyClass* keyword. The *ToString* function of the base class takes advantage of this property, as shown here:

```
Public Overrides Function ToString() As String

    If PrintTypeSetting = PrintType.Brief Then
        'Shortform: The Description property of the object is used
        'according to the original implementation in the base class
        Return MyClass.Description & vbCr & vbLf & _
            Me.NetPriceFormatted & vbTab & Me.VATAmountFormatted & vbTab & _
            Me.GrossPriceFormatted & vbCr & vbLf
    Else
        'Longform: The overridden and extended Description property
        'of the object itself is used
        Return Me.Description & vbCr & vbLf & _
            Me.NetPriceFormatted & vbTab & Me.VATAmountFormatted & vbTab & _
            Me.GrossPriceFormatted & vbCr & vbLf
    End If
End Function
```

Table 10-1 contains the keywords that specify class-level access, along with a brief description.

TABLE 10-1 Keywords for Specifying Overridden Elements of Different Inheritance Hierarchy Levels in a Class

Keyword	Description
Me	Uses the member defined in this class.
MyClass	Uses the member of the derived class that contains the *MyClass* keyword.
MyBase	Uses the member of the base class.

Abstract Classes and Virtual Procedures

If you're using Microsoft Word to edit your documents, you already know how document templates work. That means you also pretty much know what abstract classes are. Document templates in Word are used to define formatting rules for documents.

When I'm writing a normal paragraph for this book, the document template I'm using specifies that the font is "Segoe" and the font size is 9.5 points. A document created based on a document template is formatted according to the template's properties. Using a template is the only convenient way to ensure that all chapters in a book are formatted consistently.

Abstract classes work similarly; they provide prototypes of procedures, but these procedures serve exclusively as templates, forcing developers to implement certain members before they can use their derived class. These procedures are knows as virtual procedures. A virtual procedure has two tasks:

- It provides developers with a procedure signature (or the signatures for overloaded procedures).

- It forces developers to override the existing procedure(s) in a derived class and, above all, to implement them.

For this practical example, imagine that the sample application developed earlier in this chapter is deployed at a large online store such as Amazon. Of course, you'd need to include many more product groups, and for companies like Amazon that operate globally, you'd need to include many more tax rates.

Because each derived class would need to override most of the methods in the base class, it would instead make sense to create the product class *ShopItem* as an abstract class. To force team members to implement the tax-related functions, you configure the functions in question as virtual functions. That way, you ensure that the developers must program more *deliberately*, because if they don't implement the tax-related functions, the class will not compile.

> **Note** This also applies to our hypothetical example that we presented earlier in the chapter in the sidebar "Inheritance and Polymorphism—We Know How It Works, but Why Use It?" It makes a lot of sense to implement the base class *GraphicsObject* as an abstract class, because it can't implement a *Render* method by itself. What could it possibly draw, after all?

You need to make only a few changes to the example program to implement this change. You can still use object variables of the *ShopItem* type after restructuring it, but you can no longer instantiate the class directly (which you never did that in the sample program anyway).

Declaring a Class as Abstract with *MustInherit*

To create an abstract class you use the keyword *MustInherit*. If you put this keyword in front of the keyword *Class* of the *ShopItem* class in our example, nothing happens. Because the example never instantiates *ShopItem* itself, everything else stays the same—and there are no error messages. But what you have achieved is that the class can only be instantiated from a derived class; in other words, now you can't instantiate the class somewhere in the program (but you could before). Give it a try and see what happens. Enter the following line in *Sub Main*:

```
Dim locShopItemTestInstance As New ShopItem
```

An error message appears, as shown in Figure 10-10:

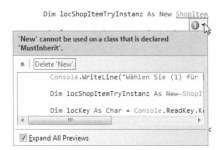

FIGURE 10-10 A class that has been defined as abstract with *MustInherit* can't be instantiated.

Declaring a Method or Property of an Abstract Class as Virtual with *MustOverride*

Developers usually don't look forward to getting errors, but it's a different story with a virtually defined method or property: in this case, an error message usually appears because a method or property in a derived class has *not* been overridden (that is, it hasn't been implemented) yet. But that's exactly what you want to achieve with virtual methods and properties.

In this example, the property *GrossPrice,* which calculates a product's gross price from the net price (taking the appropriate tax rate into account), demonstrates a virtual property clearly. Developers are forced to recognize that they are responsible for the correct calculation of the gross price when deriving from the *ShopItem* class, because they must implement a variant of this property in their derived class.

You declare a procedure as virtual with the keyword *MustOverride*. If you change the existing property *GrossPrice* of the *ShopItem* class (shown in the following code line) you will receive a few "desirable" error messages, like that shown in Figure 10-11.

```
Public MustOverride Property GrossPrice() as Double
```

```
Public MustOverride Property GrossPrice() As Double
    Get
        Return myNetPrice * 1.19
    End Get

    Set(ByVal Value As Double)
        myNetPrice = Value / 1.19
    End Set
End Property
```

Error List   9 Errors   0 Warnings   0 Messages

	Description	File	Line	Column	Project
6	'End Set' must be preceded by a matching 'Set'.	mdlMain.vb	175	9	Inventory
9	'Public Overloads Property GrossPrice As Double' cannot shadow a method declared 'MustOverride'.	mdlMain.vb	300	31	Inventory
8	Class 'DVDItem' must either be declared 'MustInherit' or override the following inherited 'MustOverride' member(s): Inventory.ShopItem : Public MustOverride Property GrossPrice As Double.	mdlMain.vb	264	7	Inventory
5	Declaration expected.	mdlMain.vb	174	13	Inventory
2	Statement cannot appear outside of a method body/multiline lambda.	mdlMain.vb	170	13	Inventory
1	Syntax error.	mdlMain.vb	169	9	Inventory
4	Syntax error.	mdlMain.vb	173	9	Inventory

FIGURE 10-11 Procedures marked as virtual with *MustOverride* must not contain any code and must be overridden in derived classes.

One error is located directly in the property procedure. This is because virtual procedures may not contain code themselves. They serve only to remind developers that they must implement the procedure in their derived classes. The following error message shows how well this works:

```
The class DVDItem must be declared as MustInherit or override the following
inherited MustOverride member:
    Inventory.ShopItem : Public MustOverride Property GrossPrice() As Double.
```

Right now, the *DVDItem* class doesn't implement this *GrossPrice* property. Suppose that videos and DVDs each have a special tax rate that differs from the reduced tax rate that applies to books. A developer might easily have overlooked this and failed to implement the property. The products in question would then have the wrong tax rate. To make this work, again, you only need make the following changes in the program:

■ First, remove the code from the property procedure *GrossPrice* in the *ShopItem* class so that only the prototype remains (the procedure head without the *End Property* statement).

- Next, insert a property procedure *GrossPrice* in the *DVDItem* class—basically the same code you removed from the *ShopItem* class, but adjusted by replacing *MyNetPrice* with *NetPrice*.

That eliminates all the errors, and your program is ready for a potential tax increase, special tax rates, and "subsidy cuts," such as the removal of the reduced tax rate for books.

> **Companion Content** Open the corresponding solution (.sln) for the example with abstract classes, which you can find in the \VB 2010 Developer Handbook\Chapter 10\Inventory02 folder.

Interfaces

The concept of interfaces offers you another possibility for standardizing classes. Similar to abstract classes, interfaces serve to create rules that regulate such things as certain members being required within classes derived from those interfaces. As opposed to abstract classes, however, interfaces contain only these rules—they do not contain code. What's interesting is that classes in .NET can inherit only from one class—but can implement any number of interfaces (unlike C++, in which multiple inheritance is possible, and sometimes confusing). You can think of interfaces in .NET as being similar to interfaces in daily life: a class (an object), for example a *Notebook* derived from the base class *Computer*, can implement several interfaces. For example, the *Notebook* class might implement the interfaces Bluetooth, VGA, USB, and so on.

Because interfaces don't contain any code, they can't be instantiated directly, just like abstract classes. However, you can create object variables with the type of an interface to reference derived classes. This behavior lets you create extremely flexible class libraries.

The .NET Framework uses these interface characteristics for two purposes:

- They force the programmers to abide by certain conventions. Programmers bind the interfaces to their classes. But the instances of those classes, into which the interfaces are bound, are never directly controlled by interface variables. This is called an *interface pattern*.

- They also serve to create valid management classes, which can then use all those objects for which the predetermined interfaces are implemented.

    Go back to the hypothetical example in the sidebar "Inheritance and Polymorphism— We Know How It Works, but Why Use It?" In that scenario, it would also make sense to describe the objects in the form of interfaces. Doing that would give the team implementing the concrete objects for drawing the utmost flexibility. They could create

code-containing base classes for the objects with the highest common denominator, but they could also create completely new special objects that simply bind the appropriate interfaces. Their implementations can therefore be individually customized yet still be inserted into the predetermined object model via interfaces.

With regard to the second bullet point, a three-tier concept is usually employed for components provided to developers. At the top tier is a class that performs the actual task (whatever that is). It can bind objects that implement a specific interface. On the lowest tier, the component provides the developer with the interface(s). So that developers who want to use the component don't have to perform the entire implementation, the component should provide abstract classes based on the interfaces that have some basic functionality (the middle tier).

Here's another example to help you understand these relationships. Suppose that you have been told to create a component that displays data in table format—call it *Table Control*. This component is mainly composed of two subcomponents: one that draws the table, gives it a grid, ensures that the user can move the cursor within the table, and so on. Ideally, this component is not responsible for drawing the table content; it leaves that task to a different class, and only binds it. The other component is responsible for drawing the content of a single cell. This second component not only saves the data for the individual cells, but also ensures that this data is drawn on the screen in a table cell, as needed. To provide users with the utmost flexibility when using the table control later on, this second class (the cell content-drawing component) should not be a coded class; instead, it should be an interface at the bottom tier. On the second tier, the table control should offer users at least one abstract class based on this interface that already implements the most important basic functionality. The component on the top tier then provides the complete cell components, which the user can begin to use immediately to fill the table with data.

If a developer notices at some point that the existing cell components don't offer every possible desirable feature, he has the following options:

- He can derive from the abstract class and develop a custom cell component that fulfills the special requirements. That's not too much work, because the abstract class already contains much of the management code, which probably just needs to be amended.

- If this approach is still too restrictive, he can take over the *complete* implementation of the cell class. In this case, he needs to bind the interface provided by the table component to ensure that the entire functionality the table component dictates is present within the custom cell class. Of course, the disadvantage of this option is that it takes a lot more work.

This chapter's example also works well for demonstrating how to use interfaces. We will implement an interface that dictates the basic functions that, until now, the main program accessed via the *ShopItem* class. The interface for the sample application will be called

IShopItem (putting the "I" for *Interface* in front is the common naming convention for inter-face classes), and the implementation takes place before the main module, as demonstrated in the following:

```
Interface IShopItem
    Property PrintTypeSetting() As PrintType
    ReadOnly Property ItemDescription() As String
    Function ToString() As String
    Property GrossPrice() As Double
End Interface
```

Next, we take care of the main program, which should now use the new interface for con-trol and no longer the abstract product base class. The only change you need to make is to declare the abstract product base class, as follows:

```
Sub Main()
    'StreamReader for reading the text files
    Dim locSr As StreamReader
    Dim locList As New DynamicList   ' Dynamic list
    Dim locElements() As String     ' Individual ShopItem elements
    Dim locShopItem As IShopItem    ' One single Shop element
    Dim locDisplayMode As PrintType ' Display mode
```

Because the interface *IShopItem* contains all the properties of the original abstract base class *ShopItem*, no other changes are necessary. But changing this one line has far reaching impli-cations, and you find yourself inundated with errors, as illustrated in Figure 10-12.

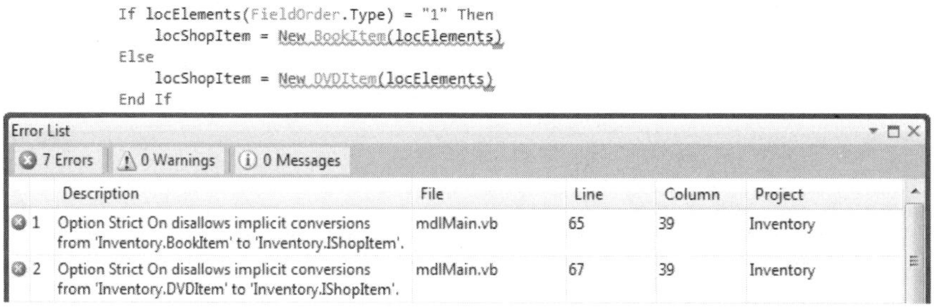

FIGURE 10-12 Since currently none of the derived classes implements the interface, it's not yet possible to reference the existing classes.

Even though the main program can now process all objects for which the new interface has been implemented, so far none of the classes implements the interfaces, and therefore, the program can't be executed. Visual Basic displays a confusing error.

Because it can't make a connection between *locShopItem* (declared as *IShopItem*) and the classes *BookItem* and *DVDItem*, it does the next best thing that seems to make sense: it tries to implicitly convert the types. Since an implicit conversion from one type to another is pro-hibited by *Option Strict On* (globally applied in the project settings), it returns an error mes-sage that initially might seem misleading.

All the classes we use in the program are derived from the *ShopItem* class. Implementing the interface *IShopItem* in the *ShopItem* class causes all classes derived from *ShopItem* to automatically implement *IShopItem*. It's therefore enough to build all required procedures into the abstract base class to help the compiler produce an executable again.

In Visual Basic there are two things you must keep in mind when implementing an interface:

- When defining a class, use *Implements* to specify which interface should be implemented.

- For each affected procedure of the class, you define individually which interface procedure it should implement. Here you also use the keyword *Implements*.

To add the *Implements* statement, enter **Implements IShopItem** below the line *MustInherit Class ShopItem*. DO NOT press Enter, but leave the line with an arrow key.

As soon as you have added the keyword *Implements* to the class definition in this manner, the error messages disappear. However, they will be replaced by other error messages right away, as shown in Figure 10-13.

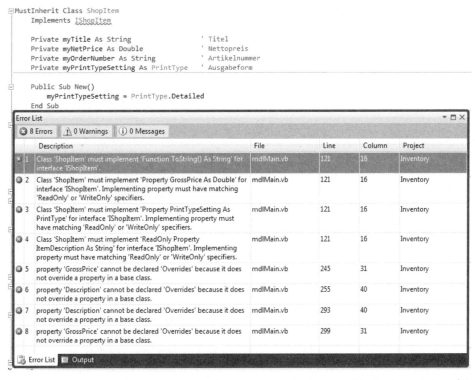

FIGURE 10-13 When you implement an interface you also must take care of the implementation of the individual interface procedures.

You might be wondering why it's not enough to give the procedure in the class the same name as the interface procedures—after all, that's sufficient when deriving classes.

In C#, that works with no problem, so the question is legitimate. But C# doesn't provide the ability to define a different name in your class procedure, one that doesn't correspond to the name of the interface procedure as you can in Visual Basic. In that respect, this feature of Visual Basic provides you with more flexibility. Also, Microsoft Intermediate Language (MSIL), into which the compiler converts each .NET application first, is conceptualized to require the explicit specification of the interface procedure that is to be implemented—in C#, the compiler does indeed implicitly perform this conversion, but exclusively implicitly.

Thanks to IntelliSense you also have an advantage in Visual Basic in the form of code input assistance: as soon as you enter the *Implements* keyword at the end of a procedure that you want to bind to an interface element, IntelliSense offers the available choices in a list, as shown in Figure 10-14.

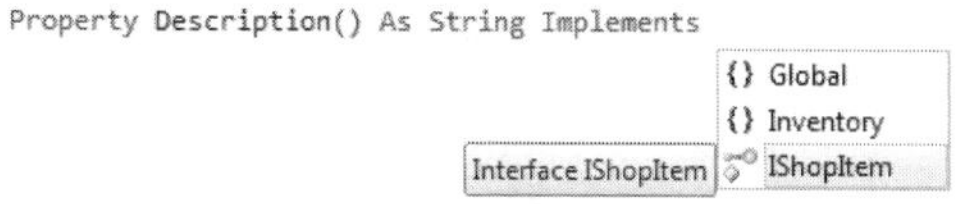

```
Property Description() As String Implements
                                    {} Global
                                    {} Inventory
                    Interface IShopItem  IShopItem
```

FIGURE 10-14 IntelliSense provides support to help you select the correct interface implementation option.

To get the sample application running again, you need to edit the following procedures and assign the correct interface procedures to them:

```
Public MustOverride Property GrossPrice() As Double Implements IShopItem.GrossPrice
    .
    .
    .
Public Overridable ReadOnly Property Description() As String
    Implements IShopItem.ItemDescription
    Get
        Return OrderNumber & vbTab & Title
    End Get
End Property

Public Property PrintTypeSetting() As PrintType Implements IShopItem.PrintTypeSetting
    Get
        Return myPrintTypeSetting
    End Get

    Set(ByVal Value As PrintType)
        myPrintTypeSetting = Value
    End Set
End Property
```

```
Public Overrides Function ToString() As String Implements IShopItem.ToString
    If PrintTypeSetting = PrintType.Brief Then
        'Shortform: The Description property of the object is used
        'according to the original implementation in the base class
        Return MyClass.Description & vbCr & vbLf & _
            Me.NetPriceFormatted & vbTab & Me.VATAmountFormatted & vbTab & _
            Me.GrossPriceFormatted & vbCr & vbLf
    Else
        'Longform: The overridden and extended Description property
        'of the object itself is used
        Return Me.Description & vbCr & vbLf & _
            Me.NetPriceFormatted & vbTab & Me.VATAmountFormatted & vbTab & _
            Me.GrossPriceFormatted & vbCr & vbLf
    End If
End Function
```

Note The second property deserves a special mention, because it binds an interface procedure with a different name. You can see that the names themselves are just hollow words here. Only with *Implements* do you specify which interface element corresponds to which class element. Of course, this feature doesn't give you carte blanche: you can't implement a property defined in an interface as a class method, but only as a property. It's also not possible to assign a method of an interface definition, which, for example, accepts a *String* as parameter, to a method of a class that expects an *Integer* as parameter. Also, note that the return types must be identical between the interface and the class that implements the interface. An incorrect assignment would corrupt the Common Type System of .NET; therefore, the background compiler won't even work if you try to do this (see Figure 10-15).

```
Public MustOverride Property GrossPrice() As Double Implements IShopItem.ItemDescription
```

Error List					− □ ×
⊗ 2 Errors	⚠ 0 Warnings	ⓘ 0 Messages			
Description		File	Line	Column	Project
⊗ 2 'GrossPrice' cannot implement 'ItemDescription' because there is no matching property on interface 'IShopItem'.		mdlMain.vb	221	68	Inventory
🗐 Error List Output					

FIGURE 10-15 Signatures, element types (property, method, event), and return types of an interface definition must correspond to those of the binding class.

After you have performed these changes, you will find only a few "errors" in the *DynamicList* class. So far, this class has only accepted *ShopItem* objects in the methods *Add* and *Item*. If you replace the used *ShopItem* objects with those of the type *IShopItem*, the program becomes executable again (the statements that need to be changed are highlighted in bold):

```
Class DynamicList

    private myStepIncreaser As Integer = 4
    private myCurrentArraySize As Integer
    private myCurrentCounter As Integer
    private myArray() As IShopItem

    Sub New()
        myCurrentArraySize = myStepIncreaser
        ReDim myArray(myCurrentArraySize)
    End Sub

    Sub Add(ByVal Item As IShopItem)

        'Check whether the current array limit has been reached.
        If myCurrentCounter = myCurrentArraySize - 1 Then
            'Create new arry with more storage,
            'and copy elements there.

            'New array becomes larger:
            myCurrentArraySize += myStepIncreaser

            'Create temporary array.
            Dim locTempArray(myCurrentArraySize - 1) As IShopItem

            'Copy elements.
            'Important: You must take care of,
            'copying yourself, unlike in VB6!
            For locCount As Integer = 0 To myCurrentCounter
                locTempArray(locCount) = myArray(locCount)
            Next

            'Assign temporary array to member array.
            myArray = locTempArray
        End If

        'Save element in the array
        myArray(myCurrentCounter) = Item

        'Increase pointer to the next element.
        myCurrentCounter += 1

    End Sub

    'Returns the number of the existing elements.
    Public Overridable ReadOnly Property Count() As Integer
        Get
            Return myCurrentCounter
        End Get
    End Property
```

```
    'Permits assignment.
    Default Public Overridable Property Item(ByVal Index As Integer) As IShopItem
        Get
            Return myArray(Index)
        End Get
        Set(ByVal Value As IShopItem)
            myArray(Index) = Value
        End Set
    End Property
End Class
```

> **Companion Content** To view the program example with the changes for interfaces, open
> the corresponding solution (.sln), which you can find in the \VB 2010 Developer Handbook\
> Chapter 10\Inventory03 folder.

Editor Support for Abstract Classes and Interfaces

It might have struck you as odd that I asked you *not* to confirm the changes for the interface
implementation with *Implements* in the *ShopItem* class by pressing Enter, but to leave the line
with one of the arrow keys instead.

If you had left the line with Enter, Editor support for the implementation of the function bodies would have been triggered. In this case, though, the routines were already present and
complete, so the support would have been a hindrance, as the following examples show.

Create a new Visual Basic console project under any name you like. Implement an interface and a class according to the template below, and then insert it above the line *Module
Module1* in the code file *Module1.vb*:

```
Interface ITest
    Property AProperty() As String
    Function AMethod() As Integer
End Interface

Public Class BindsITest

End Class
```

Move the cursor below the line *Public Class BindetITestEin*, enter **Implements ITest**, and then
press Enter. The result is displayed in Figure 10-16.

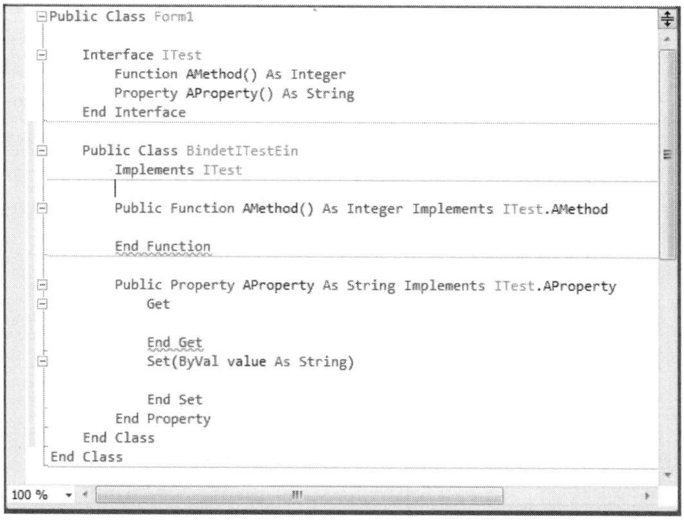

```
Public Class Form1

    Interface ITest
        Function AMethod() As Integer
        Property AProperty() As String
    End Interface

    Public Class BindetITestEin
        Implements ITest

        Public Function AMethod() As Integer Implements ITest.AMethod

        End Function

        Public Property AProperty As String Implements ITest.AProperty
            Get

            End Get
            Set(ByVal value As String)

            End Set
        End Property
    End Class
End Class
```

100 %

FIGURE 10-16 After you have bound an interface with *Implements*, the Editor inserts the complete code bodies of the required members.

This also works for appending: you can add a method, property, or event (more about events later) in the interface definition, but you first receive an error message because this new element does not exist in the implementing class. If you move the cursor behind the interface name of the *Implements* statement below the class definition and then press Enter, the element code body is appended to the end of the class again.

Give it a try. In the interface *ITest*, insert a further method with a return type of *String*, called *SecondMethod* so that your code looks like this:

```
Interface ITest
    Property AProperty() As String
    Function AMethod() As Integer
    Function SecondMethod() As String
End Interface
```

The error list displays a message informing you that the new method has not been implemented in the class that binds the interface.

To resolve this error, all you need to do is move the cursor below the line *Public Class BindsITest* behind *Implements ITest*, and then press Enter.

The error disappears immediately because the Editor inserts the code body for the method *SecondMethod*, connects it to the interface with *Implements*, and thus fulfills the implementation requirements of the interface.

The Pitfalls of Automatic Code Completion with Interfaces or Abstract Classes

Unfortunately, Editor support doesn't always work without glitches, and it can be misleading when the base class already contains methods or properties that have the same names as the implementing methods or properties, but are not yet connected to them. To correct this, remove the interface implementation *Implements ITest.SecondMethod* behind the function, as shown here:

```
Public Function SecondMethod() As String Implements ITest.SecondMethod

End Function
```

The Editor then adds a blue squiggly line beneath the following code:

```
Implements ITest
```

This is because it noticed that now the method *SecondMethod* of the interface *ITest* is no longer correctly implemented. But after that, the Editor support doesn't function so well. If you move the cursor back below the line *Public Class BindsITest* behind *Implements ITest* and then press Enter, you'll see a function body displayed at the end of the class, as shown in Figure 10-17.

```
    Public Class BindetITestEin
        Implements ITest

        Public Function AMethod() As Integer Implements ITest.AMethod

        End Function

        Public Function SecondMethod() As String

        End Function

        Public Function SecondMethod1() As String Implements ITest.SecondMethod

        End Function

        Public Property AProperty As String Implements ITest.AProperty
            Get

            End Get
            Set(ByVal value As String)

            End Set
        End Property
    End Class
End Class
```

FIGURE 10-17 When automatically completing code bodies of members that already exist with the same name, a "similar" member name is invented.

The method *SecondMethod* now basically exists twice (once with the "1" appended). So instead of completing the *Implements* statement with the corresponding interface member name behind *SecondMethod*, which would be the correct thing to do, the Editor creates a completely new method and implements the interface member in it.

Should something like this happen while you're creating your own interfaces, you need to transfer the *Implements* statement to the intended (and already existing) method and delete the method created by the Editor.

It becomes even more confusing when you are implementing a method or property that only exists in the base class. By default *ToString* belongs to this group. *ToString* is part of every new class because it represents a method of *Object*, and, as you already know, every new class is implicitly derived from *Object*, unless you specify otherwise. Of course, each new class inherits the *ToString* method (why the *ToString* method is "connected" to *Object*, is explained in the section "The Methods and Properties of Object").

Now watch what happens when you explicitly add this method to the interface. As expected, you first see an error in the program because the new interface definition requires that you implement a *ToString* function. Because *ToString* is present by default, this happens without programmer intervention. You still need to bind the inherited *ToString* function to the interface method definition *ToString* via *Implements* (refer to Figure 10-14).

With *Implements*, this wouldn't work so easily, because there is no method code to which we can append *Implements* to assign the *ToString* of the interface.

Let's find out how the Editor "helps," and how we can reach our goal.

- In the interface *ITest*, insert another method of type *String*, called **ToString**, which produces the following code:

```
Interface ITest
    Property AProperty() As String
    Function AMethod() As Integer
    Function SecondMethod() As String
    Function ToString() As String
End Interface
```

  Another message displays in the error list, stating that this new method was not implemented in the class bound to the interface.

- Try to resolve the error with Editor support: again place the cursor below the line *Public Class BindsITest* behind *Implements ITest*, and then press Enter.

  The result is the same as in the previous example, but not quite transparent. This is because the class does not contain code for the *ToString* method, which was taken over from base class *Object*.

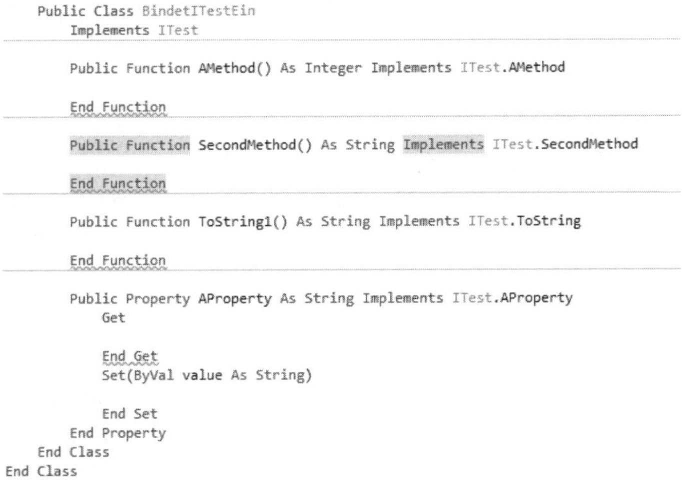

```
Public Class BindetITestEin
    Implements ITest

    Public Function AMethod() As Integer Implements ITest.AMethod

    End Function

    Public Function SecondMethod() As String Implements ITest.SecondMethod

    End Function

    Public Function ToString1() As String Implements ITest.ToString

    End Function

    Public Property AProperty As String Implements ITest.AProperty
        Get

        End Get
        Set(ByVal value As String)

        End Set
    End Property
    End Class
End Class
```

FIGURE 10-18 The Editor's behavior during code completion is more confusing if there is an inherited method or property with the same name as in the interface definition.

Basically, the Editor has the same problem. There is already a method (*ToString*), except this time it's not visible because it was inherited from the base class (*Object* in our example). Therefore, the Editor creates a version of the function name and gives the method the same name, appended by "1".

You can resolve this error by performing the following steps:

1. Override the method or property that must be implemented.

2. Call only the base method or property within the method or property.

3. Implement the interface at the overridden method or property.

In this case, the code would look as follows:

```
Public Overrides Function ToString() As String Implements ITest.ToString
    Return MyBase.ToString
End Function
```

Editor Support for Abstract Classes

The support you receive for implementing interfaces is also available for abstract classes. Add the following abstract class to the example:

```
MustInherit Class AbstractTest
    Public MustOverride Property AProperty() As String
    Public MustOverride Function AMethod(ByVal AParameter As String) As String
End Class
```

Now, create a class based on *AbstractTest*:

```
Public Class BasedOnAbstractTest
    Inherits AbstractTest

End Class
```

As soon as you press Enter after the *Inherits AbstractTest* statement, the Editor automatically completes all methods and properties that have been marked as virtual with *MustOverride*, in the form of code bodies:

```
Public Class BasedOnAbstractClass
    Inherits AbstractTest


    Public Overrides Property AProperty As String
        Get

        End Get
        Set(ByVal value As String)

        End Set
    End Property

    Public Overrides Function AMethod(ByVal AParameter As String) As String

    End Function
End Class
```

Interfaces that Implement Interfaces

In principle, interfaces can implement other interfaces. However, they do it differently than classes. Interfaces can inherit from other interfaces—just like classes can inherit from other classes, and thus reuse their entire functionality.

But because interfaces don't have any real functionality, they inherit only the implementation requirements from other interfaces. This means that an interface that inherits from another interface contains both its own rules, as well as those of the interface from which it inherits. Additionally, interfaces can inherit only from interfaces, not from classes (which, of course, can be explained because interfaces, unlike classes, cannot contain code).

Here's an example. Add the following code to the module from the previous example:

```
Interface IBaseInterface
    Property AProperty() As String
End Interface

Interface IMoreComplexInterface
    Inherits IBaseInterface

    Property SecondProperty() As String
End Interface
```

The interface *IMoreComplexInterface* contains the requirements for both interface definitions (its own and its parent's requirements).

When you implement this combined interface in a class, and then press Enter after the *Implements* statement, the Code Editor inserts the following code in the class module:

```
Public Class ComplexClass
    Implements IMoreComplexInterface

    Public Property AProperty() As String Implements IBaseInterface.AProperty
        Get

        End Get
        Set(ByVal value As String)

        End Set
    End Property

    Public Property SecondProperty() As String Implements
        IMoreComplexInterface.SecondProperty
        Get

        End Get
        Set(ByVal value As String)

        End Set
    End Property
End Class
```

Binding Multiple Interfaces in a Class

Multiple inheritance is not provided in the .NET infrastructure. In multiple inheritance, a new class is created from multiple base classes, and the inheriting class takes over the functionality of all the base classes.

In Visual Basic you can implement more than one interface in a class, and even though that's not quite as "awesome" as multiple inheritance, being able to bind multiple interfaces helps.

> **Note** Multiple inheritance is only awesome at first glance. And it will probably never exist in Visual Basic, because even one of the inventors of C++, Mr. Stroustrup, views it rather skeptically by now. (In Java it has even been left out *intentionally*.) Multiple inheritance makes for conflicts that cannot be settled, which the compiler must resolve arbitrarily (two methods of the same name in both classes with implementation, and so on). According to Stroustrup, "[...] Multiple inheritance remains understandable when only one base class truly implements member functions and the others only declare pure virtual functions [...]".

Binding multiple interfaces is very simple. Change the previous example for the interface definitions as follows, by commenting out the *Inherits* keyword for *IMoreComplexInterface*:

```
Interface IBaseInterface
    Property AProperty() As String
End Interface

Interface IMoreComplexInterface
    'Inherits was removed, both interfaces are on the "same level".
    Property SecondProperty() As String
End Interface

Public Class ComplexClass
    Implements IBaseInterface, IMoreComplexInterface

    Public Property AProperty() As String Implements IBaseInterface.AProperty
        Get

        End Get
        Set(ByVal value As String)

        End Set
    End Property

    Public Property SecondProperty() As String Implements
        IMoreComplexInterface.SecondProperty
        Get

        End Get
        Set(ByVal value As String)

        End Set
    End Property
End Class
```

The only line that needs to be changed in the code of the binding class is the line in bold. Nothing needs to be changed in the remaining code, which assigns the interface members to the class members.

The Built-In Members of the Object Type

Object itself provides several basic methods and properties, which each new class automatically inherits. The developers of the .NET Framework have thus made sure that each object has specific basic functionality that other classes can count on.

Returning the String Representation of an Object with *ToString*

The *ToString* method returns a string that "describes" a class instance. Primitive variables, for example, use the *ToString* method to convert their values into strings—usually even with formatting options. You know that the *ToString* method is the first point of reference for the implementation of simple polymorphous behavior. You only need to override the *ToString* method of a class, and leave it to the class itself how to represent the text in a *ListBox*, for example. The default implementation of the *ToString* method returns the type name of the class.

Comparing Objects

For each object, there is a method called *Equals* that checks whether the object instance referenced by an object variable is the same as one referenced by a different object variable.

Important The *Equals* method does not check whether the content of two objects is the same, if the object variables reference two *different* instances. Having said this, for Value Types—and Primitive Types like *Integer*, *Double*, *Decimal*, *String* or *Date* belong to value types as well—*Equals* tests for equality of the actual values.

Let's use an example to illustrate this. For better understanding you should first go back to Chapter 8, "Class Begins," and take a look at Figure 8-7.

Note Instead of using the *Equals* method, to which you can pass a different object to be compared to the current one, you can also use the *Is* operator (or the *IsNot* operator respectively) and achieve the same result. This second option is closer to natural language. The following example shows how to use both techniques in your code.

Companion Content Open the corresponding solution (.sln), which you can find in the \VB 2010 Developer Handbook\Chapter 10\EqualsDemo folder.

```
Module mdlMain

    Sub Main()

        'Instantiating with New and thus
        'creating storage for the Contact object
        'on the Managed Heap
        Dim objVarContact As New Contact With {
            .LastName = "Halek",
            .FirstName = "Sarah",
            .Zip = "99999",
            .City = "Musterhausen"}

        'objVarContact2 points to the same object;
        'the referenced instance is the same!
        Dim objVarContact2 As Contact
        objVarContact2 = objVarContact

        'objVarContact3 point an object of the same kind;
        'the referenced instance is not exactly the same, but just the same kind!
        Dim objVarContact3 As New Contact With {
                    .LastName = "Halek",
                    .FirstName = "Sarah",
                    .Plz = "99999",
                    .Ort = "Musterhausen"}

        'The proof:
        Console.WriteLine("The statement ""objVarContact = objVarContact2 is "" " & _
            objVarContact.Equals(objVarContact2))

        Console.WriteLine("The statement ""objVarContact = objVarContact3 is "" " & _
            objVarContact.Equals(objVarContact3))

        Console.WriteLine()

        'Alternatively with the IS keyword:
        Console.WriteLine("The statement ""objVarContact = objVarContact2 is "" " & _
            (objVarContact Is objVarContact2))

        Console.WriteLine("The statement ""objVarContact = objVarContact3 is "" " & _
            (objVarContact Is objVarContact3))

        Console.WriteLine()
        Console.WriteLine("Press key to exit")
        Console.ReadKey()
    End Sub

End Module
```

```
Class Contact

    Public Property LastName As String
    Public Property FirstName As String
    Public Property Zip As String
    Public Property City As String

End Class
```

This little demonstration is pretty much self-explanatory. It defines three object variables based on the class *Contact*. It instantiates from it two objects (from *objVarContact1* and *objVarContact3*) and fills them with the same data. The second object variable (*objVarContact2*) points to the same instance as the first object variable. Therefore, a comparison with *Equals* or *Is* returns true.

> **Tip** Follow this rule: if two object variables refer to the same instance, and therefore save the same pointers to the actual data on the Managed Heap, *Is* or *Equals* return *True* (otherwise, *False*). The data itself (the instances of the objects) is not used for this comparison.

The output of this program, therefore, looks as follows:

```
The statement "objVarContact = objVarContact2 is " True
The statement "objVarContact = objVarContact3 is " False

The statement "objVarContact = objVarContact2 is " True
The statement "objVarContact = objVarContact3 is " False

Press key to exit
```

Equals, *Is*, and *IsNot* in Real World Scenarios

So where can you use this feature? When it comes to testing for identical objects the answer is simple: almost everywhere.

At the very least, object comparison is a necessity when you are looking for a specific object in a collection, such as the *Items* collection of the *ListBox*. Perhaps you want to delete an item from the list of a *ListBox*. For this purpose you would use the *ListBox.Remove* method, which removes a specific item from the *Items* collection of the *ListBox*. The *Remove* method can accept any object, and of course, it can't compare the contents of the object instances stored

in the *ListBox* control to the object that you want to remove. But it can determine whether two object variables point to the same instance, which is exactly how *Remove* recognizes which object to remove.

The following demonstration shows how this works in practice. This familiar example fills a *ListBox* with contact data. A button lets you remove a selected item from the list.

You can find out about the reference to a selected object of a *ListBox* with the control's *SelectedItem* property. If *SelectedItem* returns *Nothing*, you are dealing with a null reference. In this case, an object variable points to no proper instance of a class.

If *SelectedItem* returns a value that is not *Nothing*, an object in the list is selected. You can then pass this object to the *Remove* method of the *ListBox.Items* collection.

> **Companion Content** Open the corresponding solution (.sln), which you can find in the
> \VB 2010 Developer Handbook\Chapter 10\EqualsRealLife folder.

The following code snippet shows the button's event handler routine, which deletes a list item, if one is selected:

```
    Private Sub btnDeleteContact_Click(ByVal sender As System.Object, ByVal e As System.
➡EventArgs) _
                Handles btnDeleteContact.Click
        Dim locContact As Object
        locContact = lstContacte.SelectedItem
        If locContact IsNot Nothing Then
            lstContacts.Items.Remove(locContact)
        End If
    End Sub
```

Internally, the *Remove* method iterates through the items comparing the item to be deleted to each list item, removing the item when it finds a match. It performs a similar comparison when you call the *Is* or the *Equals* method.

The Methods and Properties of Object: An Overview

Table 10-2 outlines the built-in methods of the class *Object*:

TABLE 10-2 Description of the *Object* Members

Member	Description
Equals	Determines whether the current instance is identical to the specified *Object*. Two objects are identical when their instances (the data on the heap to which they pointo) match. *ValueType* variables override this method and compare the individual members. Because structures automatically derive from *ValueType*, this behavior applies to all structures. And because primitive Types are based on ValueTypes as well, these types also inherit this behavior.
GetHashCode=	Produces a hash code (a kind of identifier) based on the object's contents. This hash code is used, for example, when an object is searched for in a table (an array) and the search must be performed very quickly. Therefore, *GetHashCode* should return unique values, if possible, but at the same time include content-dependent values as a basis for the hash code calculation. The algorithm implemented in *Object*, which all new classes automatically inherit, guarantees neither uniqueness nor consistency. It is therefore recommended that you develop your own hash code algorithms for derived objects, if possible, and override this method if you want to save your object frequently in hash tables.
GetType	Retrieves the type of the instance as a *Type* object. You need the type of the object as a starting point to be able to use a procedure called reflection checking which features the program contains (properties, methods, fields, and so on). More about this in Chapter 21, "Attributes and Reflection."
(Shared) ReferenceEquals	This static method corresponds to the *Equals* method, but it accepts both objects to be compared as parameters. Because this method is static, it can be called only via the type name (*Object.ReferenceEquals*).
ToString()	Returns a string that describes the current object. You can take this literally in the original version: *ToString* returns the class name, when you don't override the function. If possible, *ToString* should at least partially return the object's content as a string.
Finalize	An Object's Finalize method is exclusively called by the Garabge Collector. It signals the object that it is about to be discarded so that the object can then free resources that it no longer needs, if it hasn't done this, yet. Classes that replace *Finalize* with their own implementations should use the *IDisposable* pattern. You'll see more about this in Chapter 13, "Dispose, Finalize, and the Garbage Collector."
MemberwiseClone	Creates a *"flat copy"* of the object that provides the method. When you call *MemberwiseClone*, this method creates a copy of all value type members and returns those in a new object instance. For reference types, only address copies are created. They then point to the same objects in the Managed Heap, to which the reference types of the originals point as well. *MemberwiseClone* is *Protected* and therefore can be called only by the class itself. Classes can implement a *Clone* method and use their own *MemberwiseClone* method to do this. Classes that implement this method should also implement the *ICloneable* interface.

Shadowing of Class Procedures

Visual Basic also provides another way of replacing procedures in a base class with others of the same name in a derived class. This is called member *shadowing*.

After defining a function in a base class, a function of the same name in a derived class can completely shadow the original, as shown in the following example:

> **Companion Content**   Open the corresponding solution (.sln), which you can find in the \VB 2010 Developer Handbook\Chapter 10\Shadowing01 folder.

```
Module mdlMain

    Sub Main()
        Dim locBaseInstance As New BaseClass
        Console.WriteLine(locBaseInstance.AFunction().ToString())

        locBaseInstance = New DerivedClass
        Console.WriteLine(locBaseInstance.AFunction().ToString())

        Console.WriteLine()
        Console.WriteLine("Press key to exit!")
        Console.ReadKey()
    End Sub

End Module

Public Class BaseClass

    Protected test As Integer

    Sub New()
        test = 10
    End Sub

    Public Function AFunction() As Integer
        Return test * 2
    End Function

End Class

Public Class DerivedClass
    Inherits BaseClass

    Public Function AFunction() As Integer
        Return test * 3
    End Function

End Class
```

Without taking a close look at the class implementation, you might assume that the module will first return the value 20 and in the next line the value 30. But this example only seems like an exercise in polymorphism. Actually the single function of the base class is neither defined as overridable by the keyword *Overridable* nor does the same function of the derived class try to override this function with *Overrides*. Upon closer inspection Visual Basic displays a warning for *AFunction* of the derived class, as shown in Figure 10-19.

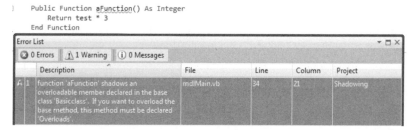

FIGURE 10-19 A function of the derived class shadows the function of the base class.

Even though Visual Basic generates a warning, it still compiles the program. The message is truly a warning, not an error; it informs you that one function is shadowed by another.

Shadowing impacts the class behavior, because the function of the base class is called, even though the object variable contains a derived instance. The shadowing processes performed by Visual Basic interrupt the inheritance order of the class and ensure that a function not marked for override cannot be overridden.

You can avoid of the warning by putting the keyword *Shadows* in front of the function in the derived class, as follows:

```
Public Shadows Function AFunction() As Integer
```

Shadows is purely cosmetic though (and this also applies in the next sections); it doesn't shadow anything by itself, it just precludes the warning. In the following sections you will find out how you can still make use of the newly defined method, which is idle right now.

Shadows as Interruptor of the Class Hierarchy

Companion Content Open the corresponding solution (.sln), which you can find in the \VB 2010 Developer Handbook\Chapter 10\Shadowing02 folder.

```
Option Explicit On
Option Strict On

Module mdlMain

    Sub Main()
        Dim locFourthClass As New FourthClass
        Dim locFirstClass As FirstClass = locFourthClass
        Dim locSecondClass As SecondClass = locFourthClass
        Dim locThirdClass As ThirdClass = locFourthClass

        Console.WriteLine(locFirstClass.AFunction)
        Console.WriteLine(locSecondClass.AFunction)
        Console.WriteLine(locThirdClass.AFunction)
        Console.WriteLine(locFourthClass.AFunction)

        Console.WriteLine()
        Console.WriteLine("Press key to exit!")
        Console.ReadKey()

    End Sub
End Module

Public Class FirstClass

    Public Overridable Function AFunction() As String
        Return "First class"
    End Function

End Class

Public Class SecondClass
    Inherits FirstClass

    Public Overrides Function AFunction() As String
        Return "Second class"
    End Function
End Class

Public Class ThirdClass
    Inherits SecondClass

    Public Overrides Function AFunction() As String
        Return "Third class"
    End Function

End Class

Public Class FourthClass
    Inherits ThirdClass
    Public Overrides Function AFunction() As String
        Return "Fourth class"
    End Function

End Class
```

Can you imagine the output you will see when you execute this program? The different object and class names might seem a little confusing in the beginning, but the result is clear: the program returns the text "Fourth class" four times. The fourth class is instantiated once and is referenced by each variable.

Each of the other object variables is defined by a class of the class inheritance hierarchy and can therefore reference each instance of a derived class, as you have learned earlier in this chapter. Now make a small change to the third class, as shown in bold in the following:

```
Public Class ThirdClass
    Inherits SecondClass

    '"Overrides" was exchanged for "Overridable Shadows":
    Public Overridable Shadows Function AFunction() As String
        Return "Third class"
    End Function

End Class
```

Guess what happens when you run the program again. The output is as follows:

```
Second Class
Second Class
Fourth Class
Fourth Class

Press key to exit!
```

Did you guess the output correctly? It's not so hard to understand the result.

The *AFunction* method of the third and fourth classes has nothing to do with the first two classes. Because of the shadowing in the third class, the function is newly implemented. Just as with a completely different function which is added in *ThirdClass*, a new *Overridable* is required, because otherwise *FourthClass* could not override the function with *Overrides*.

> **Note** The actual shadowing process is not triggered by the keyword *Shadows*, but by defining the method of the same name. The *Shadows* keyword only ensures that the warning disappears.

Maybe it's confusing that the first class returns the text "Second class." But what else should it return? "First class," you might say. But that's not correct, because it would go against the principle of polymorphism. It can't return "Fourth class," because this function is out of reach for *FirstClass*. In *ThirdClass*, this function is simply replaced by a completely new version. Basically .NET Framework salvages what can be salvaged, and tries to go forward in the inheritance order—and therefore, *SecondClass* is the last function that can be reached by polymorphism before the inheritance order is interrupted by the shadowing process in *ThirdClass*.

This behavior is desirable because if you don't want a member of a class to be overridden, it won't be overridden. The CLR always guarantees that a function that cannot be overridden retains its original capabilities, even if they shadow other functions in derived classes with the same name.

Internally, there are two different versions of *AFunction*, and if you change the sample program as follows, what actually happens becomes obvious.

Companion Content Open the corresponding solution (.sln), which you can find in the \VB 2010 Developer Handbook\Chapter 10\Shadowing03 folder.

```
Option Explicit On
Option Strict On

Module mdlMain
    Sub Main()
        Dim locFourthClass As New FourthClass
        Dim locFirstClass As FirstClass = locFourthClass
        Dim locSecondClass As SecondClass = locFourthClass
        Dim locThirdClass As ThirdClass = locFourthClass

        Console.WriteLine(locFirstClass.AFunction_a)
        Console.WriteLine(locSecondClass.AFunction_a)
        Console.WriteLine(locThirdClass.AFunction_b)
        Console.WriteLine(locFourthClass.AFunction_b)

        Console.WriteLine()
        Console.WriteLine("Press key to exit!")
        Console.ReadKey()

    End Sub

End Module

Public Class FirstClass

    Public Overridable Function AFunction_a() As String
        Return "First class"
    End Function

End Class

Public Class SecondClass
    Inherits FirstClass

    Public Overrides Function AFunction_a() As String
        Return "Second class"
    End Function
```

```
End Class

Public Class ThirdClass
    Inherits SecondClass

    Public Overridable Function AFunction_b() As String
        Return "Third class"
    End Function
End Class

Public Class FourthClass
    Inherits ThirdClass

    Public Overrides Function AFunction_b() As String
        Return "Fourth class"
    End Function

End Class
```

Don't Ignore Shadow Warnings!

Even if shadowing of methods or properties causes only warnings, not errors, don't ignore them! Especially when it comes to code generation, you should be aware of potential problems. For example, consider the generation of data layers based on an actual database, such as in *LINQ to SQL* or *LINQ to Entities* (you'll learn more about this topic in Chapter 27, "LINQ to Entities: Programming with Entity Framework"). When an object that a database table or a database view is based on has a property with the exact same name as a field in the corresponding database table, the code generation process can emit shadowing code. Suppose, for example, that you have a field named *Property* in a database table. The code generator for this entity would, among other things, generate a method composed of the prefix "On", the name of the property, and the postfix "Changed". For this example, that would become the method name *OnPropertyChanged*. Unfortunately, this method name also belongs to a crucial method of the entity's base class, which notifies other instances whenever any of its properties has been changed. Had it been overwritten (or shadowed for that matter), none of the updating notification techniques for this entity's database tables would have worked anymore. But shadowing of this important method is exactly what would happen if the code generation started, and the compilation would always succeed. So, especially when it comes to code generation, watch out for shadow warnings in the error list with particular care!

Special Form "Module" in Visual Basic

Among all the existing Microsoft .NET programming languages, only Visual Basic has *modules*. And even here a module is deceptive packaging, because what's called a module is basically just a class with static methods, properties, and members that cannot be instantiated, like a class with a constructor marked with the access modifier *Private*, or an abstract class). For the record:

- A module cannot be instantiated; neither can an abstract class or a class with a private constructor.

- A module cannot provide overridable procedures; neither can static procedures of a class.

- A module can provide only procedures, which can be accessed only directly, without an object instance. The same applies to the static procedures of an abstract class or of a class with a private constructor.

There are a few subtle distinctions. For example, modules cannot implement interfaces; classes can, but they can't define *static* interface members. In reality, this apparent difference isn't really a difference. A module can also only be defined on the top tier and can't be nested in others.

It's recommended that you use modules sparingly for OOP, because they don't create reusable code.

This book therefore uses modules only for "quick and dirty" projects, such as console applications that perform tests, or for quick demonstration applications, as you have seen in the previous chapters.

Singleton Classes and Self-Instantiating Classes

Assume you want to design a class to facilitate output to the screen or printer. What's special in this case is that you must have control over the instantiation of this class. It's not enough to leave the number of instantiations to the class itself. After all, a certain printer exists only once, and can't have multiple instances of the same class in memory.

An abstract class with static procedures (or a module) could possibly be an alternative, but the problem is that neither the functions of a module nor the static function of an abstract class can be overridden in other classes.

The solution is *Singleton* classes. Unlike the different variants of classes to which you have been introduced so far, *Singleton* classes are not "built-in" class types of the CLR or of .NET Framework, they are a so called "pattern." You need to develop them yourself—but fortunately, that's a lot easier than you might think.

> **Companion Content** Open the corresponding solution (.sln), which you can find in the
> \VB 2010 Developer Handbook\Chapter 10\Singleton folder.

```vb
Imports System.Threading

Module mdlMain

    Dim varModule As Integer = 5

    Sub New()

    End Sub

    Sub Main()
        Dim locSingleton As Singleton = Singleton.GetInstance()
        Dim locSingleton2 As Singleton = Singleton.GetInstance()

        Console.WriteLine(locSingleton Is locSingleton2)
        Console.WriteLine()
        Console.WriteLine("Press key to exit!")
        Console.ReadKey()
    End Sub

    Property test() As Integer
        Get

        End Get
        Set(ByVal Value As Integer)

        End Set
    End Property

End Module

Class Singleton

    Private Shared locSingleton As Singleton
    Private Shared locMutex As New Mutex

    'Constructor is private,
    'thus the class can only be instantiated by itself
    Private Sub New()
    End Sub

    'GetInstance retruns a Singleton instance
    'The class can only be instantated by this function
    Public Shared Function GetInstance() As Singleton
        'Make the process thread-safe
        'Waits until an different thread which
```

```
            'instantiates this class is finished
            locMutex.WaitOne()
            Try
                If locSingleton Is Nothing Then
                    locSingleton = New Singleton
                End If
            Finally
                'Instantiation complete,
                '...can continue...
                locMutex.ReleaseMutex()
            End Try

            'Return instance
            Return locSingleton

    End Function

End Class
```

The first thing you notice is that the class cannot be directly instantiated, because its constructor is private. So how do you create an instance of the class?

The answer is the static function, *GetInstance*. It ensures that the class instantiates itself, if necessary. At the same time it ensures that the instantiation process of the class is thread-safe, because .NET Framework permits the implementation of true multitasking in your programs. Multitasking involves situations wherein several tasks within a program (or several programs) can be performed simultaneously.

The private constructor prevents outside callers from instantiating the class, but because the point is to create one, and only one, instance of the singleton class, it must also prevent two different callers from calling *GetInstance* at the same time. To do that, the class uses a *Mutex* instance.

Note Mutex is derived from **mut**ual **ex**clusion.

Note Unless you are using multithreaded programming techniques, you don't need to worry about this issue. You'll see more about this topic in Chapter 28, "Programming with the Task Parallel Library (TPL)."

The main program checks the functionality of the *Singleton* class. It grabs an instance with *GetInstance* and saves it in an object variable. It repeats this process with further object variables and then compares the two "instances" with *Is*.

And indeed, the program displays *True* on the screen, because the *Singleton* class has created only *one* instance of itself—both object variables therefore point to the same instance.

Chapter 11
Developing Value Types

Chapter 8, "Class Begins," discussed designing compound value types with the *Structure* keyword as well as reference types based on custom classes. This chapter explores value types in more detail and dives a little deeper into real-life situations that involve value types. We will show you how to develop a reusable component that you can use in your own applications. also In addition, we'll discusses special details about value types, such as how to exactly control the storage sequence of field variables within a structure, and what constructors in value types are all about.

A Practical Example of Structures

A class produces a reference type, and a structure produces a value type. In principle, a structure is created exactly the same way as a class, and both have similar capabilities, as the example that follows demonstrates.

This section discusses techniques to convert values between different numeric systems. The Microsoft .NET Framework supports some conversions, but not all possible combinations. For example, you can convert a hexadecimal value into a decimal number by using the static *Parse* function, as follows:

```
Dim AnInteger As Integer = Integer.Parse("FFFF", Globalization.NumberStyles.HexNumber)
```

The other option available to you is to use the *ToInt* function or the *ToString* function of the *Convert* class, for example:

```
Dim AnInteger as Integer = Convert.ToInt32(OtherNumericSystemString, NumericSystemInteger)
```

You can also convert a string that contains a number from any supported numeric system back into an integer. However, you can only convert a number of the base-2, the base-8, and of course the base-10 and base-16 system by using *NumericSystemInteger*. The limits apply to converting an integer value into a different numeric system, which is then represented as a string. The following statement converts the integer variable *ConvertInteger* into a different numeric system defined by *NumericSystemInteger* (only 2, 8, 10, or 16 are valid values here):

```
Dim OtherNumericSystemString as String = Convert.ToString(ConvertInteger,
NumericSystemInteger)
```

But there are a few techniques for creating a value type that can handle any conversion (not just to and from the numeric systems supported by the .NET Framework).

> **Companion Content** Open the corresponding solution (.sln), which you can find in the
> \VB 2010 Developer Handbook\Chapter 11\Structure01 folder.

For example, you can even take advantage of the base-32 system.[1] You think you've never used it? Maybe you have: when installing any Microsoft product, you have to enter an installation key, which is generated, of course, with the help of an algorithm. Actually, the algorithm is probably based less on the processing of letters than with the numeric calculation of them. The *Ulong* value (64-bit, without prefix, has existed since Visual Basic 2005), which saves the result of the serial number algorithm could therefore, for example, be converted based on the duotrigesimal system (base-32 system) into a string. Thus, the number:

9.223.372.036.854.775.807

would look as follows in this numeric system:

7VVVVVVVVVVVV

And the number:

9.153.672.076.852.735.401

would appear (to show another example) as follows:

7U23085PJGBD9

---

[1] The best name would really be "duotrigesimal system," but it has no historical validation. Without any guarantee that this link will still work when this book is going to print, you can learn about the naming conventions of numeric systems at *http://tinyurl.com/35c4e6*. A little bit of info on the side: the hexadecimal system isn't named very consistently, because it was derived from a Greek and a Latin root ("Hexa" Greek; "decem" Latin). Strictly speaking it should be "sedecimal" or "sexadecimal." The abbreviation for hexadecimal is "hex," so we can be thankful for the Greek-Latin combo.

And here's the code sample for the structure *NumberSystems*, as explained previously:

```
Public Structure NumberSystems

    Private myUnderlyingValue As ULong
    Private myNumberSystem As Integer
    Private Shared myDigits As Char()

    Shared Sub New()
        myDigits = New Char() {"0"c, "1"c, "2"c, "3"c, "4"c, "5"c, "6"c, "7"c, _
                               "8"c, "9"c, "A"c, "B"c, "C"c, "D"c, "E"c, "F"c, _
                               "G"c, "H"c, "I"c, "J"c, "K"c, "L"c, "M"c, "N"c, _
                               "O"c, "P"c, "Q"c, "R"c, "S"c, "T"c, "U"c, "V"c, _
                               "W"c, "X"c, "Y"c, "Z"c}
    End Sub
```

The conversion table is saved in a static array that is initialized in the static constructor of the structure. The constructor is overloaded; you can pass an *Integer* value or a *ULong* value, or a *ULong* value and a parameter that specifies the numeric system that you want to work with (up to the base-33 system):

```
Sub New(ByVal Value As Integer)
    Me.New(CULng(Value), 16)
End Sub

Sub New(ByVal Value As ULong)
    Me.New(Value, 16)
End Sub

Sub New(ByVal Value As ULong, ByVal NumberSystem As Integer)

    myUnderlyingValue = Value
    If NumberSystem < 2 OrElse NumberSystem > 33 Then
        Dim BaseNumberSystemException As Exception = New OverflowException _
            ("Identifying number of the numeric systems outside " &
            "the valid range!")
        'No joke:
        'Throw  BaseNumberSystemException
    End If
    myNumberSystem = NumberSystem

End Sub

Public Property Value() As ULong

    Get
        Return myUnderlyingValue
    End Get
    Set(ByVal Value As ULong)
        myUnderlyingValue = Value
    End Set

End Property
```

The *Value* property only serves to newly specify or query the value saved for the conversion into the respective numeric system.

```
Public Property NumberSystem() As Integer
    Get
        Return myNumberSystem
    End Get
    Set(ByVal Value As Integer)
        If Value < 2 OrElse Value > 33 Then
            Dim BaseNumberSystemException As Exception = New OverflowException _
                ("Identifying number of the numeric systems outside the valid range!")
            Throw  BaseNumberSystemException
        End If
        myNumberSystem = Value
    End Set
End Property
```

The *NumberSystem* property is used to specify or query the numeric system into which you want to convert later on.

```
Public Overrides Function ToString() As String

    Dim locResult As String = ""
    Dim locValue As ULong = myUnderlyingValue

    Do
        Dim digit As Integer = CInt(locValue Mod NumberSystem)
        locResult = CStr(myDigits(digit)) & locResult
        locValue \= CULng(NumberSystem)
    Loop Until locValue = 0

    Return locResult

End Function
```

The *ToString* method proceeds according to the following algorithm to determine the characters (numerals) for the specified numeric system. First, it copies the original value into a temporary variable to ensure that the *Value* property isn't destroyed—that variable will be changed later. Next, the method *ToString* performs a remainder value division with the *Mod* function, which doesn't provide the result of the division, just the remainder value.

An example in the base-10 system will help you understand this operation:

If you divide the value 129 by 10, the result is 12 with a remainder of 9. This 9 is important here, because this is the least significant digit (the one on the far right) of the result. Then the value is divided by the base number of the numeric system—10 in this example—resulting in 12. Because the result of the division (not the remainder) is larger than 0, the process is repeated. The remainder value of the division is determined again, and this time it's 2. The 2 is the second least significant digit. This loop is repeated until all digits (or numerals) are calculated. The numerals are read from the *myDigits* array, the static array created by the structure's static constructor when it is used for the first time.

> **Note** In this example, you will find several conversions of value types into others with the help of Cxxx operators. Chapter 12, "Typecasting and Boxing Value Types," presents more information about those, but here's what you need for now: a conversion of the data type *Integer* into the data type *ULong* by using *CULng* is necessary in the preceding code (see the line highlighted in bold) so that the division can take place across the entire 64-bit width. Without this conversion, Visual Basic would initiate a standard 32-bit integer division—which can't work with the 64-bit wide *ULong* variable *locValue*.

```vb
Public Shared Function Parse(ByVal Value As String,
    ByVal NumberSystem As Integer) As NumberSystems

    'Here the value is constructed
    Dim locValue As ULong

    For count As Integer = 0 To Value.Length - 1
        Try
            'Current character in the string, which is processed
            Dim locTmpChar As String = Value.Substring(count, 1)

            'Use binary search to find the character in the array and
            'therefore the digit number
            Dim locDigitValue As Integer = CInt(Array.BinarySearch(
                myDigits, CChar(locTmpChar)))

            'Check whether the character is within the valid range
            If locDigitValue >= NumberSystem OrElse locDigitValue < 0 Then
                Dim BaseNumberSystemException As Exception = New FormatException _
                    ("The number '" & locTmpChar & "' is not part of the " &
                     "numeric system!")
                Throw BaseNumberSystemException
            End If

            'Create the power of the found digit number and add to the total value
            locValue += CULng(Math.Pow(NumberSystem, Value.Length - count - 1) *
                        locDigitValue)

        Catch ex As Exception
            'In case something goes wrong in between
            Dim BaseNumberSystemException As Exception = New InvalidCastException _
                ("The digit of the numeric system is outside the valid range!")
            Throw BaseNumberSystemException
        End Try
        'process next character
    Next

    Return New NumberSystems(locValue, NumberSystem)

End Function
End Structure
```

The *Parse* function is a static function (just like the *Parse* functions of many other data types in the Common Language Runtime [CLR]) that serves to convert a string, which represents a value in a specific numeric system, into a *NumberSystem*-value. It follows this formula:

NumeralValue = DigitValue × NumericSystemBaseValue$^{\text{DigitPosition}-1}$

Digit values range from 0–33 (digits from 0–9, followed by the alphabet in capital letters from A–Z). The function iterates from the beginning to the end through the characters of the string to be converted and determines the digit value with the static *BinarySearch* function of the *Array* class. It is the value of a multiplier of the product. The other multiplier results from raising the base value of the numeric system to the power of the digit position.

The example is meant to help you understand the algorithm better—this time by a conversion from the hexadecimal system:

Consider the number "F3E." To convert it, the function determines the digit value for "F," which corresponds to the value 15. Because it is the third character in the string (read back to front), 16 is raised to the power of 2 (F is the digit in position 1), which results in 256, and is multiplied by 15. The result is 3840. Now the second digit: the value is 3, and the exponent is 1, because it is the second character of the string. The result, 48, added to the previous value results in 3888. Finally, the last digit: the exponent[2] is 0, therefore the product is the digit value (multiplication by one doesn't change anything) which is 14 for "E". The "14" is added to the extension, for a total of 3902.

The main program of this sample project and the structure are located in two different files. Double-clicking NumberSystems.vb in Project Explorer opens the source code of the structure; mdlMain.vb contains the module for the main program, as shown below:

```
Module mdlMain

    Sub Main()

        Dim locLong As ULong
        locLong = &HFFFFFFFFFFFFFFFFUL
        Dim locNS As New NumberSystems(locLong)
        Console.WriteLine("{0:#,##0} corresponds to:", locLong)

        locNS.NumberSystem = 2  : Console.WriteLine("Binary: " & locNS.ToString)
        locNS.NumberSystem = 8  : Console.WriteLine("Octal: " & locNS.ToString)
        locNS.NumberSystem = 10 : Console.WriteLine("Decimal: " & locNS.ToString)
        locNS.NumberSystem = 16 : Console.WriteLine("Hexadecimal: " & locNS.ToString)
        locNS.NumberSystem = 32 : Console.WriteLine("Duotrigesimal: " & locNS.ToString)

        'Backwards:
        Console.WriteLine()
        Console.WriteLine("Counter-example:")
        Console.Write("'7U23085PJGBD9' duotrigesimal corresponds to decimal: ")
```

---

[2] Any value raised to the power of 0 is 1.

```
        locNS = NumberSystems.Parse("7U23085PJGBD9", 32)
        Console.WriteLine(locNS.Value)

        Console.WriteLine()
        Console.WriteLine("Press Return to exit")
        Console.ReadLine()
    End Sub
End Module
```

When you start the program, you see the following output:

```
18.446.744.073.709.551.615 corresponds to:
Binary: 1111111111111111111111111111111111111111111111111111111111111111
Octal: 1777777777777777777777
Decimal: 18446744073709551615
Hexadecimal: FFFFFFFFFFFFFFFF
Duotrigesimal: FVVVVVVVVVVV

Counter-example:
'7U23085PJGBD9' duotrigesimal corresponds to decimal: 9153672076852735401

Press Return to exit
```

Passing Value and Reference Parameters

You might wish to pass a value type to a procedure as a reference with the keyword *ByRef*. In this case, the data itself is not copied to the stack, but only a pointer to the corresponding storage location in the stack. Changes to other data within the procedure are directly reflected in the original variable. Changing the reference parameters within the *called* procedure changes the variable value in the *calling* program, as well. Here's an example:

```
Dim ValueType1 as New NumberSystems(10)
TakesValueType(ValueType1)
Console.WriteLine(ValueType1.Value)
Dim ValueType2 as NumberSystems = ValueType1
ValueType2.Value = 50
Console.WriteLine(ValueType1.Value)
.
.
.
Sub TakesValueType(ByRef ValueType As NumberSystems)

    ValueType.Value = 99

End Sub
```

Passing something via *ByRef* can make sense, for example, if you want to return several pieces of information to the parent program. A function returns a single value. But how would you communicate in a function with the main program when you want to pass a string to a function that converts this string into a number? On the one hand, you need to know

whether this was possible at all (the function returns *True* or *False*), but on the other hand you need to know the converted value in a number variable.

The .NET Framework solves the problem like this: The type *Int32* (the default Visual Basic *Integer* data type) provides, for example, the static method *TryParse*, which expects the convertible string as the first parameter. As the second parameter, it expects an *Integer* variable *ByRef*, which is set to the converted value within the function. The function returns *True* or *False* (whether the conversion succeeded). The following example shows how this works:

```
Dim retValue As Integer
If Integer.TryParse("456123", retValue) Then
    MessageBox.Show("String was converted:" & retValue)
End If
```

> **Note** *ByVal* and *ByRef* impact the passing of reference type parameters. They do this not when changing the object content, but when assigning object variables to other object instances. When you pass an object variable (a reference) with *ByRef* and within the procedure assign a new instance to the object variable, the instance from the calling procedure is also changed. This is not the case with *ByVal*.

Constructors and Default Instantiations of Value Types

Because no structure instances can exist without data, the CLR automatically creates a corresponding data instance when a structure is defined—regardless of whether *New* was used to instantiate the structure. The following example illustrates this point:

```
Dim AValue As NumberSystems
Dim AReference As ReferenceType

AValue.Value = 10
AReference.Value = 10
```

These lines execute with no problems until the last line, which triggers an exception because you are trying to change the property of an object that doesn't exist on the Managed Heap, as illustrated in Figure 11-1.

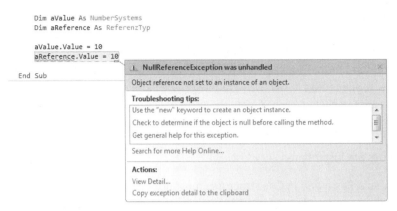

FIGURE 11-1 Trying to change a property of an object that was not instantiated causes an exception.

No Default Constructor Code for Value Types

Structures in Visual Basic have no default constructors. A default constructor in Visual Basic is a *Sub New* that doesn't accept parameters. Therefore, the following construct is faulty:

```
Public Structure TestValueType

    Private myTestProperty As String

    'Error: A constructor without parameters which is not declared as "Shared"
    'cannot be declared in a structure.
    Sub New()
        myTestProperty = "Pre-initialized"
    End Sub

    'That's OK:
    Sub New(ByVal Specification As String)
        myTestProperty = Specification
    End Sub

    Property TestProperty() As String
        Get
            Return myTestProperty
        End Get
        Set(ByVal Value As String)
            myTestProperty = Value
        End Set
    End Property

End Structure
```

Structures construct value types, and value types work very differently (when it comes to constructors and initializers) than you have seen so far with reference types, which are constructed from classes. The CLR always creates instances of value types, and there is no way to prevent that (remember that for classes a private constructor was enough). As you have seen, value types are implemented in the .NET Framework because developers need data structures that work extremely fast. In summary:

- Value types are always instantiated without initializers.

- Value types are instantiated very fast.

Therefore, in Visual Basic (and in C#), structures must not have a default constructor; otherwise, the developer might be under the impression that she has influence on *when* this default constructor is called. Because the .NET Framework can't guarantee (due to performance issues) that the constructors will be used during instantiation, developer-made default constructors are not be permitted. The instantiation of value types defined with structures happens differently than instantiation of regular classes defined with *Class*. Classes can be instantiated only with the keyword *New*, after which they can be used. Structures don't need to be instantiated with *New* when they are used for the first time—they're instantiated implicitly. The following construct is therefore permitted:

```
'No instantiation with New...
Dim tvt As TestValueType
'...but it still exists:
tvt.TestProperty = "Test"
```

As soon as a value type is defined implicitly .NET Framework ensures that all its field variables are assigned their default values (for example 0 for numeric types, *False* for *Boolean*, and so on). This doesn't necessarily happen when the data type is instantiated, but perhaps just before its first use.

An implicit default constructor might not take effect or not take effect early enough. Because the Framework controls value types, Visual Basic prohibits the use of default constructors with value types to ensure the integrity of variable values.

When to Use Value Types—When to Use Reference Types

You have already learned that value types were created primarily for better performance. For applications that need to process data extremely fast, it makes sense to use or create data types that can move easily within the computer's memory. Some examples include:

- An image requires a large amount of memory when it is loaded from the hard drive into main memory. The memory where an image is stored should of course be set up as a reference type. However, coordinates that define positions on the image and are incorporated into the algorithms for calculating the image should be stored as value types because they need to work quickly.

- Datasets that you need to keep in memory (for example, for contact management applications) require a lot of space. Therefore, they should be set up as reference types. But a data structure that simply creates a link between a dataset ID and a search key makes more sense as a value type.

- Should you be so ambitious as to program your own web browser, the data of an HTML page would, of course, be set up as a reference type. However, an element in a DNS list containing IP address and host headers might make more sense as a value type.

- Value types make sense when you want to add additional primitive data types to existing primitive data types. For example, beginning with version 2008, Microsoft SQL Server recognizes geographical data. Not only are these geographical types completely implemented in Managed .NET code, but they are also value types based on structures.

- New numeric types that represent numeric systems other than the decimal system would also make sense as value types.

It's clear that whenever you need to process small amounts of data, it makes sense to create value types based on a structure. As the data types become more complex or are themselves based on reference types, you should instead use reference types based on a class.

Targeted Memory Assignment for Structure Members with the Attributes *StructLayout* and *FieldOffset*

Structures permit a targeted placement of memory areas for field variables. It's important to mark the structure with a special attribute and thus instruct the compiler how to overlap the memory areas of the various field variables.

This possibility makes working with the different byte significance of integer values very easy. Integer numbers are composed of bytes, as you know. A number of the data type *Short* is stored in 2 bytes, an *Integer* in 4 bytes, and a *Long* in 8 bytes. For signed integer values, the highest bit is used as the sign. If that bit is set, the value is negative; otherwise, it is positive. It is relatively labor-intensive to extract numeric types from other larger numeric types. For example, a *Long* is composed of two 32-bit integer values: a high-value *DWord* (a *Word* corresponds to two bytes, and a *DWord*—a Double Word—corresponds to two *Word*s, and therefore four bytes) and a low-value *DWord*. If you want to find out the numeric value of the high-value *DWord*, you can either calculate it or read it from memory, which is much faster, of course.

So what exactly do you need this for? 32-bit graphics, for example, save 3 colors per pixel and an alpha value in four bytes altogether or as unsigned 32-bit integer value (*UInteger* in Visual Basic). In the manner explained in the following, you can, for example, create a structure that is based on an *Integer* value. Appropriate properties within the structure could return the individual color values of a pixel as bytes, without a single line of calculation.

As another common usage example, some of the Windows operating system functions you can call from .NET programs pack a combination of parameters into a single data type with many bits. One parameter is located in the high-value bytes, the other in the low-value bytes.

For example, the unsigned *Long* value *$FFFFAABB00FF* consists of two *DWord*s: *$0000FFFF* and *$AABB00FF*. To determine the value of the upper *DWord*, you need to mask it first with *$FFFFFFFF00000000* (perform a logical *AND* operation) and then move the 32 bits to the right. Alternatively, you can read the upper 32 bits directly from the memory, because you can assign this portion of the *Long* variable specifically to an *Integer* variable.

You must meet two preconditions, though. First, you must ensure that the field variables of a structure define their required memory exactly in the order in which they appear in the source code. The attribute *StructLayout* takes care of this. Second, you need to specify with the attribute *FieldOffset* exactly which place on the processor stack the memory of a field variable should start (always calculated from 0). This way you can ensure that field variables of different types can overlap, and then specifically access the memory of the field variable of a certain type, "disguised as a different type," so to speak, such as extracting the upper *DWord* of an unsigned *Long* value.

The basic approach to creating such a structure is shown in the sample program that follows. You can use it as a template and extend it to match your specific requirements.

> **Companion Content** Open the corresponding solution (.sln), which you can find in the \VB 2010 Developer Handbook\Chapter 11\StructLayout folder.

The structure defined below is called *LongEx*. It lets you define a 64-bit value and retrieve the value as a signed or unsigned long, or as a partial value in the form of high- or low-value 32-bit integer values (also either signed or unsigned):

```
'Inform that the order of the
'byte definitions must be followed strictly!
<StructLayout(LayoutKind.Explicit)> _
Public Structure LongEx
    <FieldOffset(0)> Private myUnsignedLong As ULong
    <FieldOffset(0)> Private mySignedLong As Long
    <FieldOffset(0)> Private myLowUnsignedInt As UInteger
    <FieldOffset(4)> Private myHighUnsignedInt As UInteger
    <FieldOffset(0)> Private myLowSignedInt As Integer
    <FieldOffset(4)> Private myHighSignedInt As Integer
```

The *<StructLayout>* attribute at the beginning of the structure specifies that the order of the member definitions (the order of their memory addresses) must be strictly adhered to. The *FieldOffset* attribute that appears before each member allows the memory areas for the corresponding field variables to overlap. Thus the *FieldOffset* attribute specifies the memory address in the stack where the data of a data type should be placed. This memory address is specified relative to the start position of the structure itself.

> **Important** Structures can also contain reference types. Because in this case, the structure saves pointers to the actual data, there might be a great risk of "bending" the pointer to a reference type with *FieldOffset*—and is that something .NET Framework prohibits adamantly, because such behavior would cause code to become type-unsafe and destroy the entire memory concept. Therefore, if you work with *FieldOffset*, you can use only value types as field variables. At the same time, this excludes the use of arrays, because an array variable also just represents the pointer (a reference) to the actual array data.

The remaining property procedures are only used for reading the field variable in the usual manner:

```
Sub New(ByVal Value As ULong)
    myUnsignedLong = Value
End Sub

Sub New(ByVal Value As Long)
    mySignedLong = Value
End Sub

Sub New(ByVal value As UInteger)
    myLowUnsignedInt = value
End Sub

Sub New(ByVal value As Integer)
    myLowSignedInt = value
End Sub

Public Property Value() As ULong
    Get
        Return myUnsignedLong
    End Get
    Set(ByVal value As ULong)
        myUnsignedLong = value
    End Set
End Property

Public ReadOnly Property SignedLong() As Long
    Get
        Return mySignedLong
    End Get
End Property

Public ReadOnly Property HighUnsignedInt() As UInteger
    Get
        Return myHighUnsignedInt
    End Get
End Property
```

```
    Public ReadOnly Property LowUnsignedInt() As UInteger
        Get
            Return myLowUnsignedInt
        End Get
    End Property

    Public ReadOnly Property HighSignedInt() As Integer
        Get
            Return myHighSignedInt
        End Get
    End Property

    Public ReadOnly Property LowSignedInt() As Integer
        Get
            Return myLowSignedInt
        End Get
    End Property
End Structure
```

Chapter 12
Typecasting and Boxing Value Types

In many cases, you'll need to convert variables of one type into different types. This process is called *Typecasting* (as in giving it a role to play), and it includes:

- The physical conversion of a concrete value into another type—data is processed, analyzed, and saved at a different location.

- Assigning an object variable to a different object variable of a different but derived type (a type that's based on the first variable's class). For example, an object variable of the parent class *FirstClass* can be set to reference an instance of the *SecondClass* class, which presumably inherits from the *FirstClass* class.

- The process of "*boxing*" (as in *packing into a box*) or "*unboxing.*" During boxing, a value type is converted into a reference type so that it can be referenced by an object variable of the appropriate type. Boxing becomes necessary when a value type must be handled like a reference type. It's actually possible to treat an *Integer* or *String* as an object.

Companion Content Open the corresponding solution (.sln), which you can find in the \VB 2010 Developer Handbook\Chapter 12\Casting folder.

Converting Primitive Types

In Visual Basic, there are several possibilities for converting a base data type into a different type. The easiest way to do this is to make a direct assignment, which, assuming *Option Strict* is *On*, won't work with all data types, as shown in the following example:

```
Dim AnInteger as Integer=1000
Dim ALong as Long
'An Integer value can be converted to a Long value implicitly
ALong=AnInteger
```

During this process, an implicit conversion of a value of an *Integer* variable into a *Long* variable takes place. This is possible implicitly (by a simple assignment), because during this process no accuracy is lost. The *Long* data type can store a much larger numeric range than *Intege;*. therefore, all possible *Integer* values can easily be saved as *Long* values. The Integer data type is said to be "widened," because it's now stored in a variable with larger (wider) range. With *Option Strict* set to *On*, however, you can't perform the opposite conversion, as shown here:

```
Dim AnInteger As Integer
Dim ALong As Long = Integer.MaxValue + 1L
'Long cannot be converted without loss; implicit conversion isn't possible!
AnInteger = ALong
```

When you enter this code, the Editor generates a warning after you leave the last line. The reason is that Visual Basic cannot guarantee a conversion of this type without loss of accuracy, so it issues a warning. Unlike converting an *Integer* value to a *Long*, this conversion is a narrowing one: you're trying to map a value of a type with a wider range to a type with a narrower range. Narrowing conversions are not performed automatically when *Option Strict* is *On*. You can always perform the conversion explicitly, and you have the following options with which to do it:

- You use *CInt* to convert a *Long* into an *Integer* type, like this:

  ```
  'Int cannot be converted without loss; explicit conversion is required!
  AnInteger = CInt(ALong)
  ```

- You can use the *CType* built-in function for the same process. *CType* basically works similarly to *CInt*, but it's not limited to converting to the *Integer* type. Therefore, the second parameter specifies the type into which you want to convert the object specified by the first parameter:

  ```
  'Long cannot be converted without loss; explicit conversion is required!
  AnInteger = CType(ALong, Integer)
  ```

- As a final option you can use the *Convert* class of the .NET Framework—however, this is also the slowest method. Beginning with Visual Basic 2005, the Visual Basic compiler ensures that *Cxxx* or *CType* operations always use the fastest conversion option. Visual Basic 2002 and 2003 were not as highly optimized—in some cases, using the *Convert* class was even preferable to the built-in *Cxxx* or *CType* operations. Calling with the *Convert* class, which is now at least 1.5 times slower, looks as follows:

```
'Long cannot be converted without loss; explicit conversion is required!
AnInteger = Convert.ToInt32(ALong)
```

Theoretically, you have yet one more conversion option: you can set *Option Strict* to *Off* and let Visual Basic take care of the conversion into the desired data type at runtime. However, when using this approach, the Editor does not produce a warning—even when loss of accuracy occurs during conversion. We strongly advise against using this option!

> **Note** If you change the definition of the initial value, as shown in the following statement, you will receive an exception (see Figure 12-1). That's because you are trying to convert a value that simply can't be converted, as demonstrated here:
>
> ```
> Dim ALong As Long = Integer.MaxValue + 1L
> ```
>
> The value to be converted is set to the largest possible value that can be represented by the *Integer* data type plus one. This value exceeds the capacity of the *Integer* data type, and you get a warning.
>
> ```
> Sub Main()
>
>     Dim anInteger As Integer
>     'Dim aLong As Long = 1000
>     Dim aLong As Long = Inte
>     'anInteger = aLong
>     anInteger = CInt(aLong)
>     anInteger = CType(aLong,
>     anInteger = Convert.ToIn
> ```
> ┌──┐
> │ ⓘ **OverflowException was unhandled**   ✕ │
> ├──┤
> │ Arithmetic operation resulted in an overflow.   │
> │   │
> │ **Troubleshooting tips:**   │
> │ ┌──────────────────────────────────────┐   ▲ │
> │ │Make sure you are not dividing by zero.│   │
> │ └──────────────────────────────────────┘   ▤ │
> │ Get general help for this exception.   │
> │   ▼ │
> │   │
> │ Search for more Help Online...   │
> │   │
> │ **Actions:**   │
> │ View Detail...   │
> │ Copy exception detail to the clipboard   │
> └──┘
> ```
>     Dim aStringWithDate As S
>     Dim anOtherStringWithDat
>     Dim aStringWithDouble As
>     Dim aDate As DateTime
>     Dim aDouble As Double
>
>     'An Array of possible da
>     Dim DateformattingFormat
> ```
>
> **FIGURE 12-1** When casting between data types, you need to ensure that the conversion won't generate overflow errors.

Converting to and from Strings

Of course, converting primitive data types isn't restricted to numeric types. What's more interesting is the conversion of a string into a numeric value or a date value, and vice versa. This is a very common operation, as most applications allow users to enter numeric values into *TextBox* controls, which contain strings, not numbers.

You can always perform the conversion by using the methods discussed in the preceding section. Here are a few examples:

```
Dim AStringWithDate As String = "24.12.2003"
Dim ADate As DateTime

ADate = CDate(AStringWithDate)
ADate = CType(AStringWithDate, DateTime)
ADate = Convert.ToDateTime(AStringWithDate)
```

Converting Strings by Using the *Parse* and *ParseExact* Method

There is another possibility that provides more flexibility. The *DateTime* structure[1] has a static method called *Parse*,[2] which can convert a string containing a date into a *DateTime* value. The *Parse* function contains several overloads for flexibility. Starting with its simpler form, you can specify a format provider, which defines the resulting desired date format so that the conversion method can handle days and months properly. You can use an optional third parameter to indicate a specific tolerance during string analysis.

To gain even more control, use the *ParseExact* method. With this method, you can use a string array with input patterns as a rule for the string analysis. For example, suppose that you want to create an input field in a program without strictly enforcing the date input format "dd.MM.yy" so that the field also accepts the alternative input formats "ddMMyy" or "ddMM." In this case, you would use the *ParseExact* method to convert the date value. Here the .NET Framework takes care of all the analysis work, and converts the string into a date value according to your specifications, or it generates an exception that you can catch when the user doesn't enter the date in one of the acceptable formats.

What you have learned about strings so far applies to numeric data types, as well. The numeric classes (*Integer*, *Double*, *Decimal*) each provide their own *Parse* method for converting numbers, which is much more flexible than the previously introduced alternatives.

---

[1] This structure corresponds exactly to the *Date* data type of Visual Basic; therefore, it doesn't matter whether you write *Date.Parse* or *DateTime.Parse*.

[2] To parse pretty much means to analyze.

> **Note** The *ParseExact* method is not available for numeric data types.

The next section shows how to use these methods.

Converting Into Strings by Using the *ToString* Method

The counterpart to *Parse* is the *ToString* method. Basically, you can convert any variable content with the *ToString* method into a string—at least as far as primitive data types, such as *Date, Integer, Double, Decimal*, and so on are concerned. The .NET Framework contains solid support for formatting numbers and date values—a glance at the .NET Framework Help (press F1) for how each object functions is definitely called for.

The following program sections provide you with a brief overview of the *Parse, ParseExact*, and *ToString* methods and show you how to call them in your code. You will find them in many other places in the book.

```
Dim AStringWithDate As String = "24122003"
Dim ADifferentStringWithDate As String = "2412"
Dim AStringWithDouble As String = "1.123,23 €"
Dim ADate As DateTime
Dim ADouble As Double

'An array with possible date formats for Date.ParseExact
Dim DateFormattingFormats() As String = New String() {"ddMMyyyy", "ddMM"}

'Examples for date conversion
ADate = DateTime.ParseExact(AStringWithDate, _
                            DateFormattingFormats, _
                            Nothing, _
                            Globalization.DateTimeStyles.AllowWhiteSpaces)
Console.WriteLine("Date " & ADate.ToString("ddd, dd.MMM.yyyy"))

ADate = DateTime.ParseExact(ADifferentStringWithDate, _
                            DateFormattingFormats, _
                            Nothing, _
                            Globalization.DateTimeStyles.AllowWhiteSpaces)
Console.WriteLine("Date " & ADate.ToString("ddd, dd.MMM.yyyy"))

'Number examples
ADouble = Double.Parse(AStringWithDouble, Globalization.NumberStyles.Currency)
Console.WriteLine("Value " & ADouble.ToString("#,###.## Euro"))
```

Catching Type Conversion Failures

When you unleash your application to real users, you have no idea what they might throw at it, but no matter what it is, your application should be able to handle all kinds of erroneous data gracefully. Users will input unexpected data—data that you'd never try out in your tests. Therefore it makes sense to catch any errors for entered date values or numbers and inform the user, if necessary.

You have two possibilities for doing this:

- Use the *Parse* or *ParseExact* (for date values) methods and enclose them in a *Try...Catch* block. If *Parse* or *ParseExact* trigger an exception, which would be the case with an incorrect format, you catch the exception in the *Catch* block, return an appropriate error message, and then let the user try again.

- Use the static method *TryParse*, which has also been available for all numeric data types since Visual Basic 2005. *TryParse* does not return the actual parsed value as the function result, but instead returns *True* or *False*. If the result is *True*, the parse operation was successful. *TryParse* returns the converted value through a variable passed to the method by reference. If the conversion fails, the method returns *False* and you ignore the second argument.

The following example demonstrates these two approaches:

```
'This is how you catch faulty input formats:

'Version 1: With TryParse (for date and numeric types)
If Double.TryParse("1.234,56", ADouble) Then
    Console.WriteLine("String could be parsed. Result: " & ADouble.ToString)
Else
    Console.WriteLine("String could not be parsed!")
End If

'Version 2: With exception handling
Try
    'This can't work!
    ADatum = DateTime.ParseExact("2005_12_24", _
                    DateFormattingFormats, _
                    Nothing, _
                    Globalization.DateTimeStyles.AllowWhiteSpaces)

Catch ex As Exception
    Console.WriteLine("Parsing generates an exception:" & vbNewLine & _
        ex.Message)
End Try
```

Casting Reference Types by Using *DirectCast*

When you work with custom classes, the need to convert derived reference types to their base types is quite common. Consider the *DerivedClass,* which inherits from *AClass.* You define an object variable of the type *AClass,* but assign an instance of the *DerivedClass* to it. This is what makes polymorphism such a powerful programming technique (see Chapter 10, "Class Inheritance and Polymorphism").

Now you need a function that is provided only by *DerivedClass.* Because you are dealing with an instance of this class, the necessary function is generally available—but you can't access it with the object variable that you're using. The *DirectCast* method lets you set the reference to the object instance to point to an object variable of the "correct" type. Then you can call the method of the parent class.

The following code segment demonstrates this technique:

```
'Class casting
Dim locAClass As AClass
Dim locDerivedClass As DerivedClase = New DerivedClass

'Implicit casting is possible, because in the inheritance hierarchy it moves towards base
'class
locAClass = locDerivedClass

'Doesn't work; function isn't present.
'locAClass.AddValues()

'Doesn't work either; it moves further down in the inheritance hierarchy,
'and then implicit conversion isn't possible:
'locDerivedClass = locAClass

'This works:
locDerivedClass = DirectCast(locAClass, DerivedClass)
locDerivedClass.AddValues()

Console.WriteLine("KDerived: " & locDerivedClass.ToString())
Console.WriteLine("KValuePair: " & locAClass.ToString())
```

In this example you could also use *CType* and replace the line

```
locDerivedClass = DirectCast(locAClass, DerivedClass)
```

with

```
locDerivedClass = CType(locAClass, DerivedClass)
```

However, it's recommended that you always use *DirectCast* for reference types (although there are no performance issues—internally the compiler converts *CType* into *DirectCast* anyhow). When you use *DirectCast,* you immediately realize that it is not a data conversion in the sense of primitive data types, but rather a kind of message to the compiler to regard the type in question as the type specified by the *DirectCast* method.

TryCast—Determining Whether Casting Is Possible

Because an object variable of a base class may always refer to an instance of its derivative, you might wish to find out if a specific object variable points to a derived class instance.

For example, with the *Handles* statement, you can specify that a method handles the results of several sources. In a Windows Forms application method, you can therefore process the *Click* event from several different controls in one place:

> **Companion Content** Open the corresponding solution (.sln), which you can find in the \VB 2010 Developer Handbook\Chapter 12\TryCast folder.

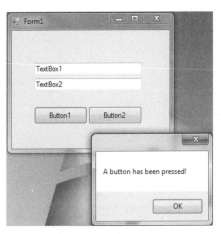

FIGURE 12-2 With *TryCast* or *IsAssignableFrom*, you can determine whether an object variable of a base class points to an instance of a type. You need this frequently when you work with controls.

When you start this example, you can click one of the text boxes or one of the buttons in the form. Each time, a message box appears informing you which type of control you clicked. So far, this is nothing special, but when you look at the code, you can see that this demo uses a common event handler to handle the *Click* event for multiple controls, as you can see in the following listing:

```
Public Class Form1

    Private Sub Control_Click(ByVal sender As Object,
                      ByVal e As System.EventArgs) _
                Handles TextBox1.Click, TextBox2.Click,
                Button1.Click, Button2.Click

        'We are handling all 4 Click events,
        'sender can point to a TextBox or a Button:
```

> **Tip** Many collections in the .NET Framework are based on *Object* arrays, and therefore, values
> are boxed during assignment. Typed collections, such as *List(Of)* or *Collection(Of)*, are based
> directly on typed arrays; thus, they don't need to box their individual elements. (You will learn
> more about collections and lists in the following chapters.) This is why they are much faster
> and consume less memory. Numeric and date values, for example, need only half the memory
> space—even less on 64-bit systems that have pointers of twice the width (8 instead of 4 bytes
> per element).

What *DirectCast* Cannot Do

DirectCast can cast reference types that box a value *back* into the value type ("unboxing"),
but it cannot cast value types. Such an operation can't work, because after all, the inheritance
hierarchy can only be cast in the direction of the parent class. Because value types cannot be
passed on, this path remains cut off.

Of course, *DirectCast* can't convert primitive data types into other primitive data types either.
Use functions *Cxxx*, *CType* (depending on data type) and the methods *Parse*, *ParseExact*, and
TryParse or (for all data types) the methods of the *Convert* class.

To Box or Not to Box

You have seen that the compiler boxes value types when they need to be converted into an
object—for example, to save then in *Object* arrays. But in some cases the boxing isn't immediately obvious. For example:

- Boxing occurs when passing a value type as a parameter to a method that expects an
  object. Its value type is first boxed into an object, and then the reference to the boxed
  value type is passed on as a parameter.

- Boxing also occurs when you implement an interface for a value type. The Common
  Language Runtime (CLR) must box the value type because interfaces are reference
  types by definition.

- Boxing occurs when you call *GetType* for a value type, because *GetType* is a method
  inherited by *Object*, which only works with reference types.

- Boxing does not occur when you call a normal method of a value type. The CLR is
  capable of jumping directly to methods that are "appended" to a value type.

■ Boxing also does not occur when you call the *ToString* function. The *ToString* function can generally be overwritten, and if this method *were* overwritten for a particular type, then of course the .NET Framework would need to call the overwritten method, not the initial method. Doing that would require a look-up in the methods table of the over-writing type, for which its type would need to be determined, which, as a reverse con-clusion, would work only if it were available as a reference type—which would mean *Boxing*! Therefore, you cannot inherit from value types, and that's the only reason why you can call the *ToString* method of a value type without first having to convert the type to a reference type.

Changing the Values of Interface-Boxed Value Types

During boxing and unboxing of value types, behaviors can occur that are hard to trace at first glance. As you saw previously, accessing a member of a value type automatically leads to the immediate boxing of the value type in question into an object. The following example demonstrates the implications of this behavior, and illustrates why such behaviors can differ significantly, even though you are dealing with the same value type instances.

> **Companion Content** Open the corresponding solution (.sln), which you can find in the
> \VB 2010 Developer Handbook\Chapter 12\Boxing folder.

```vb
Interface IMustHaveValue
    Property Value() As Integer
End Interface

Module mdlMain

    Sub Main()
        Dim AValueType As New ValueType(10)
        Dim AReferenceType As New ReferenceType(10)

        AValueType.Value = 20
        Console.WriteLine(AValueType.Value) ' 20 -> changed directly!
        ChangeValueType(AValueType)
        Console.WriteLine(AValueType.Value) ' 20 -> changed in the stack copy
        ChangeReferenceType(AReferenceType)
        Console.WriteLine(AReferenceType.Value) ' 30 -> changed on the Managed Heap

        Dim AnInterface As IMustHaveValue = AValueType
        ChangeViaInterface(AnInterface)
        Console.WriteLine(AnInterface.Value) ' 40, changed on the Managed Heap
          ' 20, but have nothing to do with each other
        Console.WriteLine(AValueType.Value)
```

```vbnet
        Console.WriteLine()
        Console.WriteLine("Press key to exit")
        Console.ReadLine()

    End Sub

    'Changes the property of the value type.
    Sub ChangeValueType(ByVal AValueType As ValueType)
        AValueType.Value = 30
    End Sub

    'Changes the property of the reference type.
    Sub ChangeReferenceType(ByVal AReferenceType As ReferenceType)
        AReferenceType.Value = 30
    End Sub

    'Changes the property via the interface.
    Sub ChangeViaInterface(ByVal AnInterface As IMustHaveValue)
        AnInterface.Value = 40
    End Sub
End Module

'Test class of the value type
Structure ValueType
    Implements IMustHaveValue

    Dim myValue As Integer

    Sub New(ByVal Value As Integer)
        myValue = Value
    End Sub

    Property Value() As Integer Implements IMustHaveValue.Value
        Get
            Return myValue
        End Get
        Set(ByVal Value As Integer)
            myValue = Value
        End Set
    End Property
End Structure

'Test class of the reference type
Class ReferenceType
    Implements IMustHaveValue

    Dim myValue As Integer

    Sub New(ByVal Value As Integer)
        myValue = Value
    End Sub
```

```
    Property Value() As Integer Implements IMustHaveValue.Value
        Get
            Return myValue
        End Get
        Set(ByVal Value As Integer)
            myValue = Value
        End Set
    End Property
End Class
```

This example defines an interface, a reference type, and a value type. Both types implement the same interface, the *IMustHaveValue* interface, which you can see at the beginning of each class.

The first value change is obvious: the property of the value type is changed directly here. Therefore, the changed value of the property is also reflected in the output.

The second value change is a bit less obvious, but you have already seen this technique in action. A copy of the value is placed on the stack. Changes to the stack are only temporary. There is no connection to the object. Therefore, the original value is kept.

It's different, however, when you change the value of the reference type with the method *ChangeReferenceType*. There is no copy of the object, only a pointer to the data in the Managed Heap. Therefore, a change in the procedure also reflects the change of the object variable in the program part, which calls the procedure.

It gets interesting when the use of an interface variable comes into play, which references a value type. Here the value type is converted into a reference type right from the beginning and the variable's value ends up on the Managed Heap. The subroutine performs the changes there, and thus they also are reflected by the original reference to the object on the Managed Heap—via the object (interface) variable *AnInterface*. But you can only access the data on the Managed Heap via this variable. The original variable, from which the copy on the Managed Heap was created, has no connection to the object variable. The original variable, *AValueType*, therefore retains its original value.

> **Note** Boxing needs to taken with a grain of salt because the processes aren't transparent at first glance and can cause seemingly inexplicable behavior. You need to be especially careful when accessing value types with interface variables, as the last example clearly demonstrated.
>
> Use value types when your primary concern is speed and when the types you are developing don't require much memory space. Furthermore, you should use these types directly. When you need to save large sets of value types in collections, don't edit a value type of the collection by using tricks; instead, cast it to a value type variable and edit the instance there. Afterward, box it back into the appropriate array element.

Chapter 13
Dispose, *Finalize*, and the Garbage Collector

Microsoft .NET Framework provides developers with an extraordinarily solid platform for creating and using a large variety of types. Developers who have struggled with memory leaks and buffer overflows will appreciate one feature of .NET: the *Garbage Collector* (GC). That's actually the correct technical expression for the part of the Common Language Runtime (CLR) that identifies unneeded objects and disposes of them—when the time is right and .NET Framework needs storage space.

To explain how that works, I'll revisit an old example used earlier to demonstrate a totally different topic. Remember the *DynamicList* class from Chapter 10, "Class Inheritance and Polymorphism"? You used that sample application to save product data sets (*ShopItems*). In addition to implementing a method that demonstrates a dynamic increase in storage requirements, this example also shows something else: the ability to free up memory space that is no longer required.

Here's the *Add* method of the *DynamicList* class:

```
Sub Add(ByVal Item As ShopItem)

    'Check whether the current array limit has been reached
    If myCurrentCounter = myCurrentArraySize - 1 Then
        'Create new array with more memory,
        'and copy elements into it.

        'New array becomes larger:
        myCurrentArraySize += myStepIncreaser

        'Create temporary array.
        Dim locTempArray(myCurrentArraySize - 1) As ShopItem
```

```
                'Copy elements
                'Important: Unlike in VB6 you must take
                'care of the copying yourself!
                For locCount As Integer = 0 To myCurrentCounter
                    locTempArray(locCount) = myArray(locCount)
                Next

                'Assign the temporary array to the member array.
                myArray = locTempArray
            End If

            'Save the element in the array.
            myArray(myCurrentCounter) = Item

            'Increase the pointer to the next element.
            myCurrentCounter += 1

        End Sub
```

Now, let's look at the code block from a different angle. You're no longer interested in the required memory space or enlarging arrays, only at the memory that becomes redundant as a result of this method.

Arrays in .NET are not value types, they're reference types. The memory required for everything derived from *System.Array* is reserved on the Managed Heap—arrays declared with *Dim* also fall into this category.

In the code snippet from the preceding sample program, there are two lines that would normally cause a memory leak if the code weren't running on the .NET Framework. Figure 13-1 illustrates the problem. There's an original array, which has a reserved memory area on the Managed Heap. However, the array has become too small. Therefore, the procedure defines a new array by using the variable *locTempArray*. Here's where the interesting part occurs: *locTempArray* is assigned to *myArray*, effectively "bending" the pointer to the memory area of the corresponding elements. Now, *myArray* points to the same array elements to which *locTempArray* had pointed earlier. The addresses of the elements that *myArray* formerly pointed to are now uselessly sitting somewhere in memory, because they are no longer referenced. So, what happens to them now?

Important Only the addresses are redundant, not the elements themselves. When copying the elements, we haven't actually copied the element contents, only the addresses to the elements. When bending the array pointer, only the four pointers to the elements remain. But we are still using the elements—now as part of the array with eight elements.

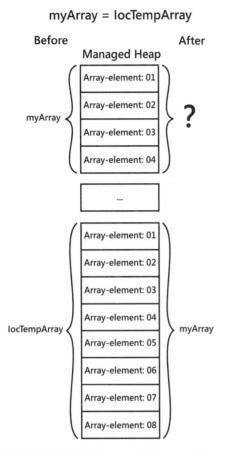

FIGURE 13-1 What happens to the array elements that "exist" in a void after assignment?

The Common Object Model (COM)—the predecessor of .NET and a technology you are still using, whether consciously or subconsciously (such as when you automate Microsoft Word or Microsoft Excel)—used a reference counter approach for each object. The initial assignment of an object to an object variable set the counter to one. Each subsequent assignment of that object to a variable (each new reference to the object) increased the counter by one. Similarly, when removing a reference—meaning a variable which used to reference the object was assigned to another object or to *Nothing*, or the program left the scope of a referencing variable so that it could no longer reference the object—the reference counter was decreased by one. When the reference counter reached 0, the object could be safely disposed of; it was no longer needed, because it was no longer referenced from any place in the program.

However, this reference-counting approach had a couple of disadvantages. First, it required significant computer time. It was also prone to a problem called *circular references*, which is when one object references another object, which in turn, points back to the first object. In such cases, the reference counter can never become 0, even when the actual program contained no more references to those objects, but they still referenced each other, which caused memory leaks.

The .NET Framework, or rather the CLR, solves this problem by using a completely different process to dispose of objects.

The Garbage Collector in .NET

The existing memory of the Managed Heap is shared by all assemblies that run in an *application domain* ("AppDomain" for short). Windows typically isolates applications by running them in strictly separate processes. Under normal circumstances a program in one process cannot access data in a different process; data can be exchanged cross-process only via proxies.

AppDomains in .NET, which are managed by the CLR, are different than Windows processes. They permit the parallel execution of several applications in *one* process. The CLR guarantees that the applications can run just as isolated and unhindered as they would in a Windows process. Each AppDomain manages a memory area that stores the data of the assemblies and programs[1] running within that AppDomain. This memory area is called the *Managed Heap*, with which you have already worked a few times and become familiar.

When memory in the Managed Heap becomes scarce (and sometimes for other reasons), the CLR starts a process that is literally like garbage collection in real life. This garbage collection process identifies objects that are no longer being used. Specifically, it identifies objects that are no longer referenced by an object variable in the application. Here's a short program that illustrates the point:

> **Companion Content** Open the corresponding solution (.sln), which you can find in the \VB 2010 Developer Handbook\Chapter 13\GCEvents folder.

---

[1] To be accurate, a program is also an assembly.

```vbnet
Public Class Form1

    Private myContact As Contact


    Private Sub Button1_Click(ByVal sender As System.Object,
                        ByVal e As System.EventArgs) Handles Button1.Click

        'Remains.
        Dim contact1 As New Contact With {.LastName = "Ardelean",
                                    .FirstName = "Adriana",
                                    .Zip = "99999",
                                    .City = "Wonttellyou"}

        'Is immediately disposed of.
        Dim contact2 As New Contact With {.LastName = "Löffelmann",
                                    .FirstName = "Klaus",
                                    .Zip = "59555",
                                    .City = "Lippstadt"}


        myContact = contact1

        'Only testing, do nothing else!
        GC.Collect()

    End Sub


    Private Sub Button2_Click(ByVal sender As System.Object,
                        ByVal e As System.EventArgs) Handles Button2.Click
        'Only testing, do nothing else!
        GC.Collect()
    End Sub
End Class

Public Class Contact
    Public Property LastName As String
    Public Property FirstName As String
    Public Property Zip As String
    Public Property City As String

    Protected Overrides Sub Finalize()
        Debug.Print("Finalizing:" & LastName)
    End Sub

End Class
```

When you start the program, you see a form with two buttons. When you click the Create Objects button, the program creates two test objects: *contact1* (*Adriana Ardelean*) and *contact2* (*Klaus Löffelmann*). The *contact1* variable is assigned to the class variable *myContact*, so even when program scope leaves the method, a reference to the object remains. If you then click *Trigger Garbage Collector*, the output window of Microsoft Visual Studio (if necessary activate it by pressing Ctrl+Alt+O) displays the text *Finalizing:Löffelmann*. There is no longer a reference to the object that was previously referenced by *contact2*, so the GC disposes of the object. To do that it calls its *Finalizer* method, which you'll see more about shortly.

> **Caution**   To do this, the class we are using as the object supplier overrides its *Finalize* method. We are kind of misusing the *Finalize* to find out when the object is disposed of. Don't do this in your own programs.

The GC functions at extremely high speed, particularly for applications that create a lot of disposable objects in a short amount of time.

How the Garbage Collector Works

The GC is fast because it classifies objects it should check into *generations*. The creators of the GC algorithm assumed that objects created at the start of an application are likely to be long-term objects that would remain in memory longer than those that are generated elsewhere, such as locally in procedures. This assumption logically leads to the conclusion that it makes sense to classify objects according to these "generations" to optimize the GC algorithm when disposing of these objects.

The GC not only marks objects for further maintenance, but it also equips them with a counter, which reports how often an object has already been checked for disposal. The more often the GC has "visited" an object without disposing of it, the older that object logically is (and the higher its generation number becomes), but the less likely it is that the object will be disposed of in the *next* GC run.

Simply explained, the process works as described in the following, and is based on the so-called "mark-and-compact algorithm."

- A new object requires memory space. The memory requirement on the Managed Heap reaches a certain size—approximately within the range of a modern processor's cache size. That triggers a GC run.

- All objects are marked as "*checked*" during this run. The GC determines determines which ones are no longer in use and can be discarded. Generation 0 objects (those created since the last run) that are still valid become generation 1 objects. As of .NET

1.0, the GC runs by default on a thread parallel to the main application thread. When objects exist that need to be disposed of, the GC moves the memory for the objects still in use to the addresses of the objects to be discarded, thus overwriting them and generating space for new objects in that segment. If it is necessary for this to end, the GC stops all running threads of the application for a short time. This process is so highly optimized that a generation 0 garbage collection usually happens in milliseconds. This is how the .NET Framework reclaims space for new objects. After the GC run, any remaining objects promoted to generation 1 are ignored during subsequent regular (short) runs for performance reasons. The GC assumes correctly that objects which weren't removed during the first pass are most likely still being used during the next run.

> **Note** As of .NET 4.0, a GC does not only perform certain tasks concurrently to your .NET Application. Concurrent Garbage Collection was implemented as early as the first version of the framework. When it was not a generation 0 or 1 GC—which were always blocking— the CLR tried to do as much as possible of the work on a dedicated thread for a full GC. The new background GC, first introduced in .NET 4.0, is an evolution of the concurrent GC. Basically, what it can do better is to run a Full GC while a generation 0 or a generation 1 GC is in progress. Also, the CLR team made noticeable improvements to the background GC's algorithm, so it can run concurrently in more situations and need to stop the application's threads less often. And it is faster.

- At some point another memory requirement threshold for new objects is reached. At this point, both generation 0 and generation 1 objects are examined more closely (remember, generation 1 objects are ignored for performance reasons during generation 0 runs). In principle the same things happen as in a generation 0 garbage collection run, but this time the GC disposes of unreferenced objects from generation 1, as well.

- The same thing happens at yet another threshold, in the region of 16 MB. Any remaining objects from generation 1 now become generation 2, and generation 0 objects become generation 1. Generation 2 is the end of the line; the .NET GC only uses 3 generations: 0, 1, and 2.

The advantages of this multi-tiered process are plain to see: the assumption that recently created objects (generation 0 objects) are typically used only briefly, provides a huge speed advantage. Truly large memory blocks need to be moved only when certain thresholds (in the megabyte range) have been crossed. Additionally these thresholds take the processor caches into consideration and are adjusted to their size.

Unfortunately the garbage collection process causes a problem of a different kind. Unlike with COM's reference counting, objects in the .NET Framework don't know *when* they will

be disposed of, because typically, only the CLR decides when a garbage collection run takes place (with one exception). Typically, the GC runs when:

- Your .NET application has finished its work and is about to close. Typically this is the time, where the CLR shuts down as well. Because several AppDomains can run in a process, and closing an AppDomain doesn't necessarily lead to shutting down the CLR, the GC is also run when an AppDomain is shut down.

- There is too little memory space, either because there are too many objects or because there is less Windows memory for whatever reason. In this case, the GC checks whether generation 0 objects can be disposed of, and does so if necessary. Windows informs the CLR about low memory conditions, so the CLR doesn't need to check itself.

- Here's the exception. The GC can be launched in the AppDomain with the *GC.Collect()* method. You saw that method earlier in the example code, but it's important to realize that that was for instructional purposes only. It is not best practice to use this method, because you wouldn't give the GC the chance to be as highly optimized by applying the generation algorithm as it could be. Only in very few exceptional circumstances does it make sense to trigger the GC yourself.

> **Note** If a certain operation needed a large amount of memory, and you want the delay for cleaning up this memory to be happening at a predictable time, calling the GC yourself can be a good idea.
>
> Another situation for which you might want to trigger the GC yourself would be, when you need to use a third-party-assembly that uses unmanged, limited resources (probably COM components) of the system, which need to be reclaimed regulary but lack the correct implementation to do so in a *Dispose* method. In such circumstances, calling *GC.Collect()* could be your "sheet anchor." And, of course, for debugging or testing purposes, it is OK to call *GC.Collect()* directly.

When it comes to disposing of an object that was no longer needed, COM had a distinct advantage: when the last reference was resolved and the reference counter reached 0, the *Terminate* event took place, and the object could initiate the required steps for disposal immediately.

Normally it's not a problem that an object doesn't know when it's being disposed of. It's only important for an object to know when it's about to be discarded so it can perform clean-up tasks beforehand—not in regard to its own memory management (because other objects referenced by it would also be disposed of by the GC), but to free resources to which the GC has no access.

In other object-oriented programming (OOP) languages, this was (and still is) taken care of by a destructor. Just like the constructor you learned about, which is run when an object is created, the destructor runs when the object is destroyed.

These are cases where, for example, an object has received a handle[2] for a certain device or operating system resource. To free this handle, the object must perform the required actions before it is discarded.

Unfortunately, that no longer works in .NET, because objects in .NET don't know if and when they will be destroyed. However, there is a way to inform objects that they will be destroyed and to then trigger the necessary steps for freeing the resources they allocate. You'll hear the term "non-deterministic destructors," which means that it is impossible to determine in advance when the destructor will be called. That occurs when the GC chooses—and objects don't know when that is.

The solution to this problem lies in the implementation of an interface called *IDisposable*. You typically need this only if you need to free resources other than those of .NET, called "unmanaged resources." You can find an example of a class that implements *Idisposable* in the section "Dispose," later in this chapter.

The Speed in Allocating Memory for New Objects

Ever since it was first released, the .NET infrastructure has had to battle a preconception that it's slow. It's the nature of preconceptions that they usually contain a kernel of truth. On-demand compilation by the Just-in-Time (JIT) compiler of the CLR is certainly a technology with many advantages—but speed is not one of them. But you can still defend the .NET infrastructure when it comes to the matter of speed.

.NET has several speed advantages, one of which is the creation of memory space for a new object. And let's be honest, in almost any imaginable scenario, it's more important to be able to create objects as quickly as possible as it is to be able to dispose of them as quickly as possible.

Why is object creation is so much faster in .NET than, for example, creating an object on the common runtime heap of a typical C-based system. Here's why: in a C runtime heap, all memory-allocated objects exist as a concatenated list. When a new object requires memory, the C runtime must iterate through this list, and when it finds enough unused memory space between two objects, it breaks the chain at that location and inserts the new object there.

Allocating memory in .NET Framework works differently. There is an address pointer that points to the memory address where the next object should be placed; new objects are therefore not just placed anywhere, they're always placed at the end of the list of objects in the Managed Heap. At any given time, this address pointer holds the memory starting point for a new object. So, allocating memory for new objects in .NET Framework doesn't take

---

[2] An identifier issued by the operating system for using a certain resource (file, screen, interfaces, special Windows operating system objects, and so on).

much time (unlike in the common C runtime systems), and that's a clear speed advantage, thanks to the CLR.

Similarly, because of the way C runtime systems allocate memory, objects that are created sequentially might end up located far away from each other in memory. Again, this doesn't happen in .NET Framework. Objects created sequentially are typically located one after another in memory.

Of course this makes sense when you consider the probabilities of how and when memory is allocated for objects. When you allocate memory for a bitmap, for example, it's also likely that related objects, such as fonts and brushes will need to be created in the same context, and these will probably be created at around the same time, as well. Above all, it's important for the memory of these objects to be physically located in one of the fast processor caches. So far, it looks like the .NET Framework memory management adds only positive features. If only not for one small problem: although modern computers have a huge amount of memory available, it isn't inexhaustible. At some point a clean-up must take place—garbage collection—and that takes time.

But you have already seen how the GC algorithm works by using generations. The generation 0 algorithm is laid out in such a way that it isn't triggered as long as the required memory lies within the processor's fast cache memory range.

The speed compromise that developers must make to enjoy this extremely fast memory allocation, coupled with the advantage that the objects reside very close to one other in memory—and therefore probably in the processor cache—is, I believe, definitely justifiable.

Finalize

When an object is marked for disposal by the GC, it usually calls that object's *Finalize* method before it ultimately frees the object memory and destroys the object. The *Object* class itself has already implemented *Finalize*, and because all classes are derived from *Object*, every object in .NET has a *Finalize* method.

 Note To be accurate, the *Finalize* method contained in *Object* is not called within the garbage collection context, because it doesn't actually perform anything. Instead, the GC algorithm determines whether the object overrides *Finalize*, and if so, it calls that overridden version.

In its basic implementation, *Object.Finalize* does... well, absolutely nothing. Basically it just exists. That means that if an object needs to implement custom functionality to prepare for its disposal, it must override the *Finalize* method.

In principle, *Finalize* is therefore the (non-deterministic) destructor for .NET classes.

> **Companion Content** Open the corresponding solution (.sln), which you can find in the
> \VB 2010 Developer Handbook\Chapter 13\Finalize01 folder.

```
Module mdlMain

    Sub Main()
        Dim locTest As New TestClass("First test class")
        Dim locTest2 As New TestClass("Second test class")
        locTest = Nothing
        locTest2 = Nothing

        'GC.Collect()

        'Wait a moment (actually a second)
        Threading.Thread.Sleep(1000)

        Console.WriteLine("Both objects are now no longer used!")
    End Sub

End Module

Class TestClass

    Private myName As String

    Sub New(ByVal Name As String)
        myName = Name
    End Sub

    Protected Overrides Sub Finalize()
        MyBase.Finalize()
        Console.WriteLine(Me.myName & " was disposed of")
    End Sub
End Class
```

> **Tip** Start this program by pressing Ctrl+F5 (without debugging) to prevent the console window
> from disappearing after you exit the program. Otherwise, you won't be able to see the result.

When you run this program, notice that the message "Both objects are now no longer used!"
is displayed first. Afterward, the texts are displayed, which indicate that both used objects
have been finalized:

```
Both objects are now no longer used!
Second test class was disposed of
First test class was disposed of
```

The reason for this is probably already obvious. The GC in this program does not run while
the program is running—and because the program requires only a few bytes of memory, it
has no reason to. Object finalization still takes place, though—when the application ends. At

this point the last line of the actual program has long since been processed—that's the line of code that renders the message "Both objects are now no longer used!" on your screen. If you remove the comment character from the line:

```
'GC.Collect()
```

you'll see a different result. Now when you run the program the output changes to:

```
Second test class was disposed of
First test class was disposed of
Both objects are now no longer used!
```

> **Caution** In the sample program, we used the *Console* class in the *Finalize* method as if it were no problem at all. Don't do that. You shouldn't perform any screen output in your *Finalize* methods; instead, complete any finalization tasks as quickly as possible. The truth is, you can't be sure whether any objects you are using in a *Finalize* method still exist at that moment.

When *Finalize* Does Not Take Place

In *Finalize* methods, under certain circumstances, you can cause new objects to be created, which themselves can create new objects, and so on. Of course, these objects must then also be finalized. In the worst-case scenario, you trigger such a huge cascade of new objects that they can never all be finalized. However, your application still won't hang, because .NET Framework has implemented some precautionary measures.

> **Companion Content** Open the corresponding solution (.sln), which you can find in the \VB 2010 Developer Handbook\Chapter 13\FinalizeNoNo01 folder.
>
> Keep in mind that this example shows what you should NEVER do to your applications!

```
Module mdlMain

    Sub Main()
        Dim locTest As New TestClass("TestClass")
    End Sub

End Module

Class TestClass

    Private myName As String

    Sub New(ByVal Name As String)
        myName = Name
    End Sub
```

```
    Sub WriteText()
        Console.Write(myName)
    End Sub

    Protected Overrides Sub Finalize()
        MyBase.Finalize()
        Dim locTemp As New TestClass("locTemp")
        WriteText()
        Console.WriteLine(" was disposed of")
    End Sub
End Class
```

When you start this program, it displays a number of messages. Unfortunately *Finalize* itself creates a new instance of *TestClass*, which it uses to issue a message. Of course, this instance must be finalized, as well. Doing that creates yet another new *TestClass* instance, and so on. After a while, the GC recognizes that the finalization process is doing exactly the opposite of what it is meant to do; it's creating more and more objects, increasing memory requirements. In such cases, the GC simply cancels the finalization after a few seconds.

The code example that follows presents another bad example (if you really want to try it out yourself, you can find it in the companion files in the \VB 2010 Developer Handbook\ Chapter 13\FinalizeNoNo02 folder). Even though this example doesn't use a large amount of memory, it takes far too much time. Again, after a relatively short period of time, the GC loses patience and cancels the finalization process. The object first declared in the sample program won't get the chance to be finalized.

```
Module mdlMain

    Sub Main()
        'A regular object which could normally be finalized without issues
        Dim locTest1 As New TestClass(False, "First test object")
        'but here's the problem: a queue loop flag is set.
        Dim locTest2 As New TestClass(True, "Second test object")
    End Sub

End Module

Class TestClass

    'This flag controls the entry into the queue.
    Private myWaitInFinalize As Boolean
    'A property for differentiating class instances
    Private myName As String
```

```
        'Flag for waiting and defining the name.
        Sub New(ByVal WaitInFinalize As Boolean, ByVal Name As String)
            myWaitInFinalize = WaitInFinalize
            myName = Name
        End Sub

        Protected Overrides Sub Finalize()
            MyBase.Finalize()

            'Only jump into the queue
            'if the flag was set at New.
            If myWaitInFinalize Then

                Dim locSecs As Integer
                Dim lastSec As Integer
                lastSec = Now.Second
                Do
                    'Issue a message every second.
                    If lastSec <> Now.Second Then
                        lastSec = Now.Second
                        locSecs += 1
                        Console.WriteLine("Waiting {0} seconds", locSecs)
                        'After 60 seconds it would end.
                        If locSecs = 60 Then Exit Do
                    End If
                Loop

            End If
            'Successfully finalized --> issue message
            Console.WriteLine("object {0} was finalized!", myName)
        End Sub
    End Class
```

If you need to implement finalization logic in your own classes, the following points are important (remember, *never* do this without implementing *IDisposable*, as described in the next section):

- Ensure that the finalization process happens as quickly as possible. Preferably, it should require hardly any time at all.

- Ensure that you never, *under any circumstances*, create new instances of any objects within the finalization process.

The .NET Framework does include some objects whose existence is guaranteed by the CLR at the time of finalization.

As the outputs you generate during finalization are most likely for testing purposes only, you can use the *Debug* class. This class provides *Write* and *WriteLine* methods, but has crucial advantages over the *Console* class: The *Debug* class is guaranteed to exist at finalization, and its output is rendered in a *Trace Listener*.

> **Note** A Trace Listener is a program that resides in the memory. It listens to special debug tasks and renders them in its own windows or protocols them in some other way. If you run programs in the development environment of Visual Studio, the task window is the preinstalled Trace Listener. All outputs you generate with *Debug.Write(Line)* are displayed in the output window.

Finalize is a method that is exclusively callable by the .NET Framework, which raises the question: what happens when you want to create objects that users can close down or destroy? It turns out that the .NET Framework provides an interface pattern, the *IDisposable* interface that you can use for this purpose. You'll learn more about this in the next section.

Dispose

The *IDisposable* interface provides an implementation rule that helps you implement a method that you can call from your code (unlike *Finalize*) to dispose of an object. If you implement this interface in your classes via *Implements*, you must also add a *Dispose* method, which is then responsible for all the necessary clean-up. You basically try to simulate the functionality of a real destructor in other OOP languages, which is typically called automatically, without your help. Calling *Dispose* is therefore a compromise that you make—it's the tradeoff for having the advantages of the GC.

> **Note** Use *Using* as a structure block to achieve an implicit *Dispose* for the used object when the program leaves the scope of the structure block.

The clean-up code you'd add to *Dispose* is basically the same kind of tasks a *Finalize* method would perform. But *Dispose* must do a bit more work, because when you clean up with *Dispose*, you must make sure that the GC doesn't repeat the clean-up work within your object when it calls *Finalize*. Therefore, the GC has a *SuppressFinalize* method. If you call this method and pass your class to it as an argument, the GC excludes that class from all further GC clean-up runs.

The actual task of the *Dispose* method is to determine whether a call has taken place via your own program by using *Dispose* (some classes use *Close*, which does the same thing as *Dispose*, but under a different name[3]) or via the GC with *Finalize*. Your *Dispose* must also recognize whether an object has been discarded, and if necessary must resolve any exceptions.

The sample application that follows shows a complete *Finalize/Dispose* implementation.

---

[3] The exception proves the rule, and the *System.Windows.Forms* class is one of those exceptions. When you close a form with *Close*, you can prevent the closing of the form in the *FormClosing* event (by setting *e.Cancel* to *True*). However, if you close the form with *Dispose*, which is also possible, then you basically kill it—it's immediately gone, destroyed, disposed of, and it no longer triggers any events. Other objects, such as those that read or write into files also use *Close*.

Implementing a High Resolution Timer as *IDisposable*

Today's computers are anything but slow. For example, the computer on which this text was written has an Intel I5 processor with a clock speed of 2.67 MHz. In just one second it can perform approximately 50,000 million instructions, which is 50 *billion* statements per second (processor instructions of course, not BASIC commands). A small program that simply uses one of the four processor cores to boot and count from 0 to 4 billion therefore requires about 11 seconds to run. That means it performs approximately 360 billion counts per second, or about 360,000 counts every millisecond:

```
Dim sw = Stopwatch.StartNew
For c As UInteger = 0 To UInteger.MaxValue - 1
Next
sw.Stop()
MessageBox.Show("Duration in ms: " & sw.ElapsedMilliseconds.ToString("#,##0"))
```

In spite of this incredible performance, .NET does not allow you to query a certain state or perform a certain task any more frequently than every one-hundredth of a second.

Let's think about that: one hundredth of a second is an eternity for a modern processor. In 10 milliseconds, it can process about 500,000,000 statements—in that time, the counter loop would have counted from 0 to 3.6 billion. So the performance to check more often is available; nevertheless this task poses a problem: When you perform state updates or state queries in an infinite loop, you are obviously blocking the performance of one entire processor core. A program with the task of implementing a stopwatch in a form (WinForms) or window (WPF) with a one-hundredth-of-a-second display, would look as shown in Figure 13-2.

> **Companion Content** Open the corresponding solution (.sln), which you can find in the \VB 2010 Developer Handbook\Chapter 13\StopWatch folder.

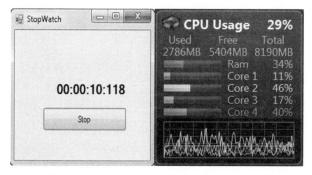

FIGURE 13-2 The simplest version of the stopwatch cracks a nut with a sledgehammer: due to the infinite loop, the program uses up an entire processor core. That's not efficient!

When you start the program, you can see the problem immediately by looking at Windows Task Manager or—as shown in the Figure 13-2—in one of the cute little processor load mini apps that you can download: the program consumes 100 percent of the processor's time because it updates the display in an infinite loop. Only every once in a while does it call *DoEvents* to give the application a chance to come up for air, update its controls, and process queries. If you develop software in this manner, you truly have nothing to write home about:

```
Public Class Form1

    Private myStopSignaled As Boolean

    Private Sub btnStartStopButton_Click(ByVal sender As System.Object,
                ByVal e As System.EventArgs) Handles btnStartStopButton.Click

        If btnStartStopButton.Text = "Start" Then
            btnStartStopButton.Text = "Stop"
            Dim sw = Stopwatch.StartNew

            Dim lastMs As Long

            Do
                'Waiting for the nex millisecond
                Do
                    If lastMs <> sw.ElapsedMilliseconds Then
                        lastMs = sw.ElapsedMilliseconds
                        elapsedMillisecondsLabel.Text =
                            TimeSpan.FromMilliseconds(lastMs).ToString(
                            "hh\:mm\:ss\:fff")
                        My.Application.DoEvents()
                        If myStopSignaled Then
                            Return
                        End If
                    End If
                Loop
            Loop
        Else
            myStopSignaled = True
            btnStartStopButton.Text = "Stop"
        End If
    End Sub
End Class
```

"Hey, no problem!" you might think. "Just implement the whole thing with a timer and set it to a 1-ms-cycle! That shouldn't require any additional processor performance, right?" Well OK, then just take a look at what happens when you add another button with the following code to the example:

```
Private myTimer As Timer

Private Sub TimerTestButton_Click(ByVal sender As System.Object,
                                  ByVal e As System.EventArgs) Handles
                                  TimerTestButton.Click
    myTimer = New Timer
    myTimer.Interval = 1
    myTimer.Start()

    Dim sw = Stopwatch.StartNew
    Dim lastms = sw.ElapsedMilliseconds

    AddHandler myTimer.Tick,
        Sub(timerSender As Object, timer_e As EventArgs)
            Dim cms = sw.ElapsedMilliseconds
            Debug.Print("Time elapsed: " & cms - lastms & " ms.")
            lastms = cms
        End Sub
End Sub
```

When you start the program after making that change and click the new button, you see a list similar to the one in the following example in the Visual Studio output window (if necessary use Ctrl+Alt+O to get to the display):

```
Time elapsed: 16 ms.
Time elapsed: 20 ms.
Time elapsed: 13 ms.
Time elapsed: 16 ms.
Time elapsed: 20 ms.
Time elapsed: 12 ms.
Time elapsed: 21 ms.
Time elapsed: 12 ms.
Time elapsed: 14 ms.
Time elapsed: 20 ms.
Time elapsed: 12 ms.
Time elapsed: 14 ms.
Time elapsed: 20 ms.
Time elapsed: 20 ms.
```

It's true that now the program uses hardly any processor time (as Task Manager shows you), but the program still misses the target. The call to update the stopwatch happens considerably less frequently than every one hundredth of a second (10 milliseconds); in fact, the interval is significantly higher. What you are observing here is a fundamental problem of a non-realtime operating system, such as Windows: you can create the timer in the example any way you like, but below 15–20 milliseconds, it's a no-go in Windows 7. Older systems are even worse: even 25–30 milliseconds can pose a problem. And some outlier times of up to 40 milliseconds are common with all Windows systems. That's partly because the Windows scheduler, which ensures that each simultaneously running thread in the system gets its turn, doesn't have a smaller resolution either.

After all, a context change for a thread is an elaborate task—a thread in Windows uses no less than 1 MB, and even in the Windows initial state, when it was just started, several hundred threads might be launched, even though they might not all be active, as is illustrated in Figure 13-3.

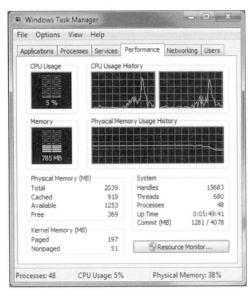

FIGURE 13-3 With Microsoft Outlook 2010, Word 2010, and Visual Studio 2010 running, even a modern, dual-core, hyper-threading Netbook has plenty to do: approximately 800 threads are more or less actively at work.

This is why the Windows scheduler doesn't toggle between threads too often—about every 15–20 milliseconds, the next-in-line of hundreds of simultaneously running threads share the available processor cores. And each one gets its turn—but no more often than that. This means that you can consider neither the regular .NET timers nor any other trick to wrangle a resolution of less than 10 milliseconds without squandering the computing power of an entire core.

Nevertheless, there is a solution: beginning with Windows XP, developers have been able to use the *multimedia-timer*, which is normally used for synchronizing playback media (such as audio and video), because those also need a higher resolution timer than regular timers can provide. Upon first use, the multimedia-timer internally changes the scheduler to the resolution of 1 millisecond, and therefore can fire every millisecond. Because .NET permits the use of operating system functions via platform invoke calls (*P/Invoke*), you can develop a class with relatively little effort that also provides such a timer in .NET.

Companion Content Open the corresponding solution (.sln), which you can find in the \VB 2010 Developer Handbook\Chapter 13\HighSpeedTimer01 folder.

A class that provides access to the multimedia-timer looks similar to the following:

```
Imports System.ComponentModel
Imports System.Runtime.InteropServices

Public Class HighSpeedTimer

    Private myTimerID As Integer              ' Multimedia-timer ID
    Private myUser As Integer                 ' Custimized parameter - not used.
    Private myTimerCapabilities As TimerCaps  ' Contains the TimeCaps that describe
                                              ' the timer resolution
    Private myMode As Integer = 1             ' 0=once, 1=periodically. 1 is
                                              ' pre-defined.

    Private myPeriodInMs As Integer           ' How often to trigger?
    Private myresolutionInMs As Integer       ' Timer resolution?
    Private myHasStarted As Boolean           ' Is the timer running?

    'Delegate necessary for the call-back from the operating system,
    'when the timer has run out...
    Private Delegate Sub TimeProc(ByVal id As Integer, ByVal msg As Integer,
                        ByVal user As Integer, ByVal reserved1 As Integer,
                        ByVal reserved2 As Integer)

    '...and is defined in this delegate variable.
    Private myCallBackTimeProc As TimeProc

    'The event triggered by the call-back routine,
    'when the timer has run out.
    Public Event Elapsed(ByVal sender As Object, ByVal e As EventArgs)
```

The lines in the code that follows show how you can call operating system methods directly from Visual Basic. The methods for controlling the multimedia-timer are located in the library winmm.dll (short for *Windows Multimedia*). The *DllImport* attribute, which is located above the method, specifies that the code of the method is not in the method body, but that you are dealing with an external call.

Tip The website *http://www.pinvoke.net* is a very useful source for determining which methods are provided by the operating system and how to call any particular method. But before you start creating large call libraries that wrap operating system functions, you should first try to find a .NET equivalent. There are very few cases for which you truly need to call operating system routines via *P/Invoke*.

```
'Determines the capabilities of the timer on this computer
<DllImport("winmm.dll")>
Private Shared Function timeGetDevCaps(ByRef caps As TimerCaps,
                            ByVal sizeOfTimerCaps As Integer) As Integer
End Function
```

```vb
'Creates and starts the multimedia-timer.
<DllImport("winmm.dll")>
Private Shared Function timeSetEvent(ByVal delay As Integer,
    ByVal resolution As Integer,
    ByVal CallBackProc As TimeProc, ByVal user As Integer,
    ByVal mode As Integer) As Integer
End Function

'Deletes a timer that is currently running.
<DllImport("winmm.dll")>
Private Shared Function timeKillEvent(ByVal id As Integer) As Integer
End Function

''' <summary>
''' Creates an instance of this class and sets the repetition frequency
''' of the timer trigger and the resolution in milliseconds.
''' </summary>
''' <param name="periodInMs">Repetition frequency - how often should
''' the timer trigger.</param>
''' <param name="resolutionInMs">Timer resolution (the value 1ms delivers
''' the most correct result).</param>
''' <remarks></remarks>
Sub New(ByVal periodInMs As Integer, ByVal resolutionInMs As Integer)
    'Determines the capabilities of the multimedia-timer which can
    'then be called via TimerCapabilities.
    Dim ret = timeGetDevCaps(myTimerCapabilities,
        Marshal.SizeOf(myTimerCapabilities))

    myPeriodInMs = periodInMs
    myresolutionInMs = resolutionInMs
    myCallBackTimeProc = AddressOf CallBackTimeProc
End Sub

''' <summary>
''' Starts the timer.
''' </summary>
''' <remarks></remarks>
Public Sub Start()

    If myHasStarted Then
        Return
    End If

    Dim ret = timeSetEvent(myPeriodInMs, myresolutionInMs,
                        myCallBackTimeProc, myUser, myMode)
    Dim hr = Marshal.GetHRForLastWin32Error
    If ret = 0 Then
        Throw New Win32Exception("The timer could not be started!")
    Else
        myTimerID = ret
        myHasStarted = True
    End If

End Sub
```

The method presented in the following code is the one that you should really rack your brains over. As long as a program that uses the multimedia-timer class always ensures that the timer is stopped, nothing can happen. But what happens when the program encounters unforeseen events that prevent the timer from being freed up? Under certain circumstances, the timer might still run when you simply don't expect it to—or worse, the program might be closed without having the opportunity to stop the timer and release it.

```
''' <summary>
''' Stops the timer.
''' </summary>
''' <remarks></remarks>
Public Sub [Stop]()
    If Not myHasStarted Then
        Return
    End If

    timeKillEvent(myTimerID)
End Sub


'The call-back routine which is called by the operating system
'when the timer has run out.
Private Sub CallBackTimeProc(ByVal id As Integer, ByVal msg As Integer,
                            ByVal user As Integer, ByVal param1 As Integer,
                            ByVal param2 As Integer)
    RaiseEvent Elapsed(Me, EventArgs.Empty)
End Sub


''' <summary>
''' Determines the possibilities the system has regarding the timer.
''' </summary>
''' <value></value>
''' <returns></returns>
''' <remarks></remarks>
Public ReadOnly Property TimerCapabilities As TimerCaps
    Get
        Return myTimerCapabilities
    End Get
End Property


''' <summary>
''' Determines whether the timer has been started.
''' </summary>
''' <value></value>
''' <returns></returns>
''' <remarks></remarks>
```

```
    Public ReadOnly Property HasStarted As Boolean
        Get
            Return myHasStarted
        End Get
    End Property

End Class

'Required for passing the parameter to the operating system routines
<StructLayout(LayoutKind.Sequential)>
Public Structure TimerCaps
    Public PeriodMin As Integer
    Public periodMax As Integer
End Structure
```

To prevent the timer from continuing to run, you implement the *IDisposable* interface. The next section shows how this works.

Visual Basic Editor Support for Inserting a Disposable Pattern

The pattern you need to keep in mind when implementing a disposable class is a lot more complex than implementing other functions by binding one or more interfaces.

You *must* adhere to the internal pattern—which of course goes far beyond the simple corresponding *Dispose* method.

For this reason Visual Studio provides special Editor support for the *IDisposable* interface. As soon as you insert it at the class header and press Enter after the line *Implements IDisposable*, the Editor not only inserts the function bodies that the interface requires into your class code (see Figure 13-4), it also adds a specific function skeleton.

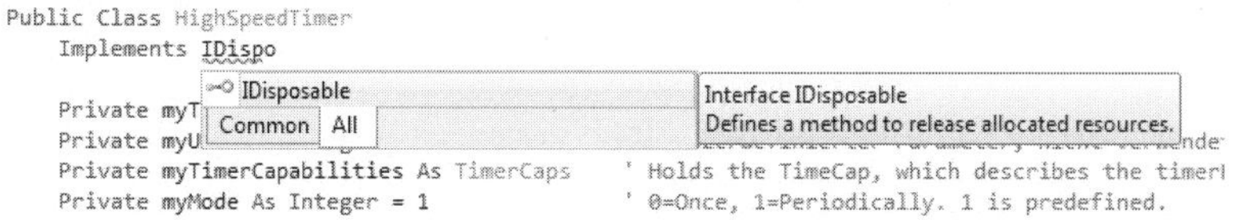

FIGURE 13-4 Implementing *IDisposable* is simple: simply press Tab to complete the line, and then press Enter to insert the interface method bodies.

You can try this yourself with our high-speed timer example. After you have performed the steps that were just described, the almost complete *IDisposable* implementation is already located at the end of the *HighSpeedTimer* class code, as shown in Figure 13-5.

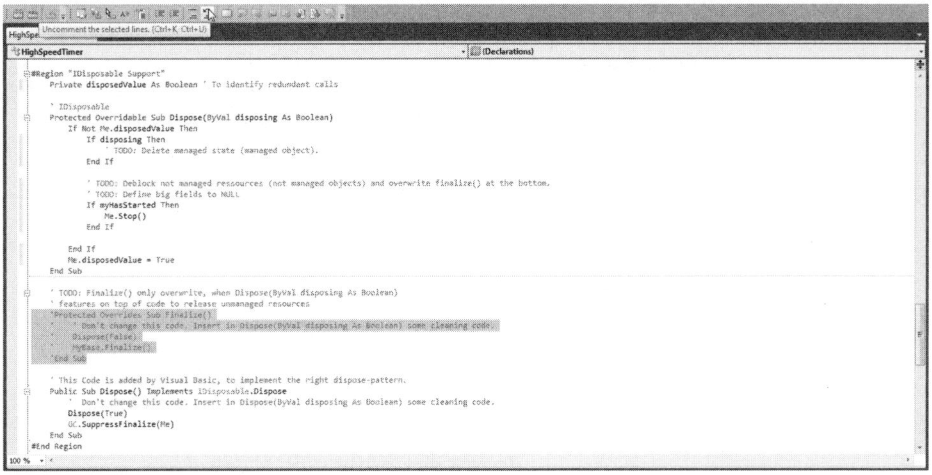

FIGURE 13-5 The Editor support for *IDispose* is quite thorough compared to its support for other interfaces: it inserts the complete *Dispose* and *Finalize* code, which you then just need to modify.

The additional code you need to add here is both quick and easy. First, follow the recommendations in the comments above the *Finalize* method. Because the timer is actually an *unmanaged* resource, remove the comment marks from the lines in question, as shown in the Figure 13-5. That way, you ensure that the *Dispose* method you are implementing can also be called with the *Finalize* method via the GC, if necessary.

And finally you just need to free the timer (if it's still active) at the crucial place in the code, which you can implement very quickly. Refer to the changes highlighted in bold in the following code:

```
#Region "IDisposable Support"
    Private disposedValue As Boolean 'This is how you identify superfluous calls

    ' IDisposable
    Protected Overridable Sub Dispose(ByVal disposing As Boolean)
        If Not Me.disposedValue Then
            'There are no managed objecte to consider,
            'so we don't need this If branch:
            'If disposing Then
            '    ' TODO: Delete managed state (managed objects).
            'End If

            'Here the timer must be released, if it's still active.
            If myHasStarted Then
                Me.Stop()
            End If

        End If
        Me.disposedValue = True
    End Sub

    ' TODO: Only override Finalize() if Dispose(ByVal disposing As Boolean)
    ' above has code for sharing unmanaged resources.
```

```
Protected Overrides Sub Finalize()
    ' Don't change this code. Insert clean-up code above in
    ' Dispose(ByVal disposing As Boolean).
    Dispose(False)
    MyBase.Finalize()
End Sub

' This code is added by Visual Basic to implement the Dispose pattern correctly.
Public Sub Dispose() Implements IDisposable.Dispose
    ' Don't change this code. Insert clean-up code above in
    ' Dispose(ByVal disposing As Boolean).
    Dispose(True)
    GC.SuppressFinalize(Me)
End Sub
```

> **Companion Content** Open the corresponding solution (.sln) for this extended example,
> which you can find in the \VB 2010 Developer Handbook\Chapter 13\HighSpeedTimer02-
> IDisposable folder.

One more important issue that needs to be addressed concerns the last line in the *Dispose*
method: the developer has used the *HighSpeedTimer* class and is now able to release the
object manually for disposal by calling *Dispose*. However, if that happens, the GC no longer
needs to perform clean-up tasks. In fact, in such a case, the GC must not be allowed to execute the clean-up code any longer; it must be informed that these tasks have already been
performed. This happens in the last line of the code sample where it calls the method *GC.
SuppressFinalize*.

Targeted Object Release with *Using*

Objects that accept information about their disposal implement a method called *Dispose*,
as you have already learned. When you call *Dispose* on an object, it simultaneously frees all
reserved system resources and signals the GC that it's free to be destroyed. You've seen how
to implement such a pattern in your own classes, but what's the best way to call *Dispose*?

The following simple code writes some text into a file, but demonstrates typical usage:

```
Dim locSw As StreamWriter
Try
    locSw = New StreamWriter("C:\Textfile1.txt")
    Try
        locSw.WriteLine("First line of text")
        locSw.WriteLine("Second line of text")
        'Empty write buffer
        locSw.Flush()
    Catch ex As Exception
        Debug.Print("Error while writing the file!")
```

```
    Finally
        'Free all system resources again
        locSw.Dispose()
    End Try
Catch ex As Exception
    Debug.Print("Error while opening the file!")
End Try
```

Because releasing allocated system resources—in this case, a file handle—is so important, the code places the *Dispose* method call in the *Finally* section of a *Try/Catch/Finally* block. This ensures that the file system resources the object uses will definitely be freed, even if the operation triggered an exception.

> **Note** Two nested *Try* blocks makes sense here, because different exceptions might occur when opening the file than when writing to it. The system resources themselves are allocated only by the *StreamWriter* object after it has been opened *successfully* and must therefore, only in this case (inner *Try/Catch* block), be freed again with *Dispose*.

The *Using* keyword gives you targeted control over the lifespan of an object that implements *Dispose*. The following code sample is functionally identical to the previous example, but *Using* simplifies dealing with the object, and the code becomes easier to read:

```
'Writing a files - Using controls the lifespan of locSw2
Try
    'Alternatively you could continue to use locSw:
    'locSw = New StreamWriter("C:\Textfile2.txt")
    'Using locSw
    Using locSw2 As New StreamWriter("C:\Textfile2.txt")
        Try
            locSw2.WriteLine("First line of text")
            locSw2.WriteLine("Second line of text")
            'Schreibpuffer leeren
            locSw2.Flush()
        Catch ex As Exception
            Debug.Print("Error while writing the file!")
        End Try
    'Here locSw.Dispose is performed automatically
    End Using
Catch ex As Exception
    Debug.Print("Error while opening the file!")
End Try
```

In this example, the *Finally* section of the inner *Try/Catch* blocks has become redundant because the program can't ignore *End Using*. Even if you were to jump out of the *Using* block with *Return*, the code would still call the *Dispose* method of the object before leaving the procedure.

Tip *Using* is frequently used in connection with Microsoft SQL Server. If you need a connection to SQL Server, use the required *Connection* object within a *Using* statement. Perform all operations you need within the *Using* block, and when you are finished, close the SQL Server connection with *End Using*. This approach means that you can safely leave such a code block without explicitly having to ensure that the SQL Server connection is closed. In addition to closing the connection (which the method *Close()* could do as well), with *Dispose()*, any *Shared Lock*[4] in the database is removed, as well. This makes your application more robust, because you avoid multiple open connections. (After all, it's easy to forget to close a connection after an early exit from a code block that processes SQL operations.)

---

[4] In order not to breach the ACID (*Atomic, Consistent, Isolated, Durable*) maxim for SQL Server, no data must be changed, for example, via a *SELECT* query while it is providing data in a connection. A Shared Lock permits several read-access connections, but ensures that no data can be changed.

Chapter 14
Operators for Custom Types

The operator procedures that were introduced with Microsoft Visual Basic 2005 could be called "convenience tools."[1] They make life easier for developers, and they don't have any negative impact on the user. They also don't provide anything to help you solve programming problems, but they help make classes or structures easier to use later on—and code easier to read.

Introduction to Operator Procedures

Operator procedures let you add operator actions to your classes. When you create a custom type, whether it's based on a class or a structure, that type provides certain functionality via methods. With the help of operator procedures, you can bind these methods to operators.

One example for this could be a *SuperString* class—a class that functions like the primitive data type *String*, but adds methods to simplify working with the various string functions. You can already use a concatenation operator with strings—the + (plus) or & (ampersand)

---

[1] The IT term "Convenience Patterns" was coined specifically for overloading methods.

character to connect two strings—but in almost all programming languages this stands for the existing string concatenation operator, not an addition. Take a look at the following lines of code:

```
'Declaration and definition of a regular string
Dim locNormalString As String
locNormalString = "When you hit your head against the wall "
locNormalString = locNormalString + "you burn 150 calories."
Console.WriteLine("Original string:")
Console.WriteLine(locNormalString)
```

When you run this, you see the following result:

```
Original string:
When you hit your head against the wall you burn 150 calories.
```

Let's follow this idea a little further. The following example multiplies a string:

```
"Klaus" * 5
```

This results in the following output:

```
KlausKlausKlausKlausKlaus
```

Take a look at the next example:

```
"Klaus Löffelmann's Internet appearance is located on http://loeffelmann.de"-"Löffelmann's"
```

If you remove "Löffelmann's," the output becomes:

```
"Klaus Internet appearance is located on http://loeffelmann.de"
```

Similarly, string "division" using a separation character could create a *String* array with the partial strings. Thus, the expression:

```
"Different|words|are|separated|like|this" : "|"c
```

would become a *String* array with these elements:

```
Different
words
are
separated
like
this
```

And finally, implicit (direct assignment) or explicit assignment (with *CType*) type conversions into other types would be possible:

```
Dim locSuperString as SuperString = "This is a string constant, not a SuperString constant"
```

Or:

```
Dim locSuperString as SuperString = CType("the same with explicit assignment", SuperString)
```

Preparing a Structure or Class for Operator Procedures

The most important thing you need to know about operator procedures is that they are exclusively implemented as static functions. That's because with many operators you must pass two arguments to the operator procedure. The following code line would also be possible without operators:

```
TypeInstance3 = TypeInstance1 + TypeInstance2
```

In that case, the line would look like this:

```
TypeInstance3 = TypeInstance.Add(TypeInstance1, TypeInstance2)
```

Therefore, when you look at the following code samples, keep in mind that implementing operator procedures is only *one* possible way to accomplish the goal (albeit a very practical one). Similarly, the code

```
Dim testString = "Klaus"
testString = testString + " shows what can be done with operators."
```

could also be written as

```
Dim testString="Klaus"
testString = String.Concat(testString, " shows what can be done with operators.")
```

and you could add:

```
testString=String.Concat(testString, " And what also works without.")
```

If you assume that the class or structure from which *TypeInstance1*, *TypeInstance2*, and *TypeInstance3* are derived is called *TypeInstance*, it becomes clear that only a static implementation makes sense. You don't need an instance of this class or structure to add two independent instances of that class or structure—you just need the code to perform the addition and return a function result of the type *TypeInstance*.

It's similar to parsing a string for conversion into a numeric variable, for example. A static function is used here, as well (*Parse*). Note that you don't need an instance; you can use *Parse* directly with this code:

```
Dim ADouble as Double = Double.Parse("123,45")
```

Because you need a corresponding set of static functions, it makes sense to implement that functionality first in the corresponding class or structure. Initially, these don't need to be static. A *SuperString* class with completely implemented functionality would look as follows:

> **Companion Content** Open the corresponding solution (.sln), which you can find in the \VB 2010 Developer Handbook\Chapter 14\OperatorOverload folder.

```vb
Public Structure SuperString

    Private myValue As String

    Public Sub New(ByVal Value As String)
        myValue = Value
    End Sub

    Public Overrides Function ToString() As String
        Return myValue
    End Function

    Public Function Add(ByVal differentString As SuperString) As SuperString
        Return New SuperString(myValue & differentString.ToString)
    End Function

    Public Function Subtract(ByVal differentString As SuperString) As SuperString
        Return New SuperString(myValue.Replace(differentString.ToString, ""))
    End Function

    Public Function Subtract(ByVal lastCharacter As Integer) As SuperString
        Try
            Return New SuperString(myValue.Substring(0, myValue.Length -
                                    (lastCharacter + 1)))
        Catch ex As Exception
            Return New SuperString(myValue)
        End Try
    End Function

    Public Function Multiply(ByVal amount As Integer) As SuperString

        'We are neat and avoid errors! ;-)
        If myValue Is Nothing Then
            Return Nothing
        End If
```

```
            If myValue = "" Or amount < 1 Then
                Return New SuperString("")
            End If

            'It's fastest with the StringBuilder!
            Dim locSB As New System.Text.StringBuilder

            'Just append the initial string as often
            'as 'amount' dictates.
            For c As Integer = 1 To amount
                locSB.Append(myValue)
            Next

            'and return!
            Return New SuperString(locSB.ToString)
        End Function

        Public Function Divide(ByVal separator As Char) As SuperString()
            Dim locStringArray As String()
            locStringArray = myValue.Split(New Char() {separator})

            Dim locSuperStringArray(locStringArray.Length - 1) As SuperString
            For z As Integer = 0 To locStringArray.Length - 1
                locSuperStringArray(z) = New SuperString(locStringArray(z))
            Next
            Return locSuperStringArray

        End Function
End Structure
```

These initial functions are implemented as normal methods (they support the later implementation of operators), so they're relatively easy to create. The code itself doesn't require
much explanation. With conventional programming—that is, without operators—using this
class is demonstrated by the *Sub Main* of the project module, as follows:

```
Module Main

    Sub Main()
        'Declaration and definition of a regular string
        Dim locNormalString As String
        locNormalString = "When you hit your head against the wall "
        locNormalString = locNormalString + "you burn 150 calories."
        Console.WriteLine("Original string:")
        Console.WriteLine(locNormalString)

        'Declaration and definition of a SuperString
        Dim locSuperString As New SuperString(locNormalString)
```

```
                'SuperString function demo: Adding (appending) other strings
                Console.WriteLine()
                Console.WriteLine("'Adding' strings - append: 'Great, isn't it?'")
                locSuperString = locSuperString.Add( _
                        New SuperString(vbNewLine + " - Great, isn't it?"))
                Console.WriteLine(locSuperString.ToString)

                'Subtracting (removing) other strings
                Console.WriteLine()
                Console.WriteLine("'Subtracting' strings - remove: ', isn't it?'")
                locSuperString = locSuperString.Subtract( _
                        New SuperString(", isn't it"))
                Console.WriteLine(locSuperString.ToString)
                Console.WriteLine()
                'Subtract is overloaded-also works with the amount
                'of the last characters which need to be removed.
                Console.WriteLine("'Subtracting' strings-subtract the final 9 characters:")
                locSuperString = locSuperString.Subtract(9)
                Console.WriteLine(locSuperString.ToString)
                Console.WriteLine()

                'Multiplying strings
                Console.WriteLine("'Multiplying' strings:")
                locSuperString = locSuperString.Multiply(4)
                Console.WriteLine(locSuperString.ToString)
                Console.WriteLine()

                'Dividing strings-a bit more tricky
                locSuperString = New SuperString(
                    "The fortune cookie was invented in 1916 by George Jung, " & _
                    "an American pasta maker.")
                Console.WriteLine("'Dividing' strings:")
                Console.WriteLine(locSuperString.ToString)
                Dim locSuperStrings() As SuperString
                locSuperStrings = locSuperString.Divide(" "c)
                For Each locSString As SuperString In locSuperStrings
                    Console.WriteLine(locSString.ToString)
                Next
                Console.WriteLine()
                Console.WriteLine("Press key to exit!")
                Console.ReadKey()
            End Sub
```

When you run this example, the following output is displayed in the console window:

```
Original string:
When you hit your head against the wall you burn 150 calories.

'Adding' strings - append: 'Great, isn't it?'
When you hit your head against the wall you burn 150 calories.
 - Great, isn't it?
```

```
'Subtracting' strings - remove: ', isn't it?'
When you hit your head against the wall you burn 150 calories.
 - Great?

'Subtracting' strings—subtract the final 9 characters:
When you hit your head against the wall you burn 150 calories.

'Multiplying' strings:
When you hit your head against the wall you burn 150 calories.When you hit your head
against the wall you burn 150 calories.When you hit your head against the wall you burn 150
calories.When you hit your head against the wall you burn 150 calories.

'Dividing' strings:
The fortune cookie was invented in 1916 by George Jung, an American pasta maker.
The
fortune
cookie
was
invented
in
1916
by
George
Jung,
an
American
pasta
maker.

Press key to exit!
```

Implementing Operators

Now that you've seen the background information, you can go on to implement some static operator procedures. You'll use standard math calculation operators in this example.

The example here differentiates between two types: actual operators, such as +, −, *, /, and so on, and operators that are used to convert types. You'll start with the calculation operators:

```
Public [Class|Structure] OpType
    Public Shared Operator OpChar(ByVal objVar1 As [OpType|Type1], ByVal objVar2 As
[OpType|Type2]) As Type3
        ' Here is the code that performs the actual operation
    End Operator
End [Class|Structure]
```

The code body illustrates what's important:

- You can apply operators to classes *and* structures.

- Which operator (+,−, *, /, and so on) is used is specified by *OpChar*. Table 14-1, at the end of this chapter, lists which calculation operators you can implement, and what they are intended to do.

- At least one of the parameters you pass to an operator procedure must have the same type as the class or structure that defines the operator procedure.

- The operator procedure must be static (defined with the modifier *Shared*).

- The return type can be anything.

Applied to this example the *Add* routine looks as follows:

```
Public Shared Operator +(ByVal sstring1 As SuperString,
    ByVal sstring2 As SuperString) As SuperString
    Return sstring1.Add(sstring2)
End Operator
```

The + (plus) operator adds the two parameters before and after it together (it concatenates them). The parameter to the left of the operator becomes the first parameter passed to the operator procedure; the one to the right of the operator becomes the second parameter.

> **Note** This type of implementation works without problems, because the *SuperString* type is based on a structure—a value type. If it were based on a reference type, problems during the implementation of the operator procedures would be pretty much pre-programmed. Before implementing operator procedures in your own classes, be sure to read the section "Implementing True and False Evaluation Operators" later in this chapter.

After adding this operator procedure to the class, you can rearrange the code in the module that adds the two strings. Thus, this older code:

```
locSuperString = locSuperString.Add( _
        New SuperString(vbNewLine + "-Great, isn't it?"))
```

becomes:

```
locSuperString = locSuperString + New SuperString(vbNewLine + " - Great, isn't it?")
```

Even that slight change makes the code easier to write and read. You can then implement the other operators, as well:

```
Public Shared Operator -(ByVal sstring1 As SuperString,
    ByVal sstring2 As SuperString) As SuperString
    Return sstring1.Subtract(sstring2)
End Operator
```

```
Public Shared Operator *(ByVal sstring1 As SuperString,
    ByVal amount As Integer) As SuperString
    Return sstring1.Multiply(amount)
End Operator

Public Shared Operator /(ByVal sstring1 As SuperString,
    ByVal separator As Char) As SuperString()
    Return sstring1.Divide(separator)
End Operator
```

Overloading Operator Procedures

The original subtraction routine exists in two overloaded versions. The first one accepts a *SuperString* as a parameter. The method searches for the parameter in the original string and removes it if found. The second option takes an *Integer* value as a parameter, which controls the number of characters to remove from the end of the string. You can't yet call this latter function by using an operator.

As with regular methods, you can use overloads for operator procedures, as well, in the same way as you did in Chapter 10, "Class Inheritance and Polymorphism," in the section, "Overloading Methods, Constructors, and Properties." The following example demonstrates an overloaded method:

```
Public Shared Operator -(ByVal sstring1 As SuperString, ByVal amount As Integer) As
➥SuperString
        Return sstring1.Subtract(amount)
End Operator
```

This changes both subtraction versions in the module to support operators, as shown in the following:

```
    .
    .
    .
        'Subtract (remove) other strings
        Console.WriteLine()
        Console.WriteLine("'Subtracting' strings - remove: ', isn't it?'")
        'locSuperString = locSuperString.Subtract( _
        '        New SuperString(", was"))
        locSuperString = locSuperString - New SuperString(", isn't it")
        Console.WriteLine(locSuperString.ToString)
        Console.WriteLine()

        'Subtract is overloaded - also works with the amount
        'of the last characters which need to be removed.
        Console.WriteLine("'Subtracting' strings—subtract the final 9 characters:")
        locSuperString = locSuperString - 9
        Console.WriteLine(locSuperString.ToString)
        Console.WriteLine()
    .
    .
    .
```

Implementing Comparison Operators

In principle, comparison operators can be implemented for custom types in a manner similar to calculation operators, with two additional conditions:

- Comparison operators must always return a *Boolean* data type as the function result. The *Boolean* value informs callers whether the comparison was successful.

- You must implement comparison operators in pairs. For example, if you implement an operator that checks for *equal*, you must also implement an operator that checks for *not equal*. If you implement a size comparison, you must also implement operators for *greater than* and *less than*. The same applies to *equal to or greater than* and *equal to or less than*.

The comparison operator implementation for the *SuperString* class appears as follows:

```
Public Shared Operator <>(ByVal sString1 As SuperString,
    ByVal sString2 As SuperString) As Boolean
    Return (sString1.ToString <> sString2.ToString)
End Operator

Public Shared Operator =(ByVal sString1 As SuperString,
    ByVal sString2 As SuperString) As Boolean
    Return (sString1.ToString = sString2.ToString)
End Operator

Public Shared Operator <(ByVal sString1 As SuperString,
    ByVal sString2 As SuperString) As Boolean
    Return (sString1.ToString < sString2.ToString)
End Operator

Public Shared Operator >(ByVal sString1 As SuperString,
    ByVal sString2 As SuperString) As Boolean
    Return (sString1.ToString > sString2.ToString)
End Operator
```

Implementing Type Conversion Operators for Use with *CType*

Type conversion operators are double-edged swords. They definitely increase the degree of convenience, but they can also lead to tremendous problems—you'll see more about these problems later.

To recap: you can use an implicit conversion to convert a small data type into a larger data type—for example an *Integer* value into a *Long* value, as demonstrated here:

```
'Here you can use an implicit conversion (type extended)
Dim aLong As Long, anInteger As Integer
anInteger = 10
aLong = anInteger
```

However, the Visual Basic compiler initially blocks a type conversion into a smaller type—at least until you explicitly finagle your way out of the situation with *CType* or a special *Cxxx* operator. Keep in mind that data can become lost during a conversion into a smaller type (or a conversion that completely changes the type). Visual Basic reminds you of this by forcing you to use *CType*. Such *explicit* conversions look as follows:

```
'This requires an explicit conversion (because it's a conversion into a smaller type)
aLong = 1000
anInteger = CType(aLong, Integer)
```

Or:

```
'This conversion must also be explicit
Dim aDouble As Double, aString As String
aString = "1,828,488,382.45"
aDouble = CType(aString, Long)
```

Of course, types aren't converted "just like that"—especially for complex type conversions, such as from a string to a numeric value. For these, a sophisticated program handles the conversion.

You can implement such a program—or rather, such a subroutine—with *Operator Ctype* procedures for your own data types. It's up to you whether to use implicit or explicit conversions. For the *SuperString* example, it would be nice if the following line worked:

```
Dim aSuperString As SuperString = "This is a string"
```

It turns out that you can make that work. The constant assigned to *SuperString* is of the type *String*. Since you don't want to have to use *CType* here (and you can, because there is no risk of data loss during the conversion), you just need to implement a conversion operator procedure that extends the data type. Here's how it works (take a close look at the modifiers of the following procedure):

```
Public Shared Widening Operator CType(ByVal normalString As String) As SuperString
    Return New SuperString(normalString)
End Operator
```

The keywords *Operator CType* show that the routine handles a type conversion. The modifier *Widening* specifies that the conversion here is *implicit*; in other words, you don't need to completely write out an explicit conversion. As you already know, *Shared* defines the routine as static. The actual conversion code is simple: The procedure creates a new *SuperString* instance based on the passed-in *String*, and returns it as the function result.

If you want to force the developer who is using your class to initiate an explicit type conversion with *CType*, you replace the modifier *Widening* (make larger) with *Narrowing* (make smaller).

Of course, the whole thing about narrowing and widening of data types is just a guideline. You are free to make each data type implicitly or explicitly convertible, regardless of whether the conversion might lose data.

By the way, the conversion you just implemented works only in one direction at the moment. For example, suppose that you try to use it the other way, as shown in the following:

```
Dim aString as String = aSuperString
```

If you do this, the following message appears in the error list:

```
The value of the type "SuperStringIntro.SuperString" cannot be converted to "String".
```

To make it work in both directions, you need to add another *CType Operator* procedure to the project, as shown here:

```
Public Shared Widening Operator CType(ByVal SuperString As SuperString) As String
    Return SuperString.ToString
End Operator
```

Implementing True and False Evaluation Operators

One way to implement true and false evaluation mechanisms is to provide implicit or explicit conversions into the data type *Boolean* for your class. But Visual Basic offers a different option for this purpose—the operators *IsTrue* and *IsFalse*. The *IsTrue* and *IsFalse* operators don't work in the usual fashion. They can't be used as names in your programs, such as *CType*.

Actually they are simply aids for defining operator procedures to specify a certain procedure for an operation which (similar to implicit data conversion) doesn't really need operators.

For example, our *SuperString* class can provide a mechanism that specifies that certain string contents return *True* when evaluated, and all others *False*. In this case, the following can be implemented:

```
Sub ExperimentsForBooleanEXpressions()
    'Here implicit (type-extended) conversion is possible
    Console.Write("Would you like to enter more data (Yes, No):")
    Dim locSupStr As SuperString = Console.ReadLine
    If locSupStr Then
        Console.WriteLine("OK, go ahead!")
    Else
        Console.WriteLine("Well, then don't...")
    End If
    Console.WriteLine()
    Console.WriteLine("Press a key to exit!")
End Sub
```

The corresponding operator procedures that make this approach possible can be structured as follows:

```
Public Shared Operator IsTrue(ByVal sString As SuperString) As Boolean
    Dim locString As String = sString
    locString = locString.ToUpper
    Select Case locString
        Case "YES"
            Return True
        Case "Y"
            Return True
        Case "CORRECT"
            Return True
        Case "TRUE"
            Return True
        Case "SELECTED"
            Return True
        Case "PRESSED"
            Return True
        Case "CONFIRMED"
            Return True
        Case "ACCEPTED"
            Return True
    End Select
    Return False
End Operator

Public Shared Operator IsFalse(ByVal sString As SuperString) As Boolean
    If sString Then
        Return False
    Else
        Return True
    End If
End Operator
```

> **Note** As with comparison operators, the operators *IsTrue* and *IsFalse* must be bound in pairs. In addition, when binding *IsTrue* and *IsFalse*, you should also consider wiring the *Not* operator; otherwise, the developer who is using your class can't use the following expression:
>
> ```
> If Not locSupStr Then
>     .
>     .
>     .
> End If
> ```

Problem Handling for Operator Procedures

When used correctly, operator procedures can make a developer's life a lot easier. But at the same time, bear in mind that there are some situations where implementing operator procedures can cause errors.

Beware When Using Reference Types!

This chapter's *SuperString* example added operator procedures to a structure, which is a value type. The operator procedures also accepted value types. Now take a closer look at one of the calculation operator procedures:

```
Public Shared Operator +(ByVal sstring1 As SuperString, ByVal sstring2 As SuperString) As
➥SuperString
    Return sstring1.Add(sstring2)
End Operator
```

Here, the *Add* function is applied to *sstring1*, and *Add* returns a new instance of *SuperString*. But it doesn't have to be this way. Some implementations are "inclined" to change the object itself. If *Add* did that (if *Add* were a method that didn't return a function result), the code of the operator procedure might look like this:

```
Public Shared Operator +(ByVal sstring1 As SuperString, ByVal sstring2 As SuperString) As
➥SuperString
    sstring1.Add(sstring2)
    Return sstring1
End Operator
```

As long as the values that are manipulated by *sstring1.Add* are value types, and as long as *sstring1* itself is a value type, such a procedure carries no risk.

But this becomes tricky when an *Add* method manipulates a reference type, and when *sstring1* itself is a reference type.

In this case, you would basically accept a pointer to the actual object data as a parameter in *sstring1*. The subsequent addition wouldn't change a copy of *sstring1*, but instead would change the existing instance—which would have originally been located in the calling code

of the operator. You would thus get the same result in the object variable which you pass as an operand as well as in the object variable to which you assign the expression.

The following code illustrates this. In this example, assume the type for which operators have been defined is a reference type:

```
Dim objVar1 As New RefType(10)
Dim objVar2 As New RefType(20)
Dim objVar3 As RefType
objVar3 = ObjVar1 + objVar2
```

Assuming *RefType* can add numbers, the result of 30 wouldn't only be in *objVar3*, but also in *objVar1*. And in the end, it's actually even worse: *objVar3* and *objVar1* point to the same data. Thus, changing *objVar1* would always lead to changing *objVar3*.

Especially with operator procedures, where you'd least expect such a behavior, you should make sure that their return value always returns a new instance of their type when they are processing reference types.

Be Careful of Ambiguities During Signature Resolution

The example class permits the following after the type conversion functions have been fully implemented:

```
aSuperString = aSuperString + "Klaus"
```

At first glance, this might seem strange, because you haven't implemented an overload version that accepts a "simple" string for the addition. Nevertheless, the Visual Basic compiler doesn't report an error. That's correct, and here's why:

The only operator procedure that permits an addition with the + operator accepts a variable of the type *SuperString* as second parameter. This parameter has an implicit type conversion mechanism that can convert a regular *String* into a *SuperString*. Therefore, the compiler does the only right thing: it implicitly converts "Klaus" into a *SuperString*, and then passes that *SuperString* to the *Addition* operator procedure.

So what happens if there is an implicit conversion of *String* into *SuperString* as well as an overloaded version of the addition operator that accepts strings? In this case, the addition operator procedure is used.

But—you guessed it—errors can creep in when the routines use different approaches to convert the string into a *SuperString*. Searching for errors in complex types can then become quite arduous.

> **Tip** Try out all possible parameter combinations. Find out where each conversion actually takes place. To do that, you need to run all the operator procedures step by step in the Visual Studio Debugger.

Implementable Operators: an Overview

You'll probably be amazed at which operators you can implement with operator procedures. Table 14-1 provides an overview.

> **Important** Note that some functions can only be implemented in pairs.

The *Intended Mathematical Function* column is just meant to provide you with an implementation guideline. In the end, nobody can stop you from subtracting your data types with +, or adding them with −. It's up to you.

TABLE 14-1 Operators in Visual Basic 2010 for the Implementation of Custom Types

Operator	Intended mathematical function	Note
+	Addition	
−	Subtraction	
\	Division without remainder	
/	Division	
^	Power	
&	Composition	
<<	Move left	Normally bit-wise with integers.
>>	Move right	Normally bit-wise with integers.
=	Test for equivalency	Not for controlling an object variable assignment, which is only possible with a *Ctype* operator. When implementing this operator, < > (not equal) must also be implemented.
< >	Test for non-equivalency	When implementing this operator, = (equal to) must also be implemented.
<	Test for less than	When implementing this operator, > (greater than) must also be implemented.
>	Test for greater than	When implementing this operator, < (less than) must also be implemented.
<=	Test for less than or equal to	When implementing this operator, > = (greater than or equal to) must also be implemented.
>=	Test for greater than or equal to	When implementing this operator, < = (less than or equal to) must also be implemented.

Operator	Intended mathematical function	Note
Like	Test for similarity	
Mod	Determining remainder	
And	Logical And composition	
Or	Logical Or composition	
Xor	Logical ExclusiveOr composition	
Not	Logical negation	
CType	Control of implicit or explicit type conversion	Use *Narrowing* for explicit and *Widening* for implicit type conversion.
IsTrue	Evaluation of boolean expressions	*IsTrue* and *IsFalse* must be implemented as a pair. You should also provide a *Not* operator here. **Important:** These operators can only be used in evaluation constructors, such as *If … Then … Else, Do While*, and so on—they do *not* provide implicit conversion into the data type *Boolean*.
IsFalse	Evaluation of boolean expressions	Same as for *IsTrue*. You can read more about this in the section "Implementing True and False Evaluation Operators," earlier in this chapter.

Chapter 15

Events, Delegates, and Lambda Expressions

You are probably familiar with events in Windows programming, from subroutines that handle common user events, such as a button click or a list item selection. However, consuming these predefined events is just the tip of the iceberg.

Classes can also trigger events that can be used by other classes. Event-raising classes should follow certain rules, which you'll examine later in more detail. You can also connect events retroactively (at runtime) to corresponding handlers, so that they're consumed only when necessary.

Behind the scenes, events are based on lists of *delegates*. Variables of type *Delegate* (and types derived from *Delegate*) function, in principle, like regular variables; however, instead of storing data, they store pointers to methods. This is why you can "call" a delegate variable; the program transfers execution to the method to which the delegate variable points.

This chapter deals with events. Not only does it introduce these technologies, but it also illustrates how you can add your own events to custom classes. These events are triggered at runtime and can then be consumed by other components.

Companion Content Open the corresponding solution (.sln), which you can find in the \VB 2010 Developer Handbook\Chapter 15\Alarm01 folder.

For this chapter, you'll use a sample program that, in its first version, imitates a simple alarm clock. When you first start this sample project you see the form shown in Figure 15-1.

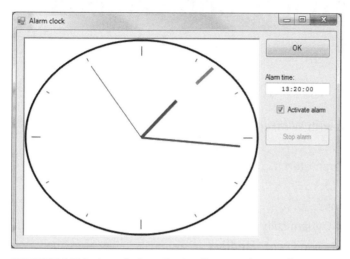

FIGURE 15-1 This alarm clock application illustrates the use of events.

This is roughly how the program functions: you can enter an alarm time in the format *HH:mm:ss* in the *Alarm Time* field. If you check the box *Activate Alarm Clock*, the program draws a small red mark on the clock face that shows the alarm time. When the clock reaches this time, it triggers an alarm clock "rings"—in this case by making the entire graphic of the clock blink red.

It's not really important here how the program draws the clock into the *PictureBox* control. What's important is the class that handles the alarm functionality. Basically, this class works like a regular alarm clock. You set the alarm time by using a property, and when that time arrives, the class triggers an event.

There are two ways to consume events:

■ Assigning the desired procedure by using a field variable of a class declared with the keyword *WithEvents*.

■ Manually adding an event handler procedure by using an *AddHandler* method at runtime.

However, there is an even faster way of consuming events. You can implement event triggers with *Onxxx* methods in a derived class. In this case, it makes more sense to override the event-raising routines and to implement the event handler in this manner. This is the preferred option with Windows Forms applications if you want to code for form events.

> **Note**   In Chapter 4, "Introduction to Windows Forms—Designers and Code Editor by Example," in the section, "The Property Window," you learned how to insert event routine bodies into your code with the help of the Editor or the Designer. This chapter takes the next step and shows you how event handlers work in more detail.

Consuming Events with *WithEvents* and *Handles*

If you insert a button into an empty form and then double-click the button, the Visual Studio IDE opens the Code Editor, displays the form code, and inserts a function body, which is later called when the user clicks the button at runtime.

To make such event handling possible, there are three required components: the object variable that provides the event must be declared with *WithEvents*; the signature[1] of the procedure that processes the event must correspond to the event signature the object provides; and finally, the procedure that uses the keyword *Handles* must be wired to the object event (or with other events of the object or with events of other objects, if their signatures are the same).

The routines that perform this kind of event handling in our sample code are as follows:

```
'Event handler routine which is caused when
'the AlarmTrigger signals an alarm, because a
'certain time has been reached.
Private Sub myAlarmTrigger_Alarm(ByVal Sender As Object, ByVal e As AlarmEventArgs) _
    Handles myAlarmTrigger.Alarm
    'Alarm clock rings!
    myAlarmStatus = True
    'And it rings for this amount of time.
    myAlarmDownCounter = myAlarmDuration
    'We should be able to turn it off.
    btnTurnOff.Enabled = True
    'And it should ring at the same time tomorrow.
    e.Reset = True
End Sub

'Event handling routine, triggered
'when the Picturebox content is redrawn.
Private Sub picAlarmClock_Paint(ByVal sender As Object, _
    ByVal e As System.Windows.Forms.PaintEventArgs) _
    Handles picAlarmClock.Paint
    If myAlarmTrigger IsNot Nothing AndAlso myAlarmTrigger.AlarmActivated Then
        DrawClock(e.Graphics, Date.Now, myAlarmTrigger.AlarmTime, myCurrentColor)
    Else
        DrawClock(e.Graphics, Date.Now, myCurrentColor)
    End If
End Sub
```

---

[1]   Remember that the signature of a procedure is composed of the types that a procedure accepts as parameters.

.
.
.

```
'Event handling routine triggered
'when the timer fires. This happens
'every 500 milliseconds, at which point we redraw
'the complete clock-taking background blinking
'into consideration if the alarm clock is going off.
Private Sub myTimer_Tick(ByVal sender As Object, ByVal e As System.EventArgs)
    Handles myTimer.Tick
    'Is the alarm going off?
    If myAlarmStatus Then
        'Yes, change colors every 500 ms
        If myCurrentColor = Color.White Then
            myCurrentColor = Color.Red
        Else

            myCurrentColor = Color.White
        End If
        'Reduce alarm duration counter
        myAlarmDownCounter -= 1
        If myAlarmDownCounter = 0 Then
            'Switch off alarm when it has run out.
            SwitchOffAlarm(True)
        End If
    End If

    'Redraw entire clock in any case
    picAlarmClock.Invalidate()
End Sub
```

You must declare the following three objects at class scope. These thus become field variables whose events are handled by the appropriate procedures:

- *myTimer*

- *picAlarmClock*

- *myAlarmTrigger*

You must declare all object variables that provide events with the keyword *WithEvents*, as shown in the sample that follows. The exception here is *picAlarmClock*, which represents a control added to the form with the Designer:

```
Public Class frmMain

    Private WithEvents myTimer As Timer
    Private WithEvents myAlarmTrigger As SimpleAlarmTrigger
```

IntelliSense shows the corresponding object events only when the procedure is followed by the *Handles* keyword, as shown in Figure 15-2.

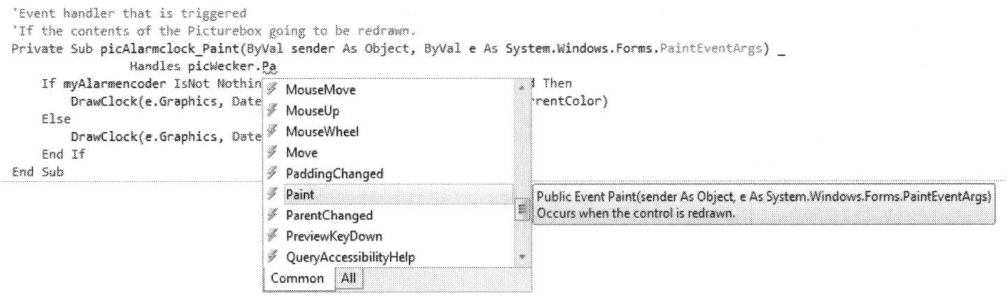

```
'Event handler that is triggered
'If the contents of the Picturebox going to be redrawn.
Private Sub picAlarmclock_Paint(ByVal sender As Object, ByVal e As System.Windows.Forms.PaintEventArgs) _
          Handles picWecker.Pa
   If myAlarmencoder IsNot Nothin                          Then
      DrawClock(e.Graphics, Date                        rrentColor)
   Else
      DrawClock(e.Graphics, Date
   End If
End Sub
```

| MouseMove |
| MouseUp |
| MouseWheel |
| Move |
| PaddingChanged |
| Paint |
| ParentChanged |
| PreviewKeyDown |
| QueryAccessibilityHelp |

Common | All

Public Event Paint(sender As Object, e As System.Windows.Forms.PaintEventArgs)
Occurs when the control is redrawn.

FIGURE 15-2 IntelliSense helps you to wire events to a procedure—when you're selecting possible event-providing objects as well as when you're selecting events.

Object variables that reference controls are bound into the form code in the same manner, but that code is not immediately visible, because the Visual Studio Designer that generates the form code divides the source code of a class into several physical files to keep the actual code file of the form "cleaner."

To see the rest of the form's code, click the *Show All Files* icon at the top frame of the tool window in Solution Explorer (use the ToolTips to help you find the correct icon). After doing that, you see a plus sign in front of every form file that has a branch that you can open by clicking it. Each form has a file called *form.Designer.vb* that contains the background code that declares the controls on the form; there you see the *WithEvents* keyword used to wire the events, as shown in the following:

```
.
.   ' At the end of the file frmMain.Designer.vb:
.
    Friend WithEvents picAlarmClock As System.Windows.Forms.PictureBox
    Friend WithEvents Label1 As System.Windows.Forms.Label
    Friend WithEvents mtbAlarmTime As System.Windows.Forms.MaskedTextBox
    Friend WithEvents chkActivateAlarm As System.Windows.Forms.CheckBox
    Friend WithEvents btnOK As System.Windows.Forms.Button
    Friend WithEvents btnTurnOff As System.Windows.Forms.Button

End Class
```

Raising Events

The code sample that follows for event handling routines shows generally how you wire events to certain procedures. The section in bold, for example, consumes an event from a class instance that is not even part of .NET Framework—we created this class specifically to demonstrate how classes trigger events.

Here's the relevant class code (in *AlarmTrigger.vb*):

```vb
Public Class SimpleAlarmTrigger

    Private WithEvents myTrigger As Timer
    Private myAlarmTime As Date
    Private myAlarmActivated As Boolean
    Private myThreshold As Integer = 2

    ''' <summary>
    ''' Is triggered when a certain time has been reached.
    ''' </summary>
    ''' <param name="Sender">The object which triggered this event.</param>
    ''' <param name="e">AlarmEventArgs which give more information about the object.</param>
    ''' <remarks></remarks>
    Public Event Alarm(ByVal Sender As Object, ByVal e As AlarmEventArgs)

    Sub New(ByVal AlarmTime As Date)
        Me.AlarmTime = AlarmTime
    End Sub

    Sub New(ByVal AlarmTime As Date, ByVal Activated As Boolean)
        Me.AlarmTime = AlarmTime
        Me.AlarmActivated = Activated
    End Sub
    .
    .
    .

    Private Sub myTrigger_Tick(ByVal sender As Object,
                               ByVal e As System.EventArgs) Handles myTrigger.Tick
        If myAlarmTime < DateTime.Now Then
            Dim locAlarmClockEventArgs As New AlarmEventArgs(AlarmTime)
            OnRing(locRingTimeEventArgs)
            If locRingTimeEventArgs.Recreated Then
                AlarmTime = locRingTimeEventArgs.AlarmTime
            Else
                AlarmActivated = False
            End If
        End If
    End Sub

    ''' <summary>
    ''' Triggers ringing.
    ''' </summary>
    ''' <param name="e"></param>
    ''' <remarks></remarks>
    Protected Overridable Sub OnRing(ByVal e As AlarmEventArgs)
        RaiseEvent Alarm(Me, e)
    End Sub
End Class
```

The class needs an aid that takes care of triggering the event at the correct time. The code must check the time at regular intervals, to find out whether the specified alarm time has been reached. For this purpose the class uses a *Timer* object called *myTrigger* that is defined

as a field variable by using *WithEvents*. The *Tick* event is wired to the procedure *myTrigger_Tick*, which is called repeatedly, as long as the timer is running.

The *Tick* event handler compares the current time with the alarm time and fires the *Alarm* event when the alarm time has been reached. The code calls the *OnRing* method, which ensures that the actual event is triggered with *RaiseEvent*. *RaiseEvent* can fire any event defined at class level with the keyword *Event*—in this example, this is the *Alarm* event.

Events Cannot Be Inherited—the Detour Via *Onxxx*

If you're asking yourself why *myTrigger_Tick* has to use the *OnRing* workaround, remember object-oriented programming (OOP) and Chapter 10, "Class Inheritance and Polymorphism."

Here's the reason. Suppose that you want to implement events in a base class, and then use them in derived classes. You want to ensure that the events are raised, but you also want to ensure that derived classes can trigger events. However, the latter is only possible by using a workaround; derived classes *cannot use the events of their base classes*, as the following example shows:

```
'Base class
Public Class BaseClass

    Public Event SomethingHappened(ByVal sender As Object, ByVal e As EventArgs)

    Protected Overridable Sub OnSomethingHappened(ByVal e As EventArgs)
        RaiseEvent SomethingHappened(Me, e)
    End Sub

End Class

'Derived class
Public Class DerivedClass
    Inherits BaseClass

    Private Sub MethodForRaisingEvent()
        'Error:
        'Derived classes cannot raise base class events
        RaiseEvent SomethingHappened(Me, EventArgs.Empty)

        'But it works this way!
        OnSomethingHappened(EventArgs.Empty)

    End Sub

End Class
```

Fortunately, you can use the workaround shown in the preceding example to raise events from within the code of a derived class. The derived class simply calls the *Onxxx* methods implemented by the base class; those methods then trigger the desired event.

It also works the other way around: the derived class doesn't need to wire the event itself during implementation. It can simply override the corresponding method of the base class that raises the event. This is the most direct path.

This is the basic principle for all event-raising components (including forms) that can be used through inheritance in the .NET Framework. How the routine in the event example works is therefore pretty much self-explanatory. The form events aren't wired to a specific procedure with *Handles*; instead the base code of the form is simply overridden. For example, the *OnResize* method triggers the *Resize* event when the form size changes:

```
'Called by the base class part of System.Windows.Forms.Form,
'when the form is resized.
Protected Overrides Sub OnResize(ByVal e As System.EventArgs)
    'Important: Call base function, otherwise the
    'Resize event is no longer raised!
    MyBase.OnResize(e)
    'Redraw content of the PictureBox,
    'when the form size has changed.
    picAlarmClock.Invalidate()
End Sub
```

Important When overriding event-raising *Onxxx* methods in derived classes, be sure to call the base method with *myBase.Onxxx*. Otherwise, you might prevent events from being triggered, because *RaiseEvent* will no longer fire, possibly causing problems for developers working with instances of your class.

Providing Event Parameters

If you examine the different event handling routines shown so far, you'll soon recognize a recurring scheme in the event signatures:

```
Private Sub myTrigger_Tick(ByVal sender As Object, ByVal e As System.EventArgs) Handles
myTrigger.Tick
    .
    .
    .
End Sub
```

- Each signature contains a parameter called *sender* of type *Object*—which provides information about the event trigger. The variable sender is declared as *Object*, because very different objects (*TextBoxes, ListBoxes*, and so on) can raise an event.

- A second parameter named *e* of type *EventArgs* (or a derivate of *EventArgs*)—either provides more data about the event or gives you control over the remaining chain of events. The base class *System.EventArgs* does not contain such additional information. However, if you implement the *KeyDown* event of a form, for example, *e* is the derived type *System.Windows.Forms.KeyPressEventArgs*, a type that provides (among others) an *e.KeyChar* property (the character produced by pressing that key).

> **Tip** When you fire an event that doesn't require individual event parameters, and therefore needs only the base implementation of *EventArgs*, just use the static method *Empty* to pass a valid *EventArgs* instance, as demonstrated in the following:
>
> ```
> RaiseEvent AnEvent(Me, EventArgs.Empty)
> ```

The Event Source: *sender*

The *sender* parameter always contains the event source as an object. This is particularly important when an event handler routine must process several events from different objects—something that was unthinkable in Visual Basic 6.0 or VBA—because you need to be able to discover which object is responsible for which event, and react accordingly.

> **Companion Content** Open the corresponding solution (.sln), which you can find in the \VB 2010 Developer Handbook\Chapter 15\EventTest folder.

When you start the *EventTest* project, you see a form with several buttons, as shown in Figure 15-3.

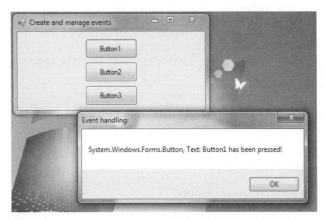

FIGURE 15-3 The example contains an event handler routine for all three buttons.

At first glance, there seems to be nothing special about this code sample. But notice that although the form handles the *Click* event for each button, there's only one event handling routine that takes care of all three events:

```
Public Class frmEvents

    Private Sub Button1And2Events(ByVal sender As System.Object, ByVal e As
        System.EventArgs) _
            Handles Button1.Click, Button2.Click, Button3.Click

        'A MessageBox is displayed when the user triggers Button1, Button2, or
        'Button3.
        MessageBox.Show(sender.ToString & " was clicked!")

    End Sub
End Class
```

That code makes it clear what *sender* is good for. To discover which button triggered the event, you inspect *sender* and take that into consideration when handling the *Click* event.

Because *sender* is not a *String* variable with descriptive text, but an actual reference to the event-raising object, you can cast *sender* back to its original type with `Dim btn As Button=CType(Sender, Button)`.

In this example, you know that type casting won't cause problems because the example uses only buttons. Therefore, you can use the following code to convert *sender* back to the original *Button* object, and then manipulate it in ways that are not possible with *sender* itself:

```
Public Class frmEvents

    Private Sub Button1And2Events(ByVal sender As System.Object, ByVal e As
System.EventArgs) _
            Handles Button1.Click, Button2.Click, Button3.Click

        'A MessageBox is displayed when the user triggers Button1, Button2, or
        'Button3.
        MessageBox.Show(sender.ToString & " was clicked!", "Event handling result:")

        'Color the clicked button red.

        'ERROR! Not possible, because Sender has the type Object:
        sender.Backcolor = Color.Red

        'This works, because there are only buttons,
        'therefore it's safe to cast in Button:
        Dim locClickedButton As Button
        locClickedButton = DirectCast(sender, Button)

        'Now it's possible to color the clicked button in red
        locClickedButton.BackColor = Color.Red
    End Sub
End Class
```

This becomes slightly more complex when *sender* might be any of several types. For example, to discover whether the *sender* type is *Button*, you use the rather clumsy syntax *If TypeOf sender Is Button Then...* in Visual Basic. Of course, you can replace *Button* with any other type for which you want to check.

Detailed Event Information: *EventArgs*

EventArgs is a class intended for sending parameters to event-receiving instances. Even if an event does not require parameters, event parameters are always passed with an *EventArgs* instance; again, if you don't need special values, use the static function *EventArgs.Empty*, which generates an *EventArgs* object without content.

When an event requires specific parameters, you just create a new class that inherits from *EventArgs* (the name of the class should also end in *EventArgs*) and extend it with the properties and constructors you need to hold the parameters for the event.

In many cases, an instance of *EventArgs* does more than just pass parameters to event-binding instances. An event-binding instance can also change the parameters of an *EventArgs* instance to signal that the rest of the event chain should be controlled in some way. For example, when you write an event procedure for the *Form_Closing* event, you can prevent the form from closing by setting e.Cancel=True. You might use this, for example, when your application still contains unsaved data, but the form closing event was triggered by shutting down Windows.

Note Take a look at the conditions in the following code line:

```
If e.ClosingReason=CloseReason.WindowsShutDown And UnsavedData=True Then e.Cancel=True
```

If all of the conditions are true, then even the Windows shutdown itself can be cancelled through the *e* argument of the *FormClosing* event. This is a special Windows characteristic, because preventing data loss has higher priority. You can also see this feature in action in other Windows programs; for example, try shutting down the computer with an open file containing unsaved text in Microsoft Word.

Having pointed all that out, why then doesn't this rule apply to the installation of a series of hotfixes or a Service Pack within the Windows operating system? When a hotfix or Service Pack has been applied, Windows tends to shut down in the middle of a work session, and it really doesn't care if documents are opened or, even worse, whether they're saved. Please, Microsoft, make Windows stop doing that!

Let's return to the alarm clock example to demonstrate this component of event programming. Take another look at the event-raising procedure:

```
Private Sub myTrigger_Tick(ByVal sender As Object, ByVal e As System.EventArgs) Handles _
                                                    myTrigger.Tick
    If myAlarmTime < DateTime.Now Then
        Dim locRingTimeEventArgs As New AlarmEventArgs(AlarmTime)
        OnRing(locRingTimeEventArgs)
        If locRingTimeEventArgs.Reset Then
            AlarmTime = locRingTimeEventArgs.AlarmTime
        Else
            AlarmActivated = False
        End If
    End If
End Sub
```

In this code, *AlarmEventArgs* is a custom class derived from *EventArgs* that provides the parameters *AlarmTime* and *Reset* for the event. The *AlarmEventArgs* class exists only to provide these two parameters; it has no other function.

```
Public Class AlarmEventArgs
    Inherits EventArgs

    Private myAlarmTime As Date
    Private myReset As Boolean

    Sub New(ByVal AlarmTime As Date)
        myAlarmTime = AlarmTime
        myResetn = True
    End Sub

    Sub New(ByVal AlarmTime As Date, ByVal Reset As Boolean)
        myAlarmTime = AlarmTime
        myReset = Reset
    End Sub

    Public Property AlarmTime() As Date
        Get
            Return myAlarmTime
        End Get
        Set(ByVal value As Date)
            myAlarmTime = value
        End Set
    End Property

    Public Property Reset() As Boolean
        Get
            Return myReset
        End Get
        Set(ByVal value As Boolean)
            myReset = value
        End Set
    End Property
End Class
```

Looking at both code snippets shows that event parameters can work in both directions. A procedure that processes the event can specify whether the alarm clock should ring the next day at the same time by setting the *Reset* property. When the event is raised and an instance of the *AlarmEventArgs* class is "passed upward," one parameter (*AlarmTime*) serves the event-binding class and the other (*Reset*) serves the event-raising class. The sample code you saw earlier (*Private Sub myTrigger_Tick*) shows how to set these parameters.

Delegates

When programming, the statements you write in a high-level language are translated into op-codes (byte command sequences) that can be interpreted and run by the different processor cores. You can get an idea of how this works by setting a breakpoint in a line of your program in the Editor by pressing F9, starting your program, running it to the break-point, and then executing the command Disassembly in the *Debug menu under Window*. Figure 15-4 shows a Visual Basic example of how this looks in the assembler.

```
        Dim t As Integer = 15
000000a9 C7 45 B8 0F 00 00 00 mov        dword ptr [ebp-48h],0Fh
        Dim product = 10 * t
000000b0 8B 45 B8           mov        eax,dword ptr [ebp-48h]
000000b3 BA 0A 00 00 00     mov        edx,0Ah
000000b8 6B C0 0A           imul       eax,eax,0Ah
```

FIGURE 15-4 The Disassembly window shows how the individual lines of your program look from the processor's point of view: These are real byte sequences that represent the Assembler op-codes (the data the processor understands as commands).

In Figure 15-4, the value 15 (hexadecimal 0F) is regarded as an integer (*dword*) and written into the memory location specified by the address [*ebp-48h*]. This corresponds to the code that assigns the value 15 to the variable *t*. The next lines are equally easy to interpret, but this book is not about learning and understanding assembly language.

What's important here is for you to recognize that programs and program parts are located at specific places in your computer's main memory, just like data. And if programs are data, then there should be something like variables to program parts, subs, or functions—in other words, methods.

The problem is that program parts such as methods must be subject to type safety. The example that follows shows why.

Companion Content Open the corresponding solution (.sln), which you can find in the \VB 2010 Developer Handbook\Chapter 15\Delegates\DelegatesDemo1 folder.

```
Module Module1

    Sub Main()
        Console.ReadKey()
        If Debugger.IsAttached Then
            Debugger.Break()
        End If
        Dim s = Square(12)
        Dim p = Power(2, 12)
        Console.WriteLine(s.ToString)
        Console.WriteLine(s.ToString)
    End Sub

    Function Square(ByVal var1 As Integer) As Integer
        Dim ret = var1 * var1
        Return ret
    End Function

    Function Power(ByVal var1 As Integer, ByVal var2 As Integer) As Integer
        For c As Integer = 1 To var2
            var1 *= var1
        Next
        Return var1
    End Function

End Module
```

You might wonder why the program starts by pressing a key before anything else happens. Don't worry: in the following, you'll look at the program from the processor's point of view and examine how it runs the program.

1. In the Debug menu, click the command Start Without Debugging, or press Ctrl+F5 to start the program with debugging disabled.

2. Launch a second instance of Visual Studio 2010.

3. From the Debug menu of the new Visual Studio instance, click the command *Attach To Process*.

    Visual Studio displays the dialog shown in Figure 15-5.

> **Note** This feature is not available in Visual Studio Express 2010; it's available only with Visual Studio 2010 Professional or higher versions.

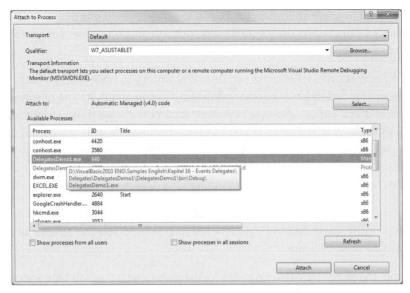

FIGURE 15-5 Using a second instance of Visual Studio, you can debug applications that you can't interrupt directly, such as custom controls in the Designer of another Visual Studio instance.

4. Select the sample application you just started from the list, and then click the Attach button.

5. Navigate back to the console application, and then press any key.

As soon as you trigger the key press, the program encounters the statement *Debugger.Break* and stops in the second instance of Visual Studio. It also shows the corresponding source code. You can now open the assembly window by going to the Debug/Window menu and clicking Disassembly. Once there you'll see the commands the processor will execute next (see Figure 15-6).

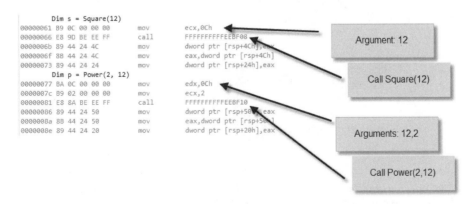

FIGURE 15-6 Parameters are passed to methods by loading the corresponding processor registers with arguments.

Ok, now you not only know how to append the debugger to any desired application to examine it from the processor's standpoint, but you also know how parameters are passed to methods in assembly language.

Looking at that code, it becomes apparent that when you want to use a data type that stores addresses of subroutines in an object variable, it's not enough for the object variable to save only an address. It must also save how many parameters were passed to this routine. If you take another look at Figure 15-6, you can probably imagine what happens if this order is not strictly followed. There is no instance that ensures that the appropriate memory addresses or processor registers are allocated the correct values. The subroutine still uses the registers— but they might contain any kind of random values, which can lead to a devastating result.

Therefore, you don't just need a new variable type that can save a program address; this variable type must also define the signature the routine uses. You can achieve all this by using the variable type *Delegate*.

To recap: the signature determines how many parameters of which type are passed to a method when it is called. Now that you possess this knowledge, here's an example that uses delegates within the context of a small Windows Presentation Foundation (WPF) application:

Companion Content Open the corresponding solution (.sln), which you can find in the \VB 2010 Developer Handbook\Chapter 15\Delegates\DelegatesDemo2 folder.

Figure 15-7 shows what you see when you start this application.

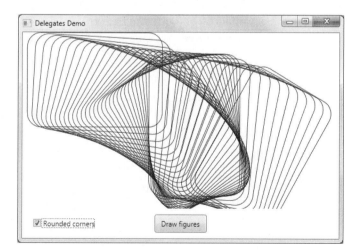

FIGURE 15-7 You can select or clear the Rounded Corners check box to change the style in which the graphic is drawn. Internally this is managed by a delegate variable.

Click the Draw Figures button to draw a graphic made of rectangles on the screen. If you select the *Rounded Corners* check box, the sample application refreshes the graphic with rounded corners. Internally, a *Delegate* variable controls which version is drawn, as the following code segment shows:

```
'Defines a new variable type for saving methods
'which fulfill this signature:
Delegate Function DrawRectangleDelegate(ByVal xLeft As Double,
   ByVal yTop As Double,
   ByVal xRight As Double, ByVal yBottom As Double) As Rectangle

Class MainWindow

   'Declare delegate variable and define with the function for determining
   'an "angular" rectangle
   Private GetRectangle As DrawRectangleDelegate= AddressOf AngularCorners
```

Because delegates, just like enums, structures, and classes, define new types, they aren't forced to assign them to a class by code, as shown in the example. (The definition of the new delegate is located in the first line of the example.) Object variables, later defined by the type *DrawRectangleDelegate,* can be used only to refer to methods that have the exact same signature as the defined delegate type—the type and order of the parameters that are later passed to the compatible methods must match those defined by the delegate. For methods that return values (functions), the return types must also match those defined by the delegate.

The example contains two methods that are signature-compatible with the delegate: *RoundedCorners* and *AngularCorners*. The following code lines show you how these two methods (or rather the *addresses* of these methods) are assigned, depending on the *CheckBox* state, using the *AddressOf* operator of the *GetRectangle* variable which was defined by the type *DrawRectangleDelegate*:

```
   'On click the graphic is drawn from rectangles.
   Private Sub DrawButton_Click(ByVal sender As System.Object,
                        ByVal e As System.Windows.RoutedEventArgs) Handles
DrawButton.Click
      Redraw()
   End Sub

   'The checkbox toggles between rounded and regular corners.
   Private Sub RoundedCornersCheckBox_ToggleCheck(ByVal sender As System.Object,
                    ByVal e As System.Windows.RoutedEventArgs) _
         Handles RoundedCornersCheckBox.Checked, RoundedCornersCheckBox.Unchecked

      If RoundedCornersCheckBox.IsChecked Then
         GetRectangle = AddressOf RoundedCorners
      Else
         GetRectangle = AddressOf AngularCorners
      End If
      Redraw()
   End Sub
```

```
'Redraws the graphic.
Private Sub Redraw()
    Dim s As New Rectangle()
    DrawAreaCanvas.Children.Clear()

    'Fan out a few rectangles, i.e. turn them during drawing...
    For c = 0 To 120 Step 3

        '...and move each next one a bit to the
        'right and down.
        Dim x1, y1 As Double
        x1 = 10 + c * 3
        y1 = c \ 2

        'Here we find out the rectangle object via the delegate
        'which contains a different "address" depending on whether
        'the checkbox was activated or not.
        Dim recToDraw = GetRectangle(x1, y1, x1 + 300, y1 + 200)
```

When the graphic is drawn, the methods are not called directly; they're called indirectly using the method that was assigned to the *Delegate* variable *GetRectangle*.

```
        'Determining the position in WPF on the canvas only works
        'via attached properties.
        Canvas.SetLeft(recToDraw, DirectCast(recToDraw.Tag, Point).X)
        Canvas.SetTop(recToDraw, DirectCast(recToDraw.Tag, Point).Y)

        'We turn the rectangle c degrees; the center of rotation
        'has been moved a bit to the left and up.
        recToDraw.LayoutTransform = New RotateTransform(c, -100, -50)

        'Adding to the children collection on the canvas
        'created the screen display.
        DrawAreaCanvas.Children.Add(recToDraw)
    Next
End Sub

'Creates a WPF rectangle object with normal corners at the specified coordinates...
Private Function AngularCorners(ByVal x1 As Double, ByVal y1 As Double,
                                ByVal x2 As Double, ByVal y2 As Double) As Rectangle

    Return New Rectangle() With {.Tag = New Point(x1, y1),
                                 .Width = x2 - x1,
                                 .Height = y2 - y1,
                                 .Stroke = New SolidColorBrush(Colors.Black)}
End Function

'...and this method creates on with rounded corners.
Private Function RoundedCorners(ByVal x1 As Double, ByVal y1 As Double,
                                ByVal x2 As Double, ByVal y2 As Double) As Rectangle
```

```
        Return New Rectangle() With {.Tag = New Point(x1, y1),
                                     .Width = x2 - x1,
                                     .Height = y2 - y1,
                                     .RadiusX = 30,
                                     .RadiusY = 30,
                                     .Stroke = New SolidColorBrush(Colors.Black)}
    End Function

End Class
```

The rest of the example is easy to understand—it contains just the two methods that are signature-compatible with the new delegate type and whose addresses are saved in the delegate variable, depending on the *CheckBox* state.

Passing Delegates to Methods

Because delegates are basically just variable types, you can pass them to methods as parameters. The following example shows the circumstances under which you can do this. The example is yet another version of the *MiniAddressBook* example from Chapter 9, "First Class Programming."

> **Companion Content** Open the corresponding solution (.sln), which you can find in the \VB 2010 Developer Handbook\Chapter 15\MiniAdressoClass V6 folder.

This version rebuilds the sorting routine of the original example, replacing the sort criteria expression (which was firmly wired to the last name of the contact in the previous version of the program) with a delegate. The delegate expects two parameters: the two *Contact* instances to be compared. The method saved in the delegate returns a value of type *Integer*, as follows: 0 when both contacts are the same, 1, when the first one is larger, and −1 if the first one is smaller. The actual *Contact* value that is compared is controlled by whichever procedure the delegate variable points to. The changes initially look like this:

```
    'Defines the type ComparerDelegate which expects two parameters of the type
    'Contact and returns an Integer.
    '-1: first contact is less
    '0: contact is the same
    '1: first contact is larger
    'Why a contact is actually larger or less is regulated by the method
    'whose address is saved in the delegate.
    'Therefore the sorting algorithm can be used more flexibly.
    Public Delegate Function ComparerDelegate(ByVal k1 As Contact, ByVal k2 As Contact) As
Integer

    'cDel is a delegate variable of the type ComparerDelegate.
    Sub SortAddresses(ByVal cDel As ComparerDelegate)
```

```
Dim numberOfElements As Integer = 101

Dim outerCounter As Integer
Dim innerCounter As Integer
Dim delta As Integer

Dim tempContact As Contact

delta = 1

'Determine the largest value of the distance order
Do
    delta = 3 * delta + 1
Loop Until delta > numberOfElements

Do
    'Cancellation criteria-therefore count down
    delta \= 3

    'Shellsort's kernel algorithmus
    For outerCounter = delta To numberOfElements - 1
        tempContact = tempContact(outerCounter)

        innerCounter = outerCounter
        Do
            'Delegate variables can either be called directly via the name
            'like methods or with the Invoke methode.
            If cDel.Invoke(tempContact, Contacts(innerCounter - delta)) = 1 OrElse _
                cDel(tempContact, Contacts(innerCounter - delta)) = 0 Then Exit Do
            Contacts(innerCounter) = Contacts(innerCounter - delta)

            innerCounter = innerCounter-delta
            If (innerCounter <= delta) Then Exit Do
        Loop
        Contacts(innerCounter) = tempContact
    Next
Loop Until delta = 0
End Sub
```

From the last line in bold, you can see that the actual method call can happen in two ways: the way you've already seen—directly via the delegate variable like a method—or through the *Invoke* method, which receives the same parameters the method would normally receive.

> **Tip** We recommend that you use the *Invoke* method, because this way you can immediately see whether a call is an actual method or a call through a delegate.

The two methods whose addresses are saved as required in the delegate variable ensure that the list is sorted differently, because they compare the contact instances they receive in different ways:

```
Function ContactLastNameComparison(ByVal k1 As Contact, ByVal k2 As Contact) As Integer
    Return String.Compare(k1.LastName, k2.LastName)
End Function

Function ContactCityComparison(ByVal k1 As Contact, ByVal k2 As Contact) As Integer
    Return String.Compare(k1.City, k2.City)
End Function
```

Now let's explore how to use the extended flexibility of this sort routine, and where the delegate variable receives a method:

```
    Sub Main()
    .
    .
    .

        'Generate random addresses
        Console.Write("Random addresses are being generated... ")
        GenerateRandomAddresses()
        Console.WriteLine("Done!")

        'Output the first 10 random addresses
        OutputAddresses(0, 10)

        'Sort the addresses by last name
        Console.WriteLine()
        Console.Write("Addresses are being sorted by last name... ")
        Dim compDelegate As ComparerDelegate = AddressOf ContactLastNameComparison
        SortAddresses(compDelegate)
        Console.WriteLine("Done!")
        Console.WriteLine()

        'Output the first 10 random addresses
        OutputAddresses(0, 10)

        'Sort the addresses by City
        Console.WriteLine()
        Console.Write("Addresses are being sorted by city name... ")
        compDelegate = AddressOf ContactCityComparison
        SortAddresses(compDelegate)
        Console.WriteLine("Done!")
        Console.WriteLine()
    .
    .
    .

    End Sub
```

At two locations, the sort routine uses the delegate parameter to call the comparison methods (which are then used for the actual sorting). The following step-by-step explanation will help you understand how it all works when the program starts up:

1. After creating a set of random addresses, the application defines a delegate variable *compDelegate*, assigning it the address of the method *ContactLastNameComparison*.

2. The *SortAddresses* method is called, passing the delegate variable as an argument.

3. *SortAddresses* runs *Invoke* on the delegate variable, which calls the method *ContactLastNameComparison* for the item comparison.

   The contact list thus is sorted by last name.

4. After that first sort occurs, back in the main module, the delegate variable *compDelegate* is assigned the address of the method *ContactCityComparison*.

5. The application again calls the *SortAddresses* method, passing it the delegate variable again—which now points to a different method than it did before.

6. *SortAddresses* again runs *Invoke* on the delegate variable, which this time calls the *ContactCityComparison* method to perform item comparisons. The contact list is thus sorted by city name during the second iteration.

Lambda Expressions

Lambda expressions combine the best of delegates with the best of methods. Lambdas originate in functional programming. They link functions with object variables. In the simplest case, the code looks like the following example.

> **Companion Content** Open the corresponding solution (.sln), which you can find in the
> \VB 2010 Developer Handbook\Chapter 15\Lambdas\SimpleLambdaDemo folder.

```
Sub Main()

    Dim expressionLambda = Function(square As Double) square * square
    Dim expressionSub = Sub(ValueToPrint As Double)
                            Console.WriteLine(ValueToPrint.ToString)

    '"The following code "prints" 144. First 12*12 is executed,
    'then the result is returned.
    expressionSub(expressionLambda(12))

    'Wait for key, so we can see something.
    Console.ReadKey()

End Sub
```

In this example, you can see lambda expressions in action. The example contains familiar keywords—*Sub* and *Function*—but they are used in an unfamiliar manner. The first thing you notice is that the methods accept parameters, but are missing a method name. This is why lambdas are also called *anonymous methods*.

> **Note** C# actually differentiates between anonymous methods and lambdas by definition, but in the end, the C# compiler turns them into the same thing.

You should learn how to read code like this—and get used to doing so—because both *expressionsLambda* and *expressionSub* are delegate variables. Both types save the addresses of single-line methods defined in-line. The biggest difference is that you don't use the *AddressOf* operator, because the methods whose addresses are saved in the delegate variables have no name. The keywords *Function* and *Sub* without a name directly return the internal memory address of the method to variable to which they're assigned, without you ever actually seeing it (not that you would be able to).

You can then use *expressionLambda* like a method; doing so executes the code behind *Function(...)* in the previous example. And when you use *expressionSub* the example executes the method *Console.WriteLine*. The example also shows that you can use such expression lambdas in a nested fashion.

Single-Line Expression Lambdas and Multi-Line Statement Lambdas

.NET differentiates between *expression lambdas* and *statement lambdas*. The distinguishing characteristic of expression lambdas is that they can consist of only a single line, as shown in the preceding example. This is because you can dynamically build *expression trees* from several lambda expressions that can be compiled at runtime. For multi-line lambda expressions, such structures would be too complicated.

Multi-line statement lambdas are most similar to anonymous methods, which can be reached only via their addresses, which are saved in delegate variables.

Visual Basic 2008 introduced single-line lambda functions as described above, and thus provides an easier way to use delegates, but they work only on *Function*—expressions. Lambdas without return values (defined by *Sub*) are not possible in Visual Basic 2008.

A method from a collection class demonstrates how flexible programming can be with multi-line lambdas. (The same example gets a bit ahead of the explanations in the book.) The *ForEach* method of the generic list *List(Of)* shows the use of lambdas in a simple and plausible way. If you need to process the items of the generic list as quickly as possible, a lambda function

makes a lot of sense, because, unlike the regular *For Each* construct, it doesn't need to take an internal detour via *GetEnumerator* to enumerate all the list items; instead, it can access the list items directly.

For example, to return the list items in the Debug window with a lambda function you can use the following code:

```
Sub LambdaDemo()
    Dim namesList As New List(Of String) From {"Peter", "Klaus", "Tanja", "Sonja"}
    'Instead of a delegate:
    Dim writeToDebugDelegate As New Action(Of String)(AddressOf WriteToDebug)
    namesList.ForEach(writeToDebugDelegate)

    'We write it directly:
    namesList.ForEach(Function(item) WriteToDebug(item))
End Sub

Shared Function WriteToDebug(ByVal text As String) As Boolean
    Debug.Print(text)
    Return True
End Function
```

In this case, *Action(Of String)* is the delegate type that the *ForEach* method expects as delegate variable, but you can also pass the lambda function of the *ForEach* method directly as a parameter.

Until Visual Basic 2010, lambdas were limited to methods with return parameters. Therefore, before Visual Basic 2010, it was impossible to specify a construct such as *Debug.Print* directly in a lambda function because *Debug.Print* represents a *Sub*—a method without a return value. However, with the advent of Visual Basic 2010, this is possible. The construct

```
namesList.ForEach(Sub(item) Debug.Print(item))
```

is permitted, as well as multi-line lambdas:

```
namesList.ForEach(Sub(item)
                      'Several lines of code can be placed here
                      Debug.Print(item)
                  End Sub)
```

Using lambdas will make you look at Visual Basic programs in a different way. Lambdas have the potential of relieving the developer's workload, because in many scenarios, they eliminate the need to use delegates, which reduces the number of lines of code and saves programming time. At the same time, the code looks cleaner, because the code itself is located at the spot where it actually happens.

This means even more in .NET Framework 4.0, because delegates are used more frequently for parallel code execution, where automatic distribution over several processors or processor cores is important, as the following example shows.

> **Note** You must import the namespace *System.Threading.Tasks* for the following code segment to compile.

```
Parallel.ForEach(namesList, Sub(item)
                                'Parallel item processing.
                                'Watch out: Due to parallelization this no longer
                                'happens sequentially, but instead without
                                'any kind of order!
                                Debug.Print(item)
                             End Sub)
```

You can find more details about parallelization in Chapter 28, "Programming with the Task Parallel Library (TPL)."

In practice, you'll more likely work with lambdas as shown in the following example. This code validates a user entry into a control, triggering an exception if validation fails. In that case, a ToolTip containing an appropriate error message should be displayed right next to the control that caused the exception, as illustrated here:

```
Protected Overrides Sub OnValidating(ByVal e As System.ComponentModel.CancelEventArgs)

    MyBase.OnValidating(e)
    If e.Cancel Then
        Return
    End If

    'ValidateInput checks whether the entry is ok, and returns
    'an exception if there is an error.
    'The exception shows the error text.
    Dim valRes = ValidateInput(myValueControl.Value.ToString)
    If valRes IsNot Nothing Then
        e.Cancel = True

        'If necessary we can also issue an audio alert.
        If myBeepOnFailedValidation Then
            Beep()
        End If

        'The error message must be displayed in a Tooltip
        'next to the control for a certain amount of time.
        Dim tt As New ToolTip()

        'We draw the control ourselves.
        tt.OwnerDraw = True

        'Fade out.
        tt.UseFading = True
        tt.UseAnimation = True
```

```vb
'Thanks to multi-line Lambdas we can pass the drawing code
'directly to the Draw event.
AddHandler tt.Draw,
    Sub(sender As Object, de As DrawToolTipEventArgs)
        Dim pen As New Pen(Brushes.Black, 1)
        'Clone Point array and adjust coordinates

        Dim path As New GraphicsPath()
        Dim p1, p2 As PointF
        p1 = PointF.Empty

        'The coordinates of the ToolTip frame are in a List(Of PointF),
        'which we iterate with the ForEach method 'and again with a
        'multi-line Lambda.
        myToolTipShapeCoordinates.ForEach(
            Sub(item)

                'Adjust the ToolTip coordinates to the control coordinates:
                Dim x = item.X
                Dim y = item.Y
                If x = -1 Then
                    x = de.Bounds.X + de.Bounds.Width - 1
                Else
                    x += de.Bounds.X
                End If

                If y = -1 Then
                    y = de.Bounds.Y + de.Bounds.Height - 1
                Else
                    y += de.Bounds.Y
                End If
                p1 = p2
                p2 = New PointF(x, y)
                If p1 <> Point.Empty Then
                    path.AddLine(p1, p2)
                End If
            End Sub)

        'Set to AntiAlias so that drawing looks softer.
        de.Graphics.SmoothingMode = SmoothingMode.AntiAlias
        path.CloseFigure()

        'Draw background, border, and text of the ToolTip:
        de.Graphics.FillPath(New SolidBrush(Color.AliceBlue), path)
        de.Graphics.DrawPath(Pens.Black, path)
        de.Graphics.DrawString(de.ToolTipText, New Font(
            FontFamily.GenericSansSerif,8, FontStyle.Regular),
            Brushes.Black, New RectangleF(de.Bounds.X + 15, de.Bounds.Y + 5,
            de.Bounds.Width - 15, de.Bounds.Height - 5))
    End Sub
```

```
                 'Issue ToolTip. This triggers the above code,
                 'because only now the Draw event of the ToolTip is triggered
                 'which was assigned this code with AddHandler.
                 tt.Show("Error in the entry:" & vbNewLine & vbNewLine &
                         valRes.Message, Me, Me.Width - 10, Me.Height \ 2,
                         Me.ExceptionBalloonDuration)
         End If
     End Sub
```

Embedding Events Dynamically with *AddHandler*

Event embedding using the keyword *WithEvents* fails when you declare the objects that provide the events at the procedure level (locally) or if they're part of an array or collection. In such
situtations, you can wire up events dynamically at runtime by using *AddHandler*.

> **Companion Content** Open the corresponding solution (.sln), which you can find in the
> \VB 2010 Developer Handbook\Chapter 15\Alarm02 folder.

This example expands the simple alarm clock application you saw earlier in the chapter by
permitting more than just one alarm time. When you start the program, you see the screen
depicted in Figure 15-8.

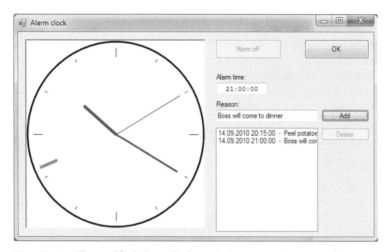

FIGURE 15-8 The modified Alarm Clock application can capture several alarm times.

Figure 15-8 shows that you can specify multiple alarm times. This version also lets you provide a message that is displayed on the clock face when the alarm goes off, as shown in
Figure 15-9.

Internally, this version has a class that manages a list of object instances, similar to *DynamicList*, which you saw in previous chapters. This time, the example uses a generic collection named *Collection*, which ships with the .NET Framework.

The tough part is that you can now no longer use a global variable within the derived *Collection* class that you would declare with *WithEvents*—now you have a *list* of *AlarmTrigger* instances.

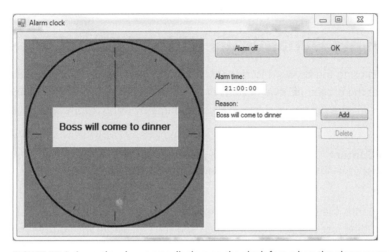

FIGURE 15-9 An optional message displays on the clock face when the alarm goes off.

Therefore, you need to follow a different path: whenever the user enters an alarm time and thus adds a new *AlarmTrigger* instance to the list with *Add*, you need to catch it in the *Collection* derivate and wire an event trigger (defined in *this* class) to the *Alarm* event of the new *AlarmTrigger* instance at runtime.

Conversely, you must ensure that when a user deletes an alarm trigger from the list that you remove the connection. You must also remove all the event connections for all existing *AlarmTrigger* instances in the list if you remove all the items in the list by using *Clear*. Here's how the code should look:

```
Imports System.Collections.ObjectModel

''' <summary>
''' Manages a list with AlarmTrigger objects, and raises an event,
''' when one of the AlarmTrigger objects requires it.
''' </summary>
''' <remarks></remarks>
Public Class AppointmentList
    Inherits Collection(Of AlarmTrigger)

    ''' <summary>
    ''' Is raised when one of the AlarmTrigger objects added to the
    ''' instance fires an Alarm event itself.
```

```
''' </summary>
''' <param name="sender">
        Reference to the AlarmTrigger object which has raised the event.</param>
''' <param name="e">AlarmEventArgs instance which contains parameters
        to the event.</param>
''' <remarks></remarks>
Public Event Alarm(ByVal sender As Object, ByVal e As AlarmEventArgs)

'Contains Nothing or the date of the next appointment.
Private myNextAppointment As Nullable(Of Date)

'Is triggered, for example, by Add or Insert of the Collection class.
'Override, because the Alarm event of the object must be wired
'to the AlarmHandler procedure.
Protected Overrides Sub InsertItem(ByVal index As Integer, ByVal item As AlarmTrigger)

    'Dynamically wire the Alarm event of the object to the prozedur AlarmHandler.
    AddHandler item.Alarm, AddressOf AlarmHandler

    'Let the basic procedure do what it needs to do
    '(namely put the item at the correct location).
    MyBase.InsertItem(index, item)

    'The list has changed-the next appointment could be different!
    UpdateNextAppointmentProperty()
End Sub

'Called via assignment of an item with the Item property.
'Override, because the Alarm event of the object must be wired
'to the AlarmHandler procedure.
Protected Overrides Sub SetItem(ByVal index As Integer, ByVal item As AlarmTrigger)

    'Remove the old item from this location:
    RemoveHandler Me(index).Alarm, AddressOf AlarmHandler

    'Wire the new item
    AddHandler item.Alarm, AddressOf AlarmHandler

    'Let the basic procedure do what it needs to do
    '(namely put the item at the correct location).
    MyBase.SetItem(index, item)
End Sub

'Is triggered, for example, by Remove or RemoveAt of the Collection class.
'Override, to remove the wired event with AlarmHandler.
Protected Overrides Sub RemoveItem(ByVal index As Integer)

    'Dynamically remove the Alarm event of the object from the procedure AlarmHandler.
    RemoveHandler Me(index).Alarm, AddressOf AlarmHandler

    'Let the basic procedure do what it needs to do
    '(namely remove the item from the list).
    MyBase.RemoveItem(index)
```

```vb
                'The list has changed-the next appointment could be different!
                UpdateNextAppointmentProperty()
        End Sub

        'When all items are cleared the events of all objects are cleared.
        Protected Overrides Sub ClearItems()

            'Remove all items.
            For Each locItem As AlarmTrigger In Me
                RemoveHandler locItem.Alarm, AddressOf AlarmHandler
            Next

            'Call basic routine.
            MyBase.ClearItems()

            'There is no next appointment.
            myNextAppointment = Nothing
        End Sub

        ''' <summary>
        ''' Raises an event as soon as this routine is executed as the
        ''' event handler routine of an item in this collection.
        ''' </summary>
        ''' <param name="sender"></param>
        ''' <param name="e"></param>
        ''' <remarks></remarks>
        Private Sub AlarmHandler(ByVal sender As Object, ByVal e As AlarmEventArgs)
            RaiseEvent Alarm(sender, e)
        End Sub

        ''' <summary>
        ''' Searches of the next appointment in the item list.
        ''' </summary>
        ''' <remarks></remarks>
        Private Sub UpdateNextAppointmentProperty()

            'No items present...
            If Me.Count = 0 Then

                '...so there is no next appointment
                myNextAppointment = Nothing
            Else

                'Search all items for the earliest
                myNextAppointment = Me(0).AlarmTime
                For Each locItem As AlarmTrigger In Me
                    If locItem.AlarmTime < myNextAppointment.Value Then
                        myNextAppointment = locItem.AlarmTime
                    End If
                Next
            End If
        End Sub
```

```
''' <summary>
''' Returns the next appointment or Nothing.
''' </summary>
''' <value></value>
''' <returns></returns>
''' <remarks></remarks>
Public ReadOnly Property NextAppointment() As Nullable(Of Date)
    Get

        'Only return value. The search for the earliest date
        'was already performed during the list change.
        Return myNextAppointment.Value
    End Get
End Property
End Class
```

Let's elaborate a bit more on the generic *Collection*, which you can reach via the namespace *System.Collections.ObjectModel* (not, as you might assume, via *System.Collections.Generics*.[2])

The *Collection* class takes the place of the older *DynamicList*. By letting the new custom class *AppointmentList* inherit from *Collection*, and subsequently overriding the methods *InsertItem*, *RemoveItem*, and *ClearItems*, you can still control how the collection adds, deletes, or clears all the items—just as if you had developed those methods yourself. It makes no difference whether adding new items happens with *Add* or *Insert*—the *Inherits Collection* statement ensures that *InsertItem* is called, so you are informed of any list changes. You'll see more about *Collections* in Chapter 19, "Arrays and Collections."

When a new *AlarmTrigger* object is added to the list, it's important to be notified, so you can raise another event when that *AlarmTrigger* object fires. In this case, though, you can't use *WithEvents*, because you're dealing with a local object variable that you "get to know" only after it is provided via *InsertItem*.

That's why you need to wire the event dynamically via *AddHandler* at runtime. The first section of the bold code in the preceding example shows how this works. *AddHandler* takes two parameters: the object event (in this case *item.Alarm*), and a delegate (as described in the last section). Later, when the *AlarmTrigger* object raises the *Alarm* event (you need to add that event to the list), the procedure passed as the second parameter of *AddHandler*—as delegate— handles that event.

To do the opposite—remove the event wiring from this procedure when the *AlarmTrigger* item is removed from the list—you use the keyword *RemoveHandler*, which works the same as *AddHandler*.

---

[2] You can find out why that's the case by reading Krzysztof Cwalina's blog at *http://tinyurl.com/3a7992z*.

> **Tip** Beginning with Visual Basic 2010, you can also take direct advantage of statement lambdas in *AddHandler*. For example, to evaluate the *Click* event of a Windows Forms button dynamically, you can use the following code:
>
> ```
> Sub aMethod()
>     Dim aButton As New Button
>     AddHandler aButton.Click, Sub(sender, e)
>     MessageBox.Show(sender.ToString & " was clicked!")
> End Sub
> ```
>
> Bear in mind that you can *no longer* remove a statement lambda handler with *RemoveHandler*. If that's necessary, you instead need to use a delegate variable, as shown in the following code:
>
> ```
> Sub aMethod()
>     Dim aButton As New Button
>     Dim handler As EventHandler = Sub(sender, e)
>     MessageBox.Show(sender.ToString & " was clicked!")
> End Sub
>
>
> AddHandler aButton.Click, handler
>
> 'Now it can be removed:
> RemoveHandler aButton.Click, handler
> ```

The same kind of change occurs when an item in the appointment list is changed by using an assignment such as this:

```
AppointmentListInstance.Item(x)=NewAlarmTriggerItem
```

In this case, you remove the current items with *RemoveHandler* and embed the newly assigned item with *AddHandler*. This way the procedure *AlarmHandler* is always called, no matter which *AlarmTrigger* object of the appointment list raises an *Alarm* event. The *AlarmHandler* procedure then raises an event that can be processed by the code in the form *frmMain*.

To make it easier for the main program—which creates an instance of *AppointmentList* to save the appointments—to display each one, the example includes a procedure that always finds the next appointment (*UpdateNextAppointmentProperty*), places it into a field variable (*myNextAppointment*), and supplies it to the main program via a property (*NextAppointment*). This variable is updated whenever the appointment list changes.

The *myNextAppointment* field variable is defined as a generic value type—*Nullable(Of)*. To anticipate what you'll read about in more detail in Chapter 18, "Advanced Types," in the section "Nullables." *Nullable* permits you to turn any value type into a *nullable* type which can save either an actual value or *Nothing* (a capability most value types don't have by default). You can then use the property *HasValue* to check whether the *Nullable* instance has a value or is *Nothing*, reading any existing value with the *Value* property. Because the appointment list can also be empty, you can take advantage of the properties of the generic *Nullable* class, because you just need to save a date or *Nothing* (if the list is empty) for each next appointment.

Processing the appointment list within *frmMain* looks as follows:

```
Public Class frmMain

    Private WithEvents myTimer As Timer
    Private WithEvents myAppointmentList As AppointmentList

    'The background color of the clock
    'which changes with a continuous alarm.
    Private myCurrentColor As Color

    'Alarm duration in 500ms steps (=25 seconds).
    Private myAlarmDuration As Integer = 50

    'Counter for the duration of the alarm remainder.
    Private myAlarmDownCounter As Integer

    'True: Alarm is currently active --> the clock blinks.
    Private myAlarmStatus As Boolean

    'If this string is Nothing, a text message is displayed
    'on the clock face, otherwise nothing.
    Private myLastAlarmMessage As String

    Sub New()

        'This call is required for the Windows Form Designer.
        InitializeComponent()

        'This timer is required for displaying the clock
        'and making it blink if the alarm continues.
        myTimer = New Timer()
        myTimer.Interval = 500
        myTimer.Start()

        'The default background color of the clock is white.
        myCurrentColor = Color.White

        'AppointmentList is still empty.
        myAppointmentList = New AppointmentList
    End Sub
```

The preceding code declares the required field variables, and *Sub New* takes care of their correct initialization and the insertion of controls by calling *InitializeComponent*. Of course the most important object is *myTimer*, which ensures that the clock display updates regularly. This timer fires every 500 milliseconds, which initiates a redraw of the *PictureBox* control's contents in the *myTimer_Tick* event handler by using *Invalidate*.

Unlike the previous version of this program, this version doesn't just use a simple *AlarmTrigger* object; it uses the newly implemented list *myAppointmentList* which was declared with *WithEvents* so that the *Alarm* event fires whenever one of the *Alarm* objects in the list raises an *Alarm* event. The following code section deals with this event:

```
'Event handling routine which is raised
'when the alarm trigger signals an alarm,
'because a certain time has been reached.
Private Sub myAlarmTrigger_Alarm(ByVal Sender As Object, ByVal e As AlarmEventArgs) _
    Handles myAppointmentList.Alarm
    'Alarm clock rings!
    myAlarmStatus = True
    'It rings this long:
    myAlarmDownCounter = myAlarmDuration
    'We must be able to turn off the ringing.
    btnTurnOffAlarm.Enabled = True

    'Set message text
    myLastAlarmMessage = e.AlarmText

    'Remove from list
    lstAppointment.Items.Remove(Sender)

    'Remove from appointment list
    myAppointmentList.Remove(DirectCast(Sender, AlarmTrigger))
End Sub
```

The *AlarmEventArgs* also haven't been edited: they supply the message text directly, as long as it needs to be displayed in the center of the clock face.

If one of the *AlarmTrigger* items has raised an *Alarm* event, you'll find out via the detour of the *AppointmentList*. To ensure that the "wake-up phase" is initiated in the display, and that the appointment message is displayed on the clock face, you set myLastAlarmMessage = e.AlarmText, which is taken into consideration when the clock is redrawn.

```
    .
    .
    .
    End Sub

    'Is called if the user clicked the Add button.
    Private Sub btnAdd_Click(ByVal sender As System.Object, _
                ByVal e As System.EventArgs) Handles btnAdd.Click

        Dim locAlarmTime As Date

        'Retrieve time and appointment reason from the TextBox control.
        If Date.TryParse(mtbAlarmTime.Text, locAlarmTime) And _
            Not String.IsNullOrEmpty(txtReason.Text) Then

            'Instantiate new AlarmTrigger object,
            'which is then added directly to the ListBox...
```

```
    Dim locAlarm As New AlarmTrigger(locAlarmTime, txtReason.Text, True)
    lstAppointment.Items.Add(locAlarm)

    '...as well as to the appointment list.
    myAppointmentList.Add(locAlarm)

    'Redraw the clock, so that the ring time for the next appointment
    'is displayed as a red line in the clock face!
    picAlarmClock.Invalidate()
  Else

    'Oops! There is no such time - TryParse
    'has failed.
    MessageBox.Show("Please check your entry for errors!")
  End If
End Sub
```

What's new here and therefore worth mentioning is the routine that ensures that a new *AlarmTrigger* object is created and added to the list when the user enters the data for a new appointment and then clicks *Add*.

By the way, it becomes apparent here that the program has to struggle with a small short-coming, because the references to the actual appointments—the *AlarmTrigger* objects—are basically saved in two lists: in the *Collection(Of AlarmTrigger)* collection and in *ListBox* control's internal list. However, you need both the *ListBox* to display of the appointments and the *Collection(Of AlarmTrigger)* collection so that you'll receive a notification when one of its *AlarmTrigger* objects raises an event. Therefore, you need to update both lists when a user captures a new appointment or deletes an already-captured appointment from the list.

One way to get around this shortcoming is to move the entire *AddHandler* logic into the main program. However, this does not comply with the OOP requirement of creating reuseable components.

Implementing Your Own Event Handlers

In some cases, it's important for you to have complete control over event registration and triggering—especially for debugging purposes.

Suppose that you have developed a complex component, and you need to check which of its instances consume a certain event and how long the execution of this event takes. This can be tricky, because the component "knows" that it raises an event, but you can't formulate the code in such a way that you are informed as to what event handlers are wired into your component.

Using *custom event handlers*, this is now possible. It's also worth mentioning that custom event handlers were available in Visual Studio 2008, but they weren't documented anywhere!

A custom event handler defines both an event and an event handler in one statement. You don't need to define the actual event separately in a class where you define a custom event handler.

You can also make use of the Editor's built-in support for event programming. Because there are three methods that process individual tasks (registering the event, unregistering the event, and raising the event), the Editor creates these as soon as you insert the custom event handler definition and press Enter, as shown in Figure 15-10.

```
Public Class WithCustomEventHandler

    Custom Event DebugClick As EventHandler
        AddHandler(ByVal value As EventHandler)

        End AddHandler

        RemoveHandler(ByVal value As EventHandler)

        End RemoveHandler

        RaiseEvent(ByVal sender As Object, ByVal e As System.EventArgs)

        End RaiseEvent
    End Event

End Class
```

FIGURE 15-10 Press Enter after inserting the custom event line. The Visual Basic Editor takes care of the rest.

Now it's easy:

- Place the code that you want to execute when some other component wires the event (which it will consume later) into *AddHandler*. The other component passes you an event handler—a special delegate—that you need to remember, because when you trigger the event, you must hit all the delegates for the various components in sequence.

- Place the code that you want to execute when a component unwires an event into *RemoveHandler*.

- Finally, insert code to resolve the events into the method *RaiseEvent*. The source of this call is, unlike the two methods just discussed in the previous bullet items, not one of the event consumers, but the event-raising class itself.

To save the event handlers added by these other components, the .NET Framework provides a special collection (more about collections in Chapter 21, "Attributes and Reflection") called *EventHandlerList*. This list also has the methods *AddHandler*, *RemoveHandler*, and *Item*, with which you can deposit different events in the list via an object key, if your component defines more than one custom event handler. You should declare the *EventHandlerList* at the beginning of your class, as shown in the following code.

```
Public Class DebugButton
   Inherits Button

   Private myEventHandlers As EventHandlerList = New EventHandlerList
```

In the corresponding event methods you can, for example, access the list items via a string key. The following code fragment shows you how to add an event handler in *AddHandler* and remove it in *RemoveHandler*:

```
AddHandler(ByVal value As EventHandler)
    myEventHandlers.AddHandler("DebugClick", value)
End AddHandler

RemoveHandler(ByVal value As EventHandler)
    myEventHandlers.RemoveHandler("DebugClick", value)
End RemoveHandler
```

The following example demonstrates custom event handlers in context. It simulates the problem posed at the beginning of this section: how to track which component takes how long to process an event, and when the event takes place.

To do this, the example provides a new control derived from *Button*, called *DebugButton*. It defines a new event called *DebugClick*, which functions exactly like the normal *Click* event except that it also defines which component the event has consumed in a static list, as shown in the sample code that follows:

> **Companion Content** Open the corresponding solution (.sln), which you can find in the \VB 2010 Developer Handbook\Chapter 15\CustomEvents folder.

```
Imports System.ComponentModel    ' EventHandlerList collection
Imports System.Threading         ' Thread.Sleep to simulate workload

Public Class Form1

    'Determines the random numbers necessary to wait
    'for certain periods of time (to simulate workload).
    Private myRandomGenerator As New Random

    'The event handler method for the Click events of all Debug buttons.
    Private Sub DebugButton_DebugClick(ByVal sender As Object,
                                ByVal e As System.EventArgs) _
        Handles DebugButton1.DebugClick, DebugButton2.DebugClick,
                DebugButton3.DebugClick

        'Simulate that the workload takes between 250 ms and 2000 ms.
        'The buttons are disabled to show when we are continuing.
        DirectCast(sender, Control).Enabled = False
```

```vb
                'Give the Windows message queue loop time to "come up for air",
                'so that the button can be disabled.
                My.Application.DoEvents()

                'Simulate workload: Thread.Sleep pauses the current thread.
                System.Threading.Thread.Sleep(myRandomGenerator.Next(250, 2000))

                'Then reactivate the button.
                DirectCast(sender, Control).Enabled = True

        End Sub

        'Triggered when the Result button is clicked,
        'and then the application displays a list of the events
        'created by clicking the various Debug buttons.
        Private Sub ResultDebugButton_Click(ByVal sender As System.Object,
                                    ByVal e As System.EventArgs) _
                                Handles ResultDebugButton.Click

            'We are now creating the event form on the fly
            Dim resultForm As New Form With {.Text = "Event list"}

            'Add the ListBox to the form
            Dim resultList As New ListBox() With {.Dock = DockStyle.Fill}

            'Starting position of the window is the center of the screen.
            resultForm.StartPosition = FormStartPosition.CenterScreen

            'Assign event list:
            resultList.DataSource = DebugButton.DebugClickInfos

            'Add ListBox to the form.
            resultForm.Controls.Add(resultList)

            'Show dialog.
            resultForm.ShowDialog()
        End Sub
End Class

'This class saves an event data set.
Public Class DebugClickInfo
    Public Property Sender As Object                    ' What triggered it?
    Public Property EventTime As Date                   ' When was it triggered?
    Public Property ExecutionDuration As TimeSpan       ' How long did the handling take?

    'ToString has been overridden, so we can directly assign a list
    'with instances of this class to a ListBox. This way the
    'DebugClickInfo class takes care of displaying the content as text.
    Public Overrides Function ToString() As String

        'Construct return string: first the event time,
        'then the duration, and finally the sender that raised the event.
        Dim retString = EventTime.ToLongTimeString & ": "
        retString &= ExecutionDuration.ToString("ss\:fff") & "    (Sender: "
```

```vb
            'If the sender is a control we issue the name,
            'otherwise whatever ToString returns.
            If GetType(Control).IsAssignableFrom(Sender.GetType) Then
                retString += DirectCast(Sender, Control).Name
            Else
                retString += Sender.ToString
            End If

            retString &= ")"
            Return retString
        End Function
    End Class

    'The DebugButton does the same as the "regular" button,
    'but it gets an additional event which protocols all
    'clicks via the custom event handler.
    Public Class DebugButton
        Inherits Button

        'The delegates list when the events are registered in other components
        '(for example by the form in this case).
        Private myEventHandlers As EventHandlerList = New EventHandlerList

        'The event list which records how long something has taken and what it is.
        Private Shared s_debugClickInfos As New List(Of DebugClickInfo)

        'This is how the component recognizes when a click has taken place.
        Protected Overrides Sub OnClick(ByVal e As System.EventArgs)
            MyBase.OnClick(e)
            RaiseEvent DebugClick(Me, e)
        End Sub

        'This code block defines the custom event.
        Custom Event DebugClick As EventHandler

            'Is called when a component which wants to consume
            'the event "wires" it.
            AddHandler(ByVal value As EventHandler)
                'Save the passed event handler in the event delegate list
                'of this instance. Here "DebugClick" is just an arbitray but
                'unique name for which we need to retrieve all handlers

                myEventHandlers.AddHandler("DebugClick", value)
            End AddHandler

            'Is called when a component removes a wired event.
            RemoveHandler(ByVal value As EventHandler)
                'Remove the EventHandler from the event delegates list.
                myEventHandlers.RemoveHandler("DebugClick", value)
            End RemoveHandler

            'Is called when an instance of this class
            'raises the DebugClick event.
            RaiseEvent(ByVal sender As Object, ByVal e As System.EventArgs)
```

```
                'Are there registers in this event?
                If myEventHandlers.Item("DebugClick") IsNot Nothing Then
                    'Iterate all handlers of the event of this instance
                    For Each delItem In myEventHandlers.Item(
                        "DebugClick").GetInvocationList

                        'Measure everything and...
                        Dim eventTime = Now
                        Dim sw = Stopwatch.StartNew
                        'Calls the actual event handler code in the target component.
                        CType(delItem, EventHandler).Invoke(sender, e)
                        sw.Stop()

                        '...write the results in the list.
                        s_debugClickInfos.Add(New DebugClickInfo With {
                            .EventTime = eventTime,
                            .ExecutionDuration =
                            TimeSpan.FromMilliseconds(sw.ElapsedMilliseconds),
                            .Sender = sender
                            })
                    Next
                End If
            End RaiseEvent
        End Event

        'Static property which contains the result list of the "event records"
        'of all instances of this class.
        Public Shared ReadOnly Property DebugClickInfos As List(Of DebugClickInfo)
            Get
                Return s_debugClickInfos
            End Get
        End Property

End Class
```

Chapter 16
Enumerations

Introduction to Enumerations

Enumerations, usually called *Enums* (not to be confused with *lists* or *collections*), are primarily meant to make life easier for programmers. Using Enums, you can define and group constant values by name. At the same time, you can restrict the values to that specific set of names and values. Suppose that you have created a small contact management application that lets you categorize your contacts. You can define a contact as a client, a friend, a business colleague, or as part of some other group. To simplify this example, further assume that a contact can only belong to *one* of these groups (supposedly, there are certain socially gifted individuals who manage to be friends with business colleagues). You have assigned a specific number to each category, and using these numbered categories, you can now call specific functions in your database application. For example, *ContactPerson* contacts can be grouped with *Company* contacts, but *Suppliers* can't, because those contacts each represent a company by themselves).

Even without Enums, you can write the code in such a way that you call the functions by the number assigned to each category (an integer), but the category numbers are hard to remember, and it would be difficult to avoid calling the functions with, for example, the number 42, which would be totally OK as an integer—the only problem is that you have no 42nd category—only 10 or so. Enums provide not only an easier way to refer to these values (by name), but they also restrict the possible values so that you can't call the functions with invalid values such as 42.

Of course, you can always create your own list to associate the contact categories/numbers. But for practicality's sake you can create an *Enum* to make the associations easier.

> **Companion Content** Open the corresponding solution (.sln), which you can find in the
> \VB 2010 Developer Handbook\Chapter 16\Enums folder.

The following example presents the *Enum* for the contact categories. Note that it's just a
simple list of names wrapped in an *Enum/End Enum* definition.

```
Public Enum ContactCategory
    Family
    Friend
    Acquaintance
    Colleague
    BusinessPartner
    Client
    Supplier
    ToAvoid
    Company
    ContactPersonAtCompanyContact
End Enum
```

Now, how can you use these *Enum* elements? Very simple. If you don't specify values for the
names, the .NET Framework assigns values in the sequence that the names appear in the
Enum block, from top to bottom, beginning with 0, in ascending order, incrementing by 1
for each name. After defining an *Enum*, you can define variables to hold instances of that
enumeration type, and then simply specify the *Enum* type (the name) rather than having to
remember the numbers:

```
Sub main()

    Dim locContacts As ContactCategory

    locContacts = ContactCategory.BusinessPartner
    Console.WriteLine(locContacts)
    Console.ReadLine()

End Sub
```

When you run this code, it displays the value 4 in the console window.

Determining the Values of Enumeration Elements

If you don't want to use the default enumeration, you can change the enumeration to specify the values that work best for you, as shown in the following example:

```
Public Enum ContactCategory
    Family = 10
    Friend
    Acquaintance
    Colleague
    BusinessPartner
    Client  = 20
    Supplier
    ToAvoid = 30
    Company
    ContactPersonAtCompanyContact
End Enum
```

Running the same program again displays the value 14.

Duplicate Values Are Allowed!

Enumeration elements do not have to be unique. In the following example, *BusinessPartner* as well as *ToAvoid* have a value of 20 in the enumeration definition.

```
Public Enum ContactCategory
    Family = 10
    Friend
    Acquaintance
    Colleague
    BusinessPartner = 20
    Client
    Supplier = 19
    ToAvoid
    Company
    ContactPersonAtCompanyContact
End Enum
```

Determining the Types of Enumeration Elements

By default, the .NET Framework creates the elements of an enumeration internally as integer values. However, you can define whether the enumeration elements should be declared as *Byte*, *Short*, or *Long*. For Intel processors, you should keep in mind that *Integer* (32 bits in .NET) is generally preferred for performance reasons because of the alignment with an even number of memory addresses. However, regardless of the numeric size you choose, it's sufficient to define the corresponding names for the *Enum*, as shown in the following:

```
Public Enum ContactCategory As Short
    Family
    Friend
    Acquaintance
    ...
End Enum
```

Retrieving the Types of Enumeration Elements at Runtime

Should you need to determine which basic data type is hiding behind an enumeration element at runtime, simply use the *GetUnderlyingType* property, as follows:

```
'Retrieves the name of the underlying basic data type of an enumeration.
Console.WriteLine([Enum].GetUnderlyingType(GetType(ContactCategory)).Name)

'Retrieves the type name using an enumeration variable.
Console.WriteLine([Enum].GetUnderlyingType(locContacts.GetType).Name)
```

If you applied these two lines to our current example, they would display the following output in the console window:

```
Int16
Int16
```

> **Important** To access the *Enum* type identifier in the source code, type the keyword *Enum* in square brackets (as shown in the previous code sample) so that the Visual Basic Editor handles it correctly as an expression.

Converting Enumerations to Other Types

In many cases, it might make sense to convert an enumeration element to its underlying type—for example, when writing the value of an *Enum* variable to a database. In certain cases, it is also necessary to determine the value of an *Enum* element based on its name, which is a string, or to convert an *Enum* element value to its associated element name (a string).

Converting to Numeric Values and Vice Versa

It's important to understand that, to the .NET Framework, an *Enum* is not a simple numeric value; it's a type. To convert an *Enum* element to its value (or back if necessary), you must do the following (the example below still assumes that the *Enum* data type is *Short*):

```
Dim locContacts As ContactCategory
Dim locShort As Short

        locContacts = ContactCategory.BusinessPartner

        'Type conversion from underlying data type of enum...
        locShort = locContacts
        locShort = ContactCategory.Company

        '...and vice versa, not difficult either:
        locContacts = CType(locShort, ContactCategory)
```

Parsing Strings into Enumerations

If you want to know the element name associated with the value of an enumeration variable, use the following:

```
Dim locContacts As ContactCategory = ContactCategory.Company
Console.WriteLine(locContacts.ToString())
```

For this example, the output window displays:

```
Company
```

The reverse procedure is a little more complicated. To carry it out, you use the *Enum.Parse* method, as shown here:

```
'Converting back to an Enum element from a string.
Dim locString As String = "BusinessPartner"
locContacts = DirectCast([Enum].Parse(GetType(ContactCategory), locString), ContactCategory)
```

Note that the static *Enum.Parse* function also lets you generate an enumeration element at runtime. *Parse* expects an *Enum* type, which you first need to retrieve by using *GetType*. Because *Parse* creates an object that contains a boxed *Enum* element, you need to then unbox it from the object by using *DirectCast*.

> **Tip** As of .NET Framework 4.0, Enums also provide a *TryParse* function based on Generics (see Chapter 17, "Developing with Generics"), which greatly simplifies the conversion of strings back to the original *Enum* value. The following example shows how the previous example would look in .NET Framework 4.0:
>
> ```
> 'With .NET Framework 4.0 it's a little easier:
> If [Enum].TryParse(locString, locContacts) Then
>     Console.WriteLine("Enum value BusinessPartner was recognized and converted!")
> End If
> ```

Flags Enumerations

Flags enumerations are ideal when you need enumerations with elements that can be combined with one another. As discussed earlier, it is quite possible that a contact in your database is a *friend* as well as a *business colleague*. The .NET Framework has a great way of supporting such situations.

When defining a *Flags* enumeration you need to keep three things in mind.

1. You should define an enumeration name for the situation of "none of the combinations" (for example, by using *None*). This item has a value of 0.

2. You need to assign values that can be combined bitwise. To do that, you count the individual values up by using powers of two.

3. You add the *Flags* attribute to the enumeration.

The classic example is the button order and question icon of the Windows *MessageBox*. You can call this ancient Windows API from User32.dll in C/C++ directly. The definition is as follows:

```
int MessageBox(HWND hWnd,LPCTSTR lpText,LPCTSTR lpCaption,UINT uType);
```

The C syntax isn't of interest to us here; however, it's worth looking at which parameter was used how, and to reach what goal. For example, if you want to display a question mark, you need to specify the value 32 as *uType*, and for the *Yes* and *No* buttons, you use *4* as the *uType*; *4+32=36* for both together. .NET provides this API as well—encapsulated in an object, as illustrated here:

```
MessageBox.Show("Hello world", "VB for ever", MessageBoxButtons.YesNo,
MessageBoxIcon.Question)
```

To make it a little easier for the user, the parameters for the buttons and question mark icon were separated. And now guess which values were assigned to *MessageBoxButtons.YesNo* and *MessageBoxIcon.Question*—could it be 4 and 32?

The following example shows how this would work for the *ContactCategories* enumeration example:

```
<Flags()> _
Public Enum ContactCategories
    None = 0
    Family = 1
    Friend = 2
    Acquaintance = 4
    Colleague = 8
    BusinessPartner = 16
    Client = 32
    Supplier = 64
    ToAvoid = 128
    Company = 256
    ContactPersonAtCompanyContact = 512
End Enum
```

After defining this *Flags* enumeration, you can perform combined assignments to a variable of the type *ContactCategories* by using the logical operator *Or*, as the following example shows:

```
Sub EnumFlags()

    Dim locContacts As ContactCategories
    locContacts = ContactCategories.Friend Or ContactCategories.BusinessPartner
    Console.WriteLine(locContacts)
    Console.WriteLine(locContacts.ToString())

    Console.ReadLine()

End Sub
```

This example generates the following output:

```
18
Friend, BusinessPartner
```

Querying *Flags* Enumerations

When querying *Flags* enumerations, you need to be careful, because combinations can yield values that do not correspond to a specific element value. Only by "masking" (retrieving a single bit value) using the operator *And* can you retrieve the correct value. The following example shows how to do that:

```
Dim locContacte As ContactCategories
locContacts = ContactCategories.Friend Or ContactCategories.BusinessPartner

'Attention using Flags! Bits must be masked!
'This query provides the wrong result!
If locContacts = ContactCategories.BusinessPartner Then
```

```
        Console.WriteLine("You are a BusinessPartner")
Else
        Console.WriteLine("You are not a BusinessPartner")
End If

'This is the correct version. This query provides the correct result:
If (locContacts And ContactCategories.Friend) = ContactCategories.Friend Then
        Console.WriteLine("You are a Friend")
Else
        Console.WriteLine("You are not a Friend")
End If

'And this is how combination queries work:
If locContacts = (ContactCategories.Friend Or ContactCategories.BusinessPartner) Then
        Console.WriteLine("You are a Friend and a BusinessPartner")
End If
```

When you run this example, you see the following result:

```
You are not a BusinessPartner
You are a Friend
You are a Friend and a BusinessPartner
```

The first line is, of course, wrong; the value of the *Enum* variable *locContacts* isn't masked, the code is simply comparing the combined value, which doesn't match a contact category, causing the incorrect result. The last two comparisons show the correct way to check a flag's *Enum* value.

> **Tip** Beginning with .NET Framework 4.0, querying *Flags* enumerations has become easier, because Enums now provide the method *HasFlag*, which works as follows:
>
> ```
>         'It's also possible in .NET Framework 4.0:
>         If locContacts.HasFlag(ContactCategories.Friend) Then
>             Console.WriteLine("You are a Friend")
>         Else
>             Console.WriteLine("You are not a Friend")
>         End If
> ```

Chapter 17
Developing with Generics

Introduction

Generics are not new to Microsoft Visual Basic 2010; they've been around since Visual Basic 2005. Generics are a way to create a single code base that can accommodate many different types, and they are an invaluable tool for developing robust applications. Many of the classes you use every day are based on generics—whether those are Nullables, generic collections such as *List(Of T)* or *Collection(Of T)*, or generic delegates like *Action(Of T)*, *Function(Of T)*, or *Tuple(Of T)*. They're also a central component of Microsoft *Language-Integrated Query* (LINQ), a querying technology that you'll explore later in this book. As important as these technologies are, not every Visual Basic programmer dares to tackle them—an unnecessary reluctance, in my opinion, because after you grasp the concepts, you can put generics to good use, and simplify your development work by producing more stable code.

Generics: Using One Code Base for Different Types

Methods and properties accept arguments of specific types, and also return values of specific types. In other words, they act on specific data types that are known at compile time. So if you want to be able to pass, say, either an integer or a string to a method or property, you would typically have to write two versions: one that accepts an integer, and a different one that accepts a string. Alternatively, you can define the method or property so that you can pass an *Object* data type, which can accommodate all possible data types—but the *Object* data type isn't type-safe and might trigger unexpected exceptions at runtime.

> **Companion Content** Open the corresponding solution (.sln), which you can find in the \VB 2010 Developer Handbook\Chapter 17\Generics01 folder.

This following example uses the by-now-familiar *DynamicList* class. First, it adds a few items to an instance of the class. Then the code iterates through the list's items by using a *For Each* loop, and then displays the items in the console window:

```
Module mdlMain
    Sub Main()
        Dim locList As New DynamicList
        locList.Add(123.32)
        locList.Add(126.32)
        locList.Add(124.52)
        locList.Add(29.99)
        locList.Add(13.54)
        'This will cause problems!
        locList.Add(#12/31/2010 4:00:00 PM#)
        locList.Add(43.32)
        For Each locItem As Double In locList
            Console.WriteLine(locItem)
        Next

        Console.WriteLine()
        Console.WriteLine("Press key to exit!")
        Console.ReadKey()
    End Sub

End Module
```

When you start this program, you see the output shown in Figure 17-1.

FIGURE 17-1 The list is only issued up to the *Date* item because it's not convertible into *Double*.

It's obvious why this happens. We tried to build a list with pure *Double* items, but a *Date* item has snuck in. Such mistakes are easily recognizable in a simple program like this, but in larger projects you should try to avoid such mistakes in the first place.

Solution Approaches

So how do you ensure that the list contains only items of a specific type? You do it by making the *DynamicList* class type-safe. In other words, by not permitting list to accept variables of the *Object* type, but only strongly typed values (doubles, integers, dates, and so on). The advantage of a strongly typed list is that assignments of the wrong type are caught at design time, rather than runtime.

Let's revisit the source code of the *DynamicList* class and perform the appropriate changes. Create a new class and call it *DynamicListDouble* (you can find it in the sample project in its own class file). The following code example marks those sections in bold where the data type *Object* has been changed to *Double*:

```
Class DynamicListDouble
    Implements IEnumerable

    Protected myStep As Integer = 4        ' Step-width by which the array is increased
    Protected myCurrentArraySize As Integer ' Current array size
    Protected myCurrentCounter As Integer   ' Pointer to the current item
    Protected myArray() As Double           ' Array with the items

    Sub New()
        myCurrentArraySize = myStep
        ReDim myArray(myCurrentArraySize - 1)
    End Sub

    Sub Add(ByVal Item As Double)

        'Save item in the array
        myArray(myCurrentCounter) = Item

        'Increase pointer to next item
        myCurrentCounter += 1

        'Check whether the current array limit has been reached
        If myCurrentCounter = myCurrentArraySize - 1 Then
            'Create new array with more memory,
            'and copy items into it.

            'New array becomes larger:
            myCurrentArraySize += myStep
```

```
            'Create temporary array
            Dim locTempArray(myCurrentArraySize - 1) As Double
            Array.Copy(myArray, locTempArray, myArray.Length)
            myArray = locTempArray
        End If
    End Sub
    .
    .
    .
End Class
```

After editing the class, you also need to change the main program so that it uses the new *DynamicListDouble* class:

```
Module mdlMain

    Sub Main()
        Dim locList As New DynamicListDouble
        locList.Add(123.32)
        locList.Add(126.32)
...
```

As soon as you attempt to add a variable that's not of the type specified in the declaration of the list, the Editor will detect the error as you type and display the appropriate error message, as shown in Figure 17-2.

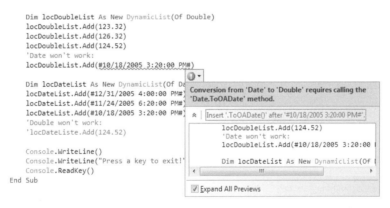

FIGURE 17-2 With type-safe classes, the Editor displays an error message at design time if you try to add a value of the wrong type to the list.

This particular error message even suggests how to convert a *Date* value into its equivalent *Double* type, but you get the idea—just getting any information about the incorrect type assignment would be sufficient. Clearly, a major advantage of type-safe classes is that the compiler can catch errors at design time so that they can be fixed immediately.

Standardizing the Code Base of a Type by Using Generics

Developing a type-safe class such as *DynamicList* is slightly more complex than developing the *Object*-based version, but eventually you might need to work with classes and structures that are much more complex. At the same time, when working with classes and structures that manage large amounts of data, you might need to store items of different data types to the same list. Using the *Object* data type might sound like a good idea, initially, but you should always insist on type safety. Until now, you had only the following possibilities:

- Create a new version of the processed class for each data type. This is a huge effort that entails an equally large problem: If you find an error in one of the classes it's likely to be in all the classes, because they differ only in the type of data they accept (such as *DynamicListDouble, DynamicListString, DynamicListDate*, and so on), so you must fix the error in all the classes you have created.

- Create a class based on an interface, letting you adjust types via inheritance. This helps with the maintenance issue, because solving an error in the base class also solves it in the class derivatives. However, implementing such classes requires extremely abstract thinking and careful planning, and you might not always have time for that.

Generic data types are different. When working with generic data types, you don't specify which type your class or structure will later process during development. Instead, you work with type parameters, which determine the actual type you're working with during runtime— thanks to the Just-in-Time (JIT) compiler.

In other words, whatever you would do manually by copying your code and adjusting types at development time, the JIT compiler and generics do for you automatically at runtime. Simply put, just like Find/Replace helps you in Microsoft Word, the JITter copies the IML code of your generic class, replacing all type parameters with the specified type at runtime.

> **Note** Of course, it's not quite that easy. The JIT compiler is able to keep segments of code that's common in generic classes and to generate new code only where there is no other option.

Here's what happens when you apply generics to a list like *DynamicList*: instead of deciding on a data type, such as *Double, Integer,* or *String*, when you declare an instance of the *DynamicList* class, you use a placeholder at those locations—a type parameter— specified with the *Of* keyword in the class's header, as follows:

```
Class DynamicList(Of flexibleDataType)
```

And instead of using a fixed data type within the class, you use the type parameters as representatives. For the *DynamicList* class this means:

```
Class DynamicList(Of flexibleDataType)
    Implements IEnumerable

    Protected myStep As Integer = 4          ' Step width by which the array is increased.
    Protected myCurrentArraySize As Integer  ' Current array size.
    Protected myCurrentCounter As Integer    ' Pointer to current items.
    Protected myArray() As flexibleDataType  ' Array with items.

    Sub New()
        myCurrentArraySize = myStep
        ReDim myArray(myCurrentArraySize - 1)
    End Sub

    Sub Add(ByVal Item As flexibleDataType)

        myArray(myCurrentCounter) = Item
        myCurrentCounter += 1
        If myCurrentCounter = myCurrentArraySize - 1 Then
            myCurrentArraySize += myStep

            'Create temporary array
            Dim locTempArray(myCurrentArraySize - 1) As flexibleDataType

            'Copy elements;
            Array.Copy(myArray, locTempArray, myArray.Length)
            myArray = locTempArray
        End If
    End Sub
    'Returns the number of the existing elements
    Public Overridable ReadOnly Property Count() As Integer
        Get
            Return myCurrentCounter
        End Get
    End Property

    'Permits assignment
    Default Public Overridable Property Item(ByVal Index As Integer) As flexibleDataType
        Get
            Return myArray(Index)
        End Get
        Set(ByVal Value As flexibleDataType)
            myArray(Index) = Value
        End Set
    End Property

    Public Function GetEnumerator() As System.Collections.IEnumerator _
                    Implements System.Collections.IEnumerable.GetEnumerator
        Dim locTempArray(myCurrentArraySize) As flexibleDataType
        Array.Copy(myArray, locTempArray, myArray.Length)
        Return myArray.GetEnumerator
    End Function
End Class
```

Now you can use *DynamicList* for any data type you like—and you don't need to give up type safety to do so. Figure 17-3 shows how you use the generic data type. The module's *Sub Main* declares the generic class with the specific type that you want to work with, in this case, the *Double data type*:

```
Dim locDoubleList As New DynamicList(Of Double)
```

Then, it creates a new *DynamicList*, this time based on the *Date* data type:

```
Dim locDateList As New DynamicList(Of Date)
```

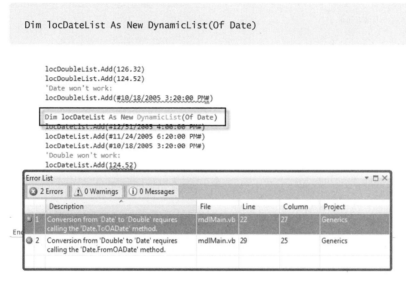

FIGURE 17-3 Using *Of*, you can specify a specific data type you want to use for an instance of you generic class.

The error list in the Figure 17-3 shows you that both "type versions" of the class are type-safe. The first list, *locDoubleList*, can store only *Double* values, whereas *locDateList* can store only *Date* values. Any attempt to add a different type to either list causes an error message at design time.

Constraints

Even though you can configure the *DynamicList* class to store values of any type, that flexibility might not always be desirable—especially when you are using generic types within a generic class, whose type you don't yet know at design time.

> **Companion Content** Open the corresponding solution (.sln), which you can find in the \VB 2010 Developer Handbook\Chapter 17\Generics02 folder.

Constraining Generic Types to a Specific Base Class

Suppose that you have created an application that calculates, manages, and displays various kinds of 3D shapes (cubes, balls, pyramids, and so on). You want to create a generic class that saves the various shapes in a list like *DynamicList*, and calculates their total volume with a method that's common to all the types.

Further, assume that all the shape classes have a common base class that saves position and color information for each shape so that you don't have to implement common shape properties repeatedly. Such a class inheritance order might look as follows:

```
Imports System.Drawing

'Provides the base properties of a body
Public MustInherit Class BodyBase

    Private myColor As Color
    Private myPosition As Point

    MustOverride ReadOnly Property Volume() As Double

    Public Property Color() As Color
        Get
            Return myColor
        End Get
        Set(ByVal value As Color)
            myColor = value
        End Set
    End Property

    Public Property Position() As Point
        Get
            Return myPosition
        End Get
        Set(ByVal value As Point)
            myPosition = value
        End Set
    End Property
End Class

Public Class Cube
    Inherits BodyBase

    Private mySideLength_a As Double
    Private mySideLength_b As Double
    Private mySideLength_c As Double

    Sub New(ByVal a As Double, ByVal b As Double, ByVal c As Double)
        mySideLength_a = a
        mySideLength_b = b
        mySideLength_c = c
    End Sub
```

```vbnet
    Public Overrides ReadOnly Property Volume() As Double
        Get
            Return mySideLength_a * mySideLength_b * mySideLength_c
        End Get
    End Property
End Class

Public Class Pyramid
    Inherits BodyBase

    Private myFootprint As Double
    Private myHeight As Double

    Sub New(ByVal Footprint As Double, ByVal Height As Double)
        myFootprint = Footprint
        myHeight = Height
    End Sub

    Public Overrides ReadOnly Property Volume() As Double
        Get
            Return (myFootprint * myHeight) / 3
        End Get
    End Property
End Class
```

Obviously, you could use the existing *DynamicList* class to store any variable of the *BodyBase* type, as shown in Figure 17-4.

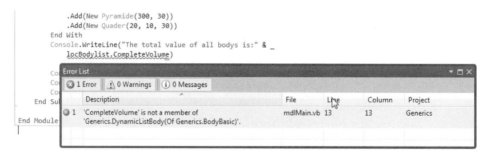

FIGURE 17-4 *DynamicList* must also provide a *TotalVolume* property, but it's not implemented yet.

But this causes a chain of problems. As Figure 17-4 shows, the application was trying to use a list property that doesn't yet exist. And typically, there's no way to implement this property, because within the generic *DynamicList* class, you would need to create a *TotalVolume* property that iterates through all the items it contains and queries their *Volume* property. Unfortunately, you can't implement this procedure, as shown in Figure 17-5.

FIGURE 17-5 The property necessary for calculating the total volume cannot be reached.

That's because iterating through the *DynamicList* items means that you must ensure that the current item has a type appropriate for the entire generic class. This means that it must be a *flexibleDataType* type (otherwise the class would no longer be generic).

However, *flexibleDataType* can be any data type you like; therefore, only the properties and methods that *all* the data types provide are available. Logically, those are the properties and methods provided by *Object,* which each new class inherits implicitly. So those are the items that IntelliSense shows you, as illustrated in Figure 17-5.

Now it's time to get to the constraints. When you inform the generic data type that it can accept only data types based on *BodyBase*, the .NET Framework can offer the methods and properties of that base class via *locItem* (of the type *flexibleDataType*)—those by *BodyBase*.

You will make these changes next, but not in the class *DynamicList* itself, because you don't want to limit our *DynamicList* so that it can only manage *BodyBase* objects. Instead, you implement these changes in a class otherwise identical to the *DynamicList* class, but that contains the required changes. Call this class *DynamicListBody*; it looks as follows (to save some space, this code shown here contains only the changes from the *DynamicList* class):

```
Class DynamicListBody(Of flexibleDataType As BodyBase)
    Implements IEnumerable

    Protected myStep As Integer = 4          ' Step width by which the array is increased.
    Protected myCurrentArraySize As Integer  ' Current array size.
    Protected myCurrentCounter As Integer    ' Pointer to current item.
    Protected myArray() As flexibleDataType  ' Array with items.

    Sub New()
        myCurrentArraySize = myStep
        ReDim myArray(myCurrentArraySize - 1)
    End Sub

    Sub Add(ByVal Item As flexibleDataType)
    .
    .
    .
    End Sub
```

```
Public ReadOnly Property TotalVolume() As Double
    Get
        Dim locVolume As Double
        For Each locItem As flexibleDataType In Me
            locVolume += locItem.Volume
        Next
        Return locVolume
    End Get
End Property
```
...

The first line of the class code shows how to implement constraints. In addition to the extension (*Of flexibleDataType*, the generic type parameter), the definition also contains the addition *As BodyBase*, meaning that only the *BodyBase* classes and classes derived from *BodyBase* can be used as the basis for creating a *DynamicListBody* instance.

Now you can implement the property *TotalVolume*. Because the data types for this generic class are limited to *BodyBase* and its derived classes, the .NET Framework knows that it can safely provide all the methods that *BodyBasis* supplies for all objects based on *flexibleDataType*.

After implementing this new class you can restructure the test program in the module mdlMain.vb:

```
Module mdlMain

    Sub Main()
        Dim locBodyList As New DynamicListBody(Of BodyBase)
        With locBodyList
            .Add(New Cube(10, 20, 30))
            .Add(New Pyramid(300, 30))
            .Add(New Pyramid(300, 30))
            .Add(New Cube(20, 10, 30))
        End With
        Console.WriteLine("The total volume of all bodies is:" & _
            locBodyList.TotalVolume)

        Console.WriteLine()
        Console.WriteLine("Press key to exit!")
        Console.ReadKey()
    End Sub

End Module
```

Figure 17-6 shows that the class can only be used when it is based on a class that inherits from *BodyBasis*.

```
Module mdlMain

    Sub Main()
        Dim locBodylist As New DynamicListBody(Of Double)
```

Error List					▾ □ ✕
🔴 1 Error ⚠ 0 Warnings ⓘ 0 Messages					
Description	File	Line	Column	Project	
🔴 1 Type argument 'Double' does not inherit from or implement the constraint type 'Generics.BodyBasic'.	mdlMain.vb	4	51	Generics	

```
        Console.WriteLine()
```

FIGURE 17-6 You can only instantiate a constrained generic class by using a data type that fulfills the constraint.

> **Note** .NET Framework does not permit you to define multiple base classes as constraints for a generic type, because that would imply multiple inheritance, which .NET 4.0 does not (and probably never will) handle.

Constraining a Generic Type to Specific Interfaces

You can design generic classes to be considerably more flexible if you constrain them to specific interfaces rather than base classes.

Another advantage of interfaces is that many of the classes built into the .NET Framework already support specific interfaces, so you can create generic classes based not only on your own types (whose constraints are easily controlled because you can access the source code), but also use types in the .NET Framework.

Suppose that you want to add a sorting method to the *DynamicList* class. The basic requirements of a sorting routine for a collection are item comparison and element swapping. To facilitate comparison of custom data types, the .NET Framework provides the *IComparable* interface. Any class that implements this interface must include a function called *CompareTo*. Moreover, when you create a generic class, you can constrain the types it supports to types that support the *IComparable* interface. Thus, the class stays generic but can still save any data type that implements the *IComparable* interface itself. When you do that, you can assume that a *CompareTo* function exists, meaning you can implement a sort function in the generic class itself. By the way, all primitive data types (such as *String*, *Long*, *Decimal*, *Date*, and so on) support *IComparable*.

> **Companion Content** Open the corresponding solution (.sln), which you can find in the \VB 2010 Developer Handbook\Chapter 17\Generics03 folder.

Here's yet another changed (and shorter) version of the *DynamicList* class, now called *DynamicListSortable*, which contains a constraint for the class name definition and a *Sort* method:

```
Class DynamicListSortable(Of flexibleDataType As IComparable)
    Implements IEnumerable

    Protected myStep As Integer = 4         ' Step width by which the array is increased.
    Protected myCurrentArraySize As Integer ' Current array size.
    Protected myCurrentCounter As Integer   ' Pointer to current item.
    Protected myArray() As flexibleDataType ' Array with items.

    Sub New()
        myCurrentArraySize = myStep
        ReDim myArray(myCurrentArraySize - 1)
    End Sub

    Sub Add(ByVal Item As flexibleDataType)
        .
        .
        .
    End Sub

    'Sorts the items which are saved by DynamicListSortable
    Public Sub Sort()
        Dim locOuterCounter, locInnerCounter As Integer
        Dim locDelta As Integer
        Dim locItemTemp As flexibleDataType

        locDelta = 1

        'Determine the greater value of the distance order
        Do
            locDelta = 3 * locDelta + 1
        Loop Until locDelta > myCurrentCounter

        Do
            locDelta \= 3

            'Shellsort's kernel algorithm
            For locOuterCounter= locDelta To myCurrentCounter - 1
                locItemTemp = Me.Item(locOuterCounter)
                locInnerCounter = locOuterCounter
                Do While (Me.Item(locInnerCounter - locDelta).CompareTo(locItemTemp) > 0)
                    Me.Item(locInnerCounter) = Me.Item(locInnerCounter - locDelta)
                    locInnerCounter = locInnerCounter - locDelta
                    If (locInnerCounter <= locDelta) Then Exit Do
                Loop
                Me.Item(locInnerCounter) = locItemTemp
            Next
        Loop Until locDelta = 0
    End Sub
```

The implementation of a sort algorithm is possible only because of the constraint implemented by the *IComparable* interface. Because the types must implement the *IComparable* interface (otherwise no instantiation of *DynamicListSortable* would be possible), the *Sort* method can rely on the *CompareTo* method without risk (see the bold highlighted line in the preceding code).

And as mentioned previously, because all primitive data types in .NET implement *IComparable*, you can now use any primitive type with the class, as shown in the following code segment:

```
Module mdlMain

    Sub Main()
        Dim locDoubleList As New DynamicListSortable(Of Double)
        locDoubleList.Add(124)
        locDoubleList.Add(1243)
        locDoubleList.Add(24)
        locDoubleList.Add(14)
        locDoubleList.Add(1)
        locDoubleList.Add(-32)
        locDoubleList.Add(231)
        locDoubleList.Add(143)

        locDoubleList.Sort()
        For Each locItem As Double In locDoubleList
            Console.WriteLine(locItem)
        Next
        Console.WriteLine()

        Dim locStringList As New DynamicListSortable(Of String)
        locStringList.Add("Klaus")
        locStringList.Add("Arnold")
        locStringList.Add("Sarah")
        locStringList.Add("Christiane")
        locStringList.Add("Jürgen")
        locStringList.Add("Uta")
        locStringList.Add("Helge")
        locStringList.Add("Uwe")

        locStringList.Sort()
        For Each locItem As String In locStringList
            Console.WriteLine(locItem)
        Next

        Console.WriteLine()
        Console.WriteLine("Press key to exit!")
        Console.ReadKey()
    End Sub

End Module
```

Examine the lines highlighted in bold in the preceding listing. On the one hand, they illustrate that a generic list can be based on different data types; on the other hand, they demonstrate that complex functions such as sorting can work, even though you don't know at design time which types the list will have to deal with later.

Executing the program produces the following output, which shows that this concept works:

```
-32
1
14
24
124
143
231
1243

Arnold
Christiane
Helge
Jürgen
Klaus
Sarah
Uta
Uwe

Press key to exit!
```

 Note Implementing a sorting algorithm in custom collection classes is just as superfluous as creating custom collection classes from scratch. .NET Framework provides a variety of collection classes to accommodate most requirements. However, it's still interesting to see how the concept of collection classes functions, and certainly an advantage for a better understanding of Chapter 21, "Attributes and Reflection," which introduces the most important collections in .NET Framework.

Constraining a Generic Type to Classes with a Default Constructor

In some cases, a generic class must be able to instantiate the type it should be based on. It won't be able to do that if the type it's based on is an abstract class, an interface, or a class where all the constructors have parameters.

If you want to exclude these cases for a type implemented as a generic class, you must define a constraint that requires that types on which it is based have a default constructor. Here's how you do that:

```
Public Class GenericClassWithInstantiableType(Of flexibleDataType As New)

    Public Sub TestMethod()
        'Only possible due to the defined constraint:
        Dim locTest As New flexibleDataType

        'And here locTest is instantiated as data type!
        Console.WriteLine(locTest.ToString)
    End Sub
End Class
```

Constraining a Generic Class to Value Types

Constraining a generic class to value types is very similar to the previous section. You constrain the item type with the *As Structure* keyword, meaning that you can store only value types (including structures) in an instance of the generic class. Here's an example:

```
Public Class GenericClassOnlyWithValueTypes(Of flexibleDataType As Structure)

    Public Sub TestMethod()
        'Is value type—no instantiation with New required!
        Dim locValueType As flexibleDataType

        'And here locTest is instantiated as data type.
        Console.WriteLine(locValueType.ToString)
    End Sub
End Class
```

Combining Constraints and Specifying Multiple Type Parameters

Visual Basic lets you combine constraints for generic data types. Unlike the constraints for base data types, you *can* specify constraints for multiple interfaces. To define multiple type constraints or several interfaces for a generic data type, you first combine the requirements in curly braces, as shown in the following code:

```
Public Class GenericConstraintCombo(Of flexibleDataType As {Structure, IComparable, IDisposable})

    Public Sub TestMethod()
        Dim locValueType As flexibleDataType
        Dim locValueType2 As flexibleDataType
```

```
        'Can be used directly, since it's a value type because of the structure
        'Comparable thanks to IComparable
        locValueType.CompareTo(locValueType2)

        'Disposable thanks to IDisposable
        locValueType.Dispose()
        locValueType2.Dispose()
    End Sub
End Class
```

Additionally you can also set up a generic class that uses multiple type parameters. For example, if you need to create a collection that functions as a dictionary, you need to specify two data types: one for the lookup value (the key) and another for the actual value. (Don't program this yourself, because it already exists in the generic class *KeyedCollection* in the *System.Collections.ObjectModel* namespace.) You can specify the constraints for each type parameter individually:

```
Public Class GenericDictionary(Of KeyType As {Structure, IComparable}, _
                    ValueType As {New, IComparable, IDisposable})

    Public Sub TestMethod()
        Dim locValueType As KeyType
        Dim locValueType2 As ValueType

        'Can be used directly, since it's a value type because of the structure
        'Comparable thanks to IComparable
        locValueType.CompareTo(locValueType2)

        'Disposable thanks to IDisposable
        locValueType2.Dispose()
    End Sub
End Class
```

Chapter 18
Advanced Types

Along with generics (which you learned about in Chapter 17, "Developing with Generics"), in 2005, the Microsoft .NET Framework 2.0 introduced a very important data type based on this technology: the *Nullable* value type. As of .NET Framework 3.5, Nullables became available to Visual Basic 2008. You were briefly introduced to Nullables in the Chapter 1, "Beginners All-Purpose Symbolic Instruction Code." This chapter takes a closer look at them.

With Microsoft Visual Basic 2010, delegates gain additional meaning as a result of the introduction of the multi-line statement lambdas that you learned about in Chapter 15 "Events, Delegates, and Lambda Expressions." The manner in which you can approach solving problems changes completely—you might almost call it a paradigm shift in program or code structure. To support this feature, there are several new classes in Visual Basic 2010 and .NET Framework 4.0 that you will soon be using on a daily basis. These classes simplify development considerably under many different circumstances—particularly when it comes to multithreaded programming, which is becoming increasingly important and benefits from lambdas and delegates. I'm talking about the classes *Action(Of T)* and *Function(Of T)*, described later in this chapter.

In addition to these classes, you will also learn about more advanced types in this chapter, which are a bit more demanding to work with than what you have used so far.

Nullable Value Types

Nullable types have existed in the .NET Framework since Visual Basic 2005, but they were implemented only half-heartedly. Even though they did receive special treatment by the Common Language Runtime (CLR), they were not yet implemented with their own type literal, unlike in C# (see the section, "Special Characteristics of Nullable During Boxing"). This changed as of Visual Basic 2008.

Nullable is a generic data type with a constraint to value types. It makes it possible for any value type to "save" an additional state in addition to its actual value—namely *Nothing*.

And what is this capability good for? As just one example, if you have any database programming experience, you know that database tables can have data fields that can "save" the value *Null*—as an indicator that nothing (not even the number 0) has been saved in that field.

CheckBox controls in Windows Forms applications are another example (see Figure 18-1). They have an intermediary state, in which they are neither checked nor unchecked, which is supposed to indicate the state "undefined." There are all kinds of states a simple *Boolean* variable can't accommodate—*True* and *False* just aren't enough. It would be a different story if you could define a variable of type *Boolean* that could also reflect the value "nothing has been saved."

FIGURE 18-1 A *Boolean* is not well suited for saving the intermediary state of a *CheckBox* control.

Well, now you can do just that. Beginning with Visual Basic 2008, you define a variable as a Nullable value type by appending a question mark (a *type literal*) to the variable name. That looks like the following line:

```
Private myCheckBoxState As Boolean?
```

It can also look like this:

```
Private myCheckBoxState? As Boolean
```

Alternatively, you can still define a Nullable in the same way that you did in Visual Basic 2005:

```
Private myCheckBoxState As Nullable(Of Boolean)
```

And don't worry, you don't need to work your way through hundreds (maybe thousands) of lines of 2005 code to make the changes for the subsequent Visual Basic versions by adding the question marks. All three variants create exactly the same result.

> **Companion Content** Open the corresponding solution (.sln), which you can find in the \VB 2010 Developer Handbook\Chapter 18\NullableAndCheckBox folder.

This following example demonstrates how you can save all the possible states of a *CheckBox* control, whose *ThreeState* property for displaying all three states has been set to *True*, in a field variable of the *Boolean?* Nullable type. Click *Save State* to save the state of the *CheckBox* control in the field variable. Next, change the state, and then recreate the original state of the *CheckBox* control with the appropriate button. The corresponding code looks as follows:

```
Public Class Form1

    Private myCheckBoxState As Boolean?

    'This would also work:
    'Private myCheckBoxState? As Boolean

    'And this too:
    'Private myCheckBoxState As Nullable(Of Boolean)

    Private Sub btnOK_Click(ByVal sender As System.Object, _
                            ByVal e As System.EventArgs) Handles btnOK.Click
        Me.Close()
    End Sub

    Private Sub btnSave_Click(ByVal sender As System.Object, _
                              ByVal e As System.EventArgs) Handles btnSave.Click

        If chkDemo.CheckState = CheckState.Indeterminate Then
            myCheckBoxState = Nothing
        Else
            myCheckBoxState = chkDemo.Checked
        End If
    End Sub

    Private Sub btnRecreate_Click(ByVal sender As System.Object, _
        ByVal e As System.EventArgs) Handles btnWiederherstellen.Click
        If Not myCheckBoxState.HasValue Then
            chkDemo.CheckState = CheckState.Indeterminate
        Else
            If myCheckBoxState.Value Then
                chkDemo.CheckState = CheckState.Checked
            Else
                chkDemo.CheckState = CheckState.Unchecked
            End If
        End If
    End Sub
End Class
```

In the preceding example, the lines in which the field variable *Boolean?* is used are highlighted in bold. Note the following:

- **Value Assignment** To assign a value of the base type to *type?*, you can use implicit conversion; in other words, simply assign the value directly, as shown in the following line:

```
myCheckBoxState = chkDemo.Checked
```

- **Reset to *Nothing***   To reset a Nullable instance to *Nothing*, just assign it the "value" *Nothing*, as shown in the following code:

```
myCheckBoxState = Nothing
```

- **Check for value**   To determine whether a Nullable instance contains a value or *Nothing*, use the *HasValue* property, as this code shows:

```
If Not myCheckBoxState.HasValue Then
    chkDemo.CheckState = CheckState.Indeterminate
Else
...
```

- **Call the base type value**   And finally, you must be able to determine the value a Nullable instance carries, when its value is not *Nothing*. The property *Value* can do this for you, for example:

```
If myCheckBoxState.Value Then
    chkDemo.CheckState = CheckState.Checked
Else
    chkDemo.CheckState = CheckState.Unchecked
End If
...
```

Alternatively, you can call the value without the *Value* property, but you must ensure that the variable contains *Nothing*; in other words, that you can only assign it to a variable of the same type (namely Nullable of the base type).

> **Note**   In this example, you might have noticed that when the *ThreeState* property of a *CheckBox* control has been set and currently has the state *Indeterminate*, it's obviously not possible to change it into a different state (*Checked* or *Unchecked*) by using its *Checked* property. However, you can use the *CheckState* property to switch the *CheckBox* control out of the *Indeterminate* state programmatically.

Be Careful When Using *Boolean* Expressions Based on Nullables

Be especially careful when working with *Boolean* expressions that are Nullables—in fact, you should generally try to avoid such uses altogether. With regular *Boolean* expressions, you can assume that if a value is not *False*, it must automatically be *True*—there is no exception to that rule. However, with Nullable *Booleans* the rules are quite different: when a value of the type *Boolean?* has the "value" *Nothing*, it is neither false nor true. However, when

the expression *Not booleanValue* has been evaluated as *False*, from experience, we tend to assume the reverse conclusion: that it is *True*. Therefore, such constructs are prone to errors, as the following example shows:

```
Dim regularBoolean As Boolean = False
If regularBoolean Then
    'In this case, if the value is not true, ...
    Console.WriteLine("Value is true!")
Else
    '... it must be false.
    Console.WriteLine("Value is false!")
End If


'Now the value is a nullable boolean and can also be Nothing.
Dim booleanNullable As Boolean? = Nothing

If booleanNullable Then
    'Therefore, if the value is not true ...
    MessageBox.Show("Value is true!")
Else
    '...it does NOT necessarily have to be false!
    MessageBox.Show("Value isn't necessarily false!")
    If Not booleanNullable Then
        'Only here do we know that it was false.
        MessageBox.Show("Value is definitely false!")
    End If
End If
```

Special Characteristics of Nullable During Boxing

The data type *Nullable* (*type?*) is what you would typically create in Visual Basic as a structure; in other words, a value type. But you wouldn't be able to exactly reproduce this particular value type through programming, because it is treated specially by the CLR—which is a good thing.

> **Companion Content** Open the corresponding solution (.sln), which you can find in the \VB 2010 Developer Handbook\Chapter 18\NullableDemo folder.

When processing an instance of any structure (any value type), you will have to box the value type in an object variable at some point—for example, if you are saving it as part of an array or a collection.

Whenever a defined value type is boxed in an object, this object can logically not be *Nothing*, no matter what "value" the structure has. For the Nullable type this is different, as the following example shows:

```
Module NullableDemo

    Sub Main()
        Dim anObj As Object
        Dim aNullOfInt As Integer? = Nothing

        'Of course, there is only one usable instance, because
        'Integer? is a value type!
        Console.WriteLine("aNullOfInt has a value: " & aNullOfInt.HasValue)

        'Nevertheless the folowing construct returns True,
        'as if anObj had no reference!
        anObj = aNullOfInt
        Console.WriteLine("Is anObj Nothing? " & (anObj Is Nothing).ToString)
        Console.WriteLine()

        'And unboxing is possible as well!
        'There is no Null exception!
        aNullOfInt = DirectCast(anObj, Integer?)

        'And this works too?-Of course!
        aNullOfInt = DirectCast(Nothing, Integer?)

        'We are boxing an Integer?
        aNullOfInt = 10
        '
        anObj = aNullOfInt
        Dim anInt As Integer = DirectCast(anObj, Integer)

        Console.WriteLine("Press key to exit!")
        Console.ReadKey()

        'This doesn't work even though Nullable
        'basically fulfills the constraint rules!
        'Dim anotherNullOfInt As Nullable(Of Integer?)

    End Sub
End Module
```

When you run this example, you see the following lines:

```
aNullOfInt has a value: False
Is anObj Nothing? True

Press key to exit!
```

What happens here is anything but a matter of course—but still clean CLR design—because even though *aNullOfInt* is not initialized (or, to use the above example, initialized with *Nothing*—which amounts to the same thing), an instance of the structure still exists, of course; it just reflects the value *Nothing*. According to the known rules, subsequently boxing that value in the variable *anObj* should also lead to *anObj* containing a pointer to an instance of the variable *aNullOfInt*, which reflects *Nothing*, rather than a Null pointer. But that's not the case, because the output of:

```
Console.WriteLine("Is anObj Nothing? " & (anObj Is Nothing).ToString)
```

displays the following on your screen:

```
Is anObj Nothing? True
```

Of course, casting *Nothing* back into Nullable is therefore also permitted, as you can see in the code. And there is another irregularity pertaining to Nullable data types when casting a boxed type (assuming it's not *Nothing*) back into its base type, as the following code snippet shows:

```
'We are boxing an Integer?
aNullOfInt = 10
'
anObj = aNullOfInt
Dim anInt As Integer = DirectCast(anObj, Integer)
```

Here the Nullable data type (*Integer?*) is boxed into an object, but is later converted back to its *base data type* (*Integer*). I think this is a logical design, even though it completely contradicts the "normal" boxing process for value types in objects.

The Difference Between *Nothing* and *Nothing* as a Default Value

In this context it's important to take another look at the following behavior, which seems inconsistent at first glance, as is illustrated in Figure 18-2.

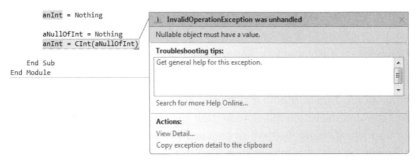

FIGURE 18-2 Although you can assign *Nothing* directly to an Integer variable, you can't assign the *Nothing* from a Nullable integer.

This raises the question: why can you assign *Nothing* directly to an *Integer* variable, but not the *Nothing* "saved" in a Nullable integer (I'm using quotes, because nothing is saved, *which is why* querying the content returns *Nothing*).

In the first case, *Nothing* actually means "the *default value* of the data type." When you assign *Nothing* to a variable, it always is assigned that type's default value. When you assign *Nothing* to a reference type, it just happens to be a 0–reference pointer, whereas for numeric data types, it's the value 0.

But in the second case—assigning the *Nothing* value from the Nullable—there is really no content—and non-existent content is not the same as the default value of the type. Therefore, Visual Basic returns an error message at runtime, and rightly so, because a value type cannot be assigned *Nothing*.

Generic Delegates

With the introduction of multi-line statement lambdas, program code will be considerably different in the future. For example, multi-line statement lambdas have the advantage of letting you write event-handling code directly at the location where the event is bound, as the following example illustrates:

```
Public Class Form1

    Sub New()

        ' This call is required for the Designer.
        InitializeComponent()

        Dim MessageText As String = "Button1 was clicked"

        ' Add initializations after the InitializeComponent() call.
        AddHandler Button1.Click, Sub(sender As Object, e As EventArgs)
                                      MessageBox.Show(MessageText)
                                  End Sub
    End Sub

End Class
```

You can see here that the *Click* event is already coded in the constructor of the form. The multi-line lambda is the argument for *AddHandler* at the location where you'd previously use the *AddressOf* operator to refer to a signature-compatible method.

The advantage of this kind of coding is that you can use local variables from the method that contains the lambda, within the lambda itself. In the preceding example, the lambda uses the local variable *MessageText*, which contains the output text for the *MessageBox* that is displayed when the user clicks the button. That this is permitted isn't self-evident, because

lambda execution happens at a different point in time than the definition of the local variables, of course.

Being able to directly specify a lambda instead of a delegate in the manner shown in the example above is a comfortable way to code, I think. But it can work even more smoothly because you can assign delegate variables of a specific signature to lambdas, and thus make them interchangeable.

Action(Of T)

Using the generic delegate *Action(Of T)*, you can create a new delegate based on it, which is compatible with method signatures that don't have return values. For example, suppose you have a method that you want to assign to a delegate that has the following signature:

```
Private Sub NightClickHandler(ByVal sender As Object, ByVal e As EventArgs)
    MessageBox.Show("Good night, dear User!" &
                    vbNewLine & "The button was clicked")

End Sub
```

Then you either create a new delegate as described in Chapter 15, or you make it easy on yourself and use the generic delegate *Action(Of T)*, as shown in Figure 18-3.

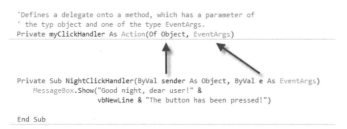

FIGURE 18-3 The type parameters of the *Action* class must have the same order as the method types that an instance of the *Action* class accepts as a delegate.

Figure 18-3 shows that by declaring *myClickHandler* as *Action(Of Object, EventArgs)* it becomes signature-compatible to the method *NightClickHandler*. If the method (*NightClickHandler*) had an additional parameter, for example, of type *String*, then you would also give the *Action(Of T)* class an extra parameter, and the definition would look as follows:

```
Private myClickHandler As Action(Of Object, EventArgs, String)
```

> **Note** The *Action(Of T)* delegate works in connection with methods that have from 0 to 16 parameters. If you ever need a delegate for a method signature with more than 16 parameters, you will need to define your own delegate type.

> **Companion Content** Open the corresponding solution (.sln), which you can find in the \VB 2010 Developer Handbook\Chapter 18\GenericDelegates folder.

From this point onward, *myClickHandler* functions just like any other delegate variable. The following example demonstrates the possible applications with multi-line statement lambdas:

```
Public Class Form1

    'Defines a delegate to a method which accepts a parameter
    'of the type Object and one of the type EventArgs.
    Private myClickHandler As Action(Of Object, EventArgs)

    'An EventHandler which is called when the current time is later than 6pm.
    Private Sub NightClickHandler(ByVal sender As Object, ByVal e As EventArgs)
        MessageBox.Show("Good night, dear User!" &
                        vbNewLine & "The button was clicked")

    End Sub

    Sub New()

        ' The call is required for the Designer.
        InitializeComponent()

        Dim MessageText As String = "Button1 was clicked"

        'Before noon, this Lambda as delegate
        If Now.TimeOfDay < New TimeSpan(12, 0, 0) Then
            'Note: the types of sender and e are derived from
            'the signature of myClickHandler (type inference).
            ' 'as Object' and 'as EventArgs' don't need to be specified.
            myClickHandler = Sub(sender, e)
                                 MessageBox.Show("Good morning, dear User!" &
                                                 vbNewLine & MessageText)
                             End Sub

            'Before 6pm, this Lambda as Delegate
        ElseIf Now.TimeOfDay < New TimeSpan(18, 0, 0) Then
            'Here also: Type inference for Lambda parameters.
            myClickHandler = Sub(sender, e)
                                 MessageBox.Show("Good day, dear User!" &
                                                 vbNewLine & MessageText)
                             End Sub
        Else
            'Otherwise assign the NightClickHandler Sub to the Action delegate.
            myClickHandler = AddressOf NightClickHandler
        End If
```

```
'Here the Click event is wired
'which calls the Action delegate.
AddHandler Button1.Click, Sub(sender, e)
                                myClickHandler(sender, e)
                            End Sub

    End Sub

End Class
```

Function(Of T)

The *Action(Of T)* class works great for methods that don't return values to the calling instance. For methods that do return values, use the generic delegate *Function(Of T)*. Unlike *Action(Of T)*, it always accepts one further type parameter that represents the return value type. Otherwise, *Function(Of T)* functions exactly like *Action(Of T)*. Figure 18-4 illustrates how you can make a delegate variable of the type *Function(Of T)* signature-compatible to a method with return value.

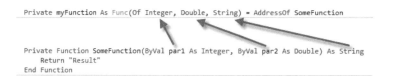

FIGURE 18-4 The type parameters of the *Func* class must have the same order as the method types that an instance of the *Func* class accepts as a delegate. The last type parameter of *Func* corresponds to the return type of the method.

Tuple(Of T)

With methods that return function results, certain situations pose a problem that usually requires a bit of extra effort; specifically, what should you do when the function returns more than just one value as the result? So far you have seen two possibilities that can avoid this problem:

- You pass parameters by reference, essentially "misusing" the passed variable as a return value. This is similar to the *TryParse* method of many primitive data types, so you can determine whether a string can be converted into a primitive data type.

- You create a support class or structure that combines the returned values.

Tuple(Of T) provides yet a third option. The generic *Tuple* class reconciles as many values as you specify parameters (up to eight) when declaring a variable. You can specify values for the *Tuple* exclusively during class instantiation in the constructor.

If you want to read the values the *Tuple* saves, use the appropriate *Item* property, which exists in numbered form for each specified type parameter—not as an index, but as a fixed name (*Item1, Item2, Item3 ...*). The following example demonstrates how to use the *Tuple* class:

```
Sub TupleTest()

    'Defines a new Tuple with three values.
    Dim t As New Tuple(Of Double, Integer, String)(3.1415926, 20, "Test")
    Debug.Print("First value of Tuple:" & t.Item1.ToString)
    Debug.Print("Second value of Tuple:" & t.Item2.ToString)
    Debug.Print("Third value of Tuple:" & t.Item3)

    t = TupleFunction
End Sub

Function TupleFunction() As Tuple(Of Double, Integer, String)
    'This function returns three values encapsulated in a Tuple.
    Return New Tuple(Of Double, Integer, String)(3.141592657, 20, "String")
End Function
```

Type Variance

Within the context of object-oriented programming, type variance means that an object variable of a certain type can also point to an instance of a derivate of this type (covariance) or that an object variable of a derived class type can point to an instance of its base class (contravariance).

You can see a simple example of covariance in polymorphism for overridden methods of a base class. For example, if a *ListBox* in your *Items* collection expects variables of the type *Object*, you can also pass types derived from *Object*. In this case, *Object* behaves as a *covariant*.

However, there is a problem with collections. Suppose that you have a base type called *BaseClass* and a type derived from it called *DerivedClass*. As you know already, you can then use base types in covariant form in many cases.

 Note To understand this section, you must be familiar with the topics of generics (see Chapter 17) and collections (see Chapter 19, "Arrays and Collections"). The information in Chapter 11, "Developing Value Types," and the functionality of polymorphism and other basic concepts covered in Chapter 12, "Typecasting and Boxing Value Types," also help with this demanding topic.

If *BaseType* can behave covariantly toward *DerivedType*, shouldn't *BaseType* in *List(Of BaseType)* then also be covariant to *List(Of DerivedType)*, such that the following line would be possible?

```
Dim baseList As List(Of AddressBase)
Dim derivedList As New List(Of Colleague)

baseList = derivedList
```

The answer is "No"—and Figure 18-5 illustrates how to find help, even if it doesn't explain *why* such an assignment is prohibited.

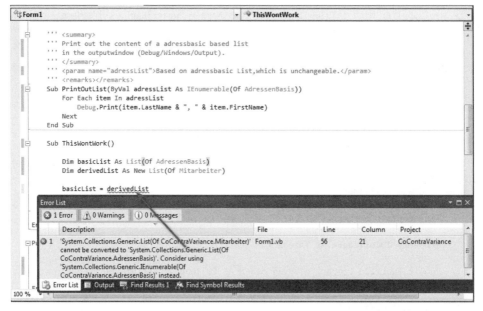

FIGURE 18-5 Even though *baseList* can be used covariantly regarding an instance of *Colleague*, because *Colleague* is derived from *AddressBase*, lists from *List(Of T)* with type parameters aren't automatically covariant.

You can explore this problem with a practical example.

> **Companion Content** Open the corresponding solution (.sln), which you can find in the
> \VB 2010 Developer Handbook\Chapter 18\CoContraVariance folder.

Here's a nice little program that distinguishes itself by virtue of one major characteristic: it doesn't run. the reason is that the program defines two lists, one with colleagues and one with suppliers, as presented in the following:

```
'Fill Colleague by using collection initializers
Dim colleagues As New List(Of Colleague) From {
    New Colleague With {.IDColleague = 1, .LastName = "Leenings", .FirstName = "Ramona"},
    New Colleague With {.IDColleague = 3, .LastName = "Calla", .FirstName = "Sarika"},
    New Colleague With {.IDColleague = 2, .LastName = "Löffelmann", .FirstName = "Klaus"},
    New Colleague With {.IDColleague = 3, .LastName = "Pusch", .FirstName = "Marcus"},
    New Colleague With {.IDColleague = 2, .LastName = "Belke", .FirstName = "Andreas"}}

Dim suppliers As New List(Of Supplier) From {
    New Supplier With {.IDSupplier = 1, .LastName = "Woerrlein", .FirstName = "Hartmut"},
    New Supplier With {.IDSupplier = 2, .LastName = "Löffelmann", .FirstName = "Klaus"},
    New Supplier With {.IDSupplier = 3, .LastName = "Grauthoff", .FirstName = "Kristin"}}
```

Both initial classes are based on a common base class, which is the class *AddressBase*:

```
Public Class AddressBase

    Property FirstName As String
    Property LastName As String

End Class

Public Class Colleague
    Inherits AddressBase
    Implements IComparable(Of Colleague)

    Property IDColleague As Integer

    Public Function CompareTo(ByVal other As Colleague) As Integer _
        Implements System.IComparable(Of Colleague).CompareTo
        Return (Me.LastName & Me.FirstName).CompareTo(other.LastName & other.FirstName)
    End Function

End Class

Public Class Supplier
    Inherits AddressBase

    Property IDSupplier As Integer
End Class
```

And now a developer gets the idea to write a *common* method that displays either suppliers or colleagues:

```
Sub OutputList(ByVal addressList As List(Of AddressBase))
    For Each item In addressList
        Debug.Print(item.LastName & ", " & item.FirstName)
    Next
End Sub
```

And that's exactly the problem right now. The method that is supposed to output these items (colleagues and suppliers) accepts a *list* of the type *AddressBase*. However, the first list it receives (see Figure 18-6) has the type *Colleague*. And of course, you can't add suppliers to it, because otherwise, type safety and homogeneity of the list would be compromised.

But if you do an all-inclusive casting of a *List(Of Colleague)* into *List(Of AddressBase)* this is exactly what could happen. There is really nothing to prevent you from adding suppliers to *List(Of AddressBase)*. Only if you call the method *OutputList* and *read* items in this method (in other words, *not* change its content), then it remains a *List(Of Colleague)*, which is processed only via the "base class."

```
'Co-Variance Demo
Public Class Form1

    Private Sub Button1_Click(ByVal sender As System.Object, ByVal e As System.EventArgs)
        'Fill employee with the listing-initializers
        Dim employee As New List(Of Employee) From {
                New Employee With {.IDEmployee = 1, .LastName = "Leenings", .FirstName = "Ramona"},
                New Employee With {.IDEmployee = 3, .LastName = "Heckhuis", .FirstName = "Jürgen"},
                New Employee With {.IDEmployee = 2, .LastName = "Löffelmann", .FirstName = "Klaus"},
                New Employee With {.IDEmployee = 3, .LastName = "Pusch", .FirstName = "Marcus"},
                New Employee With {.IDEmployee = 2, .LastName = "Belke", .FirstName = "Andreas"}}

        Dim suppliers As New List(Of suppliers) From {
                New suppliers With {.IDLieferant = 1, .LastName = "Thiemann", .FirstName = "Uwe"},
                New suppliers With {.IDLieferant = 2, .LastName = "Löffelmann", .FirstName = "Klaus"},
                New suppliers With {.IDLieferant = 3, .LastName = "Grauthof", .FirstName = "Kristin"}}

        PrintOutList(employee)
        PrintOutList(suppliers)
```

FIGURE 18-6 A variation of the same problem: *OutputList* accepts a *List(Of adressBase)*—casting the derived types as type parameters when calling the method is not possible. The type parameter of *List(Of)* is not covariant.

If there were a constraint that items could not be added to such a base class list, then—and only then—its homogeneity would be guaranteed, and then it could be used as a parameter for a method like the one used for output here.

In Visual Basic 2010, this is possible, but only for type parameters of generic *interfaces*. In the end, that doesn't matter. You don't really care whether you're using a class or an interface variable to access the list.

Using an interface is possible, because when defining interfaces in Visual Basic 2010 or .NET Framework 4.0, you have the option to define an interface for covariant use by using the keyword *Out* for type parameters, and for contravariant, use with the keyword *In*.

The keyword *Out* ensures that an interface must implement only functions or properties that can return the specified type, while *In* ensures that methods or properties only accept parameters of this type—but must not return them.

.NET Framework 4.0 does this with *IEnumerable*, the interface that dictates that a class represents a collection and can therefore be iterated with *For Each*. *IEnumerable* is defined as follows:

```
Public Interface IEnumerable(Of Out type)
    .
    .
    .
End Interface
```

The new keyword *Out* specifies that classes used to access this interface only *output* the specified type, but can't *accept* them. Therefore, the following would work:

```
Function AMethod() As type
```

But the line that follows wouldn't, because the interface receives a type:

```
Sub AnotherMethod(ByVal aParameter As type)
```

In this case, reconstructing the list output into an *IEnumerable* leads to homogenous lists. The type parameter for *IEnumerable* is, as mentioned before, defined with *Out*; therefore, the *Items* method of the interface can return items, but the interface cannot include an *Add* method which would accept this generic type. Remember that this does not mean that the class which implements the interface cannot have an *Add* method—only that the interface can't bind such a method, which is enough of a guarantor for type safety. After reconstruction the program runs exactly as we want it to:

```
Sub OutputList(ByVal addressList As IEnumerable(Of AddressBase))
    For Each item In addressList
        Debug.Print(item.LastName & ", " & item.FirstName)
    Next
End Sub
```

Note The method *Distinct* illustrates the reverse case—contravariance for generic interfaces—which basically works the same way, except that you use the keyword *In* as part of the definition, which specifies that the type parameter can be passed to the class, but must not be returned.

Extension Methods

In principle, it has always been possible to extend classes with new methods or properties. You inherited them and then added new methods or properties in the inherited class code. This worked as long as the following conditions were met:

- The types were not marked with the *NotInheritable* modifier (*Sealed* in C#).

- The types weren't value types—because types created with *Structure* are automatically value types and those are implicitly not inheritable.

To help structure your code better, Microsoft added *extension methods* in Visual Basic 2008. You can use these to add user-defined functions to already defined data types without having to create a new, inherited type. An extension method is a special kind of static method, but you can call it just like an instance method for the extended type. When writing client code in Visual Basic (or C#), there's no discernable difference between calling an extension method and the methods the type actually defines.

However, there are constraints and conventions when extending classes in this manner:

- Extension methods must be specifically marked with an attribute in Visual Basic: the *ExtensionAttribute* located in the namespace *System.Runtime.CompilerServices*.

- An extension method can only and exclusively be a *Sub* or *Function*. You can extend a class with extension methods, but *not* with properties, new field variables, or events.

- An extension method must be located in a separate module.

- The module must be imported just like any other class, if it resides in a different namespace than the instance it uses.

- An extension method has at least one parameter that specifies the type (class, structure) it extends. For example, to create an extension method for the data type *String*, the first parameter the extension method accepts must be a *String*. For this reason, you can't use an *Optional* parameter or a *ParamArray* parameter for the first parameter in the parameter list, because those vary at runtime, and the first parameter must be known to the compiler at design time.

The Main Application Area of Extension Methods

The main reason for introducing extension methods into .NET languages was to be able to create a LINQ-compatible language infrastructure for the compiler, which makes using valid generic and static functions "feel" like they match the type.

To gain a deeper understanding, you must possess a comprehensive knowledge of interfaces. You should also ensure that you understand the section on lambda expressions.

The developers of .NET Framework 3.5 faced the difficult task of incorporating additional functionality into existing types *without* changing the code of these types in any way—generic collection classes were particularly affected. That would have led to so-called *breaking changes* (changes with unpredictable impact on existing development). So the only option was to add additional functionality into static generic code, which would have felt rather "uncool."

Extension methods are basically just a sham package, because they are simple static methods that only *feel* like member methods of the corresponding types. The following code snippet should illustrate this:

> **Companion Content** Open the corresponding solution (.sln), which you can find in the \VB 2010 Developer Handbook\Chapter 18\ExtensionMethodsDemo folder.

```vb
'Important: The Extension attribute resides in this namespace
Imports System.Runtime.CompilerServices

'Important: The namespace with the extention method for a type must be imported!
Imports ExtentionMethodsDemo.MyExtentionMethod

Module MainModule

    Sub Main()

        Dim t = "This is the first line!\nAnd this is the second."
        Console.WriteLine(t.Formatted)

        'Wait for key.
        Console.ReadKey()
    End Sub

End Module

Namespace MyExtentionMethod

    Module ExtentionMethodsModule

        'The Extension attribute marks a method
        'as extension method. The type of the first parameter
        'specifies the type which must be extended.
        <Extension()> _
        Public Function Formatted(ByVal text As String) As String
            'Turn \n into CR+LF.
            Return text.Replace("\n", vbNewLine)
        End Function

    End Module
End Namespace
```

This little example extends the *String* data type with a *Formatted* method. This method converts text containing a C++ or C#-type formatting statement (namely the "\n" that represents a line break). In the example, a string that contains a line break control character can be reformatted for Visual Basic by calling the *Formatted* method. For the *String* data type to accept this new method, the conditions presented in the following list are required.

> **Important** This example isn't meant to illustrate the way control characters work in C# or C++, where the conversion of control characters happens at compilation time. This example uses processor time to perform the control character conversion at runtime.

- The method must be defined as static. Because in Visual Basic all methods located in a module are static, it's best to put extension methods into a module, as shown in the code example.

- For the method to be recognized as an extension method for the data type, you must include the *ExtensionAttribute* on the extension method. To be able to access *ExtensionAttribute*, you must reference the namespace *System.Runtime. CompilerServices*.

- For the type to be able to access the extension method, you must import the namespace that contains the extension method. Of course, this is also true if the namespace where the extended type is located is different than that of the extension method. Therefore, the corresponding *Imports* statement is located at the beginning of the code file.

Extending existing types in this fashion is convenient (see also Chapter 15). But when it comes to creating infrastructure for LINQ, extension methods become a truly brilliant trick; because extension methods all have a type as a first parameter, they can also receive interfaces as a type. This means, however, that all types that implement this interface also have the additional methods. In combination with generics and lambda expressions this is of course a pretty cool thing, because the actual functionality is controlled by one or several lambda expressions (depending on the expansion stage of overloaded versions of the static extension methods), and the actual type to be processed only sees the light of day due to the use of generics when determining the correct type later on. This little trick helps you to quickly create complete, type-safe infrastructure for grouping, sorting, filtering, determining, or mutually excluding items of all collections that implement a specific interface extended by extension methods— for example, for *IEnumerable(T)* by static methods of the *Enumerable* class.

So, let's recap: *all* collections that embed *IEnumerable(T)* are extended by member methods located in *Enumerable*, and those methods are exactly the ones required by LINQ to perform selections, sorts, groupings, and other data operations. But it only seems that way—in fact, the entire LINQ functionality is basically delegated to a purely procedurally-structured class that contains a bunch of static functions.

Using Extension Methods to Simplify Collection Initializers

With the advent of Visual Basic 2010 and the concept of collection initializers, extension methods play an additional role; they simplify using parameters passed in curly braces after the *From* clause for collection initializers. You'll explore such initializers in more detail in Chapter 19.

Part III

Programming with .NET Framework Data Structures

In this part:

Chapter 19
Arrays and Collections

Arrays have been available in almost all derivatives of BASIC for decades—and of course, they're available in Microsoft Visual Basic, as well. But the Microsoft .NET Framework wouldn't be the .NET Framework if it didn't offer arrays with many more possibilities than simple data access via a numeric index.

This means that the performance of arrays reaches far beyond the simple provision of containers for saving the elements of a data type. Because arrays are based on *Object* and therefore form a class of their own (namely *System.Array*), .NET Framework offers a broad spectrum of functions for element management via *Array* objects.

For example, you can pretty much sort an array at the press of a button. When you have an array in sorted form, you can perform a binary search or many other operations without having to write the corresponding code yourself.

Last but not least, the type *System.Array* constitutes the basis for further data types, such as *ArrayList*, which can dynamically manage data elements of all types, as well as the basis for many of the generic collection types—which themselves are the bases for *LINQ to Objects*.

This chapter shows you what you can do with arrays and the classes derived from them. It also prepares you for working with *LINQ to Objects*.

Array Basics

In the original sense of BASIC, you use arrays to hold a number of elements of the same data type, making all the elements available by using a single name. To differentiate between the individual array elements and be able to access them, arrays use an *index* (a simple numbering of elements). It's worth noting that an array index has little to nothing in common with an index for a database table.

> **Companion Content** Many of the larger examples below are combined into in various methods in the project *Arrays*. You can find this project in the \VB 2010 Developer Handbook\Chapter 19\ Arrays folder.

> **Note** You can use this project to replicate examples on your own computer or to perform your own experiments with arrays.

Here's a basic array example:

```
Sub Example1()

    'Declare an array with 10 elements.
    'Important: Unlike in C# or C++ you specify the index of the
    'last element, not the number of elements!
    'Element count starts at 0.
    'Therefore the following statement defines 10 elements:
    Dim locIntArray(9) As Integer

    'Initialize random generator.
    Dim locRandom As New Random(Now.Millisecond)

    For count As Integer = 0 To 9
        locIntArray(count) = locRandom.Next
    Next

    For count As Integer = 0 To 9
        Console.WriteLine("Element No. {0} has the value {1}", count,
locIntArray(count))
    Next

    Console.ReadLine()

End Sub
```

When you run this example, the console window shows a list of values similar to the one that follows (of course your values will be different, because they are random).

> **Note** The values actually aren't completely random—*Random* only means that the generated sequences of numbers are *distributed* randomly. Given the same starting point (defined by the parameter *Seed* which you pass to the *Random* class during instantiation) *Random* will always produce the same number sequence. In this case, because the code passes a millisecond as a base, and a second comprises 1,000 milliseconds, there is a probability of only 1:1000 that you will generate the same sequence of numbers as printed here. It's always difficult to teach a deterministic machine something as indeterministic as luck.

```
Element No. 0 has the value 1074554181
Element No. 1 has the value 632329388
Element No. 2 has the value 1312197477
Element No. 3 has the value 458430355
Element No. 4 has the value 1970029554
Element No. 5 has the value 503465071
Element No. 6 has the value 112607304
Element No. 7 has the value 1507772275
Element No. 8 has the value 1111627006
Element No. 9 has the value 213729371
```

This example demonstrates the most basic way to create and use arrays. Obviously, you are not limited to *Integer* when defining the element type. The overarching principle here is that any object in .NET can be an array element.

Initializing Arrays

Arrays are *static* in memory: once created, they can no longer be changed. But an object variable that points to a particular array type can be pointed to a different array of the same type, even one with a different number of elements. You can do this in one of several ways. The instant you define an array and specify the number of elements it will contain, the .NET Framework reserves the memory space for those elements, as shown in the following:

```
'Byte array with 11 elements (0-10)
Dim myByteArray(10) As Byte
```

This statement establishes an array of the type *Byte*, and at the same time it reserves the memory space for 11 *Byte* elements.

Changing Array Dimensions at Runtime

In some cases, it might make sense to initially define an array to be of a specific type, but to leave the number of elements open. Maybe the number of elements will be calculated later on or determined in some other way, and therefore, it should also be defined later. This is how it works (and if you now expect the very BASIC-esque *ReDim* to be introduced, you will be very disappointed):

```
Public Class ArrayInitializeDemo

    'For now just define as array of type Integer
    Private myIntegerArray() As Integer

    Sub New(ByVal ElementCount As Integer)
        'Here we know now many we need,
        'and now we reserve the elements:
        myIntegerArray = New Integer(ElementCount - 1) {}
    End Sub

End Class
```

The first bold-highlighted line shows you that *myIntegerArray* has been declared, but not yet defined. Like any other reference variable, it therefore points to *Nothing*. The second high-lighted line creates space for the appropriate number of elements.

> **Note** When defining new arrays, it's important to remember to specify the *upper limit* of the array, and not the number of elements. And don't forget to put the empty curly braces behind the dimension specification. Otherwise, the compiler sees the value inside the parenthesis as an argument for a parameterized constructor of the corresponding value type (which doesn't exist) and generates an error message.

The Magic of *ReDim*

Mainly for reasons of backward compatibility, the .NET versions of Visual Basic offer an option for dimensioning an array after its initial declaration. The following is an example:

```
Sub Example3()

    Dim locNumberStrings As Integer = 15
    Dim locStringArray As String()
    locStringArray = GenerateStrings(locNumberStrings, 30)
    Console.WriteLine("Initial size: {0} elements. Content follows:",
        locStringArray.Length)
    Console.WriteLine(New String("="c, 40))
    PrintStrings(locStringArray)
    'We need 10 more, but the old ones should remain!
```

```
        ReDim Preserve locStringArray(locStringArray.Length + 9)

        'Do the old ones really remain?
        Console.WriteLine()
        Console.WriteLine("Content check:", locStringArray.Length)
        Console.WriteLine(New String("="c, 40))
        PrintStrings(locStringArray)

        'Generate 10 further elements.
        Dim locTempStrings(9) As String

        '10 chars more per element, so we can recognize the new ones easily.
        locTempStrings = GenerateStrings(10, 40)

        'Copy into the "old" array, but only from index 15 onward.
        locTempStrings.CopyTo(locStringArray, 15)

        'And check what's really written inside!
        Console.WriteLine()
        Console.WriteLine("Content check:", locStringArray.Length)
        Console.WriteLine(New String("="c, 40))
        PrintStrings(locStringArray)

        Console.ReadLine()
    End Sub
```

The first line of code in this example capitalizes on Visual Basic's ability to separate array dimensioning and array declaration by performing those operations at different times. Initially, *locStringArray* is declared only as an array—what the size of the array will be is not yet specified. By the way, in Visual Basic, it doesn't matter whether you declare a variable to be an array by writing the statement as follows:

```
Dim locStringArray As String()
```

Or, if you write it as shown here:

```
Dim locStringArray() As String
```

The size of the array is specified in the procedure *GenerateStrings*. First, the procedure dimensions a totally different array (*locStrings*), but because that array is returned to the calling instance, the array content created here continues on under a different name (*locStringArray*). The array referenced by both object variables is the same in the original sense.

On a side note, this process actually corresponds to the re-dimensioning of an array already. As you have seen in the first array example, it doesn't matter whether you are using an array variable to accept an array as the return value of a function which is previously dimensioned

with a fixed number of elements or without the specifications of the array size. But keep in mind, by doing this you lose the content of the original array (if it exists) because the method creates a new array, and by assigning the object variable *locStringArray* internally, only a pointer is bent. The memory area of the old elements can no longer be referenced and would be removed by the Garbage Collector at the next opportunity.

> **Important** This fact has consequences, because unlike in Visual Basic 6.0 or VBA, arrays are *not* automatically copied when assigned to a different object variable. Array variables behave like any other reference type in .NET. Assigning an array variable to a different array only reassigns its pointer to the memory area of the actual data in the Managed Heap. The elements themselves remain at their location in the Managed Heap; the .NET Framework doesn't allocate new memory, nor does it copy the existing array elements to assign them to the new object variable.

You can also resize or re-dimension arrays by using the *ReDim* statement, as shown in the preceding code. By using the *Preserve* keyword, you can specify that existing elements are maintained during the resize operation. So what exactly happens when re-dimensioning with *ReDim*?

- When you call *ReDim*, the .NET Framework reserves a completely new memory area for the array.

- The object variable that pointed to the previously assigned array elements is reassigned to point to the new memory area.

- The memory area that contained the old array element pointers is reclaimed during the next Garbage Collector pass.

- When you add the *Preserve* keyword after the *ReDim* statement, the operation preserves the existing array elements.

  Here's what actually happens: with *Preserve*, the .NET Framework also creates a new memory area, reserving the space for the newly specified number of array elements. In both cases, the pointer of the array variable is switched to point to the new memory area. But with *Preserve*, the existing elements are copied into the new area before the old memory area is freed and the Garbage Collector destroys the old elements.

By the way, with *Preserve* you can only keep elements that are saved in one-dimensional arrays or elements that are addressed by the last dimension of a multidimensional array.

Pre-Allocating Values of Array Elements in Code

All the arrays used in the examples thus far are filled with data at runtime. However, in many cases you might want to create arrays that you automatically pre-fill with data hard-coded into the program:

```
Sub Example5()

    'Declaration and definition of elements with Double values
    Dim locDoubleArray As Double() = {123.45F, 5435.45F, 3.14159274F}

    'Declaration and subsequent definition of elements with Integer values
    Dim locIntegerArray As Integer()
    locIntegerArray = New Integer() {1I, 2I, 3I, 3I, 4I}
    'Declaration and subsequent definition of elements with Date values
    Dim locDateArray As Date()
    locDateArray = New Date() {#12/24/2005#, #12/31/2005#, #3/31/2006#}

    'Declaration and definition of elements in the Char array:
    Dim locCharArray As Char() = {"V"c, "B"c, "."c, "N"c, "E"c, "T"c, " "c, _
                                  "r"c, "u"c, "l"c, "e"c, "s"c, "!"c}

    'Two-dimensional array
    Dim locTwoDimensional As Integer(,)
    locTwoDimensional = New Integer(,) {{10, 10}, {20, 20}, {30, 30}}

    'Or nested (which is not two-dimensional)!
    Dim locJagged As Date()()
    locJagged = New Date()() {New Date() {#12/24/2004#, #12/31/2004#}, _
                              New Date() {#12/24/2005#, #12/31/2005#}}
End Sub
```

The most frequent error source when using array initializers is that the assignment operator is not applied correctly. The assignment operator is *required* for declaration/definition combinations. If you are only writing a new *definition*, you leave it off. Also, note the difference between multidimensional and jagged arrays (which will be covered in more detail in the section "Multidimensional and Jagged Arrays" later in this chapter).

Type Inference When Using Array Initializers

When you use arrays at a procedure level (in *Function* and *Sub* methods or property procedures), the compiler permits local type inference, which saves you many keystrokes:

```
Private Sub SomeThing()

    'String array with 5 elements (can only be defined on procedure level).
    Dim myStringArray = {"Andreas", "Ramona", "Klaus", "Adriana", "Magges"}

End Sub
```

You are looking in vain for a type definition for *myStringArray*, but nevertheless the array object variable created is strongly defined as an *Array* of strings. The compiler recognizes that the individual instances inside the curly braces are strings and therefore concludes that the whole thing is an array of strings.

For arrays, you can also capitalize on type inference when calling methods that expect an empty array of a certain type as a parameter (among others). The following example shows such a case. By using reflection (see Chapter 21, "Attributes and Reflection"), the code determines the constructor of a type and calls it with the *Invoke* method. Both methods require arrays as parameters. In the following example, the array parameters must be a specific type, but must not contain elements:

```
Dim tk = GetType(TestClass). _
        GetConstructor(New Type() {}). _
          Invoke(New Object() {})
```

First, the code calls *GetType* to determine the type object of the class *TestClass*. *GetConstructor* then determines the constructor for the type passed via the *Type* array. Finally, *Invoke* calls the constructor with the appropriate parameters. Passing an empty array of a certain type takes place the only way possible so far, with *New ArrayType() { }*.

In C#, this looks similar, including in the most recent Visual C# 2010 version:

```
var f = typeof(TestClass).
        GetConstructor(new Type[0]).
          Invoke(new Object[] { });
```

Unlike in Visual Basic (because for array definitions in C#, you specify the number of elements, not the upper limit of the array), you can define empty arrays two ways: by specifying the type and 0 in square brackets, or by passing the type and a square bracket as an array indicator as well as an empty list as an object initializer with two braces.

In Visual Basic 2010 it's even easier, as demonstrated here:

```
Dim tk = GetType(TestClass).
        GetConstructor({}).
          Invoke({})
```

The Visual Basic compiler does something remarkable here. The *GetConstructor* method defines through its signature which type of argument it expects, and derives the empty array initializer from the context to create the correct type—in this case, into an array of the type *Type*. The same happens afterward with the *Invoke* method, for which the correct type, namely an empty array of the type *Object*, is derived from the array initializer literal.

Dominant Types

Within this context, take a look at the following array definitions, which all use local type inference:

```
'New as of Visual Basic 2010
'Type inference for arrays:
Dim locWhatWillItBe = {2, 4, 8, 16, 32, 64, 128}

'One type is dominant.
Dim locAndThis = {2, 4, 5.6F, 10.266212122326667R}

'This doesn't work—Object arrays only works with Option Strict Off!
'Dim AnotherVersion = {10, "c"c, "A text", #7/24/1969#}
```

The first line is clear: because it uses only *Integer* constants, the resulting array is also of type *Integer*.

The second definition isn't as obvious, because it contains *Integer*, *Single*, and *Double* values. The defined dominant type is *Double*. Because nothing can go wrong during a conversion from *Integer* or *Single* to *Double*, that becomes the dominant type.

> **Note** Even though the *Decimal* data type is more precise than *Double*, *Double* remains the dominant type when you add *Decimal* constants to the list that are forced by a type literal (for example, 3.14159265754D). The resulting array would therefore be *Double*, even if just one *Double* value appeared in the list.

The third definition is not possible. The Visual Basic compiler would need to settle on *Object* as the dominant type, but type safety doesn't permit that. Instead, the compiler typically raises an error. However, if you turn *Option Strict* off, the Visual Basic compiler creates an array of *Object*.

Multidimensional Arrays and Jagged Arrays

When defining arrays, you are not limited to one dimension. This feature has been part of BASIC dialects for decades. You create a multidimensional array by specifying the number of elements for each dimension, separated by commas during declaration:

```
Dim ThreeDimensional(5, 10, 3) As Integer
```

If you don't want to set the number of elements during declaration of the arrays, use the following declaration statement:

```
Dim AlsoThreeDimensional As Integer(,,)
```

You can then define the array with *ReDim* or function calls, which return a correctly dimensioned array.

Alternatively, you can use the following syntax:

```
'Nested instead of Redim:
Dim AlsoSimpleJagged As Integer()()
AlsoSimpleJagged = New Integer(10)() {}
```

Jagged Arrays

Jagged arrays are different from multidimensional arrays. With jagged (or nested) arrays, each array element itself is an array. That array can also contain arrays, and so on. Unlike with multidimensional arrays, each individual element can contain differently dimensioned arrays—and those arrays can change later on.

You define jagged arrays by specifying each array dimension inside a separate pair of parentheses. By contrast, you specify the dimensions for multidimensional arrays within a single pair of parentheses, separated by commas.

The following code examples (from the *Sub Example6*) show you how to define jagged arrays and call their individual elements:

```
'Simple jagged; depth is not defined.
Dim SimpleJagged(10)() As Integer

'First element contains an Integer array with three elements.

SimpleJagged(0) = New Integer() {10, 20, 30}

'Second element contains an Integer array with eight elements.
SimpleJagged(1) = New Integer() {10, 20, 30, 40, 50, 60, 70, 80}

'Prints the third element of the second array element (30).
Console.WriteLine(SimpleJagged(1)(2))

'Assign everything in one go.
SimpleJagged = New Integer()() {New Integer() {30, 20, 10}, _
                                New Integer() {80, 70, 60, 50, 40, 30, 20, 10}}

'Prints the third element of the second array element (now 60).
Console.WriteLine(SimpleJagged(1)(2))
Console.ReadLine()
```

Important Array Properties and Methods

You saw some *Array* properties and methods in the previous code examples. This section shows you more of the possibilities of the *Array* class, which offers many powerful options that can save you a lot of programming time, if used correctly.

Determining the Number of Array Elements by Using *Length*

To ascertain the number of elements in an array, use the *Length* property. For two-dimensional and multidimensional arrays, *Length* also determines the total number of all elements. But watch out when working with jagged arrays, because *Length* determines only the number of elements of the *parent* array. You can find out the length of an element of the parent array by using the following:

```
'Jagged arrays
Dim locJagged As Date()()
locJagged = New Date()() {New Date() {#12/24/2004#, #12/31/2004#}, _
                          New Date() {#12/24/2005#, #12/31/2005#}}

Console.WriteLine("Parent array has {0} elements.", locJagged.Length)
Console.WriteLine("Array of the 1. element has {0} elements.", locJagged(0).Length)
```

Sorting Arrays with *Array.Sort*

Arrays can be sorted by using the very simple *Sort* method. The following example demonstrates how:

```
Sub Example7()

    'Create array:
    Dim locNames As String() = {"Jürgen", "Martina", "Hanna", "Gaby",
                               "Michaela", "Miriam", "Ute", "Leonie-Gundula",
                               "Melanie", "Uwe", "Andrea", "Klaus", "Anja",
                               "Myriam", "Daja", "Thomas", "José", "Kricke", "Flori",
                               "Katrin", "Momo", "Gareth", "Anne"}
    System.Array.Sort(locNames)
    PrintStrings(locNames)
    Console.ReadLine()
End Sub
```

When you run this example, it displays the following list in the console window:

```
Andrea
Anja
Anne
Daja
Flori
Gaby
Gareth
Hanna
José
Jürgen
Katrin
Klaus
Kricke
Leonie-Gundula
Martina
Melanie
Michaela
Miriam
Momo
Myriam
Thomas
Ute
Uwe
```

The *Sort* method is a static method defined in *System.Array*—and it can do a lot more than a simple sort. For example, you can sort a correlated index at the same time, or sort only part of the array, delimited by specified array indices. See the .NET Framework Help for specific information about the available *Sort* method overloads.

Reversing the Array Order with *Array.Reverse*

Another static *System.Array* method called *Reverse* inverts the order of the array elements. When used in the context of the *Sort* method, *Reverse* sorts the array in descending order. Add the following lines to the previous example:

```
Console.WriteLine()
Console.WriteLine("Sorted in descending order:")
Array.Reverse(locNames)
PrintStrings(locNames)
Console.ReadLine()
```

The names are displayed in reverse order in the console window, as shown here:

```
Sorted in descending order:
Uwe
Ute
Thomas
...
Anja
Andrea
```

Searching a Sorted Array with *Array.BinarySearch*

The .NET Framework also helps you search for specific elements of an array. To do this, the *Array* class provides the static function *BinarySearch*.

> **Important** To perform a binary search on an array, you must sort it first—otherwise the binary search will most likely return invalid results. In addition, *Array.BinarySearch* is useful only if you ensure that there are no duplicate elements; otherwise, there's no guarantee that the function will find the *first* object rather than an arbitrary object that matches the search criteria.

As an example, take a look at the following:

```
Sub Example8()

  'Create array:
  Dim locNames As String() = {"Jürgen", "Martina", "Hanna", "Gaby", "Michaela", _
                   "Miriam", "Ute", "Leonie-Gundula", "Melanie", "Uwe", _
                   "Andrea", "Klaus", "Anja", "Myriam", "Daja", "Thomas", _
                   "José", "Kricke", "Flori", "Katrin", "Momo", _
                   "Gareth", "Anne", "Jürgen", "Gaby"}
  System.Array.Sort(locNames)
  Console.WriteLine("Jürgen was found at position {0}", _
      System.Array.BinarySearch(locNames, "Jürgen"))
  Console.ReadLine()
End Sub
```

Just like *Sort*, *BinarySearch* is an overloaded function and offers further options which, as mentioned earlier, can restrict the search to certain index areas. IntelliSense and the online Help system can provide further details of its use.

Implementing *Sort* and *BinarySearch* Custom Classes

The .NET Framework lets you create arrays of any desired type—even types that you create yourself. You don't need to keep anything special in mind when creating a class intended for use as an array element.

It's a different story, however, when you want to use an element comparison function on an array, or if you want to control the criteria by which your array is sorted, or specify the criteria for a *BinarySearch*. Here's an example: *

Suppose that you have created a class that saves the addresses of a contact database. The code that follows demonstrates how it works and how to use it:

> **Companion Content** The following class code manages an address entry. You can find this code in the \\VB 2010 Developer Handbook\Chapter 19\IComparer01 folder.

```
Public Class Address

    Sub New(ByVal Name As String, ByVal FirstName As String, ByVal Zip As String,
        ByVal City As String)
        Me.Name = Name
        Me.FirstName = FirstName
        Me.ZIP = Zip
        Me.City = City
    End Sub

    'Automatically implemented properties
    Public Property Name() As String
    Public Property FirstName() As String
    Public Property ZIP() As String
    Public Property City() As String

    Public Overrides Function ToString() As String
        Return Name + ", " + FirstName + ", " + ZIP + " " + City
    End Function
```

As you can see, this is straightforward Visual Basic code. The class provides a few properties for the data it manages, and overrides the *ToString* method of the base class, so it can return an address as a single complete string.

> **More Information** If you need to refresh your knowledge regarding the process of overriding, read Chapter 10, "Class Inheritance and Polymorphism," before proceeding.

The following small sample program defines an array from this class, sets up a few addresses for experimenting, and then prints them in a custom subroutine:

```
Module ComparerExample

Sub Main()
        Dim someAddresses(5) As Address

        someAddresses(0) = New Address("Ardelean", "Adriana", "90820", "Encinitas CA")
        someAddresses(1) = New Address("Löffelmann", "Klaus", "90210", "Encinitas CA")
        someAddresses(2) = New Address("Heckhuis", "Jürgen", "90210", "Los Angeles CA")
        someAddresses(3) = New Address("Hora", "Cate", "90210", "Pompano Beach FL")
        someAddresses(4) = New Address("Hora", "Oli", "90210", "Pompano Beach FL")
        someAddresses(5) = New Address("Merkel", "Angela", "54923", "Berlin WI")

        Console.WriteLine("List of addresses:")
        Console.WriteLine(New String("="c, 40))
        PrintAddresses(someAddresses)
```

```
            Console.WriteLine()
            Console.WriteLine("List of addresses (sorted):")
            Console.WriteLine(New String("="c, 40))
            'Array.Sort(someAddresses)

            PrintAddresses(someAddresses)

            Console.ReadLine()
        End Sub
        Sub PrintAddresses(ByVal Addresses As Address())
            For Each locString As Address In Addresses
                Console.WriteLine(locString)
            Next
        End Sub

    End Module
```

You might notice that nothing particularly exciting happens here. When you run the program it returns the following output in the console window:

```
List of addresses:
========================================
Ardelean, Adriana, 90820 Encinitas CA
Löffelmann, Klaus, 90210 Encinitas CA
Heckhuis, Jürgen, 90210 Los Angeles CA
Hora, Cate, 90210 Pompano Beach FL
Hora, Oli, 90210 Pompano Beach FL
Merkel, Angela, 54923 Berlin WI
```

The displayed list is a bit of a mess though from a sorting perspective. But watch what happens when you extend the program with a *Sort* statement. To do this, uncomment the *Array. Sort* method at the beginning of the code. After starting the program, you wait for the second, sorted output of the list, but instead, the .NET Framework triggers an exception as shown in Figure 19-1.

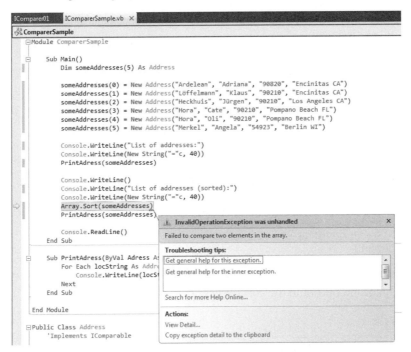

FIGURE 19-1 When you run the program, an exception is triggered as soon as the code encounters the *Array.Sort* method line. The exception details show you what went wrong.

The reason for this is that the *Sort* method of the *Array* class tries to compare the individual array elements to each other. To do this it needs a so-called *Comparer*. Because the code doesn't explicitly state that *Sort* should use a specific comparer (there isn't one yet), it creates a default comparer from an interface that classes should implement when they want to compare their elements to each other. This interface is called *IComparable*. But the class hasn't implemented this interface, and thus, it generates an exception.

At this point, you have three possible ways to resolve the problem. One option is for you to implement the *IComparable* interface to be able to compare and sort instances of this class without naming an explicit comparer.

A second option is to provide the class with an *explicit* comparer, which you name by passing it to the *Sort* (or *BinarySearch*) methods. The advantage of this comparer is that you can determine the criteria according to which the address list should be searched or sorted.

The third option is to do both. By doing this, the class becomes universally usable and you reduce the risk of an exception. And that's exactly what you'll do in the next few sections.

Implementing Class Comparability with *IComparable*

Implementing the *IComparable* interface to enable class instances to be compared to each other is relatively simple. To recap: you can use interfaces to make code more generally valid and usable. Embedding an interface into a class or structure forces the elements (properties, methods, events) that the interface requires to exist in the class. At the same time you can call, for example, one of the required interface methods for a class via an interface variable. The calling instance is no longer important here, but what it's dealing with is important—an *Integer* or a *Decimal* data type. The calling instance works solely with an interface variable to call the desired method. For example, the *Integer* data type that implements the *IComparable* interface compares *Integer* values, a *String* data type that implements *IComparable* compares strings, and so on. However, none of this is important to the *Array* class of .NET Framework. As the calling instance, it's only interested in the result.

Implementing the interface in our sample class requires only a *CompareTo* method that compares the current instance of the class with another instance. The method must be compatible with the one that the interface requires.

When you use *IComparable*, you don't have the option to specify which data field should be the comparison criteria, our criteria will be a string containing first and last name, city, and zip code—exactly the string that *ToString* already returns in the current version. Therefore, you don't even need to run the actual comparison, but you can pass it on to the standard *CompareTo* function of the *String* object that *ToString* returns. Therefore, the modifications to the class are minor, as the following code shows (shortened to reflect only the changes):

```
Public Class Address
    Implements IComparable
    .
    .
    .
    Public Function CompareTo(ByVal obj As Object) As Integer Implements
        System.IComparable.CompareTo

    Dim locAddress As Address

    Try
        locAddress = DirectCast(obj, Address)
    Catch ex As InvalidCastException
        Dim addrException As New InvalidCastException(
        "'CompareTo' of the class 'Address' cannot run comparisons " + _
        "against objects of other types!")
        Throw addrException
    End Try
    Return ToString.CompareTo(locAddress.ToString)
    End Function
End Class
```

At first glance, the code highlighted in bold in the middle might seem senseless: it catches a possible error, and then simply triggers it again, after adding a new exception message. In this case, however, the error text is important. You're essentially performing a favor for yourself or for users of your class when you customize the error text of an exception so that you know exactly who or what triggered it. When you start the program now, it returns the desired result, as shown in the following:

```
List of addresses:
=======================================
Ardelean, Adriana, 90820 Encinitas CA
Löffelmann, Klaus, 90210 Encinitas CA
Heckhuis, Jürgen, 90210 Los Angeles CA
Hora, Cate, 90210 Pompano Beach FL
Hora, Oli, 90210 Pompano Beach FL
Merkel, Angela, 54923 Berlin WI

List of addresses (sorted):
=======================================
Ardelean, Adriana, 90820 Encinitas CA
Heckhuis, Jürgen, 90210 Los Angeles CA
Hora, Cate, 90210 Pompano Beach FL
Hora, Oli, 90210 Pompano Beach FL
Löffelmann, Klaus, 90210 Encinitas CA
Merkel, Angela, 54923 Berlin WI
```

Using Lambdas with Array Methods

In Visual Studio 2010, using lambdas has become practical because you can now write lambdas made up of more than one line. This is particularly applicable to methods of the .NET Framework that expect generic delegates as parameters, because you can now use multi-line lambdas directly. The *Array* class provides several methods that turn array sorting into child's play:

```
Array.Sort(locAddresses, Function(value1, value2)
   Return value1.ToString.CompareTo(value2.ToString)
   End Function)
```

The first argument you pass to the static *Sort* method is the array that you want to sort. The second argument is a either a delegate that points to a method that accepts two parameters matching the type contained in the array, or a lambda that does this directly, as seen in the example.

The question then becomes: how do you know which signature is behind which delegate? Admittedly, it's not obvious at first glance, but you can look it up easily in the Help system, as Figure 19-2 illustrates.

FIGURE 19-2 Consult the Help system (press F1 to access it) to find out which signature a lambda must have so it can be used as parameter for a generic delegate.

According to the Help system, the correct signature of the lambda is as follows:

```
'Alternatively: Sort with Comparision delegate and Lambda:
Array.Sort(Of Address)(locAddresses, Function(value1 As Address, value2 As Address)
    Return value1.ToString.CompareTo(value2.ToString)
    End Function)
```

This line functions the same, of course, and contains all required type information in detail. Here, the Visual Basic compiler saves you a lot of work, by deriving all the types (highlighted in bold in the code) from the type of the variable that you pass as the first parameter: *locAddresses*. Because *locAddresses* has the type *Addresses*, all other type definitions and type parameters *must* result from it, and therefore, you can omit them in the appropriate locations.

Another method that you can use with lambdas is the *ForEach* method of the *Array* class. It basically does the same as a *ForEach* loop—but does it a little bit faster. The project also contains the following example:

```
'Also here: an alternative with a method which expects
'a delegate that can be written as a Lambda:
Sub PrintAddressesLambda(ByVal Addresses As Address())
    Array.ForEach(Addresses, Sub(item)
    Console.WriteLine(item.ToString)
    End Sub)
End Sub
```

You can find more examples for using lambdas in static methods and an explanation for the generic *List(Of)* collection in the section "*List(Of)* Collections and Lambda Expressions," later in this chapter.

Enumerators

It's convenient to use arrays or—as you will see later, collections—to save data, but you must also be able to access the data easily. With *indexers*, .NET Framework offers you the simplest option to access individual values: using an object variable, you provide an index value or a variable that represents an index. By changing the variable that serves as an index, you can programmatically specify which array element you want to process. What you get are typical counter loops for iterating through the array elements, such as the following:

```
For count As Integer = 0 To Array.Length - 1
    DoSomethingWith(Array(count))
Next
```

> **Note** Enumerators have nothing to do with Enums. Only the names are similar. Enums are listed/enumerated names of certain values in the program code, while enumerators work with *For Each*.

When an object implements the *IEnumerable* interface, it enables a more elegant method for iterating through the elements provided by the object. Fortunately *System.Array* implements the interface *IEnumerable*, which means that you can access array elements with *For Each*. For example:

```
'Declaration and definition of elements in the Char array
Dim locCharArray As Char() = {"V"c, "B"c, "."c, "N"c, "E"c, "T"c, " "c, _
                            "r"c, "u"c, "l"c, "e"c, "s"c, "!"c}
For Each c As Char In locCharArray
    Console.Write(c)
Next
Console.WriteLine()
Console.ReadLine()
```

If you run this example, you see the following text in the console window:

```
VB.NET rules!
```

Enumerators are supported by all type-defined arrays and most collections, but you can also use them in your own classes if you want to permit developers who are working with your classes to iterate through elements with *For Each*.

> **Important** Enumerators are vital for LINQ (see Part V, "Language-Integrated Query—LINQ," and later). You can only use collection classes in LINQ queries that implement *IEnumerable(Of T)*, so keep that in mind when you design custom collection classes.

Custom Enumerators with *IEnumerable*

Enumerators have more uses then just enumerating lists of saved elements in arrays or collections. You can use them when a class returns its enumeration elements via algorithms. Here's an example code snippet that *doesn't* work (even though you might wish that it did):

```
'This does not work:
For d As Date=#24/12/2010# To #31/12/2010#
    Console.WriteLine("Date in enumeration: {0}", d)
Next d
```

It would be useful to be able to iterate across a date range, day by day, in some applications; for example, if your program needs to find out how many of your colleagues' birthdays occur in a certain month.

If an operation doesn't work with *For Each … Next* out of the box, you might be able to create a class that provides an enumerator so that *For Each … Next* does work. This class should accept parameters during instantiation that specify the date range over which you want to iterate. To be able to iterate through the elements of a class using *For Each,* the class must embed the interface *IEnumerable.*

It can only do that if it provides a *GetEnumerator* function that delivers an object with the actual enumerator.

> **Companion Content** First, look at the base class, and then open the corresponding solution (.sln), which you can find in the \VB 2010 Developer Handbook\Chapter 19\Enumerators folder. Start the program by pressing Ctrl+F5.

```
Public Class DateEnumeration
    Implements IEnumerable
    Dim locDateEnumerator As DateEnumerator

    Sub New(ByVal StartDate As Date, ByVal EndDate As Date, ByVal StepWidth As TimeSpan)
        locDateEnumerator = New DateEnumerator(StartDate, EndDate, StepWidth)
    End Sub
    Public Function GetEnumerator() As System.Collections.IEnumerator _
                Implements System.Collections.IEnumerable.GetEnumerator
        Return locDateEnumerator
    End Function
End Class
```

The preceding example shows that the class itself doesn't do anything amazing—it just creates the framework with the parameters it receives and provides the *GetEnumerator* functions required by *IEnumerable*. The class *DateEnumerator* handles the actual task of enumeration, which is also the return value of *GetEnumerator*.

An instance of this class is created during instantiation of *DateEnumeration*. The code that follows shows what exactly happens in this class:

```
Public Class DateEnumerator
    Implements IEnumerator

    Private myCurrentDate As Date

    Sub New(ByVal StartDate As Date, ByVal EndDate As Date, ByVal StepWidth As TimeSpan)
        Me.StartDate = StartDate
        Me.EndDate = EndDate
        Me.StepWidth = StepWidth
        myCurrentDate = StartDate
    End Sub

    Public Property StartDate() As Date
    Public Property EndDate() As Date
    Public Property StepWidth() As TimeSpan

    Public ReadOnly Property Current() As Object Implements
        System.Collections.IEnumerator.Current
        Get
            Return myCurrentDate
        End Get
    End Property

    Public Function MoveNext() As Boolean Implements System.Collections.IEnumerator.MoveNext
        myCurrentDate = myCurrentDate.Add(StepWidth)
        If myCurrentDate > EndDate Then
            Return False
        Else
            Return True
        End If
    End Function

    Public Sub Reset() Implements System.Collections.IEnumerator.Reset
        myCurrentDate = StartDate
    End Sub
End Class
```

The constructor and the property procedures are not so interesting here. What's interesting is that the class implements yet another interface called *IEnumerator* that provides the actual enumeration functionality. For this purpose, it must implement three things: the *Current* property, the *MoveNext* function, and the *Reset* method.

When iterating a *For Each* loop, the class object currently being modified is determined by the *Current* property of the enumerator. *For Each* indicates to the enumerator that it's ready

to access the next object by calling the function *MoveNext*. When *MoveNext* returns *False*, signalling that no further objects are available, the surrounding *For Each* loop stops.

The *MoveNext* function in this example simply increases the internal date counter variable by the value specified during instantiation. If adding the step width to the current date counter doesn't exceed the *EndDate* value, the function returns *True*, and *For Each* can continue. When the calculated date is larger than *EndDate*, the loop exits and the iteration process stops.

The program can now use this class elegantly, as the following code shows:

```
Module Enumerators
    Sub Main()
        Dim locDateEnumeration As New DateEnumeration(#12/24/2004#,
                                                       #12/31/2004#,
                                                       New TimeSpan(1, 0, 0, 0))

        For Each d As Date In locDateEnumeration
            Console.WriteLine("Date in enumeration: {0}", d)
        Next

    End Sub
End Module
```

The preceding code displays each date as a date string in the console window.

Collection Basics

Arrays have a crucial disadvantage in .NET Framework. Even though they can be enlarged or reduced dynamically at runtime, the programming effort that goes into them is quite extensive. If you have experience with earlier versions of Visual Basic, you have surely come across a different type, called a *Collection*, to which you were first introduced in Chapter 1.

Collections permit developers to manage elements much like arrays, but collections can grow as needed. However, this also means that indexing by using numbers to identify elements can only work conditionally. For example, when an array has 20 elements, and you want to expand it to hold 21 elements, you can't just add the element—you must expand the array first. But with a collection, you can simply add the element by using the *Add* method.

Internally almost all collections are managed as arrays. When you create a new collection, the internal array initially has room for 16 elements by default. When the collection class needs more space, it creates a new array of 32 elements, copies the existing elements into the new array, and then continues working with the new array as if nothing had happened.

This initial load factor increases with each new array to minimize the memory allocation and copy processes. When the internal limit has been reached, the collection assumes that a program will likely require the same amount of memory for upcoming elements. If that's

not enough, you can assume that the number of elements in the collections will continue to grow, possibly even exponentially. To avoid excessive copy processing, collection classes increase the step width exponentially, doubling it each time. Normally this means that the step width ends up growing faster than the array. Therefore, the number of complete copy processes is reduced (and optimized). The load factor tops out at 2,048.

Very simplified, the following code illustrates a basic collection class:

```
Class DynamicList
    Implements IEnumerable

    Private myStepIncreaser As Integer
    Private myCurrentArraySize As Integer
    Private myCurrentCounter As Integer
    Private myArray() As Object

    Sub New()
        MyClass.New(16)
    End Sub

    Sub New(ByVal StepIncreaser As Integer)
        myStepIncreaser = StepIncreaser
        myCurrentArraySize = myStepIncreaser
        ReDim myArray(myCurrentArraySize)
    End Sub

    Sub Add(ByVal Item As Object)

        'Check whether the current array limit has been reached
        If myCurrentCounter = myCurrentArraySize - 1 Then
            'Create new array with more memory,
            'and copy elemente into it.

            'New array becomes larger:
            myCurrentArraySize += myStepIncreaser

            'Create temporary array
            Dim locTempArray(myCurrentArraySize - 1) As Object

            'Copy elements
            'Important: Unlike in VB6, you have to take
            'care of the copying yourself!
            Array.Copy(myArray, locTempArray, myArray.Length)

            'Assign the temporary array to the member array
            myArray = locTempArray

            'Next time more elements are reserved!
            myStepIncreaser *= 2
        End If

        'Save the element in the array
        myArray(myCurrentCounter) = Item
```

```
        'Increase the pointer to the next element
        myCurrentCounter += 1

    End Sub

    'Returns the number of the existing elements
    Public Overridable ReadOnly Property Count() As Integer
        Get
            Return myCurrentCounter
        End Get
    End Property

    'Permits assignments and queries
    Default Public Overridable Property Item(ByVal Index As Integer) As Object
        Get
            Return myArray(Index)
        End Get

        Set(ByVal Value As Object)
            myArray(Index) = Value
        End Set
    End Property

    'Returns the enumerator of the base (to the array)
    Public Function GetEnumerator() As System.Collections.IEnumerator Implements
        System.Collections.IEnumerable.GetEnumerator
        Return myArray.GetEnumerator
    End Function
End Class
```

Now you might think that this operation could lead to performance problems, because every few elements, the entire array content must be copied.

> **Companion Content** Open the corresponding solution (.sln), which you can find in the \VB 2010 Developer Handbook\Chapter 19\DynamicList folder.

How long do you think it takes to create an array with 200,000 random numbers (with decimals) in this manner? 3 seconds? 2 seconds?

```
Module DynamicListDemo

    Private Const SAMPLESIZE = 200000

    Sub Main()

        Dim locDynamicList As New DynamicList
        Dim locRandom As New Random(Now.Millisecond)
```

```
        Console.WriteLine("Creating {0} random Double elements...", SAMPLESIZE)
        Dim locTimer = Stopwatch.StartNew
        For count As Integer = 1 To SAMPLESIZE
            locDynamicList.Add(locRandom.NextDouble * locRandom.Next)
        Next
        locTimer.Stop()
        Console.WriteLine("...{0:#,##0} milliseconds!",
            locTimer.ElapsedMilliseconds)
        Console.ReadLine()
    End Sub
...
```

Find out for yourself by running the program. Here's the output:

```
Creating 200000 random Double elements...
...21 milliseconds!
```

The program took only 21 milliseconds for this operation—which is pretty impressive, and illustrates how fast Visual Basic is these days.

Note This result for the preceding example was obtained on an Intel Core 2 Quad Q6600 processor. Readers of my older book *Visual Studio 2008—The Developer Handbook* (you can download the German version for free from *http://www.activedevelop.de*) will notice that the result is actually a millisecond slower than the computer on which I wrote the Visual Basic 2005 book seven years ago. It's become apparent that newer computers can no longer significantly scale their performance "vertically" via the system clock, only horizontally via multiple processors. Running this example uses only one of four processor cores—three-quarters of the processor remains unused (and in this example even worse: *useless*!). As you can see, taking advantage of multithreading development techniques has become crucial to extract a bit more performance out of modern processors, and should *always* be considered when porting older programs, such as old Borland, MFC, or Visual Basic 6.0 applications to .NET. When I ran this code on a Samsung Notebook with a Core 2 Duo P8600 processor running at 2.4 GHz, the result under Windows 7 was no faster than 28 milliseconds. And on a brand new Core I7-2600, exactly one year later for the English translation, it still returned results between 16 and 22 milliseconds.

Nevertheless, you will never need the *DynamicList* class, because .NET Framework already offers a class that exposes its functionality—and that class is even a bit faster. It also provides features that the homemade *DynamicList* class doesn't provide. In the example project for this chapter, you can find a Sub Example2 file, which runs the same procedure that you just saw using the .NET Framework class *ArrayList*:

```
    Sub Example2()

        Dim locDynamicList As New ArrayList
        Dim locRandom As New Random(Now.Millisecond)

        Console.WriteLine("Creating {0} random Double elements...", SAMPLESIZE)
        Dim locTimer = Stopwatch.StartNew
        For count As Integer = 1 To SAMPLESIZE
            locDynamicList.Add(locRandom.NextDouble * locRandom.Next)
        Next
        locTimer.Stop()
        Console.WriteLine("...{0:#,##0} milliseconds!",
            locTimer.ElapsedMilliseconds)
        Console.ReadLine()
    End Sub
```

Here's the output:

```
Creating 200000 random Double elements...
...19 milliseconds!
```

Its speed isn't bad, either!

ArrayList basically works along the same lines as *DynamicList*; it uses the same trick to gain maximum performance—doubling the size of each new array, based on the size of the previous array, and reducing the total copying effort. Because it is part of the .NET Framework, it doesn't require the Just-in-Time (JIT) compiler at runtime, which again helps with speed.

The data of the individual elements doesn't actually move when *ArrayList* creates a new internal array. Instead, the copy operation copies the *pointers* to the data, the elements themselves remain in the same location in the Managed Heap. Chapter 8, "Class Begins," discusses this topic in the section, "New or Not New: About Objects and Reference Types."

> **Important** The speed with which *ArrayList* works for primitive and regular value types (such as *Double* in our example) actually is not optimal, because internally *ArrayList* is an array of objects, and primitive value types, as described in Chapter 12, "Typecasting and Boxing Value Types," must be boxed, which takes time and memory space. However generics has made it possible to build collections based on typed arrays rather than on *Object* arrays. The time and memory savings are huge. Generics also simplify the work of the Garbage Collector, because when the collection resizes the internal array, it no longer needs to dispose of hundreds of single, boxed elements, but only one "old" array. As mentioned earlier, this applies only to primitive value types. For regular reference types the difference is irrelevant.
>
> **Rule of Thumb:** When using value types in collections, ensure that you work with generic collections—mainly *List(Of Type)* and *Collection(Of Type)*. Don't confuse the latter with the Visual Basic 6.0/VBA-compatible *Collection* class, which is not generic.

Initializing Collections

Visual Basic 2010 has a new and elegant option that lets you initialize collections with values during declaration. This is similar to what you learned in the section "Pre-Allocating Values of Array Elements in Code." The syntax is slightly different though, as the following example shows:

```
'Collection initializers:
Dim germanDogNamesList As New ArrayList From {"Waldi", "Basko", "Hasso",
                                              "Wauzi", "Bello", "Minka"}
```

For each element that you specify in braces behind the *From* keyword, the compiler gener-ates an *Add* command that adds that element to the collection, as shown in the following:

```
Dim VB$t_ref$S0 As New ArrayList
VB$t_ref$S0.Add("Waldi")
VB$t_ref$S0.Add("Basko")
VB$t_ref$S0.Add("Hasso")
VB$t_ref$S0.Add("Wauzi")
VB$t_ref$S0.Add("Bello")
VB$t_ref$S0.Add("Minka")
Dim locDogNamesList As ArrayList = VB$t_ref$S0
```

> **Note** Just to be thorough (and to avoid a pesky litigation), if you consider getting yourself a German shepherd, Doberman, or Rottweiler, please don't call him *Waldi* (typical German dachs-hund name), *Wauzi* (only puppies are so named), or *Minka* (which is a typical German *cat* name). Actually, you would do well to not name your dog using any of these, since they're a bit of a liv-ing cliché than actual dog names. (Well, *Basko* would be OK, I suppose. Honestly!)

Using Extension Methods to Simplify Collection Initializers

Why is it so important to know how collection initializers work internally? What works so eas-ily for individual primitive data types, does not really make life easier when it comes to more complex classes, because each element you write inside the braces must be specified as a fully-initialized instance:

```
Module Module1

    Sub Main()

        Dim Addresses As New ArrayList() From
            {New Address With
                {.FirstName = "Ramona", .LastName = "Leenings"},
            New Address With
                {.FirstName = "Adriana", .LastName = "Ardelean"},
```

```
            New Address With
                {.FirstName = "Margarete", .LastName = "Schindler"}}
    End Sub


    Public Class Address
        Public Property FirstName As String
        Public Property LastName As String
        Public Property CityAndState As String
        Public Property Zip As String
    End Class
End Module
```

Now that you know that the *Add* method is crucial for adding the elements that appear in brackets behind *From*, you can simplify your use of collection initializers by controlling the form in which the *Add* method receives parameters that it will add as collection elements. As you saw in Chapter 18, "Advanced Types," extension methods make this possible, as the following example shows:

> **Companion Content** Open the corresponding solution (.sln), which you can find in the \VB 2010 Developer Handbook\Chapter 19\CollectionInitializers folder.

This code adds a module with an extension method to the previous example. Be aware that because it uses the *Extension* attribute, you must reference the *System.Runtime. CompilerServices* namespace.

```
Module AdressenCollectionInitializer
    'The Extension attribute marks a method as
    'extension method. The type of the first parameter
    'specifies the type that needs to be extended.
    <Extension()> _
    Public Sub Add(ByVal listOfAddresses As ArrayList,
                ByVal FirstName As String,
                ByVal LastName As String)
        listOfAddresses.Add(New Address With {.FirstName = FirstName,
                                        .LastName = LastName})
    End Sub
End Module
```

Because this *Add* method receives an *ArrayList* as the first parameter and the method is marked with the *Extension* attribute, it extends the class *ArrayList* with an *Add* method that accepts two *String* parameters—basically overloading the existing *ArrayList.Add* method with a new version. This new method creates and initializes an *Address* class instance and adds it

to the *ArrayList*. As a result, you can also specify the new *Add* method indirectly in collection initializers, as demonstrated here:

```
Dim otherAddresses As New ArrayList() From
    {{"Klaus", "Löffelmann"},
     {"Andreas", "Belke"},
     {"Marcus", "Pusch"}}
```

> **Note** *ArrayList* is a class purposely kept very general. It takes *Object* as its element type, which means it's not type safe. Therefore, especially when you are simplifying collection initializers with extension methods, you should always prefer the generic equivalent—in this case *List(Of Addresses)*. Using the generic *List (Of...)* collection also provides a performance advantage when using value types, because unlike with *ArrayList*, they don't need to be boxed.

Important Collections of .NET Framework

.NET Framework contains a number of collections, one of which you have already seen in action—*ArrayList*. This section introduces other important collections in the .NET Framework and explains their purpose as well as characteristics that you should beware of when using them.

ArrayList: Universal Storage for Objects

You can use *ArrayList* as a container for all kinds of objects. It's not the most modern collection type in the .NET Framework, but it is one of the most basic and longest-serving. It largely serves to illustrate the *concept* of collections, so if you understand how *ArrayList* works, you will understand the other collections, as well.

You instantiate an *ArrayList* object and assign new elements to it with the *Add* function. Using the default *Item* property, you can retrieve existing elements or replace them. *AddRange* lets you add elements from an existing *ArrayList* to a different *ArrayList*. The *Count* property returns the number of elements the *ArrayList* contains.

Clear deletes all elements of an *ArrayList*. In contrast, *Remove* deletes an object that you pass as a parameter. If several of the same objects exist in the *ArrayList* (determined by using the *Equals* method of each object), *Remove* deletes the first matching instance found. If you know the position of an element that you want to delete, you can delete it by using *RemoveAt*. You can remove a known range of elements by using *RemoveRange* by passing the starting position and the number of elements to remove.

You can convert *ArrayList* objects into simple arrays, but when doing so, there are a few things you must keep in mind. All the elements of the *ArrayList* must be of the same type

as the array into which you want to convert them. You initiate the conversion by calling the *ToArray* method of the *ArrayList* object. When you are converting a type-defined array (such as *Integer()* or *String()*), you specify the basic type (not the array type) as an additional parameter. To perform the reverse operation (convert an array into an *ArrayList*), use the appropriate *ArrayList* constructor—the constructor handles the conversion into an *ArrayList*.

> **Note** Take a look at the code example that follows, and carefully read the conversion notes for the *ArrayList* objects.

ArrayList implements the *IEnumerable* interface, providing an enumerator that you can use to iterate through the elements of the *ArrayList* by using *For Each*. Ensure that you use the correct type for the loop variable. *ArrayList* elements are not type-safe, and you can avoid a type violation only if you know with certainty which types the *ArrayList* holds (the following example demonstrates this error):

> **Companion Content** Open the corresponding solution (.sln), which you can find in the \VB 2010 Developer Handbook\Chapter 19\CollectionsDemo folder.

```
Sub ArrayListDemo()
    Dim locMaleNames As String() = {"Jürgen", "Uwe", "Klaus", "Christian", "José"}
    Dim locFemaleNames As New ArrayList
    Dim locNames As ArrayList

    'Create ArrayList from the existing array.
    locNamen = New ArrayList(locMaleNames)

    'Fill ArrayList with Add.
    locFemaleNames.Add("Adriana") : locFemaleNames.Add("Miriam")
    locFemaleNames.Add("Melanie") : locFemaleNames.Add("Anja")
    locFemaleNames.Add("Stephanie") : locFemaleNames.Add("Heidrun")


    locNamen.AddRange(locFemaleNames)

    'Insert ArrayList into an ArrayList.
    Dim locDogNames As String() = {"Hasso", "Bello", "Beamer", "Merc", "Basko", "Porsche"}
    'Insert *before* the 6th element
    locNames.InsertRange(5, locDogNames)

    'Convert ArrayList back into an array.
    Dim locAllNames As String()

    'Attention: Error!
    'locAllNames = DirectCast(locNames.ToArray, String())
```

```
'Attention: Another error!
'locAllNames = DirectCast(locNames.ToArray(GetType(String())), String())

'This is how it works.
locAllNames = DirectCast(locNames.ToArray(GetType(String)), String())

'Repeat builds an ArrayList from repeated elements.
locNames.AddRange(ArrayList.Repeat("Double name", 10))

'Change an element in the array.
locNames(10) = "Fiffi"
'It's also possible with the Item property:
locNames.Item(13) = "Miriam"

'Deleting the first elements that fits from the list.
locNames.Remove("Basko")

'Deleting an element from a certain position.
locNames.RemoveAt(4)

'Deleting a certain range from the ArrayList.
'Count determines the number of elements in the ArrayList.
locNames.RemoveRange(locNames.Count - 6, 5)

'Returning the elements with the Default property of the ArrayList (Item).
For i As Integer = 0 To locNames.Count - 1
    Console.WriteLine("Name No. {0} is {1}", i, locNames(i).ToString)
Next

'Add something other than a String object to the ArrayList,
'to prepare for the following error.
locNames.Add(New FileInfo("C:\TEST.TXT"))

'This loop cannot be run to the end,
'because there is an object that's not of the type String!
For Each aString As String In locNames
    'Here something happens with the string.
    'Not important, therefore doesn't care of the return value.
    aString.EndsWith("Peter")
Next
Console.ReadLine()
End Sub
```

When you run this example, you first see the expected results on the screen. However, the program code never reaches the statement *Console.ReadLine* to wait for your last confirmation. Instead it triggers an exception, as shown in Figure 19-3.

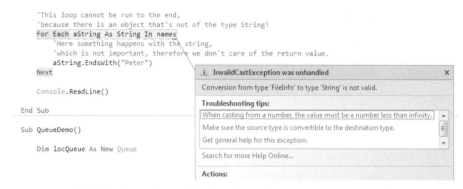

```
'This loop cannot be run to the end,
'because there is an object that's not of the type String!
For Each aString As String In names
    'Here something happens with the string,
    'which is not important, therefore we don't care of the return value.
    aString.EndsWith("Peter")
Next

    Console.ReadLine()

End Sub

Sub QueueDemo()

    Dim locQueue As New Queue
```

FIGURE 19-3 While iterating with *For Each* through a collection, you must ensure that the elements correspond to the loop variable type to avoid the exceptions shown here.

The last element in the *ArrayList* is not a string, which causes the exception to occur. Always make sure that the loop variable of a *For Each* construct corresponds to the types saved in a collection.

> **Note** Since *ArrayList* is based on *Object*, the instances of this class are not type-safe. As a result, it must box value types elaborately to save them. This is why, wherever possible, you should use the generic equivalents *List(Of Type)* or *Collection(Of Type)*, which are located in the namespaces *System.Collections.Generic* and *System.Collections.ObjectModel*.
>
> In contrast, use *ArrayList* instances with non-homogenous collections; for example, collections that save different elements of completely different types.

Type-Safe Collections Based on *CollectionBase*

You can avoid the problem presented in the previous section by forcing a collection to be homogenous (in other words, only process elements of the same type) with the help of generics. For the later use of *LINQ to Objects* (see Chapter 25), that's a requirement. However, another classic option exists that uses interfaces to implement a base class. You then use that to make derived classes type-safe without using generics. You can always fall back on this technique, if for some reason you can't use generics—for example, if you need to use an older version of .NET Framework that doesn't support generics, or if you are developing for a platform that doesn't provide generics.

To do this, the .NET Framework provides an abstract class called *CollectionBase*, which you can use as a template, and then derive and extend.

> **Companion Content** Open the corresponding solution (.sln), which you can find in the \VB 2010 Developer Handbook\Chapter 19\TypeSafeCollections folder.

The following code shows how to use the *Item* property and the *Add* method in a custom collection:

```
Public Class Addresses
    Inherits CollectionBase

    Public Overridable Function Add(ByVal Adr As Address) As Integer
        Return MyBase.List.Add(Adr)
    End Function

    Default Public Overridable Property Item(ByVal Index As Integer) As Address
        Get
            Return DirectCast(MyBase.List(Index), Address)
        End Get
        Set(ByVal Value As Address)
            MyBase.List(Index) = Value
        End Set
    End Property
End Class
```

Here's a corresponding sample program to test the class:

```
Module TypeSafeCollections

    Sub Main()
        Dim locAddresses As New Addresses
        Dim locAddress As New Address("Christian", "Sonntag", "99999", "Munich")
        Dim locOtherType As New FileInfo("C:\Test.txt")

        'No problem:
        locAddresses.Add(locAddress)

        'The Editor isn't happy!
        'locAddresses.Add(locOtherType)

        'Also no problem.
        locAddress = locAddresses(0)

        For Each anAddress As Address In locAddresses
            Console.WriteLine(anAddress)
        Next
        Console.ReadLine()
    End Sub

End Module
```

This test program shows that type safety is guaranteed in this collection. However, if you studied the object-oriented programming section of this book thoroughly, this program might raise some questions. For example, take a look at the description for *CollectionBase* in the online help; you'll see the following prototype:

```
<Serializable>
MustInherit Public Class CollectionBase
   Implements IList, ICollection, IEnumerable
  .
  .
  .
```

CollectionBase binds several interfaces, including *IList*, which requires the implementation of an *Add* function with the following signature:

```
Function Add(ByVal value As Object) As Integer
```

Did you notice the irregularity? The class inherits from *CollectionBase*, which binds *IList*—and *IList* requires an *Add* method. Therefore, your class must have an *Add* method, which you would need to override. But there isn't one, and that's a good thing, because if it existed, you would need to match its signature for the override, and the *IList.Add* signature accepts an *Object* parameter. This means your class's type safety would be gone. If you overloaded it, someone could still pass it an *Object*—and again, type safety would be gone.

You can uncover the secret by taking a closer look at the *Add* function in the new *Addresses* collection:

```
    Public Overridable Function Add(ByVal Adr As Address) As Integer
        Return MyBase.List.Add(Adr)
    End Function
```

MyBase relies on the base class, using its *Add* function, which returns the *List* property to pass on the element that needs to be added. But what does *List* do? Which object does it return? Rather confusingly, *List* returns the instance of the *Address* class being added—in other words, you're using polymorphism at its best!

> **Note** This construct presented in the preceding paragraph reminded me of a *Star Trek: Voyager* episode in which Tom Paris visits the *Holodeck* with B'Elanna Torres to watch an "antique" 3D movie using 3D glasses in a holographically projected movie theater. Her comment: "Let me get this straight: you've gone through all this trouble to program a three-dimensional environment that projects a two-dimensional image, and now you're asking me to wear these, to make it look three-dimensional again?"

Here's what the Visual Studio online Help says about *List*: "Calls an *IList* with the list of the elements in the *CollectionBase* instance."

Wow, that's informative!

The situation becomes more clear when you look at the following construct. Keep in mind that you are trying to figure out how to implement an *Add* function of an interface in a class—without preventing an embedded class from providing an *Add* function with an entirely different signature:

```
Interface ITest
    Function Add(ByVal obj As Object) As Integer
End Interface

MustInherit Class ITestClass
    Implements ITest

    Private Function ITestAdd(ByVal obj As Object) As Integer Implements ITest.Add
        Trace.WriteLine("ITestAdd:" + obj.ToString)
    End Function

End Class

Class ITestClasseDerivate
    Inherits ITestClass

    Public ReadOnly Property Test() As ITest
        Get
            Return DirectCast(Me, ITest)
        End Get
    End Property

    Public Sub Add(ByVal TypeSafe As Address)
        Test.Add(TypeSafe)
    End Sub
End Class
```

The *ITest* interface of this class requires that any class that implements the interface must implement an *Add* function. The abstract class *ITestClass* embeds this interface correctly; however, it doesn't make the function publicly available because it is defined as *Private*. In addition—and this is the crucial issue—the function isn't called *Add*, but *ITestAdd*. This is possible because Visual Basic interface embedding is always explicit, or more precisely, because of the keyword *Implements* at the end of the function declaration.

So now you have a clean interface implementation, *and* callers can't see the function assigned to the interface from the outside. But how do you call the *ITestAdd* function of the base class *ITestClass*? Here's the solution to the riddle: the function isn't quite as private as it seems, because you can access it via an interface variable. When you cast your own instance of the class into an interface variable of type *ITest*, you can still access its private *ITestAdd* function via the interface function *ITest.Add*—and there you go!

For ease of use, the class *ITestClassDerivate* provides a property (*Property Test*) that returns the current class instance as an *ITest* interface instance, which you can then use directly.

To get back to the original example, the *Addresses* class, which inherits from *CollectionBase*, does exactly the same thing. The *List* property of the class *CollectionBase* corresponds to the *Test* property of the class *ITestClass* in our example.

Hashtables: Fast Lookup for Objects

Hashtable objects are the ideal tool for building a data collection that uses a key rather than a numeric index to identify individual objects. Here's an example:

Suppose that you have developed an address management program. You want to retrieve individual addresses by using a kind of match code (a *ClientID*, *VendorID*, and so on). If you were to use an *ArrayList* to hold the addresses, you would need to put out considerable effort to retrieve a specific array element by using the match code name. To find an element in the list, you'd need to implement a *CompareTo* method for your address class, so the list could be sorted with *Sort*. Subsequently you could find the element with a *BinarySearch*, assuming the *CompareTo* method you implemented could compare address class instances via their ID values.

Hashtable objects simplify such a scenario immensely. When you add a hashtable to an object, its *Add* method not only accepts the object that needs to be saved (the value to be added), but it also accepts an additional object. This additional object (passed as the first parameter) represents a key for retrieving the object. You don't retrieve an object from a hashtable by using an index as you do with *ArrayList*:

```
Element = anArrayList(5)
```

Instead, you pass the appropriate key, such as the following:

```
Element = aHashtable("ElementKey")
```

Of course, for this example to work, you would first need to have added an element associated with the key *ElementKey*.

Using Hashtables

> **Companion Content** Open the corresponding project, which you can find in the \VB 2010 Developer Handbook\Chapter 19\HashtableDemo01 folder. This project demonstrates the use of the *Hashtable* class. That project contains a class that reflects a data structure—an address.

Using a static function, you can create any number of random addresses, which are initially saved in an *ArrayList*. Then, use the *ArrayList* to experiment with the *Hashtable* class. In the interest of being thorough (and so it will be easier to understand for you later), I want to briefly introduce this *Address* class to you.

Important You need at least 1 GB working memory in Windows XP and 2 GB in Windows Vista or Windows 7 to be able to reproduce the following hashtable examples. The example requires all this memory because you need a large number of elements to perform valid speed comparisons, given today's fast processors. At the same time, you must have enough free memory available so that memory paging to the hard disk does not occur, which would distort the results.

```
Public Class Address

    'Constructor-sets up a new instance
    Sub New(ByVal Matchcode As String, ByVal Name As String,
            ByVal FirstName As String, ByVal Zip As String, ByVal City As String)
        Me.Matchcode = Matchcode
        Me.Name = Name
        Me.FirstName = FirstName
        Me.ZIP = ZIP
        Me.City = City
    End Sub

    Public Overridable Property Matchcode() As String
    Public Overridable Property Name() As String
    Public Overridable Property FirstName() As String
    Public Overridable Property ZIP() As String
    Public Overridable Property City() As String

    Public Overrides Function ToString() As String
        Return Matchcode + ": " + Name + ", " + FirstName + ", " + ZIP + " " + City
    End Function

    Public Shared Function RandomAddresses(ByVal Amount As Integer) As ArrayList

        Dim locArrayList As New ArrayList(Amount)
        Dim locRandom As New Random(Now.Millisecond)

        Dim locLastNames As String() = {"Heckhuis", "Löffelmann", "Thiemann", "Müller",
                "Meier", "Tiemann", "Sonntag", "Ademmer", "Westermann", "Vüllers",
                "Hollmann", "Vielstedde", "Weigel", "Weichel", "Weichelt", "Hoffmann",
                "Rode", "Trouw", "Schindler", "Neumann", "Jungemann", "Hörstmann",
                "Tinoco", "Albrecht", "Langenbach", "Braun", "Plenge", "Englisch",
                "Clarke"}

        Dim locFirstNames As String() = {"Jürgen", "Gabriele", "Uwe", "Katrin", "Hans",
                "Rainer", "Christian", "Uta", "Michaela", "Franz", "Anne", "Anja",
                "Theo", "Momo", "Katrin", "Guido", "Barbara", "Bernhard", "Margarete",
                "Alfred", "Melanie", "Britta", "José", "Thomas", "Daja", "Klaus",
                "Axel", "Lothar", "Gareth"}
        Dim locCities As String() = {"Wuppertal", "Dortmund", "Lippstadt", "Soest",
                "Liebenburg", "Hildesheim", "München", "Berlin", "Rheda", "Bielefeld",
                "Braunschweig", "Unterschleißheim", "Wiesbaden", "Straubing",
                "Bad Waldliesborn", "Lippetal", "Stirpe", "Erwitte"}
```

```
    For i As Integer = 1 To Amount
        Dim locName, locFirstName, locMatchcode As String
        locName = locLastNames(locRandom.Next(locLastNames.Length - 1))
        locFirstName = locFirstNames(locRandom.Next(locLastNames.Length - 1))
        locMatchcode = locName.Substring(0, 2)
        locMatchcode += locFirstName.Substring(0, 2)
        locMatchcode += i.ToString("00000000")
        locArrayList.Add(New Address(
                    locMatchcode,
                    locName,
                    locFirstName,
                    locRandom.Next(99999).ToString("00000"),
                    locCities(locRandom.Next(locCities.Length - 1))))

    Next
    Return locArrayList
End Function

Shared Sub OutputAddresses(ByVal Addresses As ArrayList)
    For Each Item As Object In Addresses
        Console.WriteLine(Item)
    Next
End Sub

End Class
```

Creating the class to save an address is no problem. What's important is to understand the *Matchcode* property of this address class. *Matchcode* essentially represents a primary key in this class and is therefore always unique in a set of addresses. The random address-generating procedure in this example ensures that each address has a unique *Matchcode*. The Matchcode is composed of the first two letters of the last name, the first two letters of the first name, and an incrementing number. As an example, if you create and return 15 different random addresses by using the following code:

```
Sub TestAddresses()

    'Create 15 random addresses.
    Dim locDemoAddresses As ArrayList = Address.RandomAddresses(15)

    'Output addresses in the console window.
    Console.WriteLine("List with random personal data")
    Console.WriteLine(New String("="c, 30))
    Address.OutputAddresses(locDemoAddresses)

End Sub
```

You will see something like this result in the console window:

```
List with random personal data
==============================
HeMo00000001: Heckhuis, Momo, 06549 Straubing
SoGu00000002: Sonntag, Guido, 21498 Liebenburg
ThAl00000003: Thiemann, Alfred, 51920 Bielefeld
```

```
HöJü00000004: Hörstmann, Jürgen, 05984 Liebenburg
TiMa00000005: Tiemann, Margarete, 14399 München
TiAn00000006: Tiemann, Anja, 01287 Dortmund
ViGu00000007: Vielstedde, Guido, 72762 Wuppertal
RoMe00000008: Rode, Melanie, 94506 Hildesheim
TiDa00000009: Tiemann, Daja, 54134 Lippstadt
BrJo00000010: Braun, José, 14590 Soest
WeJü00000011: Westermann, Jürgen, 83128 Wuppertal
HeKa00000012: Heckhuis, Katrin, 13267 Bad Waldliesborn
TrJü00000013: Trouw, Jürgen, 54030 Lippstadt
PlGa00000014: Plenge, Gabriele, 97702 Braunschweig
WeJü00000015: Weichel, Jürgen, 39992 Unterschleißheim
```

At this point, you might be asking, "why all this setup?" The answer is that it's important for the correct use of *Hashtable* objects and to gain an understanding of how hashtables save elements. When you are saving an object in a hashtable, the key *must be unique*; otherwise, you wouldn't be able retrieve all the elements. (Which of two elements indexed by a key should the hashtable return when the keys are identical?)

Processing Speed of Hashtables

Now, you can look at a hashtable in action and see what it can do. Using the *ArrayList* that supplies us with the *RandomAddresses* function, the following program builds a hashtable containing at least 1,000,000 elements. At the same time it creates an array containing 51 random elements from the *ArrayList* and remembers the *Matchcode* for each element. Subsequently, it uses those *Matchcode*s to pick elements from the list and measures the time it takes to access them. Here's the code:

```
Module HashtableDemo

    Sub Main()

        ''For the further examples uncomment the following three lines.
        'TestAddresses()
        'Console.ReadLine()
        'Return

        Dim locNumberAddresses As Integer = 1000000
        Dim locAccessElements As Integer = 2
        Dim locMeasurements As Integer = 3
        Dim locAccesses As Integer = 1000000
        Dim locTemplateAddresses As ArrayList
        Dim locAddresses As New Hashtable
        Dim locTestKeys(locRandomElements) As String
        Dim locRandom As New Random(Now.Millisecond)

        'Waiting for start
        Console.WriteLine("Press Enter to start")
        Console.ReadLine()
```

```
'Generate many addresses:
Console.Write("Creating {0} random address entries...", locNumberAddresses)
Dim locTimer = Stopwatch.StartNew
locTemplateAddresses = address.RandomAddresses(locNumberAddresses)
locTimer.Stop()
Console.WriteLine("finished after {0} ms", locTimer.ElapsedMilliseconds)
locTimer.Reset()


'Building the hashtable
Console.Write("Building the hashtable with random address entries...",
  locNumberAddresses)
locTimer.Start()
For Each address As Address In locTemplateAddresses
    locAddresses.Add(address.Matchcode, address)
Next
locTimer.Stop()
Console.WriteLine("finished after {0} ms", locTimer.ElapsedMilliseconds)
locTimer.Reset()


'Pick n random addresses
For i As Integer = 0 To locAccessElements
    locTestKeys(i) = DirectCast(locTemplateAddresses(
        locRandom.Next(locNumberAddresses)), Address).Matchcode
Next


Dim locTemp As Object
Dim locTemp2 As Object = Nothing


'Accessing, and measuring how long it takes.
'Do it 5 times to confirm the measurement.
For z As Integer = 1 To locMeasurements
    Console.WriteLine()
    Console.WriteLine("{0}. Measurement:", z)
    For i As Integer = 0 To locAccessElements
        Console.Write("{0} accesses to: {1} in ", locAccesses,
            locTestKeys(i))
        locTemp = locTestKeys(i)
        locTimer.Start()
        For j As Integer = 1 To locAccesses
            locTemp2 = locAddresses(locTemp)
        Next j
        locTimer.Stop()
        locTemp = locTemp2.GetType
        Console.WriteLine("{0} ms", locTimer.ElapsedMilliseconds)
        locTimer.Reset()
    Next
Next

    'Access to Arraylist for comparison
    For i As Integer = 0 To locRandomElements
        Console.Write("{0} accesses to ArrayList element in ", locZugriffe)
        locTimer.Start()
```

```
                For j As Integer = 1 To locZugriffe
                    locTemp2 = locTemplateAddresses(0)
                Next j
                locTimer.Stop()
                locTemp = locTemp2.GetType
                Console.WriteLine("{0} ms", locTimer.ElapsedMilliseconds)
                locTimer.Reset()
            Next

        Console.ReadLine()
    End Sub
```

When you run the program you'll see output similar to the following:

 Note The code was run on a Notebook with a 2.5 GHz Dual Core T9300 processor with 2.5 GHz clock rate, 4 GB main memory, under the 64-bit version of Windows 7.

```
Press Enter to start

Creating 1000000 random address entries...finished after 2105 ms
Building the hashtable with random address entries...finished after 584 ms

1. Measurement:
1000000 accesses to: WeMo00182238 in 112 ms
1000000 accesses to: PlMa00662840 in 132 ms
1000000 accesses to: WeLo00244369 in 131 ms
1000000 accesses to ArrayList element in 26 ms
1000000 accesses to ArrayList element in 30 ms
1000000 accesses to ArrayList element in 27 ms

2. Measurement:
1000000 accesses to: WeMo00182238 in 142 ms
1000000 accesses to: PlMa00662840 in 134 ms
1000000 accesses to: WeLo00244369 in 111 ms
1000000 accesses to ArrayList element in 25 ms
1000000 accesses to ArrayList element in 26 ms
1000000 accesses to ArrayList element in 25 ms

3. Measurement:
1000000 accesses to: WeMo00182238 in 104 ms
1000000 accesses to: PlMa00662840 in 133 ms
1000000 accesses to: WeLo00244369 in 102 ms
1000000 accesses to ArrayList element in 25 ms
1000000 accesses to ArrayList element in 26 ms
1000000 accesses to ArrayList element in 26 ms
```

In this example, when launched, the program creates 1,000,000 test elements and adds them to the hashtable. It then picks three sample entries and measures the time required for 1,000,000 accesses to those three hashtable elements. It repeats this three times to ensure

consistency of the elapsed time results. It also performs a measurement to find out how much time an indexed access to an *ArrayList* element takes. The result is impressive: Access to an element via its key takes only about 4 times longer than direct access via the index. This result would not be possible if it had to search the entire hashtable from front to back for the key.

Why the Access Time to Hashtable Elements Is Almost Constant...

You can change the parameters at the beginning of the program to see more examples of the incredible speed of .NET. However, no matter how many experiments you perform, you will notice one thing: no matter what you do, the access speed to individual elements stays essentially constant (there could be an exception in rare cases in which element access takes twice as long as the average).

The secret for the fast-yet-constant average access speed lies in how the hashtable is constructed, and how it processes the key. The fastest way to access an element is to read it directly via its index (as the previous example proved when accessing the *ArrayList* elements). Therefore, it makes most sense to calculate the element's position number rather than searching through the hashtable elements to find a matching key. And that's exactly where the hashing concept comes into play. *Hashing* also means "chopping up," which sounds negative, but chopping up a key in a specific way has a positive purpose: Hashing a key (such as a string) results in an identification number, which provides information about the "absolute value" of the string. In this context *absolute value* means not only that identical strings result in identical hash values, but also that larger strings equate to larger hash values.

A simple example will illustrate the point. Consider an array of 26 words, all of which start with a different letter. These words are unsorted. You are using a simple hashing algorithm in which a string's hashcode corresponds to the number of the first letter of each word. Using this simplified constellation, you have already solved the problem of calculating the position, because your hashcode will correspond to the index number of each string in the array. Therefore, sorting as well as reading later happens extremely fast via the string itself (or rather via its first letter).

Of course, in practice the problem isn't quite as easy to solve. In the real world, you must take more characters (sticking with the example of strings as keys) into consideration to calculate the hashcode. Moreover, when dealing with long strings and limited hashcode precision, you can't exclude the possibility that different strings could result in the same hashcodes. So, you'd need to make provisions to handle collisions during index calculation. Fortunately, it's not that big of a problem. For example, when sorting the elements, if the index corresponding to the key's hashcode is already taken, you just take the next available one.

Now suppose that you have 26 elements that mostly start with different letters, but the list contains two words that start with A, one with B and none with C. The hash algorithm remains the same. You sort the B-word into slot 2, and then the first A-word into slot 1. Now you get the second A-word for sorting, and according to the hashcode it points to slot 1.

In this case, you start searching and are checking slot 2, which is already occupied by the B-word, but then you find the free slot 3. Theoretically it belongs to C, but in this case it isn't just free, but also will never be claimed, because there is no C-word in the list you are sorting. In the worst case, our example has a C-word, but no Z-word, and the second A-word is the last element to be sorted. Now the search runs through all elements and finally lands on last element for the *Z*.

...And Why You Should Know About It

You can avoid such cases by providing additional memory space. Assume that you reserve twice as much memory for the keys. Many slots will remain empty, but now the second A-word doesn't need to slide all the way to the Z-index. That's important.

This is a concept called *Load Factor*, which is the factor that specifies the relationship between assignment collision probabilities and memory requirements. The lower the collision probability, the higher memory requirement must be, and vice versa. You can test this relationship in the sample program.

At the beginning of the module in the *Sub Main* of the sample program you can find a block with commented-out declaration statements. Switch the commenting of the blocks to use the following parameters for the next trial run:

```
Dim locNumberAddresses As Integer = 1000000
Dim locAccessElements As Integer = 25
Dim locMeasurements As Integer = 3
Dim locAccesses As Integer = 1000000
Dim locTemplateAddresses As ArrayList
Dim locAddresses As New Hashtable(100000, 1)
Dim locTestKeys(locAccessElements) As String
Dim locTimer As New HighSpeedTimeGauge
Dim locRandom As New Random(Now.Millisecond)
```

This set of declarations increases the number of elements to be tested to 50 (and thus increases the probability of finding elements that collide during setup). It also changes the load factor of the hashtable (highlighted in bold in the code). When instantiating a hashtable you can specify the initial capacity as well as a load factor (the second parameter). Valid load factor values are between 0.1 and 1. The first run-through specifies a load factor of 1, relinquishing memory space at the expense of a higher collision rate, and therefore, at the expense of speed. (This value corresponds to the default setting that's in effect when you don't specify a parameter for the load factor).

Start the program with these settings and *don't* exit it after the measurement run has completed. Depending on your computer's performance, the test results will show measurements such as those presented here:

```
1000000 accesses to: BrFr00803543 in 127 ms
1000000 accesses to: HoKl00971779 in 105 ms
1000000 accesses to: TiAn00984539 in 160 ms
1000000 accesses to: TiKl00353084 in 104 ms
1000000 accesses to: HoKa00471671 in 109 ms
1000000 accesses to: ViBe00059525 in 106 ms
1000000 accesses to: WeKa00412662 in 119 ms
1000000 accesses to: TiBr00982230 in 153 ms
1000000 accesses to: BrBa00457658 in 103 ms
1000000 accesses to: HoAn00031026 in 106 ms
1000000 accesses to: TrMo00777434 in 177 ms
1000000 accesses to: ThMi00652362 in 112 ms
1000000 accesses to: WeUw00237110 in 117 ms
1000000 accesses to: HeBr00835839 in 106 ms
1000000 accesses to: VüBr00254760 in 134 ms
1000000 accesses to: LöMa00309629 in 127 ms
1000000 accesses to: ScUt00344455 in 102 ms
1000000 accesses to: WeBa00812888 in 104 ms
```

This example demonstrates that access to the list elements varies quite a bit—sometimes requiring twice as as much time as the average.

Now bring up Task Manager without exiting the program (right-click an empty area on your task bar, and then click Task Manager).

In the Task Manager dialog, click on the *Processes* tab. Look for the entry *HashtableDemo* (see Figure 19-4), and remember the value for memory usage.

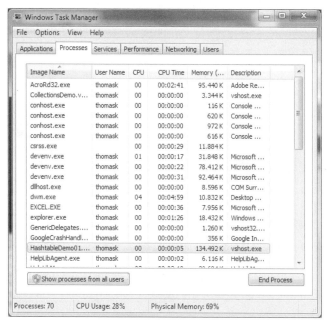

FIGURE 19-4 Using a high value for the load factor parameter of a hashtable reduces memory requirements but causes more assignment collisions.

Exit the program. Now change the load factor of the hashtable to 0.1 using the following code line, and then repeat the process:

```
Dim locAddresses As New Hashtable(100000, 0.1)
```

Watch how the smaller load factor impacts the element access speed (see also Figure 19-5):

```
1000000 accesses to: MüA100837928 in 103 ms
1000000 accesses to: HoDa00414300 in 103 ms
1000000 accesses to: JuGu00310325 in 105 ms
1000000 accesses to: A1Br00045195 in 104 ms
1000000 accesses to: NeUw00268129 in 103 ms
1000000 accesses to: TrFr00286598 in 104 ms
1000000 accesses to: HöJü00041436 in 106 ms
1000000 accesses to: HeJü00963087 in 108 ms
1000000 accesses to: WeCh00740139 in 104 ms
1000000 accesses to: A1Ga00720899 in 104 ms
1000000 accesses to: BrUw00572080 in 104 ms
1000000 accesses to: WeRa00608848 in 102 ms
1000000 accesses to: AdMi00350918 in 107 ms
1000000 accesses to: TrKa0095
```

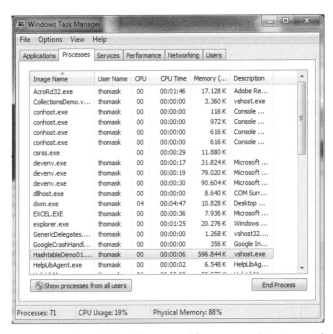

FIGURE 19-5 A smaller load factor provides more consistent access times, but at the expense of memory.

Compared to the previous example, the access times are nearly constant. Of course, it's still possible that one or two won't fit the norm, but the number of such outliers has shrunk considerably.

Also note the memory usage in Task Manager in Figure 19-5, which tells you immediately that the more consistent access speed was gained at the expense of memory: memory usage is almost five times as high as the previous version!

Now that you know the principles behind how hashtables work, you will have an easier time remembering these concepts and keeping them in mind when programming with *Hashtable* objects.

Using Custom Classes as Key

All the examples of hashtables so far have used strings as keys, meaning that the table index was created from the hashcode of these key strings.

The .NET Framework actually determines a string's hashcode by using an algorithm that's too complicated and time-consuming for this book. But in the example, because each Address has a hidden unique "client number" as its *Matchcode*, you could theoretically use that number as the index directly. Element access speed should then remain constant (independent of the load factor) because the client number is always unique (in contrast, the *hashcode* of the Matchcodes might easily result in duplicates—and thus in collisions when sorting the hashtable).

You can use members of custom classes as keys, but you must keep the following points in mind:

- The class must override its *Equals* function so that the *Hashtable* class can check whether two keys match.

- The class must override the *GetHashcode* function so that the *Hashtable* class can determine a *hashcode*.

> **Important** When overriding the *Equals* function, be sure to override the correct overloaded version of this function. Because the base function (the *Equals* function of *Object*) is implemented as non-static and static function, you must use the *Overloads* keyword. Because you want to override the function you must also use *Overrides*. The compiler doesn't permit *Overrides* by itself, because the function is already overloaded in the base class. But—and this is what's dangerous—it permits a single *Overloads*, and that leads to overshadowing the base function *without* overriding it. The result: the compiler doesn't generate an error message (not even a warning, even though it should!), but your function won't be treated as polymorphism and therefore will never be called.

Armed with this knowledge, you can now tackle a custom *Key* class. In this simplified example, a part of the Matchcode string lends itself to serve directly as *hashcode*. Because the continuous number of an address is part of the Matchcode, you can use that as a *hashcode*, resulting in the code that follows for the custom *Key* class.

Companion Content   Open the corresponding solution (.sln), which you can find in the
\VB 2010 Developer Handbook\Chapter 19\HashtableDemo02 folder.

```
Public Class AddressesKey

    Private myMatchcode As String
    Private myKeyValue As Integer

    Sub New(ByVal Matchcode As String)
        myKeyValue = Integer.Parse(Matchcode.Substring(4))
        myMatchcode = Matchcode
    End Sub

    'Required to find the correct
    'key during collisions.
    Public Overloads Overrides Function Equals(ByVal obj As Object) As Boolean
        'If Not (TypeOf obj Is AddressesKey) Then
    '     Dim errAddressKey As New InvalidCastException(
            "AddressesKey can only be compared to objects of the same type")
        '    Throw errAddressKey
        'End If
        Return myKeyValue.Equals(DirectCast(obj, AddressesKey).KeyValue)
    End Function

    'Required to "calculate" the index.
    Public Overrides Function GetHashcode() As Integer
        Return myKeyValue
    End Function
    Public Overrides Function ToString() As String
        Return myKeyValue.ToString
    End Function

    Public Property KeyValue() As Integer
        Get
            Return myKeyValue
        End Get
        Set(ByVal Value As Integer)
            myKeyValue = Value
        End Set
    End Property

End Class
```

You need to make only minor changes to the original test program to implement the new
Key class. The *Address* class doesn't need to be changed at all. The main program has a few
altered lines.

```
Module HashtableDemo

    Sub Main()

        Dim locNumberAddresses As Integer = 1000000
        Dim locAccessElements As Integer = 50
        Dim locMeasurements As Integer = 3
        Dim locAccesses As Integer = 1000000
        Dim locTemplateAddresses As ArrayList
        Dim locAddresses As New Hashtable(100000, 0.1)
        Dim locTestKeys(locZugriffsElemente) As AddressesKey
        Dim locRandom As New Random(Now.Millisecond)


        'Waiting for start
        Console.WriteLine("Press Enter to start")
        Console.ReadLine()

        'Generate many addresses:
        Console.Write("Creating {0} random address entries...", locNumberAddresses)
        Dim locTimer = Stopwatch.StartNew
        locTemplateAddresses = address.RandomAddresses(locNumberAddresses)
        locTimer.Stop()
        Console.WriteLine("finished after {0} ms", locTimer.ElapsedMilliseconds)
        locTimer.Reset()

        'Building the hashtable
        Console.Write(
            "Building the hashtable with random address entries...",
            locNumberAddresses)
        locTimer.Start()
        For Each address As Address In locTemplateAddresses
            'Change: Don't use the string, but a Key object instead
            locAddresses.Add(New AddressesKey(address.Matchcode), address)
        Next
        locTimer.Stop()
        Console.WriteLine("finished after {0} ms", locTimer.ElapsedMilliseconds)
        locTimer.Reset()

        'Pick 51 random addresses.
        'Change: The keys are saved, but not the Matchcode
        For i As Integer = 0 To locAccessElements
            locTestKeys(i) = New AddressesKey(
                DirectCast(locTemplateAddresses(locRandom.Next(
                locNumberAddresses)), Address).Matchcode)
        Next

        'Change: No more object, but instead directly an AddressesKey
        Dim locTemp As AddressesKey
        Dim locTemp2, locTemp3 As Object
```

```
                    'Access and measure how long it takes
                    'Do it 5 times to confirm the measurement.
                    For z As Integer = 1 To locMeasurements
                        Console.WriteLine()
                        Console.WriteLine("{0}. Measurement:", z)
                        For i As Integer = 0 To locAccessElements
                            Console.Write("{0} accesses to: {1} in ", locAccesses,
                                locTestKeys(i))
                            locTemp = locTestKeys(i)
                            locTimer.Start()
                            For j As Integer = 1 To locAccesses
                                locTemp2 = locAddresses(locTemp)
                            Next j
                            locTimer.Stop()
                            'Better is better: Note that the compiler notices
                            'that locTemp2 is not necessary, and it is optimized out!
                            locTemp3 = locTemp2.GetType
                            Console.WriteLine("{0} ms", locTimer.ElapsedMilliseconds)
                            locTimer.Reset()
                        Next

                        'Access to ArrayList for comparison
                .
                .
                .
            End Sub
```

The crucial line in the example was not changed. *locTemp* still serves as an object variable for the key, but it is no longer of type *String*; it's an *AddressesKey* instead. The variable *locTemp3* (previously *locTemp*) ensures that the compiler doesn't remove the inner loop as part of optimization[1] and distort the measurement results that way.

When you start this program, you notice two things: access to the data has become noticeably faster, and access to the data always happens at the same speed, independent of the load factor. Because the key values are now unique, hashtables no longer need to be concerned about collisions—they simply can't happen. Therefore, there is no appreciable advantage to changing the load factor—in fact, doing so would waste memory, because it would never be used.

In this example, the data sets weren't very large. If you think about how many accesses to the hashtable objects were actually necessary to reach a measurable value, it becomes clear that the effort wasn't really worth it. However, keep in mind that the computers on which your software will be run later are usually not as powerful as the computer on which you develop them.

---

[1] This is just a precautionary measure. I admit that I didn't actually check whether the line would be removed as part of optimization. However, considering the intelligence of modern (JIT) compilers, it seems quite possible.

Keys Must Be Immutable

If you have decided to develop custom classes to manage hashtable keys, bear in mind that keys must be immutable. Ensure that users of your class cannot change the content of a *Key* object from the outside while it is assigned to a hashtable. Otherwise, you run the risk that the *GetHashcode* function will return an incorrect hashcode for a *Key* object, meaning the hashtable lookup algorithm would not be able to find the object in the data table.

Enumerating Data Elements in a Hashtable

In principle, hashtable enumeration (iterating through it with *For Each*) is possible. However, there are two considerations:

Data elements are not saved sequentially in a hashtable. Because the hashcode of an object that must be saved is crucial to the position of the object within the data table, the actual position of an object can be predicted only with very simple hashcode algorithms. If you are using a *String* object as a key—which will most frequently be the case—the objects to be saved will be distributed in the table more randomly.

Objects are saved within a hashtable in so-called *Bucket* structures. A key belongs inseparably to its object, and both are deposited in a *Bucket* element in the table. An iteration through the data table can therefore only take place by using a special object, of the type *DictionaryEntry*.

For the example program, iterating through the hashtable might look like this:

```
'Iterating through the hashtable
For Each locDE As DictionaryEntry In locAddresses
    'in our example for the key
    Dim locAddressesKey As AddressesKey = DirectCast(locDE.Key, AddressesKey)
    'in our example for the object
    Dim locAddress As Address = DirectCast(locDE.Value, Address)
Next
```

> **Tip** You can implement fast, type-safe collections by using the *KeyedCollection* class, which .NET Framework has provided since version 2.0 as a base class. You can find an example of using *KeyedCollection* later in this chapter.

The *DictionaryBase* Class

The hashtable collection supports only type-unsafe *Object* collections, such as *ArrayList* itself. Until .NET Framework 2.0, you could implement a type-safe hashtable collection through inheritance by using the *DictionaryBase* class. That approach is similar to the one described

earlier in this chapter (*CollectionBase*), but it uses a hashtable collection as the *InnerList* instead of an *ArrayList*.

Since .NET Framework 2.0, thanks to generics (see Chapter 17, "Developing with Generics") there's a much more comfortable option for creating type-safe dictionary/hashtable implementations. The generic *Dictionary* collection (*Dictionary Of* in Visual Basic) and the *KeyedCollection* are both useful. You can implement the latter only through inheritance; it ensures a homogenous key/element collection by determining the key from the element which is added to the collection.

You can find a *KeyedCollection* example later in this chapter. Ensure that you are aware of the implementation "inadequacies" explained there in connection with *KeyedCollection* serializations.

Queue: the FIFO Principle

"First in, first out" is the principle of the *Queue* class of .NET Framework. You have probably used this principle yourself when printing several documents in a row under Windows. Printing in Windows works according to the queue principle. The document which was enqueued (added to the queue) first is processed and printed first and then dequeued *(removed from the queue)*. You use the aptly named methods *Enqueue* to add elements to the queue, and *Dequeue* to simultaneously get them back and remove them from the queue.

> **Companion Content** If you want to experiment with the *Queue* class, use the *CollectionsDemo* project, which you can find in the \VB 2010 Developer Handbook\Chapter 19\CollectionsDemo folder. Open the corresponding solution (.sln) and change the program so that it calls *Sub QueueDemo* to be able to reproduce the example in the code that follows.

```vb
Sub QueueDemo()

    Dim locQueue As New Queue

    'The type-safe version with generics would be:

    Dim typeSafeQueue As New Queue(Of String)

    Dim locString As String

    locQueue.Enqueue("First element")
    locQueue.Enqueue("Second element")
    locQueue.Enqueue("Third element")
    locQueue.Enqueue("Fourth element")

    'Check what's at the beginning without removing it.
    Console.WriteLine("Element at beginning of queue:" + locQueue.Peek().ToString)
    Console.WriteLine()
```

```
    'Iterating works too.
    For Each locString In locQueue
        Console.WriteLine(locString)
    Next
    Console.WriteLine()

    'Remove all elements from the queue and show the result in the console window.
    Do
        locString = CStr(locQueue.Dequeue)
        Console.WriteLine(locString)
    Loop Until locQueue.Count = 0
    Console.ReadLine()
End Sub
```

When you run the program, it returns this output in the console window:

```
Element at beginning of queue:First element

First element
Second element
Third element
Fourth element

First element
Second element
Third element
Fourth element
```

> **Note** The type-safe version of this collection is called *Queue(Of Type)*. By being type-safe (thus ensuring the code is more robust), it has considerable speed advantages for value types. Internally, it's based on value type arrays, whose elements don't need to be boxed.

Stack: the LIFO Principle

The *Stack* class works according to the "Last in, first out" principle—exactly the reverse of the FIFO principle of the *Queue* class. You add an element at the top of the stack with the *Push* method, and remove and retrieve it with *Pop*. *Pop* removes and retrieves the element most recently placed on the stack with *Push*.

> **Companion Content** You can find the following demonstration in the same project as the previous one (\VB 2010 Developer Handbook\Chapter 19\CollectionsDemo folder). Change the program to call the *Sub StackDemo* to replicate the example in the code that follows.

```
Sub StackDemo()
    Dim locStack As New Stack

    'The type-safe version with generics would be as follows:
    Dim typeSafeStack As New Stack(Of String)
```

```
        Dim locString As String

        locStack.Push("First element")
        locStack.Push("Second element")
        locStack.Push("Third element")
        locStack.Push("Fourth element")

        'Check what's on the stack without removing the element.
        Console.WriteLine("Top element on the stack: " + locStack.Peek.ToString)
        Console.WriteLine()

        'Iteration works too.
        For Each locString In locStack
            Console.WriteLine(locString)
        Next
        Console.WriteLine()

        'Remove all elements form the stack and display the result in the console window.
        Do
            locString = CStr(locStack.Pop)
            Console.WriteLine(locString)
        Loop Until locStack.Count = 0
        Console.ReadLine()
    End Sub
```

When you run the program, it shows the following output in the console window:

```
Top element on the stack: Fourth element

Fourth element
Third element
Second element
First element

Fourth element
Third element
Second element
First element
```

> **Note** The type-safe version of this collection is called *Stack(Of Type)*. By being type-safe
> (thus ensuring the code is more robust), it has considerable speed advantages for value types.
> Internally, it's based on value type arrays, whose elements don't need to be boxed.

SortedList: Keeping Elements Permanently Sorted

When you want to sort your elements as soon as you add them to the collection, the
SortedList class is the right tool. But keep in mind: of all the collections classes introduced so
far, the *SortedList* class consumes the most resources. With applications for which speed is
of the essence, you might want to organize your data differently, for example, by using an
unsorted hashtable or even an *ArrayList*.

SortedList is somewhat of a mixture of *ArrayList* and *Hashtable* functionality (even though algorithmically speaking it has nothing whatsoever to do with *Hashtable*). You can access the elements of *SortedList* either via a key or via an index. The next example shows how *SortedList* is generally used.

> **Companion Content** Open the corresponding files, which you can find in the \VB 2010 Developer Handbook\Chapter 19\SortedListDemo folder.

The example consists of three code files. The file *Data.vb* contains the *Address* class (with which you should be familiar from the previous sections in this chapter)—but in slightly changed form. In this version, the *Matchcode* of the random addresses starts with the incremented number and ends with the letter combination of the last and first names. This way, we avoid some problems: first, sorting the *Matchcode* also sorts the addresses by last and first names, and second, you can't perform certain confirmations of program behaviors.

```
Module SortedListDemo
    Sub Main()
        Dim locRandomAddresses As ArrayList = Address.RandomAddresses(6)
        Dim locAddresses As New SortedList

        Console.WriteLine("Original sort:")
        For Each locAddress As Address In locRandomAddresses
            Console.WriteLine(locAddress)
            locAddresses.Add(locAddress.Matchcode, locAddress)
        Next

        'Access per index:
        Console.WriteLine()
        Console.WriteLine("Access per index:")
        For i As Integer = 0 To locAddresses.Count - 1
            Console.WriteLine(locAddresses.GetByIndex(i).ToString)
        Next

        Console.WriteLine()
        Console.WriteLine("Access per enumerator:")
        'Access per enumerator
        For Each locDE As DictionaryEntry In locAddresses
            Console.WriteLine(locDE.Value.ToString)
        Next
        Console.ReadLine()
    End Sub
End Module
```

When you start this program, it generates output similar to the following in the console window:

```
Original sort:
00000005PlKa: Plenge, Katrin, 26201 Liebenburg
00000004PlKa: Plenge, Katrin, 93436 Liebenburg
00000003AlMa: Albrecht, Margarete, 65716 Bad Waldliesborn
00000002HoBa: Hollmann, Barbara, 96807 Liebenburg
00000001LöLo: Löffelmann, Lothar, 21237 Lippetal
00000000AdKa: Ademmer, Katrin, 49440 Unterschleißheim

Access per index:
00000000AdKa: Ademmer, Katrin, 49440 Unterschleißheim
00000001LöLo: Löffelmann, Lothar, 21237 Lippetal
00000002HoBa: Hollmann, Barbara, 96807 Liebenburg
00000003AlMa: Albrecht, Margarete, 65716 Bad Waldliesborn
00000004PlKa: Plenge, Katrin, 93436 Liebenburg
00000005PlKa: Plenge, Katrin, 26201 Liebenburg

Access per enumerator:
00000000AdKa: Ademmer, Katrin, 49440 Unterschleißheim
00000001LöLo: Löffelmann, Lothar, 21237 Lippetal
00000002HoBa: Hollmann, Barbara, 96807 Liebenburg
00000003AlMa: Albrecht, Margarete, 65716 Bad Waldliesborn
00000004PlKa: Plenge, Katrin, 93436 Liebenburg
00000005PlKa: Plenge, Katrin, 26201 Liebenburg
```

You can see that the list was re-sorted according to the key, which affects access to elements via an index as well as via the enumerator with *For Each*.

Note Since .NET Framework 2.0, the generic collection class *SortedList(Of Key, Type)* is available as a type-safe alternative. Ensure that you don't confuse it with the generic class *SortedSet(Of Type)* which provides a sorted set of elements in which duplicates are not allowed.

Generic Collections

Compared to "regular" collections, generic collections offer a significant advantage: they are always type-safe. Because they are not based on *Object* like the "normal" collections, such as the *ArrayList* class, they don't accept any data type for elements; instead, they limit the collection items to whatever data type you specified when defining the collection.

For example, suppose that you define a *Collection* based on *Integer* with this code:

```
Dim locGenColl As New Collection(Of Integer)
```

Now you no longer run the risk of accidentally adding an element to your collection that is not an *Integer*. In other words, the following line would be marked as an error in the Editor at design time:

```
locGenColl.Add("An element")
```

Using generic collections in your programs makes them more robust and reduces design time because you don't have to deal with runtime errors; you can correct any errors at design time, so there's less to test. And fewer tests translate to shorter design times and reduced cost.

> **Important** Many generic collections can process value types—That is, primitive data types such as *Integer*, *Date*, *Double*, or *Decimal* and value types like *Point* or *Size*—much faster than non-generic collections. That's because generic collections can usually access strongly typed arrays internally, while non-generic collections base the data carriers on *Object* arrays. Therefore, the elements must be boxed (as described in Chapter 12), which is an elaborate and time-consuming process that also requires additional memory.

There are many generic collections in .NET Framework 2.0 and later, but to describe them all in detail would take too long and isn't really necessary, because other than their original definitions, most of them work just like their non-generic counterparts. Therefore, this section focuses on the important characteristics of non-generic collections.

Table 19-1 lists important generic collections and describes what you can do with them. The collections you will work with most frequently are described in more detail and include examples in the rest of this chapter.

TABLE 19-1 The Most Important Generic Collection Types

Namespace	Collection	Description
System.Collections.ObjectModel	*Collection(Of Type)*	Provides a default collection for simple, unsorted management of elements of a certain type.
		Characteristics: Contrary to *List(Of Type)* this class exposes overridable methods so that you can change the behavior during element insert, delete, and update operations in derived classes. Internally, *Collection(Of Type)* is based on a *List(Of Type)*—so it's only marginally slower than using the *List(Of Type)* directly. This class is useful for situations in which you want to be notified when elements are added or removed—for example, you might bind to remove events or to maintain a *Parent* property so that an object knows to which collection it was added.

Namespace	Collection	Description
System.Collections.ObjectModel	*KeyedCollection(Of Key, Type)*	Provides a collection of elements that permits lookup via a strongly-typed key or via an index. **Characteristics:** This collection can be used only in derived classes, because the type you are saving generates a default key, and that must be defined in the derived class. **Important:** Avoid using *Integer* keys, because they cause problems during collection serialization.
System.Collections.ObjectModel	*ReadOnlyCollection(Of Type)*	Provides a collection whose elements are read-only. **Characteristics:** You can pass elements from a different generic collection of the same type to this collection only during instantiation—through its constructor. After that, the elements are read-only, so you cannot change them after instantiation.
System.Collections.Generic	*Dictionary(Of Key, Type)*	Provides a collection of keys and values. **Characteristics:** Assigns a set of keys to a set of values. Each addition to the dictionary consists of a value and its assigned key. A value can be retrieved very quickly via its assigned key, because the *Dictionary* class is implemented in the form of a hashtable. You can find more about this concept later in this chapter.
System.Collections.Generic	*LinkedList(Of Type)*	Provides a double-linked list. **Characteristics:** This is a linked list with individual nodes of the type *LinkedListNode*; adding and removing individual elements is extremely fast.
System.Collections.Generic	*List(Of Type)*	Provides a default collection for simple, unsorted management of elements of a certain type. **Note:** This class is not suitable for inheritance in custom collection classes where you need to use code to edit the list. Use the *Collection(Of)* collection instead (described previously in this table).

Namespace	Collection	Description
System.Collections.Generic	*Queue(Of Type)*	Provides a FIFO *(first in, first out)* collection of objects. **Note:** In principle this collections works like its non-generic relative. You can find more about the non-generic version of this collection earlier in this chapter in the section "Queue: The FIFO Principle."
System.Collections.Generic	*SortedDictionary(Of Key, Type)*	Provides a collection of key/value pairs whose order is specified with a key sort.
System.Collections.Generic	*SortedList(Of Key, Type)*	Manages a sorted list whose elements can be called via a key. **Note:** In principle, this collection works like its non-generic relative. You can find more about the non-generic version of this collection earlier in this chapter in the section "SortedList: Keeping Elements Permanently Sorted." Contrary to *SortedDictionary*, the sort takes place via the element, not via the key.
System.Collections.Generic	*Stack(Of Type)*	Provides a LIFO *(last in, first out)* collection of objects. **Note:** In principle, this collection works like its non-generic relative. You can find more about the non-generic version of this collection earlier in this chapter in the section "Stack: the LIFO Principle."
System.Collections.Generic	*SortedSet(Of Type)*	Manages a sorted set of elements that must not have duplicates. **Note:** Adding an element that already exists in the collection does *not* trigger an exception; the element just isn't inserted.

List(Of) Collections and Lambda Expressions

The *List(Of)* class is one of the most frequently used generic collection class. The class does not need to box and unbox elements, so it's faster than its non-generic counterparts. Therefore, when performance is a concern, use *List(Of Type)* instead of other collection classes when saving primitive data types in a collection.

List(Of Type) provides support for the lambda functions that became available in Visual Basic 2008. The following example assumes that you understand lambda functions. If you are not familiar with lambdas, you should read Chapter 15, "Events, Delegates, and Lambda Expressions," to gain a basic understanding. Notice that multi-line statement lambdas are especially suitable when working with many *List(Of Type)* class methods.

> **Companion Content** Open the corresponding solution (.sln), which you can find in the \VB 2010 Developer Handbook\Chapter 19\ListOfDemo folder.

When you start the program, you see a dialog similar to Figure 19-6. The form contains a *ListView* filled with 50 random addresses. You can sort the list by clicking the column headers.

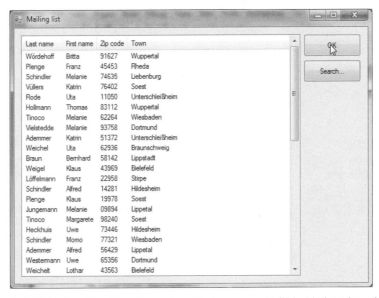

FIGURE 19-6 In this address list, sort and lookup are controlled with the column headers.

You can search the list by clicking the Search button. The search function searches through the entries by the most recently sorted column, looking for text that matches the search text.

So far, this example is nothing special. But after you take a look at the conversion, you will realize that this is quite a different approach. It begins with the way the list writes the random addresses

ForEach and the Generic Action Delegate

If you want to display the content in an array or a collection in a list, the process is pretty straight-forward: you iterate with a *For Each* construct through the collections, process each element, and then use the appropriate methods or properties to display items in the list. The following example uses a different approach:

```
'The following Lambda is called for each element of the list.
myAddresses.ForEach(Sub(element)
                    Dim locLvwItem As New ListViewItem(element.Name)

                    'Specify sub entries
                    With locLvwItem.SubItems
                        .Add(element.FirstName)
                        .Add(element.ZIP)
                        .Add(element.City)
                    End With

                    'Put reference in tag to find it again
                    locLvwItem.Tag = element

                    'Add to Listview
                    lvwAdressen.Items.Add(locLvwItem)

                End Sub)
```

You can use the *ForEach* method to iterate through a collection. At the same time, the code calls a delegate for each element. In this case, the delegate builds the *ListView* items. Beginning with version 2010, Visual Basic can process multi-line lambdas, therefore you no longer need to specify a delegate, instead, you can use a lambda directly, which provides the code to be used by *ForEach* for each element.

Of course, you can still use "manual" delegate variables here, as well. Depending on the program state, they use different procedures, which makes this approach so appealing.

Either way, it's important that the methods fulfill the signature demands of the *Action* delegate which *ForEach* requires. It must be a method that doesn't have a function result (a *Sub*) and that takes as a parameter an element whose type corresponds to the base type of the generic list. In this example, that's the *Address* type.

As a result, for each element in the *myAddresses* list, the loop calls the lambda function (highlighted in bold in the preceding code example).

Sort and the Generic Comparison Delegate

Basically, the next pairing works in a similar fashion. You use it to sort an array with the *Sort* method without using a special *Comparer* class. The difference here is that the code uses a

lambda expression to avoid having to delegate to a separate sort function. The code snippet in the following example shows you how to work with single-line and multi-line expression lambdas in this context:

```
'Called when one of the columns is clicked.
Private Sub lvwAddresses_ColumnClick(ByVal sender As Object,
    ByVal e As System.Windows.Forms.ColumnClickEventArgs) Handles
    lvwAddresses.ColumnClick

    'Convert column number of e.Column into SortAddressesBy
    mySortBy = CType(e.Column, SortAddressesBy)

    Select Case mySortBy
    Case SortAddressesBy.Name
        myAddresses.Sort(Function(adr1, adr2) String.Compare(adr1.Name, adr2.Name))

    Case SortAddressesBy.FirstName
        myAddresses.Sort(Function(adr1, adr2) String.Compare(
            adr1.FirstName, adr2.FirstName))

    Case SortAddressesBy.ZIP
        myAdressen.Sort(Function(adr1, adr2) String.Compare(adr1.ZIP, adr2.ZIP))

    Case SortAddressesBy.City
        'Multi-line would work also,...
        myAddresses.Sort(Function(adr1, adr2)
                                    '...but don't forget Return!
                                    Return String.Compare(adr1.City, adr2.City)
                                End Function)

    End Select

    'Display the elments resorted
    DisplayElements()
End Sub
```

In this example, *Sort* works with lambda expressions, each of which sorts according to a different *Address* property, depending by which of the four columns the *ListView* is sorted.

Find and the Generic Predicate Delegate

You use this last generic "dream team"—*Find* and a delegate set up with the generic *Predicate* class—when you want to find a specific object in a generic list. Again, the basic approach is similar to those you've already seen, as the following example shows, with the results illustrated in Figure 19-7:

```
Private Sub btnSearch_Click(ByVal sender As System.Object, ByVal e As System.EventArgs) _
                    Handles btnSearch.Click

    'Query search text
    Dim searchForm As New frmSearch
    Dim currentSearchText As String     'The most recently queried search text
```

```vb
'Remember the search text, so the Predicate delegate
'can access it.
currentSearchText = searchForm.SearchText
If String.IsNullOrEmpty(currentSearchText) Then
    Return
End If


'Here the search begins!
Dim locFoundAdr As Address = Nothing

Select Case mySortBy
    Case SortAddressesBy.Name
        locFoundAdr = myAddresses.Find(Function(adr) adr.Name = currentSearchText)
    Case SortAddressesBy.FirstName
        locFoundAdr = myAddresses.Find(Function(adr) adr.FirstName = currentSearchText)
    Case SortAddressesBy.ZIP
        locFoundAdr = myAddresses.Find(Function(adr) adr.ZIP = currentSearchText)
    Case SortAddressesBy.City
        'Multi-line would work here also,...
        locFoundAdr = myAddresses.Find(Function(adr)
                                        '...but, again, don't forget Return!
                                        Return adr.City = currentSearchText
                                      End Function)
End Select

'When an element was found, mark it.
If locFoundAdr IsNot Nothing Then

    'Search all ListView element, and check whether...
    For Each locLvwItem As ListViewItem In Me.lvwAdressen.Items

        '... the Tag reference corresponds to the reference of the searched object.
        If locLvwItem.Tag Is locFoundAdr Then

            'Found! Mark ListView element...
            locLvwItem.Selected = True

            '...and make sure that is is located in the visible range.
            locLvwItem.EnsureVisible()
            Return
        End If
    Next
End If
End Sub
```

FIGURE 19-7 The search text always refers to the last-sorted column.

Here too, lambda expressions (highlighted in bold in the preceding code), make searching through the various parts of the addresses relatively easy. The code uses different lambda expressions depending on the last-sorted column. The lambdas handle the comparison to your search text.

Selecting the found text in the list represents a small challenge—which is why the example saves a reference to each element in the *Tag* property of each *ListViewItem* when building the list. When *Find* matches the search text, the code retrieves the corresponding *Address* object, which it then uses to iterate through the *ListViewItem* collection, testing each Address object by comparing it to its *Tag* property. The effort is necessary because there is no other way to identify the correct *ListViewItem* element, and you need the *ListViewItem* to select the correct line in the list, by using its *Select* property.

KeyedCollection: Key/Dictionary Collections with Additional Index Queries

We have to admit that we're big fans of *KeyedCollection*—along with *Collection(Of Type)*. *KeyedCollection* has two crucial advantages:

- It lets you specify any desired type (well—*almost* any desired type, but more about that later) as a key, meaning that you can use it as a dictionary collection and query its elements via a key.

- But you can also treat it like a regular *Collection*, meaning that you can iterate through its elements with *For Each* or request individual elements via a numeric index.

Because *KeyedCollection* requires a key value to retrieve elements, it needs a way to generate a key from the elements you add. Therefore, the *KeyedCollection* class is also an abstract base class: to use it, you derive a new class from *KeyedCollection* and override its *GetKeyForItem* method. That method controls how the class generates a key when you add an element. Therefore, you should use a *KeyedCollection* class only to manage elements that have at least one unique property, such as a personnel number, a client ID, a unique code, or something similar.

Important *KeyedCollection* also has one notable disadvantage, or rather, a design issue. When you try to serialize its content (for example, save it as an XML file by using a built-in .NET Framework feature) you cannot use an *Integer* data type as key, because the .NET Framework "bails" with an exception. Chapter 21 has more information about this problem and provides a workaround.

Companion Content Open the corresponding files, which you can find in the \VB 2010 Developer Handbook\Chapter 19\KeyedCollectionDemo folder.

This example project contains two code files, *Data.vb* and *KeyedCollection.vb*. The first one contains the by-now-familiar *Address* class from earlier in this chapter, which saves address data and exposes a static function that generates any number of random addresses, returning them in an *ArrayList*.

In this example, you can think of the *Address* class as a management element for the *KeyedCollection*. As stated, the one requirement is that the *Address* class must have a unique property value that distinguishes one *Address* element from another.

> **Note** The functionality for checking uniqueness cannot be implemented by the *Address* class itself because it doesn't know the other elements of the collection. Therefore, the specification of such a data property is only a theoretical definition here. The main program must ensure that no duplicate keys exist in the collection when adding a new element.

KeyedCollection is an *abstract* base class, so you can't use it directly. You must inherit from it, instead. Therefore, you create a new class name, as you have seen for abstract classes:

```
Public Class Addresses
```

And add the code to inherit from *KeyedCollection*:

```
    Inherits KeyedCollection(Of String, Address)
```

This line both derives from *KeyedCollection* and specifies that the key type will be *String* and the type for the elements that you want to manage will be *Address*.

When you press Enter, the Visual Basic Editor automatically inserts the following stub method body that you must override:

```
    Protected Overrides Function GetKeyForItem(ByVal item As Address) As String

    End Function
```

This is the function that *KeyedCollection* uses to retrieve the key value (which must be of the key type) whenever you add a new element to the collection or replace an element. This ensures that each element has its own unique key.

In this example, the *Address* class *Matchcode* property value is unique to each *Address* instance. This property has the type *String*—therefore, the key type for the *KeyedCollection* is also String. The completely implemented *KeyedCollection* looks as follows:

```
''' <summary>
''' Manages objects of the type Address as dictionary collection.
''' Derived from the abstract base class KeyedCollection.
''' </summary>
''' <remarks></remarks>
```

```vb
Public Class Addresses
    Inherits KeyedCollection(Of String, Address)

    'This method must be overridden to make sure
    'that each element has a key.
    Protected Overrides Function GetKeyForItem(ByVal item As Address) As String
        'Here we specify that the unique key is the Matchcode.
        Return item.Matchcode
    End Function
End Class
```

This sort of implementation is all you need to work with a *KeyedCollection*. The main module, *KeyedCollection.vb*, demonstrates how to use the collection and shows how to call the elements of a class derived from *KeyedCollection* by using either keys or indexes, as shown here:

```vb
Imports System.Collections.ObjectModel

Module KeyedCollection

    Sub Main()
        'First define a normal ArrayList
        'which contains 100 random addresses.
        Dim locArrayList As ArrayList = Address.RandomAddresses(100)

        'This is the "self-made" KeyedCollection
        Dim locKeyedAddresses As New Addresses

        'We fill the KeyedCollection with the elements of the ArrayList
        For Each locAddressItem As Address In locArrayList
            locKeyedAddresses.Add(locAddressItem)
        Next

        'Call the elements from the KeyedCollection:
        'Variation No. 1: via the index
        For c As Integer = 0 To 10
            Console.WriteLine(locKeyedAddresses(c).ToString)
        Next

        'Empty line-to make it easier to read:
        Console.WriteLine()

        'Pick one to get to the Matchcode:
        Dim locMatchcode As String = locKeyedAddresses(10).Matchcode

        'Variation No. 2: An address can also be called via the key
        '(in this case via the Matchcode).
        Dim locAddress As Address = locKeyedAddresses(locMatchcode)
        Console.WriteLine("The address with the Matchcode " & locMatchcode & " is:")
        Console.WriteLine(locAddress.ToString)
        Console.WriteLine()
```

```
        Console.WriteLine("Press key to exit!")
        Console.ReadKey()
    End Sub

End Module
```

Linking Elements with *LinkedList(Of)*

The generic *LinkedList(Of)* class was first introduced in .NET Framework 2.0, and it is worth mentioning here because it gives you the ability to manage elements in the form of linked lists.

LinkedList(Of) provides a list of nodes, each of which is an instance of the type *LinkedListNode*. Each element "points" to its next and previous element. You can insert or delete elements very fast. You can imagine a chain that just needs to be opened at the correct spot to add or remove a new link.

Internally, *LinkedList(Of)* does not save elements directly; instead, they're placed in a node object called *LinkedListNode*, which manages the links to the preceding and following nodes in the list.

Because it manages elements differently than other collections, *LinkedList(Of)* offers methods and properties other collections don't have. Table 19-2 lists special methods and properties of the *LinkedList* class.

TABLE 19-2 **The Special Methods and Properties of the *LinkedList* Class**

Method	Description
AddAfter	Adds a new node or value after an existing node in the *LinkedList*.
AddBefore	Adds a new node or value before an existing node in the *LinkedList*.
AddFirst	Adds a new node or value at the beginning of the *LinkedList*.
AddLast	Adds a new node or value at the end of the *LinkedList*.
Find	Finds the first node that contains a specified value.
FindLast	Finds the last node that contains a specified value.
First	Retrieves the first node of the *LinkedList*. This property is read-only.
Last	Retrieves the last node of the *LinkedList*. This property is read-only.
Remove	Removes the first node or value from the *LinkedList*.
RemoveFirst	Removes the node at the beginning of the *LinkedList*.
RemoveLast	Removes the node at the end of the *LinkedList*.

> **Companion Content** Open the corresponding solution (.sln), which you can find in the \VB 2010 Developer Handbook\Chapter 19\LinkedList folder.

```vb
Module LinkedList

    Sub Main()
        Dim locLinkedList As New LinkedList(Of Address)
        Dim locAddresses As ArrayList = Address.RandomAddresses(50)
        Dim locAddress As Address = Nothing

        'Append eight addresses to the respective end of the LinkedList
        For c As Integer = 0 To 49

            'We'll remember the 25. for the later search in the list
            If c = 25 Then
                locAddress = DirectCast(locAddresses(c), Address)
            End If
            locLinkedList.AddLast(DirectCast(locAddresses(c), Address))
        Next

        Dim locLinkedListNode As LinkedListNode(Of Address)
        'Find the node which corresponded to the 25. address entry.
        locLinkedListNode = locLinkedList.Find(locAddress)
        Console.WriteLine("Before " & locLinkedListNode.Value.ToString & _
            " comes " & locLinkedListNode.Previous.Value.ToString & _
            " and then comes " & locLinkedListNode.Next.Value.ToString)
        Console.WriteLine()

        'Insert a new addess before the 25.:
        Console.WriteLine("Insert Sarah Halek in front!")
        locLinkedList.AddBefore(locLinkedListNode, _
                New Address("SasiMatch", "Halek", "Sarah", "99999",
                            "Musterhausen"))

        Console.WriteLine()

        'Return the same thing again. It should now reflect the changes.
        Console.WriteLine("Before " & locLinkedListNode.Value.ToString & _
            " comes " & locLinkedListNode.Previous.Value.ToString & _
            " and then comes " & locLinkedListNode.Next.Value.ToString)
        Console.WriteLine()
        Console.WriteLine("Press key to exit.")
        Console.ReadKey()
    End Sub
End Module
```

When you run this program now, you see something similar to the following on your screen:

```
Before "Hörstmann, Hans" comes "Englisch, Margarete" and then comes "Löffelmann, Katrin"

Insert Sarah Halek in front!

Before "Hörstmann, Hans" comes "Halek, Sarah" and then comes "Löffelmann, Katrin"


Press key to exit.
```

Chapter 20
Serialization

As you develop applications, you will eventually need to save the objects that you use to manage data so that you can retrieve and use them later, or you'll need to pass them to a different instance for further processing. In such cases, you basically need to create a snapshot of the current "state" of an object, saving all properties and all child objects at the same time. Of course, initially it doesn't matter how you save data; you can read objects in byte-by-byte fashion directly from the memory or write them into a file. You could also compress the data by using appropriate algorithms and then save the result to a file. Yet another option is to first convert the object data, such as numbers or date values, into a format that can be read by the intended recipient, specially formatted so that they can be transferred via the Internet to a different server, perhaps by a web service.

No matter how you retrieve data from an object and move it to a different location, the process that performs the task can follow only one specific procedure: It must query all the properties and variables of the object *sequentially*, process them, and then do something with the processed data. This procedure is called object *serialization*.

Of course, the procedure must be reversible; for example, if you have serialized a number of address objects in a text file, you need to be able to reconstitute them. To retrieve saved address data after exiting an address program and turning off the computer, the reverse process must occur when a user turns on the computer, starts the address management program, and wants to continue working with the previously stored addresses. In this case, the objects must assume the same state that they had before serialization—they must be *deserialized* from the text file.

Fortunately, the .NET Framework supports both serialization and deserialization. You don't need to manually read each individual object property and write it into a text file, nor do you need to re-instantiate address objects yourself from their serialized state. The .NET Framework provides several ingenious tools that you will get to know in this chapter. You should study these closely, because they can make your work a lot easier—and not just when you want to save addresses to your hard drive.

> **Note** To serialize instances of classes and then deserialize them somewhere else, you need the class definition in both entities. With the techniques introduced here, you can't transfer the entire class code, only the states within an object.

Introduction to Serialization Techniques

Before exploring the serialization techniques .NET Framework offers, here's a very simple example. This program does one thing: it accepts user input for an address and then serializes (saves) it to a file when the user clicks a button, as illustrated in Figure 20-1.

> **Companion Content** Open the corresponding solution (.sln), which you can find in the \VB 2010 Developer Handbook\Chapter 20\Serialization01 folder.

FIGURE 20-1 The read-only properties are not applied during serialization.

To begin, this example doesn't use any .NET Framework serialization techniques yet. Instead, it reads the individual properties manually and saves them as text in a file. When a user clicks the Serialize button, the *Click* event handler generates an *Address* object from the contents of the controls in the dialog, and passes it to another procedure that opens a file for writing, reads the *Address* object's properties sequentially, and then writes them into the file as a string, as demonstrated in the following:

```
Private Sub btnSerialize_Click(ByVal sender As System.Object, ByVal e As System.EventArgs) _
       Handles btnSerialize.Click
       Dim locAddress As New Address(txtFirstName.Text, _
                                     txtLastName.Text, _
                                     txtStreet.Text, _
                                     txtZIPCity.Text)
       'Use an "impossible" file name, to make sure that no other
       'important file by the same name will override it.
       Address.SerializeToFile(locAddress, "C:\serializedemo_f4e3w21.txt")

       'Display info about the data set.
       txtCreatedOn.Text = locAddress.CapturedOn.ToString("dd.MM.yyyy HH:mm:ss")
       txtCreatedBy.Text = locAddress.CapturedBy
    End Sub
```

In this case, the *Address* class provides the elements for saving the address data and a static procedure for serializing the object data in a file, as shown here:

```
Imports System.IO

Public Class Address

    Private myCapturedOn As DateTime
    Private myCapturedBy As String

    Sub New(ByVal FirstName As String, ByVal LastName As String,
        ByVal Street As String, ByVal ZIPCity As String)
        'The contructor sets up all member data
        Me.LastName = LastName
        Me.FirstName = FirstName
        Me.Street = Street
        Me.ZIPCity = ZIPCity
        myCapturedOn = DateTime.Now
        myCapturedBy = My.User.Name
    End Sub

    'Write all public fields into the file
    Public Shared Sub SerializeToFile(ByVal adr As Address, ByVal Filename As String)
        Dim locStreamWriter As New StreamWriter(Filename, False,
            System.Text.Encoding.Default)
        With locStreamWriter
            .WriteLine(adr.FirstName)
            .WriteLine(adr.LastName)
            .WriteLine(adr.Street)
            .WriteLine(adr.ZIPCity)
            .Flush()
            .Close()
        End With
    End Sub

    'Read from the file and create a new address object from it
    Public Shared Function SerializeFromFile(ByVal Filename As String) As Address
        Dim locStreamReader As New StreamReader(Filename,
            System.Text.Encoding.Default)
        Dim locAddress As Address
        With locStreamReader
            locAddress = New Address(.ReadLine, .ReadLine, .ReadLine, .ReadLine)
        End With
        locStreamReader.Close()
        Return locAddress
    End Function

    Public Property LastName() As String
    Public Property FirstName() As String
    Public Property Street() As String
    Public Property ZIPCity() As String
```

```
    'The following two properties have a read-only status, because
    'even the developer is not allowed to manipulate the creation date!
    Public ReadOnly Property CapturedOn() As DateTime
        Get
            Return myCapturedOn
        End Get
    End Property

    Public ReadOnly Property CapturedBy() As String
        Get
            Return myCapturedBy
        End Get
    End Property
End Class
```

This code example has two read-only properties; they can be read, but must not be written. These properties hold information about who created the *Address* object, and when it was created. The values can be defined only during object creation.

Standard serialization, as shown in the preceding example, already poses a problem: when you end the program, restart it, and then click the Deserialize button, a new *Address* object is created, but this object isn't exactly the same as the original one. The creation date and the creator of the object could have been saved along with the rest, but because these two properties are read-only, the deserialization algorithm can't restore the original property values.

This program reflects this fact. When you deserialize the saved object by clicking the Deserialize button, the Created At field doesn't contain the original creation date, it contains the date at the time of deserialization.

Serializing with *SoapFormatter* and *BinaryFormatter*

Performing serialization and deserialization with the .NET Framework is a different story. You don't need to read the object properties yourself—the .NET Framework does it for you automatically. But there's more; some classes of the .NET Framework that handle serialization can even serialize and deserialize private class properties.

> **Important** The following rule applies to all objects that you want to serialize: they must be marked with a special attribute called *Serializable*. After adding the *Serialize* attribute, you can use two of the *Serializer* classes to serialize and deserialize the marked object instance, which also take private class field variables into account.

- **SoapFormatter Class**   Provides serialization and deserialization to and from SOAP format. The data content of an object is converted into pure text which can be easily displayed and read in a text editor and can also be transported over the Internet without problems as a SOAP message. The disadvantage is that it's not terribly efficient because of the conversion of data to a text representation.

- **BinaryFormatter Class**   Provides serialization and deserialization to and from binary format. The data content of an object is stored in the same form used in working memory. For example, if the data of an object is saved in a file using this serializer, the data is compact. However, files generated in this manner are not directly readable because the object data is in binary format, not stored as text representations.

The following example demonstrates how to use both of these classes, and Figure 20-2 displays the new interface.

Companion Content Open the corresponding solution (.sln), which you can find in the \VB 2010 VB 2010 Developer Handbook\Chapter 20\Serialization02 folder.

FIGURE 20-2 In this version, you can choose either SOAP or binary serialization. The read-only properties are retained during deserialization.

When you start this program, you select the desired format for serialization or deserialization. If you choose the SOAP format, the *SoapFormatter* class generates a file similar to the one below (assuming you entered the same data as shown in Figure 20-2):

```
<SOAP-ENV:Envelope xmlns:xsi="http://www.w3.org/2001/XMLSchema-instance"
xmlns:xsd="http://www.w3.org/2001/XMLSchema" xmlns:SOAP-ENC="http://schemas.
xmlsoap.org/soap/encoding/" xmlns:SOAP-ENV="http://schemas.xmlsoap.org/soap/
envelope/" xmlns:clr="http://schemas.microsoft.com/soap/encoding/clr/1.0" SOAP-
ENV:encodingStyle="http://schemas.xmlsoap.org/soap/encoding/">
<SOAP-ENV:Body>
```

```
<a1:Address id="ref-1" xmlns:a1="http://schemas.microsoft.com/clr/nsassem/
Serialization02/Serialization02%2C%20Version%3D1.0.0.0%2C%20Culture%3Dneutral%2C%20
PublicKeyToken%3Dnull">
<myName id="ref-3">Thiemann</myName>
<myFirstName id="ref-4">Uwe</myFirstName>
<myStreet id="ref-5">Autorenstraße 34</myStreet>
<myZIPCity id="ref-6">99999 Buchhausen</myZIPCity>
<myCapturedOn>2008-10-15T09:43:45.1295355+01:00</myCapturedOn>
<myCapturedBy id="ref-7">NOTEVISTA\Uwe</myCapturedBy>
</a1:Address>
</SOAP-ENV:Body>
</SOAP-ENV:Envelope>
```

Universal SOAP File Serializer and Deserializer

You'd be surprised how little coding effort it takes to perform the serialization in the program. In Solution Explorer, there are two additional class files that contain the encapsulations of *SoapFormatter* and *BinaryFormatter* for serialization (and deserialization) of the objects in files. The class *SoapSerializer* looks as follows:

```
Imports System.Runtime.Serialization
Imports System.Runtime.Serialization.Formatters.Soap
Imports System.IO

Public Class SoapSerializer

    Shared Sub SerializeToFile(ByVal FileInfo As FileInfo, ByVal [Object] As Object)

        Dim locFs As FileStream = New FileStream(FileInfo.FullName, FileMode.Create)
        Dim locSoapFormatter As New SoapFormatter(Nothing, _
                New StreamingContext(StreamingContextStates.File))
        locSoapFormatter.Serialize(locFs, [Object])
        locFs.Flush()
        locFs.Close()

    End Sub

    Shared Function DeserializeFromFile(ByVal FileInfo As FileInfo) As Object

        Dim locObject As Object

        Dim locFs As FileStream = New FileStream(FileInfo.FullName, FileMode.Open)
        Dim locSoapFormatter As New SoapFormatter(Nothing, _
                New StreamingContext(StreamingContextStates.File))
        locObject = locSoapFormatter.Deserialize(locFs)
        locFs.Close()
        Return locObject

    End Function
End Class
```

If you want to use *SoapFormatter*, you must add a reference to your project. To do this, right-click the project name or the folder References (if the icon *Show All Files* is active) in Solution Explorer, and then select Add Reference from the context menu. In the dialog box that appears, select the entry System.Runtime.Serialization.Formatters.Soap (see Figure 20-3) by double-clicking it. Click OK to close the dialog, and then be sure to place the following statements as the first lines in the code file in which you want to use *SoapFormatter*.

```
Imports System.Runtime.Serialization
Imports System.Runtime.Serialization.Formatters.Soap
```

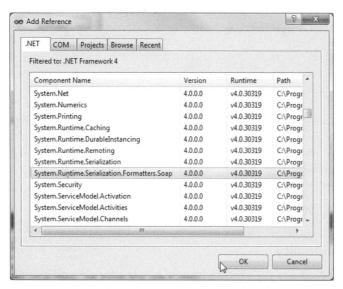

FIGURE 20-3 To serialize object files in the SOAP format with the class *SoapFormatter*, you must embed this reference into your project.

Universal Binary File Serializer and Deserializer

The *BinarySerializer* class looks like this:

```
Imports System.Runtime.Serialization
Imports System.Runtime.Serialization.Formatters.Binary
Imports System.IO

Public Class BinarySerializer

    Shared Sub SerializeToFile(ByVal FileInfo As FileInfo, ByVal [Object] As Object)

        Dim locFs As FileStream = New FileStream(FileInfo.FullName, FileMode.Create)
        Dim locBinaryFormatter As New BinaryFormatter(Nothing, _
                New StreamingContext(StreamingContextStates.File))
```

```
            locBinaryFormatter.Serialize(locFs, [Object])
            locFs.Flush()
            locFs.Close()

    End Sub

    Shared Function DeserializeFromFile(ByVal FileInfo As FileInfo) As Object

        Dim locObject As Object

        Dim locFs As FileStream = New FileStream(FileInfo.FullName, FileMode.Open)
        Dim locBinaryFormatter As New BinaryFormatter(Nothing, _
                    New StreamingContext(StreamingContextStates.File))
        locObject = locBinaryFormatter.Deserialize(locFs)
        locFs.Close()
        Return locObject

    End Function
End Class
```

Be sure to place the following statements as the first lines in the code file in which you want to use *BinaryFormatter*:

```
Imports System.Runtime.Serialization
Imports System.Runtime.Serialization.Formatters.Binary
```

Unlike with *SoapFormatter*, you don't need to add a reference to your project.

File Serializer Functionality

Both classes function according to the exact same principle, but they use different formatters (classes that provide data processing logic) to generate different formats or to recreate the original object.

When performing a serialization, you first open a file stream, which the formatter uses to transfer data from the object to a file. When the class instantiates the formatter, it passes a *StreamingContext* instance to the constructor. In this case, the object data is serialized into a file. The serialization of the object itself occurs with just this one line:

```
locSoapFormatter.Serialize(locFs, [Object])
```

The rest is obligatory: the stream data is cleared from the internal buffer with *Flush*, and then the file is closed. The result is that the object data is written into the file, including data from private members. The same thing happens in the opposite direction during deserialization.

Tip To perform this kind of file serialization in your own programs, just copy the code files *BinarySerializer.vb* or *SoapSerializer.vb* into your project folder, and then add them to your project. You can then use them exactly as they are used in the example address object project.

```
<Serializable()> _
Public Class Address

    Private myCapturedOn As DateTime
    Private myCapturedBy As String

    Sub New(ByVal FirstName As String, ByVal LastName As String, ByVal Street As String,
            ByVal ZIPCity As String)
        'The contructor sets up all member data
        Me.LastName = LastName
        Me.FirstName = FirstName
        Me.Street = Street
        Me.ZIPCity = ZIPCity
        myCapturedOn = DateTime.Now
        myCapturedBy = My.User.Name
    End Sub

    'Write all public fields into the file-Soap format
    Public Shared Sub SerializeSoapToFile(ByVal adr As Address, ByVal Filename As String)
        SoapSerializer.SerializeToFile(New FileInfo(Filename), adr)
    End Sub

    'Read from the file and create a new address object from it-Soap format
    Public Shared Function SerializeSoapFromFile(ByVal Filename As String) As Address
        Return DirectCast(SoapSerializer.DeserializeFromFile(New FileInfo(Filename)), Address)
    End Function

    'Write all public fields into the file-Binary format
    Public Shared Sub SerializeBinToFile(ByVal adr As Address, ByVal Filename As String)
        BinarySerializer.SerializeToFile(New FileInfo(Filename), adr)
    End Sub

    'Read from the file and create a new address object from it - Binary-Format
    Public Shared Function SerializeBinFromFile(ByVal Filename As String) As Address
        Return DirectCast(BinarySerializer.DeserializeFromFile(New FileInfo(Filename)), Address)
    End Function
```

Important When using object serialization, ensure that all objects that you want to serialize have the *Serializable* attribute, as shown in the first two lines of the previous code sample. If the class you want to serialize, or an object instance that contains this class, does *not* have this attribute, .NET Framework triggers an exception, as shown in Figure 20-4.

FIGURE 20-4 If a class you want to serialize, or an object which embeds it, is not marked with the attribute *Serializable*, .NET Framework throws an exception during the serialization attempt.

Shallow and Deep Object Cloning

The advantage of serializing with .NET Framework functions is that serialization algorithms are capable of automatically creating so-called *deep clones* (complete copies) of an object.

Before we proceed, here's a bit of background. Suppose that you have an object that saves some application data. This object has a property that provides an *ArrayList* that contains further elements. To create a complete copy of this object, it wouldn't be sufficient to copy the elements contained in the *ArrayList*, as the following example shows:

> **Companion Content** Open the corresponding solution file (.sln), which you can find in the
> \VB 2010 Developer Handbook\Chapter 20\DeepCloning folder.

```
Module mdlMain

    Sub Main()
        Dim locAddrOriginal As New Address("Marcus", "Pusch", "Musterstraße 22",
            "59555 Lippstadt")
        Dim locAddrCopy As Address
        locAddrOriginal.FriendsWith = New List(Of Address) From {
            New Address("Ramona", "Leenings", "Autorstr. 33", "49595 Buchhausen"),
            New Address("Cate", "Hora", "Autorstr. 34", "49595 Buchhausen"),
            New Address("Gabriele", "Löffelmann", "Autorstr. 35",
                "49595 Buchhausen")}

        'Output original address
        Console.WriteLine("Original:")
        Console.WriteLine("=========")
        Console.WriteLine(locAddrOriginal)
```

```
            'Create copy
            With locAddrOriginal
                locAddrCopy = New Address(.FirstName, .Name, .Street, .ZIPCity)
                locAddrCopy.Name += " (copy)"
                locAddrCopy.FriendsWith = .FriendsWith
            End With

            'Output copy
            Console.WriteLine("Copy:")
            Console.WriteLine("=========")
            Console.WriteLine(locAddrCopy)

            'Changes to the original:
            CType(locAddrOriginal.FriendsWith(1), Address).Name = "Löffelmann-Beck"
            CType(locAddrOriginal.FriendsWith(2), Address).Name = "Löffelmann-Beck"

            'Copy after changes to the original
            Console.WriteLine("Copy after changes to the original:")
            Console.WriteLine("===============================")
            Console.WriteLine(locAddrCopy)
            Console.ReadLine()

        End Sub

End Module
```

This example uses the slightly changed *Address* class from the previous example. It has an additional property called *FriendsWith*, which corresponds to the generic list (*List(Of Address)*) with the purpose of accepting other addresses that specify who the contact's friends are:

```
<Serializable()> _
Public Class Address

    Private myCapturedOn As DateTime
    Private myCapturedBy As String

    Sub New(ByVal FirstName As String, ByVal Name As String, ByVal Street As String,
            ByVal ZIPCity As String)
        'The constructor sets up all member data
        Me.Name = Name
        Me.FirstName = FirstName
        Me.Street = Street
        Me.ZIPCity = ZIPCity
        myCapturedOn = DateTime.Now
        myCapturedBy = Environment.UserName
    End Sub

    Public Property Name() As String
    Public Property FirstName() As String
    Public Property Street() As String
    Public Property ZIPCity() As String
```

```
   Public ReadOnly Property CapturedOn() As DateTime
      Get
         Return myCapturedOn
      End Get
   End Property

   Public ReadOnly Property CapturedBy() As String
      Get
         Return myCapturedBy
      End Get
   End Property

   Public Property FriendsWith() As List(Of Address)

   Public Overrides Function ToString() As String
      Dim locTemp As String
      locTemp = Name + ", " + FirstName + ", " + Street + ", " + ZIPCity + vbNewLine
      locTemp += "--- Friends with: ---" + vbNewLine
      For Each locAddr As Address In FriendsWith
         locTemp += "   * " + locAddr.ToShortString() + vbNewLine
      Next
      locTemp += vbNewLine
      Return locTemp
   End Function

   Public Function ToShortString() As String
      Return Name + ", " + FirstName
   End Function
End Class
```

This class also contains two functions—*ToString* and *ToShortString*—that convert an *Address* instance into a string, to simplify output.

The program now creates an original address and adds "friend" address objects to it, which are stored in the *FriendsWith* list. It then generates an identical copy of the original address in the object *locAddrCopy*.

The problem is that the identical copies are "shallow" copies of the objects. The copy takes only the top-level properties, which becomes apparent when you run the example program, as illustrated in the following:

```
Original:
=========
Pusch, Marcus, Musterstraße 22, 59555 Lippstadt
--- Friends with: ---
   * Leenings, Ramona
   * Hora, Cate
   * Löffelmann, Gabriele
```

```
Copy:
=========
Pusch (copy), Marcus, Musterstraße 22, 59555 Lippstadt
--- Friends with: ---
   * Leenings, Ramona
   * Hora, Cate
   * Löffelmann, Gabriele


Copy after changes to the original:
=================================
Pusch (copy), Marcus, Musterstraße 22, 59555 Lippstadt
--- Friends with: ---
   * Leenings, Ramona
   * Löffelmann-Beck, Cate
   * Löffelmann-Beck, Gabriele
```

The preceding example shows that when you change the *FriendsWith* property of the original object, the friends of the copy change, as well. That's because the *FriendsWith* property doesn't actually represent an instance of *List(Of Address)*; it just references the list. The elements exist only once in the generic list. As a result, this example creates only a shallow copy (or shallow clone) of the *Address* object.

It's different when you generate a deep copy (or deep clone). In the deep copy, the *ArrayList* elements are actually copied; after the copy, you have two completely independent objects with equally independent elements.

While it's relatively easy to perform a deep copy on a simple object as presented in the Address example, it's quite a different story to create deep copies of truly complex objects—and implementing a *DeepCopy* routine yourself can quickly become an enormous effort. In addition, you would not be able to design such a routine such that it works universally. It would only be useful for a specific type. If you derived a class to supplement that base class and added additional properties, you would need to modify the *DeepCopy* routine again.

Fortunately, you don't need to go to all that trouble, because you can use the .NET Framework serialization functions to handle the entire process. During serialization, the .NET Framework creates a deep copy. And because serialization doesn't necessarily mean storing the object in a file, you can use a little trick to create a universal *DeepCopy* routine that works with any serializable object, as the example in the next section illustrates.

Note The statement regarding the .NET Framework creating a deep copy during serialization is not entirely correct, because it doesn't actually create a copy of the object. It just reads its data during serialization. However, it does read down to the lowest level; thus, the combined process of serializing an object into a data stream and deserializing this data stream into a new object can be called "deep-copying" the object.

The Universal *DeepClone* Method

The following example uses the *BinarySerializer* to serialize and deserialize an object, as you've already seen, but it uses a different carrier. Rather than writing the object to be serialized into a file, it serializes the object into a *MemoryStream*, which then is converted into a *Byte* array. For deserialization, the *BinarySerializer* recreates the original object from the *Byte* array (which it first converts into a *MemoryStream* object). Because the *BinarySerializer* processes nested properties, it's easy to create a class from it that can generate a deep copy of any object marked as serializable and that contains only serializable objects.

> **Companion Content** Open the corresponding solution (.sln), which you can find in the \VB 2010 Developer Handbook\Chapter 20\UniversalDeepCloning folder.

```
Imports System.Runtime.Serialization
Imports System.Runtime.Serialization.Formatters.Binary
Imports System.IO

Public Class ADObjectCloner

    Public Shared Function DeepCopy(ByVal [Object] As Object) As Object
        Return DeserializeFromByteArray(SerializeToByteArray([Object]))
    End Function

    Shared Function SerializeToByteArray(ByVal [Object] As Object) As Byte()

        Dim retByte() As Byte
        Dim locMs As MemoryStream = New MemoryStream
        Dim locBinaryFormatter As New BinaryFormatter(Nothing, _
                    New StreamingContext(StreamingContextStates.Clone))
        locBinaryFormatter.Serialize(locMs, [Object])
        locMs.Flush()
        locMs.Close()
        retByte = locMs.ToArray()
        Return retByte

    End Function

    Shared Function DeserializeFromByteArray(ByVal by As Byte()) As Object

        Dim locObject As Object

        Dim locFs As MemoryStream = New MemoryStream(by)
        Dim locBinaryFormatter As New BinaryFormatter(Nothing, _
                    New StreamingContext(StreamingContextStates.File))
        locObject = locBinaryFormatter.Deserialize(locFs)
        locFs.Close()
        Return locObject

    End Function

End Class
```

In the following example, the main program no longer uses custom code to copy the object; it uses the *DeepCopy* function of the class (the changed passage is highlighted in bold):

```vb
Module mdlMain

    Sub Main()
        Dim locAddrOriginal As New Address("Hans", "Mustermann", "Musterstraße 22",
            "59555 Lippstadt")
        Dim locAddrCopy As Address
        locAddrOriginal.FriendsWith = New List(Of Address) From {
            New Address("Ramona", "Leenings", "Autorstr. 33", "49595 Buchhausen"),
            New Address("Cate", "Hora", "Autorstr. 34", "49595 Buchhausen"),
            New Address("Gabriele", "Löffelmann", "Autorstr. 35", "49595 Buchhausen")}

        'Output original address
        Console.WriteLine("Original:")
        Console.WriteLine("=========")
        Console.WriteLine(locAddrOriginal)

        'Create copy
        locAddrCopy = DirectCast(ADObjectCloner.DeepCopy(locAddrOriginal), Address)

        'Output copy
        Console.WriteLine("Copy:")
        Console.WriteLine("=========")
        Console.WriteLine(locAddrCopy)

        'Changes to the original:
        DirectCast(locAddrOriginal.FriendsWith(1), Address).LastName =
            "Löffelmann-Beck"
        DirectCast(locAddrOriginal.FriendsWith(2), Address).LastName =
            "Löffelmann-Beck"

        'Copy after changes to the original
        Console.WriteLine("Copy after changes to the original:")
        Console.WriteLine("==================================")
        Console.WriteLine(locAddrKopie)
        Console.ReadLine()

    End Sub

End Module
```

When you run this version of the program, you can see the difference from the previous example. The two generated objects truly are completely independent of each other. Changes to the *FriendsWith* list of the original object no longer have any impact on the copy, as is illustrated in the output here:

```
Original:
=========
Mustermann, Hans, Musterstraße 22, 59555 Lippstadt
--- Friends with: ---
    * Leenings, Ramona
    * Hora, Cate
    * Löffelmann, Gabriele


Copy:
=========
Mustermann, Hans, Musterstraße 22, 59555 Lippstadt
--- Friends with: ---
    * Leenings, Ramona
    * Hora, Cate
    * Löffelmann, Gabriele


Copy after changes to the original:
===================================
Mustermann, Hans, Musterstraße 22, 59555 Lippstadt
--- Friends with: ---
    * Leenings, Ramona
    * Hora, Cate
    * Löffelmann, Gabriele
```

Serializing Objects with Circular References

Circular references usually cause the most trouble for memory algorithms. You might be familiar with circular references from table calculations. For example, they occur when cell A references cell B, cell B references cell C, and cell C references cell A (which is not allowed in table calculations). However, the .NET Framework does permit circular references in objects. Going back to this chapter's example, such references can easily occur, because it's likely that person A considers person B a friend and person B considers person A a friend as well.

The example that follows shows the usual effects of circular references.

> **Companion Content**   Open the corresponding solution (.sln), which you can find in the
> \VB 2010 Developer Handbook\Chapter 20\CircularReferences folder.

This example contains the following changes to the *Address* class: the *ToString* function itself no longer uses the short form of the addresses to output the *FriendsWith* property. Instead, it generates the output string directly with a slightly changed version of *ToString*. You can see the change when you run the program and look at the result, as follows:

```
First address:
==============
Hora, Cate, Musterstraße 24, 32132 Buchhausen
--- Friends with: ---
    Doe, Joan, Autorenstr. 12, 32132 Buchhausen

    Leenings, Ramones, Autorenstr. 22, 32132 Buchhausen
    --- Friends with: ---
        Hora, Oli, Autorenstr. 22, 32132 Buchhausen



Second address:
==============
Leenings, Ramones, Autorenstr. 22, 32132 Buchhausen
--- Friends with: ---
    Hora, Oli, Autorenstr. 22, 32132 Buchhausen
```

The program that brought about this output looks like this:

```
Module mdlMain

    Sub Main()
        Dim locFirstAddr As New Address("Cate", "Hora", "Musterstraße 24",
            "32132 Buchhausen")
        Dim locSecondAddr As New Address("Ramones", "Leenings", "Autorenstr. 22",
            "32132 Buchhausen")
        locFirstAddr.FriendsWith = New List(Of Address) From
            {New Address("Joan", "Doe", "Autorenstr. 12", "32132 Buchhausen"),
             locSecondAddr}

        locSecondAddr.FriendsWith = New List(Of Address) From
            {New Address("Oli", "Hora", "Autorenstr. 22", "32132 Buchhausen")}

        'If you add this line, you create a circular reference
        'locSecondAddr.FriendsWith.Add(locFirstAddr)

        'Output original address
        Console.WriteLine("First address:")
        Console.WriteLine("==============")
        Console.WriteLine(locFirstAddr)

        Console.WriteLine("Second address:")
        Console.WriteLine("==============")
        Console.WriteLine(locSecondAddr)
```

```
        'Create copy
        Dim locAddrCopy As Address = DirectCast(ObjectCloner.
            DeepCopy(locFirstAddr), Address)
        Console.ReadLine()
    End Sub
End Module
```

The result and the program text tell you that the program takes nested data in the property *FriendsWith* (as well as the *List(Of Address)* behind it) into consideration. When it creates the list of people who are friends, and that person has friend entries, those also appear in the output.

However, such a programmatic approach can have fatal consequences. If person A is friends with person B, and person B is friends with person A (which certainly isn't unusual), you are dealing with a circular reference.

The *ToString* algorithm fails in this case, because it continues to call itself forever, due to the circular reference. You can test this behavior by uncommenting the bold line. When you run the program you'll eventually get this message in the output window:

```
Process is terminated due to StackOverflowException
```

The program "hangs" for a while. Depending on how well your system deals with insufficient available stack memory, you might see the exception depicted in Figure 20-5.

Caution Don't ever let a circular reference get this far. When a *StackOverflowException* occurs, it's already too late—you can rarely catch this kind of exception, and only then if you triggered it yourself. If the Common Language Runtime (CLR) triggers the exception, you've already lost. Therefore, be very careful, and avoid recursions without exit conditions at all costs.

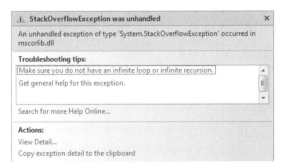

FIGURE 20-5 *ToString* of the example class fails because of the circular reference. It keeps calling itself and uses up all available stack memory.

Many serialization algorithms fail due to circular references. However, you can test whether the *DeepCopy* method works by commenting out all the *Console.WriteLine* commands. After restarting, the program goes past the following line without problems, ends properly, and therefore proves that the.NET Framework serialization algorithm handles circular references:

```
Dim locAddrCopy As Address = DirectCast(ObjectCloner.
                            DeepCopy(locFirstAddr), Address)
```

Serializing Objects of Different Versions When Using *BinaryFormatter* and *SoapFormatter* Classes

There is one important serialization issue that you need to keep in mind: when using *BinaryFormatter* or *SoapFormatter* to serialize objects to files, you might run into version conflicts when updating a program.

As an example, suppose that your application has some data represented by an object. This object encapsulates all the data of your application. Because you want to provide users with the option to save the data in a file, you are using the .NET serialization functions.

At some later date, you update your program and add some properties to the data class. But the deserialization functions of both serialization classes now expect data for some properties which did not exist in the old object model, so the attempt to deserialize data stored with the earlier version fails with an exception.

You can prevent this is by using the *SerializationBinder* class, which offers a version problem solution. You can find out more about this object in the Visual Studio Online Help.

Another way to tackle the version problem is by using XML serialization, which is discussed in the next section.

XML Serialization

XML serialization generally follows the same principles as the *BinaryFormatter* and *SoapFormatter* classes that you've already seen. But XML serialization has some important advantages:

- The "different class versions" problem does not apply to XML deserialization; the deserialization process simply assigns existing data to matching properties of the class that you want to deserialize.

- XML code is easy to read and can be imported and processed by many different programs.

Nevertheless, you must make certain compromises when creating classes for XML serialization:

- Like other classes with which you want to use .NET serialization, they must be marked with the *Serializable* attribute.

- The class you want to serialize in XML format must have a constructor (*Sub New()*) that takes no parameters.

- You can serialize only field variables or properties that have *public* access.

If your classes fulfill these requirements, nothing stands in your way.

Companion Content Open the corresponding solution (.sln), which you can find in the \VB 2010 Developer Handbook\Chapter 20\XMLSerialization folder.

This example XML serialization project is very similar to the *List(Of Type)* example from Chapter 19, "Arrays and Collections." It generates some random addresses and displays them as a list. Unlike to the example in Chapter 19, however, this version contains a menu with which you can invoke some additional functionality, as demonstrated in Figure 20-6.

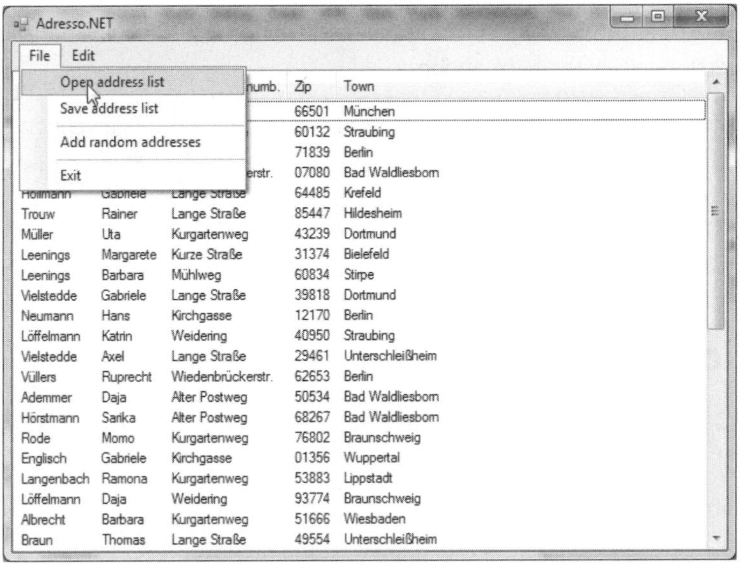

FIGURE 20-6 This update of our address management program "Adresso.NET" permits you to generate random addresses, save your created lists in files, and then load them.

You can click File | Add Random Addresses to create any desired number of random addresses. Click File | Save Address List to store the generated address list as an XML file. Similarly, you can load an XML file containing a serialized address list by clicking File | Open Address List menu item. The loaded objects then appear in the *ListView* control.

Apart from the list display and some code to handle the menu events, the example code has two central classes. You already know one of these, the *Address* class, from previous examples. Here are the changes to this version:

```
<Serializable()>
Public Class Address

    ''' <summary>
    ''' Creates a new instance of this class.
    ''' </summary>
    ''' <remarks>A constructor without parameters is required,
    ''' to make XML serialization possible.</remarks>
    Sub New()
        MyBase.New()
    End Sub

    'Constructor-creates a new instance
    Sub New(ByVal Matchcode As String, ByVal Name As String, ByVal FirstName As String, _
            ByVal Street As String, ByVal Plz As String, ByVal City As String)
        Me.Matchcode = Matchcode
        Me.Name = Name
        Me.FirstName = FirstName
        Me.Street = Street
        Me.ZIP = ZIP
        Me.City = City
    End Sub

    Public Overridable Property Matchcode() As String
    Public Overridable Property Name() As String
    Public Overridable Property FirstName() As String
    Public Overridable Property Street() As String
    Public Overridable Property ZIP() As String
    Public Overridable Property City() As String

    Public Overrides Function ToString() As String
        Return Matchcode & ":" & Name & ", " & FirstName
    End Function
End Class
```

You need three things to make XML serialization work with collections of elements of this type:

- You must apply the *Serializable* attribute to the class (see the first bolded line in the code).

- The class must have a constructor without parameters (see the next highlighted line)

- All the properties you want to serialize must be publicly accessible. In this example, the properties therefore have a *Public* modifier.

The individual *Address* elements are saved in a collection called *Addresses*, which is derived from the generic class *List(Of Address)*. (You can find more detail about generic collections in Chapter 19.) This class looks as follows:

```
<Serializable()>
Public Class Addresses
    Inherits List(Of Address)

    ''' <summary>
    ''' Creates a new instance of this class.
    ''' </summary>
    ''' <remarks></remarks>
    Sub New()
        MyBase.New()
    End Sub

    ''' <summary>
    ''' Creates a new instance of this class
    ''' and permits accepting an existing collection into it.
    ''' </summary>
    ''' <param name="collection">The generic Address collection whose elements
    ''' must be entered into this collection instance.</param>
    ''' <remarks></remarks>
    Sub New(ByVal collection As ICollection(Of Address))
        MyBase.New(collection)
    End Sub

    ''' <summary>
    ''' Serializes all elements of this collection into an XML file.
    ''' </summary>
    ''' <param name="FileName">The file name of the XML file.</param>
    ''' <remarks></remarks>
    Sub XMLSerialize(ByVal FileName As String)
        Dim locXmlWriter As New XmlSerializer(GetType(Addresses))
        Dim locXmlFile As New StreamWriter(FileName)
        locXmlWriter.Serialize(locXmlFile, Me)
        locXmlFile.Flush()
        locXmlFile.Close()
    End Sub

    ''' <summary>
    ''' Generates a new instance of this collection class from an XML file.
    ''' </summary>
    ''' <param name="FileName">Name of the XML file from which the data for
    ''' this collection instance should be taken.</param>
    ''' <returns></returns>
    ''' <remarks></remarks>
    Public Shared Function XmlDeserialize(ByVal FileName As String) As Addresses
        Dim locXmlReader As New XmlSerializer(GetType(Addresses))
        Dim locXmlFile As New StreamReader(FileName)
        Return CType(locXmlReader.Deserialize(locXmlFile), Addresses)
    End Function

    ''' <summary>
```

```
''' Returns an instance of this class with random addresses.
''' </summary>
''' <param name="Anzahl">Number of random addresses which are to be generated.</param>
''' <returns></returns>
''' <remarks></remarks>
Public Shared Function RandomAddresses(ByVal Number As Integer) As List(Of Address)
.
.   ' Left out code which is not necessary here.
.
    End Function
End Class
```

The class that saves the *Address* elements fulfills the requirements for XML serialization—it has the required attribute, a constructor without parameters, and public properties. The only public property that counts for this class (the *Items* property) is defined by the base *List(Of Address)* class and is of course available through inheritance in the derived *Addresses* class. The *Items* property provides the XML serializer with access to the individual *Address* elements and, therefore, also access to each *Address* object's data fields.

At first it might seem confusing that the method for serializing the class content is not static, but the method for deserializing it *is* static. It makes sense, though when you consider that during deserialization, no instance of the *Addresses* class exists yet; therefore, there's no member method that you could call, either, because the instance with the *Address* elements results from the deserialization process.

Serialization, though, is different, because the individual elements already exist, stored in the *Addresses* instance, so serialization can be a member (rather than static) method. Each *Address* instance accesses its own elements during serialization.

Using the two methods is simple. The two event handler methods below, which handle user menu selections, make it easy (the relevant code is highlighted in bold):

```
'Is called when the user selects File/Open Address List.
Private Sub tsmLoadAddressList_Click(ByVal sender As System.Object,
                ByVal e As System.EventArgs) Handles tsmLoadAddressList.Click

    Dim fileOpenDialog As New OpenFileDialog
    With fileOpenDialog
        .CheckFileExists = True
        .CheckPathExists = True
        .DefaultExt = "*.xml"
        .Filter = "Adresso XML files" & _
            " (" & "*.adrxml" & ")|" & "*.adrxml" & "|All Files (*.*)|*.*"
        Dim dialogboxResult As DialogResult = .ShowDialog
        If dialogboxResult = Windows.Forms.DialogResult.Cancel Then
            Exit Sub
        End If

        'Deserialize addresses
        myAddresses = Addresses.XmlDeserialize(.FileName)
```

```
                    'Display list again
                    DisplayElements()
            End With
        End Sub


        'Is called when the user selects File/Open Address List.
        Private Sub tsmSaveAddressList_Click(ByVal sender As System.Object, _
                        ByVal e As System.EventArgs) Handles tsmSaveAddressList.Click

            Dim fileSaveDialog As New SaveFileDialog

            With fileSaveDialog
                .CheckPathExists = True
                .DefaultExt = "*.xml"
                .Filter = "Adresso XML files" & " (" & "*.adrxml" & ")|" & _
                    "*.adrxml" & "|All Files (*.*)|*.*"
                Dim dialogboxResult As DialogResult = .ShowDialog
                If dialogboxResult = Windows.Forms.DialogResult.Cancel Then
                    Exit Sub
                End If

                'Serialize addresses
                myAddresses.XMLSerialize(.FileName)
            End With
        End Sub
End Class
```

Checking the Version Independence of the XML File

The XML file this program generates looks similar to Figure 20-7. You can look at your version with Notepad.

Even if you remove a data field from this XML file (as shown in Figure 20-7) and then save the file, you can still deserialize this XML file—the *Address* object created for that entry simply receives a *City* assignment during deserialization, but the deserialization process does not fail.

FIGURE 20-7 Even if you remove a data field from the XML file, the file can still be deserialized.

You can also add an additional property to the *Address* class and still use older versions of the serialization files.

Serialization Problems with *KeyedCollection*

The generic *KeyedCollection* class is ideally suitable as a collection basis for business objects for the following reasons:

- It's type-safe, because it's generic.

- You can retrieve objects either via an index *or* a key. The object itself must provide the key, as discussed in Chapter 19.

- Because the *KeyedCollection* has an index, it provides an enumeration function for *ForEach* and at the same time it also implements dictionary functionality.

For flexibility, this class is hard to beat. However, that flexibility can be a problem when the key data type and indexer get in each other's way. Suppose that you have a class like the one shown in the following example, which provides a unique key of a business object via an ID. This type of application is quite common, because database programs often contain tables that use an *Integer* as a primary key and main index.

> **Companion Content** Open the corresponding solution (.sln), which you can find in the \VB 2010 Developer Handbook\Chapter 20\KeyedCollection folder.

```
Public Class Address
.
.
.

    Sub New(ByVal IDAddress As Integer, ByVal LastName As String, ByVal FirstName As String)
        myIDAddress = IDAddress
        myLastName = LastName
        myFirstName = FirstName
    End Sub
.
.
.

    Public Property IDAddress() As Integer
.
.
.

    Public Property LastName() As String
.
.
.

    Public Property FirstName() As String
.
.
.
End Class
```

This business object saves a simple address (some properties have been omitted to save space).

The important point here is that each business object of this type is uniquely identifiable by its *IDAddress* property—and the problem is that this property has the type *Integer*. A *KeyedCollection* collection implementation based on this class illustrates why this poses a problem. The *IDAddress* property is ideal for creating a unique key:

```
Public Class Addresses
    Inherits System.Collections.ObjectModel.KeyedCollection(Of Integer, Address)

    Protected Overrides Function GetKeyForItem(ByVal item As Address) As Integer
        Return item.IDAddress
    End Function
End Class
```

It's perfectly possible to build a *KeyedCollection* in this structure without problems

```
    Protected Overrides Sub OnLoad(ByVal e As System.EventArgs)
        MyBase.OnLoad(e)
        myAddresses.Add(New Address(2, "Löffelmann", "Klaus"))
        myAddresses.Add(New Address(4, "Leenings", "Ramona"))
        myAddresses.Add(New Address(6, "Sonntag", "Miriam"))
        myAddresses.Add(New Address(8, "Dröge", "Ruprecht"))
        myAddresses.Add(New Address(10, "Vielstedde", "Anja"))
    End Sub
```

Unfortunately, retrieving the elements is problematic when the key has the *Integer* data type, as shown in Figure 20-8.

```
Private Sub btnPrintObjects_Click(ByVal sender As System.Object,
    For count As Integer = 0 To 4
        Debug.Print(myAddress(
    Next
    End Sub
```
Item**(key As Integer)** As KeyedCollection.Address
Gets the element with the specified key.
key: *The key of the element to get.*

FIGURE 20-8 When the key is an *Integer* type, the *KeyedCollection* only offers a single signature for retrieving elements.

So far this makes sense. Because the indexer and the key are the same data type, neither the compiler nor .NET Framework can determine which "version" of the retrieval function to use (the indexer or the key). The method signature determines which version is used, and because in this case both use the same type, there's no difference between the signatures. Therefore, there is only one way to get to the element.

It would be different if the key were the *Long* data type.[1] In this case, the indexer executes when you pass an *Integer* and the key executes when you passed a *Long*. IntelliSense would then offer you two possibilities for retrieving the elements (see Figure 20-9).

---

[1] Please read this section all the way through, before switching all your *KeyedCollection*-based collection classes to the data type *Long* as key!

```
Private Sub btnPrintObjects_Click(ByVal sender As System.Object, ByVal e As System.EventArgs)
    For count As Integer = 0 To 4
        Debug.Print(myAddress(
    Next
End Sub
```

▲ 1 of 2 ▼ Item(**index As Integer**) As KeyedCollection.Address
Gets or sets the element at the specified index.
index: The zero-based index of the element to get or set.

```
Private Sub btnObjectS
    Dim writer As New X
    Dim file As New Str
    writer.Serialize(file, myAddress)
    file.Close()
End Sub
```

▲ 2 of 2 ▼ Item(**key As Long**) As KeyedCollection.Address
Gets the element with the specified key.
key: The key of the element to get.

FIGURE 20-9 If key and indexer have different data types, the *KeyedCollection* provides two possibilities for reaching an individual element.

This *Integer* vs. *Integer* issue isn't actually such a big deal, because thanks to the enumerator implemented by *KeyedCollection*, you can still either retrieve the objects via the key or retrieve them one after the other in a *ForEach* loop.

It does become problematic, however, when you try to serialize the data. Take a look at what's happening in Figure 20-10.

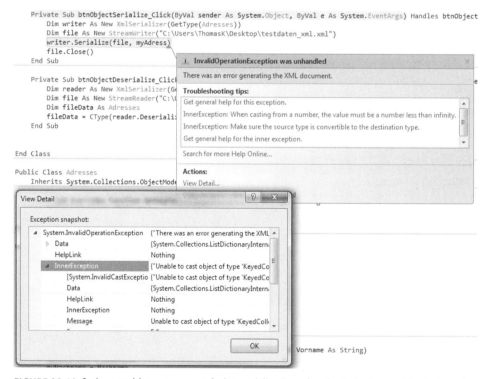

FIGURE 20-10 Serious problems can occur during serialization when both the key and the indexer have the *Integer* type.

The serialization algorithm is obviously unable to handle having two of the same data types. It tries to access the objects sequentially via a counter variable, which the indexer of *KeyedCollection* misinterprets as a key. Because in this example the IDs don't correspond to the numbering sequence of the objects, the attempt fails and the program exits with an exception, as shown in the preceding figure.

The takeaway is: when using *KeyedCollection*, if your key has an *Integer* value, ensure that you use the data type *Long* for the key so that the compiler can recognize *Integer* as the indexer. Alternatively, you can write a key helper class to access the elements.

Chapter 21
Attributes and Reflection

If you are developing larger applications, you're likely to use attributes. Attributes are special classes that don't perform any function themselves; instead, they advise other code that an element in your application must be handled in a specific way.

You can use both attributes that the Microsoft .NET Framework provides along with those that you design on your own. If you build your own, you must understand the techniques that make attribute recognition at runtime possible—that's where *reflection* comes into play.

Reflection techniques in the .NET Framework basically represent a code analyst; they help you gain information about assemblies, classes, methods, properties, and other elements at runtime. Attributes are among these elements. You can use reflection to determine whether a certain method of a class or class instance has a certain attribute. In particular, custom attributes and reflection are closely connected, which is why they're both included in this chapter.

Here are a few practical examples that illustrate the enormous number of options attributes and reflection have to offer:

- You want a class in your database application to automatically synchronize to existing database fields: Some classes represent tables; the properties of these classes represent the individual data fields. Thanks to attributes, you can mark these classes and synchronize them with the database at runtime.

- Forms can create themselves based on certain classes and take over input or the job of changing a class instance.

- A class derived from the *ListView* control can automatically display an array containing instances of specially marked classes. Attributes then specify which properties of an array element should be used as columns. You can control the order of the columns with other attributes.

These are just some examples of the power of attributes. You saw another in the *Serializable* attribute, which you learned about in Chapter 20, "Serialization." That attribute specifies that a class or property can be serialized. These are wide-ranging examples that are intended to give you a broad idea of the power of attributes and reflection.

Introduction to Attributes

You use attributes very differently than regular classes (even though they are created the same way). Attributes give classes or procedures special properties. Just like the bold high-lighted lines in the code examples of this book don't change the meaning of the code, the bold attribute still fulfills its purpose; **it draws your attention to the marked text**, essentially telling you to read that code more carefully.

You "mark" a class or procedure in Microsoft Visual Basic with an attribute, by putting it in front of the class or procedure definition, enclosed in less-than and greater-than (<>) characters. The specific syntax is as follows:

```
<MyAttribute(OptionalParameter)> Class MyClass

End Class
```

Because lines with attributes can become unnecessarily long and difficult to read, it's best to wrap the line as shown below. Remember that as of Visual Basic 2010, you no longer need to use the underscore character (_) to wrap the line (see also Chapter 4, "Introduction to Windows Forms—Designers and Code Editor by Example"):

```
<MyAttribute(OptionalParameter)>
Class MyClass

End Class
```

The impact of an attribute to the code that follows is not controlled by the attribute class itself; it's controlled exclusively by instances that examine the elements that have attributes. Attribute classes are usually classes that don't provide any real functionality—they are just containers for information. Remember this important concept when you're planning to use attributes.

Important Attribute classes always end with *"Attribute"*, but you don't need to append the name *Attribute* to be able to use an attribute-based class for marking purposes.

Using Attributes with *ObsoleteAttribute*

The purpose of the *ObsoleteAttribute* class is to mark a procedure as *deprecated* (a procedure that might no longer be available in future versions). Suppose that you developed a class library for .NET a year ago. Now, you want to make an updated and reengineered version available to your customers. During the class overhaul, you realized that certain functions are no longer necessary, because your class library is now much more automated, or because it makes sense to replace certain functions with newer, more efficient ones.

Of course, you can't just remove the redundant functions in the new version. Even if users of your class library compile their programs with your new version, any calls to the older functions will fail (or the program won't compile in the first place). By using the *Obsolete* attribute, you warn the user not to use the deprecated functions. Just put the *ObsoleteAttribute* in front of the respective class or procedure and add a comment.

> **Companion Content** Open the corresponding solution (.sln), which you can find in the
> \VB 2010 Developer Handbook\Chapter 21\AttributesDemo folder.

After you have loaded the sample program, take a look at the source code and how the error list responds to using a certain property. Figure 21-1 shows the resulting Error List.

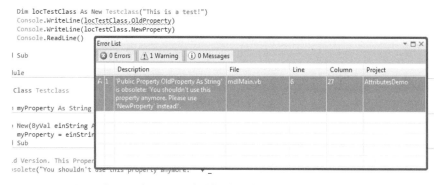

FIGURE 21-1 Removing an element marked by the *Obsolete* attribute triggers a warning

In the example, the property *OldProperty* of the class *TestClass* has been marked with the *Obsolete* attribute. The Visual Basic compiler recognizes this attribute and displays a warning in the error list. The *ObsoleteAttribute* class itself has nothing to do with the text output, other than providing the text for it. The actual text output is triggered by the Visual Basic Compiler or the development environment.

Tip In the preceding example, even though *OldProperty* was marked with the *ObsoleteAttribute* class, the property can still be used and the program will compile and run. If you so choose, you can force a marked obsolete member to generate a compiler error—ensuring that any program that uses the marked member no longer compiles or runs. To do that, change the second (*Boolean*) parameter behind the message string in the *ObsoleteAttribute* constructor to *True*.

Visual Basic-Specific Attributes

You have already encountered many of the most important attributes in previous chapters; however, there are a few special attributes just for Visual Basic, These special attributes are listed in Table 21-1.

Note The special attributes are not restricted to use only in Visual Basic—and of course you can use any .NET Framework attributes in your own Visual Basic applications, as well. To get a list of all the attributes in the .NET Framework, visit the Online Help for the *Attribute* class and display all the derived classes.

TABLE 21-1 Visual Basic-Specific Attributes

Attribute	Purpose
COMClassAttribute class	Instructs the compiler to display the class as a Component Object Model (COM) object.
VBFixedStringAttribute class	Specifies the size of a string with a fixed length in a structure intended for use in file input and output functions. Visual Basic-specific.
VBFixedArrayAttribute class	Specifies the size of a fixed array in a structure, which should be used with file input and output functions. Visual Basic-specific.
SerializableAttribute class	Specifies that the class can be serialized.
MarshalAsAttribute class	Specifies how to marshal a parameter between Visual Basic-managed code and unmanaged code of, for example, a Windows API. Managed by the Common Language Runtime (CLR).
AttributeUsageAttribute class	Specifies how an attribute can be used.
DllImportAttribute class	Specifies that the method marked with the attribute is implemented in an unmanaged DLL, for example, for *P/Invoke* operating system calls.

Introduction to Reflection

Before connecting the topics of reflection and attributes in the next sections, it's worth exploring what the reflection classes have to offer by themselves.

Reflection refers to techniques a program can use to obtain more information about classes, analyze classes, and create class instances programmatically.

Of course, the latter is no great feat. After all, you do it all the time by using the constructor of a class. But that's not what this is about. The goal here is to be able to use classes that your program is unaware of when you start it.

For example, assume that you need to provide a function that accepts an arbitrary object as a parameter and returns the value of each property of that object on the screen. Normally, you wouldn't be able to do this because you can't know in advance which object type to expect, so you also don't know its property names. Therefore, you can't retrieve the values of these properties.

So to make that scenario work, you must find a way to analyze an object and discover what properties it has. After determining the property names, you need to be able to retrieve the value of each property, and then finally, display those values on the screen.

> **Companion Content**   Open the corresponding solution (.sln), which you can find in the
> \VB 2010 Developer Handbook\Chapter 21\Reflection01 folder.

The *Address* class that you know from Chapter 20 forms a central part of this example. The *Main* procedure of this console application creates a new *Address* instance and displays the results of examining that instance in the console window, as the following output shows:

```
Attributes of class:Reflection01.Address
Standard attributes:
    *AutoLayout, AnsiClass, Class, Public, Serializable

List of Members:
    *get_LastName, Method
    ------------
    *set_LastName, Method
    ------------
    *get_FirstName, Method
    ------------
    *set_FirstName, Method
    ------------
    *get_Street, Method
    ----------
    *set_Street, Method
    ----------
    *get_ZipCity, Method
    ------------
    *set_ZipCity, Method
```

```
     ------------
*get_IsFriendWith, Method
     ----------------
*set_IsFriendWith, Method
     ----------------
*get_DateCreated, Method
*get_CreatedBy, Method
*ToString, Method
*ToShortString, Method
*Equals, Method
     ------
*GetHashCode, Method
     -----------
*GetType, Method
     -------
*.ctor, Constructor
*.ctor, Constructor
*LastName, Property
 Value: Ardelean
*FirstName, Property
 Value: Adriana
*Street, Property
 Value: Book Ave. 100
*ZipCity, Property
 Value: De 32154 Publish Valley
*IsFriendWith, Property
 Value: System.Collections.Generic.List'1[Reflection01.Address]
*DateCreated, Property
 Value: 7/2/2011 2:17:42 PM
*CreatedBy, Property
 Value: klauslo
```

This program is capable not only of retrieving an (almost) complete member list for the passed-in object instance, but it can also display the values of those properties.

Before taking a closer look at how this program works, we'll explain a few basics about types and reflection that can assist you in understanding the rest of this discussion.

The Type Class as the Origin for All Type Examinations

The classes and methods located in the *Reflection* namespace of .NET Framework are key here. The starting point for all reflection operations is the *Type* class, which can determine the type of an object variable at runtime.

You can't instantiate the *Type* class itself, because it's an abstract class; however, you can use it to determine the type of an existing object. The *Type* class itself doesn't belong to the *Reflection* namespace—but you need it to retrieve (along with other classes in this namespace) information about the type declarations of an object that you want to examine, for example constructors, methods, fields, properties, and events. You also use these functions to retrieve information about the module and the assembly in which the class is defined.

Each object in the .NET Framework provides a *GetType* function with which you can determine the *Type* object upon which it is based. You can also use the static version of this function to create a *Type* object when you know the fully-qualified name of the type. By using *TypeOf* in conjunction with the *Is* operator, you can perform type comparisons. Alternatively, the *Is* operator also works with *GetType*, which you can also use as an operator. The following code snippets demonstrate typical usage of these functions:

```
'A few Type experiments:
Dim locFriend As New Address("Adriana", "Ardelean", "Book Ave. 100", "De 32154
➥Publisher Valley")

Dim locTest As New Address("Klaus", "Löffelmann", "One Microsoft Way", "WA 99999
➥Redmond")
Dim locType1, locType2 As Type
locType1 = locTest.GetType

'Important: TypeOf works only together with the Is operator:
If TypeOf locTest Is Reflection01.Address Then
    Console.WriteLine("Address type recognized!")
Else
    Console.WriteLine("Address type not recognized!")
End If

'And this is also an alternative with does the same:
If locTest.GetType Is GetType(Reflection01.Address) Then
    Console.WriteLine("Address type recognized!")
Else
    Console.WriteLine("Address type not recognized!")
End If

'This is how it works when two type object
'must be compared to each other:

locType2 = GetType(Address)                     ' Standard: GetType as operator
locType2 = GetType(Reflection01.Address)        ' Alternative: with namespace
locType2 = Type.GetType("Reflection01.Address") ' Alternative: from string

Console.WriteLine("The type " + locType1.FullName + _
    CStr(IIf(locType1 Is locType2, " corresponds to ", " does not correspond to ")) +
    "the type " + locType2.FullName)

'Find out whether a type variable (e.g. base class or interface)
'is compatible to the actual instantiated object.
Dim addressWithBirthDate As New DerivedAddress With
    {.Name = "Leenings", .FirstName = "Ramona", .Street = "Irgendwoweg 12",
     .ZIPCity = "Someplace-Hausen",
     .FriendsWith = New List(Of Address) From {locTest, locFriend},
     .BirthDate = #7/24/1991#}

If GetType(Address).IsAssignableFrom(addressWithBirthDate.GetType) Then
    Console.WriteLine(addressWithBirthDate.ToShortString &
                      " can be saved in the type 'Address'.")
End If

Console.ReadLine()
```

This program produces the following output:

```
Address type recognized!
Address type recognized!
The type Reflection01.Address corresponds to the type Reflection01.Address
Leenings, Ramona can be saved in the type 'Address'.
```

> **Note** The sample project also contains this code snippet (directly after the *Main* procedure which ends in *Exit Sub*). If you want to experiment with it, just comment out *Exit Sub*.

After you have obtained a *Type* object in this manner, you can retrieve further information about that type by using its functions.

Class Analysis Functions Provided by a Type Object

Table 21-2 provides an overview of the most important functions and class types provided by the *Type* class, which help you to get more details about the type:

TABLE 21-2 The Most Important Functions for Retrieving Information About a Type

Type class function	Task
Assembly	Retrieves the assembly which defines the type. Return type: *System. Reflection.Assembly*
AssemblyQualifiedName	Retrieves the fully-qualified assembly name. Return type: *String*
Attributes	Retrieves a bit combination (*Flags Enum*) that provides information about all non-custom attributes. Return type: *TypeAttributes*
BaseType	Retrieves the type from which the specified type inherits directly. Return type: *Type*
FullName	Retrieves the fully-qualified name (including namespace) of the specified type. Return type: *String*
GetCustomAttributes	Retrieves an array with all the custom attributes. If no custom attributes were defined for the type, the function returns *Nothing*. Return type: *Object()*
GetEvent	Retrieves the *EventInfo* object of a known event. The event name is passed as a string. Return type: *EventInfo*
GetEvents	Retrieves a list (an array) containing all the object events. Return type: *EventInfo()*

Type class function	Task
GetField	Retrieves the *FieldInfo* object of a known public field. The field name is passed as a string. Return type: *FieldInfo*
	Important: Frequently, fields are not defined as *public*, or (unlike properties) aren't available when there is an instance of the class you are examining. Therefore it's important that you use the so-called *BindingFlags* (which control what you are determining) to specify that you are examining an instance of the class (*Reflection.Binding Flags.Instance*) and that you want to retrieve non-public elements (*Reflection.BindingFlags.NonPublic*). Otherwise, you won't get a result for the defined private field variables of an instance:
| | ```
Dim retField=ClassInstance.GetType().GetField(
        Reflection.BindingFlags.NonPublic Or Reflection.
BindingFlags.Instance)
``` |
	Note: If you want to retrieve everything other than private fields, just leave out the *BindingFlags* parameter.
GetFields	Retrieves a list (as array) with all the public fields of the object. Return type: *FieldInfo()*
	Important: (see *GetField*) You must specify *BindingFlags*, to query for instance and non-public members. A loop that iterates through fields looks as follows:
| | ```
For Each item In Me.GetType().GetFields(
        Reflection.BindingFlags.NonPublic Or Reflection.
BindingFlags.Instance)
    Debug.Print(item.ToString)
Next
``` |
GetMember	Retrieves the *MemberInfo* object of a *member* (whose name you know) of the object. A *member* is a parent category of an object element, and can therefore be a property, method, event, or field. Using the *MemberType* property of a *MemberInfo* object, you can determine what kind of object element it is. Return type: *MemberInfo*
GetMembers	Retrieves a list (an array) containing all elements (*member*) of the object. Return type: *MemberInfo()*
GetProperty	Retrieves the *PropertyInfo* object of a property whose name you know. The property name is passed as a string. Return type: *PropertyInfo*
GetProperties	Retrieves a list (an array) of all properties of the object. Return type: *PropertyInfo()*

With that information in hand, take a look at the example program that follows. In essence, it uses the *Type.GetMembers* function to retrieve information about any desired object.

```
Module mdlMain

    Sub Main()
        Dim locAddress As New Address("Adriana", "Ardelean", , "Book Ave. 100",
            "De 32154 Publisher Valley") With
            {.FriendsWith = New List(Of Address) From
                {New Address "Klaus", "Löffelmann", "One Microsoft Way",
                "WA 99999 Redmond")}}

        PrintObjectInfo(locAddress)
        Console.ReadLine()
    End Sub

    Sub PrintObjectInfo(ByVal [Object] As Object)
        'Find out the object type to access the object content
        Dim locTypeInstance As Type = [Object].GetType

        'Return the attributes that are not custom:
        Console.WriteLine("Attributes of the class:" + locTypeInstance.FullName)
        Console.WriteLine("Default attribute:")
        Console.WriteLine("    *" + locTypeInstance.Attributes.ToString())
        Console.WriteLine()

        'Find out members and their optional attributes
        Dim locMembers() As MemberInfo

        'Gets everything (except for non-public elements);
        'BindingFlags can be left out:
        locMembers = locTypeInstance.GetMembers(BindingFlags.Default)

        'Makes sure that only non-public fields are retrieved:
        'locMembers = locTypeInstance.GetMembers(
        '    BindingFlags.Instance Or BindingFlags.NonPublic)
        Console.WriteLine("Member list:")
        For Each locMember As MemberInfo In locMembers
            Console.WriteLine("    *" + locMember.Name + ", " _
                            + locMember.MemberType.ToString)
            If locMember.GetCustomAttributes(True).Length > 0 Then
                Console.WriteLine("    " + New String("-"c, locMember.Name.Length))
            End If

            'If we are dealing with properties, we are also retrieving the value.
            If locMember.MemberType = MemberTypes.Property Then
                Dim locPropertyInfo As PropertyInfo = DirectCast(locMember,
                    PropertyInfo)
                Dim value = locPropertyInfo.GetValue([Object], Nothing)
                If value IsNot Nothing Then
                    Console.WriteLine("    Value: " + value.ToString)
                End If
            End If
```

```
                'Return field information when the appropriate
                'Bindingflags were specified.
                If locMember.MemberType = MemberTypes.Field Then
                    Dim locFieldInfo As FieldInfo = DirectCast(locMember, FieldInfo)
                    Dim value = locFieldInfo.GetValue([Object])
                    If value IsNot Nothing Then
                        Console.WriteLine("     Value: " + value.ToString)
                    End If
                End If
            Next
        End Sub
End Module
```

Tip To determine all elements of a type, you can use the function *GetMembers*, as shown in the preceding example (the first highlighted block). You can then examine the *MemberType* of each single element to find out what element type you are dealing with (property, method, and so on).

Note Keep in mind that each property also has methods. Within .NET Framework, properties are treated as such. They use either a *set_* or *get_* prefix to differentiate the manner of access. Therefore, the element list you determine with *GetMembers* contains three elements for each property (two methods and one property—assuming, of course, that it's not a read-only or write-only property).

Important With a *BindingsFlag* enum/flag combination, you can specify which elements that you want to investigate. For example, the code example has two lines that call *GetMembers*, but one is commented out. When you uncomment the second definition, `locMembers = locTypeInstance.GetMembers(BindingFlags.Instance Or BindingFlags.NonPublic)`, the function returns all non-public members of the instance and their contents—including all non-public field variables, in addition to the two methods defined as *Protected*, which inherit *Address* from *Object*. This is interesting, because it illustrates how the Visual Basic compiler has set up the appropriate backing fields all by itself, by using automatically implemented properties in the *Address* test class:

```
Attributes of class:Reflection01.Address

Standard attributes:

    *AutoLayout, AnsiClass, Class, Public, Serializable


List of Members:

    *Finalize, Method

    --------

    *MemberwiseClone, Method
```

```
             --------------

 *myDateCreated, Field

  Value: 7/2/2011 2:26:30 PM

 *myCreatedBy, Field

  Value: klauslo

 *_LastName, Field

   ---------

  Value: Ardelean

 *_FirstName, Field

   ----------

  Value: Adriana

 *_Street, Field

   -------

  Value: Book Ave. 100

 *_ZipCity, Field

   ---------

  Value: De 32154 Publisher Valley

 *_IsFriendWith, Field

   -------------

  Value: System.Collections.Generic.List'1[Reflection01.Address]
```

Object Hierarchy of *MemberInfo* and Casting to a Specific Info Type

MemberInfo is the base class for all, more specific reflection-*XXXInfo* objects. Derived from it are:

- *EventInfo*, which saves information about class events.

- *FieldInfo*, which saves information about the public fields of a class.

- *MethodInfo*, which saves information about class methods.

- *PropertyInfo*, which saves information about class properties.

When retrieving information about a class or an object with the *GetMembers* function, the more specific info objects in the individual *MemberInfo* objects of the *MemberInfo* arrays are

boxed. However, using a *CType* or *DirectCast* statement, you can convert them back into the actual info type, which allows you to access the properties of the info type:

```
If locMember.MemberType = MemberTypes.Property Then
    Dim locPropertyInfo As PropertyInfo = DirectCast(locMember, PropertyInfo)
End If
```

Determining Property Values with *PropertyInfo* at Runtime

Having obtained a *PropertyInfo* object in this manner, you can then retrieve the property value. When doing so, there are two preconditions: such a type must exist, and it must have been previously instantiated. To retrieve the property value, call the *PropertyInfo.GetValue* method. The example program uses *GetValue* to display the current content of a property as text.

> **Tip** Because every class has at least a default implementation of the *ToString* function, requesting the string value is safe (although whether *ToString* returns a usable result depends on the implementation of the *ToString* method of that particular class).

The following example program also contains code that determines the values of properties or field variables for objects of a previously unknown type:

```
'If we are dealing with properties, we are also retrieving the value.
If locMember.MemberType = MemberTypes.Property Then
    Dim locPropertyInfo As PropertyInfo = DirectCast(locMember, PropertyInfo)
    Dim value = locPropertyInfo.GetValue([Object], Nothing)
    If value IsNot Nothing Then
        Console.WriteLine("    Value: " + value.ToString)
    End If
End If

'Return field information when the appropriate
'Bindingflags were specified.
If locMember.MemberType = MemberTypes.Field Then
    Dim locFieldInfo As FieldInfo = DirectCast(locMember, FieldInfo)
    Dim value = locFieldInfo.GetValue([Object])
    If value IsNot Nothing Then
        Console.WriteLine("    Value: " + value.ToString)
    End If
End If
```

To call *GetValue* for properties, you need to pass at least two parameters: the first parameter specifies the object from which the specified property value should be retrieved. Because some properties take parameters, in such cases you need to pass an *Object* array that contains the parameters as the second parameter. If you are using a property that does not require parameters, pass *Nothing* as the second parameter, as shown in the example.

For fields, *GetValue* requires only one parameter—an object variable that points to the object whose field value you want to determine.

Creating Custom Attributes and Recognizing Them at Runtime

Next to manual data serialization, recognizing and reacting to custom attributes at runtime is probably the most frequent way of using reflection techniques. As mentioned earlier, attributes serve to mark classes or class elements. Attribute classes normally don't have any real functionality, because only very rarely is their class code executed.

> **Companion Content** Open the corresponding solution (.sln), which you can find in the \VB 2010 Developer Handbook\Chapter 21\Reflection02 folder.

The code file mdlMain.vb contains the definition of an *Attribute* class, which appears as follows:

```
'Create custom attribute
<AttributeUsage(AttributeTargets.All)>
Public Class MyAttribute
    Inherits Attribute

    Private myName As String

    Public Sub New(ByVal name As String)
        myName = name
    End Sub 'New

    Public ReadOnly Property Name() As String
        Get
            Return myName
        End Get
    End Property
End Class
```

You can restrict an *Attribute* class so that it can be used on only specific elements of a class, which is the purpose of the *AttributeUsageAttribute*. By choosing one or more of the values from enum *AttributeTargets*, as shown in the preceding code example, you specify the class elements to which your *Attribute* class applies.

It's important that you derive custom *Attribute* classes from the *Attribute* base class with *Inherits*, so that reflection functions can later recognize them as attributes.

This following extended example program again uses the *Address* class with *Attribute* decorations in specific places. It also uses the new *MyAttribute* class shown in the previous example. As you can see in the code, the *MyAttribute* class accepts a parameter, a name, that's purely for informative purposes here. The *Address* class uses the *String* parameter, to determine the context in which the attribute is used. The *Address* class containing the custom attribute looks as follows (the *Attribute* usage is highlighted in bold).

Note The example proves that you can leave off the *"Attribute"* appendix from an attribute's name, as long as the attribute class correctly ends in *Attribute* (as mentioned earlier).

```vb
<Serializable(), My("Above the class")> _
Public Class Address

    Private myCapturedOn As DateTime
    Private myCapturedBy As String

    <My("Above the constructor")>
    Sub New(ByVal FirstName As String, ByVal Name As String,
            ByVal Street As String, ByVal ZIPCity As String)
        'Constructor inserte all member data
        Me.Name = Name
        Me.FirstName = FirstName
        Me.Street = Street
        Me.ZIPCity = ZIPCity
        myCapturedOn = DateTime.Now
        myCapturedBy = Environment.UserName
    End Sub

    <My("Above a property ")>
    Public Property LastName() As String
    Public Property FirstName() As String
    Public Property Street() As String
    Public Property ZIPCity() As String
    Public Property FriendsWith() As List(Of Address)

    Public ReadOnly Property CapturedOn() As DateTime
        Get
            Return myCapturedOn
        End Get
    End Property

    Public ReadOnly Property CapturedBy() As String
        Get
            Return myCapturedBy
        End Get
    End Property

    <My("Above a method")>
    Public Overrides Function ToString() As String
        Dim locTemp As String
        locTemp = Name + ", " + FirstName + ", " + Street + ", " + ZIPCity + vbNewLine
        locTemp += "--- Friends with: ---" + vbNewLine
        For Each locAdr As Address In FriendsWith
            locTemp += "  * " + locAdr.ToShortString() + vbNewLine
        Next
        locTemp += vbNewLine
        Return locTemp
    End Function
```

```
    Public Function ToShortString() As String
        Return Name + ", " + FirstName
    End Function
End Class
```

In this case, the goal of reflection is to recognize the attributes at runtime. The evaluation program itself, which finds attributes, becomes easier to understand if you first look at the result. When you run the program, it generates the following screen output:

```
Attributes of class:Reflection02.Address
Standard attributes:
    *AutoLayout, AnsiClass, Class, Public, Serializable

Custom attributes:
    * System.SerializableAttribute
    * Reflection02.ThatsMyAttribute

List of members:
    *get_LastName, Method
     ------------
         * System.Diagnostics.DebuggerNonUserCodeAttribute
           TypeId: System.Diagnostics.DebuggerNonUserCodeAttribute
    *set_LastName, Method
     ------------
         * System.Diagnostics.DebuggerNonUserCodeAttribute
           TypeId: System.Diagnostics.DebuggerNonUserCodeAttribute
    *get_FirstName, Method
     -------------
         * System.Diagnostics.DebuggerNonUserCodeAttribute
           TypeId: System.Diagnostics.DebuggerNonUserCodeAttribute
    *set_FirstName, Method
     -------------
         * System.Diagnostics.DebuggerNonUserCodeAttribute
           TypeId: System.Diagnostics.DebuggerNonUserCodeAttribute
    *get_Street, Method
     ----------
         * System.Diagnostics.DebuggerNonUserCodeAttribute
           TypeId: System.Diagnostics.DebuggerNonUserCodeAttribute
    *set_Street, Method
     ----------
         * System.Diagnostics.DebuggerNonUserCodeAttribute
           TypeId: System.Diagnostics.DebuggerNonUserCodeAttribute
    *get_ZipCity, Method
     -----------
         * System.Diagnostics.DebuggerNonUserCodeAttribute
           TypeId: System.Diagnostics.DebuggerNonUserCodeAttribute
    *set_ZipCity, Method
     -----------
         * System.Diagnostics.DebuggerNonUserCodeAttribute
           TypeId: System.Diagnostics.DebuggerNonUserCodeAttribute
    *get_IsFriendWith, Method
     ----------------
         * System.Diagnostics.DebuggerNonUserCodeAttribute
           TypeId: System.Diagnostics.DebuggerNonUserCodeAttribute
    *set_IsFriendWith, Method
```

```
----------------
       * System.Diagnostics.DebuggerNonUserCodeAttribute
         TypeId: System.Diagnostics.DebuggerNonUserCodeAttribute
*get_DateCreated, Method
*get_CreatedBy, Method
*ToString, Method
 --------
       * Reflection02.ThatsMyAttribute
         Name: Above a method
         TypeId: Reflection02.ThatsMyAttribute
*ToShortString, Method
*Equals, Method
 ------
       * System.Runtime.TargetedPatchingOptOutAttribute
         Reason: Performance critical to inline across NGen image boundaries
         TypeId: System.Runtime.TargetedPatchingOptOutAttribute
*GetHashCode, Method
 -----------
       * System.Runtime.TargetedPatchingOptOutAttribute
         Reason: Performance critical to inline across NGen image boundaries
         TypeId: System.Runtime.TargetedPatchingOptOutAttribute
*GetType, Method
 -------
       * System.Security.SecuritySafeCriticalAttribute
         TypeId: System.Security.SecuritySafeCriticalAttribute
*.ctor, Constructor
*.ctor, Constructor
 -----
       * Reflection02.ThatsMyAttribute
         Name: Above the constructor
         TypeId: Reflection02.ThatsMyAttribute
*LastName, Property
 --------
       * Reflection02.ThatsMyAttribute
         Name: Above a property
         TypeId: Reflection02.ThatsMyAttribute
 Value: Ardelean
*FirstName, Property
 Value: Adriana
*Street, Property
 Value: Book Ave. 100
*ZipCity, Property
 Value: De 32154 Publisher Valley
*IsFriendWith, Property
 Value: System.Collections.Generic.List'1[Reflection02.Address]
*DateCreated, Property
 Value: 7/2/2011 3:16:29 PM
*CreatedBy, Property
 Value: klauslo
```

The passages that refer to the attribute itself, as well as its valid parameter, appear in bold type.

Determining Custom Attributes at Runtime

To discover custom attributes, call the function *GetCustomAttributes*. You can apply this function to either a type (the class or structure itself) or a single member. It takes a *Boolean* value as a parameter, which specifies whether it should also examine types in the object inheritance tree for attributes (when *True*).

Because the parameters of an attribute class are usually retrievable as properties, you can use *GetType* to retrieve its type instance (after you have determined the attribute), and then list its properties with *GetProperties*. Finally, you can call *GetValue* to read the actual value of the attribute property.

The modified sample program shows how this works. Initially it reads a possible custom attribute that applies to the entire class, and then it examines each individual class member for attributes:

```
Module mdlMain


    Sub Main()

        Dim locAddress As New Address("Adriana", "Ardelean", "Book Ave. 100", "De
    ➥32154 Publisher Valley") With
            {.IsFriendWith = New List(Of Address) From
                {New Address("Klaus", "Löffelmann", "One Microsoft Way", "WA 99999
    ➥Redmond")}}

        PrintObjectInfo(locAddress)
        Console.ReadLine()

    End Sub
    Sub PrintObjectInfo(ByVal [Object] As Object)
        'Find out the object type to access the object content
        Dim locTypeInstance As Type = [Object].GetType

        'Return the attributes that are not custom:
        Console.WriteLine("Attribute of the class:" + locTypeInstance.FullName)
        Console.WriteLine("Default attribute:")
        Console.WriteLine("    *" + locTypeInstance.Attributes.ToString())
        Console.WriteLine()

        'Determine custom attributes of the class
        '(*Only* custom attributes can be determined this way)
        Console.WriteLine("Custom attributes:")
        For Each locAttribute As Attribute In
            locTypeInstance.GetCustomAttributes(True)
            Console.WriteLine("    * " + locAttribute.ToString())
        Next
        Console.WriteLine()
```

```
        'Find out members and their optional attributes
        Dim locMembers() As MemberInfo
        locMembers = locTypeInstance.GetMembers()
        Console.WriteLine("Member list:")
        For Each locMember As MemberInfo In locMembers
            Console.WriteLine("    *" + locMember.Name + ", " _
                            + locMember.MemberType.ToString)
            If locMember.GetCustomAttributes(True).Length > 0 Then
                Console.WriteLine("    " + New String("-"c, locMember.Name.Length))
                For Each locAttribute As Attribute In _
                    locMember.GetCustomAttributes(False)
                    Console.WriteLine("        * " + locAttribute.ToString())
                    For Each locPropertyInfo As PropertyInfo In _
                        locAttribute.GetType.GetProperties
                        Console.Write("        " + locPropertyInfo.Name)
                        Console.WriteLine(": " + locPropertyInfo.GetValue( _
                            locAttribute, Nothing).ToString)
                    Next
                Next
            End If

            If locMember.MemberType = MemberTypes.Property Then
                Dim locPropertyInfo As PropertyInfo = CType(locMember, PropertyInfo)
                Console.WriteLine("    Value: " + locPropertyInfo.GetValue( _
                    [Object], Nothing).ToString)
            End If
        Next
    End Sub

End Module
```

 Note *GetCustomAttributes* returns only *custom* attributes. If you want to find out, for example, whether a class is serializable, you can retrieve this information either through an *IsXxx* function of your *Type* object (*IsSerializable* for example) or with the *Attributes* property.

Part IV
Development Simplifications in Visual Basic 2010

Chapter 22
Using *My* as a Shortcut to Common Framework Functions

Microsoft Visual Basic 2010 has a few language-specific features (some would use the term "peculiarities") that at first glance seem to circumvent the object-oriented programming (OOP) concepts on which the Microsoft .NET Framework is based. For example, it seems as if you can access forms directly without having to first instantiate them. Visual Basic 6.0 had functionality like this (VBA still does!), but it's exclusive to the .NET version of Visual Basic; looking for this functionality in C# is fruitless. In addition, you'll find Visual Basic code in which the compiler acts as if it were being programmed by a ghostly developer behind the scenes.

Those things belong to the list of complaints from OOP purists and were aimed at the old Visual Basic 6.0/VBA squad. The purists concluded that these features never should have been implemented in Visual Basic .NET to begin with, because they threw Visual Basic 2005 back into the pool of "baby programming languages" and that "one should not support the stubbornness of the procedural fraction [of developers]." (Whoa! I'm just quoting an unnamed source here; please don't shoot the messenger.)

I admit that for a while I saw myself more at home with the OOP purists than with the old procedural Visual Basic 6.0 league. I didn't want my beautiful, new, and finally grown-up .NET version of Visual Basic to be spoiled with "replicated" Visual Basic 6.0 features that might damage its reputation—after all, Visual Basic hasn't had an easy time establishing itself as a professional programming language in certain circles.

But in truth, this entire discussion is moot, because Visual Basic has everything you need for OOP programming. Personally, I can get by in C# and Visual Basic equally well, but I prefer programming in Visual Basic, because I think that the Editor and background compiler in Visual Basic let you to work faster and more efficiently than their C# equivalents. If some people prefer not to use the functionality discussed in this part of the book, such as the Application Framework or the *My* namespace, nobody is forcing them to do so. If they want to make their work more difficult than necessary, so be it; it'll just take them longer to finish the job.

One of the most frequently used arguments is that Visual Basic uses components that actually don't belong to .NET Framework to simplify programming tasks. This simply isn't true. All these features intended to attract the "old" Visual Basic 6.0 squad to switch to .NET are implemented in the file *VisualBasic.dll*, which *is* a part of the .NET Framework. Some people argue that you should avoid these simplifications based on rumors that Visual Basic-specific features might be banished from .NET Framework in the future. But (and this is an important "but") keep in mind that without the *VisualBasic.dll* file, no Visual Basic program can be executed, no matter what approach you take (Visual Basic-specific or .NET-purist) or which .NET Framework components you use. Once you realize that the file *VisualBasic.dll* is an integral part of the .NET Framework, just like all other .NET assemblies, and that Visual Basic-specific simplifications (such as the Application Framework and *My* namespace) are located there, you should read the following pages. You can solve a lot of problems both quickly and easily by using these features—the examples will prove it!

Important There really is an assembly that contains the name *VisualBasic*, and it's called the *VisualBasic.Compatibility* assembly. From the outset, it was designed for the .NET Framework 1.0 and 1.1 and intended exclusively for 32-bit platforms. It contains support functions for backward compatibility with Visual Basic 6.0. This is why all of its methods are also marked with the *Obsolete* attribute. You should definitely try to avoid using this DLL (even for 32-bit applications).

Apart from that, it's also possible that in the future that Visual Basic 6.0-style functions will no longer work the way they are supposed for technical reasons. The *FileOpen* method, which uses file handles is one example: the file handles must work in a coordinated fashion across multiple assemblies. Because of the very aggressive inline behavior of the 64-bit Just-in-Time (JIT) compiler, it's possible, for example, that the assembly from which a call originated can't be cleanly determined; therefore, file handle assignment can't be guaranteed reliably. You must then be prepared for the possibility that these methods might no longer be usable in the future, so you should avoid using them, as well.

Visual Basic 2010 Simplifications Using the Example of the DotNetCopy Backup Tool

Anyone who regularly generates many new and important files—and realistically, that means all software developers belong to this group—know how important data backup is. But even developers don't always do the right thing or follow our own recommendations. Personally, I copy my data every night to an external drive using a simple batch file that runs at a Windows command prompt. A proper differentiating band backup with a band for each day of the week is something I only recommend to my clients. To be fair, in my case that would have been hard to do, because over 60 percent of this book was conceived about 9000 kilometers from home (remember, I still originally come from Germany) in a beautiful apartment in the Belltown district of Seattle. For historical data backup to an external hard drive, the following example was a big help.

As an alternative to my batch copy file, it would be an enormous improvement if there were a program that didn't just copy files from certain folders, but would also create backup histories of the files that would need to undergo a version increment before any previously-updated file was backed up again, similar to Figure 22-1.

DotNetCopy does exactly that. And it can do much more: you can set up DotNetCopy in such a way that it only copies files that don't exist in the target directory or files where the target directory are older than the files you need to save.

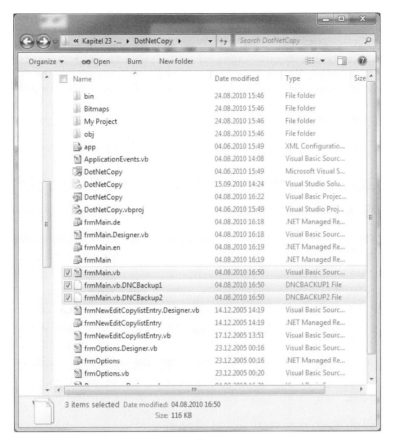

FIGURE 22-1 DotNetCopy only copies files when they are newer than the versions in the target directory or don't yet exist there. For files that already exist, the program automatically creates backup histories.

Tip Even if this tip has nothing to do with .NET, Visual Basic, Visual Studio, or Application Development, I find it so important that I simply have to mention it: as of Windows Vista, you can also locally (not in a server environment) access "shadow copies" of files. This is the default setting on the boot drive (normally the C drive). If you want to use shadow copy for additional drives, you can configure that in a dialog that you can access via the Control Panel or by clicking System | Advanced. Once there, click the System Protection tab (see Figures 22-2 and 22-3).

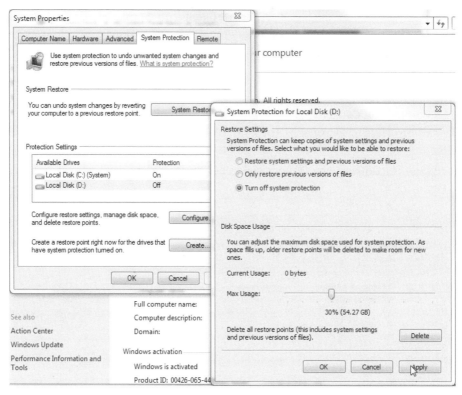

FIGURE 22-2 Beginning with Windows Vista, you can set up part of your hard drive for shadow copies.

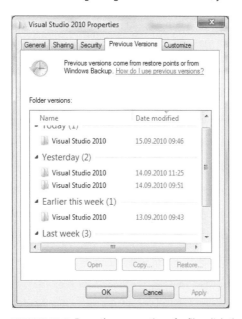

FIGURE 22-3 From the properties of a file, click the Previous Versions tab. From there, you can call up the different versions of your files. Unfortunately, this doesn't work (or doesn't work reliably) on external backup disks—DotNetCopy represents a good alternative here.

With shadow copies, the files in the target directory aren't simply replaced, losing their old version forever. Instead, you can specify the number of backup levels you want the program to keep automatically for older files. (Figure 22-1 shows how this will look on the backup drive later, as a backup history.)

> **Companion Content** Open the file DotNetCopy.sln, which you can find in the \VB 2010 Developer Handbook\Chapter 22\DotNetCopy folder.

You use the DotNetCopy Options dialog box to control the copy behavior, as illustrated in Figure 22-4.

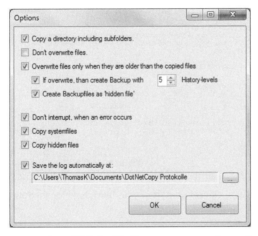

FIGURE 22-4 With DotNetCopy, you can configure the copy settings in the Options dialog box.

With DotNetCopy, you then create a *copy list* that instructs the program regarding the source and destination folders (what should be backed up and where). Figure 22-5 shows how you can save and load copy lists, which makes the program quite flexible.

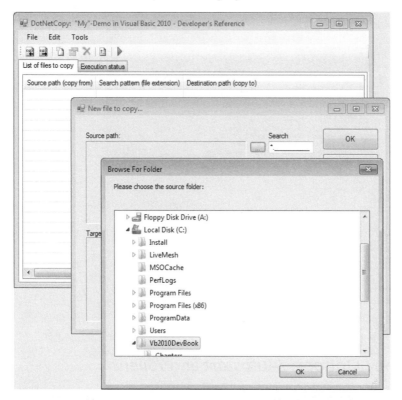

FIGURE 22-5 With DotNetCopy, you can create, save, and load copy lists that contain multiple source and target paths.

After you have created and saved a copy list, you can begin the process by clicking the Start Copying button, as shown in Figure 22-6.

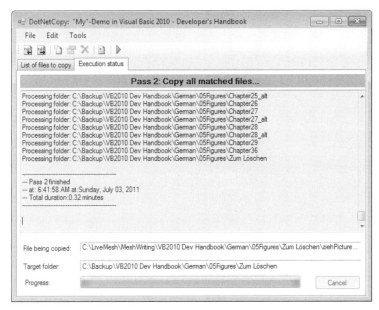

FIGURE 22-6 DotNetCopy after a successful backup run.

DotNetCopy Options: */Autostart* and */Silent*

This tool is particularly useful for administrators who might want to embed batch files, because it can be started in two modes: Autostart mode and Silent mode.

- Use Autostart mode to specify a copy list file when the program starts. The program loads the copy list file and launches the backup process immediately. You can launch DotNetCopy in copy list mode from the command prompt or via the Start menu by specifying the */autostart:copylistfile.ols* option, where copylistfile.ols is the copy list you want to use. For example:

```
Dotnetcopy /autostart:backup.ols
```

- You can also launch DotNetCopy with no visual user interface by using */silent* option (you can combine */silent* with the */autostart* option). For example, to use the backup.ols copy list file shown in the preceding command line, you would use the following:

```
Dotnetcopy /autostart:backup.ols /silent
```

Now that you have learned how DotNetCopy functions, here's a look at how the other chapters in the book come into play.

You don't need to dig deep into the .NET Framework to understand this program—far from it. Thanks to some Visual Basic-specific features, DotNetCopy requires surprisingly little code.

Even if you're a new Visual Basic 6.0/VBA convert, you'll only encounter two new classes from the .NET Framework; the rest of the application's functionality is almost entirely based on features provided by the *My* namespace and the Application Framework.

Maintaining Directories and Files with the *FileInfo* and *DirectoryInfo* Classes

The .NET Framework provides two classes called *FileInfo* and *DirectoryInfo* that provide access to files and folders available to your computer.

The *FileInfo* class lets you "edit" files much the way you would in Windows Explorer, while the *DirectoryInfo* class provides the same functionality for folders. Just imagine both classes as providing Windows File Explorer functionality, but without a visible user interface: The *FileInfo* class lets you retrieve file attributes, rename files, move files, test whether files exist, and so on. *DirectoryInfo* works basically the same way, but applies to folders.

After you know the exact path and name of a file, it's easy to work with that file, such as building a path correctly, extracting the file name only from the full path name, and determining the file extension. The two classes *FileInfo* and *DirectoryInfo* help you here, as well. When creating a new subfolder, you don't need to worry whether its parent folders already exist. For example, if you use the *DirectoryInfo* class to create a path called *C:\Folder1\SubFolder\ActualFolder*, it creates the required parent folders (*Folder1* and *SubFolder*), as well, if they don't already exist. The following code shows a few examples of using the *FileInfo* and *DirectoryInfo* classes:

DirectoryInfo Object:

```
'Create a new DirectoryInfo object from the path string:
Dim aDirInfo As New DirectoryInfo("C:\Folder1\SubFolder")
'Does the folder exist?
If Not aDirInfo.Exists Then
    Debug.Print("Folder does not exist - is being created:")
    'Create the folder with all required subfolders
    aDirInfo.Create()
End If
```

FileInfo Object:

```
'Create a new FileInfo object from the path / file name string
Dim aFileInfo As New FileInfo("c:\Folder1\SubFolder\textfile.txt")
'Each FileInfo object also contains a DirectoryInfo object
'which can be retrieved with the Directory property:
If Not aFileInfo.Directory.Exists Then
'Create path to the file, if necessary
    aFileInfo.Directory.Create()
End If
```

```
'Does the file exist?
If Not aFileInfo.Exists Then
'Create a simple text file.
    My.Computer.FileSystem.WriteAllText(aFileInfo.FullName, "File content", False)
End If
Debug.Print("File extension: " & aFileInfo.Extension)
Debug.Print("Pure file name: " & aFileInfo.Name)
Debug.Print("Complete path and file name: " & aFileInfo.FullName)
Debug.Print("File attributes: " & aFileInfo.Attributes)
Debug.Print("Copying the file to the main directory...!")
'Important: Both path and new file name must be specified as target!
aFileInfo.CopyTo("C:\" & aFileInfo.Name)
Debug.Print("Deleting the original file...!")
aFileInfo.Delete()
```

This code displays the following output:

```
File extension: .txt
Pure file name: textfile.txt
Complete path and file name: c:\Ordner1\Unterordner\textfile.txt
File attributes: 32
Copying the file to the main directory...!
Deleting the original file...!
```

The Principle Functionality of DotNetCopy

DotNetCopy demonstrates some special features of Visual Basic as compared to other .NET Framework programming languages. The Application Framework provides some of these features, and the *My* namespace, which helps resolve certain thematically categorized problems you will encounter frequently as you program, provides the rest.

DotNetCopy uses the following features in connection with the Application Framework: the Visual Styles of Windows XP and later operating systems, application events, and a function that prevents a second instance of DotNetCopy from being started when an instance of DotNetCopy is already active.

> **Note** Whether it is actually essential to avoid multiple instances of DotNetCopy (so it can function correctly) is debatable. You might like to be able to run multiple instances of DotNetCopy at the same time. However, the program is definitely suitable for demonstrating how the Application Framework works.

Because DotNetCopy recognizes the option */silent*, you need a mechanism that kicks in before the first form is displayed, which (in this mode) also prevents the first form from being displayed. The Application Framework provides a number of events for this purpose, one of which fires as soon as the program has been started. This event-handling routine controls whether the main form is displayed. It's called *MyApplication_Startup*. You'll find the code in the file ApplicationEvents.vb.

After that event, the program launches the main form (frmMain.vb, which contains the code for the backup process) in *Silent* mode, without displaying it. This has no negative impact on the program's functionality. The code that updates the form (the update progress bar and protocol output, the folder currently being edited, and so on.) still works—you just can't see the updates because the form itself it not displayed.

From that point on, the application works the same in all modes. First, it loads the copy list by using the function *LoadCopyEntryList*. That function is triggered either from the *HandleAutoStart* method (called by *MyApplication_Startup*) or when a user selects the menu entry or icon to load a copy list. Next, the copy process starts in the method *CopyFiles*, either when it's called from *HandleAutoStart* or when a user selects the menu entry or clicks the icon button.

Both *CopyFiles* and all the methods it calls use functions from the *My* namespace extensively.

The project files are heavily commented, but you'll see the important code sections in this and in Chapter 23, "The Application Framework."

DotNetCopy is a good example for demonstrating how easily you can develop complex applications with Visual Basic and its simplified features—and it's also a useful tool that you might actually use. In my case, DotNetCopy replaced my old batch file processes, and I've made good use of the data backup history it generates.

One last comment about OOP and the Visual Basic simplifications: DotNetCopy is definitely not the best example of OOP, but it is useful and stable, and it was developed quickly. To create the same tool in C# without the Visual Basic simplifications would have taken at least a day longer. OOP is a must-have for larger applications, and that rule applies when working in Visual Basic, as well, even though *My* and the Application Framework exist. However, OOP tempts you to do more than is strictly necessary. Remember that you don't need to construct a skyscraper foundation to build a single-family home. Keep this analogy in mind when tackling class planning for larger projects.

There is nothing wrong with using the Visual Basic-specific simplifications. If they save you time and you can foresee that they won't stand in the way of future extensions, use them! And ignore the C# or Visual Basic developers who tell you differently.

The *My* Namespace

Microsoft introduced the *My* namespace in Visual Basic 2005 to simplify access to specific functionalities. It basically uses features of the .NET Framework to create "shortcuts" to certain targets that can otherwise be reached only circuitously.

If you worked through the example in Chapter 5, "Introduction to Windows Presentation Foundation," you have already seen some of these shortcuts. For example, you saw how easy it is to use *My.Settings* to access application settings, which automatically save your work.

But the *My* namespace offers many more cool features. It's hard to define exactly which ones at any given point, because the features *My* provides depend on the project type that you are currently editing. Generally, however, you can group the functionalities in the *My* namespace into the following categories:

- **My.Application**   Provides access to information about the current application, such as the path to the executable file, the program version, current cultural information, or the user authentication mode.

- **My.Computer**   Provides access to several child objects, through which you can retrieve computer-related information, including information about the file system, audio and video specifications, connected printers, general I/O hardware (such as mouse and keyboard), memory, network environment, serial interfaces, and so on.

- **My.Forms**   Use this to retrieve the default instances of all forms of a Windows Forms application.

- **My.Resources**   Provides easy access to embedded resources, such as string tables, bitmaps, and so on.

- **My.Settings**   Provides access to application settings and helps to ensure that you can restore those settings at program start, if necessary, and save them at program end.

- **My.User**   Provides access to information about the currently logged on user, and helps you implement custom authentication mechanisms.

- **My.WebServices**   Provides a property for each web service referenced by the current project, thus giving you access to the web services without having to create an explicit proxy class for each one.

Here's one example of why *My* functionality is project specific. In console applications, which don't use forms, the category *My.Forms* obviously won't be available to you. Table 22-1 lists *My* functionality by project type.

TABLE 22-1 Availability of the *My* Namespace Features in Important Project Types

My object	Windows Forms application	Class library	Console application	Windows Forms control library	Windows service
My.Application	Yes	Yes	Yes	Yes	Yes
My.Computer	Yes	Yes	Yes	Yes	Yes
My.Forms	Yes	No	No	Yes	No

My object	Windows Forms application	Class library	Console application	Windows Forms control library	Windows service
My.Resources	Yes	Yes	Yes	Yes	Yes
My.Settings	Yes	Yes	Yes	Yes	Yes
My.User	Yes	Yes	Yes	Yes	Yes
My.WebServices	Yes	Yes	Yes	Yes	Yes

It doesn't make much sense to exhaustively cover a complete reference list of all the *My* functionalities for each individual area. After all, *My* exists so that you can avoid having to look up too much information—you can just rely on IntelliSense and dynamic help instead to quickly get to the functionality that you need. Instead, a developer handbook should teach you about software development, as you saw earlier in the demonstration code for *My*. The *My* functionalities in the following sections are therefore not complete and aren't meant to be. It's more important to teach you the general processes in connection with the *My* namespace. You can use IntelliSense and the Online Help later on to find other functions on your own.

However, there are a few things worth mentioning about the *My* namespace and its functionalities that you won't find in the Online Help. You'll cover those in the sections that follow. You'll find many of these features in the DotNetCopy example and the code snippets.

Calling Forms Without Instantiation

In Visual Basic 6.0 and VBA, you had to instantiate an object that you wanted to work with. For example, if you used a *Collection* to store other objects, you had to create it first by using the following code:

```
Dim collection As Collection
Set collection = New Collection
collection.Add 5
```

It's clear that simply using the following line by itself would not have worked:

```
Collection.Add 10
Collection.Add 15
Collection.Add 20
```

But that's exactly how Visual Basic 6.0 seems to have treated forms: both the class name and instance could be identical. This version, which instantiates a *Form1* instance works:

```
Dim f As Form1
f.Show
```

But you could also just use the class *Form1* as instance variable directly:

```
Form1.Show
```

Of course, this does not follow the rules of OOP, but it was probably easier to understand for many Visual Basic 6.0 programmers. That's why the Visual Basic compiler was designed to make such form class usage possible.

When compiling a Windows Forms application, the Visual Basic compiler ensures that some hidden source code is compiled into your application. Basically, the Visual Basic compiler generates this source code and adds it (invisibly) to the Windows project.

So in Visual Basic 2010, you can use the following line to set up a form created under the class name *Form2* as a modal dialog:

```
Form2.ShowDialog
```

But it only *looks* as if you were using a static class method directly, because *Form2* is actually a property that returns an *instance* of the type *Form2*. What really happens here is that the compiler alters this line, instead compiling the following source code to generate the executable file:

```
My.Forms.Form2.ShowDialog
```

Internally the compiler builds *MyProject.Forms* from this construct. The class *MyProject*, however, is a class that is unreachable under that name, because it has attributes that mark it in such a way that the compiler can't "see" it. It does exist though. For each form that you add to your project, the compiler creates a property that has the type of the respective form in the My*Forms* class (which is also invisible). *MyForms* is an embedded class in the *MyProject* class whose instance you can retrieve via the *Forms* property of the *MyProject* class. And finally, this property—which uses the name of the form—ensures that you can instantiate the desired form class and then use it without problems or *NullReference* exceptions.

To illustrate, let's look at the definition of the following line:

```
My.Forms.Form2.ShowDialog
```

This basically translates to: *(MyProject class).(Forms property of the MyProject class of the type MyForms). (Form2 property of the MyForms class of the type Form2).(ShowDialog method of the Form2 class).*

Reading Command-Line Arguments with *My.Application.CommandLineArgs*

Applications in Windows can be started in multiple ways. The simplest and most commonly encountered way is by double-clicking a shortcut (for example from the desktop). You can also start any Windows or command-line application directly by typing the name of the executable file at the command prompt or by using the *Run* command from the Start menu. Many applications let you specify additional options via their command lines. These options

control the application's runtime behavior. For example, you can start Windows Explorer with a drive parameter:

```
Explorer c:\
```

This command not only launches Windows Explorer, but it also immediately displays the contents of the root directory on the C drive.

Parameters passed to applications in this manner are called *command-line arguments*. Using the *My* namespace, you can easily detect any command-line arguments used to launch your own programs.

As discussed earlier, the DotNetCopy application uses such command-line arguments to put the application into the Autostart or the Silent mode. The following code, located in the *StartUp* event of the *MyApplication* object, runs when the application starts, and demonstrates the usage of command-line arguments:

> **Note** You can find this code in the file ApplicationEvents.vb of the project. You'll see more about application events in Chapter 23.

```
Partial Friend Class MyApplication

    Private Sub MyApplication_Startup(ByVal sender As Object, ByVal e As _
        Microsoft.VisualBasic.ApplicationServices.StartupEventArgs) Handles Me.Startup

        'Set the directory for the log file first...
        If String.IsNullOrEmpty(My.Settings.Option_AutoSaveProtocolPath) Then
            My.Settings.Option_AutoSaveProtocolPath = _
                My.Computer.FileSystem.SpecialDirectories.MyDocuments & _
                    "\DotNetCopy protocols"
            Dim locDi As New DirectoryInfo(My.Settings.Option_AutoSaveProtocolPath)

            'Examine and...
            If Not locDi.Exists Then
                '...create, if necessary
                locDi.Create()
            End If

            'Save settings
            My.Settings.Save()
        End If

        Dim locFrmMain As New frmMain

        'Read command line
        'Are there any command line arguments?
        If My.Application.CommandLineArgs.Count > 0 Then
            'Iterate through each command line argument
            For Each locString As String In My.Application.CommandLineArgs
```

```
                        'Remove all unnecessary empty characters and
                        'make it case-insensitive.
                        'NOTE: This only works under Windows;
                        'if the copy list file comes from a Unix server,
                        'make sure that the file name is all caps,
                        'because Unix (and Linux) derivates are case-sensitive!!!
                        locString = locString.ToUpper.Trim

                        If locString = "/SILENT" Then
                            locFrmMain.SilentMode = True
                        End If

                        If locString.StartsWith("/AUTOSTART") Then
                            locFrmMain.AutoStartCopyList = locString.Replace("/AUTOSTART:", "")
                            locFrmMain.AutoStartMode = True
                        End If
                Next
        End If
```

.
.
.

Targeted Access to Resources with *My.Resources*

Resource files save application elements such as bitmaps, icons, strings, and so on in separate files. You can read these elements from the resource files by using *My.Resources* at runtime.

The advantage of using such external resources is that it makes applications more flexible—you can update the resources without having to alter the actual application code. For example, consider the localization feature of a Microsoft Office program such as Microsoft Word into another language. If the text for each application message were hard coded, Microsoft would need to provide the entire source code to translators, who would then have to identify translatable text embedded somewhere in the source. That would also result in multiple versions of the source code, each of which would need to be updated for changes or bug fixes—an effort which is simply unsupportable for larger projects.

Creating and Managing Resource Elements

The sample application retrieves the strings for the column headers of the *ListView* control that contains the copy list entries from a resource file. You manage the resource file itself the same way you saw earlier in the sample application for Chapter 5, as described in the following:

1. To edit an application's resource file, open the project properties by right-clicking it in Solution Explorer to open the context menu.

2. Select the Resources tab.

3. Using the drop-down list (see Figure 22-7), select the type of resource that you want to use.

For strings, you can assign and edit values in the form of a table. For other resource types, such as bitmaps, icons, or audio clips, click the Add Resource button to add the corresponding file to the resource file.

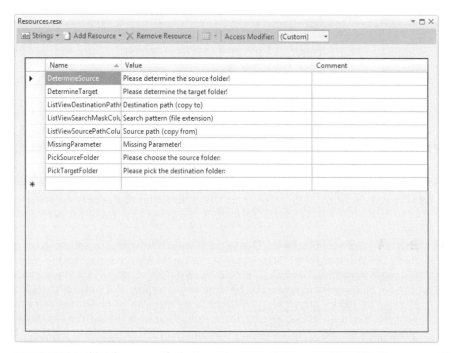

FIGURE 22-7 In this tab you specify the type of resource that you want to add to the resource file. For types other than strings, use the Add Resource button to save bitmaps, icons, audio clips, and other resources in your resource file.

Retrieving Resources with *My.Resources*

If you have added resources to your project as described above, retrieving them at runtime is simple, thanks to *My*. The DotNetCopy project does this in the form's *form_Load* event handler. Here's how it sets up the *ListView* column headers:

```
''' <summary>
''' Is called when the form is loaded and contains the initialization
''' of the ListView and is starting the copy process
''' (and necessary loading of the copy list), when the program
''' runs in Autostart (but not in Silent) mode.
''' (Silent mode is handled in ApplicationEvents.vb).
```

```
'''  </summary>
'''  <param name="sender"></param>
'''  <param name="e"></param>
'''  <remarks></remarks>
Private Sub frmMain_Load(ByVal sender As Object, ByVal e As System.EventArgs) _
        Handles Me.Load
    'Set up the ListView
    With Me.lvwCopyEntries.Columns
        'Retrieve the texts for the ListView columns from the resource file
        .Add(My.Resources.ListViewSourcePathColumnName)
        .Add(My.Resources.ListViewSearchMaskColumnName)
        .Add(My.Resources.ListViewDestinationPathColumnName)
        'Align the columns
        AlignColumns()
    End With
```

.
.
.

You could, of course, extend this process to control the messages in the backup log; however, for simplicity's sake, this example limits string resources to the *ListView* column headers:

Note WinForms applications implicitly use resource files when you add strings or picture files to them. The Windows Forms Designer might not use the *My* namespace for the generated code, but retrieving bitmap files from a resource, for example, to add an icon to something like an icon bar button, functions basically the same way as a string. You can explore this for yourself by showing the hidden project files with the *Show All Files* icon in Solution Explorer (the ToolTip will help you find it). Check out the code that creates the form in the file frmMain.Designer.vb, which is located in the branch below the form file frmMain.vb.

.
.
.

```
'
'tsbLoadCopyList - a snippet from the file generated by the FormsDesigner for
'assigning an image to an icon in DotNetCopy:
Me.tsbLoadCopyList.DisplayStyle =
    System.Windows.Forms.ToolStripItemDisplayStyle.Image
Me.tsbLoadCopyList.Image = CType(resources.GetObject("tsbLoadCopyList.Image"), _
                System.Drawing.Image)

Me.tsbLoadCopyList.ImageTransparentColor = System.Drawing.Color.Magenta
```

.
.
.

Assigning an icon with the *My* namespace would look as follows:

```
Me.tsbLoadCopyList.Image = My.Resources.LoadCopyList
```

The precondition for this would be that you had added the corresponding image file to the resource file in the manner just described, as shown in Figure 22-8.

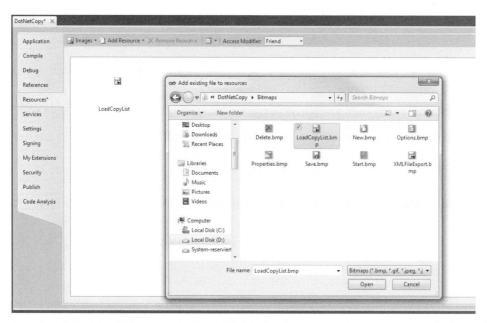

FIGURE 22-8 Click the Add Resource button (click the triangle next to the button name, not the button itself), and then in the drop-down list, select Add File to add a bitmap to the resource file, which you can then assign at runtime with *My.Resource* and load the elements.

Writing Localizable Applications with Resource Files and the *My* Namespace

Using resource files explicitly makes sense only when you are planning to make your application available in more than one language. This is a process called "localization." To make your application localizable, you need to create named resource files that follow a specific convention.

Unfortunately, Visual Studio 2010 for Windows Forms applications does not offer Designer support to help you create new resource files for other cultures that match the ones that already exist. Instead, you need to create them manually and trick the integrated development environment (IDE) a little. Designer support is limited to forms. You use the *Localizable* property to specify whether a form should be localized.

> **Tip** If you want to perform the following steps, we recommend that you copy the project files to a different location on your hard drive so that you can play around with them without risking the original project files. If something does go wrong during your experiments, you can copy the source project again and start over without losing anything.

1. Open your "experimental copy" of DotNetCopy, and then open Solution Explorer by pressing Ctrl+Alt+L.

2. Click the Show All Files icon in Solution Explorer to display all the project files.

   Open the branch next to the now-visible My Project entry. You should see the file Resources.resx, which stores the German culture resources.

3. Right-click this Resources.resx to open its context menu, and then select Copy.

4. In this next step, you'll play a little trick on the IDE: add the file at the same location where the original file resides, thus creating a copy of the resource file.

   If you right-click it, the context menu contains no *Add* entry. Therefore *left*-click the file Resources.resx to select it, and then choose Insert from the Edit menu of the Visual Studio IDE. This places the desired copy into the branch *My Project*.

5. Rename the copied resource file.

   Later, when .NET Framework executes your program, it will choose which file to use for which culture, based on the resource file name. For example, if you develop an application on a German Windows platform, at runtime on German systems, the application will always use the resource file with which you developed it. For English and United States systems, you need a resource file named Resources.en.resx; for a French system, you need a Resources.fr.resx file; for an Italian one, Resources.it.resx, and so on.

> **Tip** The common language abbreviations correspond to the ones that you would use for culture-dependent format providers.

6. Double-click the unnamed file so that you can localize the entries it contains, as shown in Figure 22-9.

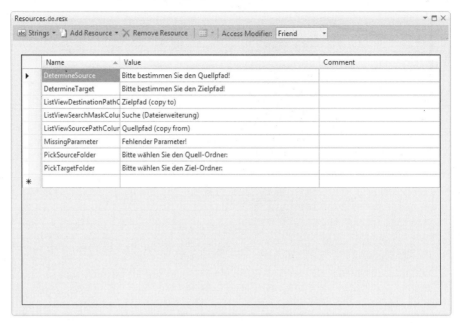

FIGURE 22-9 After copying an additional resource file into your project, you can begin localizing the resources.

7. Save your changes, and then rebuild the entire project.

You will notice that a new subfolder has been added to the directory of the project's executable (by default that path is *Project\bin\Debug*). This new subfolder contains a *satellite assembly* that holds the localized resources for each original resource file. The .NET Framework uses this subfolder/assembly automatically if the name of the subfolder corresponds to the cultural abbreviation of the operating system's culture (*en* for English, *fr* for French, and so on). The upshot is that if you created the satellite assemblies as described here, you're done—you don't need to do anything else yourself, except to ensure that the appropriate subfolders exist.

On a German system the application automatically appears as shown in Figure 22-10 (note the labels of the *ListView* columns extracted from the DotNetCopy resource file, as shown in Figure 22-9).

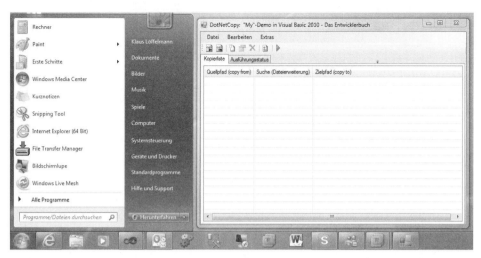

FIGURE 22-10 This German-language OS uses the German satellite assembly automatically (assuming it exists). Text localized in the resource file is displayed in German.

Localization versus Simple Translation

The type of resource file in this description contains only the localization of those elements that you would use in your applications directly from code. But there are other UI elements that also need to be localized: the forms themselves. You can local-ize Windows Forms quite easily (see Figure 22-11). Open and select the form in the Windows Forms designer. Set its localizable property to *True*. Next, in the Properties window, find the appropriate language property for the localization. As soon as you open the drop-down list and select the language item, the whole Design view for that form switches to the selected language. From that point on, you are designing every-thing on the form for that language. This means that not only can you translate the *Text* property for every UI element to the corresponding language, the localization also includes such things as repositioning or resizing the controls on the form, as the current language or culture demands. German captions, for example, are usually some 1.15 times longer than their English counterparts, which is why in most cases the cap-tions of the UI elements need to be resized and repositioned as well. This is why the process is called *localization,* and not simply *translation*. Localization takes many more design factors into account than does translation. In this respect, Windows Forms still has a huge advantage for the localization of user interfaces over Windows Presentation Foundation (WPF) (see Chapter 5), because the WPF localization tooling is (as of this writing) nowhere near as advanced as in Windows Forms.

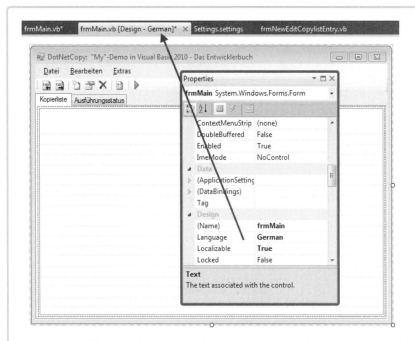

FIGURE 22-11 When you've changed the language settings for a form, you can identify for which language you are localizing at the moment by looking at the tab's caption.

As soon as you switch the language property back to standard, the designer switches the Design view back to the language in which you started. It is good practice, when you design forms for more than one language, to finalize your original language first, and only then start working on the next language, to make sure that every UI element is already in place.

Simplified File Operations with *My.Computer.FileSystem*

FileInfo and *DirectoryInfo* already provide considerable assistance for file operations. But the *My* namespace contains functions that do an even better job; these are responsible for the fact that the backup tool DotNetCopy doesn't need much code, even though it's quite flexible.

DotNetCopy uses functions from *My.Computer.FileSystem* extensively when it performs the actual backup tasks. Especially noteworthy are functions such as *GetFiles*, which you can use to read the contents of entire directory structures recursively. Optionally, you can retrieve just the files names they contain. This is similar to using the *Dir* command at a Windows command prompt. Launching *Dir* with the */S* option returns not only the current or named directory and files, but also its subfolders and files.

The actual copy routine in DotNetCopy uses the *GetFiles* function to identify and cache all subfolders and their files. It then copies files based on that list. The following code snippet demonstrates how this works:

```
' '' <summary>
''' The copy routine which is controlled by the My.Settings options.
''' </summary>
''' <remarks></remarks>
Public Sub CopyFiles()
.
.   'Shortened to save space
.

    'In this loop first all files are determined which need to be
    'examined whether they should be copied or not.
    For locItemCount As Integer = 0 To lvwCopyEntries.Items.Count - 1
        Dim locCopyListEntry As CopyListEntry
        'CType is required, so .NET knows which type
        'was save in the Tag property.
        locCopyListEntry = CType(lvwCopyEntries.Items(locItemCount).Tag, CopyListEntry)
        'Update UI
        lblCurrentPass.Text = "Pass 1: Copy preparation by assembling the paths..."
        lblSourceFileInfo.Text = "Look for subfolders in:"
        lblDestFileInfo.Text = ""
        lblProgressCaption.Text = "Progress preparation:"
        lblCurrentSourcePath.Text = locCopyListEntry.SourceFolder.ToString
        LogInProtocolWindow(locCopyListEntry.SourceFolder.ToString)
        pbPrepareAndCopy.Value = locItemCount + 1

        'Allow Windows to update the controls
        My.Application.DoEvents()

        'GetFiles from My.Computer.FileSystem supplies the names of all
        'the files in the root and its subfolders.
        Dim locFiles As ReadOnlyCollection(Of String)
        Try
            locNotCaught = False
            locFiles = My.Computer.FileSystem.GetFiles( _
                    locCopyListEntry.SourceFolder.ToString, _
                    FileIO.SearchOption.SearchAllSubDirectories, _
                    locCopyListEntry.SearchMask)
        Catch ex As Exception
            LogError(ex)
            'If there were any errors during the assembling of the files,
            'the directory must be skipped, and this important fact must
            'be protocolled in the application log file!
            My.Application.Log.WriteException(ex, TraceEventType.Error, _
                "DotNetCopy could not search the " & _
                locCopyListEntry.SourceFolder.ToString & " directory., " & _
                "Therefore this directory was not included!")

            ' Like "Catch", there also should be a "NotCaught" branch...
            locNotCaught = True
        End Try
.
.
.
```

My.Computer.FileSystem provides another functionality that is also very practical, namely the *CopyFile* method. Unlike the *CopyTo* method of the *FileInfo* class, this one uses the exact same operating system function of Windows, which Windows Explorer uses, as well. This means that if you are using *CopyFile* from the *My* namespace, you can automatically have the well-known progress bar displayed. (DotNetCopy does not use it in this example.)

```
''' <summary>
''' Internal copy routine which performs the actual copy job.
''' </summary>
''' <param name="SourceFile">Source file to be copied.</param>
''' <param name="DestFile">Source path where the file must be copied.</param>
''' <remarks></remarks>
Private Sub CopyFileInternal(ByVal SourceFile As FileInfo, ByVal DestFile As FileInfo)
    'In case the target file doesn't exist yet,
    'copy anyway.
    If Not DestFile.Exists Then
        Try
            'Copy file without displaying the Windows UI.
            My.Computer.FileSystem.CopyFile(SourceFile.ToString, DestFile.ToString)
            LogInProtocolWindow("Copied, OK: " & SourceFile.ToString)
        Catch ex As Exception
            LogError(ex)
        End Try
        Exit Sub
    End If
    'Only copy file if it is newer then the one it overwrites
    If My.Settings.Option_OnlyOverwriteIfOlder Then
        If SourceFile.LastWriteTime > DestFile.LastWriteTime Then
            'If history backup is enabled...
            If My.Settings.Option_EnableBackupHistory Then
                '...then perform it.
                ManageFileBackupHistory(DestFile)
            End If
            Try
                'Copy file.
                My.Computer.FileSystem.CopyFile(SourceFile.ToString, DestFile.ToString)
                LogInProtocolWindow("Copied, OK: " & SourceFile.ToString)
            Catch ex As Exception
                LogError(ex)
            End Try
        End If
    End If
End Sub
```

Note Unfortunately, when using *CopyFile* in Windows applications, where forms are bound to a message queue (which is the default for Windows Forms applications), error messages are also displayed as modal dialogs. This is especially problematic and undesirable when errors occur. However, it's important to realize that for applications that don't initiate a message queue, error messages are not displayed by the operating system in a visible modal dialog. In other words: If your program has no visible user interface, no visible error message appears, even if *CopyFile* triggers an error.

For the DotNetCopy program, that means when it's started in Silent mode, you don't want visible error messages—and that won't happen, because in this mode, it has no visible UI. It uses the same form class as when DotNetCopy runs normally (not in Silent mode), but the form doesn't display.

The following code, located in the *StartUp* event of the *MyApplication* object and triggered immediately when the application starts, demonstrates this:

```
'Note: locFrmMain was already instantiated further up in the code,
'but not displayed!
'Silent mode only remains "on", if AutoStart is enabled.
locFrmMain.SilentMode = locFrmMain.SilentMode And locFrmMain.AutoStartMode

'And when in Silent mode, the form is not bound to the application context!
If locFrmMain.SilentMode Then
    'Everthing is performed in the invisible instance of the main form,
    locFrmMain.HandleAutoStart()
    'and has completed before the "actual" program
    'is started with the main form.
    e.Cancel = True
Else
    'In non-silent mode the form is bound to the application,
    'and off we go!
    My.Application.MainForm = locFrmMain
End If
    End Sub
End Class
```

Using Application Settings with *My.Settings*

DotNetCopy uses application settings to retain settings after a program exits. You typically specify these settings by clicking Tools | Options. Because application settings were discussed in detail in Chapter 5, the following is just a summary of what you already know:

You maintain application settings (just like the string tables of the resources) in a table that you access via the project properties, as shown in Figure 22-12.

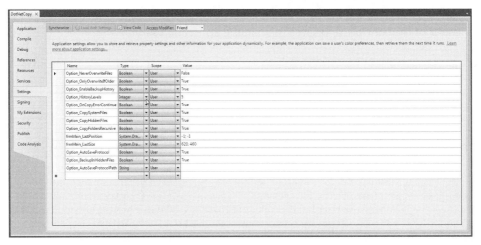

FIGURE 22-12 You can retrieve application settings with *My.Settings*. You maintain them just like resources, on the Settings tab in the project properties.

For each name you define in the table, the application creates an object variable of the type you have specified under *Type*, which you can then retrieve by using *My.Settings*. You can also select between two scopes for each variable: choose *User* scope when you want to be able to change the variable content at runtime and save that new content automatically when the program ends. Choose *Application* when you want the setting to be a constant that can be set only at design time, and that never changes at runtime (see Figure 22-12).

Saving and reading application settings is easy. The program uses application settings extensively, when users make changes through the options dialog. The routine below is called when the options dialog loads, ensuring that the dialog controls reflect the current application settings:

```
    Private Sub frmOptions_Load(ByVal sender As Object, ByVal e As System.EventArgs) Handles
➥Me.Load
        'Reflect the application settings in the dialog:
        'My.Settings is used for this as well.
        chkCopyFoldersRecursive.Checked = My.Settings.Option_CopyFoldersRecursive
        chkCopyHiddenFiles.Checked = My.Settings.Option_CopyHiddenFiles
        chkCopySystemFiles.Checked = My.Settings.Option_CopySystemFiles
        chkEnableBackupHistory.Checked = My.Settings.Option_EnableBackupHistory
        nudHistoryLevels.Value = My.Settings.Option_HistoryLevels
        chkNeverOverwriteFiles.Checked = My.Settings.Option_NeverOverwriteFiles
        chkOnCopyErrorContinue.Checked = My.Settings.Option_OnCopyErrorContinue
        chkOnlyOverwriteIfOlder.Checked = My.Settings.Option_OnlyOverwriteIfOlder
        chkBackupInHiddenFiles.Checked = My.Settings.Option_BackupInHiddenFiles
        chkAutoSaveProtocol.Checked = My.Settings.Option_AutoSaveProtocol
        lblProtocolPath.Text = My.Settings.Option_AutoSaveProtocolPath
    End Sub
```

When users close the dialog, the reverse process occurs; the program reads the values or states of the controls, and saves them in the application settings.

```
Private Sub btnOK_Click(ByVal sender As System.Object, ByVal e As System.EventArgs)
➥Handles btnOK.Click
    'Save the settings for the Options dialog in the application settings.
    'My.Settings is used for this as well.
    My.Settings.Option_CopyFoldersRecursive = chkCopyFoldersRecursive.Checked
    My.Settings.Option_CopyHiddenFiles = chkCopyHiddenFiles.Checked
    My.Settings.Option_CopySystemFiles = chkCopySystemFiles.Checked
    My.Settings.Option_EnableBackupHistory = chkEnableBackupHistory.Checked
    My.Settings.Option_HistoryLevels = CInt(nudHistoryLevels.Value)
    My.Settings.Option_NeverOverwriteFiles = chkNeverOverwriteFiles.Checked
    My.Settings.Option_OnCopyErrorContinue = chkOnCopyErrorContinue.Checked
    My.Settings.Option_OnlyOverwriteIfOlder = chkOnlyOverwriteIfOlder.Checked
    My.Settings.Option_BackupInHiddenFiles = chkBackupInHiddenFiles.Checked
    My.Settings.Option_AutoSaveProtocol = chkAutoSaveProtocol.Checked
    My.Settings.Option_AutoSaveProtocolPath = lblProtocolPath.Text

    'Setting the dialog result with a modally called dialog
    'causes it to be closed!
    Me.DialogResult = Windows.Forms.DialogResult.OK
End Sub
```

You can add information to the application settings; the Windows Designer and the controls do this, as well. For example, to specify or change a form label (such as the *Text* property of a Windows Forms class) without hard coding the change in code, you can do this easily via the settings interface. Open any desired form, and then open its property window (press F4). If you are displaying the properties by category, go to the Data category. The first entry there is *(Application Settings)*. You can enter the most important class properties directly, such as the value of the *Text* property. Select *(New)* at the bottom of the list. (Using *PropertyBinding*, you can swap almost all properties.) In the ensuing dialog box, enter a name for the property. In the Scope field, you can specify whether the settings should always apply to the entire application, or whether they can be specific to each user (you'll read about this in Chapter 23).

Saving Application Settings with *User* Scope

The code to save application settings isn't in the Options dialog; in fact, it doesn't exist, because in the end, it isn't really necessary. If you exit a Windows Forms application, and its Application Framework and the *Save My.Settings Upon Shutdown* option in the project properties (under the *Application* category) is enabled, then the .NET Framework automatically takes handles saving the application settings specified with *User* scope.

In some cases, you might want to save the application settings *before* exiting the program. DotNetCopy does this the very first time you launch the program, saving the settings for the position and size of the main form in the method *My.Settings.Save* (as shown in the following):

```
Private Sub frmMain_Load(ByVal sender As Object, ByVal e As System.EventArgs) _
.
. ' Left out to save space
.

    'Restore window size and position
    'when not in Silent mode
    If Not mySilentMode Then
        'When first called the size is -1, the default position
        'remains the same, the settings are immediately applied...
        If My.Settings.frmMain_LastPosition.X = -1 Then
            My.Settings.frmMain_LastPosition = Me.Location
            Me.Size = My.Settings.frmMain_LastSize
            My.Settings.Save()

            'otherwise the settings are applied
            'to the form position
        Else
            Me.Location = My.Settings.frmMain_LastPosition
        End If
        Me.Size = My.Settings.frmMain_LastSize
    End If
```

Chapter 23
The Application Framework

What Microsoft calls the "Application Framework" is actually a set of features. Among other things, the Application Framework ensure that application settings are saved when a program exits, and provides application events, which you'll see in the section, "Implementing a Code File that Handles Application Events (Start, End, Network Status, and General Exceptions)" later in this chapter.

As you've read several times already, the Visual Basic compiler amends your own source code with additional source code that you never actually get to see. This is the source code saved by the compiler. When your program uses specific features in the Application Framework (which you enable with the Application Framework options in the project properties of your project), the compiler amends the source code at compilation time to ensure that your program provides those features. Visual Basic also requires certain function calls provided by the.NET Framework file VisualBasic.dll.

For Windows applications, the Application Framework is enabled by default. You can control whether the Application Framework is enabled or disabled by using the Application tab in the project properties, as presented in Figure 23-1.

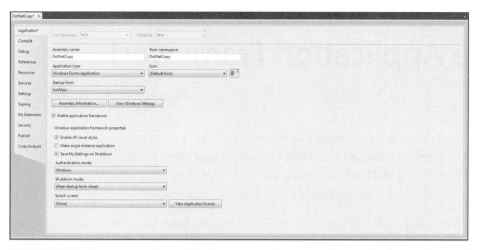

FIGURE 23-1 The features described in this chapter are available only when the Application Framework is enabled. For Windows Forms applications, the Application Framework is enabled by default.

When you select the Enable Application Framework check box, your application uses a "hidden" *Sub Main*, so to speak (which the compiler injects into your project via hidden source code), which the application uses at startup. All the other Application Framework options depend on this hidden function. For applications like this, you must select a *Start Form* that this hidden. *Sub Main* will call after it completes the preparations required to provide all the other Application Framework functions.

When you clear the check box, the application uses the custom *Sub Main* that you specified with *Start Form*, and which you must place into a module of your project. You can specify either a start object (a custom *Sub Main* in a method or class) or a form. The options in the section *Windows Application Framework Properties* are not available, in this case.

Application Framework Options

Using the following settings you can configure the section *Windows Application Framework Properties* in the project properties. Remember: these options are available only when the Enable Application Framework check box is selected.

A Windows XP Look and Feel for Your Applications—Enabling Visual XP Styles

You can enable or disable the Windows XP visual styles, also called Windows XP Designs. These provide such features as controls with rounded corners and dynamic colors. This option is enabled by default. You can also visually adjust your program to match the Vista or Windows 7 UI.

> **Note** Neither Visual Basic 2010 nor .NET Framework 4.0 support any of the new Aero design or Windows 7 operating features, such as the new taskbar, the new Common Dialogs, power-management, or technologies such as Direct2D out of the box. If you want your .NET applications to support these features, take a look at the Windows API Code Pack, which you can download here: *http://tinyurl.com/6cydcne.*

Preventing Multiple Application Starts—Creating a Single Instance Application

Select this check box to prevent users from running multiple instances of your application. This option is disabled by default, which means that, by default, users can run several instances of your application at once.

Save *My.Settings* Automatically on Shutdown

Selecting this check box specifies that the Application Framework should save any custom settings for your application (*My.Settings*) when the computer shuts down. This option is enabled by default. If you disable it, you can set it manually (programmatically) by calling *My.Settings.Save.*

Specifying the User Authentication Mode

Select Windows (the default setting) under Authentication Mode to specify that your application should use Windows Authentication to identify the currently logged-on user. You can retrieve this information at runtime by using the *My.User* object. Select Application-Defined when you prefer to use a custom user authentication code rather than the Windows default methods.

Specifying the End of Your Application—the Shutdown Mode

Select When Startup Form Closes (the default setting) to specify that the application has ended when the form set as the start form has been closed (note that this also applies if other forms are open.) Alternatively, select When Last Form Closes to ensure that the application ends when the last open form closes, or after an explicit call to *My.Application.Exit* occurs, or the *End* statement executes.

Displaying a Splash Dialog when Starting Complex Applications—Start Screen

To display a splash (start) screen, you just need to create an appropriate screen by using a form or a template. One way to do that is to right-click your project in Solution Explorer, and then click Add | New Element | Splash Screen. Then, to make the application display the splash screen, identify which form that you want to use as the splash screen in the project properties Application tab.

Adding a Code File to Handle Application Events (*Start*, *End*, Network Status, Global Exceptions)

You probably deduced in the previous sections that it must be possible to "listen to" certain application events. DotNetCopy, for example, latches itself to the program start event, and even controls the way in which the program works, based on options you pass via the command line.

To designate that your own code runs when these application events occur, you need to perform some prep-work:

1. Open the project properties, and then select the Application tab.

2. Click the View Application Events button (see Figure 23-1).

   The Visual Studio IDE immediately generates and adds a code file named ApplicationEvents.vb to your project, and then opens it in the Editor.

3. To insert the function body for the handler into one of the five existing application events, switch to the Code Editor and select the entry (MyApplication events) from the top left drop-down list.

4. From the top right drop-down list, select the event that you want to handle. Selecting an event automatically inserts a stub function body into the code. Figure 23-2 illustrates how to do this.

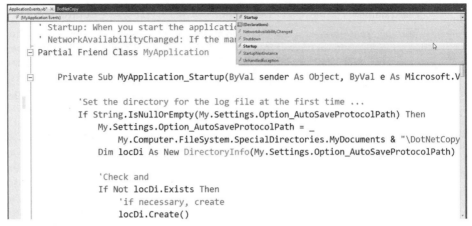

FIGURE 23-2 To insert the event handler body, select one of the five existing events from the list box.

5. Write the handler code itself.

> **Note** Some events pass special inherited versions of the *EventArgs* class as an instance, which you can use to influence the program behavior. Table 24-1 provides more information about the existing events and how they can influence your program.

TABLE 24-1 Events Provided by the Application Framework

Event name	Description	Control options
Startup	Triggered at application start before the start form is created and bound to the application context.	Yes. You can prevent application start by setting the *Cancel* property of the *StartupEventArgs* instance to *True*. In *CommandLineArgs* of this instance the command-line arguments are passed to the application as a *String* array.
Shutdown	Triggered after all applications forms have been closed, unless the application is not closed properly (such as because of an error that caused an exception).	No

Event name	Description	Control options
StartupNextInstance	Triggered at the start of a single instance application, if it is already active. **Note:** You can specify that an application can have only one active instance (cannot have multiple active instances) by enabling the option *Create Single Instance Application* on the *Application* tab in the project properties of your Windows Forms project.	Yes. By setting the *BringTo Foreground* property of the *StartupNextInstanceEventArgs* instance you can specify that the currently running application instance becomes the active application again after the event handler routine has been exited. In *CommandLineArgs* of this instance the command line arguments are passed to the application as a *String* array (the command-line arguments of the call which led to the new start attempt and therefore to the triggering of the event).
NetworkAvailabilityChanged	Triggered when a network connection has been created or closed.	No, but you can use the read-only property to query *IsNetworkAvailable* to discover whether the network is available or not.
UnhandledException	Triggered when an error is not caught. This causes an exception that is not handled	Yes. You can prevent your application from closing due to an unanticipated and unhandled error by setting the *Cancel* property of the *UnhandledExceptionEventArgs* instance to *True*. Additionally, the *Exception* property makes an *Exception* object available to you. The exception contains information about the unhandled exception that occurred.

The following example code demonstrates how to use application events:

```
Private Sub MyApplication_NetworkAvailabilityChanged(ByVal sender As Object, _
    ByVal e As Microsoft.VisualBasic.Devices.NetworkAvailableEventArgs) _
        Handles Me.NetworkAvailabilityChanged
    MessageBox.Show("The network availability has changed!" & _
        "The network is " & IIf(e.IsNetworkAvailable, "available", _
        "not available").ToString)
End Sub

Private Sub MyApplication_Shutdown(ByVal sender As Object, ByVal e As System.EventArgs) _
    Handles Me.Shutdown
```

```
      Debug.Print("The application is shutting down!")
   End Sub

   Private Sub MyApplication_StartupNextInstance(ByVal sender As Object, _
      ByVal e As Microsoft.VisualBasic.ApplicationServices.StartupNextInstanceEventArgs) _
      Handles Me.StartupNextInstance

      MessageBox.Show("You cannot start a second instance of this application!")
      e.BringToForeground = True
   End Sub

   Private Sub MyApplication_UnhandledException(ByVal sender As Object, _
      ByVal e As Microsoft.VisualBasic.ApplicationServices.UnhandledExceptionEventArgs) _
      Handles Me.UnhandledException

      'An unhandled exception has occured!
      Dim locDr As DialogResult = _
      MessageBox.Show("An unhandled exception has occured!" & _
         vbNewLine & "Do you want to exit the application?", _
         "Unhandled exception", MessageBoxButtons.YesNo, _
         MessageBoxIcon.Error, MessageBoxDefaultButton.Button1)
      If locDr = DialogResult.No Then
         e.ExitApplication = False
      End If
   End Sub
```

The program DotNetCopy contains a heavily commented example for the *StartUp* event, which fires when a Windows Forms application starts. Here's the complete code for this event handler:

> **Companion Content** You can take a look at many of the features directly in the DotNetCopy example (see Chapter 22) or open the file DotNetCopy.sln, which you can find in the \VB 2010 Developer Handbook\Chapter 23\DotNetCopy folder.

```
   Private Sub MyApplication_Startup(ByVal sender As Object,
      ByVal e As Microsoft.VisualBasic.ApplicationServices.StartupEventArgs)
      Handles Me.Startup

      'Setting the folder for the log file at first start...
      If String.IsNullOrEmpty(My.Settings.Option_AutoSaveProtocolPath) Then
         My.Settings.Option_AutoSaveProtocolPath = _
            My.Computer.FileSystem.SpecialDirectories.MyDocuments & _
            "\DotNetCopy protocols"
         Dim locDi As New DirectoryInfo(My.Settings.Option_AutoSaveProtocolPath)

         'Check and create if necessary
         If Not locDi.Exists Then
            locDi.Create()
         End If
```

```vb
            'Save settings
            My.Settings.Save()
        End If

        Dim locFrmMain As New frmMain

        'Read command line
        If My.Application.CommandLineArgs.Count > 0 Then
            For Each locString As String In My.Application.CommandLineArgs
                'Remove all unnecessary empty characters and
                'make it case-insensitive.
                'NOTE: This only works under Windows;
                'if the copy list file comes from a Unix server,
                'make sure that the file name is all caps,
                'because Unix (and Linux) derivates are case-sensitive!!!
                locString = locString.ToUpper.Trim

                If locString = "/SILENT" Then
                    locFrmMain.SilentMode = True
                End If

                If locString.StartsWith("/AUTOSTART") Then
                    locFrmMain.AutoStartCopyList = locString.Replace("/AUTOSTART:", "")
                    locFrmMain.AutoStartMode = True
                End If
            Next
        End If

        'Silent mode only remains "on", if AutoStart is enabled.
        locFrmMain.SilentMode = locFrmMain.SilentMode And locFrmMain.AutoStartMode

        'And when in Silent mode, the form is not bound to the application context!
        If locFrmMain.SilentMode Then
            'Everything is performed in the invisible instance of the main form,
            locFrmMain.HandleAutoStart()
            'and has completed before the "actual" program
            'is started with the main form.
            e.Cancel = True
        Else
            'In non-silent mode the form is bound to the application,
            'and off we go!
            My.Application.MainForm = locFrmMain
        End If
    End Sub
End Class

End Namespace
```

Part V
Language-Integrated Query— LINQ

Chapter 24

Introduction to LINQ (Language-Integrated Query)

Programs process data. In a manner of speaking, the whole purpose of programs can be reduced to this common denominator.

However, not all data is the same. Data might all be the same in principle, but developers spend a great deal of time transforming data values to make them usable. These transformations are time-intensive. Here's an example:

- When you load data from a XML file, you need to parse the data, extracting it from the original XML format and placing it into another format, saving the data you need in fields, arrays, listings, or class instances so that you can perform further processing in your application.

- When you retrieve data from hardware devices such as cameras, scanners, or multi-IO cards, you must query a driver—or implement a driver yourself to identify and convert the data into a usable format.

- When you need data saved in a database, you need to connect to the database, define appropriate queries, send these queries to the database, and then process and save the returned data so that you can perform further processing in your application.

This list is essentially endless. Whenever you write code, you're handling data. Unfortunately, prior to Microsoft Visual Studio 2008, the process was potentially different for each data source, and was often not type safe. For example, to retrieve data from a Microsoft SQL Server (or any other SQL server) table in Microsoft Visual Basic 2005, you had to send the query as a string to the SQL server. The integrated development environment (IDE) provided some help: you could use some dialog boxes to help define the query so that it selected the correct field and table names. But in the Code Editor, you were completely on your own.

Since 2003, Microsoft's goal was to provide type security for .NET developers for data queries written within the Editor. The first approach goes back to *ObjectSpaces*—before the first version of .NET. (Take a couple of minutes and do an online search: Dino Esposito, for example, reveals in an article (at *http://msdn.microsoft.com/en-us/library/ms971512.aspx*) that *ObjectSpaces* wasn't too far off from what we know today as *Linq to Entities*). The goal was to integrate data queries regardless of the data source into the programming language that was used to query the data, essentially a *Language-Integrated Query* (*LINQ*) language.

The idea was to more or less equalize data sources so that querying databases would feel almost like querying an array or collection data. Just as database providers handle differences between databases, a LINQ provider would handle differences between various types of data sources.

LINQ providers were intended to ensure that queries of in-memory data objects (collections or arrays) were carried out using search loops. On the other hand the LINQ provider had to generate Transact-SQL (T-SQL) statements for database queries; in turn, those queries were sent to the SQL server, which performed the actual (SQL) query. For that reason, today, LINQ is used for the following purposes:

- **LINQ to Objects**   You can run SQL-like queries against arrays and collections that implement the *IEnumerable* interface (most collections do). You can use collections consisting of instances or classes such as small local databases whose engines are directly integrated into the application.

- **LINQ to SQL**   You can run SQL-related queries directly against a SQL server. *LINQ to SQL* is a fast way to query Microsoft SQL Server databases. First, you use a tool that generates object/relational (O/R) code, which maps object classes that correspond to data tables in SQL Server. The Visual Basic Editor and IntelliSense recognize the database schema (structure) and can help write such LINQ queries. *LINQ to SQL* not only allows you to convert LINQ queries to T-SQL queries but also provides the ability to easily add or update data in a SQL Server table. However, since Visual Studio 2008 SP1, *LINQ to SQL* has a competing technology: going forward, *LINQ to Entities* is the technology that will be developed further. Therefore, this book does not describe *LINQ to SQL* in detail.

> **Note** While *LINQ to SQL* will no longer be a focus of further development, that doesn't mean that it will be removed from the .NET Framework. It will probably continue to exist because it offers some advantages over *LINQ to Entities*: it's more streamlined, and can query large amounts of data from SQL server faster. In fact, it seems that the first database platform that finds its way into the Windows Phone will base its API on *LINQ to SQL*. But *LINQ to SQL* is limited to Microsoft Server technologies only, and it is not nearly as flexible as *LINQ to Entities*.

- **LINQ to XML**   With this provider, you can query XML documents directly to retrieve a collection of desired elements. Chapter 26, "LINQ to XML," explains how this works in more detail.

- **LINQ to DataSets**   This works much the same as *LINQ to Objects* but queries *DataSets*. It provides additional queries that return a data set or a data table. For space reasons, this book does not explain this technology in detail. However, if you have experience with ADO.NET, you will be able to use *LINQ to DataSets* without problems after you read this and Chapter 25, "LINQ to Objects."

- **LINQ to Entities**   In principle, this provider works much like *LINQ to SQL* but with the advantage that there are more ADO.NET providers and it's not limited to SQL Server as a source. This LINQ provider offers more detailed mapping scenarios between an object model (conceptual model) and a database model (storage model). This book covers *LINQ to Entities* in more detail in Chapter 27, "LINQ to Entities: Programming with Entity Framework."

Getting Started with LINQ

LINQ extends .NET languages with query expressions. The query result depends on the LINQ provider, as explained in the last section, but *how* LINQ works is more important, because it works the same way for all LINQ-enabled entities (objects, XML, SQL, and so on).

> **Companion Content**   Open the corresponding solution (.sln), which you can find in the \VB 2010 Developer Handbook\Chapter 24\FirstLinqDemo folder.

The program creates a customer list. The collection elements are saved in business objects whose schema is identical with the table in Figure 24-1. The program also defines a second table that contains details of purchased articles. This second table doesn't contain the customer's name; it uses an ID that you can use to look up the customer data in the first table.

Relation between Customer and Product tables

ID	LastName	FirstName	Street	ZIP	City
1	Ardelean	Adriana	101 Publisher Ave.	WA 98052	Redmond
2	Löffelmann	Klaus	Wiedenbrücker Str. 47	DE-59555	Lippstadt
3	Belke	Andreas	Douglas-Adams-Str. 42	DE-10000	Hamburg
4	Calla	Sarika	One Microsoft Way	WA 98052	Redmond
5	Heckhuis	Jürgen	One Developer Ave.	DE-59555	Lippstadt
6					

IDCustomer	ProductNo	ProductTitle	Category	UnitPrice	Amount
1	6-666	The Rose Killer	Books, Novels	19,90	2
3	2-7053	Microsoft® Visual Basic® 2010 Developer's Handbook	Books, IT	59,99	2
3	3-123	The Social Network	DVD/Blue Ray	29,90	1
5	5-312	Writing Developer Handbooks 101	Books, Misc	39,90	2

FIGURE 24-1 The LINQ sample program creates two tables that are logically linked through their column ID.

And here's the actual problem or task: the program must process the data to ensure that customers are not only sorted by last name but also by the amount that they spend. In addition, the program must be able to display details of purchased articles. The program should include only customers who spent more than $1,000 and live in a specified ZIP code. It looks like this:

```
95: Clarke, Katrin - 7 Products for total 1124.20 $
    Details:
    4-444: Harry Potter and the Deathly Hallows(2 Piece(s) in total 119.90 $)
    4-324: Transporter 3(1 Piece(s) in total 39.95 $)
    4-444: The Da Vinci Code(2 Piece(s) in total 149.90 $)
    5-436: The Cathedral of the Sea(3 Piece(s) in total 254.85 $)
    5-436: The Cathedral of the Sea(3 Piece(s) in total 239.85 $)
    7-321: Pride and prejudice(3 Piece(s) in total 239.85 $)
    9-423: The Social Network(2 Piece(s) in total 79.90 $)
28: Cruise, Anja - 7 Products for total 1039.20 $
    Details:
    2-321: The Jungle Book(1 Piece(s) in total 84.95 $)
    2-424: 24 - Season 7(2 Piece(s) in total 19.90 $)
    4-324: Transporter 3(2 Piece(s) in total 129.90 $)
    5-401: How We Test Software at Microsoft(2 Piece(s) in total 189.90 $)
    5-401: How We Test Software at Microsoft(3 Piece(s) in total 254.85 $)
    5-401: How We Test Software at Microsoft(3 Piece(s) in total 89.85 $)
    5-506: Parallel Programming with Microsoft Visual Studio 2010 Step by Step
➡(3 Piece(s) in total 269.85 $)
19: Schindler, Britta - 9 Products for total 1018.90 $
    Details:
    2-134: Being John Malkovich(2 Piece(s) in total 29.90 $)
    3-123: Bodyguard(3 Piece(s) in total 89.85 $)
    3-333: Der Schwarm (German Edition)(3 Piece(s) in total 89.85 $)
    3-333: Der Schwarm (German Edition)(1 Piece(s) in total 24.95 $)
    3-534: The Maiden Heist(3 Piece(s) in total 209.85 $)
    4-444: The Da Vinci Code(1 Piece(s) in total 64.95 $)
```

```
      9-009: A tale of two cities(3 Piece(s) in total 254.85 $)
      9-445: Eclipse (The Twilight Saga, Book 3)(3 Piece(s) in total 44.85 $)
      9-646: Castaway(3 Piece(s) in total 209.85 $)
96: Spoonman, Theo - 9 Products for total 1079.15 $
      Details:
      2-321: The Jungle Book(1 Piece(s) in total 69.95 $)
      2-424: 24 - Season 7(1 Piece(s) in total 74.95 $)
      4-444: The Da Vinci Code(2 Piece(s) in total 139.90 $)
      5-506: Parallel Programming with Microsoft Visual Studio 2010 Step by Step
➡(3 Piece(s) in total 74.85 $)
      5-506: Parallel Programming with Microsoft Visual Studio 2010 Step by Step
➡(2 Piece(s) in total 59.90 $)
      5-513: Microsoft SQL Server 2008 R2 - Developer's Handbook
➡(3 Piece(s) in total 269.85 $)
      9-445: Eclipse (The Twilight Saga, Book 3)(1 Piece(s) in total 59.95 $)
      9-445: Eclipse (The Twilight Saga, Book 3)(2 Piece(s) in total 159.90 $)
      9-646: Castaway(2 Piece(s) in total 169.90 $)
...
```

LINQ lets you create *one* new collection from two collections (combining collections) by using the schema information (see Figure 24-1) to return a single-collection output, based on specified conditions. The listing looks like this:

```
Module LinqDemo


Sub Chapter24Demo()

        Dim adrListGrouped = From adrElement In adrList _
                        Join artElement In prdList _
                        On adrElement.ID Equals artElement.IDPurchasedBy _
                        Select adrElement.ID, adrElement.LastName, _
                                adrElement.FirstName, adrElement.ZipAndCountry, _
                                artElement.ProductNo, artElement.ProductName, _
                                artElement.Amount, artElement.UnitPrice, _
                                ItemPrice = artElement.Amount * artElement.UnitPrice

                        Order By LastName, ProductNo _
                        Where (ZipAndCountry > "0" And ZipAndCountry < "50000") _
                        Group ProductNo, ProductName, _
                                Amount, UnitPrice, ItemPrice _
                        By ID, LastName, FirstName _
                        Into ProductList = Group, ProductCount = Count(), _
                                TotalPrice = Sum(ItemPrice)
                        Where TotalPrice > 1000

        For Each CustomerItem In adrListGrouped
            With CustomerItem
                Console.WriteLine(.ID & ": " & .LastName & ", " & .FirstName & " - " &
                    .ProductCount & " Products for total " & .TotalPrice & " $")
                Console.WriteLine("     Details:")
```

```
                    For Each ArtItem In CustomerItem.ProductList
                        With ArtItem
                            Console.WriteLine("        " & .ProductNo & ": " & .ProductName & _
                                        "(" & .Amount & " Piece(s) in total " _
                                        & (.UnitPrice * .Amount).ToString("#,##0.00") & " $)")
                        End With
                    Next
                End With

            Next
            Console.ReadKey()


        End Sub

End Module
```

When you inspect this list, you will likely have two questions:

- How do I define a query to retrieve exactly the data that I want?

- How does LINQ work, and how does the compiler implement the LINQ query, given the class concepts and language elements of the .NET Framework?

Let's answer the last question first—because that answer will also address the first question once you understand how the compiler processes this query type and what happens with the query. You don't necessarily *need* to know this. But in the long run if you are familiar with the functionality, you can create queries faster and more efficiently.

LINQ and LINQ queries use lambda expressions. To fully understand LINQ, you should be familiar with lambda expressions (see Chapter 15, "Events, Delegates, and Lambda Expressions"), generics (see Chapter 17, "Developing with Generics," and Chapter 18, "Advanced Types"), and collections and generic lists (see Chapter 19, "Arrays and Collections").

Remember that while LINQ uses an expression syntax that includes some reserved words familiar to many people from SQL (such as *Select*, *From*, and so on), it is not T-SQL or indeed any SQL idiom. Also, the logic behind defining complex queries is very different from SQL.

LINQ: Based on Extension Methods

As mentioned in Chapter 18, LINQ is primarily based on functions implemented as extension methods. Developers use extension methods to create custom functions that extend already defined data types without the need to create a new inherited type. Extension methods are a special type of static method that you can call in the same way you call instance methods for an extended type. There is no real difference between calling an extension method and calling the methods defined in a type from client code written in Visual Basic or C#.

To extend existing types in this way is certainly convenient (see the section, "Using Extension Methods to Simplify Collection Initializers" in Chapter 19). But as far as the infrastructure for LINQ is concerned, you can use the following neat trick: because extension methods can include *all* types as a first parameter, you can also pass interfaces as types. This inevitably results in all types implementing this interface to contain these additional methods. In combination with generic and lambda expressions, this is interesting, because the actual functionality is controlled by one or more lambda expressions and the type to be processed appears only when the type is used. This trick allows you to quickly create a complete type-safe infra-structure to group, sort, filter, identify, or exclude elements in all collections that implement a specified interface containing extension methods, such as *IEnumerable(Of T)*, together with the static methods of the *Enumerable* class. In a nutshell, *all* collections that implement *IEnumerable(Of T)* are supplemented by methods in *Enumerable*, and these are the methods required by *LINQ to Objects* to select, sort, and group data, and to process data in other ways. Confusingly, that only appears to be the way it works; in fact, the entire functional-ity of LINQ is ultimately delegated to a purely procedural class that includes several static functions.

This works similarly for queries that are managed by other *LINQ to Object* providers, except that they use the *IQueryable(Of T)* interface. The extension methods that create a query use "expression trees." Simply put, these trees contain a to-do list for each query the provider can use to create a new query that Microsoft SQL Server or another Oracle server system can understand.

Before getting into the details of LINQ query syntax, it's worth taking a closer look at the extension methods for *LINQ to Objects*, based on *IEnumerable(Of T)*.

The following sections describe only a few of the extension methods. The sections serve to explain the functionality but make no claim to be complete. Instead, the goal is to provide an understanding of the context in which the methods are used by the Visual Basic compiler in proper LINQ syntax and to prepare you for Chapter 25.

The *Where* Method

The first example illustrates the most important extension method of the *IEnumerable* inter-face: the *Where* method. Because normal arrays implement *IEnumerable*, the *Where* method is available for use with these arrays. The method iterates through all the elements, calling a *Predicate* delegate for each element in the collection (the description of *List(Of Type)* in Chapter 19 contains more information). Instead of a delegate variable, you can also specify a lambda expression. If this expression evaluates to *True*—in other words, the corresponding condition is met—the affected element is put in a new result collection that has the generic *IEnumerable* type that matches the source type. In the first example, the source type is an *Integer*, and in the second example, it is a *String*:

```
Public Sub WhereExample()
    ' Where iterates through all elements in the specified
    ' listing and evaluates each element in the Lambda function.
    ' If it applies the corresponding element is put in the new
    ' listing.
    ' The first try with Integer elements ...
    Dim fnums = numbers.Where(Function(oneIntElement) oneIntElement < 6)
    Console.WriteLine("numbers < 6")
    For Each intElement In fnums
        Console.WriteLine(intElement)
    Next
    Console.WriteLine("----------------")

    ' ... another try with Strings.
    Dim fStrings = Namen.Where(Function(oneName) oneName.StartsWith("K"c))
    Console.WriteLine("names starting with 'K'")
    For Each strElement In fStrings
        Console.WriteLine(strElement)
    Next
End Sub
```

The *Select* Method

The next method is *Select*. This method can replace an element in a collection with a corresponding element from a second collection with a different type, based on its ordinal number. The following example uses two arrays of different types:

```
Private numbers As Integer() = New Integer() {9, 1, 4, 2, 5, 8, 6, 7, 3, 0}
Private NumberNames As String() = New String() {"zero", "one", "two", "three",
                                                "four", "five", "six", "seven",
                                                "eight", "nine"}
```

With those collections, you can create a collection by using the *Select* statement to retrieve elements in the second array, based on the content of elements in the first array.

```
Public Sub SelectBeispiel()
    ' Here Select is used to replace an element based on its
    ' value with an element in another listing.
    Dim numberList = numbers.Select(Function(oneIntElement) NumberNames(oneIntElement))

    Console.WriteLine("numbers:")
    For Each s As String In numberList
        Console.WriteLine(s)
    Next
End Sub
```

The preceding method returns this result:

```
Numbers:
nine
one
four
```

```
two
five
eight
six
seven
three
zero
```

Notice that this is identical to the order of the content in the first array.

Anonymous Types

Now we can play with the *Select* method some more to learn about using anonymous types efficiently. Anonymous types are unnamed classes that can be defined directly as return types, for example, within a *Select* method.

You might wonder how you can define a variable or collection based on a type that has no name. It's possible because of *local type inference* (see Chapter 1, "Beginners All-Purpose Symbolic Instruction Code") and generics (see Chapter 17). As you might recall, local type inference defines types during declaration, based on their initial assignment. That also works for types without a name: anonymous types (see Figure 24-2).

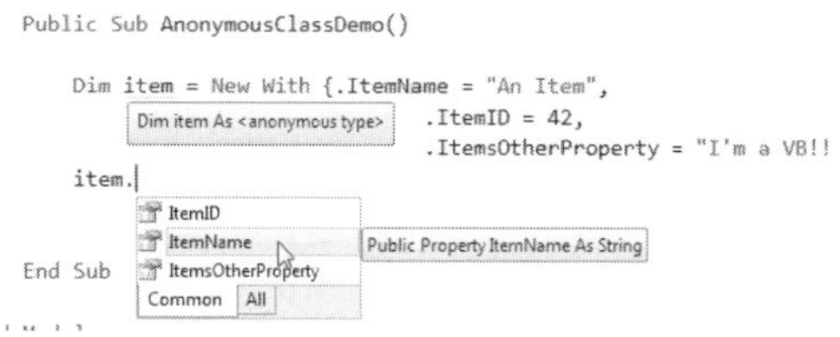

FIGURE 24-2 Anonymous classes allow you to define types without a name. Due to local type inference, you can still assign those types to object variables.

Type Inference for Generic Type Parameters

For this extended *Select* example, we use a similar technique called "type inference for generic type parameters." This concerns generic functions that infer type via passed parameters, as shown in the following method:

```
Public Function ListWithOneElement (Of TSource)(ByVal theOneElement As TSource) As _
                         List(Of TSource)
    Dim lst As New List(Of TSource)
    lst.Add(theOneElement)
    Return lst
End Function
```

You could argue whether this routine makes sense, because it can be passed an instance of any type, creating a collection (for example a list) of that type, adding the passed element, and returning the list. But this isn't about the example code in the method; it's about the way you can pass parameters. For example, to create such a routine without type inferences for generic parameters, you need to write code such as the following:

```
Dim theOneElement As Integer = 10
Dim list As List(Of Integer) = ListWithOneElement(Of Integer)(theOneElement)
```

This code defines *theOneElement* as an *Integer*. The fact that you pass an *Integer* variable to the method is sufficient for the compiler to make an *Integer* method out of the generic method. In fact, the following slightly simplified version works just as well:

```
Dim theOneElement As Integer = 10
Dim list As List(Of Integer) = ListWithOneElement(theOneElement)
```

Using type inference you can take this basic concept a step further. The type definitions in the above list are also redundant: the constant 10 already defines *theOneElement* as an *Integer*. Therefore, the type inference for generics also works for assigning the returned collection type. With this, you get an informative version of the example, as follows:

```
Dim theOneElement = 10
Dim list = ListWithOneElement(theOneElement)
```

The preceding example demonstrates that you can eliminate all explicit type settings, which means that this version also works for anonymous types, as shown in Figure 24-3.

```
Dim list = ListWithOneElement(New With {.ID = 42, .Elementname = "Adams"})
    Dim list As System.Collections.Generic.List(Of <anonymous type>)
```

FIGURE 24-3 If the passed parameter is an anonymous type, the generic type parameter of the generic method is also anonymous—like the listing that returns the method depending on the type.

Knowing that, you should also understand the following routine. Try running the following example:

```
Public Sub SelectExampleAnonymous()
    ' The Select is used to replace one element based on it's value
    ' with a second anonymous element in another listing.
    Dim anonymousList = numbers.Select(Function(oneIntElement) New With
        {.originalValue = oneIntElement,
         .numberName = numberNames(oneIntElement)})
    Console.WriteLine("content of th anonymous class elements:")
    For Each anonymousType In anonymousList
        Console.WriteLine(anonymousType.originalValue & ", " & anonymousType.numberName)
    Next
End Sub
```

Here's what you see for a result:

```
Content of the anonymous class elements:
9, nine
1, one
4, four
2, two
5, five
8, eight
6, six
7, seven
3, three
0, zero
```

If you want to know how methods like *Select* are implemented, check out the following example, which shows a method that you can use to number the elements in a collection of any type:

```
    Public Function ItemNumberer(Of TSource, TResult)(ByVal source As IEnumerable(Of
➡TSource),
        ByVal selector As Func(Of TSource, Integer, TResult)) As IEnumerable(Of TResult)

        Dim retColl As New List(Of TResult)
        Dim count = 1
        For Each item In source
            retColl.Add(selector(item, count))
            count += 1
        Next
        Return retColl.AsEnumerable
    End Function
```

This method takes a generic *IEnumerable* collection of any type and a lambda expression to return an *IEnumerable* collection that was defined by the return value of the lambda expression. The goal is to iterate through all elements in the source list and to allow the calling method to integrate an actual element number (*count*) by using the lambda expression. With an anonymous type, the method could look like the following:

```
    Public Sub ItemNumbererDemo()
        Dim numList = ItemNumberer(New String() {"one", "two", "three", "four", "five",
            "six", "seven", "eight", "nine", "ten"},
            Function(element, count) New With {.ID = count,
                .Element = element})

        For Each numListItem In numList
            Console.WriteLine(numListItem.ID & ": " & numListItem.Element)
        Next

    End Sub
```

This method is also called by inferring generic type parameters. The method *ItemNumberer* is not specified with (*Of Any, Any*). Instead the *TSource* type is derived from the passed *String*-array, and the return value is derived from the passed anonymous type. When you run the method, you see the following result:

```
1: one
2: two
3: three
4: four
5: five
6: six
7: seven
8: eight
9: nine
10: ten
```

Combining LINQ Extension Methods

As you are by now familiar with a few of the most important LINQ extension methods, here's a brief look at how these methods interact.

All these methods return collections that have something in common; just like the source collections on which they are based, the methods implement *IEnumerable(Of T)*. Serendipitously, that also means that the result collection returned by the extension methods can be used as the argument for *another* LINQ extension method; in other words, you can chain them together, as illustrated in the following example:

```
Public Sub CombinedExtensionmethods()

    Dim resultList = contacts.Where(
       Function(oneContact) oneContact.location = "Bremen").Select(Function(oneContact)
       New With {.ID = oneContact.ID,
                 .LastName = oneContact.LastName,
                 .FirstName = oneContact.FirstName,
                 .City = oneContact.location}
                 ).OrderBy(Function(Contact) Contact.LastName)

    For Each contactItem In resultList
        Console.WriteLine(contactItem.ID & ": " & _
               contactItem.LastName & ", " & _
               contactItem.FirstName & " living in " & _
               contactItem.City)

    Next
End Sub
```

When you look at the extension methods in this example, you might already suspect what really happens with the LINQ queries introduced at the beginning of this chapter.

Let's not take two steps at once, though. Take a closer look at the method combinations highlighted in bold in the preceding example:

- First, the program processes the original *contacts* list by using the *Where* extension method. In this concrete example, the *Where* method generates a new collection (again a *List(Of)* in this case) that implements *IEnumerable(Of T)*, but contains only the elements whose *Location* property contains *"Bremen."*

- The resulting list is called with the next extension method: *Select*. This method replaces an element in the first list with another element and incorporates this element in a new list. The *Select* method in this example creates an anonymous class that—in principle—is similar to the original *Contact* elements but contains property names. The old objects based on the *Contact* class are used as the foundation for a series of new objects that the *Select* method creates. The result is a collection containing anonymous class instances that expose property names.

- That collection is also the object of the *OrderBy* extension method. The method sorts the anonymous class instances by last name (*Contact.LastName*). The result, again, is a new collection.

That final generated collection is assigned to the *resultList* object variable and is then used in the *For Each* loop, as illustrated here:

```
4: Ardelean, Adriana living in Bremen
2: Leenings, Ramona living in Bremen
11: Löffelmann, Klaus living in Bremen
7: Nicklaussen, Marcus 'Magges' living in Bremen
```

Note Some of the bullet items aren't entirely true. The extender methods don't return actual collections; instead, they return execution plans for *generating* the collections. (But I didn't tell you that, yet—for now, the explanations in the bullet points are sufficient.)

Simplified Use of LINQ Extension Methods with the LINQ Query Syntax

There is not much left to say. I hope you enjoyed this chapter even if I possibly put the cart before the horse—and if you are familiar with the Porsche 911, you know that that is not necessarily a bad thing to do! You'll probably need only a brief glance to understand what the Visual Basic compiler does with a LINQ expression and how it changes the expression in combined extension methods (at least with *LINQ to Objects*).

The query in the following example uses the same method combination as the example in the previous section, but uses a simplified SQL-like syntax:

```
Public Sub combinedExtensionMethods_à_la_LINQ()

    Dim resultList = From oneContact In Contacts
                     Where oneContact.location = "Bremen"
                     Select ID = oneContact.ID,
                            LastName = oneContact.LastName,
                            FirstName = oneContact.FirstName,
                            City = oneContact.location
                     Order By LastName

    For Each contactItem In resultList
        Console.WriteLine(contactItem.ID & ": " & _
                contactItem.LastName & ", " & _
                contactItem.FirstName & " living in " & _
                contactItem.City)

    Next

End Sub
```

And of course, you get the same result. Try it!

Chapter 25
LINQ to Objects

Getting Started with *LINQ to Objects*

After reading Chapter 24, "Introduction to LINQ (Language-Integrated Query)," you should be familiar with the basic functionality of *LINQ to Objects*. In fact, you might be wondering what else there is to say about it. As far as the internal workings of LINQ, not much more, really; however, there is a lot more to learn about the effect of *LINQ to Objects* on your daily work.

After all, you don't primarily use *LINQ to Objects* to recreate a database containing business objects in your .NET application's Managed Heap—even if the examples in this chapter might imply that. Instead, you can use *LINQ to Objects* to take advantage of the SQL-like query language introduced in Chapter 24 for all sorts of purposes that you might not yet have considered. To use it effectively, though, you need to know which components of a query return the desired results. This chapter helps you to absorb that.

This chapter uses simple object collections as examples (just as in Chapter 24), so you can concentrate on LINQ and avoid being distracted by more complex examples. However, you should realize that you can use LINQ not only for your own business classes and collections, but also to edit and organize other real-world collections, such as files, graphics, or controls.

> **Note** This chapter is not exhaustive; LINQ is too powerful and extensive to cover in just a few chapters. However, you'll get enough information, examples, and suggestions to be able to augment your knowledge with the Online Help. For further reading, I recommend the book *LINQ in Action*, by Fabrice Marguerie, Steve Eichert, and Jim Wooley (Manning, 2008). You can find it online at *http://www.amazon.com/LINQ-Action-Fabrice-Marguerie/dp/1933988169*.

Anatomy of a LINQ Query

LINQ queries always start with this syntax:[1]

```
From rangeVariable In DataList
```

Frankly, from a programmer's point of view, we didn't understand at first why queries had to start with *From*. What is actually taken or used *from* the *range* variable?

The Visual Basic team has the following answer:

"'From' indicates source or origin. The 'From' clause is where you specify the query source (i.e. a data context, in-memory collection, xml, etc.). Thus, we felt the term was appropriate. 'FROM' is also a keyword in SQL. We tried to maintain as much continuity as possible from SQL to LINQ, so that newcomers to LINQ who had experience with SQL would sense the familiarity.

One interesting difference from SQL we had to make is the ordering of the query clauses. In SQL, SELECT comes before FROM. In LINQ, it is the other way around. One of the great advantages of LINQ is that you get to work with various data sources in a common model. Within the query, you really just work with objects and we can provide intelliSense for those objects.

The reason we require FROM first is that we need to know what you are querying over before we can start giving that IntelliSense information."[2]

In the context of the first query expression—*From (*rangeVariable *in the collection)*—*From* refers to more than the range variable.

Let's summarize this:

From initiates a LINQ query. In layman's terms, this means: run through all items after the keyword *In* and use the range variable after *From* to determine how the data in the collection can be selected, sorted, grouped, and transferred into a new collection, based on their properties (with instances of other item classes, if needed).

---

[1] Pure aggregate queries which start with the *Aggregate* clause are an exception (see the corresponding section of this chapter).

[2] *Source:* Lisa Feigenbaum email, sent 01/02/2008. Lisa Feigenbaum is community manager on the Visual Basic team, and a colleague of Sarika Calla, co-author of this book.

> **Important** The following is important for Transact-SQL (T-SQL) professionals: LINQ queries never start with *Select* and don't even have to contain *Select in Visual Basic*. Also, there are no *DELETE*, *INSERT*, and *UPDATE* keywords (see Chapter 27, "LINQ to Entities: Programming with Entity Framework").

Look at the following two queries and note how their results differ.

> **Companion Content** Open the sample console application, which uses business objects to illustrate other possibilities of *LINQ to Objects*. You can find the file in the \VB 2010 Developer Handbook\Chapter 25\LinqToObjectSamples folder.

This program is similar to the example in Chapter 24; it generates two random collections of the generic type *List(Of)* by using business objects (a customer list and an order list, which are related). See Chapter 24 for more information about the structure of this example.

First, look at the following listing from the program example:

```vb
Sub LINQQueryStructure()

    Console.WriteLine("Result list 1:")
    Console.WriteLine("----------------")

    Dim resultList = From adrElement In adrList
                     Order By adrElement.LastName, adrElement.FirstName
                     Select ContactId = adrElement.ID,
                            adrElement.LastName,
                            adrElement.FirstName,
                            ZipCityComb = adrElement.ZIP & " " & adrElement.City
                     Where ContactId > 50 And ContactId < 100 And
                           LastName Like "L*"

    For Each resultItem In resultList
        With resultItem
            Console.WriteLine(.ContactId & ": " & _
                            .LastName & ", " & .FirstName & _
                            " - " & .ZipCityComb)
        End With
    Next

    Console.WriteLine()
    Console.WriteLine("Result list 2:")
    Console.WriteLine("----------------")


    Dim resultList2 = From adrElement In adrList
                      Where adrElement.ID > 50 And adrElement.ID < 100 And
                            adrElement.LastName Like "L*"
```

```
                    Select ContactId = adrElement.ID,
                           adrElement.LastName,
                           adrElement.FirstName,
                           ZipCityComb = adrElement.ZIP & " " & adrElement.City
                    Order By LastName, FirstName

        For Each resultItem In resultList2
            With resultItem
                Console.WriteLine(.ContactId & ": " & _
                                  .LastName & ", " & .FirstName & _
                                  " - " & .ZipCityComb)
            End With
        Next
    End Sub
```

Notice that the queries don't match syntactically. However, when you start the example, you see the following output:

```
Result list 1:
----------------
76: Löffelmann, Katrin - 86937 Dortmund
82: Löffelmann, Bernhard - 76593 Dortmund
69: Löffelmann, Axel - 82786 Cologne
53: Lowel, Katrin - 98830 Cologne
55: Lowel, Alfred - 36272 Los Angeles

Result list 2:
----------------
69: Löffelmann, Axel - 82786 Cologne
82: Löffelmann, Bernhard - 76593 Dortmund
76: Löffelmann, Katrin - 86937 Dortmund
55: Lowel, Alfred - 36272 Los Angeles
53: Lowel, Katrin - 98830 Cologne
```

According to the code example, this output collection is based on two different result collections, generated from two different queries. Still, the results are apparently identical. Coincidence? No. If anything, it is intended that way.

This example code shows how LINQ queries work, but it also serves to show that despite syntactic similarities to SQL, LINQ queries have nothing to do with classic SQL database queries.

By analyzing both queries, you'll see why they have different syntax but produce the same result:

- Like any other LINQ query, the first query begins with a *From* clause that defines *adrElement* as an *range variable* for all the parameters that follow, up to the first *Select*. The *range* variable is (until the first *Select* command) the variable that internally iterates through the whole collection; it is the one on which the properties or public fields of the collection items depend.

- Next is the *Order By* function (but of course it doesn't necessarily have to be next) that receives the fields or properties by which the elements should be sorted as arguments from the range variable. This example uses *adrElement.LastName* and *adrElement. FirstName*. The *range* variable accesses the properties through the *Order By* clause to determine the fields by which the collection is sorted.

> **Tip** If not specified otherwise, *Order By* sorts in ascending order; however, by using the keyword *Descending*, you can change the sort expression to sort the items of the collection in descending order. To sort the first collection by last name in ascending order and by first name in descending order use the following LINQ query expression:
>
> ```
> Dim resultList =
>         From adrElement In adrList
>             Order By adrElement.LastName, adrElement.FirstName Descending
>                 Select ContactId = adrElement.ID,
>                     adrElement.LastName,
>                     adrElement.FirstName,
>                     ZipCityComb = adrElement.ZIP & " " & adrElement.City
>                 Where ContactId > 50 And ContactId < 100 And
>                     LastName Like "L*"
> ```

- Next comes a *Select*. But be careful: as you have learned in Chapter 24, *Select* is used to replace an item in a collection with another item that is specified by the *Select* statement. In the sample, the item that is replaced becomes an instance of a new anonymous class with the same fields that you specify after the *Select*.

> **Tip** Using a *Select* function for a query that refers to only one table and doesn't create groups is basically a waste of time, because you can simply work with the original items, which are selected by default in Visual Basic. Unlike SQL queries, you don't need the *Select* keyword for LINQ in Visual Basic[3] for queries that filter, select, or group items. You only need it to create a new collection that contains items of a new anonymous type, which reveals only the properties you specify as field names. Pay attention to the information regarding *Select* in the next section.

- Now that you've moved on from *Select* and informed the query that you want to continue, but only with *ContactId*, *LastName*, *FirstName* and *ZipCityComb* fields, LINQ can only create new query elements that refer to the new anonymous class established by *Select*. Therefore, an *adrElement.Id* argument after the *Where* clause wouldn't work anymore. *Select* replaced the *adrElement* with instances of an anonymous class that have only a *ContactId* property. The *Where* function filters that new collection with the elements of the anonymous class, including only elements where *ContactId > 50* and *ContactId < 100* and whose *LastName* property begins with the letter "L."

---

[3] You need it in C# though, at the end of each LINQ query.

That completes the first query. Here's a closer look at the second query:

- After setting the collection and *range* variable that serves as the item iterator, the query has a *Where* clause that limits the element to IDs between 50 and 100 and whose *LastName* property begins with the letter "L." *Where* can access these properties directly through the *range* variable because they match an element in the original collection.

- The *Select*, however, puts an end to this, performing a replace operation (unnecessarily and only for demonstration purposes) to replace the elements in the existing collection with new elements belonging to an anonymous class that also has the specified properties (in fact, the old collection is, of course, never actually touched; "replace" here means that new items in the new collection is generated *instead* of the corresponding items in the old collection).

- *Where* limits the collection in the same way as in the first example, but the element type it limits is different.

> **Important** You need to keep in mind that LINQ queries always run in a delayed fashion, never directly. This means that the actual query isn't responsible for starting the processing; instead, only the first access to an element in the result collection initiates the actual query. To learn more read the section "Concatenating LINQ Queries and Delayed Execution," later in the chapter.

As you have seen, including a *Select* clause doesn't make a lot of sense if you return only elements of a type that are already the base types of the list you run your query against. Having said that, *Select*, of course, does make perfect sense for those occasions for which you have to exchange a certain type against another type, such as the anonymous type in the previous example. But be careful: if you need to exchange one type against the other, this always costs computing time. In cascading queries or applications where you constantly have to execute queries, this can mean a hit in your application's performance, although in the current version of the framework, *Select* is quite fast. The following example, although a little bit stilted, shows why *Select* can consume unnecessary computing power without providing a reasonable advantage.

This example uses a high-speed timer to measure the execution time for various queries. It creates a list with 2,000,000 customer elements, both with and without a *Select* clause.

> **Note** When setting up this example, ensure that you change the first lines of the example project as follows:
>
> Module LinqDemo
>
> ```
>     Private adrList As List(Of Contact) = Contact.RandomContacts(2000000)
>     Private artList As List(Of Article) = Article.RandomArticles(adrList)
> ```
>
> Remember to revert these lines for the other examples.

The method containing the example looks like this:

```
Sub SelectSpeedCompare()

    Dim sw = Stopwatch.StartNew
    Console.WriteLine("Start Test")
    sw.Start()
    Dim resultList = From adrElement In adrList
                        Order By adrElement.LastName, adrElement.FirstName
                        Select ContactId = adrElement.ID,
                                adrElement.LastName,
                                adrElement.FirstName,
                                ZipCityComb = adrElement.ZIP &
                                " " & adrElement.City

    Dim firstCount = resultList.Count
    sw.Stop()
    Dim duration1 = sw.ElapsedMilliseconds

    sw.Reset()
    sw.Start()
    Dim resultList2 = From adrElement In adrList
                        Order By adrElement.LastName, adrElement.FirstName

    Dim secondCount = resultList2.Count
    sw.Stop()
    Dim duration2 = sw.ElapsedMilliseconds

    Console.WriteLine("Query duration with Select: " & duration1 &
        " for " & firstCount & " resultElements.")
    Console.WriteLine("Query duration without Select: " & duration2 &
        " for " & secondCount & " resultElements.")
End Sub
```

The test results show the difference. Using 2,000,000 elements, the difference is about one second, as shown in the output that follows:

```
Start Test
Query duration with Select: 16939 for 2000000 Elements.
Query duration without Select: 16061 for 2000000 Elements.
```

Of course, this isn't a real-world value; the example lacks relevance, because if you saved two million records you would likely use a database. However, the point is to show how not to waste processor power on unnecessary tasks.

By the way (the transition to the next section couldn't be better), if you take a closer look at the list, you should notice something that will surprise you. You can't see it? Is it a coincidence that the *Count* property is called within the time measurement? That was done

intentionally; otherwise, the results would be completely different. Now move the *Count* call, changing the example as shown here:

```
Sub SelectSpeedCompare()

...

        sw.Stop()
        Dim firstCount = resultList.Count
        Dim duration1 = sw.ElapsedMilliseconds

        sw.Reset()
        sw.Start()
        Dim resultList2 = From adrElement In adrList
                          Order By adrElement.LastName, adrElement.FirstName

        sw.Stop()
        Dim secondCount = resultList2.Count
        Dim duration2 = sw.ElapsedMilliseconds
    .
    .
    .
    End Sub
```

The resulting output should appear as follows:

```
Start Test
Query duration with Select: 1 for 2000000 Elements.
Query duration without Select: 0 for 2000000 Elements.
```

An error? No, this is exactly the result that should be returned.

LINQ Query Performance

By the way, the demonstration in the previous section is a prime example of using query expression combinations. Look at the following example and consider what might happen:

```
Sub PerformanceTest()

    Console.WriteLine("run query:")
    Console.WriteLine("--------------------")

    Dim sw = Stopwatch.StartNew
    Dim resultList = From adrElement In adrList
                     Order By adrElement.LastName, adrElement.FirstName
                     Where adrElement.ID > 50 And adrElement.ID < 100 And
                           adrElement.LastName Like "L*"

    Dim aList = resultList.ToList
    sw.Stop()
    Console.WriteLine("The query required: " & sw.ElapsedMilliseconds.ToString &
                      " milliseconds.")
    End Sub
```

First, all elements are sorted and then filtered. That's silly, because if you filter the elements first, then there are fewer elements to sort. Always consider the order of the query expressions to improve the performance.

For 200,000 elements, the preceding query expression takes about 1,400 milliseconds on an I7 notebook equipped with a Q720 processor. However, the query takes only a sensational 90 milliseconds—about 14 times faster—if you change the query expression so that the program filters first and then sorts, as shown in the following:

```
Dim resultList = From adrElement In adrList
                 Where adrElement.ID > 50 And adrElement.ID < 100 And
                       adrElement.LastName Like "L*"
                 Order By adrElement.LastName, adrElement.FirstName
```

 Tip When possible, filter *before* you add other query criteria to the query.

Concatenating LINQ Queries and Delayed Execution

As mentioned earlier, LINQ query execution is always delayed. The title of this section could be misleading because it implies that you have a choice when using LINQ queries. But you don't.

If you define a query, such as in the following example, and then run it, the query is not executed immediately:

```
Dim adrGroupedList = From adrItem In adrList
                     Join productItem In prdList
                     On adrItem.ID Equals productItem.IDPurchasedBy
                     Select adrItem.ID, adrItem.LastName,
                            adrItem.FirstName, adrItem.ZIP,
                            productItem.ProductNo, productItem.ProductName,
                            productItem.Amount, productItem.UnitPrice,
                            ItemPrice = productItem.Amount * productItem.UnitPrice
                     Order By LastName, ProductNo
                     Where (ZIP > "0" And ZIP < "50000")
                     Group ProductNo, ProductName,
                           Amount, UnitPrice, ItemPrice
                     By ID, LastName, FirstName
                     Into Artikelliste = Group, ProductCount = Count(),
                          TotalPrice = Sum(ItemPrice)
                     Where TotalPrice > 1000
```

Instead, in *adrGroupedList*, only a kind of *execution plan* is generated—a list of the methods that run successively as soon as you access an element from the result list (which still needs to be generated) or access any properties or functions of the result list are initiated, such as the *Count* property.

But it gets even better: As shown in the example that follows, you can arrange LINQ queries in successive order.

> **Note** To use this example, you need to change the first lines as follows:
>
> ```
> Module LinqDemo
>
>     Private adrList As List(Of Contact) = Contact.RandomContacts(500000)
>     Private artList As List(Of Article) = Article.RandomArticles(adrList)
> ```
>
> Remember to revert these lines for the other examples.

```
Sub SerialLinqsCompare()

    Dim sw = Stopwatch.StartNew
    Console.WriteLine("Start Test")
    sw.Start()
    Dim resultList = From adrElement In adrList
                     Order By adrElement.LastName, adrElement.FirstName

    Dim resultList2 = From adrElement In resultList
                      Where adrElement.LastName Like "L*"

    resultList2 = From adrElement In resultList2
                  Where adrElement.ID > 50 And adrElement.ID < 200

    Dim firstCount = resultList2.Count
    sw.Stop()
    Dim duration1 = sw.ElapsedMilliseconds

    sw.Reset()
    sw.Start()
    Dim resultList3 = From adrElement In adrList
                      Order By adrElement.LastName, adrElement.FirstName
                      Where adrElement.LastName Like "L*" And
                      adrElement.ID > 50 And adrElement.ID < 200
    Dim secondCount = resultList3.Count
    sw.Stop()
    Dim duration2 = sw.ElapsedMilliseconds
    Console.WriteLine("Duration of concatenated query: " & duration1 & " for " &
        firstCount & " items in the result set.")
    Console.WriteLine("Duration of single query: " & duration2 & " for " & secondCount &
        " items in the result set.")
End Sub
```

The second block (highlighted in bold) basically matches the first block except that the queries are chained, but are not executed. Execution occurs only when the code accesses the generated item list. In this example, execution occurs when the code accesses the *Count* property.

The following result shows that with 500,000 elements, there's a difference of only 35 milliseconds between the two execution plans:

```
Starting Test
Starting Test2
Duration of concatenated query: 2569 for 9 items in the result set.
Duration of simple query: 2535 for 9 items in the result set.
```

That's not really a noteworthy difference and falls in the category of insignificant error of measurement.

> **Important** Execution plans created with queries run every time you access a result list. Repeat the last bold formatted line in the above list
>
> ```
> ...
>         Dim secondCount = resultList3.Count
>         secondCount = resultList3.Count
>         hsp.Stop()
>         Dim duration2 = hsp.DurationInMilliSeconds
> ...
> ```
>
> to get the following result:
>
> ```
> Starting Test
> Starting Test2
> Duration of concatenated query: 2617 for 7 items in the result set.
> Duration of simple query: 5451 for 7 items in the result set.
> ```

Cascading Queries

The last example contains two commented-out lines that demonstrate the cascading capabilities of queries. Consider the result of the two additional lines shown in the following:

```
        'Add an item which "would" match the query
        adrList.Add(New Contact(51, "Löffelmann", "Klaus", "Wiedenbrücker Straße 47",
            "59555", "Lippstadt"))
        Console.WriteLine("Items count of simple query: " & resultList2.Count)
```

If you understand those, you also understand the concept of LINQ:

```
Starting Test
Starting Test2
Duration of concatenated query: 3422 for 12 items in the result set.
Duration of simple query: 3276 for 12 items in the result set.
Items count of simple query: 13
```

The preceding code adds another item to the original collection: the criteria list of the cascaded query. When you call the *resultList2.Count* property, it becomes obvious that LINQ initiates the entire query cascade, because the result now contains eight elements rather than seven. This wouldn't be true if LINQ had only evaluated the last result (*resultList2*) because at that point, the new element had not yet been added to the collection.

Parallelizing LINQ Queries with *AsParallel*

Because LINQ in .NET 4.0 allows query parallelization, a single query can run on several processors, when available. But be careful: if you simply add *AsParallel* to the data source, it doesn't make the query faster when more than one processor is available. When and how a query can be parallelized and distributed across several processors or processor cores depends on a multitude of factors.

For time-critical queries, you should definitely experiment. Use the stopwatch class to get a feel for the optimization possibilities.

The following example shows how you can use *AsParallel* to distribute a query to several processor cores:

```vb
Module LinqDemo

    Private Const ELEMENTCOUNT = 20000000

    Private adrList As List(Of Contact) = Contact.RandomContacts(ELEMENTCOUNT)
    Private artList As List(Of Article) '= Article.RandomArticles(adrList)
...

    Sub AsParallel()

        Dim sw = Stopwatch.StartNew
        Console.WriteLine("Starting 1st query (as parallel)")
        Dim resultList1 = From adrElement In adrList.AsParallel
                          Where adrElement.LastName Like "L*"
                          Order By adrElement.LastName, adrElement.FirstName

        Dim firstList = resultList1.ToList
        Dim lastElement = firstList(firstList.Count - 1)
        Console.WriteLine("Finished 1st query.")
        Console.WriteLine()
        sw.Stop()
        Dim duration1 = sw.ElapsedMilliseconds
        sw.Reset()

        'Rebuild the list
        adrList = Contact.RandomContacts(ELEMENTCOUNT)
        sw.Start()
        Console.WriteLine("Starting 2nd query 2 (serial)")

        Dim resultList2 = From adrElement In adrList
                          Where adrElement.LastName Like "L*"
                          Order By adrElement.LastName, adrElement.FirstName

        Dim secondList = resultList2.ToList
        sw.Stop()
        Dim duration2 = sw.ElapsedMilliseconds
```

```
      Console.WriteLine("Duration of the parallalized query: " & duration1 &
         " for " & firstList.Count & " items in the result set.")
      Console.WriteLine("Duration of the serial query: " & duration2 & " for " &
         secondList.Count & " items in the result set.")
   End Sub
```

This example reveals that the coding process to parallelize a query is a breeze. You simply attach the *AsParallel* extension method to the data source to convert the collection into a parallelized query.

Figure 25-1 shows a modern I7-2600K processor that is extremely busy: as many as 20,000,000 records had to be sorted, and the processor used up to 5 GB.

Such amounts of data are quite common in the real world, maybe not when managing contacts or customers, but quite likely when capturing measurement data, time data or operations data. And all that data needs to be filtered, sorted, and processed.

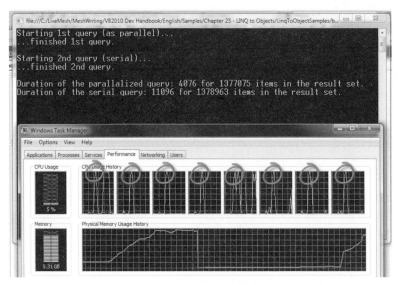

FIGURE 25-1 The processor history shows that the first query was parallelized. All eight cores show a second long peak and the query runs on all cores and processors.

In the figure, all processors are temporarily busy. Parallelizing the query makes it execute significantly faster for that amount of data. Only one core/processor is 100 percent busy working on the second non-parallelized query. The Windows scheduler distributes the 100 percent to more physical cores, but these cores are working with only half—or no—load. Only one thread, and therefore, one core is working with full load. The thread jumps back and forth between the cores and never adds up to 100 percent.

> **Caution** Parallelized queries can backfire. A parallelized query can take *longer* than a non-parallel query because the overhead caused by dividing the data into several threads can become larger than the parallel execution of the query. To discover when to use parallel techniques, it's essential that you test thoroughly with different amounts of data. To become familiar with this topic, read Chapter 28, "Programming with the Task Parallel Library (TPL)," which explains parallelization in more detail.

Guidelines for Creating LINQ Queries

The guidelines for creating queries are as follows:

- LINQ queries consist only of execution plans. The actual queries are not triggered by their definitions.

- When you use the result of a query as the result list for another query, the first query plan is not executed, but LINQ combines both query plans.

- The query is initiated and the result list generated only when you access an element of the result list (through *For Each* or the indexer).

- When you access an element-dependent property, or the elements themselves, the result list is generated again. This also applies to cascaded queries with several clauses.

- Ensure that the query is arranged correctly: filter (*Where*) before you sort, select, or group.

- Try to parallelize queries, but always test to determine whether that's actually more efficient.

Forcing Query Execution with *ToArray* or *ToList*

You've learned so far that every time you access the result variable (for example in a loop with *For Each*) of a LINQ Query—which is, in fact, of type *IQueryable*—the actual query behind it will be executed only then. So, a LINQ query is actually a kind of a sham package. This gives you the impression that the result (the resulting object variable) will contain the items as soon as the program scope reaches the query code. But that's not the case. The truth is that your query simply generates something that SQL Server guys would consider to be an execution plan—and that plan is what's actually stored in the assigned "result" variable. And as the example in the previous sections showed, this policy can be useful at times; however, in many cases it can cause serious performance issues. If, by the way, you really wanted to look at the actual types returned by the various LINQ query methods, they would look something like this (there is a method in the *LinqToObjectsSamples* demo called *TypesOfConcatenatedLinqQueries* that produces this output):

```
Analyzing types:
```

```
Although resultList is of type IEnumerable it actually is of type
System.Linq.Enumerable+WhereSelectListIterator'2[LinqToObjectSamples.Contact,Lin
qToObjectSamples.Contact]
```

```
Although resultList is of type IEnumerable it acually is of type
System.Linq.OrderedEnumerable'2[LinqToObjectSamples.Contact,System.String]
```

```
Although resultList is of type IEnumerable it acually is of type
System.Linq.Enumerable+WhereEnumerableIterator'1[LinqToObjectSamples.Contact]
```

```
Although resultList is of type IEnumerable it acually is of type
System.Linq.Enumerable+WhereEnumerableIterator'1[LinqToObjectSamples.Contact]
```

```
Although resultList is of type IEnumerable it acually is of type
System.Collections.Generic.List'1[LinqToObjectSamples.Contact]
```

But this is just to take a deep look under the hood. Is it necessary to know about those things in detail? Not really—not as long as you don't want to create LINQ queries at runtime via Reflection. And you don't want to do that. Believe me, you just don't. Having said that, if you wanted to create LINQ queries at runtime (which is something you are allowed to want), by all means, you should take a look at *http://tinyurl.com/62s7bbg*.

Therefore, the LINQ developers implemented special methods that convert a result collection based on *IEnumerable* into a "real" collection or a "real" array.

Of these, the most commonly used is the *ToList* method, which converts the result of any LINQ query into a generic *List(Of t)*. Conveniently, this works whether you're using *LINQ to Objects*, *LINQ to SQL*, *LINQ to XML* or *LINQ to something else*. When you run *ToList* for a result list like this, two things happen:

- The LINQ query is executed
- The call returns a `List(Of {original type|Select-anonymous-type})`

The returned elements are "uncommitted." You can index into the list, iterate it with *For Each,* or query the *Count* property as often as you want. The list returned by *ToList* no longer has anything to do with the original LINQ query. *ToList* is extremely simple:

```
Dim pureGenericList = resultList.ToList
```

ToList is not the only method you can use to separate a result list from the original query. With different result collections you can also use the following methods. The designation *t* is always the type of an element in the original list or an anonymous type (for example, created with the *Select* clause within the query).

- *ToList*   Converts the query result collection into a generic *List(Of t)*
- *ToArray*   Converts the query result collection into an array of the type *t*

- *ToDictionary*   Converts the query result collection into a generic dictionary of the type *Dictionary(Of t.key, t)*. You must specify *t.key* by using a lambda expression similar to the example that used an ID as a look up key:

```
Dim pureGenericList = resultList.ToDictionary(Function(oneContact) oneContact.ID)
```

- *ToLookup*   Converts the query collection into a generic lookup collection of the type *Lookup(Of t.key, t)*. Again, you must specify *t.key* with a lambda expression similar to the following:

```
Dim pureGenericList = resultList.ToLookup(Function(oneContact) oneContact.ID)
```

Note The *ToLookup* method returns a generic *Lookup* element—a *1:n* ratio *Lookup*, which assigns keys to value collections. A *Lookup* differs from *Dictionary*, which assigns a *1:1* ratio of keys to values.

Combining Multiple Collections

LINQ provides several options to combine collections. Of course, it doesn't make sense to do that randomly. The collections should have some form of logical relationship. But using the correct expression can save you a lot of time. The section, "How LINQ Works," in Chapter 24, explains a relationship between two collections. That relationship is also the topic of this section (see Figure 25-2).

Relation between Customer and Product tables

ID	LastName	FirstName	Street	ZIP	City
1	Ardelean	Adriana	101 Publisher Ave.	WA 98052	Redmond
2	Löffelmann	Klaus	Wiedenbrücker Str. 47	DE-59555	Lippstadt
3	Belke	Andreas	Douglas-Adams-Str. 42	DE-10000	Hamburg
4	Calla	Sarika	One Microsoft Way	WA 98052	Redmond
5	Heckhuis	Jürgen	One Developer Ave.	DE-59555	Lippstadt
6	Somebody	Else	Grit he Road Street	DE-28300	Bremen

IDCustomer	ProductNo	ProductTitle	Category	UnitPrice	Amount
1	6-666	The Rose Killer	Books, Novels	19,90	2
3	2-7053	Microsoft® Visual Basic® 2010 Developer's Handbook	Books, IT	59,99	2
3	3-123	The Social Network	DVD/Blue Ray	29,90	1
5	5-312	Writing Developer Handbooks 101	Books, Misc	39,90	2

FIGURE 25-2 The LINQ sample program generates two tables that are logically connected through two column IDs.

Combining Collections Implicitly

You can use the *From* clause to combine two collections. The result gives you a new collection in which each item in the first collection is combined with the items in the second collection. Figure 25-3 shows how this is perhaps the easiest way to group collections.

```
Sub CombiningCollections()

    Dim resultList = From adrElement In adrList, artElement In prdList
    'Where adrElement.ID = artElement.IDPurchasedBy

    For Each item In resultList
        item.
        With
                adrElement          Public ReadOnly Property adrElement As LinqToObjectSamples.Contact
                artElement          (.adrElement.ID & ": " & .adrElement.LastName &
                Equals              ", " & .adrElement.FirstName & ": " &
                GetHashCode         .artElement.IDPurchasedBy & ": " & .artElement.ProductName)
                GetType
        End W   ReferenceEquals
    Next        ToString
End Sub          Common  All
```

FIGURE 25-3 Using the *From* clause, you can combine two source collections.

The output of this list includes two properties that provide access to the original elements, and contains results that look like the following (abbreviated to conserve space):

```
4: Walker, Melanie: 7: The Maiden Heist
4: Walker, Melanie: 7: Pride and prejudice
4: Walker, Melanie: 7: Parallel Programming with Microsoft Visual Studio 2010
   Step by Step
4: Walker, Melanie: 8: Microsoft Visual C# 2010 - Developer's Handbook
4: Walker, Melanie: 8: Being John Malkovich
4: Walker, Melanie: 8: The Da Vinci Code
4: Walker, Melanie: 8: Microsoft SQL Server 2008 R2 - Developer's Handbook
4: Walker, Melanie: 8: The Social Network
4: Walker, Melanie: 9: Eclipse (The Twilight Saga, Book 3)
4: Walker, Melanie: 10: A tale of two cities
5: Trouw, Barbara: 1: Microsoft SQL Server 2008 R2 - Developer's Handbook
5: Trouw, Barbara: 2: The Maiden Heist
5: Trouw, Barbara: 2: The Social Network
5: Trouw, Barbara: 2: The Maiden Heist
5: Trouw, Barbara: 2: Transporter 3
5: Trouw, Barbara: 3: How We Test Software at Microsoft
5: Trouw, Barbara: 3: How We Test Software at Microsoft
5: Trouw, Barbara: 4: The Cathedral of the Sea
5: Trouw, Barbara: 4: Pride and prejudice
5: Trouw, Barbara: 4: Being John Malkovich
5: Trouw, Barbara: 4: The Da Vinci Code
5: Trouw, Barbara: 4: How We Test Software at Microsoft
5: Trouw, Barbara: 4: Microsoft Visual C# 2010 - Developer's Handbook
5: Trouw, Barbara: 4: The Da Vinci Code
5: Trouw, Barbara: 5: Runaway Jury
5: Trouw, Barbara: 5: Parallel Programming with Microsoft Visual Studio 2010
   Step by Step
5: Trouw, Barbara: 5: The Da Vinci Code
```

```
5: Trouw, Barbara: 5: Parallel Programming with Microsoft Visual Studio 2010
   Step by Step
5: Trouw, Barbara: 5: Microsoft Visual C# 2010 - Developer's Handbook
5: Trouw, Barbara: 5: The Cathedral of the Sea
5: Trouw, Barbara: 5: Microsoft SQL Server 2008 R2 - Developer's Handbook
5: Trouw, Barbara: 6: Visual Basic 2010 - Developer's Handbook
5: Trouw, Barbara: 6: Harry Potter and the Deathly Hallows
5: Trouw, Barbara: 6: Visual Basic 2010 - Developer's Handbook
5: Trouw, Barbara: 6: Catch me if you can
5: Trouw, Barbara: 6: Catch me if you can
5: Trouw, Barbara: 6: The Maiden Heist
```

The result shows how redundant and uninformative this list is, because it simply combines each product item in the product collection with each contact in the contact collection. It would be far more useful to be able to explicitly assign the purchased products to their matching contacts. Here's how you can do that:

```
Sub CombiningCollections()

    Dim resultList = From adrElement In adrList, artElement In prdList
                     Where adrElement.ID = artElement.IDPurchasedBy

    For Each item In resultList

        With (item)
            Console.WriteLine(.adrElement.ID & ": " & .adrElement.LastName &
                             ", " & .adrElement.FirstName & ": " &
                             .artElement.IDPurchasedBy & ": " & .artElement.
ProductName)
        End With
    Next
End Sub
```

This version already includes a *Where* clause that matches elements in one collection (*ID*) with a correlating item in the other collection (*IDBoughtFrom*). The resulting output makes a lot more sense because it shows which customer bought which article:

```
1: Trouv, Bob: 1: Transporter 3
1: Trouv, Bob: 1: Visual Basic 2010 - Developer's Handbook
1: Trouv, Bob: 1: Pride and prejudice
1: Trouv, Bob: 1: The Da Vinci Code
2: Wallace, Thomas: 2: Transporter 3
3: Spoonman, Anne: 3: The Maiden Heist
3: Spoonman, Anne: 3: Transporter 3
3: Spoonman, Anne: 3: Microsoft SQL Server 2008 R2 - Developer's Handbook
3: Spoonman, Anne: 3: The Cathedral of the Sea
4: Russell, Dianne: 4: The Cathedral of the Sea
4: Russell, Dianne: 4: The Cathedral of the Sea
4: Russell, Dianne: 4: Parallel Programming with Microsoft Visual Studio 2010
   Step by Step
4: Russell, Dianne: 4: How We Test Software at Microsoft
5: Feigenbaum, Thomas: 5: Der Schwarm (German Edition)
5: Feigenbaum, Thomas: 5: The Social Network
```

```
5: Feigenbaum, Thomas: 5: 24 - Season 7
5: Feigenbaum, Thomas: 5: Castaway
5: Feigenbaum, Thomas: 5: The Cathedral of the Sea
5: Feigenbaum, Thomas: 5: Catch me if you can
5: Feigenbaum, Thomas: 5: 24 - Season 7
6: Trouw, Thomas: 6: Being John Malkovich
7: Beckham, Peter: 7: The Social Network
7: Beckham, Peter: 7: The Cathedral of the Sea
7: Beckham, Peter: 7: Harry Potter and the Deathly Hallows
7: Beckham, Peter: 7: 24 - Season 7
7: Beckham, Peter: 7: Der Schwarm (German Edition)
7: Beckham, Peter: 7: Pride and prejudice
7: Beckham, Peter: 7: 24 - Season 7
7: Beckham, Peter: 7: Castaway
8: Lowel, Anja: 8: Der Schwarm (German Edition)
8: Lowel, Anja: 8: The Cathedral of the Sea
8: Lowel, Anja: 8: The Da Vinci Code
8: Lowel, Anja: 8: The Cathedral of the Sea
8: Lowel, Anja: 8: 24 - Season 7
8: Lowel, Anja: 8: Visual Basic 2010 - Developer's Handbook
```

Note The combination of two or more collections with *In* as part of the *From* clause of a query is called an implicit combination of collections. This is because the compiler is not told which list based on what element has to be combined with another list. An explicit combination is created by using *Join*. This is explained in the next section. In this example, explicit and implicit produce the same result.

Combining Collections Explicitly

Unlike implicit list combinations that are specified with *In* as part of the *From* clause, the *Join* clause allows you to set *explicit* list combinations. The *Join* clause uses the following syntax:

```
Dim resultList = From rangeVariable In first list
                 Join combinationElement In second list
                 On rangeVariable.JoinKey Equals combinationElement.secondJoinKey
```

Join combines the first collection with the second collection via a certain key (*JoinKey*, *secondJoinKey*) that creates a relationship between the two collections. In the example, each order in the product collection defines a key (*Key*, *ID*) that corresponds to the *ID* in the contact collection.

Compared with the implicit combination of tables the result is the same. The previous example updated to use *Join* looks like this:

```
Sub JoinDemo()
    Dim resultList = From adrElement In adrList
                     Join artElement In prdList
                     On adrElement.ID Equals artElement.IDPurchasedBy
```

```
            For Each item In resultList
                With item
                    Console.WriteLine(.adrElement.ID & ": " & .adrElement.LastName &
                                    ", " & .adrElement.FirstName & ": " &
                                    .artElement.IDPurchasedBy & ": " & .artElement.
ProductName)
                End With
            Next
        End Sub
```

Using the *Group Join* clause combination, you can group several collections. To learn how this works read the section "Group Join," later in this chapter.

Grouping Collections

The *Group By* clause lets you group duplicates of items or multiple collections. Suppose that you want to group a contact list by last names. Later, in a nested loop, you want to iterate through the names and the contacts assigned to the names. You can do this with the *Group By* clause, as shown in the following example:

```
        Sub GroupByDemo()
            Dim resultList = From adrElement In adrList
                                Group By adrElement.LastName Into listOfContacts = Group
                                Order By LastName

            For Each item In resultList
                With item
                    Console.WriteLine(item.LastName)
                    For Each contact In item.listOfContacts
                        With contact
                            Console.WriteLine(.ID & ": " & .LastName & ", " & .FirstName)
                        End With
                    Next
                    Console.WriteLine()
                End With
            Next
        End Sub
```

In this example, the *Group By* clause does the following: "Create a list with all last names (*Group By adrElement.LastName*) and make the names accessible with the *LastName* property.[4] Include all elements from the original list in the respective collections that belong to the last name (*Into ... = Group*) and make this list available through the *listOfContacts* property."

---

[4] Unless otherwise stated, the field or the property used for grouping has the same name as the original field. If you want to use a different name add a new name before the original one (for example, Group By lastName = adrElement.lastName Into contactList = Group –). In contrast to the previous example, you could not use the *lastName* property to query the last names.

> **Note** You must assign an alias name to the group, as shown in the following:
>
> ```
>         Dim resultList = From adrElement In adrList
>                          Group By adrElement.LastName Into Group
>                          Order By LastName
> ```
>
> Otherwise, *Group* would be the property you would use to access the elements later.

When you start this example, you see the desired result, as shown in the following (abbreviated to conserve space):

```
Baur
37: Baur, Bernhard
50: Baur, Bob

Beckham
27: Beckham, Margarete

Brown
47: Brown, Gabriele

Cruise
17: Cruise, Melanie

Feigenbaum
14: Feigenbaum, Peter
38: Feigenbaum, Gareth

Heckhuis
7: Heckhuis, Britta

Huffman
40: Huffman, Christian
44: Huffman, Barbara
45: Huffman, Guido

Jones
3: Jones, Jürgen
20: Jones, Curt
46: Jones, Bernhard
48: Jones, Katrin
```

Grouping Collections from Multiple Collections

You can also use *Group By* to group and evaluate collections combined with *Join*. Suppose that you need to create a contact list to access a product list to find out which customer bought what product. The query and the iteration through the result elements would look as in the following example:

```vb
Sub GroupByJoinedCombined()
    Dim resultList = From adrElement In adrList
                     Join artElement In prdList
                     On adrElement.ID Equals artElement.IDPurchasedBy
                     Group artElement.IDPurchasedBy, ProductNo = artElement.
ProductNo,
                         artElement.ProductName
                     By artElement.IDPurchasedBy, adrElement.LastName,
                         adrElement.FirstName
                     Into listOfProducts = Group, ProductCount = Count() Order
                         By LastName

    For Each contactItem In resultList
        With contactItem

            Console.WriteLine(.IDPurchasedBy & ": " & .LastName & ", " & .FirstName)
            For Each productItem In .listOfProducts
                With productItem
                    Console.WriteLine("   " & .ProductNo & ": " & .ProductName)
                End With
            Next
            Console.WriteLine()
        End With
    Next
End Sub
```

Here you see a summary of what we learned in the last sections. The query starts with *Join* and combines products and the customer list in a flat list that contains the customer names as well as the purchased products for each customer (name). Then the grouping follows. Unlike the first grouping example that included all elements in the child list, this example specifies the fields that should appear as properties in the inside list between *Group* and *By*. Therefore, the code changes (in a manner similar to the *Select* command) the schema of the inside list. The elements specified after *By* are the elements used for grouping and are available in the outside list. The result (hopefully!) matches your expectations:

```
26: Heckhuis, Bob
    5-436: The Cathedral of the Sea
    5-401: How We Test Software at Microsoft
    4-444: The Da Vinci Code
    5-506: Visual Basic 2010 - Developer's Handbook
    4-324: Transporter 3
    9-646: Castaway

13: Huffman, José
    9-445: Eclipse (The Twilight Saga, Book 3)
    9-423: The Social Network
    5-436: The Cathedral of the Sea
    9-445: Eclipse (The Twilight Saga, Book 3)
    2-424: 24 - Season 7
```

```
6: Jones, Dara
    4-444: Harry Potter and the Deathly Hallows
    5-554: Runaway Jury
    2-321: The Jungle Book
    3-123: Bodyguard
    4-444: Harry Potter and the Deathly Hallows
    9-646: Castaway
    4-444: The Da Vinci Code

7: Löffelmann, Frank
    5-436: The Cathedral of the Sea
    3-333: Der Schwarm (German Edition)

16: Löffelmann, Barbara
    5-506: Visual Basic 2010 - Developer's Handbook
    4-324: Transporter 3
    3-333: Der Schwarm (German Edition)
    4-444: Harry Potter and the Deathly Hallows
    9-423: The Social Network
```

Group Join

You achieve exactly the same result (but with a lot less effort) if you use the *Group Join* clause, which combines *Join* and *Group By*, as shown in the following example:

```
Sub GroupJoin()
    Dim itemList = From adrElement In adrList
                   Group Join artElement In prdList
                   On adrElement.ID Equals artElement.IDPurchasedBy
                   Into listOfProducts = Group

    For Each contactItem In itemList
        With contactItem

            Console.WriteLine(.adrElement.ID & ": " &
                              .adrElement.LastName & ", " &
                              .adrElement.FirstName)
            For Each productItem In .listOfProducts
                With productItem
                    Console.WriteLine("   " & .ProductNo & ": " & .ProductName)
                End With
            Next
            Console.WriteLine()
        End With
    Next
End Sub
```

Aggregate Functions

Aggregate functions are functions that *aggregate* (add, average, calculate maximum or minimum, or count) the elements in a collection. Unlike normal queries, aggregations pass all items in the collection to an aggregate function that calculates all items, but treats them as a batch.

> **Note** LINQ queries always start with the *From* clause—except those that aggregate collections. To run an aggregation of a collection, start the LINQ query with the *Aggregate* clause instead with the *From* clause, as shown in the examples in this section.

This first example aggregates the product list into a total, apparently calculating the total sales of articles:

```
Sub AggregateDemo()

        Dim feignedSales = Aggregate artElement In prdList
                        Into TotalSum = Sum(artElement.UnitPrice)
        Console.WriteLine("Apparent total sales are {0:#,##0.00} $", feignedSales)
```

The following is the output:

```
Apparent total sales are 47.117,60 $
```

But this result only *seems* to be accurate because the query added up only the product prices in a *decimal* variable (*apparentSales*) without taking the number of articles sold into account. The next example corrects that shortcoming:

```
        Dim realSales = Aggregate artElement In prdList
                        Let productSales = artElement.UnitPrice * artElement.Amount
                        Into TotalSum = Sum(productSales)
        Console.WriteLine("Actual sales are {0:#,##0.00} $", realSales)
```

The preceding code introduces a new variable using the *Let* clause that calculates the product of articles sold and article price, and then totals the result—accurately, this time:

```
  Actual sales are 93.306,00 $
```

Returning Multiple Different Aggregations

When an aggregate query uses only a single aggregate function, it returns only a single variable that corresponds to the return type of the aggregate function. For example, when the

Sum aggregate function returns a result with the *Decimal* type, the query result also has the *Decimal* type. But you can include multiple aggregates within a single query, as demonstrated here:

```
Dim multipleInfo = Aggregate artElement In prdList
                Let productSales = artElement.UnitPrice * artElement.Amount
                Into TotalSum = Sum(productSales),
                                priceMin = Min(artElement.UnitPrice),
                                priceMax = Max(artElement.UnitPrice)

Console.WriteLine("Total sales are {0:#,##0.00} $" & vbNewLine &
                "Minimum and maximum prices are " &
                "{1:#,##0.00} and {2:#,##0.00} $",
                multipleInfo.TotalSum, multipleInfo.priceMin,
                multipleInfo.priceMax)
```

This example calculates the product total, the maximum price, and the minimum price all in one go. In such cases, the return variable is an anonymous class type that exposes the properties defined by using the corresponding aggregate variables within the query (in this case, *Sum*, *MinimumPrice*, and *MaximumPrice*). If those variable definitions were excluded and only the aggregate functions were specified, the compiler would have named the properties of the anonymous return types by using the names of the aggregate functions.

> **Important** The last three examples illustrate how aggregate queries are not delayed like standard queries; they execute immediately.

Combining Grouped Queries and Aggregations

If you group queries, you can use aggregate functions because they combine different elements, over which you can run the various aggregate functions.

Suppose that you want to know how much a customer spent for purchases. In this case, you group the query by article using the *IDPurchasedBy* field that represents the customer. For the result list to return not only a number for the customer's total but also a first name and last name, you link the product collection and the customer collection with a *Join* clause or—even better—combine the collection grouping and summary by using a *Group Join*. Finally, you can include an *Order By* clause in the *Group Join* query to sort the result list by the calculated sales volume. If you use the *Descending* keyword on top, you can sort in descending order to display a top-ranked sales list. The actual sales aggregation happens in the clause after *Into,* which determines the property used to iterate through the internal list (*JoinedList*),

if necessary (to return single *artList product* elements). The required aggregate function, *Sum*, adds up the total price that corresponds to sales for each customer.

> **Tip** In this example, the query uses the *Take* clause to limit the result list to 10 elements. There are other clauses that you can use to limit the list, such as *Take While* or *Skip*. *Take* and *Skip* are meant for paging; use this if you want to give the user of your application the option to thumb through a list of result pages. This example should show you how they work, but you can also find more information about these clauses in the Online Help.

```
Sub JoinAggregateDemo()
    Dim resultList = From adrElement In adrList
                     Group Join artElement In prdList
                     On adrElement.ID Equals artElement.IDPurchasedBy
                     Into JoinedList = Group,
                     customerSales = Sum(artElement.UnitPrice * artElement.Amount)
                     Order By customerSales Descending
                     Take 10

    For Each item In resultList
        With item.adrElement
            Console.WriteLine(.ID & ": " & .LastName & ", " & _
                              .FirstName & " --- Sales:" & _
                              item.customerSales.ToString("#,##0.00") & _
                              " $")
        End With
    Next
End Sub
```

When you run this example, you see the following result:

```
48: Beckham, Anja --- Sales:1,269.10 $
49: Feigenbaum, Bob --- Sales:1,194.00 $
3: Beckham, Dianne --- Sales:1,134.20 $
4: Walker, Frank --- Sales:1,099.30 $
1: Picard, Gabriele --- Sales:1,049.15 $
8: Baur, Dara --- Sales:1,044.25 $
29: Tinoco, Anja --- Sales:1,019.20 $
12: Huffman, Gabby --- Sales:999.30 $
31: Trouw, Guido --- Sales:974.05 $
22: Clarke, Dara --- Sales:959.25 $
```

Chapter 26
LINQ to XML

Getting Started with *LINQ to XML*

Extensible Markup Language, or XML, is a subset of SGML (Standard Generalized Markup Language) that was standardized by the World Wide Web Consortium (W3C) in 1986.

Markup languages, together with a set of attributes, create a contextual document structure, or define the presentation of document content—or both. Today, *HyperText Markup Language* (*HTML*) is probably the most popular markup language in the world because it's used to store and display content on the web. (Another markup language you've seen in this book is *Extensible Application Markup Language* [XAML], which is used in connection with the *Windows Presentation Foundation* [WPF].) Generally, you can use simple XML documents to store basic data, such as addresses or products, in a structured way. The X, or *eXtensible*, in XML specifies that the Extensible Markup Language is merely the basis for concrete implementations for markup languages. But XML also has another purpose: it can describe and transfer all types of data.

Briefly, *LINQ to XML* is a LINQ provider that lets you process and select data saved in XML documents by using a Language-Integrated Query (LINQ) syntax.

Before exploring *LINQ to XML*, here's a brief review of XML itself. A typical XML document consists of *elements*, *attributes*, and *values*.

Companion Content Open the corresponding solution (.sln), which you can find in the \VB 2010 Developer Handbook\Chapter 26\LinqToXml folder.

Here's an example of an element:

```
<software Installable ="Yes">Visual Studio 2010</software>
```

The name of this element type is *software*. Elements in XML begin with the start tag *<name>* and finish with the end tag *</name>*, where *name* can be any value (be aware that spaces are not allowed in the name). The element has one attribute, *Installable*, which has the value *Yes*. Elements typically (but not always) have both an opening and closing tag, each enclosed in angle brackets (<>). In this example, the opening tag is followed by the element's content: *Visual Studio 2010*.

When an element has content, the content appears between the opening *<name>* and closing *</name>* tags. When an element has no value, you can use a shorthand syntax, wherein you end the opening tag with a forward slash (*<name/>*) instead of writing out both tags (*<name></name>*). An element's content can be simple text like this example, or it can include other elements.

Attributes within the element are followed by an "=" (equals) character, and the attributes value is enclosed in quotes:

```
<person name="Miller" firstName="Jack"/>
```

This example defines an element without a value—it uses the shorthand form that ends with a forward slash. The element includes two attributes: *name* and *firstName*.

These previous examples are XML fragments, not complete XML documents. An XML document must start with a declaration that specifies that the document is an XML document, as shown here:

```
<?xml version="1.0"?>.
```

More Information A complete description of XML is beyond the scope of this book. To learn more about it, visit SELFHTML at *http://de.selfhtml.org/* or the W3C website at *http://www.w3.org/*.

Processing XML Documents—Yesterday and Today

To create or change an XML structure in Microsoft Visual Basic 2005 and earlier versions required significant developer efforts. For example, here's what you had to do to extend the following XML structure that saves vehicle data by adding a *modelYear* element:

```
<fleet>
  <licensePlate>MS - VB 2010</licensePlate>
  <load amount="10 Tons">Salt</load>
  <manufacturer>Mack</manufacturer>
  <modelYear>1998</modelYear>
</fleet>
```

In Visual Basic 2005, the code is:

```
Dim xml As New XmlDocument
xml.Load(Application.StartupPath + "\fleet1.xml")
Dim nodeList As XmlNodeList = xml.GetElementsByTagName("fleet")

'In case there are more: loop
For Each node As XmlNode In nodeList
    Dim xmlElement As XmlElement = xml.CreateElement("modelYear")
    xmlElement.InnerText = "1998"
    node.AppendChild(xmlElement)
Next
```

However, beginning with Visual Basic 2008, XML processing was simplified when the .NET Framework was extended with several powerful classes. The most important of these classes are *XDocument*, *XElement*, and *XAttribute*.

Using these new classes you can create the preceding XML example document by using the following code:

```
Dim xml As New XDocument
xml.Add(New XElement("fleet", _
            New XElement("licensePlate", "MS - VB 2010"), _
            New XElement("load", _
                            New XAttribute("amount", "10 Tons"), _
                            "Salt" _
                            ), _
            New XElement("manufacturer", "Mack") _
))
```

The elements *licensePlate*, *load,* and *manufacturer* are saved as the content of the *fleet* element. The *load* element receives an attribute named *amount*. Now, to add a new *modelYear* element, you can simply use the *Add* method, as follows:

```
xml.Element("fleet").Add(New XElement("modelYear", 1998))
```

To retrieve the value of a *XElement* element (such as the model year, *1998*), use the *Value* property, as shown here:

```
'Retrieve values with the Value property
'Total "value":
Console.WriteLine(xml.Element("fleet").Value)

'Only the ModelYear:
Console.WriteLine(xml.Element("fleet").Element("modelYear").Value)
Console.ReadKey()
```

The last lines in this example return the following output:

```
MS - VB 2010SaltMack1998
1998
```

XML Literals: Using XML Directly in Code

It gets even better. Again, beginning with Visual Basic 2008, you can create documents that work with *XDocument* and *XElement* objects directly in code. These inline XML documents are called *XML literals*. The following example shows how this works:

```
Dim fleet As XElement = <fleet>
                              <licensePlate>MS - VB 2010</licensePlate>
                              <load amount="10 Tons">Salt</load>
                              <manufacturer>Mack</manufacturer>
                        </fleet>
```

The *fleet* object is a simple *Xelement*. You can add the *modelYear* element as usual:

```
fleet.Add(New XElement("modelYear", 1998))
```

And it's even easier with XML literals:

```
fleet.Add(<modelYear>1998</modelYear>)
```

Including Expressions in XML Literals

Inline XML documents don't need to be completely static; they can include dynamic elements, as well. This means that you can embed expressions delimited with <%= and %> into the inline XML code, as illustrated in the following two lines:

```
Dim myModelYear As Integer = 1998
fleet.Add(<modelYear><%= myModelYear %></modelYear>)
```

When the *Add* method executes, the value of the *modelYear* element is replaced with the value of the *myModelYear* variable.

Creating XML Documents with LINQ

You can also create XML documents by using LINQ. For example, suppose that you have a list that was created by using the following code lines:

```
Dim vehiclelist As New List(Of Vehicle)
vehiclelist.Add(New Vehicle With {.LicensePlate = "MS-VB 2010",
    .Manufacturer = "Mack", _
    .Load = New Vehicle.LoadDescription With
                                {.Amount = 10000, .goods = "Salt"}})
```

```vb
            vehiclelist.Add(New Vehicle With {.LicensePlate = "MS-C# 2010", . 
                Manufacturer = "Mercedes-Benz",
                .Load = New Vehicle.LoadDescription With
                                         {.Amount = 20000, .Goods = "Peanuts"}})
            vehiclelist.Add(New Vehicle With {.LicensePlate = "MS-F# 2010",
                .Manufacturer = "Peterbilt",
                .Load = New Vehicle.LoadDescription With
                                         {.Amount = 5000, .Goods = "Bobbleheads"}})


    Private Class Vehicle
        Public Class LoadDescription

            Public Property Amount() As Double

            Public Property goods() As String
        End Class


        Public Property LicensePlate() As String

        Public Property Load() As LoadDescription

        Public Property Manufacturer() As String
    End Class
```

Now, you need to create the following XML element from that list:

```xml
<fleet>
  <vehicle>
    <licensePlate>MS-VB 2010</licensePlate>
    <manufacturer>Mack</manufacturer>
    <load amount="10000">Salt</load>
  </vehicle>
  <vehicle>
    <licensePlate>MS-C# 2010</licensePlate>
    <manufacturer>Mercedes-Benz</manufacturer>
    <load amount="20000">Peanuts</load>
  </vehicle>
  <vehicle>
    <licensePlate>MS-F# 2010</licensePlate>
    <manufacturer>Peterbilt</manufacturer>
    <load amount="5000">Bobbleheads</load>
  </vehicle>
</fleet>
```

You create the XML structures by using *XElement* and *XAttribute*:

```vb
        Dim fleet = New XElement("fleet", _
              From fzg In vehiclelist _
              Select New XElement("vehicle", _
                            New XElement("licensePlate", fzg.LicensePlate), _
                            New XElement("manufacturer", fzg.Manufacturer), _
                            New XElement("load", fzg.Load.Goods,
                                New XAttribute("amount", fzg.Load.Amount)) _
                            )
                    )
```

This adds a list of (*vehicle*) *XElements* to the *XElement* called *fleet*. This list (which, to be accurate, is an *IEnumerable(Of XElement)*) was created with *LINQ to Objects*. The code adds child elements to the *vehicle* element, as well. You can also use expressions, such as those shown in the following:

```
fleet = <fleet>
            <%= From vcl In vehiclelist _
                Select <vehicle>
                           <licensePlate><%= vcl.LicensePlate %></licensePlate>
                           <manufacturer><%= vcl.Manufacturer %></manufacturer>
                           <load amount=<%= vcl.Load.Amount %>>
                               <%= vcl.Load.Goods %>
                           </load>
                       </vehicle> _
            %>
        </fleet>
```

Querying XML Documents with *LINQ to XML*

LINQ to XML also provides query support for XML structures. Here's another example:

```
Dim fleet = <?xml version="1.0"?>
                <fleet>
                    <vehicle>
                        <licensePlate>MS-VB 2010</licensePlate>
                        <manufacturer>Mack</manufacturer>
                        <load amount="10000">Salt</load>
                    </vehicle>
                    <vehicle>
                        <licensePlate>MS-C# 2010</licensePlate>
                        <manufacturer>Mercedes-Benz</manufacturer>
                        <load amount="20000">Peanuts</load>
                    </vehicle>
                    <vehicle>
                        <licensePlate>MS-F# 2010</licensePlate>
                        <manufacturer>Peterbilt</manufacturer>
                        <load amount="5000">Bobbleheads</load>
                    </vehicle>
                </fleet>
Dim mackVehicles = From vehicle In fleet...<vehicle> _
Where vehicle.<manufacturer>.Value = "Mack"
For Each vehicle In mackVehicles
    Console.WriteLine(vehicle)
Next
```

The *fleet* variable is an *XDocument*. The query's *From* clause retrieves all *XElements* with the name *vehicle*. The *Where* clause filters the list, selecting only vehicles for which the vehicle manufacturer is "Mack." You retrieve the value of an *XElement* by using the *Value* property.

There are two ways to access elements:

To access immediate child elements, use *<Elementname>*. But you can also access underlying elements by using the syntax ...*<Elementname>*. Elements that you access in this manner can reside at any level within the XML structure.

If you want to access the content of an attribute, use the syntax .@<Attributename>.

As an example, to retrieve all vehicles capable of carrying heavy loads, you might write:

```
Dim heavyLoad = From vehicle In fleet...<vehicle> _
                Where Cdbl(vehicle.<load>.@amount) > 15000
For Each vehicle In heavyLoad
    Console.WriteLine(vehicle)
Next
```

The output appears as follows:

```
<vehicle>
  <licensePlate>MS-C# 2010</licensePlate>
  <manufacturer>Mercedes-Benz</manufacturer>
  <load amount="20000">Peanuts</load>
</vehicle>
```

> **Caution** Even if you defined the document types with an XML schema (XSD) file for your XML document, LINQ queries always return values as strings. This applies to both elements and attributes. As shown in the example, you must always use the matching cast operators to query the actual type. Of course, this can cause errors.
>
> Therefore, you should pay special attention to type safety with *LINQ to XML*. You must enable *Option Strict*; otherwise, you risk processing strings even if you wanted to compare numeric types—and suddenly 4,500 is larger than 15,000.

IntelliSense Support for *LINQ To XML* Queries

When working with XML data, it is very useful to have IntelliSense support in the integrated development environment (IDE). Visual Basic 2010 adds this support, as shown in Figure 26-1.

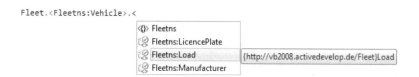

FIGURE 26-1 XML IntelliSense support.

You can use this support by importing an XML Schema Definition (XSD) file via Import in the code files. But let's start at the beginning. Microsoft Visual Studio can create an XSD file for you. First, you create the XML file that contains all the required characteristics, as illustrated in Figure 26-2).

```
fleet2.xml*  ×
    <?xml version="1.0"?>
  <Fleet>
    <vehicle>
      <LicencePlate>MS-VB 2010</LicencePlate>
      <Manufacturer>Mack</Manufacturer>
      <Goods Amount="10000">Salt</Goods>
    </vehicle>
    <vehicle>
      <LicencePlate>MS-C# 2010</LicencePlate>
      <Manufacturer>Mercedes-Benz</Manufacturer>
      <Goods Amount="20000">Peanuts</Goods>
    </vehicle>
    <vehicle>
      <LicencePlate>MS-F# 2010</LicencePlate>
      <Manufacturer>Peterbilt</Manufacturer>
      <Goods Amount="5000">Bobbleheads</Goods>
    </vehicle>
  </Fleet>
```

FIGURE 26-2 An XML file in Visual Studio.

Next, you use the Create Schema command in the XML menu (see Figure 26-3) to create a schema.

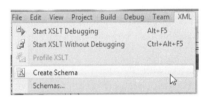

FIGURE 26-3 Creating a XML Schema Definition (XSD).

Save the created schema in the project directory and include it in the project, as depicted in Figure 26-4.

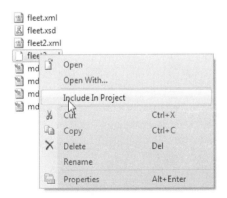

FIGURE 26-4 Including a file in Solution Explorer.

You must also specify a target namespace in the XSD file that you just created. The namespace doesn't need to exist; it's used solely for identification purposes. This example uses the namespace *http://mysample.local.de/fuhrpark2* (see Figure 26-5).

```
fleet2.xsd  X  fleet2.xsd [Design]      fleet2.xml*
    <?xml version="1.0" encoding="utf-8"?>
  <xs:schema attributeFormDefault="unqualified"
             elementFormDefault="qualified"
             xmlns:xs="http://www.w3.org/2001/XMLSchema"
             targetNamespace="http://mysample.local.de/Fleet2">
```

FIGURE 26-5 Adding a target namespace to an XSD file.

You then import the target namespace into the Visual Basic file where you want to enable XML support, as shown in Figure 26-6.

```
(General)
   Imports <xmlns=
                        <> ""
 Module XmlWithL    <> "http://mysample.local.de/Fleet2"      A target names
                        <> "http://vb2008.activedevelop.de/Fleet"
   Sub Demo()
```

FIGURE 26-6 Adding an *Imports* statement for XML schema files.

If you use several namespaces, you should add a prefix to the namespace, right after the *xmlns*, separated by a colon. The prefix acts as shorthand so that you don't need to identify elements with the full namespace name. The following example uses the prefix *fleet*. You don't need to add a prefix if you import only one namespace in a Visual Basic code file.

```
Imports <xmlns:fleet="http://mysample.local.de/fleet2">
Imports <xmlns:article="http://mysample.local.de/article">
```

Using Prefixes (*fleet* and *article*)

Now, append the prefixes to your XML structures, as follows, with the results displayed in Figure 26-7:

```
        Dim fleet = <fleet:fleet>
                        <fleet:vehicle>
                            <fleet:licensePlate>MS-VB 2010</fleet:licensePlate>
                            <fleet:manufacturer>Mack</fleet:manufacturer>
                            <fleet:load amount="10000">Salt</fleet:load>
                        </fleet:vehicle>
                        <fleet:vehicle>
                            <fleet:licensePlate>MS-C# 2010</fleet:licensePlate>
                            <fleet:manufacturer>Mercedes-Benz</fleet:manufacturer>
                            <fleet:load amount="20000">Peanuts</fleet:load>
                        </fleet:vehicle>
```

```
<fleet:vehicle>
    <fleet:licensePlate>MS-F# 2010</fleet:licensePlate>
    <fleet:manufacturer>Peterbilt</fleet:manufacturer>
    <fleet:load amount="5000">Bobbleheads</fleet:load>
</fleet:vehicle>
</fleet:fleet>
```

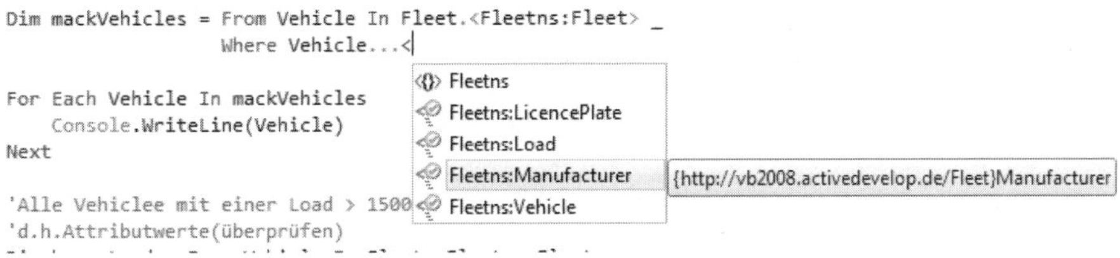

```
Dim mackVehicles = From Vehicle In Fleet.<Fleetns:Fleet> _
            Where Vehicle...<

For Each Vehicle In mackVehicles
    Console.WriteLine(Vehicle)
Next

'Alle Vehiclee mit einer Load > 1500
'd.h.Attributwerte(überprüfen)
```

<{}>	Fleetns
⬦	Fleetns:LicencePlate
⬦	Fleetns:Load
⬦	Fleetns:Manufacturer
⬦	Fleetns:Vehicle

{http://vb2008.activedevelop.de/Fleet}Manufacturer

FIGURE 26-7 XML support for the IDE.

Chapter 27
LINQ to Entities: Programming with Entity Framework

An *entity* in data modeling is a unique object that can hold information. This abstract definition already implies that *LINQ to Entities* must be a rather flexible process. But what does it do?

These days, developers create most data-oriented applications by using relational databases as the data store. The logical structure of database tables and data views in a standard database system, such as Microsoft SQL Server, Oracle Database, or IBM's DB2 represents a less-than-optimal match to the conceptual models typically used in object-oriented applications. This problem is referred to in the industry as an *impedance mismatch*. Attempts to map data to objects between the different worlds of objects and database schema will always be incomplete until the database that stores application objects is truly object oriented—and that's not the case for these large, commercial database systems.

The *Entity Data Model* (EDM) can help here because it describes a *conceptual* data model, that lets you build a bridge between the two worlds, thanks to its flexible mapping capabilities.

LINQ to SQL takes the same approach. It helps you to create business objects oriented toward the schema of a database table or view. For developers designing medium-size database systems, this is often just the kind of assistance that's required, and in many cases it's sufficient.

However, the options for mapping data between the logical, relational data model of data-bases and the conceptual, object-oriented model in applications just don't go far enough in *LINQ to SQL*, neither in assigning tables to business objects nor in the data provider(s) abstractions behind them. *LINQ to SQL* works only with Microsoft SQL Server platforms (SQL Server 2000, 2005, and 2008), and table and view mapping to an object model occurs only in a 1:1 fashion.

> **Note** *LINQ to SQL* was re-engineered for Microsoft .NET Framework 4.0 and will probably continue to be maintained in upcoming Service Packs. For some purposes, *LINQ to SQL* is more suitable than *LINQ to Entities*; for example, in the current .NET Framework version, it is notice-ably faster than *LINQ to Entities* when transferring larger amounts of data from a SQL server to a client. But unfortunately, it can transfer that data only from Microsoft SQL Server. Unlike *LINQ to Entities* or the Microsoft ADO.NET Entity Framework, .NET Framework 4.0 added no significant new functionality to *LINQ to SQL*.

LINQ to Entities gets around this shortcoming by introducing an additional layer between the generated business objects and the original database, known as a *conceptual layer*. This makes *LINQ to Entities* much more flexible than *LINQ to SQL*—but it also makes it somewhat more difficult to use.

You need to understand a few additional concepts to be able to use *LINQ to Entities* cor-rectly, and these concepts are best learned by practicing them. Therefore, you'll first explore how you use ADO.NET Entity Framework to create a conceptual entity model for a database, and after that, you'll see how to use it to query data. That way, you'll encounter the new ele-ments in the appropriate context.

Prerequisites for Testing the Examples

To perform the examples in this chapter, you need a functional instance of SQL Server 2008, or even better, the newer R2 Edition of SQL Server 2008. The Express Edition is sufficient; it's free and usually enough for most database applications. You can even distribute it along with your applications.

> **Note** Unfortunately, you can't use the version of SQL Server 2008 Express that is installed with Visual Studio 2010, because the Microsoft example database *AdventureWorks* is not compatible with this one. SQL 2008 (R2) Express with Advanced Services is a better version anyway, because it also installs SQL Server Management Studio Basic for managing SQL Server instances and databases.

If you have already installed SQL Server 2008 Express as part of your Visual Studio 2010 installation, you should uninstall it via the Control Panel (Programs And Functions). But in this

case, you don't need to re-install the required software as described in the Caution reader aid that follows.

Downloading and Installing SQL Server 2008 R2 Express Edition with Advanced Services

You can download SQL Server 2008 R2 Express Edition with Advanced Services from *http://tinyurl.com/4342ovd*.

> **Caution** Depending on the version and the components already installed on your computer, you will need to download and install the following components *before* installing SQL Server 2008 Express Edition with Advanced Services:
>
> - Ensure that .NET Framework 3.5 with Service Pack 1 is installed. The link is: *http://tinyurl.com/5wkyzun*. If you are using Windows 7 or Windows Server 2008 R2, these are already installed.
>
> - Download Microsoft Installer 4.5 from *http://tinyurl.com/3qjkqqp* and install it. Ensure that you download the correct file: for Windows Vista and Windows Server 2008, download the relevant version for your processor architecture, which begins with *Windows 6.0*. Windows XP, and Windows Server 2003 versions are marked differently (by processor architecture: *x64* for 64-bit operating systems, *x86* for 32-bit operating systems). For example, for a Vista 64-bit operating system, download the file *Windows6.0-KB942288-v2-x64.msu*.
>
> - For Windows Server 2003, Download the PowerShell component, which is part of the Management Framework Core package, from *http://tinyurl.com/3vy48v3*, and install it. PowerShell is required even if you have already installed Visual Studio 2010. If you are running Windows Server 2008 R2 or Windows 7, you don't need to download PowerShell, because it's is already part of the system. For every other supported Operating System (Vista x64, x86, XP, 2008) see *http://support.microsoft.com/kb/968930* and find the corresponding download on that page.

After you have installed all the required components, you can install SQL Server 2008 Express Edition with Advanced Services. Unfortunately, if you go for SQL Server 2008 (Express) and not the R2 Version, Windows 7 triggers messages about compatibility issues when running the installation package. You can perform the installation regardless, but you must ensure that you install Service Pack 1 for SQL Server 2008 afterward.

1. To install SQL Server 2008 (R2) Express Edition with Advanced Services, launch the installation file that you downloaded.

    The SQL Server Installation Center dialog box opens, as shown in Figure 27-1.

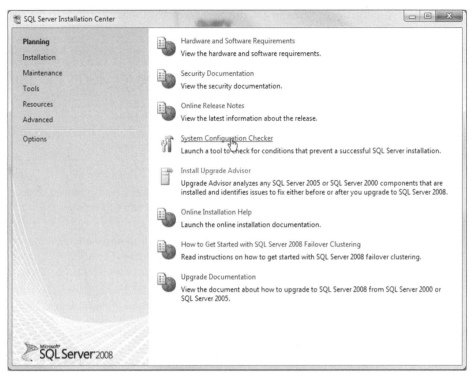

FIGURE 27-1 The SQL Server Express installation file first takes you to the SQL Server Installation Center. First, run a system configuration check before starting the actual installation (don't do this if you are using Windows 7; just skip that step).

2. Click the System Configuration Check link, to ensure that your target system meets all the installation requirements, and add any missing components.

Note You can ignore this step for Windows 7. You should have already received a warning about problems. Ignore this message for now and start the installation anyway. Afterward, you must install Service Pack 1 for SQL Server 2008, which you can find at *http://tinyurl.com/ 26k52uy.*

3. In the left pane of the dialog (see Figure 27-1), click Installation.

The dialog changes accordingly, as shown in Figure 27-2.

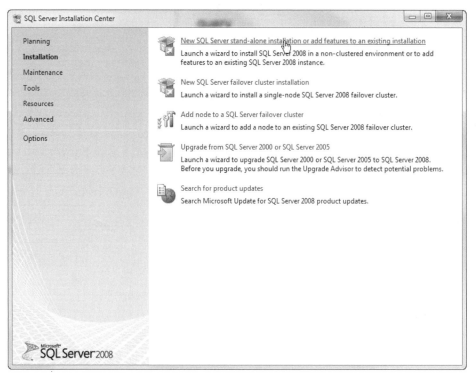

FIGURE 27-2 In the left pane of the dialog, click Installation, and then in the right pane, click the upper link to commence installation of the Express Edition of SQL Server 2008.

4. Click New SQL Server Stand-Alone Installation Or Add Features To An Existing Installation to start installing the Express Edition.

5. The installation starts checking the setup support rules.

You shouldn't get any more errors. Close the dialog by clicking OK.

6. The SQL Server 2008 Setup Wizard opens (it might appear in the original dialog, which you might need to bring to the foreground).

Click Continue, accept the licensing terms in the next step, and then click Continue again.

The Setup Support Files dialog box opens.

7. In the Setup Support Files dialog box (see Figure 27-3), click Install.

This process can take a few minutes.

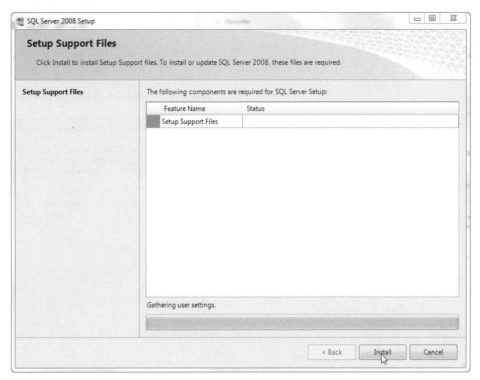

FIGURE 27-3 In the step Setup Support Files, click Install to install the setup support files.

In the summary that displays, you should see only a Windows Firewall warning. You can ignore this warning as long as you are running your SQL Server databases locally, on your computer. You only need to open the appropriate Windows Firewall ports (SQL Server default port is 1433) if you want to access the SQL Server instances from a different computer via the network. Therefore, click Continue to proceed to the next step.

8. Use the Feature Selection dialog box (Figure 27-4) to specify which features you want to install along with the main installation.

Be sure to include the Database Model Services and the Management Tools. Optionally, you can select SQL Server Replication if you want to copy the contents of the database regularly to other databases for replication purposes.

Important   You must select the Full-Text Search option for the *AdventureWorks* database to work correctly.

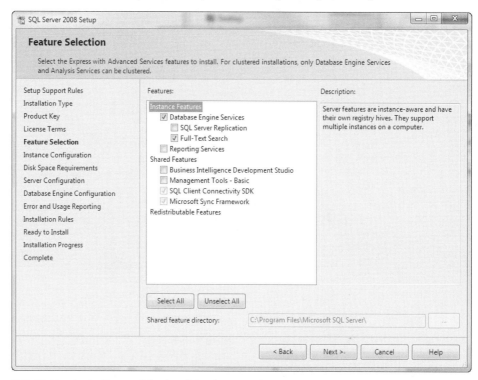

FIGURE 27-4 In the Feature Selection dialog box, you choose additional components that the setup should install. At minimum, you must select the components that are selected here. Selecting Management Tools is also strongly recommended.

9. Click Next.

10. In dialog box that opens, enter a name for the SQL Server instance that will manage your databases.

    You can keep the default *Named Instance*: *SQLExpress*, as long as there is no SQL Server instance with this name on the same computer (for example, you might have previously installed a version of SQL Server 2005 Express Edition together with Visual Studio). Otherwise, enter a different name of your choice.

11. Click Next.

12. A summary of the installation parameters appears. If you agree with the summary, confirm by clicking Next.

13. The Server Configuration dialog box opens. So that you can find your SQL Server instance later (for example, when using the Connections dialog in Visual Studio Server Explorer), set SQL Server Browser to *Automatic*, as shown in Figure 27-5.

14. In this same dialog, specify the system accounts that the database engine as well as the browser service should use, and then click Next.

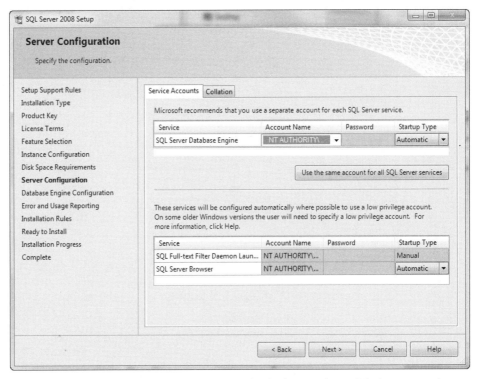

FIGURE 27-5 Specify the accounts in whose context the database engine and the browser service should run.

15. In the Database Engine Configuration dialog box (Figure 27-6), specify the authentication mode that clients will use to log on to the instance and the databases it manages.

If you're developing applications exclusively on the same computer that is running the SQL Server instance, or you're running SQL Server on a computer that belongs to an Active Directory domain, select the Windows Authentication Mode option. If no domain exists, you must transfer login information for a SQL Server instance login; this only works if you switch the instance to Mixed Mode. In this case, you must also specify a system administrator ("sa") password that you'll later use to log on to the instance.

Note A well-known virus called "SQL Slammer" used to take advantage of the understandable human weakness of not using a password for the *sa* account with SQL Server 2000; this is why the setup now warns you to choose a password. Therefore, ensure that you use a secure password composed of at least six characters, using both uppercase and lowercase characters, special characters, and numbers.

16. Click Next.

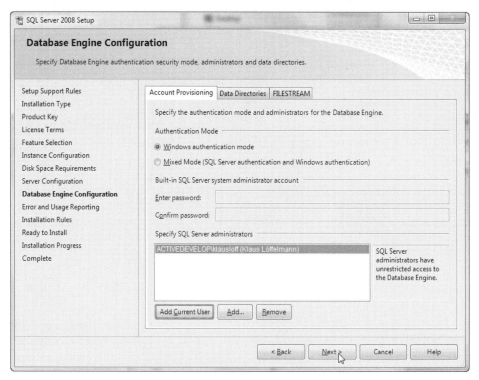

FIGURE 27-6 In the Database Engine Configuration dialog box, you specify the authentication mode the instance should use and add a user as SQL Server administrator to the database instance.

17. Set up the dialog as desired for your installation, and then click Next. (The dialog options on this screen are explained in detail in the available Help system.)

At this point, the installation rules check should be complete, as shown in Figure 27-7. The database services are now ready to be installed.

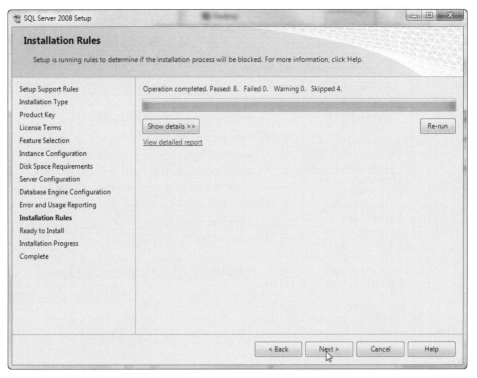

FIGURE 27-7 The installation rules have been confirmed successfully, and you're ready to install the database services.

18. Before starting the installation and clicking *Install*, review the summary in the previous dialog.

The installation takes a while. When it completes, you usually need to restart your computer. Confirm The Setup Process Is Complete dialog by clicking Continue. Click OK in the final dialog (Figure 27-8), and then click Close. Your computer doesn't restart automatically; you need to do that yourself.

> **Tip** From painful experience, if you're in the process of writing a book, ensure that you save your chapter before restarting the computer. Otherwise, you might have to rewrite the chapter. Of course, this also goes for any other work on your computer that you want to keep.

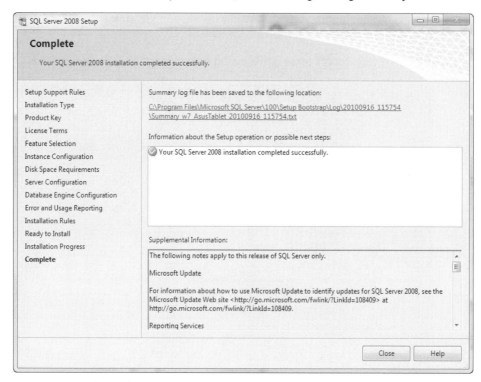

FIGURE 27-8 It's done! After restarting the computer you can use SQL Server 2008 Express with Advanced Services.

Installing the *AdventureWorks* Sample Databases

For the examples in this chapter, you also need to install the sample *AdventureWorks* database.

Note You can install the 2008 version of the *AdventureWorks* examples only on a full SQL Server 2008 or on SQL Server 2008 Express with Advanced Services, because the full-text search required for installation only works on those versions.

More Information You can find the sample databases for SQL Server 2008 at *http://tinyurl. com/adworkdb*. As mentioned earlier, you can only install them if you are using one of the full SQL Server versions or SQL Server 2008 with Advanced Services, and you have installed the full-text search component. If you download the *AdventureWorks* sample database from somewhere else, you get the *AdventureWorks 2008R2 RTM*, but you can install that version using the "regular" SQL Server 2008 with Advanced Services, as well. With R2, they are working fine, anyway.

1. After downloading the *AdventureWorks* installation file, start the installer by double-clicking it.

   The *AdventureWorks* license terms dialog box appears, as illustrated in 27-9.

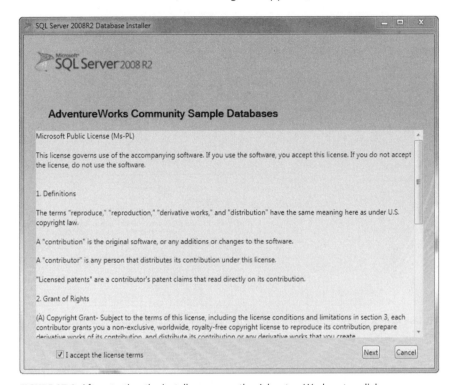

FIGURE 27-9 After starting the installer, you see the *AdventureWorks* setup dialog.

2. Accept the license terms, and then click Next.

   The Database Selection dialog opens, as shown in Figure 27-10.

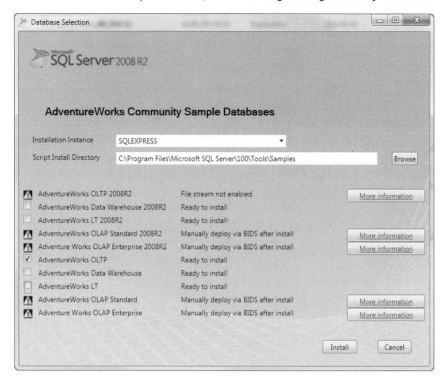

FIGURE 27-10 Set the database instance and script install directly where you want to install the *AdventureWorks* database and scripts. Ignore the warnings; they are not important for this book.

3. Using the Installation Instance drop-down list, select the instance where you want to install *AdventureWorks*. In the Script Install Directory field, specify where to save the scripts for the initial database installation.

4. Clear all the entries except AdventureWorks OLTP, and then click Install.

   The installation begins and the Installation Execution window appears (see Figure 27-11), in which you can monitor the installation progress.

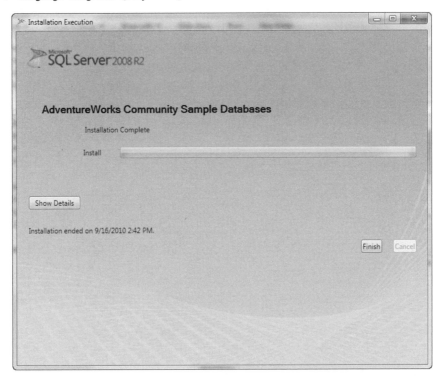

FIGURE 27-11 The last window of the *AdventureWorks* database installation.

The Working Principle of an Entity Data Model

Using *LINQ to Entities*, you can query data entities described by the Entity Data Model (EDM) using LINQ query technology. Of course, *LINQ to Entities* is *not* the EDM, and *LINQ to Entities* does not include the tools to create a model.

An entity data model belongs to the Entity Framework—or more precisely—to the ADO.NET Entity Framework. You insert an element template of this type, to add such a model to your project.

The Entity Framework model encompasses the following lofty goals:

- The data provider responsible for communication between your application and the database server must be exchangeable, without affecting queries made against the entity model.

- Users must be able to select the tables that provide the database model. These tables must not require a 1:1 mapping against the business objects that result from them.

Therefore the entity model is based on three individual models:

- The **physical storage model**, which maps everything that results from the database schema (tables, views, stored procedures), communicates with the data platform.

- The **conceptual model**, from which business objects are generated later that you query with *LINQ to Entities*.

- **Mapping**, which regulates and defines data transfer between the two models.

Important The three models (or more accurately, the two models and the mapping) are stored as an XML file when you create the EDM. This XML file has the extension *.edmx*—for *Entity Data Model eXtended markup language*. When you create a project, three different XML files are automatically added to your .NET assembly as embedded resources. This way the definitions are not freely accessible, but can be edited by exchanging the resources. And that's not all: there can be several definitions, because the actual mapping process between the two models doesn't take place at compilation, but at runtime. The practice section below shows how these three files are "specified" for use.

In the default settings, the three files have the same name as the container, except for their extensions:

- **.CSDL** Contains the XML file that describes the conceptual model (*Conceptual Schema Definition Language*)

- **.SSDL** Contains the XML file that describes the physical storage model (*Store Schema Definition Language*)

- **.MSL** Contains the mapping file (*Mapping Specification Language*)

Tip Separate creation of the three model files: If you prefer to place these three files as project output in separate files, because you might need them for additional projects, for example, open them in the EDM Designer. Select the model by clicking an empty area in the Designer, and then set the *Processing of Metafile Artifacts* property to *Copy to Output Directory in the Properties window*, as shown in Figure 27-12.

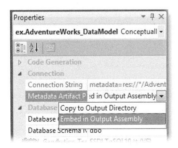

FIGURE 27-12 Select these settings to force Visual Studio to embed the three model files in the output assembly.

Now you know enough to begin building your first practical example.

LINQ to Entities: the First Practical Example

Now you're ready to explore *LINQ to Entities* by using a practical example, which will help you become familiar with its individual elements.

 Note Remember that you must have access to a SQL Server instance with *AdventureWorks* installed to perform these examples.

1. Create a new Visual Basic Console Application project.

2. Use Solution Explorer to add a new element to the solution (you get to this dialog by right-clicking the project name) and select the ADO.NET Entity Data Model template for the new element, as shown in Figure 27-13.

3. Give the new data model the name **AdventureWorks.edmx**.

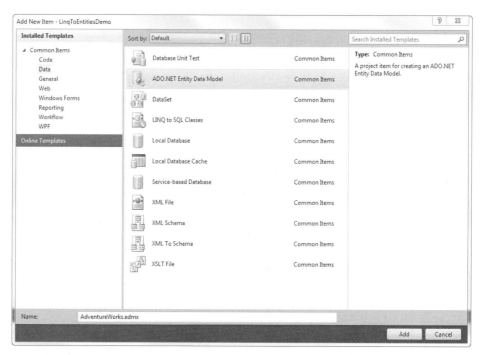

FIGURE 27-13 Adding an ADO.NET EDM.

4. Finish the dialog by clicking Add.

5. The Entity Data Model Wizard opens (see Figure 27-14) to help you either generate the model contents from a database or create an empty model.

For this exercise, select Generate From Database, and then click Next.

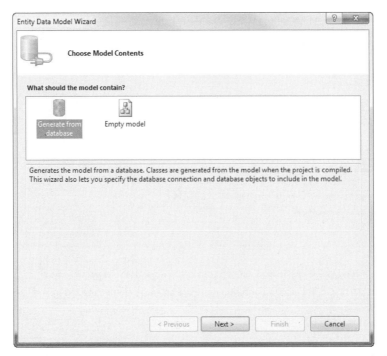

FIGURE 27-14 On the first wizard page, you specify whether to generate a model from the database or to use an empty model.

6. On the next page of the wizard, choose a connection to your data provider (Figure 27-15).

With other drivers, you can click the New Connection button to use other database plat-forms as the SQL Server data provider. Set up your connection to the database instance, and then select the database that you want to use as the basis for creating the schema creation of your new entity model. For this example, choose the instance of the *AdventureWorks* database that you installed at the beginning of this chapter.

FIGURE 27-15 On this wizard page, you generate an entity connection string and specify how it should be saved.

Note In the entity connection string preview, you can see how the schema or specification files of the entity model and the physical database instance are combined in a connection string. The connection string for the EDM determines the conceptual model, the storage model and the mapping, as well as the database that's being used.

If you prefer, you can save the entity connection string in your *App.Config* file. That way you don't have to worry about passing a super-long string when you later instantiate the object context (which manages the connection to the database instance, among other things). You should only do that if your connection string contains no sensitive logon information. If you are using integrated Windows Security to log on to a Microsoft SQL Server system, you're safe; however, if you are running SQL Server in mixed mode and you need to provide logon information in the SQL Server connection string, it makes more sense to save the connection string in the application, or to encrypt any sensitive sections of the file *App.Config*.

More Information To see other important security tips, read the MSDN article, which is available at *http://tinyurl.com/2vt9yko*.

7. Click Next to move on to the next page in the wizard.

8. On the Choose Your Database Objects page, specify which database objects you want to use for schema creation and mapping files (see Figure 27-16).

In the simplest case, the conceptual model will have a 1:1 mapping; in other words, it corresponds exactly to the storage model. Otherwise, the next task is to specify a more appropriate mapping for the generated object model you'll use in your application. For this example, select the following tables:

- ○ **Address** (address details table)
- ○ **Product** (product details table)
- ○ **ProductVendor** (supplier product table)
- ○ **Vendor** (supplier table)
- ○ **VendorAddress** (supplier address table)

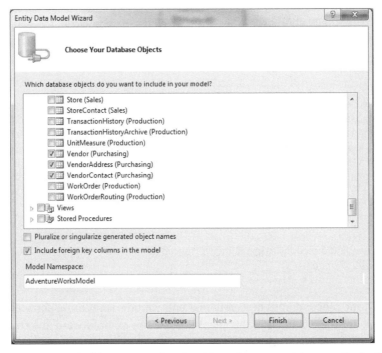

FIGURE 27-16 In this step, you select the objects that you want to use as the basis for schema creation and mapping files.

9. Select or leave clear the *Pluralize Or Singularize Generated Object Names* check box (which no doubt could have been given a better name).

Visual Studio 2008 still uses pluralization. If this check box is selected, entity *types* are singular, while entity collections (entity sets) are given plural names (such as Customer/ Customers). Note that this only makes sense for English entity names; you should not select this check box if you are working in a different language.

10. If you select the option to Include Foreign Key Columns In The Model, related child objects will include their foreign key IDs as well as the navigation property.

   This is always the case when a referenced table is not included in the entity model. The table *VendorAddress* is a good example. The table *AddressType* isn't used in the model; and the table *VendorAddress* contains the field *AddressTypeID*. If you now include the table *AddressType* into the model, the field *AddressTypeID* would be generated only if Include Foreign Key Columns In The Model is enabled. However, the navigation property—*AddressType*—is always included.

11. Click Finish when you have completed your selections.

In the Designer, the display of individual entity properties is much more transparent than in *LINQ to SQL*. The navigation properties are displayed separately from the scalar properties that map to individual fields (columns) of the database. Using an entity's navigation properties, you can access linked tables when programming with business objects.

Note The Designer is smart enough to completely resolve pure help tables (whose sole purpose in the database is to create a n:m connection) using the settings in the mapping assignment details. Unfortunately, that doesn't work when the help table contains an additional field that contains a scalar value, as is unfortunately the case with the *AdventureWorks* database which includes a *ModifiedDate* column in each table. With the *Northwind* database, which you can still install on a SQL Server 2008 instance despite its age, you can see this automatic mapping resolution in action.

Tip You can find directions to install the *Northwind* database with SQL Server 2008 on *http:// tinyurl.com/2574mao*.

With these basic preconditions met, your first entity model is set up, as shown in Figure 27-17, and available for the examples in this chapter. From this point forward, the chapter concentrates on the programmatic aspects.

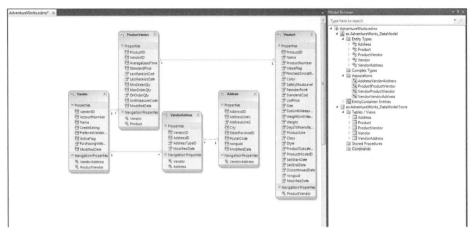

FIGURE 27-17 Unlike the O/R Designer for *LINQ to SQL*, when editing the entity model you can change assignments between the conceptual and the storage model to meet your needs.

Changing the Name of the Entity Set

You can change the name of the entity set by using the Entity Designer. For example, if you don't like the property *Vendor*, (which originated from a table called *Vendor*), and you'd rather use the plural form, you can just change the name. To do that, perform the following:

1. Double-click the EDM in Solution Explorer to open the Designer.

2. Click the entity (for example, *Vendor*).

3. Change the property *Entity Set Name* in the property window to a different name (see Figure 27-18).

Note To follow the examples below, you should *not* change the names. If you decide to rename your entities, you will need to adjust the source code accordingly.

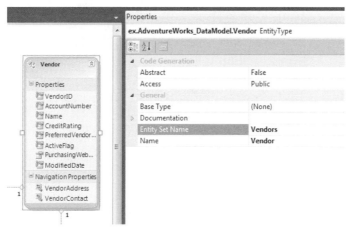

FIGURE 27-18 The name of an entity set can be changed quickly in the EDM Designer.

Note As discussed earlier, you can control automatic pluralization in the Entity Data Model Wizard via the option "Pluralize Or Singularize Generated Object Names." Currently, the wizard only works with English pluralization; it simply adds an "s" to the name, which doesn't always work with foreign names.

Changing the Entity Container Name Retroactively

While you often want to give an EDM the same name as the database that it models, it sometimes makes sense to change the name of the entity container. The programmatic context that you use to access the entity objects of the conceptual model (for example, when creating queries with *LINQ to Entities*) is created from the entity container.

Changing the name is a relatively simple process. First, open the EDM Designer, click an empty area to highlight the model itself, and then specify a new name in the Properties window in the Entity Container Name property (see Figure 27-19).

FIGURE 27-19 Changing the name of an entity container in the EDM Designer.

If you saved the connection string in the App.Config file, you might need to adjust it there too, as illustrated by the bold highlighted text in the following listing:

```
<!--<add name="EventLog" type="System.Diagnostics.EventLogTraceListener"
      initializeData="APPLICATION_NAME"/> -->
  </sharedListeners>
</system.diagnostics>
<connectionStrings><add name="AWEntities" connectionString="metadata=res://*/
AdventureWorks.csdl|res://*/AdventureWorks.ssdl|res://*/AdventureWorks.msl;provider=System.
Data.SqlClient;provider connection string=&quot;Data Source=V64_LOEFFELDEV\
SQL2008EXPRESS;Initial Catalog=AdventureWorks;Integrated Security=True;MultipleActiveRes
ultSets=True&quot;" providerName="System.Data.EntityClient" /><add name="AWEntities" con
nectionString="metadata=res://*/AdventureWorks.csdl|res://*/AdventureWorks.ssdl|res://*/
AdventureWorks.msl;provider=System.Data.SqlClient;provider connection string=&quot;Data
Source=V64_LOEFFELDEV\SQL2008EXPRESS;Initial Catalog=AdventureWorks;Integrated Security
=True;MultipleActiveResultSets=True&quot;" providerName="System.Data.EntityClient" /></
connectionStrings>
</configuration>
```

Editing the .edmx-File as XML Outside the Designer

The Designer is sufficient for most tasks, but if you get to a point at which the Designer is no longer of any help, you can just edit the .edmx file in an XML Editor.

- To do this, select *Open With* from the context menu of the *edmx* file.

- In the dialog that opens select *XML Editor* from the list (Figure 27-20), and then click *OK* to edit the model as an XML file.

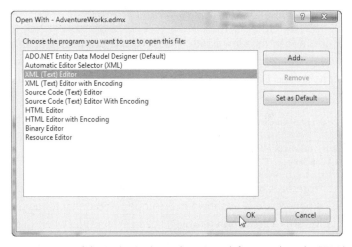

FIGURE 27-20 If the Entity Designer doesn't work for you, close the EDM in Design view, and then open the .edmx file (which contains conceptual model, storage model, and mapping) with the XML Editor.

Caution Figure 27-21 shows the sections in which you can edit the contents of the SSDL (storage model), CSDL (conceptual model), and MSL (mapping) files without risk. Be sure that you don't touch the part below the comment, *EF Designer content (DO NOT EDIT MANUALLY BELOW HERE)*. You should take this warning very seriously!

```
AdventureWorks.edmx  X   LinqToEntitiesDemo
    <?xml version="1.0" encoding="utf-8"?>
  <edmx:Edmx Version="2.0" xmlns:edmx="http://schemas.microsoft.com/ado/2008/10/edmx">
     <!-- EF Runtime content -->
  <edmx:Runtime>
     <!-- SSDL content -->
     <edmx:StorageModels>...</edmx:StorageModels>
     <!-- CSDL content -->
     <edmx:ConceptualModels>...</edmx:ConceptualModels>
     <!-- C-S mapping content -->
     <edmx:Mappings>...</edmx:Mappings>
  </edmx:Runtime>
     <!-- EF Designer content (DO NOT EDIT MANUALLY BELOW HERE) -->
     <edmx:Designer>...</edmx:Designer>
  </edmx:Edmx>

100 %
```

FIGURE 27-21 You can view and edit the conceptual model, storage model, and mapping directly in XML, if necessary. However, do not make any changes below the section labeled EF Designer content.

Querying an Entity Model

You'll find the classes generated from the conceptual model in the entity model in a code file located below the data model in Solution Explorer. It's normally hidden, but you can see it if you select show all files in Solution Explorer.

Entity Framework uses a "central administrator" class for the business objects created from the conceptual model. This central administrator class is (contrary to what you might know from *LINQ to SQL*) not called *DataContext*; it's called *ObjectContext*.

```
'''<summary>
''' No Metadata Documentation available.
'''</summary>
Partial Public Class AdventureWorksEntities
    Inherits ObjectContext
```

The object context represents business object query collections in the form of *ObjectSet(Of Type)*[1] classes. Such a generic class, as shown in the code sample that follows, therefore represents a query that returns a collection of objects of a certain type when this query is created or performed with an Entity SQL statement or a LINQ query. It runs the queries when in the following circumstances:

---

[1] The class *ObjectSet(of Type)* is based on *ObjectQuery(of Type)*, which was still the basis for *Linq to Entities* under Visual Studio 2008/.NET Framework 3.5.

- You use its iterator. For example, when you use *For Each* to iterate through the elements of a collection.

- It is assigned to a generic list (*List(Of Type)*).

- Its *Execute* method has been called explicitly, as shown here:

```
''' <summary>
''' No Metadata Documentation available.
''' </summary>
Public ReadOnly Property Product() As ObjectSet(Of Product)
    Get
        If (_Product Is Nothing) Then
            _Product = MyBase.CreateObjectSet(Of Product)("Product")
        End If
        Return _Product
    End Get
End Property
```

The bold highlighted line shows that the business objects are defined so that at first use, an instance automatically runs a query that retrieves all the elements of the assigned entity (table, view). (This, by the way, is a perfect example of the Lazy Loading pattern).

The object context also controls the database structure, manages change tracking, and provides an infrastructure for concurrency checks.[2]

Querying Data with *LINQ to Entities* Queries

The following code sample shows a simple query. It is located in Module1.vb of the sample project.

Companion Content Open the corresponding solution file (.sln), which you can find in the \VB 2010 Developer Handbook\Chapter 27\LinqToEntitiesDemo folder.

```
Module Module1

    Sub Main()

        'In the examples we are using the connections string from App.Config.
        'Change the string in the section ConnectionStrings to adjust the examples
        'to your SQL Server instance. To do this, you just need to adjust the
        'provider ConnectionString within the total ConnectionStrings.

        Dim awContext As New AWEntities()
```

---

[2] It checks whether modified data, which should now be written back to the database, has already been changed by somebody else *and* has already been written back to the database.

```
        Dim suppliers = From supplier In awContext.Vendor _
                        Where supplier.Name.StartsWith("H") _
                        Order By supplier.Name

        For Each supplier In suppliers
            Console.WriteLine(supplier.AccountNumber & ": " & supplier.Name)
            Console.WriteLine(New String("="c, 70))

            'Deliver the products to each supplier
            For Each product In supplier.ProductVendor
                Console.Write("ID:" & product.ProductID & " ")
                Console.WriteLine("Name:" & product.Product.Name)
            Next
            Console.WriteLine()

        Next

    End Sub

End Module
```

When you run the program, you notice that it displays only the following output on the screen:

```
HILLBIC0001: Hill Bicycle Center
======================================================================

HILLSBI0001: Hill's Bicycle Service
======================================================================

HOLIDAY0001: Holiday Skate & Cycle
======================================================================

HYBRIDB0001: Hybrid Bicycle Center
======================================================================
```

The inner loop is not executed (or doesn't return results). This is due to the pre-setting of *lazy loading,* which is disabled by default. With lazy loading, data from child tables are loaded automatically at first access—but not until then. Without lazy loading, nothing happens—you had to call a special method to get the data. The reason for this pre-setting might lie in the fact that Visual Studio 2008 and .NET Framework 3.5 SP 1 Designers did not support lazy loading at all; you needed to configure it manually. Microsoft probably recognized the need for a bit of touch-up and provided this remedy. You'll see more details about lazy loading behavior later in this chapter.

 Note We recommend that you have the Developer Edition of SQL Server on hand for professional development projects—it's available as part of a MSDN or TechNet subscription.

Finally, the Entity Framework unfortunately doesn't let you simply display debug output in the console. If you're lucky enough to work with the Ultimate Edition of Visual Studio, you can use IntelliTrace to record a history of ADO queries, which were triggered by your *LINQ to Entity* queries. As an alternative, you can help yourself (if you have the Developer Edition of SQL Server, for example) by using the SQL Profiler. You can find out how to use the SQL Profiler to view generated SQL in the section "A Closer Look at Generated SQL Statements."

> **Note** Just as with LINQ, *LINQ to Entities* queries also delay execution and can be chained. Chapter 25, "LINQ to Objects," contains a number of examples. With *LINQ to Entities*, you can resolve a query result list—for example, with *ToList* or *ToArray*—from its query object. However, unlike *LINQ to SQL*, the resulting list is not automatically disconnected from its data context, but only from the query chain.

How Queries Get to the Data Provider—Entity SQL (eSQL)

Unlike *LINQ to SQL*, queries in Entity Framework LINQ are not sent directly to the data provider (whose full name is *ADO.NET Entity Client Data Provider*, by the way). Instead, the developers at Microsoft created a dialect called *Entity SQL* (eSQL), which queries the conceptual model of an EDM. Because eSQL doesn't work directly against the data provider, it's data platform-independent—if you later need to change data providers, the code that queries the conceptual model of the EDM is not affected. In the worst possible case, your current data provider might not be able to translate the eSQL queries into SQL. However, this shouldn't happen with providers for the large database systems (for instance, Oracle and IBM).

A Closer Look at Generated SQL Statements

Automatically logging Transact SQL (T-SQL) queries generated by running a query in *LINQ to SQL* requires hardly any effort. Unfortunately, it's not quite as easy in *LINQ to Entities*, but you have two possibilities:

- You can cast your query into the original query object of the object context and then call the method *ToTraceString* to find out which commands the Entity Framework is *planning* to send to the data provider. For example, you could add the following high-lighted code to the sample program shown earlier:

```
...
        Dim awContext As New AWEntities()

        Dim suppliers = From supplier In awContext.Vendor _
                    Where supplier.Name.StartsWith("H") _
                    Order By supplier.Name
```

```
'With this statement we can find out
'which SQL text will be used.
Console.WriteLine(CType(suppliers, ObjectQuery(Of Vendor)).ToTraceString)
Console.WriteLine()
...
```

Doing that adds the following lines to the output:

```
SELECT
[Extent1].[VendorID] AS [VendorID],
[Extent1].[AccountNumber] AS [AccountNumber],
[Extent1].[Name] AS [Name],
[Extent1].[CreditRating] AS [CreditRating],
[Extent1].[PreferredVendorStatus] AS [PreferredVendorStatus],
[Extent1].[ActiveFlag] AS [ActiveFlag],
[Extent1].[PurchasingWebServiceURL] AS [PurchasingWebServiceURL],
[Extent1].[ModifiedDate] AS [ModifiedDate]
FROM [Purchasing].[Vendor] AS [Extent1]
WHERE [Extent1].[Name] LIKE N'H%'
ORDER BY [Extent1].[Name] ASC


HILLBICO001: Hill Bicycle Center
=======================================================================


HILLSBIO001: Hill's Bicycle Service
=======================================================================


HOLIDAYO001: Holiday Skate & Cycle
=======================================================================


HYBRIDBO001: Hybrid Bicycle Center
=======================================================================


Press key to exit
```

- A more reliable way (and more elaborate one because it reflects the actual state) is to use the SQL Profiler tool from a full SQL Server version. For example, if you can access a complete version of SQL Server via Remote Desktop in your company, you can connect the Profiler to your local SQL Express version instance. The Profiler tool provides details about any data sent between the database instance and the open client session, as depicted in Figure 27-22. As previously mentioned, you can alternatively also use a locally installed SQL Server 2008 *Developer Edition*, which has every feature of the Enterprise Edition (and therefore also features the profiler). The Developer Edition of SQL Server 2008 is especially for software developers and can, in contrast to the Enterprise Edition, be installed not only on server computers, but on Windows workstations like XP, Vista, or Windows 7.

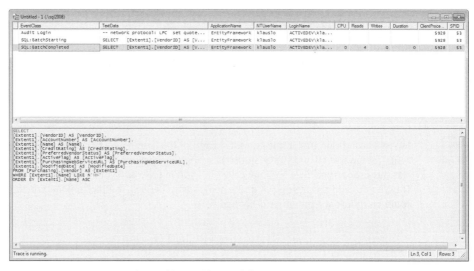

FIGURE 27-22 You can use the Profiler tool from a full SQL Server version with your Express instance. The Profiler doesn't even need to reside on your computer—as long as your network and firewall settings permit it.

Tip To connect the Profiler of the full Visual Studio with your Express instance, your firewall settings must allow the connection, and of course your network protocols must be set up accordingly. This book won't go into detail about this topic, but you can find plenty of information on the Internet by searching using the keyword *SQL Server Configurations Manager*. Also, if you have Reporting Services installed, you might want to filter those messages out. To do that, pause the profiling, and then click the Properties icon in the toolbar. In the ensuing dialog box, click the Column Filters button. You'll see an Edit Filter dialog. Apply the changes shown in Figure 27-23.

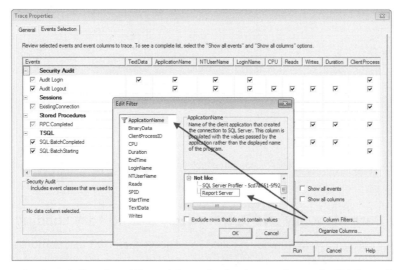

FIGURE 27-23 If you have Microsoft Reporting Services running on the SQL Server instance with which you're working, you might want to filter those messages out for better transparency.

Lazy Loading and Eager Loading in Entity Framework

Loading behavior in the .NET Framework 3.5 SP1 differed tremendously between *LINQ to SQL* and *LINQ to Entities*. The .NET Framework 4.0 extended the generator so that it can also generate code for lazy loading. To "load data only when necessary" (to paraphrase the term *lazy loading*), you need to change some Designer settings.

> **Note** Having said this, in the current version of the Entity Framework (after Service Pack 1 for .NET Framework 4.0 and Visual Studio/Basic 2010), although not the default setting, the designer sets this property to *True* automatically after you initially add your entity model to the project. Thus, if you didn't avail yourself of the companion files, the results from the previous sample could be different from those described here.

Navigate to the Model Designer in your example project, and then click an empty area to select the model itself. The property window now shows the properties of the conceptual entity model (*AdventureWorksModel* in this example).

When you change Lazy Loading Enabled to *True* (as shown in Figure 27-24) the data is loaded automatically (although, to be accurate, the generator creates code to load the data upon first access to the corresponding navigation properties). If for some reason you prefer not to use this setting, you can always retroactively load the data yourself, as described in the following section.

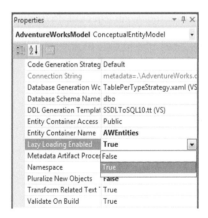

FIGURE 27-24 As of .NET Framework 4.0, you can enable lazy loading for the entire entity model in the Entity Designer.

Loading Data Manually and Retroactively During Lazy Loading

The sample project contains a module called LazyEagerLoading.vb that demonstrates how to load data from table relations manually.

Note For the sample project to start with this *Main* method, in LazyEagerLoading.vb, you need to set the appropriate start object in the project properties. In Solution Explorer, right-click the project name, select *Properties* from the context menu, and then change the Start Object, as shown in Figure 27-25.

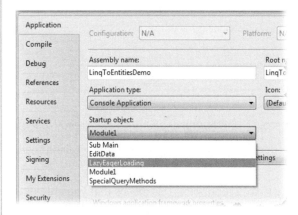

FIGURE 27-25 This is how you specify which *Sub Main* the application should call upon startup.

```vb
Imports System.Data.Objects

Module LazyEagerLoading

    Sub ManualLoading()
        Dim awContext As New AWEntities()

        Dim suppliers = From supplier In awContext.Vendor _
                        Where supplier.Name.StartsWith("H") _
                        Order By supplier.Name

        For Each supplier In suppliers
            Console.WriteLine(supplier.AccountNumber & ": " & supplier.Name)
            Console.WriteLine(New String("="c, 70))

            If Not supplier.ProductVendor.IsLoaded Then
                supplier.ProductVendor.Load()

                'Deliever the products to each supplier
                For Each product In supplier.ProductVendor
                    If Not product.ProductReference.IsLoaded Then
                        product.ProductReference.Load()
                        Console.Write("ID:" & product.ProductID & " ")
                        Console.WriteLine("Name:" & product.Product.Name)
                    End If
                Next
                Console.WriteLine()
            End If
```

```
        Next

        Console.WriteLine()
        Console.WriteLine("Press key to exit")
        Console.ReadKey()

    End Sub

End Module
```

Three things are important:

- Using *IsLoaded* lets you discover whether related entities are already loaded.

- If the related entities are not already loaded, you load them by calling the Load method.

- There is always a reference to a ":1" endpoint. This means that you are not using the actual entity name property to retroactively load the data, instead you're using the name that ends in *Reference*. Because the *ProductVendor* table (all supplier products) is connected in a 1:1 relationship to the *Product* table (product details), you need to use *ProductReference* to load the contents. But because *Vendor* and *ProductVendor* are connected in a 1:*n* relationship (the first highlighted code block in the preceding example) you *don't* use the postfix *Reference there*.

Using Eager Loading for Certain Relationships

An option that makes more sense in certain situations—especially if you only want to make relatively small amounts of data available at the beginning—is to instruct the Entity Framework to load the data for the child tables all at one time by using a *Join* connection.

To do this, call the *Include* method and pass it the path of the child table, separated by a period. For example, if you query the table *Vendor*, and you want *ProductVendor* data and the *Product* data assigned to it to be returned automatically, as well, the search path would be "ProductVendor.Product."

 Important You must not specify the original table (*Vendor* in this case) in the search path.

The changed example looks like this:

```
    Sub EagerLoading()
        Dim awContext As New AWEntities()

        Dim suppliers = From supplier In awContext.Vendor.Include("ProductVendor.
Product") _
```

```
                        Where supplier.Name.StartsWith("H") _
                        Order By supplier.Name

        'With this statement we can find out
        'which SQL text will be used.
        Console.WriteLine(CType(suppliers, ObjectQuery(Of Vendor)).ToTraceString)
        Console.WriteLine()

        For Each supplier In suppliers
            Console.WriteLine(supplier.AccountNumber & ": " & supplier.Name)
            Console.WriteLine(New String("="c, 70))


            'Deliever the products to each supplier
            For Each product In supplier.ProductVendor
                Console.Write("ID:" & product.ProductID & " ")
                Console.WriteLine("Name:" & product.Product.Name)
            Next
            Console.WriteLine()

        Next

        Console.WriteLine()
        Console.WriteLine("Press key to exit")
        Console.ReadKey()
    End Sub
```

The generated SQL text changes accordingly (this is a shortened version):

```
SELECT
[Project1].[VendorID] AS [VendorID],
[Project1].[AccountNumber] AS [AccountNumber],
… <Output shortened> …
 [Project1].[rowguid] AS [rowguid],
[Project1].[ModifiedDate2] AS [ModifiedDate2]
FROM ( SELECT
        [Extent1].[VendorID] AS [VendorID],
 … <Output shortened> …
        [Extent1].[ModifiedDate] AS [ModifiedDate],
        [Join1].[ProductID1] AS [ProductID],
         … <Output shortened> …
        [Join1].[ModifiedDate2] AS [ModifiedDate2],
        CASE WHEN ([Join1].[ProductID1] IS NULL) THEN CAST(NULL AS int) ELSE 1
ND AS [C1]
        FROM  [Purchasing].[Vendor] AS [Extent1]
        LEFT OUTER JOIN  (SELECT [Extent2].[ProductID] AS [ProductID1],
        [Exten].[VendorID] AS [VendorID], [Extent2].[AverageLeadTime] AS [AverageLeadTime],
… <Output shortened> …
]
VendorID]
        WHERE [Extent1].[Name] LIKE N'H%'
) AS [Project1]
ORDER BY [Project1].[Name] ASC, [Project1].[VendorID] ASC, [Project1].[C1] ASC
```

```
HILLBIC0001: Hill Bicycle Center
======================================================================
ID:524 Name:HL Spindle/Axle

… <Output shortened> …

HYBRIDB0001: Hybrid Bicycle Center
======================================================================
ID:910 Name:HL Mountain Seat/Saddle


Press key to exit
```

Avoiding Anonymous Result Collections in Join Queries via Select

With *LINQ to Entities*, you can use *Join* queries to merge data from several tables in a flat result list. In many cases, however, you only want to access tables with relations to select data from the main table. *Join* can do the job, but it has one problem, because it mixes the schema from both tables and therefore automatically returns a result list based on an anonymous class. We have the same problem, when we're combining the tables implicitly as Chapter 25 showed. But usually, you want a result list that's based on one concrete entity class.

The solution here, again, is to use *Select*. Recall that *Select* exchanges a given item with another item, which can be of a completely different type, and returns a new collection of that item's type.

> **Note** For demonstration purposes, the following example uses manual reloading of the related table data, as discussed in the previous section.

In the sample that follows, located in the module *SpecialQueryMethods.vb*, we solve this problem by nesting multiple *From* queries and uses *Distinct* to ensure that there are no duplicates in the result list. Constructing this query partly with *Join* would work here equally well. In both cases, the final *Select* statement is essential for determining the right type for the returned result collection.

> **Note** Be sure to change the start object to the corresponding module in the sample project, for example, to *SpecialQueryApproaches* in this case.

```vb
Sub AvoidingAnonymousResultCollections()

    Dim awContext As New AWEntities()

    'Queries all suppliers who have products
    'whose names begins with "W" in the product details.
    Dim suppliers = From supplierItems In awContext.Vendor _
                    From supplierProductItem In supplierItems.ProductVendor _
                    From productItem In awContext.Product _
                        Where supplierItems.VendorID = supplierProductItem.VendorID _
                        Where productItem.ProductID = supplierProductItem.ProductID _
                        Where productItem.Name.StartsWith("W") _
                            Select supplierItems Distinct

    'Again, with this statement we can find out
    'which SQL text will be used.
    Console.WriteLine(CType(suppliers, ObjectQuery(Of Vendor)).ToTraceString)
    Console.WriteLine()

    'Use manual reloading for the output.
    For Each supplier In suppliers
        Console.WriteLine(supplier.AccountNumber & ": " & supplier.Name)
        Console.WriteLine(New String("="c, 70))

        If Not supplier.ProductVendor.IsLoaded Then
            supplier.ProductVendor.Load()
        End If

        'Deliver the products to each supplier
        For Each produkt In supplier.ProductVendor
            If Not produkt.ProductReference.IsLoaded Then
                produkt.ProductReference.Load()
                Console.Write("ID:" & produkt.ProductID & " ")
                Console.WriteLine("Name:" & produkt.Product.Name)
            End If
        Next
        Console.WriteLine()
    Next

    Console.WriteLine()
    Console.WriteLine("Press key to exit.")
    Console.ReadKey()

End Sub
```

When you run the method, it returns the desired result list, as shown in the following:

```
GREENLA0001: Green Lake Bike Company
======================================================================
ID:870 Name:Water Bottle - 30 oz.
ID:871 Name:Mountain Bottle Cage

… <Output shortened> …
```

```
ID:854 Name:Women's Tights, L
ID:855 Name:Men's Bib-Shorts, S
ID:856 Name:Men's Bib-Shorts, M
ID:857 Name:Men's Bib-Shorts, L


Press key to exit
```

Compiled Queries

With *LINQ to Entities* you can create pre-compiled, *optimized queries* to improve performance. An optimized query is essentially a delegate to a pre-compiled instance of an *ObjectQuery(Of Type)* object, which returns the corresponding result list as an *IQueryable(Of Type)*. By including specific parameters in the lambda statement that you pass to the *CompiledQuery* class constructor when setting up the query, you can design reusable compiled queries for various query parameters.

The example that follows demonstrates how to use a compiled query. This example finds suppliers with a certain first letter in their name. Note that this query is compiled with parameters and can be reused repeatedly by passing it a first letter as an argument.

```vb
Sub CompiledQueries()

    Dim awContext As New AWEntities()

    Dim compiledSupplierQuery = CompiledQuery.Compile(Of AWEntities, _
                                        String, IQueryable(Of Vendor))( _
                Function(context, FirstLetter) From supplier In context.Vendor _
                    Where supplier.Name.StartsWith(FirstLetter) _
                    Order By supplier.Name _
                    Select supplier)

    Dim queryFor_H = compiledSupplierQuery(awContext, "H")

    For Each supplier In queryFor_H
        Console.WriteLine(supplier.AccountNumber & ": " & supplier.Name)
        Console.WriteLine(New String("="c, 70))

        'Deliver the products to each supplier
        For Each product In supplier.ProductVendor
            Console.Write("ID:" & product.ProductID & " ")
            Console.WriteLine("Name:" & product.Product.Name)
        Next
        Console.WriteLine()
    Next

    Dim queryFor_W = compiledSupplierQuery(awContext, "W")

    For Each supplier In queryFor_W
        Console.WriteLine(supplier.AccountNumber & ": " & supplier.Name)
        Console.WriteLine(New String("="c, 70))
```

```
        'Deliver the products to each supplier
        For Each product In supplier.ProductVendor
            Console.Write("ID:" & product.ProductID & " ")
            Console.WriteLine("Name:" & product.Product.Name)
        Next
        Console.WriteLine()
    Next


    Console.WriteLine()
    Console.WriteLine("Press key to exit")
    Console.ReadKey()

End Sub

End Module
```

The first highlighted line creates the compiled query through the *CompiledQuery* class.
You pass its constructor the object context type, the parameter type, and the return type.
The lambda expression defines the actual query in accordance with that type schema. The
lambda expression defines the query as a LINQ query.

> **Note** In this step, you didn't actually define the query itself, just a function delegate that *returns*
> a query when you pass the corresponding parameters.

Now, to use the query, you define an additional query variable that will have the type
IQueryable(Of Type)), which returns the precompiled query to which the function delegate
points. During that assignment, you pass the parameters to run the query. The highlighted
code lines in the previous listing show how this looks in practice.

> **Tip** By now you will surely already have noticed that LINQ to Entities differs from T-SQL tre-
> mendously. It is not always intuitive to grasp how a certain query in T-SQL would look like in
> LINQ. And, of course, not everything might be possible without tweaking here or there a little
> bit. Unfortunately, LINQ is a topic which easily fills whole books, and we have just some 60 pages
> at our disposal. This is why I strongly encourage you to take a look at the best book about the
> Entity Framework—in my opinion—written by my fellow MVP, Julia Lerman, which you can find
> more about at *http://oreilly.com/catalog/9780596807269*.

Modifying, Saving, and Deleting Data

As you've seen, querying data with *LINQ to Entities* is not terribly difficult. Modifying the data
is a different story though. The following sections discuss all data-changing operations.

With *LINQ to SQL*, the data context with the appended *Table(Of)* collections takes care of tracking the changes. With *LINQ to Entities*, the entity objects themselves fulfill the tracking tasks. They can do this because they are not just POCOs (*Plain Old CLR Objects*— simple business objects derived from *Object*), but they are derived from the *EntityObject* class (if you are working with the default project templates.)

> **More Information** You can also work with POCOs within the ADO.NET entity framework model, but explaining that is beyond the scope of this chapter. To learn more, go to *http://tinyurl. com/28jo4bo.*

The following sections describe how you can use Entity Framework to programmatically perform data modifications in the EDM object model, and how to save these changes in the database.

Saving Data Modifications to the Database by Using *SaveChanges*

Look at the example in the module *EditData*.

> **Note** Remember to change the start object to the corresponding module in the sample project: in this case, *EditData.*

The following example retrieves a supplier (the only one whose name begins with the string "hybrid"), but instead of displaying it as a collection item, it retrieves it as an instance of the class *Vendor* by using the *First* method.

> **Note** You cannot use *Single* (as in *LINQ to SQL*) with *LINQ to Entities* queries. Instead, you use the *First* method. That method ensures that the SQL Server entity data provider uses the *TOP (1)* clause in the *SELECT* query.

```
Sub ChangeData()

    Dim awContext As New AWEntities()

    Dim supplier = (From supplierItem In awContext.Vendor _
                    Where supplierItem.Name.ToLower.StartsWith("hybrid") _
                    Order By supplierItem.Name).First

    'Change back and forth, so this example will work more than once:
    If supplier.Name = "Hybrid Bicycle Center" Then
        supplier.Name = "Hybrid Cycle Center"
```

```
        Else
            supplier.Name = "Hybrid Bicycle Center"
        End If

        awContext.SaveChanges()

        Console.WriteLine()
        Console.WriteLine("Press key to exit")
        Console.ReadKey()

    End Sub
```

After making the query, the code changes the *Vendor.Name* property. Basically, all you need to do is change the property that corresponds to the property in the conceptual model—the Entity Framework takes care of mapping the change to the actual database.

To write the changes back to the database, call the *SaveChanges* method of the object context. The ADO.NET Entity Data Provider then generates the required *UPDATE* commands by itself.

Currently, you can only view commands generated by *LINQ to Entities* by using the SQL Profiler tool (see the section "A Closer Look at Generated SQL"). For the target dataset, the initial query looks like this:

```
SELECT TOP (1)
[Extent1].[VendorID] AS [VendorID],
[Extent1].[AccountNumber] AS [AccountNumber],
[Extent1].[Name] AS [Name],
[Extent1].[CreditRating] AS [CreditRating],
[Extent1].[PreferredVendorStatus] AS [PreferredVendorStatus],
[Extent1].[ActiveFlag] AS [ActiveFlag],
[Extent1].[PurchasingWebServiceURL] AS [PurchasingWebServiceURL],
[Extent1].[ModifiedDate] AS [ModifiedDate]
FROM [Purchasing].[Vendor] AS [Extent1]
WHERE LOWER([Extent1].[Name]) LIKE N'hybrid%'
ORDER BY [Extent1].[Name] ASC
```

When you call *SaveChanges*, the update uses the following statement, generated by the Entity Framework:

```
exec sp_executesql N'update [Purchasing].[Vendor]
set [Name] = @0
where ([VendorID] = @1)
',N'@0 nvarchar(50),@1 int',@0=N'Hybrid Bicycle Center',@1=52
```

Inserting Related Data into Data Tables

You insert data into tables by using either the object context or the navigation properties of the entity objects. This means:

- You add a data set to an entity object by creating an instance and calling the *AddObject* method of the object context's entity (actually: typed ObjectSet) to insert it. For example, you would add a supplier with *context.Vendor.AddObject(newVendor)* and a client with *context.Customer.AddObject(newCustomer)*, where *context* is your object context of the corresponding entity.

> **Note** To make you're applications compatible with future Entity Framework versions, don't use the old approach with *AddTo<EntityName>* directly on an object context.

- Using a navigation property, you simply insert a new instance by using the *Add* method. For example, to add a product to the table *ProductVendor*, and at the same time create the relation to the vendor table, you create a new *ProductVendor* instance by calling the *Add* method *Vendor.ProductVendor* navigation property of a *Vendor* entity instance.

So basically, you first build connections between the new data sets, and only at the very end do you call the *SaveChanges* method of the object context to place the new objects into the database with a generated SQL *INSERT* statement:

```
Sub InsertRelatedData()

    Dim awContext As New AWEntities()

    Dim newSupplier As New Vendor With {.Name = "ActiveDevelop", .CreditRating = 1, _
                            .AccountNumber = "ACTDEV00001", .ModifiedDate = Now}

    'Create the new product
    Dim newProduct As New Product With {.Name = "Visual Basic 2010-Developer Handbook", _
                            .ProductNumber = "", _
                            .ListPrice = 59, _
                            .ModifiedDate = Now, _
                            .DiscontinuedDate = #12/31/2011#, _
                            .SellStartDate = #12/10/2008#, _
                            .SellEndDate = #12/31/2011#, _
                            .SafetyStockLevel = 5, _
                            .ReorderPoint = 2}

    'Create new supplier product, connect with the product,
    'and connect with the supplier
```

```
Dim newSupplierProduct = New ProductVendor With {.Product = newProduct, _
                                  .StandardPrice = 59, _
                                  .ModifiedDate = Now, _
                                  .UnitMeasureCode = "PC", _
                                  .AverageLeadTime = 19, _
                                  .MinOrderQty = 1, _
                                  .MaxOrderQty = 10}


      'Note: This approach has been deprecated
      'awContext.AddToVendor(newSupplier)
      'Use new approach:
      awContext.Vendor.AddObject(newSupplier)           newSupplier.ProductVendor.
Add(newSupplierProduct)
      awContext.SaveChanges()

    Console.WriteLine()
    Console.WriteLine("Press key to exit")
    Console.ReadKey()
  End Sub
```

As you can see, creating and adding the individual new entity objects in the example happens in a direction that seemingly breaks the database's relationship rules. Inserting the new data sets in this order on the database level would immediately lead to a foreign key relationship violation. But you don't need to worry about that in Entity Framework, because the object context knows the table relationships defined by the storage model and generates the *INSERT* statements in an appropriate order that can't violate the relationships. As the Profiler shows, the above example produces the following *INSERT* statements:

```
exec sp_executesql N'insert [Production].[Product]([Name], [ProductNumber], [MakeFlag],
[FinishedGoodsFlag], [Color], [SafetyStockLevel], [ReorderPoint], [StandardCost],
[ListPrice], [Size], [SizeUnitMeasureCode], [WeightUnitMeasureCode], [Weight],
[DaysToManufacture], [ProductLine], [Class], [Style], [ProductSubcategoryID],
[ProductModelID], [SellStartDate], [SellEndDate], [DiscontinuedDate], [rowguid],
[ModifiedDate])
values (@0, @1, @2, @3, null, @4, @5, @6, @7, null, null, null, null, @8, null, null, null,
null, null, @9, @10, @11, @12, @13)
select [ProductID]
from [Production].[Product]
where @@ROWCOUNT > 0 and [ProductID] = scope_identity()',N'@0 nvarchar(50),@1
nvarchar(25),@2 bit,@3 bit,@4 smallint,@5 smallint,@6 decimal(19,4),@7
decimal(19,4),@8 int,@9 datetime2(7),@10 datetime2(7),@11 datetime2(7),@12
uniqueidentifier,@13 datetime2(7)',@0=N'Visual Basic 2010-Developer Handbook',@1
=N'',@2=0,@3=0,@4=5,@5=2,@6=0,@7=59.0000,@8=0,@9='2008-12-10 00:00:00',@10='2011-12-31
00:00:00',@11='2011-12-31 00:00:00',@12='00000000-0000-0000-0000-000000000000',@13='2010-07-
02 16:24:07.6920277'

exec sp_executesql N'insert [Purchasing].[Vendor]([AccountNumber], [Name], [CreditRating],
[PreferredVendorStatus], [ActiveFlag], [PurchasingWebServiceURL], [ModifiedDate])
values (@0, @1, @2, @3, @4, null, @5)
select [VendorID]
from [Purchasing].[Vendor]
```

```
where @@ROWCOUNT > 0 and [VendorID] = scope_identity()',N'@0 nvarchar(15),@1
nvarchar(50),@2 tinyint,@3 bit,@4 bit,@5 datetime2(7)',@0=N'ACTDEV00001',@1=N'ActiveDevel
op',@2=1,@3=0,@4=0,@5='2010-07-02 16:24:07.1139699'
```

```
exec sp_executesql N'insert [Purchasing].[ProductVendor]([ProductID], [VendorID],
[AverageLeadTime], [StandardPrice], [LastReceiptCost], [LastReceiptDate], [MinOrderQty],
[MaxOrderQty], [OnOrderQty], [UnitMeasureCode], [ModifiedDate])
values (@0, @1, @2, @3, null, null, @4, @5, null, @6, @7)
',N'@0 int,@1 int,@2 int,@3 decimal(19,4),@4 int,@5 int,@6 nchar(3),@7 datetime2(7)',@0=1003
,@1=107,@2=19,@3=59.0000,@4=1,@5=10,@6=N'PC ',@7='2010-07-02 16:24:07.6930278'
```

If you take a look at the sample code file, you will notice that more things happen than are shown above. Before adding a linked dataset, all previously entered data is deleted. This is necessary, because, for example, you don't want a second supplier to be added with the same data. The example also does something that should *never* occur in a live system without consulting your team: it disables a trigger.

Deleting Data from Tables

Deleting entity objects from existing collections couldn't be easier—just as when inserting data, the order in which you remove entity objects from their parent entities isn't really important, because Entity Framework takes care of generating the correct sequence of SQL *DELETE* statements to ensure that no foreign key violations occur.

Generally, you have already used or will use a query to retrieve an object that you want to delete from a database table. Often, deleting one entity means that you have to delete related rows (child entities) in other tables, as well.

Conveniently, the Entity Framework supports cascading deletes. If you are deleting a data set in a main table, data sets in child tables linked via foreign keys are deleted, too (with the default settings).

The following example first retrieves a supplier product by name. It uses a cascaded *From* LINQ query as discussed earlier, in the section "Avoiding Anonymous Result Collections," to determine an entity object. This time the query criteria appear in a linked table. (You know the product name, but you want to retrieve an entity from the supplier product table. The supplier products don't contain a product name field, that's in a linked product table, which contains details). The result of this query is a supplier product. But remember, the goal is to not only delete the supplier product, but also the related details from the *Product* table as well as the supplier from the *Vendor* table.

To determine the entity objects, the query uses manual loading again, but this time it caches the references to the *Product* and *Vendor* objects. Here's why: you are deleting objects with *DeleteObject* from the navigation properties or from the object context, and you will trigger the *DELETE* statements to the database later, using *SaveChanges*. But when you

call *DeleteObject* object references[3] to the navigation property, objects are lost, as well. Therefore, it makes sense to save the .NET references by using helper variables and then pass them to *DeleteObject* via those temporary object variables. Otherwise you would trigger an exception in the example that follows.

```
Sub DeleteData()

    Dim awContext As New AWEntities()

    'Determine the entiy objects which result from the specified product:
    Dim supplierProduct = (From supplierProductItem In awContext.ProductVendor _
                           From productItem In awContext.Product _
                           Where productItem.ProductID = supplierProductItem.ProductID _
                           Where productItem.Name =
                               "Visual Basic 2010-Developer Handbook" _
                           Select supplierProductItem).First

    'Just to make sure
    Console.WriteLine(supplierProduct.ProductID)

    'Load the parent entity objects.
    'First the supplier product which is assigned
    'to the determined product.
    supplierProduct.ProductReference.Load()

    'And we are loading the parent supplier just as easily.
    supplierProduct.VendorReference.Load()

    'We will temporarily have to remember the references
    'to the entities, because DeleteObject destroys them
    'with the parent table.
    Dim tmpProduct = supplierProduct.Product
    Dim tmpVendor = supplierProduct.Vendor

    'The deletion order is now ...
    awContext.DeleteObject(tmpVendor)

    '... no longer important.
    awContext.DeleteObject(tmpProduct)

    'Entity Framework establishes the correct order!
    awContext.SaveChanges()

    Console.WriteLine()
    Console.WriteLine("Press key to exit")
    Console.ReadKey()
```

This is a good place to observe how the cascading deletions maintain the correct order of work: even though the code deletes only two entities with *DeleteObject*, doing so

___
[3] I'm discussing the .NET references here on purpose, to avoid any confusion between the logical references between data tables and references to objects from the CLR's point of view.

requires three *DELETE* statements according to the SQL Profiler. The supplier product of the *ProductVendor* table is dependent on its supplier in the *Vendor* table. Therefore, the supplier product must be deleted first, before the supplier can be deleted from the *Vendor* table— Entity Framework takes care of that automatically. Here's the generated SQL:

```
exec sp_executesql N'delete [Purchasing].[ProductVendor]
where (([ProductID] = @0) and ([VendorID] = @1))',N'@0 int,@1 int',@0=1005,@1=109

exec sp_executesql N'delete [Production].[Product]
where ([ProductID] = @0)',N'@0 int',@0=1005

exec sp_executesql N'delete [Purchasing].[Vendor]
where ([VendorID] = @0)',N'@0 int',@0=109
```

Note For the deletion in this example to work, you must disable the trigger that's connected to the *Vendor* table. This happens in the method *InsertRelatedData*. This method has run once before because it first generates the data that you want to delete. You can also disable or delete the trigger by using SQL Server Management Studio.

Tip Sometimes it is rather awkward (at the least) to load records from the database just to delete them. *LINQ to SQL* was much better in that discipline—you could have a real delete query. Unfortunately, up to this date, the Entity Framework doesn't really support that. There are many workarounds, though. One of your options is to create a new Entity Object just with the Key ID and add that to the object context. You can then delete that object as described previously. Another method is to directly execute a delete statement against the database with the *ExecuteStoreCommand* of the object context. But this way, an previously existing entity context wouldn't be updated. There are some other approaches that you can find on the Web, of which this is one of the promising ones: *http://tinyurl.com/6ylyey5*.

Concurrency Checks

As long as you're only changing data from a single SQL Server client, your application should not encounter any problems during data updates. But what happens when multiple users are changing data in a network environment at the same time?

By default the Entity Framework uses an *optimistic concurrency* checking model. The object services save changes to the in-memory objects without running a concurrency check.

For some properties, it makes sense to adjust this setting. You can change the default behavior easily by using the Designer in the conceptual model. You just select the property in the entity and set its *ConcurrencyMode* to *Fixed* (see Figure 27-26).

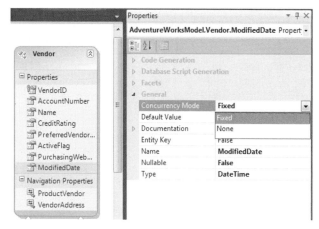

FIGURE 27-26 To enable the concurrency check for certain entity properties, set the Concurrency Mode to *Fixed*.

With the *Fixed* setting in effect, the object services perform a modification check before saving any changes to the database. When the check discovers conflicts, your application will raise an *OptimisticConcurrencyException*.

If your application saves changes to a database and modification conflicts are possible, Microsoft recommends that you use the *Refresh* method of the object context frequently in between saves. *Refresh* defines the effect of the modifications. If you pass the option *StoreWins* (where "store" stands for: *the storage unit*, in other words, the database wins), object services overwrites existing data in the entity object with fresh data from the database. Alternatively you can pass the option *ClientWins*, so that values in the entity objects are copied to the database:

```
Sub ChangeDataWithConcurrencyCheck()

        Dim awContext As New AWEntities()

        Dim supplier = (From supplierItem In awContext.Vendor _
                    Where supplierItem.Name.ToLower.StartsWith("hybrid") _
                    Order By supplierItem.Name).First

        'Change back and forth, so it works more than once:
        If supplier.Name = "Hybrid Bicycle Center" Then
            supplier.Name = "Hybrid Bicycle Center"
        Else
            supplier.Name = "Hybrid Cycle Center"
        End If
        'Set time stamp for the last change
        supplier.ModifiedDate = Date.Now

        Console.WriteLine("You can now change the data set with the VendorID {0} with SQL
Server Management Studio.", supplier.VendorID)
```

```
        Console.WriteLine("Don't forget to change at least one field and set its concurrency
mode to fixed (typically ModifiedDate).")
        Console.WriteLine("Or simply start the program again (e.g. with the Windows Explorer
from the Bin directory)")
        Console.WriteLine("Press any key")

        Console.ReadKey()
        Console.WriteLine("")
        Console.WriteLine("")

        Try
            Dim amount = awContext.SaveChanges()
            Console.WriteLine("No conflict during saving. " _
                            & amount & " updates saved.")
        Catch ex As OptimisticConcurrencyException
            awContext.Refresh(RefreshMode.ClientWins, supplier)

            awContext.SaveChanges()
            Console.WriteLine("Conflict errors were caught. Changes were saved!")
        End Try

        'Save changes
        awContext.SaveChanges()

        Console.WriteLine()
        Console.WriteLine("Press key to exit")
        Console.ReadKey()

End Sub
```

For this example to work, you must set the *ConcurrencyMode* for the *ModifiedDate* field of the *Vendor* entity object to *Fixed* beforehand, as shown in Figure 27-25.

Start the program twice: once in the Visual Studio debug mode, and once with Windows Explorer from your project's Bin directory. In one of the running program instances, press a key immediately after the message *Press any key* is displayed, wait until the program has completed and displays the message *Press key to exit*, and then press a key in the other program window. The program alerts you about a collision.

Updating a Data Model from a Database

Updating the ADO.NET Entity Data Model from a database works well in Visual Studio 2010 (that can't be said about its predecessors). Microsoft has made some improvements that make .NET Framework 4.0 much more comfortable to work with.

To start an update, display the Designer context menu, and select Update Model from Database. Figure 27-27 shows the dialog box that opens and its three tabs: Add, Update, and Delete.

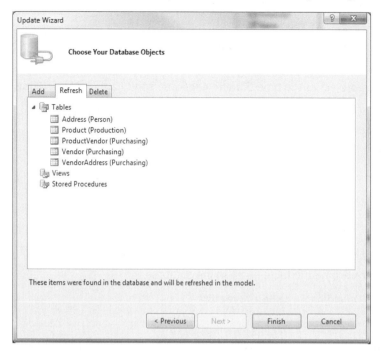

FIGURE 27-27 During a data model update, you can add new tables, views, or stored procedures. Using the Update Wizard, you can see which objects have been updated and which were deleted when they no longer exist in the database

- Use the Add tab to add new tables, views, and stored procedures to the model.

- The *Refresh* tab shows tables, views, and stored procedures that were updated in your project.

- The *Delete* tab shows objects that were removed from the model because they no longer exist in the database.

Don't try to use the Delete tab to delete elements from the entity model. That's not what it is intended to do. You can delete an entity from the model by selecting the entity in the Designer, and then clicking Delete. Alternatively, you can open the entity context menu and select Delete.

Model-First Design

In Visual Studio 2008, you could create a model from a database, but not a database from a model. But with Entity Framework 4.0, you can now create a database from a model, as well, by using a process called *model-first design*. The following steps first create a model with projects and Employees, and then they create database structures from that model.

> **Companion Content** Open the corresponding solution (.sln), which you can find in the
> \VB 2010 Developer Handbook\Chapter 27\ModelFirst folder.

1. Create a new project of the type *Console Application* and name it **ModelFirst**.

2. Add a new ADO.NET Entity Data Model element to the project, and name it
    modelFirst.edmx.

3. In the wizard, select Empty Model, and then click Finish.

    You'll see an empty Entity Data Model Designer.

4. From the Toolbox, select the Entity tool and drag it into the Designer.

5. In the Properties pane, change the name of the entity to **Employee**.

6. Change the entity set name from EmployeeSet to **Employee**.

    This will later become the table name in the database.

7. Change the ID field name to **EmployeeID**.

> **Tip** When you use the Designer context menu to create a new entity, you can specify
> the names of the entity, the entity set, and the primary key, as well as the data type of the
> entity.

8. Add some additional fields to the *Employee* entity. To do this, open the context menu
    of the *Employee* entity, and then select Add | Scalar Property (Figure 27-28).

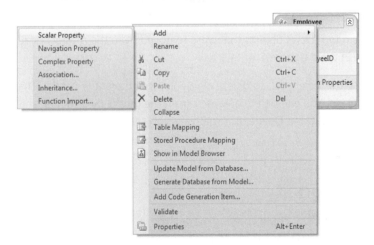

FIGURE 27-28 Adding fields in the Entity Data Model Designer.

9. In the Property window, set the data types for the new entity: for LastName and
    FirstName select String; for Birthday and CreatedOn, select DateTime.

10. Create a new entity called **Project**.

11. Change it's ID field to **ProjectID**.

12. Add the additional fields.

At this point, you need to consider foreign keys and navigation properties. These are easy to create by using the Assignment object in the Toolbox.

13. Select the Assignment tool from the Toolbox.

14. Click the *Employee* entity.

The mouse pointer changes as you move it over the *Employee* entity area.

15. Click the *Project* entity to create a new navigation property for each of the two entities.

The navigation property now represents the project manager for a project. Each project has one manager that can control 0-*n* projects. Because you clicked the employee entity first when assigning the navigation property, it becomes your "End1" point. The Project become the "End2" point, resulting in a relationship meaning *one Employee can manage several projects*. As soon as you rename the "End2" navigation property to **Manager**, the *Project* entity changes the navigation property to *Manager*. Also change the navigation property of the Employee from *Project* to **Manages**.

When working with the entity model later, this means you will be able to access the project manager from a project via the navigation property *Manager*. Similarly, from an *Employee* entity later on, you can see from the navigation property *Manages* whether this person is a project manager, and if so, use the *Manages* navigation property to access the project.

In the next steps, we want to map the assignment of Employees (who are not managers) to Projects.

One Employee can work on several projects, and several Employees can work on one project. In this case it makes more sense to start the assignment with the Employee.

16. Select the Assignment tool, click first on the *Employee* entity, and then click on the *Project* entity, which defines the following assignment: End1 multiplicity is "1 (one of Employee)" and End2 is "* (Collection of Project)".

You can read this assignment as follows: *One Employee can work on several projects and* (incorrectly!*) a project is composed of one Employee*. The assignment is therefore not yet complete.

17. Complete the assignment by selecting it and changing the End1 multiplicity from "1 (one of Employee)" to "* (Collection of Employee)".

By making this change, you're specifying that multiple Employees can work on one project. To make it easier to read, change the names of the navigation properties you just created: on the project side, call the navigation property **Employees**, and on the Employee side rename the navigation property to **WorksOn**.

> **Tip** Assignment configuration, with its End1 and End2 properties, is not very clear. You can also select each navigation property and specify the multiplicity (also called cardinality) there.

> **Note** When creating a conceptual model, the error list might show errors and warnings about unmapped entities. You can ignore these messages because they will disappear when you generate the database.

Next, from our conventional data model (ADO.NET Entity Data Model), we are going to create a database model via the required Data Definition Language (DDL) statements.

18. Click an empty area of the conceptual model, and then select the menu item Generate Database From Model.

> **Note** To generate database creation statements, you must have administrator rights in the database instance. If you are an administrator, you have administrative rights in the database by default. In Windows Vista and Windows 7, you might need to start Visual Studio as an administrator. Alternatively, you can log on to the database with the *sa* user, if you have configured the database for mixed-mode authentication.

19. The generator now creates a script that can create the new database. However, it doesn't actually generate the tables in the database instance—it simply creates and saves a file with the *instructions* to create the database. Select the desired database connection or click the New Connection button to establish a new connection, as shown in Figure 27-29.

FIGURE 27-29 Connection settings for the conceptual data model.

20. From the Server Name drop-down list, select the database instance that you want to use (see Figure 27-30).

If you want to create a new database, enter the new database in the Select Or Enter A New Database Name field, or select an existing database.

FIGURE 27-30 Entering a name for the new database.

21. The last wizard dialog (Figure 27-31) displays the code that generates the database structures. (You have already created the database itself with the Connection Manager, but it's still empty). In the Save DDL As field, enter a file name where you want to save the creation script.

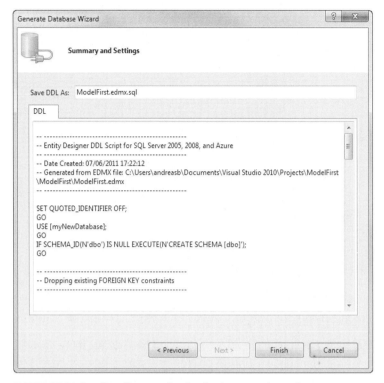

FIGURE 27-31 Specify a file name for the database creation script.

22. Navigate to the newly created creation script file. You can now connect to the database in the menu bar (the icon on the far left), select the target database, and then run the script by clicking the "Play" icon.

> **Note** If you now make changes to the table names (in the entity set) and need to regenerate the database, the wizard generates delete statements for the old tables automatically. However, it's up to you to save any existing test data before regenerating the database, and then transfer the saved values to the new model.

You might notice the table *EmployeeProject* in the created tables. That was generated because of the *m*-to-*n* connection between Employees and projects. The table field names are generated automatically from a combination of the names of the two navigation properties or IDs (such as *WorksOn_ProjectID*).

Your model should now look appear as presented in Figure 27-32.

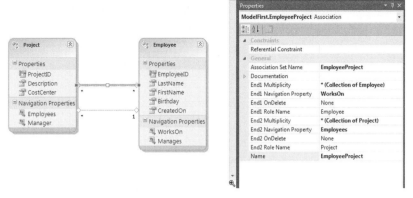

FIGURE 27-32 The final data model of the *ModelFirst* example.

Inheritance in the Conceptual Data Model

The inheritance feature in the conceptual data model can save you a lot of work. You can inherit entities in a manner similar to that of standard object-oriented programming.

For example, you can define an *Employee* entity and then derive more specific entities such as developers, project managers, and so on from the base *Employee* type. Then you can expand the derived classes with specific fields which store specific information like the developer's skills.

The transparency of this inheritance process lets you work with, for example, a *Developer* instance—without the need to know that it is derived from an *Employee*. You only need to know the inheritance hierarchy when adding the *Developer* Instance to the object context. You add this new created Developer to the context by using the existing *AddEmployee* method.

> **Companion Content** Open the corresponding solution (.sln), which you can find in the \VB 2010 Developer Handbook\Chapter 27\Inheritance folder.

If you take a look at the properties of the .edmx file (see Figure 27-33), you see that you have two options for controlling data script generation.

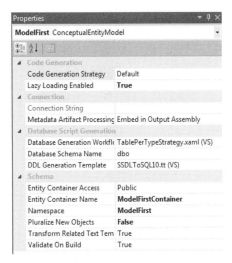

FIGURE 27-33 Setting for the code generation of the data model.

The DDL generation template, SSDLToSQL10.tt, is a T4 template for model-first table creation using the conceptual model.

> **Note** You can create your own T4 templates if you like. They are a combination of static text and program code, and they create a code file. If you are familiar with PHP or JavaServer Pages, you will find them easy to use and straightforward to create and modify. Visual Studio already provides one template. You can integrate it into the project via the model's context menu by selecting Add New Code Generation Element.

The second setting is called *Database Generation Workflow*. Currently the only option is *TablePerTypeStrategy*. When using table inheritance, this setting creates one table for each type. In conjunction with the base classes, this results in a complete entity mapping.

From the Designer context menu, you can add a new entity to the conceptual model and simultaneously select its base entity (see Figure 27-34) to get the entities *Employee* and *Developer*. With the *TablePerTypeStrategy* set, this results in two tables:

- Employee (set)
- Developer (set)

FIGURE 27-34 Adding the entity *Developer* derived from *Employee* via the context menu of the Designer.

The *Employee* table consists of the fields *EmployeeID*, *FirstName*, and *LastName*. The *Developer* table has no additional fields yet; it has only one foreign-key column, which holds the primary key of the *Employee* table, namely *EmployeeID*.

The complete *Developer* data set of an inherited table results from a *join* query between the *Employee* table and the *Developer* table. You don't need to worry about creating the join-query because the Entity Framework (or the generated code) handles that.

It's also possible to swap the *Developer* entity into the *Employee* table so that you create a single table to hold both *Employee* and *Developer*. However, in that case, you can't create the database from the model (Model First), unless you are using a custom DDL generation template or a strategy other than the *TablePerTypeStrategy*.

However, you can create the database structures manually and then import the conceptual model (select Update Model From Database from the model's context menu).

Afterward, you need to create the inheritance hierarchy in the conceptual model and distribute the data across the various entities. To do this, you need at least one field that lets you differentiate the various entity types. For example, in the *Employee-Developer* example, that differentiating field could be *ProgrammingLanguage* (type: *String*). Using the *Mapping Details* you can then distribute the data to the entity types. If the field is *Null*, the row holds an Employee; if it's not null, the row holds a developer. Another strategy might be to use an *EmployeeType* field, as demonstrated in Figure 27-35.

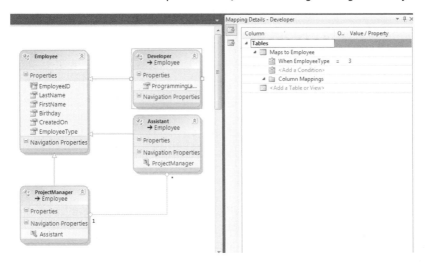

FIGURE 27-35 In the *Mapping Details* for a developer: *EmployeeType=3* describes a developer, *EmployeeType=1* a project manager, and an assistant has *EmployeeType=2*. Additional fields for the project managers, developers, and assistants are still missing (such as programming languages for the developer, and so on).

In this example, *Employee*, *Developer*, *Assistant* and *Project Manager* are all mapped to the table *Employee*.

To revisit the *TablePerTypeStrategy*: the original Model First example created an Employee entity and a *Project* entity. Then the example was extended with a *Developer* entity, which inherits from *Employee*. *Developer* has an additional field: *ProgrammingLanguage*.

> **Note** Using the form of inheritance to create multiple entities in one table requires a lot of manual work. Unfortunately, the Designer, code generator, and so on still contain errors. Perhaps an update or patch will soon become available that will make this functionality a little easier to handle.

Executing T-SQL Commands Directly in the Object Context

As you saw in the sample project *LinqToEntitiesDemo*, with the ADO.NET Entity Framework, you can use T-SQL commands directly, sending them to SQL Server for execution. For example, the method *LinqToEntitiesDemo* disables the trigger on the *Vendor* table by using the following T-SQL statement:

```
awContext.ExecuteStoreCommand("disable trigger Purchasing.dVendor on Purchasing.Vendor")
```

> **Important**   When using T-SQL commands directly, you lose one of the great advantages of the
> Entity Framework—separation of the conceptual data model from the database. Using T-SQL
> statements directly can compromise your application's compatibility with other databases.

Entity Framework 4.0 adds some new methods to the object context:

- **ExecuteFunction**   Runs a stored procedure.

- **ExecuteStoreCommand**   Runs any desired command.

- **ExecuteStoreQuery**   Runs a *SELECT* statement.

With the exception of *ExecuteStoreCommand*, these methods are overloaded; at least one
overload provides a type-safe generic function that returns an *ObjectResult(of T)*. The framework handles conversion of the return value into the type *T* by using the *Translate* method of
the object context. Any passed parameters must be specified as database-specific, as the following *AdventureWorks* database example shows:

```
Dim awContext As New AWEntities()

Dim ret = awContext.ExecuteStoreQuery(Of Vendor) _
    ("SELECT * FROM Purchasing.Vendor where
     AccountNumber=@accountNr",
     New System.Data.SqlClient.SqlParameter("accountNr", "METROSP0001")
     )
For Each ds As Vendor In ret
    Console.WriteLine("Ret:" & ds.Name)
Next
```

Within the *SELECT* statement, the parameter has an "@" (ampersand) character as a prefix.
But note that for the *SqlParameter* instance, the parameter name has no ampersand character. The parameter value is specified next (*METROSP0001* in the preceding code).

Statement parameterization offers significant performance advantages for a database management system. Whenever the database management system runs a new statement, that
statement must be parsed, and then the DBMS must create and save an execution plan.
Obviously, if you're running *exactly* the same statement repeatedly, that statement no longer needs to be parsed and no new execution plan needs to be created, which is a huge
advantage.

Working with Stored Procedures

You can also embed stored procedures or functions into the conceptual model. To do that,
select Stored Procedures in the Update Model From The Database Wizard.

These stored procedures and methods appear in the storage model of the Model Browser. From there you can add them to the conceptual data model through the context menu (Add Function Import—only available for stored procedures). After a successful import, you find the methods in the Model Browser in the *EntityContainer* under *Function Imports*, as shown in Figure 27-36.

FIGURE 27-36 In the Model Browser, you can view entities in the conceptual model and tables from the storage model as well as function imports, complex types, and much more

Note You can create function imports only for stored procedures. The terminology is rather ambiguous. Below Stored Procedures, the Model Browser not only shows procedures created with the SQL command *CREATE PROCEDURE*, but also functions created with *CREATE FUNCTION*. The simplest way to get an overview is to use the Server Explorer (see Figure 27-37).

FIGURE 27-37 The Server Explorer view helps you to identify the true stored procedures from stored functions.

You can also use stored procedures for *Insert*, *Update*, and *Delete* statements against the respective tables. The *Mapping Details* pane provides the required settings (see Figure 27-38).

FIGURE 27-38 In the Mapping Details pane, you can specify that the object context should use stored procedures for *Insert*, *Update*, or *Delete* statements for a specific entity.

Note If you are using automatically generated (primary) keys, you must configure them as return values.

Looking Ahead

With the second version (4.0) of Entity Framework, it's apparent that Microsoft listened to and implemented many developer community requests. In the future, we will certainly see the Framework add great features that will make it even easier to create professional-quality databases. But there's still work to be done, particularly when working with extremely large databases. For example, the option of distributing a large entity model over multiple files or views to make it easier to handle when working as a team still needs improvement, as does check-in and check-out with Team Foundation Server or other systems that include source code version control and collaborative features.

This book can't cover all the features of the Entity Framework; there simply isn't room to cover use of stored procedures, table inheritance, or extended mapping functionalities in detail here. The same is true of transactions. But you can implement transactions fairly easily using the *TransactionScope* objects from the .NET Framework Enterprise Services. Again, Julia Lerman's book (*http://oreilly.com/catalog/9780596807269*) would be the one with which you would want to continue.

Nevertheless, this chapter should have provided you with a good foundation on which to build. You should now be able to develop powerful databases based on the Entity Framework. If there's only one takeaway that you should remember from this chapter, it's that the Entity Framework helps future-proof your applications. The entire concept of object-relational mapping is still under development, so there's a lot left to discover and to try out—not just for you, but also for us authors.

Part VI
Parallelizing Applications

Chapter 28
Programming with the Task Parallel Library (TPL)

Introduction to Threading

With his theory of relativity, Einstein proved that simultaneity is actually an illusion. A modern computer gives the impression that it really can do multiple things at the same time. For example, my computer is playing *The Black Eyed Peas* in the background while defragging the hard drive, all while I'm writing this chapter in Microsoft Word. On the surface, these actions might seem as if they're happening simultaneously, but they're not, really. The computer divides these three actions (and more) into tiny tasks and then distributes these tasks among its processor cores. And it's not only those three tasks; it's a lot more. Some of the tasks are basically processed one after the other. But because of the speed at which the computer processes those tiny tasks, you get the impression that it's handling all the tasks at the same time.

Gordon Earle Moore, one of the founders of Intel, formulated the idea now known as "Moore's Law," which states that the number of integrated circuits and performance of chips doubles every 18 months.

Note Mr. Moore denies predicting the 18-month cycle. He says this statement was made by his colleague, David House.

Until 2002, better chip performance primarily meant operating the chip at a higher clock rate. This was comparatively easy for software developers, because they didn't need to change their code. If their code was too slow, developers would simply wait 18 months and run it on a faster processor.

But those times are gone. Since 2003, processor speed has leveled off; the maximum clock rate has remained between 3.4 and 3.8 GHz. Processors have continued to become faster, but this is due to internal design changes, not increased clock rate. The speed improvement wasn't keeping up with Moore's Law. In fact, if the law applied solely to clock rate, processors today would run at 20 to 30 GHz.

Pulse frequency has peaked because of such factors as power loss, tunnel effects, and so on. Thus, processors cannot become significantly faster; they can only be taught to do more things at the same time. While writing the first version of this chapter back in 2003 (and no, it hasn't taken me that long to write the chapter; it was for a previous edition of this book), I assumed that this would be the trend, and since then, that assumption has proven right. I took my first steps in multithreading on the first hyperthreading processors available at the time (Intel Pentium 4 with 3.06 GHz—I paid a fortune for them!). Today, when my company wants to deliver parallelization to customers, the computer performance looks like Figure 28-1.

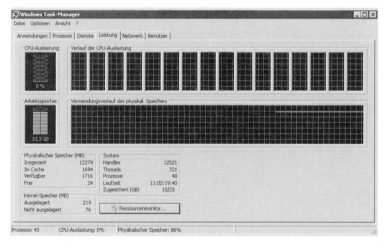

FIGURE 28-1 Modern computer systems provide a great deal of computing power. And while two processors with four cores are impressive, they only mark the beginning of the multicore trend. This image was taken on a German Windows multicore server system, but you'll get the picture, anyway. Literally.

Unfortunately, this doesn't mean that a processor with two or four cores automatically has twice or quadruple the power of a single-core chip. In fact, multiple cores are useful only when developers write software that can take advantage of those cores by dividing tasks among threads that can then run on several processor cores. Only then do users (and developers of time-critical systems) start to benefit from this new multicore technology.

With that said, it's clear that this chapter covers one of the truly important topics of both the past and the future.

> **Note** In the last figure, you might have noticed that some of the labels are in German. This is also true of several other illustrations throughout this chapter. The lead author's origin explains that mystery; he worked on this book's translation by using an English language virtual machine. However, some of the features he wanted to show here simply can't be put into that virtual computer—showing a server system with 16 cores is one of them. Unfortunately, the need for a second 16-core server with an English operating system was unanticipated when the author bought his German system, and as such, he wishes to extend his apologies for any confusion caused by these labels.

Everyone who works with computers should know the term *multitasking*. Multitasking is a juxtaposition of the words "multi" and "task," which when combined denotes something that women are usually better at than men: the ability to do more than one thing at a time.[1]

> **Note** This theory appears to extend to finding lost stuff, although I'm convinced that this is the result of a parallel universe that's cleverly concealed in my refrigerator. Whenever a woman opens the door, it makes a swap to this alternate universe. In that universe, the butter resides in the right place. In *my* universe, not only am I unable to find the butter—it simply doesn't exist.

Another similar term that's less well known than multitasking is *multithreading*. But what does that term mean exactly? Here's some background information: when you start a Windows application it consists of a process which in turn consists of a thread. In this context, "thread" is an abstract term for a certain action in a program. A thread runs a specific task, and stops after that task completes. If the task is computationally intensive, it uses all the available processor time; during that period, the program appears to be unusable. That's because when a thread uses all of a processor core's computing power (and if the computer has only one processor core, that means *all* the computing power) there's no free time for the computer to respond to user actions. The example program that follows illustrates the problem.

> **Companion Content** Open the corresponding solution (.sln), which you can find in the \VB 2010 Developer Handbook\Chapter 28\SingleThreadDemo folder.

This sample program lets you search for prime numbers below a given maximum value. The algorithm to check whether a number is a prime number is not well optimized. That's necessary for this example, because it's about creating a long-running task. When you start the program, give it some initial values, and initiate the prime number search (the length of time

---

[1] This is treated as common knowledge. Who knows if it's true?

the search requires varies, depending on your computer). You see a result similar to that shown in Figure 28-2.

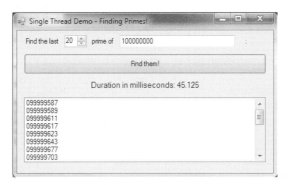

FIGURE 28-2 An Atom processor (Atom 330 Dual Core, Hyperthreading) on a netbook, calculating the last 20 prime numbers below 100 million in 45,000 milliseconds.

```
Private Sub btnStartCounting_Click(ByVal sender As System.Object,
                              ByVal e As System.EventArgs)
                              Handles btnStartCounting.Click

    'Delete list if it already contains items:
    PrimesListBox.Items.Clear()

    Dim sw = Stopwatch.StartNew

    Dim PrimesFound = 0
    Dim StartNumber = Integer.Parse(LastPrimeBeforeTextBox.Text)
    Dim leadingZeros = StartNumber.ToString.Length
    For numberToTest = StartNumber To 2 Step -1
        Dim isPrime = True

        InfoLabel.Text = "Testing: " & numberToTest.ToString("#,##0")
        InfoLabel.Refresh()

        For valueToTest = 2 To numberToTest - 1
            If (numberToTest / valueToTest) = (numberToTest \ valueToTest) Then
                isPrime = False
                Exit For
            End If
        Next
        If isPrime Then
            'Little trick (poor but easier):
            'for ListBox to sort numerically we insert leading zeroes.
            PrimesListBox.Items.Add(numberToTest.ToString(New String("0"c,
leadingZeros)))
            PrimesListBox.Refresh()

            PrimesFound += 1
```

```
                If PrimesFound = PrimesToFindUpDown.Value Then
                    Exit For
                End If
            End If
        Next

        sw.Stop()
        InfoLabel.Text = "Time in milliseconds: " & sw.ElapsedMilliseconds.ToString("#,##0")
    End Sub
```

If you launch Task Manager before the prime number calculation begins, two critical problems occur while using the program:

- While it's calculating the prime numbers, the program's interface is frozen.

- It uses the entire capacity of a processor core. Unfortunately, the program uses only one of the available processor cores. Figure 28-3 shows what that means.

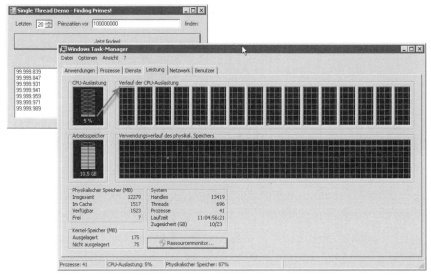

FIGURE 28-3 If you call a computationally intensive method on a multicore system, only one processor core is used. This is a disaster for systems with many cores since only a fraction of the possible performance is utilized. This image was captured on a German Windows multicore server.

The two problems are closely related. A Windows application regularly executes a loop to check whether anything has happened, such as when a user clicks a button or tries to move the window. This loop is called a *message loop*, and in principle, it looks like this:

```
Sub WindowsProc()
    Do
        Dim result = DoEvents()
        If Not result Then
            Exit Do
        End If
```

```
        Loop
    End Sub

    Function DoEvents() As Boolean

        Dim msg = GetWindowsMessage

        If msg = WM_CLOSE Then
            Return True
        End If

        If msg = WM_MOVEWINDOW Then
            'Triggers the move window event
            OnMoveWindow()
        End If
    End Function
```

As long as the application can process the message queue, everything is OK. But if any event fires a long-running method call, the message loop is blocked. In Microsoft Visual Basic, you can often solve the problem by calling *DoEvents* within the blocking method to allow the system to process messages periodically.

Of course, that's not a very elegant solution. The only logical solution is to make the long-running method execute in a separate thread. That way, the UI thread can continue to run the message loop and—most important—the task can be executed on more than one processor. One core, running the main thread, ensures that the application remains usable, while another core runs the long-running task.

Threads are useful in many scenarios, such as those presented in the following list:

- Your program creates and prints an extensive data analysis. You can run this task in a separate background thread without interrupting program execution.

- Your program creates extensive data backups. A thread can create snapshots of the data and then copy them to another location in the background.

- Your program records the states of hardware components, such as logging production data. This function can also run in the background. However, users must also be able to use these functions while production data-capture runs as a background thread.

- For complex calculations and evaluations, two or more threads can take over. In this case, the processing speed for the task would significantly increase with hyperthreading or multiprocessor systems that each use their own thread.

- For image processsing (for example, converting and filtering and scaling images) you can divide an image into smaller chunks. These chunks can then be processed in parallel on different threads.

Obviously, using multiple threads can be useful. But there are also other considerations. For example, using multiple threads raises the possibility that they can interfere with each other. You'll see more detail about that problem later.

First you'll explore the basics to see how you configure the .NET Framework to run certain portions of an application as separate threads.

Various Options for Starting a Thread

The Microsoft .NET Framework offers several options for starting a task on a single thread:

- Call the method that runs the task asynchronously by using a delegate. This is the easiest method to start a thread—but it is also the one that offers the least control.

- Use one of the special parallelization methods in the *Parallel* class, such as *Parallel.For* or *Parallel.ForEach*.

- Create a LINQ query and parallelize it by adding *AsParallel*.

- In Windows Forms applications, you can use the *BackgroundWorker* component. This helps with updating the user interface because in Windows Forms applications—and Windows Presentation Foundation (WPF) applications—you can access UI controls only from the thread on which those controls were created—usually the thread started by default when you launch the application. Therefore, this thread is also called the *user interface thread* or *UI thread*.

- You can use a thread from the thread pool. The thread pool provides several predefined *Thread* objects. Alternatively, you can create and use a new *Thread* object. However, threads are resource-intensive. Managing a new thread requires both processor time and at least a megabyte of virtual memory. Even a CLR thread uses one megabyte of real memory. You can use a *Task* object, available since .NET 4.0., to control a thread from the thread pool. If you work with earlier versions of the .NET Framework you can access the *ThreadPool* class directly.

- You can use the *Thread* class directly. Creating a new thread with an instance of this class is the most time consuming way to create threads, and it uses the most resources. That's fine for threads like the UI thread that take a long time to execute. In fact, when the standard scheduler is being used, the *Task* class doesn't take a thread from the thread pool but creates a *Thread* object if you configure the options to use a long running thread.

> **Note** If you use *Parallel.For* or *Parallel.ForEach* or parallelize LINQ queries to execute a task on several processor cores, the .NET Framework uses threads from the thread pool.

> **Companion Content**   Open the corresponding solution (.sln), which you can find in the
> \VB 2010 Developer Handbook\Chapter 28\SimpleThread01 folder.

Figure 28-4 depicts the *SimpleThread* example with which you can select from the various
options to start a thread.

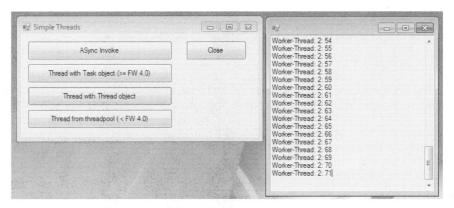

FIGURE 28-4 The *SimpleThread* demonstration shows the different options for starting threads.

```
'This is the actual worker thread that takes over the
'counting and value output
Private Sub ComplexCalculation()
    Thread.CurrentThread.Name = "Worker-Thread: " + myWorkerThreadNr.ToString
    For c As Integer = 0 To LOOPCOUNT
        'Displays the value. TSWriteLine is a static procedure
        'that displays the window
        'if used for the first time.
        TextOutput.TSWriteLine(Thread.CurrentThread.Name + ": " + c.ToString)
        'The current thread is delayed by 100ms so the
        'execution doesn't happen too fast.
        Thread.Sleep(100)
    Next
End Sub
```

This application simulates a method with a high workload in a simple way:
ComplexCalculation (as shown in the preceding code) loops a specified number of times,
incrementing the counter variable (*c*) each time. The counter variable value displays in a special output window. The figure shows two threads that run this routine at the same time.

> **Note** To output a string, such as in a text box or a label, requires more effort in Windows forms and WPF. For example, the following code always causes an exception:
>
> ```
> OutputLabel.Text = "New Label"
> ```
>
> Therefore, the sample applications use the component *ThreadSafeTextWindowComponent* for these experiments. When you add this component to a Windows forms application (drag it onto the form, you can use the methods *TSWrite* and *TSWriteLine*, which open another window containing the output text. These methods are thread-safe, so you can call them from any thread without triggering an exception. You can find more information about accessing controls in Windows Forms and WPF in the section "How to Access Windows Controls from Non-UI Threads," later in this chapter.
>
> When you use the *BackgroundWorker* component, you don't need to worry about accessing the controls of other threads because it handles such access internally.

Using the Thread Class

The typical way to start a new thread is through the *Thread* instance. This option is available in all versions of the .NET Framework and the Compact Framework. To test the example program, click the Start Thread With Thread Object button. The following code runs, executing the *ComplexCalculation* method in its own thread:

```
Private Sub btnThreadStart_Click(ByVal sender As System.Object, _
    ByVal e As System.EventArgs) _
    Handles ThreadWithThreadButton.Click

    'This object encapsulates the actual thread
    Dim locThread As Thread
    'You need this object to determine the procedure
    'that runs the thread.
    Dim locThreadStart As ThreadStart

    'Procedure to run the thread
    locThreadStart = New ThreadStart(AddressOf ComplexCalculation)

    'ThreadStart object is passed to the thread
    locThread = New Thread(locThreadStart)

    'Create a thread that will end when the main application ends:
    locThread.IsBackground = True

    'Start thread
    locThread.Start()
    'Countner to distinguish the threads by name
    myWorkerThreadNo += 1
End Sub
```

This is the long version: you define a new *ThreadStart* delegate (see Chapter 15, "Events, Delegates, and Lambda Expressions") that points to the method that you want to run in a separate thread. You pass that *ThreadStart* delegate to the *Thread* object's constructor.

Background Threads Always End When the Main Application Ends

This example sets the *IsBackground* property of the *Thread* object to *True*. This new thread then becomes a background thread, which means that the thread will end when the main application ends. Otherwise, the thread could continue to run, causing the application to become "stuck" in memory.

> **Important** *Thread* objects whose *IsBackground* property is *not* set to *True* continue to run until their tasks are done. Even if the application was shut down and its UI has disappeared, the process ends only when the last thread completes.
>
> By enabling the *IsBackground* property, you ensure that the thread either finishes or is cancelled when the main application thread shuts down.

Simplifying Thread Start With Multi-Line Lambdas

As discussed earlier in this book, Visual Basic 2010 introduced multi-line lambdas. These contain code that is assigned directly to a delegate variable or can be passed to a method instead of a delegate variable. By using property initializers, you can shorten the code to run the *ComplexCalculation* method:

```
'Since Visual Basic 2010 the compiler saves a lot of typing
'with multi-statement Lambdas:
Private Sub ThreadStartShortVersion()

    Dim locThread As New Thread(
           Sub()
               'Same loop as in the 'Complex calculation' method.
               For c As Integer = 0 To LOOPCOUNT
                   TextOutput.TSWriteLine(Thread.CurrentThread.Name +
                       ": " + c.ToString)
                   Thread.Sleep(100)
               Next
           End Sub) With
                       {.IsBackground = True, .Name = "Worker Thread: " +
                           myWorkerThreadNo.ToString}
    locThread.Start()
    myWorkerThreadNo += 1
End Sub
```

Here the working method is passed directly as a lambda to the thread constructor instead of the delegate. The thread properties are passed with the keyword *With* as property initializers. The instantiation of the *Thread* object occurs according to the extensive version but saves a lot of typing and time because a lot of the code is generated by the compiler.

Calling Delegates Asynchronously

You call delegate variables that point to valid methods just like methods, as shown in the following example:

```
Dim helloWorldAction As Action = Sub()
                                      Debug.Print("Hello World!")
                                  End Sub

helloWorldAction()

'Alternative does the same:
helloWorldAction.Invoke()
```

You already saw this in Chapter 15. You can also call a delegate asynchronously by using the *BeginInvoke* method instead of the *Invoke* method. This automatically retreives a thread from the thread pool and executes the method on that thread. You pass a delegate along with its parameters to *BeginInvoke*. As shown in the Visual Basic 2010 example, the delegate can also be a lambda, which simplifies matters. The delegate runs as soon as the asynchronous operation completes.

It's important to understand that when you call a method by using *BeginInvoke*, it returns an object that contains the result parameter of an asynchronous operation, and therefore integrates the *IAsyncResult* interface:

```
Dim aDelegate As action = AddressOf ComplexCalculation

Dim asyncres As IAsyncResult = Nothing
asyncres = aDelegate.BeginInvoke(Sub(value As Object)
                                     'This code is executed
                                     'after the task is completed.
                                     TextOutput.TSWriteLine("Worker Thread done!")
                                     'Important: Always end with EndInvoke!
                                     aDelegate.EndInvoke(asyncres)
                                     TextOutput.TSWriteLine("EndInvoke done!")
                                 End Sub, New Object)
myWorkerThreadNr += 1
```

You can control the operation by using these objects, but this book doesn't go into detail here because the *Task* class is much better suited for this purpose. You should ensure that you use the *IAsyncResult* object with *EndInvoke* to complete the asynchronous operation correctly (see the bold-highlighted line in the previous listing). Ideally, *EndInvoke* should happen in the method called after the actual worker method completes.

 Note In .NET Compact Framework, asynchronous method calls in this manner are not available.

Using the Task Class

It makes the most sense to use the *Task* class to execute a method on its own thread. But that class is available only in the Task Parallel Library (TPL), which is now a part of the Common Language Runtime (CLR) in .NET Framework 4.0.

A task corresponds to a thread in the thread pool. But tasks can also create a new *Thread* instance if you use the standard scheduler and specify that the operation will be time consuming. Usually, you don't need to worry about those implementation details.

You create a *Task* instance either through *Task* class or by calling the factory method *Task.Factory.StartNew*. The factory method not only generates a new task, it also starts the task. When you instantiate the task manually, you need to start the corresponding thread with the *Start* method. For this example, you have the following options:

```
Dim t = Task.Factory.StartNew(AddressOf ComplexCalculation)
```

Alternatively, to create the *Task* instance yourself, you would write:

```
'Alternative:
Dim t2 = New Task(Sub()
                        'Same loop as in the 'Complex calculation' method'.
                        For c As Integer = 0 To LOOPCOUNT
                            TextOutput.TSWriteLine(Thread.CurrentThread.Name + ":: " +
                                c.ToString)
                            Thread.Sleep(100)
                        Next
                    End Sub)
t2.Start()
```

By using the alternative method, you can specify the address of the *ComplexCalculation* method. But as shown in the example, in Visual Basic 2010, it's easier to include the code in a multi-line lambda.

Note Using the *ContinueWith* method, you can queue another task for execution. The method specified after *ContinueWith* starts after the task completes. You can specify several tasks as *Task* objects. This example passes a lambda to the *ContinueWith* method. The lambda simply displays a message that the worker method is done, as shown here:

```
t.ContinueWith(Sub()
                    TextOutput.TSWriteLine("Worker Thread completed!")
                End Sub)
```

Using a Thread Pool's Thread directly

If you work with a version of the .NET Framework prior to 4.0, the *Task* class is unavailable, but you can still use the threads in the thread pool. You pass a delegate by using the *QueueUserWorkItem* method, and the next available thread in the thread pool processes the method:

```
ThreadPool.QueueUserWorkItem(Sub(value)
                                 ComplexCalculation()
                             End Sub)
```

> **Note** *QueueUserWorkItem* expects a delegate that corresponds to a method signature with the parameter type *Object*. Therefore, you cannot pass *ComplexCalculation* with *AddressOf* directly at this point.

How to Access Windows Controls from Non-UI Threads

If you want to access controls in your main application from a different thread, consider the following: because controls are not thread-safe, you can use them only through the thread that initially created the controls. This is usually the main thread of the application that contains the user interface. This thread is also called the UI thread.

Remember that each Windows application runs in an infinite loop that terminates only after the main window is closed. For the application to manage events properly, it can't let multiple threads access a control and change its properties—such changes must occur successively on a single thread. If you use a different thread to update a control, the main UI thread must wait until the update is complete. But this operation can create dependencies, which in turn can cause everything to come to a halt. For example, the thread updating a control is waiting for data from another control, used by a different thread. Therefore, the thread doesn't release the control. Meanwhile, the UI thread is waiting for the control to be released, so the entire message queue is blocked. Neither thread can proceed. This condition is called a *deadlock*. You must avoid deadlocks at all costs. In this circumstance, you do this by making sure that only the thread that created the controls can update them—that's the only way to ensure that the application won't freeze.

For another thread to use a form control, it needs to tell the message queue (which runs on the UI thread) to call the method to update the control as soon as possible. By calling the method indirectly, the update occurs on the correct thread (the UI thread).

Control provides one of the few thread-safe procedures: *Invoke*. You pass a delegate as a parameter that points to the actual procedure called by the thread.

But how does this look in practice? Since you know how to launch threads, you can use the *Task* class to move the prime number calculation operation to its own thread. This doesn't make the application faster, but it's useful because the UI thread and its queue are no longer required to wait for the calculation to complete. You'll also see what happens when you don't redirect control updates to the UI thread.

> **Companion Content** Open the corresponding solution (.sln), which you can find in the \VB 2010 Developer Handbook\Chapter 28\InvokeDemo folder.

```vb
Dim calcPrimesTask = Task.Factory.StartNew(
        Sub()
            For numberToTest = Integer.Parse(LastPrimeBeforeTextBox.Text) To 2 Step -1
                Dim isPrime = True

                InfoLabel.Text = "Testing: " & numberToTest.ToString("#,##0")
                InfoLabel.Refresh()

                For valueToTest = 2 To numberToTest - 1
                    If (numberToTest / valueToTest) = (numberToTest \ valueToTest) Then
                        isPrime = False
                        Exit For
                    End If
                Next
                If isPrime Then
                    PrimesListBox.Items.Add(numberToTest.ToString("#,##0"))
                    PrimesListBox.Refresh()

                    PrimesFound += 1
                    If PrimesFound = PrimesToFindUpDown.Value Then
                        Exit For
                    End If
                 End If
            Next

            sw.Stop()
            InfoLabel.Text = "Time in milliseconds: " & _
                sw.ElapsedMilliseconds.ToString("#,##0")
        End Sub)
```

The method code between *Sub* and *End Sub* is now a command lambda, passed as a delegate to the *Task* object that is instantiated and immediately started by the *Task Factory* class. Prime number calculation now runs on a second thread. For a few seconds, everything in this example works fine—until the task tries to update the user interface. At that point, it blows up and throws an exception, as shown in Figure 28-5.

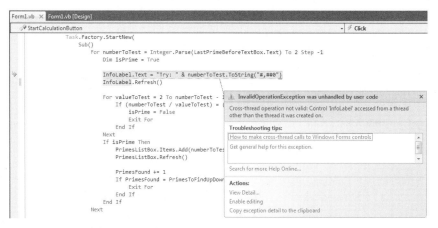

FIGURE 28-5 The attempt to access a control from a different thread fails.

To solve this problem, you need to ensure that the code that updates the controls runs in the UI thread, not the worker thread. You do this by calling the *Invoke* method, which is available for all controls. This method takes at least one delegate parameter that points to the method that you want to run in the UI thread. The example proves that you need to redirect control update to the UI thread by calling *Invoke*. But you might not need to call *Invoke* every time the update method is called—the method might be called by code already running on the UI thread. The solution is to check whether redirection to the UI thread is required, by calling *InvokeRequired*. Again, the simplest way to create the following pattern is to recycle. (Of course, you need to modify the lambda code for your specific controls and properties.)

 Note Don't forget to import the *System.Threading.Tasks* namespace if you're working with the TPL that includes the *Task* class used in the following code:

```
Imports System.Threading.Tasks
```

```
Dim labelUpdaterDel =
    Sub(numToTest As Integer)
        InfoLabel.Text = "Teste: " & numToTest.ToString("#,##0")
        InfoLabel.Refresh()
    End Sub

    If Not InfoLabel.InvokeRequired Then
        labelUpdaterDel(numberToTest)
    Else
        InfoLabel.Invoke(labelUpdaterDel, {numberToTest})
    End If
```

This part of the method defines a delegate variable that points to the lambda expression. The lambda expression takes the current value displayed in the label as a parameter.

> **Note** When parallelizing methods, you should avoid accessing loop variables that change within the loop but outside a lambda that resides in the loop, because you cannot predict the value of the counter variable with absolute certainty. Sometimes the compiler recognizes this and displays an appropriate warning. This topic is explained in further detail in the section "Avoiding Errors When Parallelizing Loops," later in this chapter.

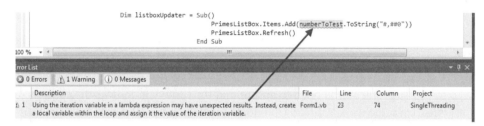

FIGURE 28-6 If possible, don't use an iteration variable in a lambda expression within a loop, because the lambda might run after the loop is completed and the iteration value at that point can be incorrect.

The modified calculation method looks similar to the following. Note that the changed lines appear highlighted in bold.

```
Private Sub StartCalculationButton_Click(ByVal sender As System.Object,
                            ByVal e As System.EventArgs) Handles
StartCalculationButton.Click

        Dim sw = Stopwatch.StartNew

        'For the threading version we query the value
        'of the control from the UI thread so we don't
        'have to delegate later.
        Dim primesToFind = PrimesToFindUpDown.Value
        Dim StartNumber = Integer.Parse(LastPrimeBeforeTextBox.Text)
        Dim leadingZeros = StartNumber.ToString.Length

        Dim PrimesFound = 0
        Dim calcPrimesTask =
            Task.Factory.StartNew(
                Sub()
                    For numberToTest = StartNumber To 2 Step -1
                        Dim isPrime = True

                        Dim labelUpdaterDel = Sub(numToTest As Integer)
                                    InfoLabel.Text = "Test: " &
                            numToTest.ToString("#,##0")
                                    InfoLabel.Refresh()
                                End Sub
```

```
If Not InfoLabel.InvokeRequired Then
    labelUpdaterDel(numberToTest)
Else
    InfoLabel.Invoke(labelUpdaterDel, {numberToTest})
End If

For valueToTest = 2 To numberToTest - 1
    If (numberToTest / valueToTest) = (numberToTest \
        valueToTest) Then
        isPrime = False
        Exit For
    End If
Next
If isPrime Then

    Dim listBoxUpdater = Sub(numToTest As Integer)
     PrimesListBox.Items.Add(numToTest.ToString(New String(
       "0"c, leadingZeros)))
     PrimesListBox.Refresh()
    End Sub

    If Not PrimesListBox.InvokeRequired Then
        listBoxUpdater(numberToTest)
    Else
        PrimesListBox.Invoke(listBoxUpdater, {numberToTest})
    End If

    PrimesFound += 1
    If PrimesFound = primesToFind Then
        Exit For
    End If
End If
Next

sw.Stop()
'Here we do it directly without asking:
InfoLabel.Invoke(
    Sub()
        InfoLabel.Text = "Time in milliseconds: " &
            sw.ElapsedMilliseconds.ToString("#,##0")
    End Sub)
End Sub)
End Sub
```

Try it. These changes don't make the program run faster than it did before, but because it performs the calculation and UI operations on different threads, the program remains responsive and the UI doesn't freeze.

> **Tip** The *Invoke* method is a blocking method. This means it runs during any event until the passing method in the UI thread completes. If the UI thread becomes blocked for any reason, the thread that calls *Invoke* is also blocked at that point. It's even possible that the UI thread is blocked by the invoked thread, in which case you have a deadlock situation that can't be resolved. It becomes truly ugly if the UI thread waits with a *Task.WaitXXX* method (see the section "How To Avoid Freezing the User Interface While Waiting For Tasks To Finish") until the thread that's trying to update the user interface with *Control.Invoke* completes. This condition ensures a deadlock.
>
> Sometimes it can make sense to specify that redirection of a thread to the UI thread is not a blocking thread. In this case, use the control's *BeginInvoke* method instead. In contrast to *Invoke*, *BeginInvoke* is not deterministic, which means you can never be sure exactly when the method will be called.

> **Note** In WPF, you must also delegate threads to the UI thread in a different way than in Windows Forms applications. In the companion files, you will find an application called *InvokeDemo_WPF* that is the WPF-equivalent of the Windows Forms example you just saw:
>
> ```
>             Dim labelUpdaterDel = Sub(numToTest As Integer)
>                                       InfoLabel.Text = "Test: " &
>                                       numToTest.ToString("#,##0")
>                                   End Sub
>
>
>     If InfoLabel.Dispatcher.CheckAccess() Then
>         labelUpdaterDel(numberToTest)
>     Else
>         InfoLabel.Dispatcher.Invoke(labelUpdaterDel, numberToTest)
>     End If
> ```
>
> *CheckAccess* corresponds to the Windows Forms *InvokeRequired* method, and *Invoke* works the same way. *BeginInvoke* is available through the control's *Dispatcher* object, and you use it the same way as in Windows Forms.
>
> But be careful: don't be surprised if you don't get IntelliSense support for the method in Visual Basic 2010 and the .NET Framework 4.0. The method is still there and is accepted by the compiler!

Parallelization with *Parallel.For* and *Parallel.ForEach*

Loop operations that repeat more than a thousand times in loops use the most processor time. Therefore, when looking for places in your application that can benefit from parallelization, start by evaluating loops. The goal is to distribute the workload to as many processor cores as possible.

Remember the example in Chapter 5, "Introduction to Windows Presentation Foundation," that reduced image size by decreasing the number of pixels within it? A processor core had to iterate through an image, line by line, and transfer only each *x* pixel into a new smaller

image. This procedure is amenable to distribution across several processor cores. Suppose that you have a system with four cores (not unusual for modern computers and notebooks). The first core can process the first line, the second core can process the second line, and so on, repeatedly, so that each core processes successive individual lines.

This is similar to the way that *Parallel.For* and *Parallel.ForEach* work. The methods try to distribute the method block that executes once for each element in an iteration over all the available cores. Doing this means that all elements are processed, but the sequence in which that occurs cannot be predicted.

Parallel.For

That sounds good so far—and you would probably be happy to shift all your program loops to *Parallel.For* so that they could run 2, 4, 8, or even 16 times as fast. However, it is not that simple.

The big problem, as mentioned, is that loop iterations don't occur in sequence; some number of them can execute at the same time. When the algorithm within the loop can iterate through all the values independently (even if the values are not in sequence) there's no problem. The sequence 1, 4, 6, 8, 7, 2, 3, 5, 9, 10 contains all the numbers—but not in sequential order. Try this with a simple console application:

> **Note** Remember to import the *System.Threading.Tasks* namespace when working with the TPL that includes the *Task* class used in the following code. The code also uses the *Sleep* method within the *Thread* class from the *System.Threading* namespace.
>
> ```
> Imports System.Threading
> Imports System.Threading.Tasks
> ```

```
Module Module1

    Sub Main()
        Parallel.For(1, 21, Sub(i)
                            Console.WriteLine(i.ToString)
                            'Pretend it takes 500 ms:
                            Thread.Sleep(500)
                        End Sub)
        Console.Read()
    End Sub
End Module
```

> **Note** *Thread.Sleep* ensures that the thread (and the task you initiate is just a thread in the thread pool) sleeps for the specified number of milliseconds. The task doesn't add to the processor load, and it wakes up by itself.

> **Note** An empty loop such as that in the following example consumes the same processor power as a complex algorithm executed within a loop to compute a new biggest prime number:
>
> ```
> For z=1 To 1000000000 ' 1 billion loop interations
>     'Do nothing
> Next z
> ```
>
> If you want to simulate processor load you should use *Thread.SpinWait* because it uses the thread to capacity (similar to iterating a long lasting *For* loop).

When running this simple example you see something similar to the following result. Why only something similar? The answer is that the exact sequence depends on how many processor cores are available for the program at any given time:

```
1
6
11
16
2
3
7
12
17
5
4
8
13
18
9
14
19
10
15
20
```

Just a glance at this code is probably enough for you to realize that *Parallel.For* basically works like the usual *For … Next* loop, but the internal code block is parallelized.

The TPL *scheduler* decides what iteration value to use and at what point the delegate is called. One way is to split the loop into blocks; each core is then responsible for iterating through one of these blocks. For example, in a loop from 0–99, core 1 might iterate items 0–24; core 2 might process items 25–49; core 3, items 50–74; and core 4, items 75–99. This simplistic example can help you understand the broad concept, but the scheduler is much more powerful and doesn't need to distribute the tasks so rigidly. In fact, loop distribution across cores depends on several factors. For example, some loops might take longer than others, in which case the schedule dynamically re-distributes the remaining loops.

> **Companion Content** Open the corresponding solution (.sln), which you can find in the
> \VB 2010 Developer Handbook\Chapter 28\SimpleParallelFor folder.

By making a small modification to the last program, you can get a vague idea of what the
distribution looks like. The result shows which thread was iterating which part, and how long
the execution took.

```vb
Imports System.Threading
Imports System.Threading.Tasks

Module Module1

    Private myThreadCount As Integer
    Private myList As System.Collections.Concurrent.ConcurrentBag(Of ItemLogEntry)

    Sub Main()
        myList = New System.Collections.Concurrent.ConcurrentBag(Of ItemLogEntry)
        Dim sw = Stopwatch.StartNew

        Parallel.For(1, 50,
                Sub(i)
                    myList.Add(New ItemLogEntry With {
                        .TickTime = sw.ElapsedMilliseconds,
                        .value = i,
                        .threadid = Thread.CurrentThread.ManagedThreadId})
                    'Pretend it takes a long time but the
                    'high numbers take a lot more time:
                    Console.Write(".")
                    Thread.SpinWait(i * 200000)
                End Sub)
        Console.WriteLine()
        Console.WriteLine("Sorted by thread ID:")
        Dim sortedById = From item In myList
                   Order By item.ThreadId, item.TickTime

        sortedById.ToList.ForEach(Sub(item)
                                     Console.WriteLine(item.ToString)
                                  End Sub)
        Console.WriteLine("Return")
        Console.ReadLine()

        Console.WriteLine()
        Console.WriteLine("Sort by time:")
        Dim sortedByTime = From item In myList
                   Order By item.TickTime

        sortedByTime.ToList.ForEach(Sub(item)
                                       Console.WriteLine(item.ToString)
                                    End Sub)
```

```
            Console.WriteLine("Return")
            Console.ReadLine()

    End Sub

    Public Structure ItemLogEntry
        Public TickTime As Long
        Public ThreadId As Long
        Public Value As Integer

        Public Overrides Function ToString() As String
            Return String.Format(
                "ThreadId {0:0000}: @{1:000000} ms - Value:{2:000000}",
                ThreadId, TickTime, Value)
        End Function
    End Structure
End Module
```

This program creates a list showing the duration of each loop iteration. It simulates a longer operation by using the *Thread.SpinWait* command. The code ensures that the duration of a loop iteration is not linear; higher iteration values takes longer. The program displays the measuring values once by thread and once by duration. The second list that displays when you press Enter is interesting. The output shows that on multiprocessor systems, loop iterations are done not only simultaneously (see the two entries at 67 ms), but also that the threads are distributed dynamically, depending of the load and the point at which they are released. You can also see that instead of creating any number of threads, the thread count depends on the number of processor cores in the system.

```
Sorted by duration:
ThreadId 0009: @000004 ms - Value:000001
ThreadId 0006: @000030 ms - Value:000013
ThreadId 0011: @000060 ms - Value:000025
ThreadId 0012: @000067 ms - Value:000037
ThreadId 0010: @000067 ms - Value:000049
ThreadId 0009: @000074 ms - Value:000002
ThreadId 0006: @000133 ms - Value:000014
ThreadId 0009: @000152 ms - Value:000003
ThreadId 0011: @000204 ms - Value:000026
ThreadId 0006: @000206 ms - Value:000015
ThreadId 0012: @000211 ms - Value:000038
ThreadId 0006: @000263 ms - Value:000016
ThreadId 0009: @000285 ms - Value:000004
ThreadId 0011: @000298 ms - Value:000027
ThreadId 0009: @000300 ms - Value:000005
ThreadId 0010: @000301 ms - Value:000008
ThreadId 0009: @000318 ms - Value:000006
ThreadId 0006: @000338 ms - Value:000017
ThreadId 0009: @000341 ms - Value:000007
ThreadId 0010: @000363 ms - Value:000009
ThreadId 0009: @000367 ms - Value:000010
```

```
ThreadId 0010: @000396 ms - Value:000020
ThreadId 0011: @000398 ms - Value:000028
ThreadId 0009: @000406 ms - Value:000011
ThreadId 0006: @000407 ms - Value:000018
ThreadId 0009: @000445 ms - Value:000012
ThreadId 0011: @000501 ms - Value:000029
ThreadId 0006: @000504 ms - Value:000019
ThreadId 0010: @000515 ms - Value:000021
ThreadId 0012: @000543 ms - Value:000039
ThreadId 0009: @000571 ms - Value:000024
ThreadId 0006: @000576 ms - Value:000032
ThreadId 0011: @000609 ms - Value:000030
ThreadId 0010: @000623 ms - Value:000022
ThreadId 0009: @000664 ms - Value:000040
ThreadId 0010: @000702 ms - Value:000023
ThreadId 0011: @000720 ms - Value:000031
ThreadId 0009: @000816 ms - Value:000041
ThreadId 0006: @000865 ms - Value:000033
ThreadId 0009: @000966 ms - Value:000042
ThreadId 0006: @000989 ms - Value:000034
ThreadId 0006: @001112 ms - Value:000035
ThreadId 0009: @001114 ms - Value:000043
ThreadId 0006: @001238 ms - Value:000036
ThreadId 0009: @001263 ms - Value:000044
ThreadId 0009: @001407 ms - Value:000045
ThreadId 0009: @001555 ms - Value:000046
ThreadId 0009: @001715 ms - Value:000047
ThreadId 0009: @001869 ms - Value:000048
Return
```

This list shows an important characteristic of parallelized loops: you cannot use *Parallel.For* in scenarios in which later loop iterations depend on the results of previous loop iterations.

> **Note** *Parallel.For* loop iterators count only up, and only in increments of 1. The first parameter specifies the start value, and the second parameter specifies the end value +1 (this is different than for *For … Next exclusive*). The third parameter is an *Action(Of Type)* delegate. The value passed to that delegate is an iteration variable. For each loop iteration, the loop executes the corresponding *Action(Of Type)* delegate (similar to *List.ForEach* in Chapter 19, "Arrays and Collections"), and each time the parameter value is different.

Example: Parallelizing the *ImageResizer*

As an example, let's go back to the *ImageResizer* in Chapter 5. The resizer has the ability to run on several cores. The code that follows is essential.

> **Companion Content** Open the corresponding solution (.sln), which you can find in the \VB 2010 Developer Handbook\Chapter 28\ImageResizer folder.

```
For y = 0 To mySmallWbm.WriteableBitmap.PixelHeight-1
    For x = 0 To myReduceToX - 1
        mySmallWbm.SetPixel(x, y,
            currentPicture.GetPixel(CInt(Math.Truncate(pixelFakt * x)),
                CInt(Math.Truncate(pixelFakt * y))))
    Next
Next
```

It could make sense to parallelize the algorithm that actually changes the size. Of course, everything parallelized with *Parallel.For* has to take long enough so that the overhead of setting up the threads doesn't take longer than simply running the task in non-parallel fashion. So it wouldn't make sense to parallelize the content of both loops. Suppose that you wanted to reduce an image from 12 to 4 megapixels. If you parallelize both loops, you would have to get a thread from the thread pool for every single target pixel, meaning you'd have to start at least four million threads. But parallelizing the outer loop, to process each line in parallel is different. Here's some code that you can try:

```
Parallel.For(0, pixelHeight,
    Sub(y)
        For x = 0 To myReduceToX - 1
            mySmallWbm.SetPixel(x, y,
                currentPicture.GetPixel(CInt(
                    Math.Truncate(pixelFakt * x)),
                    CInt(Math.Truncate(pixelFakt * y)))))
        Next
    End Sub)
```

Note If you want to try this on your own computer, at the beginning of the event handler routine for the *StartButton_Click*, you'll find the following comment (highlighted in bold):

```
Private Sub StartButton_Click(ByVal sender As System.Object,
                              ByVal e As System.Windows.RoutedEventArgs)
                              Handles StartButton.Click

    'Start_DedicatedTaskParallelFor()
    'Return
```

Uncomment the lines to start the *Parallel.For* version.

Tip If you want to use *Math.Truncate* instead of *Cint*, read the section "Methods Common to all Numeric Types" and the subsection "Performance and Rounding Issues," in Chapter 6, "The Essential .NET Data Types."

And indeed, as is clearly seen in the following table, the result is noticeable for processing 47 images, reducing them from 12 to 3 megapixels. On a dual-core notebook with 2.4 GHz the parallel operation is about 40 percent faster (66 seconds as opposed to 85 seconds).

Processor/Cores	Without parallelization	Parallel.For	Parallel.ForEach and ParallelFor
Atom 330 / 4 cores/ 2 × HT	85 seconds	66 seconds	58 seconds
47 images with 4,000 × 3,000 pixel horizontally reduzed to 1,280			

Parallel.ForEach

Parallel.ForEach works much like *Parallel.For* except that it calls a delegate for each list element. Again the TPL scheduler tries to run as many loop iterations as possible, depending on the available processors. The following example is modified to use *Parallel.ForEach*.

> **Companion Content** Open the corresponding solution (.sln), which you can find in the \VB 2010 Developer Handbook\Chapter 28\SimpleParallelForEach folder.

```vb
Imports System.Threading
Imports System.Threading.Tasks

Module Module1

    Private myThreadCount As Integer
    Private myList As System.Collections.Concurrent.ConcurrentBag(Of ItemLogEntry(Of
String))

    Sub Main()
        Dim Elements As New List(Of String) From {
                "Peter", "Ramona", "Lisa", "Sarika", "Jürgen",
                "Adriana", "Marcus", "Andreas", "Gabriele",
                "Silja", "Uta", "Oli", "Cate", "Arnold"}

        myList = New System.Collections.Concurrent.ConcurrentBag(Of ItemLogEntry(
            Of String))
        Dim sw = Stopwatch.StartNew
        Dim iterator As Integer
        Parallel.ForEach(Elements,
                Sub(element As String)
                    iterator += 1
                    myList.Add(New ItemLogEntry(Of String)() With {
                        .TickTime = sw.ElapsedMilliseconds,
                        .value = element,
                        .threadid = Thread.CurrentThread.ManagedThreadId})

                    'Pretend it takes a long time. The more
                    'elements the longer it takes.
                    Console.Write(".")
                    Thread.SpinWait(iterator * 2000000)
                End Sub)
```

```
            Console.WriteLine()
            Console.WriteLine("Sorted by thread ID:")
            Dim sortedById = From item In myList
                        Order By item.ThreadId, item.TickTime

            sortedById.ToList.ForEach(Sub(item)
                                        Console.WriteLine(item.ToString)
                                    End Sub)
            Console.WriteLine("Return")
            Console.ReadLine()

            Console.WriteLine()
            Console.WriteLine("Sorted by duration:")
            Dim sortedByTime = From item In myList
                        Order By item.TickTime

            sortedByTime.ToList.ForEach(Sub(item)
                                          Console.WriteLine(item.ToString)
                                      End Sub)
            Console.WriteLine("Return")
            Console.ReadLine()

        End Sub

        Public Structure ItemLogEntry(Of vType)
            Public TickTime As Long
            Public ThreadId As Long
            Public Value As vType

            Public Overrides Function ToString() As String
                Return String.Format("ThreadId {0:0000}: @{1:000000} ms - Value:{2}",
                                ThreadId, TickTime, Value)
            End Function
        End Structure
End Module
```

When you run this application, you see the following output:

```
. . . . . . . . . . . . .
Sorted by thread ID:
ThreadId 0009: @000118 ms - Value:Peter
ThreadId 0009: @000385 ms - Value:Ramona
ThreadId 0009: @000714 ms - Value:Lisa
ThreadId 0010: @000119 ms - Value:Sarika
ThreadId 0010: @000285 ms - Value:Jürgen
ThreadId 0010: @000471 ms - Value:Adriana
ThreadId 0010: @000915 ms - Value:Arnold
ThreadId 0011: @000132 ms - Value:Marcus
ThreadId 0011: @000303 ms - Value:Andreas
ThreadId 0011: @000647 ms - Value:Gabriele
ThreadId 0012: @000133 ms - Value:Silja
```

```
ThreadId 0012: @000329 ms - Value:Uta
ThreadId 0012: @000857 ms - Value:Oli
ThreadId 0013: @000343 ms - Value:Cate
Return


Sorted by duration:
ThreadId 0009: @000118 ms - Value:Peter
ThreadId 0010: @000119 ms - Value:Sarika
ThreadId 0011: @000132 ms - Value:Marcus
ThreadId 0012: @000132 ms - Value:Silja
ThreadId 0010: @000285 ms - Value:Jürgen
ThreadId 0011: @000303 ms - Value:Andreas
ThreadId 0012: @000329 ms - Value:Uta
ThreadId 0013: @000343 ms - Value:Cate
ThreadId 0009: @000385 ms - Value:Ramona
ThreadId 0010: @000471 ms - Value:Adriana
ThreadId 0011: @000647 ms - Value:Gabriele
ThreadId 0009: @000714 ms - Value:Lisa
ThreadId 0012: @000857 ms - Value:Oli
ThreadId 0010: @000915 ms - Value:Arnold
Return
```

The preceding output demonstrates how the application processes several elements at the same time, and you cannot predict which element will be processed at any given point.

The same applies for *Parallel.ForEach* and *Parallel.For*: you cannot use *Parallel.ForEach* for scenarios in which the loop iteration depends 100 percent on the result of a previous loop iteration.

Using *ParallelLoopStates—Exit For* for *Parallel.For* and *Parallel.ForEach*

Both *Parallel.For* and *Parallel.ForEach* are methods that run processes on other threads. After launching the threads, the methods have no influence over what happens within the methods that those threads are executing. It is obvious that being able to terminate a loop prematurely is significant. A common error for *Parallel.For* is code that relies on early loop termination by simply using *Return*. Because *Return* exits the method called *for each loop iteration*, it corresponds to a *Return* for the *Continue For* method, but not as an *Exit For*.

And there is something else to consider. If you really had something like the *Exit For* equivalent, how exactly should it react? Had it reached, in a *Parallel.For* for example, a certain iteration value, then you can't assume that the range up to this value has been processed in this loop completely. Why? The truth is simple: several loops are running. One could have counted from 1 to 5, another from 12 to 16, and yet another from 20 to 25. You see, even if one of the "sub-loops" got to 25, this doesn't ensure that every value from the beginning to the current value where you wanted to break the loop was already covered.

So, what you need is some special mechanism for loops, and *Parallel.For* and *Parallel.ForEach* provide those over the *ParallelLoopState*. Basically, here is how this works: you pass an additional parameter to the delegate that represents the body of the loop to parallelize, and with a lambda that looks something like this:

```
Parallel.For(startValue, endValue,
    Sub(i As Integer, parLoopState As ParallelLoopState)
        'Loop Body
    End Sub)
```

parLoopState now provides two Methods, *Break* and *Stop*, with which you can control how to break or stop the loop.

> **Note** You can find the following in the sample code under the *CancelableVersion* methods. Simply comment out the first two lines in *Sub Main* to run this method instead.

```
Sub CancelableVersion()

    myList = New System.Collections.Concurrent.ConcurrentBag(Of ItemLogEntry)
    Dim sw = Stopwatch.StartNew

    Dim flagWhichControlsThatAllValuesBelowTheCurrentGetProcessesed = True

    Try
        Parallel.For(1, 50,
            Sub(i, parLoopState)
                myList.Add(New ItemLogEntry With {
                    .TickTime = sw.ElapsedMilliseconds,
                    .value = i,
                    .threadid = Thread.CurrentThread.ManagedThreadId})
                'Pretend it takes a long time but the
                'high numbers take a lot more time:
                Console.Write(".")
                Thread.SpinWait(i * 200000)

                'Knock off at 25!
                If i = 25 Then
                    If flagWhichControlsThatAllValuesBelowTheCurrentGetProcessesed Then
                        'Every parallel iteration which processes values below 25 will
                        'continue until there are only values left above 25.
                        parLoopState.Break()
                    Else
                        'Alternatively, with stop, all iterations will stop immediately.
                        parLoopState.Stop()
                    End If
                End If
            End Sub)
```

```
        Catch ex As Exception
            Console.WriteLine("Exited For!")
        End Try


        Console.WriteLine()
        Console.WriteLine("Sorted by Thread-ID:")
...
    End Sub
```

When you run this application and set the flag with its unspeakable name to false, you see the following result:

```
.............Exited for!.
Sorted by Thread-ID:
ThreadId 0009: @000001 ms - Value:000001
ThreadId 0009: @000052 ms - Value:000002
ThreadId 0009: @000080 ms - Value:000003
ThreadId 0010: @000009 ms - Value:000007
ThreadId 0010: @000074 ms - Value:000008
ThreadId 0010: @000095 ms - Value:000009
ThreadId 0011: @000015 ms - Value:000013
ThreadId 0011: @000074 ms - Value:000014
ThreadId 0012: @000042 ms - Value:000019
ThreadId 0013: @000042 ms - Value:000037
ThreadId 0014: @000042 ms - Value:000025
ThreadId 0015: @000042 ms - Value:000031
ThreadId 0016: @000074 ms - Value:000043
ThreadId 0017: @000075 ms - Value:000049
Return


Sorted by Duration:
ThreadId 0009: @000001 ms - Value:000001
ThreadId 0010: @000009 ms - Value:000007
ThreadId 0011: @000015 ms - Value:000013
ThreadId 0012: @000042 ms - Value:000019
ThreadId 0014: @000042 ms - Value:000025
ThreadId 0015: @000042 ms - Value:000031
ThreadId 0013: @000042 ms - Value:000037
ThreadId 0009: @000052 ms - Value:000002
ThreadId 0010: @000074 ms - Value:000008
ThreadId 0011: @000074 ms - Value:000014
ThreadId 0016: @000074 ms - Value:000043
ThreadId 0017: @000075 ms - Value:000049
ThreadId 0009: @000080 ms - Value:000003
ThreadId 0010: @000095 ms - Value:000009
Return
```

The output illustrates the problem with just breaking a parallelized loop: even though the 25th element is the exit criterion, that doesn't mean that all 24 preceding elements were processed. It is important to remember this.

This procedure also applies to *Parallel.ForEach*. In the following example, the changes compared to the version that cannot be terminated are highlighted in bold:

```
Sub CancelableVersion()
    Dim Elements As New List(Of String) From {
                                "Peter", "Ramona", "Lisa", "Sarika", "Jürgen",
                                "Adriana", "Marcus", "Andreas", "Gabriele",
                                "Silja", "Uta", "Oli", "Cate", "Arnold"}

    myList = New System.Collections.Concurrent.ConcurrentBag(Of ItemLogEntry(Of String))
    Dim sw = Stopwatch.StartNew
    Dim iterator As Integer

    Dim ctSource As New CancellationTokenSource()
    Dim cancelToken = ctSource.Token

    Try
        Parallel.ForEach(Elements, New ParallelOptions With {
            .CancellationToken = cancelToken},
                Sub(element As String)
                    iterator += 1
                myList.Add(New ItemLogEntry(Of String)() With {
                    .TickTime = sw.ElapsedMilliseconds,
                    .value = element,
                    ].threadid = Thread.CurrentThread.ManagedThreadId})

                    If element = "Jürgen" Then
                        ctSource.Cancel()
                    End If

                        'Pretend it takes a long time. The more
                        'elements the longer it takes.
                    Console.Write(".")
                    Thread.SpinWait(iterator * 2000000)
                End Sub)
        Catch ex As OperationCanceledException
            Console.WriteLine("Exited For!")
        End Try

    Console.WriteLine()
    Console.WriteLine("Sorted by thread ID:")
    Dim sortedById = From item In myList
                Order By item.ThreadId, item.TickTime
    .
    .
    .
    End Sub
```

When you run this application, you see something like the following result:

```
Sorted by duration:
ThreadId 0010: @000009 ms - Value:Peter
ThreadId 0007: @000009 ms - Value:Adriana
ThreadId 0011: @000024 ms - Value:Marcus
ThreadId 0013: @000033 ms - Value:Silja
ThreadId 0012: @000033 ms - Value:Cate
ThreadId 0013: @000237 ms - Value:Uta
ThreadId 0012: @000274 ms - Value:Arnold
ThreadId 0010: @000312 ms - Value:Ramona
ThreadId 0011: @000391 ms - Value:Andreas
ThreadId 0007: @000418 ms - Value:Jürgen
Return
```

Here, it's also obvious that the original list sequence has nothing to do with the result. While the list element for the exit criterion (in this example, the name "Jürgen") is the 5th element in the list, the loop has processed 10 list elements before all loop iterations have been stopped.

All of this can be fixed when you use *Break* instead of *Stop*. Break in *Parallel.For* guarantees that every value below the current value in the current thread has been or will be processed before the loop (or—plural—the *loops*, for that matter) will be exited. With *Parallel.ForEach*, *Break* ensures that every item in the *iterator* collection prior to the current item in the current thread has been or will be processed. On the other hand, that means *Break* doesn't stop immediately. Depending on the range of values or items that your parallelized loop is processing, it could take some time to reach or actually meet the exit condition.

Avoiding Errors When Parallelizing Loops

When parallelizing loops, you can all-too-easily introduce errors that cause the program not only to slow down, but might cause it to fail or to behave in a way that fails to solve the problem. You have already seen a few of these problems:

- Loops don't run sequentially but in parallel. With *Parallel.For*, you always need to take into account that a loop with a smaller counter variable is not necessarily processed before one with a higher counter variable. Where a loop iteration runs and what loop iteration value it's using are non-deterministic. The same applies to *Parallel.ForEach* and the iteration order of elements. You never know which element is processed when, what elements are already processed, or which elements still need to be processed.

- The parallelized loop runs in several tasks at the same time, but with different values, and on different threads. Threads can never update controls directly. Later in this chapter, in the section "How to Access Windows Controls from Non-UI Threads," you'll see that you must send a delegate to the UI thread to update controls on the UI thread.

- Deadlocks can occur easily if you use parallelized loops that update the user interface, because a thread waits while the UI thread runs a delegate, and the UI thread waits for all current threads to complete. The section "How To Avoid the Freezing of the User Interface While Waiting For Tasks To Finish," earlier in this chapter, discussed that topic.

- Sometimes you might need to restrict the maximum number of parallelizations. For example, if parallel loops are nested, the TPL thread scheduler in .NET 4.0 might initiate significantly more tasks than there are cores available for a *Parallel.For* or *Parallel.ForEach* operation. When run with full load, the computer then seems to stop—or a memory problem can occur if the operations require a lot of memory (such as for image processing). These problems multiply with the level of parallelization.

- You should avoid accessing counter variables or iteration elements of loops directly in lambdas. This is particularly a problem in nested loops. The Visual Basic compiler (usually) displays a warning for this problem.

The following example should clarify this. Loop designs that rely on the actual loop variables are pretty common.

```
Const SPINVALUE = 20000000

Dim innerIndex As Integer
Dim outerIndex As Integer

For i = 0 To 3
    innerIndex = 0
    For j = 0 To 3
        Thread.SpinWait(SPINVALUE)
        Console.WriteLine("iIndex:{0} ;oIndex:{1}",
                innerIndex, outerIndex)
        innerIndex += 1
    Next
    outerIndex += 1
Next
```

When you run this, the following output appears in this console window:

```
iIndex:0 ;oIndex:0
iIndex:1 ;oIndex:0
iIndex:2 ;oIndex:0
iIndex:3 ;oIndex:0
iIndex:0 ;oIndex:1
iIndex:1 ;oIndex:1
iIndex:2 ;oIndex:1
iIndex:3 ;oIndex:1
iIndex:0 ;oIndex:2
iIndex:1 ;oIndex:2
iIndex:2 ;oIndex:2
iIndex:3 ;oIndex:2
iIndex:0 ;oIndex:3
iIndex:1 ;oIndex:3
iIndex:2 ;oIndex:3
iIndex:3 ;oIndex:3
```

Here is the same version parallelized with *Parallel.For*:

```
innerIndex = 0
outerIndex = 0

Parallel.For(0, 4,
            Sub(i)
                innerIndex = 0
                Parallel.For(0, 4,
                            Sub(j)
                                Thread.SpinWait(SPINVALUE)
                                Console.WriteLine("iIndex:{0} ;oIndex:{1}",
                                        innerIndex, outerIndex)
                                innerIndex += 1
                            End Sub)
                outerIndex += 1
            End Sub)
Console.ReadKey()
```

This results in the following output:

```
iIndex:0 ;oIndex:0
iIndex:1 ;oIndex:0
iIndex:2 ;oIndex:0
iIndex:3 ;oIndex:0
iIndex:4 ;oIndex:0
iIndex:5 ;oIndex:0
iIndex:6 ;oIndex:0
iIndex:0 ;oIndex:0
iIndex:1 ;oIndex:1
iIndex:2 ;oIndex:1
iIndex:3 ;oIndex:1
iIndex:4 ;oIndex:2
iIndex:5 ;oIndex:2
iIndex:6 ;oIndex:2
iIndex:7 ;oIndex:3
iIndex:8 ;oIndex:3
```

This problem occurs because the iteration variables are further processed by another thread and can change while the task accessing the variables is running. For this reason, you should only use iteration variables within parallelized *For* loops, if you have to parallelize certain methods with new tasks and pass the iteration variables as parameters.

The last problem cannot be solved easily. You need to think about the measures that you can take to create a parallelized version of the algorithm. You should also run a lot of tests to ensure that you're getting the correct results.

The same applies for the parallelization in the earlier prime number example that calculates the last *x* prime numbers below a specified threshold. Here the following problems occur:

- The prime number algorithm counts backward, which is not possible with *Parallel.For*. And you can't just reverse the array and process the numbers in the order *MaxCount-currentValue*, because the distribution to the parallel executed loop

areas would be too large for the range of values. For example, when we parallelize 0–99, the first range (assuming the value is reversed) would iterate from 99 to 50, and the second range from 49 to 0. But you want the first parallelized block to calculate 99, the second block to calculate 98, the third block to calculate 97, and so on. Each new thread should get the next *number* not the next block, because we don't want to calculate the 30 prime numbers below 100,000 with the threads that calculate the prime numbers from 20,000 to 30,000, which are not included in the 30 numbers below 100,000.

- You can't write the resulting values directly to the *ListBox* because they are not necessarily received in the correct order. The second-to-last prime number below the threshold might be calculated sooner than the third-to-last prime number and arranged in order. But then the order of the prime numbers would be wrong. Because of this, you must enable automatic sorting for the *ListBox*, which wastes computing power (although not a lot). That also means the *ListBox* is sorted alphabetically, so you'd need to go through a balancing act, adding leading zeros again to ensure that the list of numbers is sorted correctly, and then write the whole list into the *ListBox* when a prime number is found.

- You can't be sure that you won't overshoot the mark. Suppose that you want to calculate the last 20 prime numbers and test the candidates. Those could include numbers 10, 11, and 12 at the same time. If 11 and 12 complete before 10, you still need to test 10, meaning that 11 and 12 were calculated in vain because those numbers were already determined. There is no cure for that problem. You have to take this additional effort into account, because even with all that overhead, the parallel version is still faster.

- We must restrict the maximum parallelization even though the 8th or 9th prime number test is not started if only two numbers are missing.

> **Companion Content**   Open the corresponding solution (.sln), which you can find in the \VB 2010 Developer Handbook\Chapter 28\PrimesParallelFor folder.

> **Note**   Because of space restrictions the listing doesn't appear in print here. To learn more, load the example in Visual Studio, and then read the appropriate comments. In any case, look at Figure 28-7 and compare it with Figure 28-3.

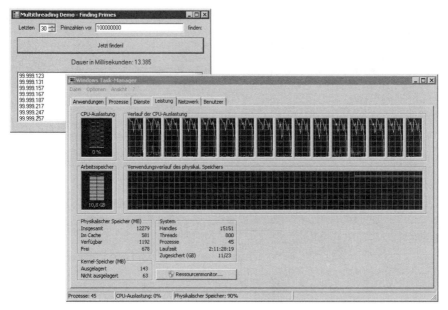

FIGURE 28-7 Thanks to the TPL of .NET Framework 4.0, you can fully utilize the performance of a modern multicore/multiprocessor system. Again, this image was captured on a German Windows multicore system.

For some algorithms, speed improvements factors of 5–10 are not exceptional. In this example, execution took only 13.5 seconds, compared to 58 seconds when using a single-threading version (a factor of almost 4.5).

Working with Tasks

At the beginning of this chapter, you saw that there are many possibilities to initiate and run methods on separate threads. As already mentioned, *tasks* have been available only since the release of .NET Framework 4.0, and they are not included in the .NET Compact Framework. A task corresponds to a thread in the thread pool. Using a task, you can easily run a method on its own thread. To create a *Task* instance, you can either use the *TaskFactory* static class (available through the *Task* class) or create one just like any other class.

> **Companion Content**   Open the corresponding solution (.sln), which you can find in the \VB 2010 Developer Handbook\Chapter 28\SimpleTask folder.

```vb
'Always remember to perform these imports
'when working with task and thread objects!
Imports System.Threading
Imports System.Threading.Tasks

Module Module1

    'Constant that determines the number of loops in the tasks.
    Private Const LOOPS As Integer = 8

    Sub Main()

        'Creates a task but doesn't start it.
        Dim firstTask As New Task(
            Sub()
                Console.WriteLine("Starting Task ID: " & Task.CurrentId.ToString)
                Console.WriteLine("Equals Thread ID: " &
                Thread.CurrentThread.ManagedThreadId.ToString)
                For count = 0 To LOOPS
                    Console.WriteLine(
                        String.Format("ThreadId: {0:000} - Count equals: {1}",
                            Thread.CurrentThread.ManagedThreadId, count))
                    'Simulate work load
                    Thread.SpinWait(8000000)
                Next
            End Sub)

        'Creates a task with the Factory class and starts the task.
        '(With the Factory class this cannot be done differently.)
        Dim taskByFactory = Task.Factory.StartNew(
            Sub()
                Console.WriteLine("Starting Task ID: " & Task.CurrentId.ToString)
                Console.WriteLine("Equals Thread ID: " &
                    Thread.CurrentThread.ManagedThreadId.ToString)
                For count = 0 To LOOPS
                    Console.WriteLine(String.Format(
                                "ThreadId: {0:000} - Count equals: {1}",
                                Thread.CurrentThread.ManagedThreadId,
                                count))
                    'Simulate work load
                    Thread.SpinWait(10000000)
                Next
            End Sub)

        'The first task is started now:
        firstTask.Start()

        'If you press a key while the other tasks are still
        'running the application will still exit.
        Console.WriteLine("main thread is done and waiting!")
        Console.Read()

    End Sub
End Module
```

When you run this application, the console window displays the following result:

```
Main thread is finished and waiting!
Starting Task ID: 1
Equals Thread ID: 11
ThreadId: 011 - Count equals: 0
Starting Task ID: 2
Equals Thread ID: 10
ThreadId: 010 - Count equals: 0
ThreadId: 011 - Count equals: 1
ThreadId: 010 - Count equals: 1
ThreadId: 011 - Count equals: 2
ThreadId: 010 - Count equals: 2
ThreadId: 011 - Count equals: 3
ThreadId: 010 - Count equals: 3
ThreadId: 011 - Count equals: 4
ThreadId: 011 - Count equals: 5
ThreadId: 010 - Count equals: 4
ThreadId: 011 - Count equals: 6
ThreadId: 010 - Count equals: 5
ThreadId: 011 - Count equals: 7
ThreadId: 010 - Count equals: 6
ThreadId: 011 - Count equals: 8
ThreadId: 010 - Count equals: 7
ThreadId: 010 - Count equals: 8
```

The first thing that stands out is the message *Main Thread Is Finished And Waiting!* that displays first. This is correct because the main thread will continue to run independently of the two lambdas passed to the *Task* instances. The tasks execute while the main thread waits for you to press a key.

If a key is pressed, the loop processing is terminated: tasks correspond to threads in the thread pool and thread pool threads always run as background threads (for a *Thread* object you would set its *IsBackground* property to *True* to achieve the same result).

This demonstration also shows the additional output lines. You can see that the task created by using the *Factory* class starts working first and returns the message for the first loop iteration just before the second task starts up (this task was already created but not started).

> **Tip** If you define a task via a multi-line statement lambda and write the following line, you don't need to type as much:
>
> `Dim someTask = Task.Factory.StartNew(Sub())`
>
> Then, position the insertion point between the last and second-to-last parentheses of the code line and press Return

Waiting on Task Completion—*WaitOne*, *WaitAny*, and *WaitAll*

Starting a task is comparatively simple. But when several tasks are running at the same time, you often need to know what task completed at what point. You might also want to be able to wait for the first (or second or third) task or maybe all the running tasks to complete before doing something else.

You can use the *WaitOne*, *WaitAny*, and *WaitAll* methods to cause *Task* instances to wait.

WaitOne is different from *WaitAny* and *WaitAll* because it is a member method, whereas *WaitAny* and *WaitAll* are static methods of the *Task* class. This means that you can use *WaitOne* to apply to the *Task* instance that calls the method. If a task is running and you call the *WaitOne* method from the thread that initiated this task, the thread will wait until the task is complete.

> **Caution** If you call *WaitOne* from the UI thread, it's completely blocked and cannot run its message queue. In certain scenarios you need to cascade (nest) tasks to prevent UI threads from freezing.

WaitAny and *WaitAll* are static methods that expect an array containing *Task* objects as a parameter. *WaitAny* waits on the current thread until *any one* of the tasks in the array completes, whereas *WaitAll* waits for all tasks in the array to finish.

The following example illustrates this. This modification of the last example waits for the task that is finished first to be identified. After the second task has finished its work, the example displays a second message.

```
Sub WaitingForTasks()

    Dim firstTask As New Task(
        Sub()
            .
            .
            .
        End Sub)

    'Creates a task with the Factory class and starts it.
    '(With the Factory class it's the only thing possible.)
    Dim taskByFactory = Task.Factory.StartNew(
        Sub()
            .
            .
            .
        End Sub)

    'The first task starts only now:
    firstTask.Start()
```

```
            'If you press a key while the other tasks are stilln
            'running the application will still exit.
            Console.WriteLine("Main thread has finished and is waiting for the results!")

            'Put the tasks the application should wait for into a task array
            '(The local type inference automatically creates a task array!)
            Dim tasksToWaitFor = {firstTask, taskByFactory}

            'Wait until the first task is finished:
            Dim taskFirstFinishedIndex = Task.WaitAny(tasksToWaitFor)

            'Identify what task is finished: the index is specified
            'in the return vaulue of WaitAny.
            Console.WriteLine(If(tasksToWaitFor(taskFirstFinishedIndex) Is taskByFactory,
                            "Factory task has finished first!",
                            "Manual task has finished first!"))

            'Wait until all (remaining) tasks are finished:
            Task.WaitAll(tasksToWaitFor)
            Console.WriteLine("All tasks are finished.")
            Console.Read()
    End Sub
```

The changed example returns the following result:

```
The main thread is finished and waits for the results!
Starting Task ID: 1
Equals Thread ID: 11
Starting Task ID: 2
Equals Thread ID: 12
ThreadId: 012 - Count equals: 0
ThreadId: 011 - Count equals: 0
ThreadId: 012 - Count equals: 1
ThreadId: 011 - Count equals: 1
ThreadId: 012 - Count equals: 2
ThreadId: 012 - Count equals: 3
ThreadId: 011 - Count equals: 2
ThreadId: 012 - Count equals: 4
ThreadId: 011 - Count equals: 3
ThreadId: 012 - Count equals: 5
ThreadId: 011 - Count equals: 4
ThreadId: 012 - Count equals: 6
ThreadId: 011 - Count equals: 5
ThreadId: 012 - Count equals: 7
ThreadId: 011 - Count equals: 6
ThreadId: 012 - Count equals: 8
Manual task was finished first!
ThreadId: 011 - Count equals: 7
ThreadId: 011 - Count equals: 8
All tasks are finished.
```

Tasks with and Without Return Values

Until now, you've seen only tasks that perform some work, but don't return results. That's fine, but it isn't sufficient, because sometimes parallelized methods need to return function values, just as normal functions do. But how and when do you obtain the function result of a task? And how do you pass parameters to a task?

When using lambdas, passing parameters is fairly simple. Tasks placed in code blocks in lambdas access the surrounding local variables, as shown in the following:

```
Dim localVariable As String = "This string"

Dim someTask = New Task(Sub()
                            localVariable &= " followed by this"
                        End Sub)

localVariable &= " is not bad"
someTask.Start()
someTask.Wait()
Console.WriteLine(localVariable)
```

Don't take the output for granted, because the *localVariable* within the lambda doesn't execute in the same sequence as the code lines. If you run this example, it returns the following:

```
This string is not bad followed by this
```

If you start the task *before* adding text to the local variable value, it returns a completely different result:

```
someTask.Start()
someTask.Wait()
localVariable &= " is not bad"
Console.WriteLine(localVariable)
```

In both cases, the order of the code that defines the string concatenations stays the same:

```
This string followed by this is not bad
```

This demonstrates that using local variables in lambdas is a bit tricky, but it's also easy and convenient. And of course, it is absolutely legitimate. (Honestly, I love lambdas. Aren't they beautiful?) But using the same code base in several tasks to pass parameters in this way is not suitable.

With tasks, you can define and pass a parameter if you want to call the method as a task. The following example shows how to pass a parameter to a task, and also how a method started as a task can return a value. First of all, here's the method to do the actual work as a task:

```
'Method that runs as a task and accepts a parameter:
'(The method that was the Lambda statement before).
Function WorkingProc(ByVal spinValue As Integer) As Long

    Dim sw = Stopwatch.StartNew

    Console.WriteLine("Starting Task ID: " & Task.CurrentId.ToString)
    Console.WriteLine("Equals Thread ID: " &
        Thread.CurrentThread.ManagedThreadId.ToString)
    For count = 0 To LOOPS
        Console.WriteLine(String.Format("ThreadId: {0:000} - Count equals: {1}",
                        Thread.CurrentThread.ManagedThreadId,
                        count))
        'Simulate work load
        Thread.SpinWait(spinValue)
    Next

    sw.Stop()
    Return sw.ElapsedMilliseconds
End Function
```

> **Note** This works only if you allow dynamic types with *Option Strict* off. If you want to enforce type safety, you need a few extra steps, such as this version of *WorkingProc*, which requires a single argument of type *object*:
>
> ```
> 'Method that runs as a task and accepts a parameter:
> '(The method that was the Lambda statement before).
> Function WorkingProc(ByVal spinValue As Object) As Long
>     Dim actualSpinValue = CInt(spinValue)
>     Dim sw = Stopwatch.StartNew
>
>     Console.WriteLine("Starting Task ID: " & Task.CurrentId.ToString)
>     Console.WriteLine("Equals Thread ID: " &
>             Thread.CurrentThread.ManagedThreadId.ToString)
>     For count = 0 To LOOPS
>         Console.WriteLine(String.Format("ThreadId: {0:000} - Count equals: {1}",
>                         Thread.CurrentThread.ManagedThreadId,
>                         count))
>         'Simulate some workwork load
>         Thread.SpinWait(actualSpinValue)
>     Next
>
>     sw.Stop()
>     Return sw.ElapsedMilliseconds
>
> End Function
> ```

An *Integer* parameter is passed to the method, which returns the elapsed processing time as the function result.

The (multiple) usage of this method works like this: Instead of a lambda, you pass the method pointer together with the operator *AddressOf* to the task—through the constructor or the *Factory* class. At the same time, you use the generic *Task* class (*Task(Of Type)*) that accepts the type of the function result as its type parameter. The modified example looks like this:

```
'Creates the first task but doesn't run it yet.
Dim firstTask As New Task(Of Long)(AddressOf WorkingProc, SPIN_ONE)

'Creates and starts a second task through the Factory class.
Dim taskByFactory = Task.Factory.StartNew(Of Long)
    (AddressOf WorkingProc, SPIN_TWO)

'The first task starts now:
firstTask.Start()
```

You pass the parameter for the method as the second argument. In this case, replace the actual method parameter for the first task (the constant *SPIN_ONE* with the corresponding value for the work load simulation) with *Thread.SpinWait* (see above) and the constant *SPIN_TWO*. But remember: The only argument you can pass is always of type *object*—*Integer* variables, for example, at this point get boxed, and must be unboxed in the calling method.

If you want to pass more than one parameter to the actual working proc and still keep type-safety enabled, there is more effort involved—you need a wrapper class for that. But thanks to the beauty of lambdas, you can get the compiler to do the work for you. So if you had the following *WorkingProc*:

```
Function WorkingProcMoreArguments(Arg1 As String, Arg2 As Integer,
    Arg3 As Double) As Long
    Return 42
End Function
```

You would call it via a task like this:

```
Dim var1 = "Testvar"
Dim var2 = 42
Dim var3 = 42.42
Dim taskMoreParameters As New Task(Of Long)(
    Function() As Long
        Return WorkingProcMoreArguments(var1, var2, var3)
    End Function)
```

The compiler generates the wrapper class (which actually implements a pattern called *state machine* required for this call) for your convenience.

Back to original sample. Of course, unlike a direct method call, starting the task doesn't return a function result because the method has to do its work first. Instead, you retrieve the function result through the *Result* property of the *Task* instance. When the result isn't

yet there, calling *Result* pauses the querying thread until the method within the task delivers the result. Essentially querying the *Result* property behaves like the *WaitOne* method of the task object. To query the result from the first task or from several tasks, you need to combine *Result* and *WaitAny*, as shown in the following example:

```
Console.WriteLine("The main thread is finished and waits for the results!")

'Put the tasks the application should wait for into a task array
'(The local type inference automatically creates a task array!)
Dim tasksToWaitFor = {firstTask, taskByFactory}

'Wait for the first task to finish:
Dim taskFirstFinishedIndex = Task.WaitAny(tasksToWaitFor)

'Identify what task is finished: the index is specified in the
'return vaulue of WaitAny.
Console.WriteLine(If(tasksToWaitFor(taskFirstFinishedIndex) Is taskByFactory,
            "Factory task was finished first after ",
            "Manual task was finished first after ") &
        tasksToWaitFor(taskFirstFinishedIndex).Result.ToString &
            " ms.")

'Wait for all (remaining) tasks to be finished:
Task.WaitAll(tasksToWaitFor)
Console.WriteLine("Alle Tasks wurden beendet.")
Console.Read()
```

The result in this example differs from the previous example only in as much as it specifies the time for the task that completed first:

```
...ThreadId: 012 - Count equals: 8
Manual task was finished first after 659 ms.
ThreadId: 011 - Count equals: 8
```

How To Avoid Freezing the User Interface While Waiting For Tasks To Finish

As already described earlier in the chapter, deadlocks can occur while updating the user interface. This is especially bad if the UI thread goes into a waiting state because it's waiting for another thread—that's updating the user interface with *Invoke*—to complete. This scenario occurs in the following example.

Companion Content Open the corresponding solution (.sln), which you can find in the \VB 2010 Developer Handbook\Chapter 28\WpfNonBlockingUi folder.

When you run this application and click the Start Working! button, strangely enough, every-thing stops working. The reason is not obvious.

```
Private Sub StartWorkingButton_Click(ByVal sender As System.Object,
                            ByVal e As System.Windows.RoutedEventArgs) _
                        Handles StartWorkingButton.Click

    MainProgress.Maximum = MAXVALUE

    Dim t As New Task(Sub()
                For z = 0 To MAXVALUE
                        Thread.SpinWait(SPINVALUE)

                        'Delegate to UI thread to update the
                        'ProgressBar. But it doesn't work
                        'because Invoke requires a working
                        'message loop that is blocked by
                        't.Wait!
                        Dispatcher.Invoke(
                            Sub(insideValue As Integer)
                                MainProgress.Value = insideValue
                            End Sub, z)
                Next
                End Sub)

    'Start task
    t.Start()

    'Blocks the UI thread
    t.Wait()

    'We will never see this...:-(
    MessageBox.Show("Task finished!")
End Sub
```

If you interrupt the demo application in this frozen state by clicking the Pause button in the Visual Studio Toolbar or by pressing Ctrl+Alt+Pause, and then open the Threads window by clicking the Threads command in the Debugging menu (or press Ctrl+Alt+H), you can see what went wrong (see Figure 28-8).

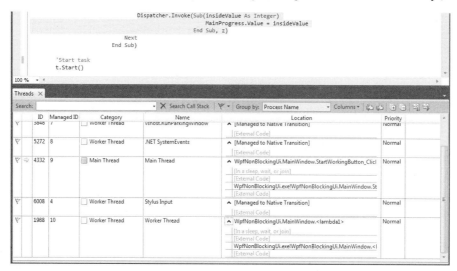

FIGURE 28-8 In the Threads window, you can see that the Worker Thread and the Main Thread are waiting for each other. This is a typical deadlock situation.

The Threads window shows that the thread of our task and the thread of the main application are in a waiting state. *Invoke* waits for the Windows message queue of the UI thread to forward the message to run the delegate. And the UI thread (Main Thread in the window) waits because of *t.Wait,* causing the message queue to stop working.

One reasonable way to solve this problem is to embed the task running the lengthy operation into another task, which, in turn, waits for the first task to finish and then displays a corresponding message on the screen (or updates the user interface in another way). In this case, updating the user interface or displaying the *MessageBox* must be reverted to the UI thread. The following example shows the solution to this problem:

```
Private Sub StartWorkingButton_Click(ByVal sender As System.Object,
                        ByVal e As System.Windows.RoutedEventArgs) _
                    Handles StartWorkingButton.Click


    MainProgress.Maximum = MAXVALUE

    Dim t2 As New Task(
        Sub()
            Dim t As New Task(Sub()
                        For z = 0 To MAXVALUE
                            Thread.SpinWait(SPINVALUE)

                            'Delegate to UI thread to update
                            'the ProgressBar.
```

```
                              Dispatcher.Invoke(
                                      Sub(insideValue As Integer)
                                          MainProgress.Value = insideValue
                                      End Sub, z)
                              Next
                          End Sub)

            'Start Worker task
            t.Start()

            'The UI thread will not be frozen because it runs in its own task.
            t.Wait()

            'This is how it works:
            Dispatcher.Invoke(Sub()
                                  MessageBox.Show("Task finished!")
                              End Sub)

        End Sub)

    'Start parent task.
    t2.Start()

End Sub
```

Cancelling Tasks by Using *CancellationToken*

You can cancel tasks to end them prematurely. If you use a class variable accessible to all
tasks, you can let the threads know to finish their work. This is usually necessary if a task runs
a time consuming operation (such as within a loop) and needs to prematurely cancel or exit
the loop, as demonstrated in the following:

```
Private myCancelEverything As Boolean

Private Sub AbbrechenButton_Click(ByVal sender As System.Object,
            ByVal e As System.Windows.RoutedEventArgs)
            Handles OkButton.Click
    myCancelEverything = True
End Sub

Sub StartTasks()
    Dim t = Task.Factory.StartNew(Sub()
                                      For tCount = 0 To Long.MaxValue
                                          Thread.SpinWait(SPINVALUE)
```

```
                            If myCancelEverything Then
                                Exit For

                                'or
                                Exit Sub
                            End If
                        Next
                    End Sub)
```

```
        End Sub
```

But a closer look reveals that this code has nothing to do with cancelling a task, because essentially it uses logic that ensures that the method ends in a different, but proper, way.

In most cases, this is the easiest and fastest solution. But you might have additional considerations, such as:

- You might need to know which tasks terminated prematurely, and which tasks completed properly.

- If you run a wait method such as *Task.WaitAll*, you might need to cancel both the running tasks and the waiting tasks—without having to wait until all the tasks complete. The waiting thread should still run after the first thread is cancelled.

In this case, you must use a *Cancellation Token*. By using the token's *IsCancellationRequested* property, you can discover whether a running task should be cancelled prematurely, or if necessary, cancel the task by triggering an *OperationCanceledException* with the *ThrowIfCancellationRequested* method of the *CancellationToken* instance. Phew! Here's a summary of how that works:

- You create a *CancellationTokenSource* instance that delivers a *CancellationToken* and lets you change the token to "exit request mode." You cannot configure this mode directly in the token itself; you must use the *CancellationTokenSource* instance, as shown here:

```
myCtSource = New CancellationTokenSource()
```

- You get a *CancelletionToken* from the *CancellationTokenSource* instance and provide the token to each task you create, as illustrated here:

```
        myCToken = myCtSource.Token

        Dim aTask As New Task(Sub()
                        'Loop
                        Do
                            myCToken.ThrowIfCancellationRequested()
                        Loop
                    End Sub, myCToken)
```

- If an operation takes a very long time and therefore can be cancelled, call the *ThrowIfCancellationRequested* method at regular intervals (such as within the loop). You should do this for all concurrent time-consuming tasks that should terminate at the same time when cancelled.

- If you want to wait for such tasks to completely cancel (for example, with *WaitAll*), specify a *Try ... Catch* block for the method call and catch an *AggregateException*. In this way, you wait until all tasks are cancelled:

```
Try
    Task.WaitAll({aTask, anotherTask, task3})
Catch ex As AggregateException
    For Each item In ex.InnerExceptions
        Debug.Print(item.Message)
    Next
End Try
```

- Or, if you want the main thread or the thread calling the different tasks to keep running after the first task was cancelled, pass a *CancellationToken* to *WaitAll* and change the *Exception* type you want to catch to *OperationCanceledException*:

```
Try
    Task.WaitAll({aTask, anotherTask, task3}, myCToken)
Catch ex As OperationCanceledException
    'Corresponding action.
End Try
```

- To terminate the tasks, use the *CancellationTokenSource*, as follows:

```
Private Sub CancelButton_Click(ByVal sender As System.Object,
                ByVal e As System.Windows.RoutedEventArgs)
                Handles CancelButton.Click
    myCtSource.Cancel()
End Sub
```

- If you want to find out whether a task completed normally or was cancelled prematurely, check its *Status* property.

The following example is a variation of the demonstration program and shows everything in context. In contrast to the example in the previous sections, this example starts several tasks to show coordinated actions. The user can click the Stop! button while the program is running to cancel both running tasks. After the first two tasks complete, a third task starts only if the user didn't click the Stop! button. When the program ends, the Debug window shows whether the tasks completed normally or the user cancelled them prematurely.

In the following example, the relevant positions for the coordinated cancellation of the tasks appear in bold text:

```
Private Sub StartWorkingButton_Click(ByVal sender As System.Object,
                ByVal e As System.Windows.RoutedEventArgs) _
                Handles StartWorkingButton.Click
```

```vb
If StartWorkingButton.Content.ToString = "Stop!" Then
    If myCtSource IsNot Nothing Then
        myCtSource.Cancel()
        Exit Sub
    End If
End If

StartWorkingButton.Content = "Stop!"

MainProgress.Maximum = MAXVALUE

myCtSource = New CancellationTokenSource()
myCToken = myCtSource.Token

Dim sw = Stopwatch.StartNew

Dim tMain As New Task(
    Sub()
        Dim t As New Task(
            Sub()
                For z = 0 To MAXVALUE
                    Thread.SpinWait(SPINVALUE)

                    'Delegate to UI thread to refresh
                    'the progress bar.
                    Dispatcher.Invoke(Sub(insideValue As Integer)
                                          MainProgress.Value = insideValue
                                      End Sub, z)
                    If myCToken.IsCancellationRequested Then
                        Debug.Print(
                            "Throwing Cancellation Requested Exception:" &
                                sw.ElapsedMilliseconds.ToString)
                        myCToken.ThrowIfCancellationRequested()
                    End If
                Next
            End Sub, myCToken)

        Dim t2 As New Task(
            Sub()
                For z = 0 To MAXVALUE \ 10
                    Thread.SpinWait(SPINVALUE * 10)

                    'Delegate to UI thread to refresh
                    'the progress bar.
                    Dispatcher.Invoke(
                        Sub(insideValue As Integer)
                            Label1.Content = "Task 2 is also active:" &
                            insideValue.ToString
                        End Sub, z)
```

```vb
                            If myCToken.IsCancellationRequested Then
                                Debug.Print(
                                    "Throwing Cancellation Requested Exception:" &
                                    sw.ElapsedMilliseconds.ToString)
                                myCToken.ThrowIfCancellationRequested()
                                'Throw New OperationCanceledException(
                                '    "Thrown manually")
                            End If
                        Next
                    End Sub, myCToken)


        'Start Worker tasks
        t.Start()
        t2.Start()

        Try
            'In this version the exception occurs when the
            'first task is cancelled.
            Task.WaitAll({t, t2}, myCToken)
            'In this version the AggregateException occurs
            'after all tasks were cancelled.
            'Task.WaitAll({t, t2})

            'This already intercepts the first cancellation.
        Catch ex As OperationCanceledException
            Debug.Print("Caught Exception: " &
                sw.ElapsedMilliseconds.ToString)
            Dispatcher.Invoke(Sub()
                                  MessageBox.Show("Task cancelled!")
                              End Sub)
            'Version waiting without CancellationToken.
            'Catch ex As AggregateException
            '    Dispatcher.Invoke(Sub()
            '                          MessageBox.Show("All tasks cancelled!")
            '                      End Sub)
        End Try


        'If the previous tasks were cancelled this task doesn't start
        'because this is also controlled by myCToken.
        Dim t3 = Task.Factory.StartNew(
                        Sub()
                            Dispatcher.Invoke(
                                Sub()
                                    MessageBox.Show("Task 3 Start!")
                                End Sub)
                        End Sub, myCToken)

        Dispatcher.Invoke(Sub()
                              If myCToken.IsCancellationRequested Then
                                  Label1.Content = "Cancelled."
                                  StartWorkingButton.Content = "Start!"
                              Else
                                  Label1.Content = "Done."
                                  StartWorkingButton.Content = "Start!"
                                  MessageBox.Show("Task finished!")
                              End If
                          End Sub)
```

```
            Debug.Print("Status Task 1:" & t.Status.ToString)
            Debug.Print("Status Task 2:" & t2.Status.ToString)
            Debug.Print("Status Task 3:" & t3.Status.ToString)

        End Sub, myCToken)

    'start parent task.
    tMain.Start()
End Sub
```

Synchronizing Threads

There are many situations in which threads cannot run simultaneously and access the existing resources of an application. Remember synchronous access to lists: when thread A queries the *Count* property of a listing at the same time that thread B completes adding a new element, thread A reaches a state in which further processing is not correct. This is not supposed to happen; access to the methods and properties should be thread-safe and synchronized. In other words, you can query the c*ount* property, but once that query starts, other threads must wait until the query completes. The same logic applies for operations that modify the list: threads querying the *Count* property of a listing must wait until threads modifying the list are complete.

The next example is similar to the first example in this chapter but is a bit more eloquent. Just to show how an unsynchronized threading operation can go wrong, it modifies the output method of the thread routine as follows:

> **Companion Content** Open the corresponding solution (.sln), which you can find in the
> \VB 2010 Developer Handbook\Chapter 28\SimpleThread02 (SyncLock) folder.

```
Imports System.Threading

Public Class frmMain

    'Field variable to number the threads.
    'Serves only to differentiate the running threads to
    'display results in the output window.
    Private myWorkerThreadNr As Integer = 1

    'Field variable to mess things up...
    Private myThreadString As String

    Private Sub btnThreadStart_Click(ByVal sender As System.Object,
        ByVal e As System.EventArgs) _
        Handles btnThreadStart.Click
```

```
'Create a new thread. The worker thread is executed as Lambda:
Dim locThread As New Thread(
    Sub()
        Dim strTemp As String

        For c As Integer = 0 To 50
            strTemp = Thread.CurrentThread.Name + ":: " + c.ToString
            'Remove the comment for SyncLock
            'so fix the program error
            'SyncLock Me
            myThreadString = ""
            For z As Integer = 0 To strTemp.Length-1
                'Simulate creating the string ...
                myThreadString += strTemp.Substring(z, 1)
                '... with a little bit more effort.
                Thread.SpinWait(1000000)
            Next
            ThreadSafeTextWindow.TSWriteLine(myThreadString)
            'End SyncLock
        Next
    End Sub)

    'In this case the thread will exit with the application:
    locThread.IsBackground = True
    'Thread has a name:
    locThread.Name = "Worker thread: " + myWorkerThreadNr.ToString
    'start thread
    locThread.Start()
    'Counter to distinguish the threads by name
    myWorkerThreadNr += 1

End Sub

Private Sub btnEnd_Click(ByVal sender As System.Object,
                         ByVal e As System.EventArgs) Handles btnExit.Click
    'Threads are background threads; there is no problem.
    Me.Close()
End Sub

End Class
```

The following happens: *myThreadString* is a class field variable used as an accumulator for each character displayed in the output window. The *TSWriteLine* method displays this string after the entire string has been assembled.

When you start the program and click the button to run a single thread once, nothing changes. But if you dare to start a second thread while the first thread is running, chaos reigns. You can see this in Figure 28-9.

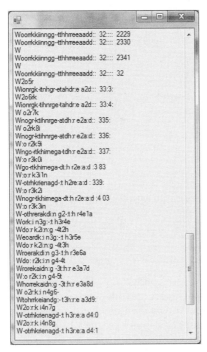

FIGURE 28-9 Two threads fighting for a field variable—and the resulting and unsatisfactory output.

The problem is that you cannot predict the point at which a thread procedure runs because with *pre-emptive multitasking* the operating system determines that point. In this case, the operating system thinks that a thread can run whenever another thread starts waiting with the *Sleep* method—this is what both threads do at regular intervals.

Synchronizing Threads with *SyncLock*

You can solve this problem by blocking code sections. The *SyncLock* statement is the key to the solution. The result is fine if you change the code as follows:

```
.
.
.
        For c As Integer = 0 To 50
            strTemp = Thread.CurrentThread.Name + ":: " + c.ToString
            'Remove the comment for SyncLock
            'to solve the program error
            SyncLock Me
                myThreadString = ""
```

```
                        For z As Integer = 0 To strTemp.Length—1
                            'Simulate the composition of the string...
                            myThreadString += strTemp.Substring(z, 1)
                            '...with a little bit more effort.
                            Thread.SpinWait(1000000)
                        Next
                        ThreadSafeTextWindow.TSWriteLine(myThreadString)
                    End SyncLock
                Next
            End Sub)
```
.
.
.

SyncLock uses an object to protect a block of code for all other threads that point to the same object. Therefore, you shouldn't change the object during access; that causes the protection to be unreliable or not work at all.

> **Important** Contrary to common belief, *SyncLock* doesn't protect the object itself against changes; it simply ensures that another thread cannot access the code simultaneously. The specified object serves only as a "tag" to protect the code. You must ensure that the object is not already being used to lock another code section. Many developers use the type object of a specified class as a *SyncLock* argument, for example:
>
> ```
> SyncLock GetType(Me)
>     .
>     .
>     .
> End SyncLock
> ```
>
> This might be good practice if the resulting object (the type) initiates different code blocks throughout the application and those code blocks cannot run at the same time. Yet it also carries a high risk of the following scenario. If *Me* is a form and you have a *SyncLock* defined in this way at several places (the same object—(*Form.GetType*)—is used over and over again), you might experience a state in which one *SyncLock* waits until another *SyncLock* completes and vice versa. The application freezes and you find yourself in a typical deadlock situation.
>
> If possible, use an object instance that only applies to *SyncLock* in the correct context for *SyncLock* objects. Only use static object instances for threads that also need to be blocked in the static context. The rule is: if you need to protect certain members of a class instance from simultaneous access, use instance objects for *SyncLock*. If you have to protect static resouces (for example, hardware components), use static objects that are marked *Shared* in Visual Basic (*Me* is not always suitable, because the form could be used at another place for SyncLock, which could result in a deadlock).
>
> A word to the wise: because *SyncLock* uses a *Try ... Catch* block, and the block could be unprotected if an exception occurs, you cannot jump into the *SyncLock* block with a *Goto* statement.

What happens when this routine executes? As soon as the first thread reaches the block it disables access to the code for all other threads by using the synclocked object. This object must meet the following conditions:

- It must be an object that references a valid address in the Managed Heap—it cannot be *Nothing*.

- It must be a reference type (because value types don't reside in the Managed Heap).

- It may not be changed by the protected routine.

The example achieves this by using a separate *Me* instance. *Me* always meets these conditions. Create static instances to protect static routines where you cannot use *Me*, such as in the following:

```
Public Class SomeClass

    Private Shared S_SyncObject as New Object.
.
        SyncLock (S_SyncObject)

            'The code for the protected routine is added here

        End SyncLock
.
.
End Class
```

If a second thread reaches the protected part of the program, it must wait for *SyncLock* until the thread executing this part of the program reaches the *End SyncLock* statement.

In this example, the member string can be created and processed without causing a problem. The member string cannot be changed by another thread because that thread has to wait until the first thread finishes executing the protected block.

> **Note** A part of a program requiring special synch protection is called a "critical section."

The Monitor Class

The *SyncLock* function has one big disadvantage: it is relentless. If a thread iterates through a critical section, *all* other threads wait at the beginning of the critical section (whether you want that to happen or not). There is nothing you can do about it. At this point, the *Monitor* class offers the highest flexibility because it can draw on a few additional methods. As soon as the thread reaches a critical section it recognizes whether it has to wait. This is illustrated in the example that follows.

> **Companion Content** Open the corresponding solution (.sln), which you can find in the \VB 2010 Developer Handbook\Chapter 28\SimpleThread03 (Monitor) folder.

```vbnet
Private Sub btnThreadStart_Click(ByVal sender As System.Object,
                                 ByVal e As System.EventArgs) _
                                 Handles btnThreadStart.Click

    'This object encapsulates the actual thread
    Dim locThread As New Thread(
        Sub()

            'This is the worker thread responsible for
            'incrementing and the value output

            Dim strTemp As String

            For c As Integer = 0 To 50
                strTemp = Thread.CurrentThread.Name + ":: " + c.ToString
                'The thread waits for 1 second. If it cannot access the code
                'in this time it exits.
                If Not Monitor.TryEnter(Me, 1) Then
                    ThreadSafeTextWindow.TSWriteLine(
                            Thread.CurrentThread.Name +
                            " informs: Already in use!")
                    Thread.Sleep(50)
                Else
                    'Access was granted. Now the worker thread starts
                    'working
                    myThreadString = ""
                    For z As Integer = 0 To strTemp.Length - 1
                        myThreadString += strTemp.Substring(z, 1)
                        Thread.Sleep(5)
                    Next
                    ThreadSafeTextWindow.TSWriteLine(myThreadString)
                    Monitor.Exit(Me)
                End If
            Next

        End Sub)

    'Determine thread name
    locThread.Name = "Worker Thread: " + myWorkerThreadNr.ToString

    'Determine background thread:
    locThread.IsBackground = True

    'Start thread
    locThread.Start()
    'Counter to distinguish the threads by their names
    myWorkerThreadNr += 1

End Sub
```

In this version, worker thread synchronization occurs through the *Monitor* class. The thread that has to wait for its predecessor is a bit impatient. If the thread cannot access the critical section within a millisecond, it displays the message *Thread Name informs: Already In Use!*, as shown in Figure 28-10.

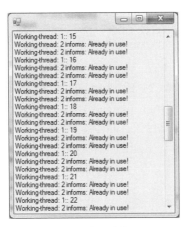

FIGURE 28-10 A thread that cannot access a critical section within a millisecond displays a succinct, if not impatient message.

The thread calls the *TryEnter* method of the *Monitor* static class to see if it can enter the critical section. You don't need to instantiate the *Monitor* class (that's not even possible). When entry is possible, the method returns *True*; otherwise, it returns *False*.

When you run the program, you see the output shown in Figure 28-10. But the *Monitor* class can do more, as you'll see in the next example.

Monitor—Wait—Pulse

Suppose that you want the worker task in the example program performed in groups of five. For a little while the first thread runs (5 iterations), and then the second thread, and so on. For this you'll need three more features:

■   You need a method to put a thread into a waiting state if it is within a critical section.

■   You need a method to wake up a thread in a waiting state. If several threads are waiting, the function should be able to bring all the waiting threads back to life.

The methods to do this are *Monitor.Wait*, *Monitor.PulseAll*, and *Monitor.Pulse*. But you also need a technique to be able to distinguish between one and several running threads. If only a single thread is running, it cannot go into sleep mode, because there is no other thread to wake it up. Implementing this is easy: the only thing you need is a basic static thread counter variable. As soon as a new thread starts, you increment the counter. When the worker routine completes, you decrement the counter. The thread goes into sleep mode only when at least one other thread is running. True to the motto, "The last one turns off the light," each thread must check whether other threads are available and wake up the last thread before it exits its worker procedure.

> **Companion Content** Open the corresponding solution (.sln), which you can find in the
> \VB 2010 Developer Handbook\Chapter 28\SimpleThread04 (Monitor Wait Pulse) folder.

When you start this program and click the button to start the thread two times, you'll see a
result similar to Figure 28-11.

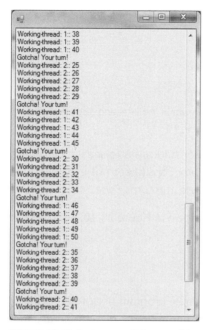

FIGURE 28-11 Exchange of blows: waiting threads can only stay in the critical section for a short while. They
will be replaced by the next waiting thread, which, in turn, works for a little while, and so on. Each thread
counts to 50—but not consecutively, because in between, each has to yield to other threads.

The corresponding listing for the worker thread looks like this:

```
'We need these to detect how many threads there are.
Private myThreadCount As Integer

'This is the worker thread responsible for
'incrementing and the value output.
Private Sub extensive calculation()

    Dim strTemp As String
    Dim stepCount As Integer

    'New thread: count!
    myThreadCount += 1
```

```vbnet
    'The critical section starts here.
    Monitor.Enter(Me)
    For c As Integer = 0 To 50
        strTemp = Thread.CurrentThread.Name + ":: " + c.ToString
        'The thread waits for 1 second. If it cannot access the code
        'in this time it exits.
        'Access was granted. Now the worker thread starts
        'working.
        myThreadString = ""
        For z As Integer = 0 To strTemp.Length - 1
            myThreadString += strTemp.Substring(z, 1)
            Thread.Sleep(1)
        Next
        ThreadSafeTextWindow.TSWriteLine(myThreadString)
        'The thread can only go to sleep if at least one
        'other thread is available to wake it up again.
        If myThreadCount > 1 Then
            stepCount += 1
            If stepCount = 5 Then
                stepCount = 0
                'Relief is on the way!
                Monitor.Pulse(Me)
                ThreadSafeTextWindow.TSWriteLine("Hey, it's you")
                'The replaced thread goes to sleep.
                Monitor.Wait(Me)
            End If
        End If
    Next
    If myThreadCount > 1 Then
        'All other threads are sleeping now.
        'At least one thread has to wake up before this thread leaves.
        'Otherwise the other threads will sleep until the next power outage...
        Monitor.Pulse(Me)
    End If
    'The critical section ends here.
    Monitor.Exit(Me)
    'Decrement thread counter.
    myThreadCount -= 1
End Sub
```

Synchronizing Limited Resources with Mutex

For working threads that don't have to interact with the outside world, it's almost immaterial how many threads are running at the same time. (Of course, you should consider using only as many threads as you need because switching between threads requires additional computing power.) When applications require access to limited hardware components, the operating system has to share use of those components between the different threads.

Here the *Mutex* class comes into play. This class basically works like the *Monitor* class but can be instantiated. That means you can define a distributor by using *Mutex* instances that depend on the available hardware components. The distributor is responsible for assigning the next available hardware component.

The following example demonstrates how to handle *Mutex* classes. This example differs from the examples that you have seen so far because it demonstrates the *Mutex* class independent of the hardware on any given computer. Three output fields in the form serve to emulate three different hardware components. The objective of the program is to divide the running threads across the three components, simulating how to use them in an optimal way.

> **Companion Content** Open the corresponding solution (.sln), which you can find in the \VB 2010 Developer Handbook\Chapter 28\SimpleThread05 (MutexDemo) folder.

When you start the program and click the Start threads button, the program searches for the first available "hardware resource" (a text output field). Another click on this button starts another thread that uses the next available output window. When you start the fourth thread while all previous threads are still running, it waits for the next free window. As soon as one of the already-running threads completes, this thread takes over the now-available output window (see Figure 28-12). The worker thread routine is designed to ensure that a single operation within the thread takes a varying amount of time to finish. This is the only way to create a realistic emulation of a simulated hardware component. Therefore, the program's initializes a *Random* object that generates random values for the *Sleep* method of the worker thread.

> **Note** The program doesn't display the screen messages directly (as in previous examples); instead, it uses three *TextBox* controls to display the text.

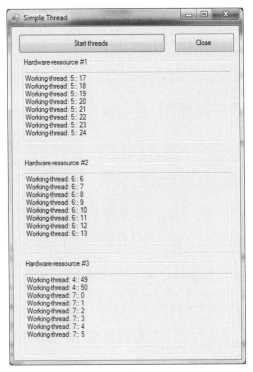

FIGURE 28-12 Three output areas simulate three hardware resources. By using a *Mutex* object array, the application recognizes which resource is available. Each thread runs in the next available window.

The following code listing demonstrates how to use instances of the *Mutex* class to implement this functionality:

```
'Field variable to number the threads.
'Serves only to differentiate the running threads to
'display results in the output window.
Private myWorkerThreadNr As Integer = 1

'Memory for Mutex objects
Private myMutexes() As Mutex

'Memory for TextBox controls
Private myTxtBoxes() As TextBox

'Random generator for artificial waiting times in the
'worker thread. The duration of the thread can be different.
Private myRandom As Random

Public Sub New()
    MyBase.New()
```

```vb
        ' This call is required for the Windows Form Designer.
        InitializeComponent()
        'Mutexes definieren
        myMutexes = New Mutex() {New Mutex, New Mutex, New Mutex}
        'Assign Textbox array
        myTxtBoxes = New TextBox() {txtHardware1, txtHardware2, txtHardware3}
        'Initialize the random generator
        myRandom = New Random(DateTime.Now.Millisecond)

    End Sub

    Private Sub btnThreadStart_Click(ByVal sender As System.Object,
                                     ByVal e As System.EventArgs) _
                                     Handles btnThreadStart.Click

        Dim locThread As New Thread(
            Sub()
                Dim locMutexIndex As Integer
                Dim locTextBox As TextBox

                'The critical section starts here
                'Wait until a TextBox is available
                locMutexIndex = Mutex.WaitAny(myMutexes)

                'Search for Textbox that matches the available mutex
                locTextBox = myTxtBoxes(locMutexIndex)
                For c As Integer = 0 To 50
                    SyncLock Me
                        If Me.IsHandleCreated Then
                            'Display text in the found TextBox
                            '(Because it is delegates to the UI thread,
                            'the detour through Invoke is necessary).
                            Me.BeginInvoke(Sub(tb As TextBox, txt As String)
                                               tb.Text += txt
                                               tb.SelectionStart = tb.Text.Length - 1
                                               tb.ScrollToCaret()
                                           End Sub, {locTextBox,
                                           Thread.CurrentThread.Name + ":: " +
                                               c.ToString + vbNewLine})
                        End If
                    End SyncLock
                    'Wait for any length of time
                    Thread.Sleep(myRandom.Next(50, 400))
                Next
                'Here the critical section ends.
                'Release the used TextBox (Mutex)
                myMutexes(locMutexIndex).ReleaseMutex()
            End Sub)

        locThread.IsBackground = True
        locThread.Name = "Worker Thread: " + myWorkerThreadNo.ToString
```

```
'Start thread
locThread.Start()
'Counter to distinguish the threads by their names
myWorkerThreadNo += 1

End Sub
```

A few additional explanations regarding this program are in order. First, it creates a *Mutex* array as a class member to manage the available resources. Using the static function *WaitAny* that receives a *Mutex* array, a thread waits until one of the *Mutex* objects in the array is available. In this case, *WaitAny* returns the index to the available *Mutex* object and changes its state to "blocked." It uses the returned index to find the corresponding *TextBox* assigned to that *Mutex*. The thread uses this *TextBox* (referenced through *locTextBox*) for the output. *WaitAny* doesn't only wait for an available *Mutex* but blocks it for the requesting thread. The *Mutex* remains in the blocked state until the thread calls the *ReleaseMutex* method.

What's Next?

Many entire books have been written about threading. The 60-odd pages in this chapter make it one of the longest chapters in this book, but it's still only an introduction, intended only to give you a brief overview of basic threading techniques.

A good starting point for sources regarding programming with the TPL is *http://Channel9. msdn.com*, where you can find many videos—including some from TPL guru and developer, Stephen Toub. The TPL team has a blog where you can find references to more information (*http://blogs.msdn.com/b/pfxteam/*) and many example applications (*http://code.msdn. microsoft.com/ParExtSamples*).

Index

Symbols

+ (addition) operator, 523–524, 532
+= (addition) operator, 54
& (ampersand), 149
<> (angle brackets)
  attribute marking, 722
  non-equivalency operator, 532
  XML document elements, 824
' (apostrophe), 169
* (asterisk), 227
<< bit shift operator, 55–56, 532
>> bit shift operator, 55–56, 532
& (composition) operator, 532
&= (concatenation) operator, 54
{} (curly braces), 619
/ (division) operator, 523–524, 532
/= (division) operator, 54
\ (division) operator, 532
= (equal sign)
  assignment operator, 37
  comparison operator, 36, 37
  equals operator, 337, 532
> (greater than) operator, 532
>= (greater than or equal to)
  operator, 532
< (less than) operator, 532
<= (less than or equal to)
  operator, 532
* (multiplication) operator, 523–524
*= (multiplication) operator, 54
^ (power) operator, 532
^= (power) operator, 54
[ ] (square brackets), 85
- (subtraction) operator, 523–524,
  532
-= (subtraction) operator, 54
_ (underscore)
  attributes and, 722
  field variables and, 349
  line continuation and, 163

A

abbreviation operators, 54
Absolute size type, 137
absolute value, defined, 665
abstract classes
  declaring methods, 427–429
  declaring properties, 427–429
  deriving from, 25–26
  Editor support for, 436–441
  interfaces and, 436–441
  MustInherit keyword, 427
  MustOverride keyword, 427–429
  virtual procedures and, 426–429
accelerator keys
  defined, 149
  specifying, 149–151
AcceptButton property
  (controls), 151
access modifiers
  about, 348, 376
  classes and, 376
  constructors, 364
  procedures and, 377
  property accessors and, 378–380
  specifying variable
    scope, 376–380
  variables and, 378
Action delegate, 683
Action(Of T) generic
  delegate, 609–611
AddAfter method (LinkedList(Of
  Type) class), 689
AddBefore method (LinkedList(Of
  Type) class), 689
AddFirst method (LinkedList(Of
  Type) class), 689
AddHandler method
  (EventHandlerList class), 536,
  561–569, 570
Add-Ins Refactor tool, 175
addition (+) operator, 523–524, 532
addition (+=) operator, 54
AddLast method (LinkedList(Of
  Type) class), 689
Add method
  ArrayList class, 650–652, 652
  Collection class, 565
  Collection(Of Type) class, 656
  ComboBox controls, 236
  Decimal structure, 281
  Hashtable class, 659
  IList interface, 657–659
  MeshGeometry3D class, 218
  XML literals and, 826
Add New Item dialog box
  about, 83
  Generate New Type dialog box
    and, 118
  managing templates, 83–84
  multitargeting and, 89
Add New Reference dialog box, 89
Add Random Addresses command
  (File menu), 712
AddRange method (ArrayList
  class), 652
Add Reference dialog box
  about, 97
  ImageResizer example, 245
  selecting assemblies, 69
AddressOf operator, 551, 557
Add Service Reference dialog
  box, 89
ADO.NET Entity Client Data
  Provider, 859
ADO.NET Entity Data Model.
  See EDM
ADO.NET Entity Framework.
  See Entity Framework
AdventureWorks sample database
  Database Selection dialog
    box, 844
  first practical example, 848–856
  Full-Text Search option, 838
  installing, 843–846
  license terms dialog box, 844
  querying entity models, 856–869
Aero design, 775
Aggregate clause (LINQ), 798, 820
aggregate functions, 820–822
alarm clock example
  about, 536
  consuming events, 537–539
  delegates and, 547–556
  embedding events
    dynamically, 561–569
  event parameters, 542–547
  implementing event
    handlers, 569–574
  lambda expressions, 556–561
  raising events, 539–542
Algol programming language, 13
alias names, 817
Alt key, 158
Alt+F6 keyboard shortcut, 100
Alt+< keyboard shortcut, 117, 402
Alt+> keyboard shortcut, 117, 402
ampersand (&), 149
Anchor property (controls), 133,
  134–135, 140–141
AndAlso keyword, 41–42
AND logical operator, 38, 82, 533,
  581

GC class
  Collect method, 496
  SuppressFinalize method, 503, 513
GDI+
  drawing considerations, 197
  .NET graphic commands and, 199
GDI (Graphics Device Interface)
  drawing considerations, 197–198
  graphic cards and, 194
Generate From Usage feature
  about, 117
  Generate New Type option, 117–118
Generate New Type dialog box
  about, 117–118
  Access option, 118
  File name option, 118
  Kind option, 118
  Project location option, 118
generations of objects, 494–497
generic collections
  about, 678
  Collection(Of Type) class, 649, 655
  KeyedCollection class, 686–689
  LinkedList(Of Type) class, 689–691
  listing of important, 679–681
  List(Of Type) class, 649, 655, 681–686
generic delegates
  about, 608
  Action delegate, 683
  Action(Of T), 609–611
  Comparer class and, 683–684
  Function(Of T), 611
  as parameters, 640
  Predicate class and, 684–686
  Tuple(Of T), 611–612
generics
  about, 583–585
  anonymous types and, 791
  building collections, 649
  combining constraints, 598–599
  constraining to classes with default constructors, 597–598
  constraining to specific base classes, 590–594
  constraining to specific interfaces, 594–597
  constraining to value types, 598, 602
  Garbage Collector and, 649
  homogenous collections and, 655
  solution approaches, 585–586
  standardizing code bases of types, 587–589
Get accessors (property procedures), 347, 378–380

GetConstructor method (Type class), 630
GetCustomAttributes method
  Attribute class, 738, 739
  Type class, 728, 739
GetEnumerator method
  IEnumerable interface, 643
  String class, 296
GetEvent method (Type class), 728
GetEvents method (Type class), 728
GetField method (Type class), 729
GetFields method (Type class), 729
GetFiles method (My.Computer.FileSystem), 765
GetHashcode method
  Hashtable class, 669
GetHashCode method
  Object class, 448
GetInstance static function, 457
GetKeyForItem method (KeyedCollection class), 686
Get keyword, 346
GetMember method (Type class), 729
GetMembers method (Type class), 729, 730, 732
GetProperties method (Type class), 729, 738
GetProperty method (Type class), 729
GetType method
  Attribute class, 738
  Enum class, 579
  Object class, 448, 485
  Type class, 630, 727, 738
GetUnderlyingType method (Enum class), 578
GetValue method (PropertyInfo class), 733
GOTO statement, 13
graphic cards
  about, 198–199
  games and, 199
  GDI support, 194–195
Graphics Device Interface. See GDI
greater than (>) operator, 532
greater than or equal to (>=) operator, 532
Grid controls
  ColumnSpan property, 232, 239
  default in windows, 222
  defining columns and rows, 225–237
  Margin property, 232
  row numbering, 228
  RowSpan property, 239
Group By clause (LINQ), 816–819

grouping
  collections, 816–819
  queries, 821–822
Group Join clause (LINQ), 816, 819, 821
GUID data type, 313–315

H

HandleAutoStart method, 753
Handles keyword, 214, 480, 537–539
HasFlag method (Enum class), 582
hashcode, 665, 669–670
hashing concept, 665
Hashtable class
  about, 659
  Add method, 659
  GetHashcode method, 669
  random data example, 659–669
hashtables
  about, 659
  access time considerations, 665–666
  enumerating data elements in, 673
  load factor concept, 666–669
  processing speed considerations, 662–665
  type-safe collections, 673
  unique key values and, 672
HasValue property, 566, 604
Header property (MenuItem class), 240
Height property
  for controls, 215
  for windows, 207
hexadecimal system, 460
hierarchies
  MemberInfo class and, 732–733
  shadowing and, 450–454
  XAML, 217, 218
Highlighted Reference feature
  about, 107–109
  changing highlighted color, 109
  disabling, 110
Hill, Murray, 14
homogenous collections, 655
HorizontalContentAlignment property (controls), 234
House, David, 897
HTML (HyperText Markup Language), 823
HTML-Reference help files, 172
HyperText Markup Language (HTML), 823
hyperthreading processors, 898

Klaus Löffelmann

Klaus Löffelmann is a Microsoft MVP for Visual Basic .NET, and has been a professional software developer for over 20 years. He has written several books about Visual Basic and is the owner and founder of ActiveDevelop in Lippstadt, Germany, a company specializing in software development, localization, technical literature, and training/coaching with Microsoft technologies.

Sarika Calla Purohit

Sarika Calla Purohit is a Software Design Engineer Test Lead on the Visual Studio Languages team at Microsoft. She has been a member of the Visual Studio team for over eight years and has contributed to Visual Basic .Net since version 1.1. Most recently, her team was responsible for testing the Visual Basic IDE in Visual Studio 2010.

What do you think of this book?

We want to hear from you!

To participate in a brief online survey, please visit:

microsoft.com/learning/booksurvey

Tell us how well this book meets your needs—what works effectively, and what we can do better. Your feedback will help us continually improve our books and learning resources for you.

Thank you in advance for your input!

Microsoft®
Press

Stay in touch!

To subscribe to the _Microsoft Press_® _Book Connection Newsletter_—for news on upcoming books, events, and special offers—please visit:

microsoft.com/learning/books/newsletter